22 SEP 1982

AUTOMOTIVE
CHASSIS AND BODY

**Other Books and Instructional Materials
by William H. Crouse and *Donald L. Anglin**

Automotive Chassis and Body*
   Workbook for Automotive Chassis and Body*
Automotive Electrical Equipment
   Workbook for Automotive Electrical Equipment*
Automotive Engines*
   Workbook for Automotive Engines*
Automotive Fuel, Lubricating, and Cooling Systems*
   Workbook for Automotive Fuel, Lubricating, and
   Cooling Systems*
Automotive Transmissions and Power Trains*
   Workbook for Automotive Transmissions and Power
   Trains*
Automotive Service Business: Operation and
   Management
Automotive Emission Control
Automotive Engine Design
Workbook for Automotive Service and Trouble
   Diagnosis
Workbook for Automotive Tools
Automotive Mechanics
   Study Guide for Automotive Mechanics
   Testbook for Automotive Mechanics*
   Workbook for Automotive Mechanics*
   Automotive Troubleshooting Cards
The Auto Book
   Auto Shop Workbook*
   Auto Study Guide
   Auto Test Book*
   Auto Cassette Series
General Power Mechanics (with Robert Worthington
   and Morton Margules*)
Small Engines: Operation and Maintenance
   Workbook for Small Engines: Operation and
   Maintenance

**Automotive Transparencies
by William H. Crouse and Jay D. Helsel**

Automotive Brakes
Automotive Electrical Systems
Automotive Engine Systems
Automotive Transmissions and Power Trains
Automotive Steering Systems
Automotive Suspension Systems
Engines and Fuel Systems

AUTOMOTIVE CHASSIS AND BODY

SUSPENSION
STEERING
ALIGNMENT
BRAKES
TIRES
AIR CONDITIONING

William H. Crouse

Donald L. Anglin

Fifth Edition

McGRAW-HILL BOOK COMPANY
GREGG DIVISION
NEW YORK
ST. LOUIS
DALLAS
SAN FRANCISCO
AUCKLAND
DÜSSELDORF
JOHANNESBURG
KUALA LUMPUR
LONDON
MEXICO
MONTREAL
NEW DELHI
PANAMA
PARIS
SÃO PAULO
SINGAPORE
SYDNEY
TOKYO
TORONTO

ABOUT THE AUTHORS

William H. Crouse

Behind William H. Crouse's clear technical writing is a background of sound mechanical engineering training as well as a variety of practical industrial experience. After finishing high school, he spent a year working in a tinplate mill. Summers, while still in school, he worked in General Motors plants, and for three years he worked in the Delco-Remy Division shops. Later he became Director of Field Education in the Delco-Remy Division of General Motors Corporation, which gave him an opportunity to develop and use his natural writing talent in the preparation of service bulletins and educational literature.

During the war years, he wrote a number of technical manuals for the Armed Forces. After the war, he became Editor of Technical Education Books for the McGraw-Hill Book Company. He has contributed numerous articles to automotive and engineering magazines and has written many outstanding books. He was the first Editor-in-Chief of the 15-volume McGraw-Hill Encyclopedia of Science and Technology.

William H. Crouse's outstanding work in the automotive field has earned for him membership in the Society of Automotive Engineers and in the American Society of Engineering Education.

Donald L. Anglin

Trained in the automotive and diesel service field, Donald L. Anglin has worked both as a mechanic and as a service manager. He has taught automotive courses and has also worked as curriculum supervisor and school administrator for an automotive trade school. Interested in all types of vehicle performance, he has served as a racing-car mechanic and as a consultant to truck fleets on maintenance problems.

Currently he serves as editorial assistant to William H. Crouse, visiting automotive instructors and service shops. Together they have coauthored magazine articles on automotive education and several books in the McGraw-Hill Automotive Technology Series.

Donald L. Anglin is a Certified General Automotive Mechanic and holds many other licenses and certificates in automotive education, service, and related areas. His work in the automotive service field has earned for him membership in the American Society of Mechanical Engineers and the Society of Automotive Engineers. In addition, he is an automotive instructor at Piedmont Virginia Community College, Charlottesville, Virginia.

Library of Congress Cataloging in Publication Data

Crouse, William Harry (date)
   Automotive chassis and body.

   (McGraw-Hill automotive technology series)
   Includes index.
   1. Automobiles—Bodies.   2. Automobiles—Chassis.
I. Anglin, Donald L., joint author.   II. Title.
TL255.C7 1976   629.2′4   75-4922
ISBN 0-07-014653-5

AUTOMOTIVE CHASSIS AND BODY

      6 7 8 9 0   WCWC   8 3 2 1

The editors for this book were Ardelle Cleverdon and Susan Berkowitz, the designer was Dennis G. Purdy, and the production supervisor was Rena Shindelman. The cover illustrator was Shelley Freshman. It was set in Melior by York Graphic Services, Inc.
Printed and bound by Webcrafters, Inc.

CONTENTS

This is the fifth edition of *Automotive Chassis and Body*. The book has undergone many changes in its five editions. These changes parallel the many changes in the automotive chassis. "Safety" has become the watchword of the automotive industry. Today's cars have energy-absorbing bumpers, reinforcing side bars in the doors, seat-belt starter interlock systems, and open-door warning-buzzer systems; some have air bags. These and other safety features are designed to protect the driver and passengers from the hazards of the highway.

But there have been many other developments in chassis design. Among these are steering gears and steering-linkage joints that require no lubrication, ball-joint-wear indicators, new disk-brake designs, antiskid controls, MacPherson suspension systems, and new shock absorbers. Also, many of the servicing procedures on chassis components have been simplified. For example, the service procedures on air conditioning no longer require pumping down the system.

The present edition of *Automotive Chassis and Body* covers these new designs and procedures. The book has been substantially rewritten, and hundreds of new illustrations have been added. During the preparation of the new edition, the latest technical and service literature issued by automotive manufacturers, both here and abroad, was analyzed to ensure good coverage of the latest developments. The authors visited and were in touch with many service facilities to assess servicing techniques under development, and new developments are incorporated in the new edition.

One special feature of this edition is the introduction of the metric system of measurements. When a United States Customary measurement is used, it is usually followed by its metric equivalent in brackets; for example, 0.002 in. [0.051 mm].

A new edition of the *Workbook for Automotive Chassis and Body* has also been prepared. It includes the basic chassis service jobs recommended by the Motor Vehicle Manufacturers Association—American Vocational Association Industry Planning Council. Together, the textbook and the workbook provide the background information and "hands-on" experience needed to prepare a student to become a qualified and certified automotive chassis mechanic.

To assist the automotive instructor, the *Instructor's Planning Guide for Automotive Chassis and Body* is available from McGraw-Hill. The instructor's guide was prepared to help the automotive instructor do the best possible job of teaching by most effectively utilizing the textbook, workbook, and other related instructional materials. The instructor's guide contains suggestions on student motivation, classroom instruction and related shop activities, program evaluation, and much more. In addition, it includes the answer key for the tests at the end of each jobsheet in the *Workbook for Automotive Chassis and Body*.

Also in the instructor's guide is a list of various related textbooks and ancillary instructional materials available from McGraw-Hill. Used singly or together, these items form a comprehensive student learning and activity package. They provide the student with meaningful learning experiences and help the student develop job competencies in automotive chassis and body and related fields. The instructor's guide explains how the various available materials can be used, either singly or in combination, to satisfy any teaching requirement.

WILLIAM H. CROUSE
DONALD L. ANGLIN

Automotive Chassis and Body is one of eight books in the McGraw-Hill Automotive Technology Series. These books cover in detail the construction, operation, and maintenance of automotive vehicles. They are designed to give you the complete background of information you need to become successful in the automotive service business. The books satisfy the recommendations of the Motor Vehicle Manufacturers Association—American Vocational Association Industry Planning Council. The books also meet the requirements for automotive mechanics certification and state vocational educational programs, and recommendations for automotive trade apprenticeship training. Furthermore, the comprehensive coverage of the subject matter in the books make them valuable additions to the library of anyone interested in automotive engineering, manufacturing, sales, service, and operation.

Meeting the Standards

The eight books in the McGraw-Hill Automotive Technology Series meet the standards set by the Motor Vehicle Manufacturers Association (MVMA) for an associate degree in automotive servicing and in automotive service management. These standards are described in the MVMA booklet "Community College Guide for Associate Degree Programs in Auto and Truck Service and Management." The books also cover the subjects recommended by the American National Standards Institute in their detailed standard D18.1-1972, "American National Standard for Training of Automotive Mechanics for Passenger Cars and Light Trucks."

In addition, the books cover the subject matter tested by the National Institute for Automotive Service Excellence (NIASE). The tests given by NIASE are used for certifying general automotive mechanics and automotive technicians working in specific areas of specialization under the NIASE voluntary mechanic testing and certification program.

Getting Practical Experience

At the same time that you study the books, you should be getting practical experience in the shop by handling automotive parts, automotive tools, and automotive servicing equipment and by performing actual servicing jobs. To assist you in your shop work, there is a shop workbook for each textbook in the Automotive Technology Series. For example, the *Workbook for Automotive Chassis and Body* includes the jobs which cover every basic servicing procedure on the automotive chassis. If you do every job in the workbook, you will have "hands-on" experience on all chassis servicing work.

If you are taking an automotive mechanics course in a school, you will have an instructor to guide you in your classroom and shop activities. But even if you are not taking a course, the workbook can act as an instructor. It tells you, step-by-step, how to do the various servicing jobs. A garage or service station is a good source of practical information. If you can get acquainted with the automotive mechanics there, you will find they have a great deal of practical information. Watch them at their work if you can. Make notes of important points for filing in your notebook.

Service Publications

While you are in the service shop, study the various publications received at the shop. Automobile manufacturers, as well as suppliers of parts, accessories, and tools, publish shop manuals, service bulletins, and parts catalogs. All these help service personnel do a better job. In addition, numerous automotive magazines are published which deal with problems and methods of automotive service. All these publications will be of great value to you; study them carefully.

These activities will help you get practical experience in automotive mechanics. Sooner or later this experience, plus the knowledge that you have gained in studying the books in the McGraw-Hill Automotive Technology Series, will permit you to step into the automotive shop on a full-time basis. Or, if you are already in the shop, you will be equipped to step up to a better and a more responsible job.

Checking Up on Yourself

You can check up on your progress in your studies by answering the questions given every few pages in the book. There are two types of tests, progress quizzes and chapter checkups, the answers to which are given at the back of the book. Each progress quiz should be taken just after you have completed the pages preceding it. The progress quizzes allow you to check yourself as you finish a lesson. On the other hand, the chapter checkups may cover several lessons, since they are review tests of entire chapters. Because they are review tests, you should review the entire chapter by rereading it or at least paging through it to check important points before trying the test. If any of the questions stump you, reread the pages in the book that will give you the answer. This sort of review is valuable; it will help you to remember the information you need when you work in an automotive shop.

Keeping a Notebook

Keeping a notebook is a valuable part of your training. Start it now, at the beginning of your studies of the automotive chassis. Your notebook will help you in many ways. It will be a record of your progress. It will become a storehouse of valuable information you will refer to time after time. It will help you learn. It will help you organize your training program so it will do you the most good.

When you study a lesson in the book, have your notebook open in front of you. Start with a fresh notebook page at the beginning of each lesson. Write the lesson or textbook page number and date at the top of the page. As you read your lesson, jot down the important points.

In the shop, make your notes on a small scratch pad or cards. You can transfer these notes to your notebook later.

You can also make sketches in your notebook showing wiring or hose diagrams, brake circuits, and so on. Save articles and illustrations from technical and hot-rod magazines. File them in your notebook. Also, save instruction sheets that come with service parts. Attach these to sheets of paper and file them in your notebook.

Your notebook will become a valued possession—a permanent record of what you learned about the automotive chassis.

Glossary and Index

There is a glossary (a definition list) of automotive terms in the back of the book. Whenever you have a question about the meaning of a term or what purpose some automotive-chassis part has, you can refer to this list. There is also an index at the back of the book. It will steer you to the page in the book where you will find the information you are seeking.

And now, good luck to you. You are studying a fascinating, complex, and admirable machine—the automobile. Your studies can lead you to success in the automotive field, a field where opportunities are nearly unlimited.

ACKNOWLEDGMENTS

During the preparation of this new edition of *Automotive Chassis and Body*, the authors were given invaluable aid and inspiration by many people in the automotive industry and in the field of education. The authors gratefully acknowledge their indebtedness and offer their sincere thanks to these many people. All cooperated with the aim of providing accurate and complete information that would be useful in the training of automotive mechanics.

Special thanks are owed to the following organizations for information and illustrations that they supplied: Akron Equipment Company; Alemite Division of Stewart-Warner Corporation; Alexander Milburn Company; American Motors Corporation; Ammco Tools, Incorporated; B. F. Goodrich Company; Barrett Equipment Company; Bear Manufacturing Company; Bendix-Westinghouse Automotive Air Brake Company; British Ford; British Motor Corporation; Buick Motor Division of General Motors Corporation; Burman and Sons, Limited; Cadillac Motor Car Division of General Motors Corporation; Chevrolet Motor Division of General Motors Corporation; Chrysler Corporation; Clayton Manufacturing Company; Fiat; Firestone Rubber Company; Fisher Body Division of General Motors Corporation; Ford Motor Company; General Motors Corporation; Goodyear Tire and Rubber Company; Hunter Engineering Company; International Harvester Company; Jack P. Hennessy Company, Inc.; John Bean Division of FMC Corporation; Kent-Moore, Incorporated; Mobil Oil Corporation; Monroe Auto Equipment Company; Oldsmobile Division of General Motors Corporation; Pontiac Motor Division of General Motors Corporation; Robinair Manufacturing Corporation; Simca; Thompson Products, Incorporated; Toyota Motor Sales, Limited; Warner Electric Brake Manufacturing Company; and Weaver Manufacturing Division of Dura Corporation. To all these organizations and the people who represent them, sincere thanks.

WILLIAM H. CROUSE
DONALD L. ANGLIN

chapter 1

FUNDAMENTAL PRINCIPLES

This chapter discusses the fundamental principles of the various operating components of the automobile. These principles will help you to understand why and how the engine, brakes, steering system, and other components operate.

⊘ **1-1 Purpose of This Book** *Automotive Chassis and Body* is about the part of the automobile called the *chassis*. The chassis includes the frame, wheels and supporting springs, steering mechanism, brakes, engine, and power train (the mechanisms that carry the engine power to the wheels). Other books in the McGraw-Hill Automotive Technology Series describe the engine (*Automotive Engines*) and the power-train components (*Automotive Transmission and Power Trains*). The remainder of the chassis components are described in this book: springs, shock absorbers, steering systems (including power steering), brakes (including power brakes), tires, and frames. There are also chapters on automotive body repair and automotive air conditioning.

⊘ **1-2 Why We Talk about Principles First** Before we describe the various chassis components, let's discuss the principles, or physical laws, that make these components operate. When we release a stone from our hand, it drops to the ground. When a vacuum exists in an engine cylinder, air rushes in as the intake valve opens. When we step on the brake pedal, liquid is forced through tubes into the brake mechanisms at the wheels so that braking action takes place. But if air gets into the tubes, the braking effect will be poor. Why do these and many other things happen? Because of certain *physical laws*. Because, for instance, air acts one way and a liquid another when pressure is applied.

The principles discussed below explain why the chassis components work. And when we understand *why* a mechanism works, it is much easier to remember *how* it works and how to service and repair it. Actually, we are all acquainted with these physical principles. There's really nothing very complicated about them.

⊘ **1-3 Gravity** Take gravity, for example. Gravity makes the stone we release from our hand fall to the earth. Gravity is the attractive force that all objects have toward each other. The earth attracts the stone and pulls it toward the earth. When a car is driven up a hill, a good part of the engine power is used to overcome gravity so the car can move up the hill. Likewise, a car can coast down a hill with the engine off because of the gravitational attraction of the earth on the car.

We usually measure gravitational attraction in terms of *weight*. When we say that an object weighs 10 pounds [4.54 kg (kilograms)], we mean that the object has enough mass for the earth to register that much pull on it. It is the gravitational attraction, or the pull of the earth, that gives an object its weight.

⊘ **1-4 Atmospheric Pressure** The air has weight, just as any other material object has weight. Normally we do not think of air as having weight because we cannot see it and because we have become accustomed to feeling its weight and movement—as we do, for instance, when it blows in our face.

However, since air is an "object," it does have weight; that is, air is pulled toward the earth by gravitational attraction.

At sea level, and at average temperature, a cubic foot [0.028 m³ (cubic meter)] of air weighs about 0.08 pound [0.036 kg] (Fig. 1-1). This seems like a very small weight. However, the blanket of air (the atmosphere) that surrounds the earth is many miles thick. This means that there are, in effect, many thousands of cubic feet of air, piled one on top of another, all adding their weight. The actual weight of this air, or its downward push, at sea level is about 15 psi (pounds per square inch) [1.05 kg/cm² (kilograms per square centimeter)]. This is another way of saying that the atmospheric pressure (the pressure, or downward push, of the air) is 15 psi. And 15 psi means 2,160 pounds per square foot (psf)[1] (Fig. 1-2). In other words, atmospheric pressure at sea level amounts to more than a ton on every

---

[1] 1 square foot = 144 square inches. 144 × 15 = 2,160.

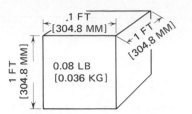

Fig. 1-1. One cubic foot of air at sea level and at average temperature weighs about 0.08 pound [0.036 kg].

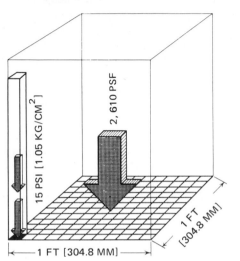

Fig. 1-2. A pressure of 15 psi [1.05 kg/cm²] means 2,160 psf (pounds per square foot).

square foot [919 kg per 0.093 m³ square meter] of the earth's surface or on any object on the earth at sea level. Since the human body has a surface area of several square feet, atmospheric pressure on the body amounts to several tons!

You may wonder why several tons of atmospheric pressure on your body doesn't crush you. The reason is that the internal pressure of your body balances the external pressure of the air. Fish are subjected to much greater pressure—more than 100,000 psi [7,030 kg/cm²] at several thousand feet down in the ocean. But their internal pressure also balances the outside pressure. They manage to live and swim about, just as we live and walk about on earth, even though a great weight of air exerts its pressure on us.

⊘ **1-5 Changes in Atmospheric Pressure** Atmospheric pressure is continually changing. It changes with the weather. It also changes as you move up from sea level by climbing a mountain or by flying in a plane. In the next section, on vacuum, we shall learn how atmospheric pressure is measured so that people can predict the weather. The reason changing atmospheric pressure is tied in with the weather is that the changing pressure helps to get the air moving from one place to another. For instance, air over the ocean picks up a great deal of moisture. Suppose that to the east of this moist air there is a sunshiny area of dry land. The sun heats the air above the

dry land. As air is heated, it expands and becomes lighter. (It contracts, or becomes heavier, when it is cooled.[2]) The lighter air tends to rise, the heavier air to sink. As the lighter air rises, the heavier, cooler, moister air from the ocean moves in under it. This brings rain and changing weather to the land.

When you climb a mountain or fly upward in an airplane, the atmospheric pressure is reduced. You put more and more of the air below you as you go up. There is less and less air above you to press down on you. At 30,000 feet [9,144 m (meters)] above the earth's surface the air pressure is less than 5 psi [0.352 kg/cm²]. At 100,000 feet [30,480 m] the air pressure is only about 0.15 psi [0.011 kg/cm²]. You could not live at this height unless you wore a space suit which maintained a pressure around you and kept you supplied with enough air to breathe.

⊘ **1-6 Vacuum** Vacuum is the absence of air or other matter. When astronauts travel hundreds of miles or more into space, they find no atmosphere at all. No air. At this distance from the earth there are only a very few particles of air, widely scattered. This is a vacuum.

But we do not need to leave the earth to find a vacuum. We can produce a vacuum anywhere on earth with a long glass tube closed at one end, plus a dish of mercury (a very heavy metal that is liquid at normal temperatures). To produce a vacuum, completely fill the tube with mercury and close the top end tightly. Next, turn the tube upside down, put the end into the dish of mercury, and open this end. When you open the end in the dish, some of the mercury will run out of the tube, leaving the upper part of the tube empty (Fig. 1-3). Since this upper part of the tube is closed, no air can get in. The upper part of the tube contains nothing; that is, it contains a vacuum.

The device shown in Fig. 1-4 is a barometer; it can be used to measure atmospheric pressure. You might wonder why all the mercury doesn't run out of the tube when it is turned upside down. The reason is that atmospheric pressure holds some mercury up in the tube. The atmospheric pressure presses down on the surface of the mercury in the dish, and this push, transmitted through the mercury, holds the mercury up in the tube (Fig. 1-4). You could compare this to putting your hand, palm down, into soft mud. As you push down on the mud, the downward pressure causes some of the mud to squirt up between your fingers.

The barometer indicates atmospheric pressure. When air pressure goes up, the air pushes harder on the mercury and forces it higher up in the tube. But when air pressure goes down, there is a weaker push and the mercury settles to a lower level in the tube. The barometer can foretell the coming of a

[2] A cubic foot of air at 100°F weighs 0.070 lb. A cubic foot of air at 0°F weighs 0.085 lb. As the air is cooled, it contracts, so there is more air in a cubic foot (actually 0.015 lb more).

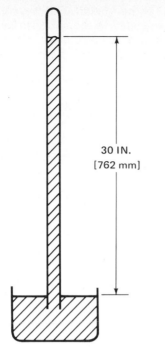

Fig. 1-3. Barometer. The mercury in the tube will stand at about 30 inches [762 mm] above the surface of the mercury in the dish when atmospheric pressure is 15 psi [1.05 kg/cm²].

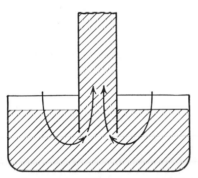

Fig. 1-4. In a barometer, the pressure of the air acts on the surface of the mercury and through the mercury to hold the mercury up in the sealed tube.

storm. A storm is normally accompanied by a lower atmospheric pressure brought on by the presence of heated, lighter, air. Thus, when the barometer "drops" (mercury goes down in the tube), chances are a storm is coming.

⊘ **1-7 Vacuum Machines** The barometer is one "machine" for producing vacuum. There are a great many devices (pumps of one sort or another) that produce vacuum. The automobile engine is, in one sense, a vacuum machine. A partial vacuum is created in the engine cylinders by the downward-moving pistons during intake strokes. As the pistons move down, atmospheric pressure pushes air toward the vacuum. The air passes through the carburetor, where it picks up a charge of fuel, and this air-fuel mixture moves on to the cylinders. Thus, the vac-

uum causes a charge of air-fuel mixture to be delivered to the engine cylinders during the intake stroke.[3]

While we are talking about the automobile engine, we might add that the engine is also a compression machine. After the intake stroke, the piston moves up during the compression stroke and compresses the air-fuel mixture to one-eighth or less of its original volume.

⊘ **1-8 Characteristics of Air** We have seen that air can expand, or thin out. We have also noted that air can be compressed, or packed into a smaller volume. Air is a mixture of several gases: about 20 percent is oxygen, and the rest is mostly nitrogen. Air, or any gas or mixture of gases, is composed of tiny particles called *molecules* (combinations of atoms). These atoms or molecules are so tiny that there are literally billions upon billions of them in a cubic inch of gas. For example, in a cubic inch [16.387 cm³ (cubic centimeters)] of hydrogen gas at atmospheric pressure and 32 degrees Fahrenheit [0°C (degrees Celsius, or centigrade)], there are about 880 billion billion atoms (Fig. 1-5). That is, 880,000,000,000,000,000,000 atoms. Yet, the cubic inch of hydrogen is almost empty because the atoms are so very tiny.

We can prove that the area is almost empty by increasing the pressure on the gas. Suppose we put the cubic inch of hydrogen gas in a rigid box and fitted a square piston to the box. Then suppose we pushed down on the piston with a force of 150 pounds [68.04 kg] (Fig. 1-6). We would find that the pressure would squeeze the atoms of hydrogen closer together so that the volume would be reduced to 1/10 cubic inch [1.6 cm³]. We would also find that the temperature of the hydrogen gas would increase. Why do these things happen?

⊘ **1-9 Pressure** The atoms or molecules of gas are in constant motion. They have a relatively large space to move around in, so they dart about in a constant turmoil. If the gas is enclosed in a con-

[3] See *Automotive Engines* for a discussion of the way the engine operates.

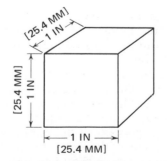

Fig. 1-5. One cubic inch of hydrogen gas at atmospheric pressure (15 psi) [1.05 kg/cm²] and at 32 degrees Fahrenheit [0°C] contains about 880 billion billion atoms.

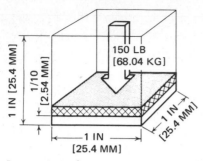

Fig. 1-6. Increasing the pressure to 150 lb (pounds) [68.04 kg] decreases the volume of gas to $\frac{1}{10}$ in³ [1.6 cm³].

tainer, molecules of the gas are constantly bumping into the inner sides of the container. There will be billions of these bumps every second in our cubic-inch container (Fig. 1-5). These billions of bumps—this constant bombardment—add up to the total push we know as *pressure*. Now, when we compress the cubic inch into one-tenth of a cubic inch (Fig. 1-6), we have squeezed the gas molecules much closer together. Since the molecules are closer together and have much less room to move around in, they bump into the walls of the container more often. In fact, they bump into the walls 10 times as often. This means that the pressure has increased by 10 times as much. We started with a pressure of 15 psi [1.055 kg/cm²] (Fig. 1-5) and increased it 10 times—to 150 psi [10.55 kg/cm²] (Fig. 1-6).

⊘ **1-10 Heat** We have noted that increasing the pressure on a gas decreases its volume. Increasing the pressure on a gas also increases its temperature. For actually, temperature, or heat, is nothing more than speed of molecular motion. When the molecules move fast, the object is hot. When the molecules move slowly, the object is cold. In a piece of ice, the molecules are moving so slowly that they all more or less hang together. The ice remains a solid. But if the ice is heated, it melts. The molecules begin to move a little faster, and they can no longer hang together to form a solid: the ice turns to water. If the water is heated, the molecules are set into even more rapid motion. Finally, they move so fast that they begin to jump clear of the liquid: the water boils, or turns to vapor.

When the cubic inch of gas is compressed to one-tenth of a cubic inch [1.6 cm³], not only are the molecules pushed more closely together but they are set into more rapid motion. This is because of the more frequent collisions between molecules and more frequent collisions with the walls of the container. Since the gas molecules are in more rapid motion, the gas is hotter. The rapidly moving gas molecules, as they bombard the walls of the container, set the molecules of the container into more rapid motion; that is, the container is heated. Outside molecules of air, as they pass the container or bump into the outer walls of the container, are then set into more rapid motion by the container mole-

cules. Soon, the heat produced by compressing the gas has all dissipated to the container walls and then to the outside air.

⊘ **1-11 Pressure Increase with Heat** If we heat a container of air, we find that the pressure inside the container increases. Suppose we start again with a cubic inch of air (Fig. 1-5). At 32 degrees Fahrenheit [0°C], this cubic inch of air is at atmospheric pressure, or 15 psi [1.05 kg/cm²]. If we heated the container of gas to 100 degrees Fahrenheit [37.8°C], we would find that its pressure would increase to about 17 psi [1.20 kg/cm²]. In heating the gas, we have caused the molecules to move faster. They bombard the walls of the container harder and more often, thus registering a higher push, or pressure.

Check Your Progress[4]

Progress Quiz 1-1 The following questions have two definite purposes. First, they give you a chance to review what you learned as you read the past few pages. Second, they give you a chance to check up on yourself to find out how well you are remembering what you read. It is much like the battery technician with a battery on charge. The technician checks periodically to see how the battery is taking the charge. Likewise, there are quizzes throughout the book that let you check yourself to see how you are taking your "charge" of information. If you don't do too well on the following checkup, don't be discouraged. It simply means that you should review the past few pages. Most good students reread their "lessons" several times to make sure they remember the important points covered.

Completing the Sentences The sentences below are incomplete. After each sentence there are several words or phrases, only one of which will correctly complete the sentence. Write each sentence in your notebook, selecting the proper word or phrase to complete it correctly.

1. The attractive force that all objects have toward each other is called: (*a*) pressure, (*b*) vacuum, (*c*) gravity, (*d*) heat.
2. At sea level and at average temperature, 1 ft³ [0.0283 m³] of air weighs about: (*a*) 0.008 lb [0.0036 kg], (*b*) 0.08 lb [0.036 kg], (*c*) 0.8 lb [0.36 kg], (*d*) 8.0 lb [3.6 kg], (*e*) 15 lb [6.81 kg].
3. At sea level and at average temperature, the atmospheric pressure is about: (*a*) 0.08 psi [0.006 kg/cm²], (*b*) 0.15 psi [0.0105 kg/cm²], (*c*) 1.5 psi [0.105 kg/cm²], (*d*) 15.0 psi [1.05 kg/cm²].
4. At sea level and at average temperature, the atmospheric pressure is about: (*a*) 2 psf, (*b*) 15 psf, (*c*) 2,160 psf.
5. As air is heated, it tends to: (*a*) contract and be-

[4] Answers to questions in the quizzes and chapter checkups are given at the end of the book.

come heavier, (b) expand and become lighter, (c) expand and become heavier.

6. Absence of air or other matter is called: (a) gravity, (b) vacuum, (c) pressure, (d) volume.

7. When the pressure on a gas is increased, the gas is: (a) cooled, (b) expanded, (c) compressed, (d) atomized.

8. The pressure of a gas against the walls of a container is the result of: (a) gravity, (b) vacuum, (c) bombardment of molecules, (d) contraction.

9. When the pressure on a gas is increased so that the gas is compressed, it is also: (a) cooled, (b) heated, (c) expanded.

10. If we heated a sealed container of gas, we would find that the pressure inside the container: (a) is reduced, (b) is increased, (c) does not change.

Hydraulics

⊘ **1-12 Meaning of Hydraulics** In its simplest sense, hydraulics has to do with certain characteristics of liquids, such as water and oil. Our special interest, so far as the automotive chassis is concerned, is related to the effects of pressure applied to a liquid. This is called *hydraulic pressure*. Hydraulic pressure is used in the brake system, in shock absorbers, and in power-steering systems. It is also used in automatic transmissions (control circuits, fluid coupling, and torque converter), in engines (hydraulic valve lifters, oil pump, fuel pump, water pump), and so on.

⊘ **1-13 Incompressibility of Liquids** We have seen that increasing the pressure on a gas will compress the gas into a smaller volume (Fig. 1-6). However, increasing the pressure on a liquid will not reduce its volume; its volume stays the same even though the pressure on it is greatly increased (Fig. 1-7). A liquid cannot be compressed into a smaller volume; it is incompressible. This might be explained as follows. The molecules of the liquid are rather close together—as opposed to a gas, in which the molecules are relatively far apart. Putting pressure on a gas can "squeeze out" some of the space between the molecules. But in a liquid, there is no extra space that can be "squeezed out" by the application of pressure. The molecules are already as close together as we can get them; putting pressure on the molecules of a liquid will not force them closer together.

⊘ **1-14 Transmission of Motion by Liquid** Since liquid is not compressible, it can transmit motion. For example, Fig. 1-8 shows two pistons in a cylinder, with a liquid separating them. When the applying piston is pushed into the cylinder 8 inches [203.2 mm], as shown, the output piston will be pushed along in the cylinder for the same distance, or 8 inches [203.2 mm]. In this illustration, you could

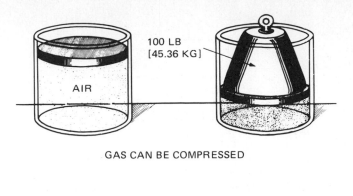

GAS CAN BE COMPRESSED

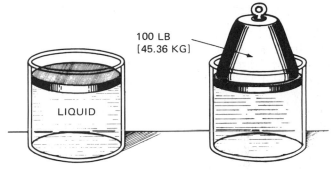

LIQUID CANNOT BE COMPRESSED

Fig. 1-7. Gas can be compressed when pressure is applied. However, liquid cannot be compressed when pressure is applied. (*Pontiac Motor Division of General Motors Corporation*)

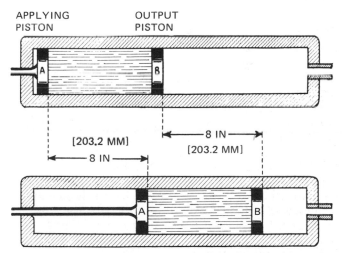

Fig. 1-8. Motion can be transmitted by liquid. When the applying piston is moved 8 inches [203.2 mm] in the cylinder, the output piston is also moved 8 inches [203.2 mm]. (*Pontiac Motor Division of General Motors Corporation*)

substitute a solid connecting rod between piston A and piston B and get exactly the same effect.

The motion can also be transmitted from one cylinder to another by a tube, or pipe (Fig. 1-9). Here, the applying piston is in cylinder A, and the output piston is in cylinder B. As the applying piston is moved into its cylinder, liquid is forced from cylinder A into cylinder B. This causes the output piston

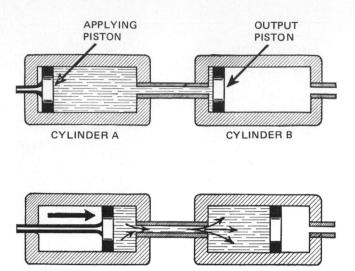

Fig. 1-9. Motion can be transmitted through a tube from one cylinder to another by liquid, or hydraulic, pressure. (*Pontiac Motor Division of General Motors Corporation*)

to be moved in its cylinder. If both pistons are of the same size, the output piston will move the same distance as the applying piston.

⊘ **1-15 Transmission of Pressure by Liquid** The pressure that is applied to a liquid is transmitted by the liquid in all directions and to every part of the liquid. For example, in Fig. 1-10 a piston with an area of 1 square inch is shown applying a force of 100 pounds. This is a force of 100 psi. If we attached pressure gauges to various parts of the system, as shown, to measure the pressure on the liquid, we would find the pressure on the liquid the same at all points. Note that regardless of the point where the pressure measurement is taken, we get the same reading.

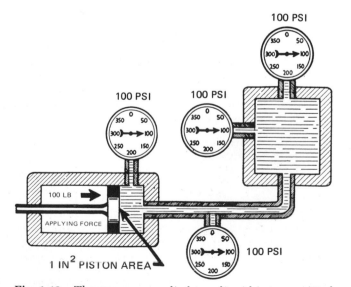

Fig. 1-10. The pressure applied to a liquid is transmitted equally in all directions. (*Pontiac Motor Division of General Motors Corporation*)

The pressure is usually referred to in terms of pounds per square inch (psi) or kilograms per square centimeter [kg/cm²] in the metric system. Thus, when a piston is applying pressure to a liquid, we can calculate the pressure in pounds per square inch if we know the force being applied by the piston and the area of the piston in square inches. For instance, in Fig. 1-11, when a 1 square inch piston applies a force of 100 pounds, the pressure on the liquid is 100 psi. But if the area of the piston is 2 square inches and the piston is applying a force of 100 pounds, the pressure on the liquid is only 50 psi. That is, each square inch of the piston is applying only 50 pounds. So the psi is determined by dividing the applied force by the area of the piston in square inches.

When we have an input-output system (Fig. 1-12), we can determine the force applied to any output piston by multiplying the pressure in psi by the area of the output piston in square inches. For example, the pressure shown in Fig. 1-12 is 100 psi. The output piston at the left has an area of 0.5 square inch. Thus, the output force on this piston is 100 × 0.5, or 50 pounds. The center output piston has an area of 1 square inch, and its output force is therefore 100 pounds. The right-hand output piston has an area of 2 square inches, and its output force is therefore 200 pounds (100 × 2). If the area of the output piston were 500 square inches, the output force, with 100 psi applied, would be 50,000 pounds. You can see that hydraulic pressure can be used to apply tremendous loads by making the output piston much larger than the input piston. In big presses used in manufacturing automotive and airplane parts, pressures of hundreds of thousands of pounds are produced by this means.

Friction and Lubrication

⊘ **1-16 Friction** Friction is the resistance to motion between two objects in contact with each other. Friction prevents one object from sliding on another. In the automobile, many parts are sliding on or rota-

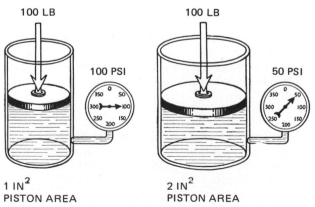

Fig. 1-11. Pressure in the system is determined by dividing the applying force by the area of the applying piston. (*Pontiac Motor Division of General Motors Corporation*)

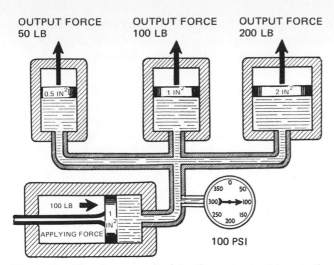

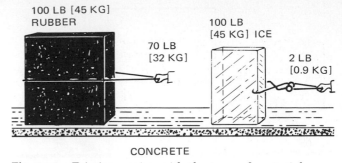

CONCRETE

Fig. 1-14. Friction varies with the type of material.

Fig. 1-12. The force applied to the output piston is the pressure in the system (in pounds per square inch [kg/cm²]) times the area of the output piston. (*Pontiac Motor Division of General Motors Corporation*)

ting within other parts. Thus, some of the power developed by the engine must be used up in overcoming this friction. This power is, in effect, wasted because it does not contribute to moving the car. On the other hand, friction is very valuable in the car brakes; here the friction between brake drums and brake shoes slows or stops the car when the brakes are applied.

⊘ **1-17 Characteristics of Friction** Friction varies with the pressure applied between the sliding surfaces, the roughness of the surfaces, and the material of which the surfaces are made. Suppose, for example, that a platform with its load weighs 100 pounds [45 kg] and that it takes 50 pounds [23 kg] of pull to move it along the floor (Fig. 1-13). If you reduced the load so that the platform with load weighed only 10 pounds [4.5 kg], you would find that it required only 5 pounds [2.3 kg] pull to move it along the floor. *Friction varies with the load.*

If you smoothed off the floor and the sliding part of the platform with sandpaper, you would find that it would require less pull to move the platform on the floor. *Friction varies with the roughness of the surfaces.*

Friction varies with the type of material, too. For example, if you dragged a 100 pound [45 kg] bale of rubber across a concrete floor, you might find that it required a pull of 70 pounds [32 kg] (Fig. 1-14). But to drag a 100-pound [45 kg] cake of ice across the same floor might require a pull of only 2 pounds [0.9 kg].

⊘ **1-18 Coefficient of Friction** Engineers need a more exact way to express frictional differences than to say that one surface has a high friction and another surface a low friction. They therefore developed the idea of the *coefficient of friction.* This is simply a figure that accurately states how much friction there is between two surfaces. For example, wood dragged on cast iron has a fairly high friction. A 100-pound [45.3 kg] block of wood might require a pull of 50 pounds [22.7 kg] to be moved over a cast-iron slab (Fig. 1-15). To state this in terms of the coefficient of friction, you divide the pull by the weight, or 50 divided by 100. This gives a coefficient of 0.5. Knowing the coefficient, you could then determine how much force would be required to pull a wood block of any weight over cast iron. All you have to do is multiply the weight by the coefficient. For instance, a 250-pound block would require a pull of 125 pounds (250 × 0.5 = 125).

The other example in Fig. 1-15 is that of a 100-pound [45.3 kg] block of bronze being dragged over a cast-iron slab. Here, the pull required is 20 pounds [9.1 kg]. This gives a coefficient of friction of 0.2. If the bronze block weighed 40 pounds [18.1 kg], you could determine how much pull would be required to move it, knowing the coefficient of friction. It would be 40 × 0.2, or 8 pounds [3.6 kg].

⊘ **1-19 Friction of Rest and Motion** More force is required to start an object than to keep it in motion (Fig. 1-16). In the example shown, two men are needed to get the object started, but once it is started, one man alone can keep it moving. Thus, the friction of an object at rest is greater than the friction of an object in motion.

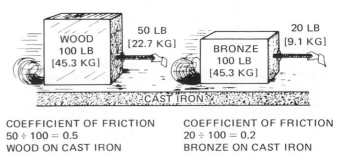

COEFFICIENT OF FRICTION
50 ÷ 100 = 0.5
WOOD ON CAST IRON

COEFFICIENT OF FRICTION
20 ÷ 100 = 0.2
BRONZE ON CAST IRON

Fig. 1-15. The coefficient of friction is the force required to move an object divided by the weight of the object.

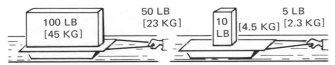

Fig. 1-13. Friction varies with the load applied between the sliding surfaces.

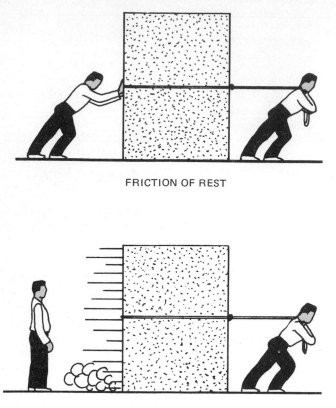

FRICTION OF REST

FRICTION OF MOTION

Fig. 1-16. Friction of rest is greater than friction of motion. In the example shown, it takes two men to overcome the friction of rest. But one man can keep the object moving, by overcoming the friction of motion.

Engineers do not usually refer to these two kinds of friction as friction of rest and friction of motion. Instead, they call them *static friction* and *kinetic friction*. "Static" means at rest; "kinetic" means in motion, or moving. Thus, static friction is friction of rest, and kinetic friction is friction of motion.

⊘ **1-20 Causes of Friction**   One explanation of friction is that it is caused by surface irregularities. The high spots on the two surfaces in contact tend to catch on each other and hinder the motion between the two objects. When the surfaces are smoothed off, the high spots are cut down and there is less tendency for them to catch on each other; friction is reduced. On the other hand, if the force between the two surfaces is increased, the high spots are pressed harder against each other, so the friction is increased.

The fact that static friction is greater than kinetic friction can be explained along the same lines. When the surfaces are at rest, the force or weight between them tends to press the high spots of one surface into the other surface. Then it takes considerable pull to move all the high spots of one surface up and out of the low spots of the other surface. But once moving, the high spots do not have a chance

to "settle" into the opposing surface; less force is required to keep the surfaces moving. That is, kinetic friction is less than static friction.

⊘ **1-21 Friction in the Car Brakes**   We have mentioned that friction is used in the car brake system. The friction between the brake drums and brake shoes slows or stops the car. This friction slows the rotation of the wheels, and then friction between the tires and road slows the motion of the car. Note that it is the friction between the tires and road that results in the car's stopping. That being the case, would the car stop more quickly if the wheels were locked (so that the tires skidded on the road)? The answer is that the car would not. If the brakes are applied so hard that the wheels lock, the friction between the tires and road is kinetic friction (friction of motion as the tires skid on road). When the brakes are applied a little less hard, so the wheels are permitted to continue rotating, the friction between the tires and road is static friction. The tire surface is not skidding on the road but is rolling on it. Since this produces static friction between the road and tires, there is considerably greater braking effect. The car will stop more quickly if the brakes are applied just hard enough to get maximum static friction between the tires and road. If the brakes are applied harder than this, the wheels will lock, the tires will slide, and the lower kinetic friction will result.

⊘ **1-22 Classes of Friction**   Up to now, we have been discussing *dry* friction, or the friction between two dry surfaces. There are two other classes of friction: greasy friction and viscous friction. The latter two are the ones we find most often in the moving parts of the automobile.
1. *GREASY FRICTION*   If we thinly coat the moving surfaces of two objects with grease or oil, we find that the friction is greatly reduced. It is assumed that this thin coat tends to fill in the low spots of the surfaces. Therefore, the surface irregularities have less tendency to catch on each other. However, high spots will still catch and wear as the two surfaces move over each other. In automobile engines, greasy friction may occur when starting. At this time, most of the lubricating oil has drained away from bearings, piston rings, and cylinder walls. Thus, when these surfaces first start to slide over each other, there is only a thin film to protect them against wear. Of course, the lubricating system quickly starts to pump oil to the moving surfaces to provide additional protective lubrication.
2. *VISCOUS FRICTION*   "Viscosity" refers to the tendency of liquids, such as oil, to resist flowing. A heavy oil is thicker, or more viscous, than a light oil. The heavy oil flows more slowly (has higher viscosity, or higher resistance to flowing). Viscous friction is the friction, or resistance to motion, between adjacent layers of liquid. As applied to ma-

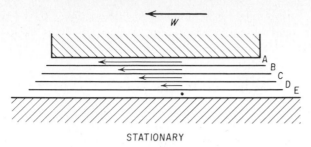

Fig. 1-17. Viscous friction is the friction between layers of liquid moving at different speeds. In the illustration, viscous friction is the friction between layers A, B, C, D, and E. W represents a moving object.

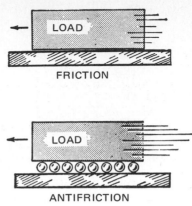

Fig. 1-18. Graphic representation of friction and antifriction bearings.

chines, viscous friction occurs during relative motion between two lubricated surfaces (see Fig. 1-17). This figure illustrates, in greatly exaggerated view, an object W moving over a stationary object, the two being separated by lubricating oil. The oil is shown in five layers, A to E, for simplicity.

Layer A adheres to the moving object W and moves at the same speed as W (as indicated by the arrow). A layer of oil E adheres to the stationary object and is therefore stationary. Thus, there must be relative motion between the layers of oil A and E. This can be pictured as a slippage between many layers of oil between A and E. The nearer a layer is to the stationary layer E, the less it moves. This is shown by the progressively shorter arrows in layers B, C, and D. There is slippage between these layers. But there is resistance to this slippage, and this is called *viscous friction.*

⊘ **1-23 Friction and Wear** When dry or greasy friction exists, the moving parts are in contact with each other, as we mentioned. This means that the high spots are interfering with each other. They catch on each other, and particles of the material are torn off. In other words, wear takes place. These tiny particles then add to the wear by scratching and gouging the moving surfaces. Soon, the roughness of the surfaces is increased, and wear goes on at a progressively swifter pace. To prevent this sort of wear, moving parts in machines are covered with coatings of oil (or grease). The oil holds the moving surfaces apart so that only viscous friction results; wear is kept to a minimum.

⊘ **1-24 Bearings** Various devices, called *bearings,* are used to support the moving parts in machines and at the same time supply the moving parts with lubricating oil. Machine bearings are classified as either friction bearings or antifriction bearings. These two names are somewhat misleading, since they seem to indicate that one type has friction while the other has not. Actually, the friction bearing does have greater friction, but both are low-friction devices. Figure 1-18 shows graphically the difference between friction and antifriction bear-

ings. In the friction bearing, one body slides over another; the load is supported on layers of oil, as shown in Fig. 1-17. In the antifriction bearing, the surfaces are separated by balls or rollers, so there is rolling friction between the two surfaces and the balls or rollers.

⊘ **1-25 Friction Bearings** Friction bearings have sliding contact between the moving surfaces. The load is supported by layers of oil. There are three types of friction bearing (Fig. 1-19): journal, guide, and thrust. The journal type is symbolized by two hands holding a turning shaft, as shown in the upper left. The hands support the shaft just as the surrounding bearing supports a shaft journal in an engine. Crankshaft, connecting rod, camshaft, and piston-pin bearings are but a few examples of this type of bearing used in the engine.

The bearing surface between the piston and cylinder wall is of the guide type (center, Fig. 1-19).

The thrust type of friction bearing checks endwise movement of the shaft (right, Fig. 1-19). The flats on the ends of the bearing are parallel to flats at the ends of the shaft journal. As the shaft attempts to move endwise, the flats, or thrust faces, prevent it.

⊘ **1-26 Antifriction Bearings** Figure 1-20 shows three types of antifriction bearing: the ball, roller, and tapered roller. There are other types, including a spherical roller, thrust, and double-row ball. But all operate on the same principle of interposing a rolling object between the moving surfaces.

The ball bearing has an inner and an outer race in which grooves have been cut. Balls roll in these two race grooves and are held apart by a spacer assembly. When one race is held stationary (for instance, by mounting it in a housing) and the other rotates (as it might when on a shaft), the balls roll in the two races to permit low-friction rotation.

The roller bearing is similar to the ball bearing except that it has rollers, either plain or tapered. The rollers roll between the inner and the outer races.

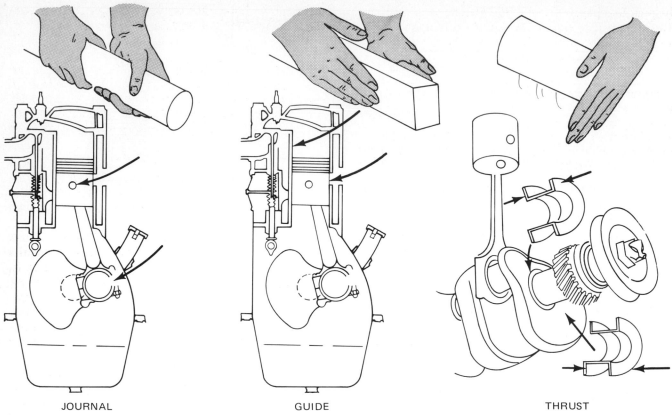

JOURNAL   GUIDE   THRUST

Fig. 1-19. Three types of friction-bearing surfaces in an automobile engine.

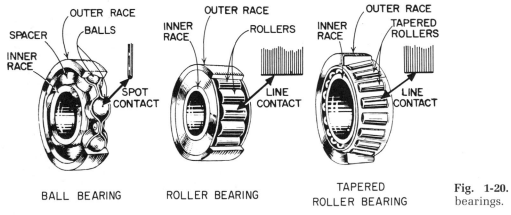

BALL BEARING   ROLLER BEARING   TAPERED ROLLER BEARING

Fig. 1-20. Antifriction bearings.

In the ball bearing, there is spot contact between the balls and races. In the roller bearing, there is line contact between the rollers and races.

Antifriction bearings are usually lubricated by grease, which is essentially oil mixed with a solidifying agent (called *soap*). The solidifying agent does not contribute directly to the lubricating of the balls or rollers. But it does hold the oil in the bearing so that the bearing receives proper lubrication.

Check Your Progress

Progress Quiz 1-2 Here is your chance to check up on yourself once again to find out how well the facts you have been reading have stuck with you. The past few pages have covered some principles that are directly related to the operation of certain chassis units. Understanding these principles will help you understand how the chassis units work. Reread the past few pages if any of the questions that follow stump you. Remember that most good students re-read their lessons several times to make sure they have memorized the important facts.

Completing the Sentences   The sentences below are incomplete. After each sentence there are several words or phrases, only one of which will correctly complete the sentence. Write each sentence in your notebook, selecting the proper word or phrase to complete it correctly.

1. Air is compressible but liquid is not because, in the liquid, the molecules are about as close together as: (*a*) in the air, (*b*) they can be, (*c*) in a vacuum.
2. Since it is incompressible, liquid can be used to transmit: (*a*) pressure and motion, (*b*) pressure and friction, (*c*) static and kinetic friction.
3. When a pressure is applied to a liquid, it will be found that the pressure: (*a*) increases with distance, (*b*) is reduced with distance, (*c*) is the same at all points.
4. The resistance to motion between two objects in contact with each other is called: (*a*) friction, (*b*) braking, (*c*) coefficient, (*d*) static friction.
5. Friction between two surfaces varies with the: (*a*) thickness and pressure; (*b*) pressure, weight, and pull; (*c*) pressure, roughness, and material.
6. The pull required to move an object, divided by the weight of the object, is called: (*a*) static friction, (*b*) kinetic friction, (*c*) coefficient of friction.
7. Two kinds of friction are: (*a*) at rest and static, (*b*) moving and kinetic, (*c*) static and kinetic.
8. Three classes of friction are: (*a*) dry, greasy, and viscous; (*b*) greasy, thin, and thick; (*c*) dry, wet, and viscous.
9. In a comparison of friction and antifriction bearings, the one with the lower friction is the: (*a*) friction bearing, (*b*) antifriction bearing.
10. Two types of antifriction bearings are: (*a*) guide and thrust, (*b*) ball and sleeve, (*c*) ball and roller.

CHAPTER 1 CHECKUP

NOTE: Since the following is a chapter review test, you should review the chapter before taking it.

You have completed a chapter in the book and have taken an important step forward into a better future. The chapter you have just finished may seem somewhat abstract and less interesting than the following chapters that deal with specific chassis units. But the general principles we have been discussing are important for you to know. When you know them, you will find you can answer many puzzling questions about how and why the chassis units perform as they do. The following test will help you to review, and remember, the important facts you have just read in the chapter. Write your answers in your notebook. The act of writing down the answers is another aid to your memory.

Completing the Sentences   The sentences below are incomplete. After each sentence there are several words or phrases, only one of which will correctly complete the sentence. Write each sentence in your notebook, selecting the proper word or phrase to complete it correctly.

1. Atmospheric pressure results from: (*a*) absence of vacuum, (*b*) compression of gas, (*c*) gravity.
2. As a solid, a liquid, or a gas is heated, its molecules: (*a*) move faster, (*b*) stop moving, (*c*) move slower.
3. Since the pressure in a closed container of gas results from the bombardment of the container walls by the gas molecules, crowding more molecules in a container (by compressing the gas) will increase the: (*a*) pressure, (*b*) vacuum, (*c*) gravity, (*d*) volume.
4. In view of the statement in the previous question, increasing the speed of the molecules—by heating the gas—will increase the: (*a*) pressure, (*b*) vacuum, (*c*) gravity.
5. Because in a liquid, there is no extra space between the molecules that can be squeezed out, liquid is: (*a*) compressible, (*b*) incompressible, (*c*) incompatible, (*d*) solid.
6. The pressure applied to a liquid by a piston, in pounds per square inch, is the force on the piston divided by the: (*a*) distance it moves, (*b*) piston area in square inches, (*c*) piston diameter.
7. Comparing the two kinds of friction (static and kinetic), other things being equal, static friction is always: (*a*) less, (*b*) equal, (*c*) greater.
8. When you apply the brakes on your car so hard that you lock the wheels so they do not turn (and the tires thus skid), the friction between the tires and road is: (*a*) static friction, (*b*) kinetic friction.
9. In a comparison of the three classes of friction, other things being equal, the class that offers the lowest friction is: (*a*) dry friction, (*b*) greasy friction, (*c*) viscous friction.
10. In comparing the actions of friction and antifriction bearings, you will note that the main difference is between: (*a*) sliding and slipping contact, (*b*) spot and line contact, (*c*) sliding and rolling contact.

Problems   Work out the following problems in your notebook.

1. If the air pressure is 20 psi, how much pressure is there per square foot?
2. A piston with an area of 5 in^2 is forced into a cylinder filled with liquid with a force of 100 lb. What is the pressure in psi?
3. A piston with an area of $\frac{1}{2}$ in^2 is forced into a cylinder filled with liquid with a force of 100 lb. What is the pressure in psi?
4. A pressure of 200 psi is applied to an output pis-

ton which has an area of 3 in². What is the force on the output piston?

5. A pressure of 200 psi is applied to an output piston which has an area of $\frac{1}{2}$ in². What is the force on the output piston?

6. An input piston of $\frac{1}{2}$ in² area is forced into a liquid-filled cylinder with a force of 400 lb. An output piston in a connected cylinder has an area of 3 in². What is the force on the output piston?

7. The coefficient of friction between a certain type of brass and cast iron is 0.25. How much force would be required to pull a block of brass weighing 100 lb over a cast-iron slab?

8. It requires a force of 75 lb to move a block of wood weighing 150 lb across a metal slab. What is the coefficient of friction?

Definitions   In the following, you are asked to define certain terms. Write the definitions in your notebook, and then check your answers with the textbook.

1. Explain what atmospheric pressure is in terms of gravity; in terms of molecular motion.

2. Explain how the barometer works.
3. Why does increasing the temperature of the gas in a closed container increase the pressure?
4. In what way does a liquid differ from a gas, so far as compressibility is concerned?
5. Friction varies with what three conditions?
6. Give an explanation of the causes of friction.
7. List and explain the three classes of friction.

SUGGESTIONS FOR FURTHER STUDY

If you are interested in the basic principles discussed in the chapter, you may wish to study them further. Almost any modern high school physics textbook will give you much additional information on the principles covered in the chapter. Your local library probably has several physics textbooks you will find of interest. If you have a chance, you could talk over various points that may not be clear to you with your high school science or physics teacher. Teachers are always willing to help anyone who is really interested in gaining more knowledge.

chapter 2

CHASSIS FUNDAMENTALS

This chapter introduces the various components, or subassemblies, that make up the automobile. In effect, it establishes the relationship between these various parts and shows how they work together in the complete car. Later chapters describe the chassis components, explain how they operate, and tell how to service and repair them.

⊘ **2-1 Components of the Automobile** Before we begin our studies of the chassis units, we might take a quick look at the complete automobile. It is made up of five basic parts, or components:

1. The power plant or engine, which is the source of power that makes the car wheels rotate and the car move. (This includes the electric, fuel, cooling, and lubricating systems.)
2. The frame, which supports the engine, wheels, and body.
3. The power train, which carries the power from the engine to the car wheels and which consists of the clutch, transmission, propeller shaft, differential, and axles.
4. The car body.
5. The car body accessories, which include the heater, lights, radio, windshield wiper, convertible-top raiser, and so on

Figure 2-1 shows, in outline, the essential parts of an automobile. Figure 2-2 shows an automotive chassis. The chassis is made up of the engine, frame, power train, wheels, and steering and brake systems. Other books in the McGraw-Hill Automotive Technology Series (*Automotive Engines* and *Automotive Transmissions and Power Trains*) cover the engine and power-train components. The other chassis parts are covered in the pages that follow.

⊘ **2-2 Frame** The frame (Fig. 2-3) supports the engine, body, wheels, and power-train members. It is usually made of box, tubular, and channel members carefully shaped and then welded or riveted together. Cross members reinforce the frame and also support the engine and wheels. The frame is extremely rigid and strong so that it can withstand the shock blows, twists, vibrations, and other strains to which it is put on the road.

In recent years, automotive manufacturers have done many things to make their cars safer to drive. For example, the frame used in many cars has been redesigned so that it will help to absorb crash forces. If the frame absorbs part of the forces resulting from a front-end collision, these absorbed forces will not be carried to the passengers. This design has holes and notches which permit the front end of the frame to collapse during a front-end collision, as shown. As it collapses, it takes up part of the shock of the collision. For a comparison, think of hitting a brick wall with your bare fist, and then of hitting it with a boxing glove on. The glove padding will cushion the blow so it is much less of a shock to your fist.

A similar arrangement is used in the British Ford sports car (Fig. 2-4), which has a front end designed to collapse progressively if the car is involved in a front-end collision.

The engine is attached to the frame in three or four places. Noise and some vibration are inherent in engine operation. To prevent this noise and vibration from passing to the engine frame, and from there to the occupants of the car, the engine is insulated from the frame by some form of rubber pad or washer at each point of support. One type of engine mounting support is shown in Fig. 2-5. In this engine, there are two rubber mountings at the front, and a single, long, narrow, rubber mounting pad at the back. Engine mounting lugs are supported in the rubber, and the mounting bolts pass through these rubber mountings so that there is no metal-to-metal contact. As a result, the rubber absorbs vibration and engine noise so that they are not carried to the car frame.

⊘ **2-3 Springs** The car wheels are suspended on springs that support the weight of the vehicle (Figs. 2-6 and 2-7). The springs absorb road shock as the

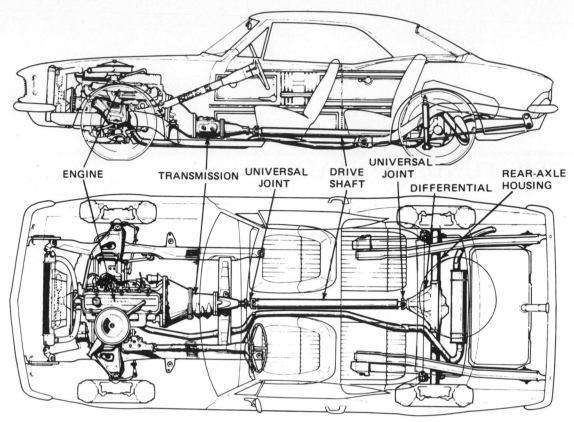

Fig. 2-1. Outline view of an automobile, showing essential parts. (*Chevrolet Motor Division of General Motors Corporation*)

Fig. 2-2. Chassis of a passenger car. The chassis contains the source of power, or engine; the frame, which supports the engine, wheels, and body; the power train, which carries the engine power to the rear wheels; and the steering and braking systems. (*Oldsmobile Division of General Motors Corporation*)

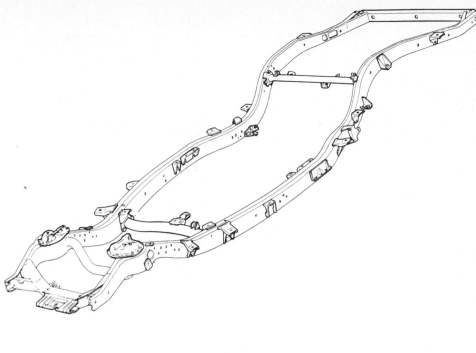

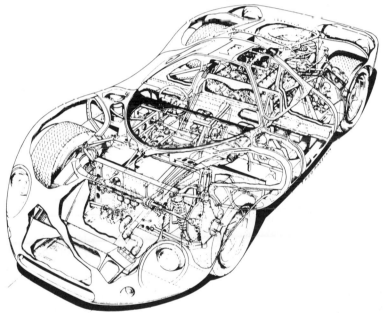

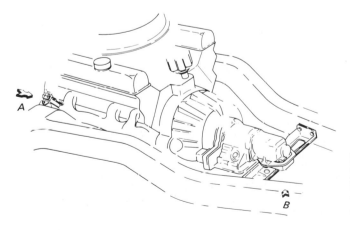

Fig. 2-3. Typical automobile frame. The frame curves upward at the rear (*to right*) to provide room for the rear springs. The frame narrows at the front (*to left*) to permit the front wheels to turn for steering. (*Ford Motor Company*)

Fig. 2-4. Mid-engine British Ford sports car. It has a front end designed to collapse progressively in case of a front-end collision. (*Ford Motor Company of England*)

Fig. 2-5. Engine supports, indicated by arrows. (*Buick Motor Division of General Motors Corporation*)

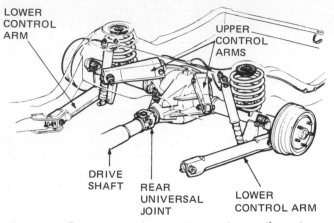

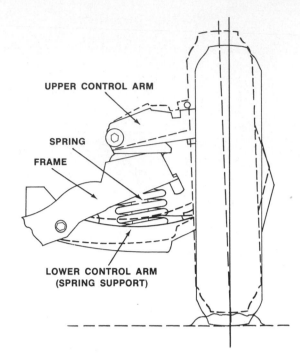

Fig. 2-6. Rear-suspension system using coil springs. (*Buick Motor Division of General Motors Corporation*)

wheels encounter holes or bumps and prevent, to a large extent, any consequent jarring action or up-and-down motion from being carried through the frame and body. Springs are coil type, leaf type, torsion bar, or air suspension. Figure 2-7 shows one of the coil springs used in a front-suspension system. The coil spring is a heavy steel coil. The weight of the frame and body puts an initial compression on the spring. The spring will further compress when the wheel passes over an obstruction in the road (Fig. 2-8). It will expand if the wheel encounters a hole in the road (Fig. 2-9).

The leaf spring has been made in a number of forms, but the one most commonly used is the semi-elliptical type (Figs. 2-10 and 2-11). The leaf spring is made up of a series of flat plates, or leaves, of graduated length, one on top of another. The spring assembly acts as a flexible beam and is usually fas-

Fig. 2-8. Front suspension at one wheel, showing the action as the wheel meets a bump in the road. Note how the upward movement of the wheel, shown in dashed lines, raises the lower control arm, causing the spring to compress.

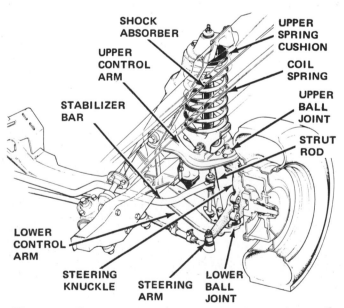

Fig. 2-7. Passenger-car front suspension using coil springs. The frame, wheel, and other components are partly cut away to show suspension parts. (*American Motors Corporation*)

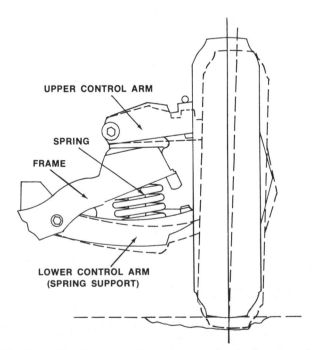

Fig. 2-9. Front suspension at one wheel, showing the action as the wheel meets a hole in the road. Note how the downward movement of the wheel, shown in dashed lines, lowers the lower control arm, permitting the spring to expand.

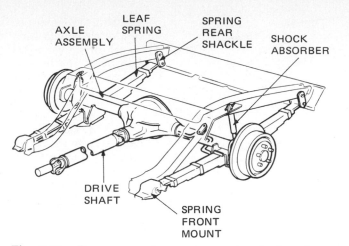

Fig. 2-10. Rear-suspension system using leaf springs. (*Chevrolet Motor Division of General Motors Corporation*)

tened at the two ends to the car frame and at the center to the wheel axle. Some cars have used only one leaf spring at the rear and one at the front, each spring supporting two wheels. With this design, the center of the spring is attached to the frame, and each end of the spring supports a wheel. The action is similar on all leaf springs. When the wheel encounters a bump, the spring bends upward to absorb the blow. When the wheel drops into a hole, the spring bends downward. Thus, the leaf spring does the same job as the coil spring in the vehicle.

The torsion-bar suspension system (Fig. 2-12) uses bars connected between the suspension or control arms and the frame. Movement of the wheels up and down twists the bars more or less to provide the springing action.

Springs are usually insulated mechanically from the frame by means of rubber bushings and pads to prevent road vibration from being transmitted to the frame and body.

⊘ 2-4 Shock Absorbers Springs alone cannot provide a satisfactorily smooth ride. Therefore, an addi-

tional device, called a *shock absorber,* is used with each spring. To understand why springs alone would not give smooth riding qualities, let us consider the action of a coil spring. The same actions would take place with a leaf type of spring. The spring is under an initial load provided by the car weight, and this gives the spring an original amount of compression. When the wheel passes over a bump, the spring becomes further compressed. After the bump is passed, the spring attempts to return to its original position. However, it overrides its original position and expands too much. This behavior causes the car frame to be thrown upward. Having expanded too much, the spring attempts to compress so that it will return to its original position; but in compressing it again overrides. In doing this the wheel may be raised clear of the road, and the car frame consequently drops. The result is an oscillating motion of the spring that causes the wheel to rebound, or bounce up and down several times after a bump has been encountered. If, in the meantime, another bump is encountered, a second series of reboundings will be started. On a bumpy road, and particularly in rounding a curve, the oscillations might be so serious as to cause the driver to lose control of the car.

Shock absorbers (Fig. 2-7) prevent these spring oscillations. Figure 2-13 shows one type of shock absorber in sectional view. This is the direct-acting, or telescope, shock absorber. One end of the shock absorber is attached to the frame, the other to the lower control arm (at front as shown in Fig. 2-7) or to the axle housing or spring (at rear, as shown in Figs. 2-6 and 2-10). Thus as a wheel moves up or down in relation to the frame, the shock absorber will shorten or lengthen (see Fig. 2-13). When the shock absorber shortens, the piston rod forces the piston down into the cylinder tube, thereby putting the fluid below the piston under high compression. The fluid is forced through small orifices, or openings in the piston, and into the upper part of the cylinder tube. On rebound, when the wheel moves downward after passing a bump or dropping into a hole in the road, the shock absorber is extended

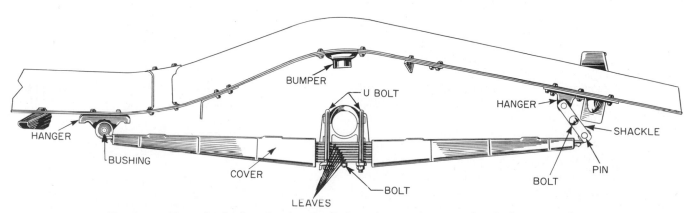

Fig. 2-11. How the leaf spring is attached to the car frame and axle housing. This is a rear spring. (*Chevrolet Motor Division of General Motors Corporation*)

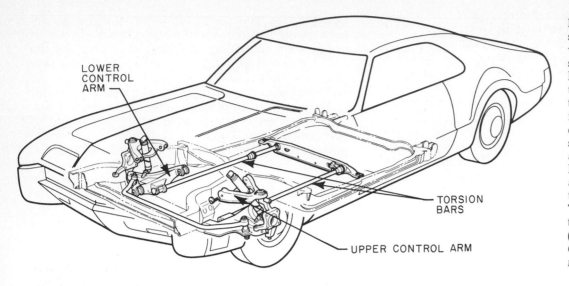

LOWER
CONTROL
ARM

TORSION
BARS

UPPER CONTROL ARM

Fig. 2-12. Front suspension of a car with front-wheel drive using torsion bars. The bars are locked to the frame at the rear. They are attached at the front to the inner ends of the lower control arms. The torsion bars twist varying amounts as varying loads are applied. This allows the front wheels to move up and down. The action is similar to that of other springs. (*Oldsmobile Division of General Motors Corporation*)

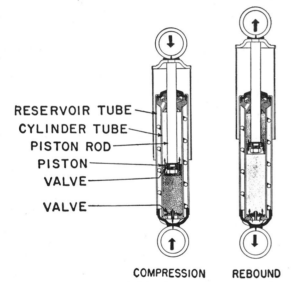

RESERVOIR TUBE
CYLINDER TUBE
PISTON ROD
PISTON
VALVE
VALVE

COMPRESSION   REBOUND

Fig. 2-13. Direct-acting shock absorber in sectional view, showing what happens during compression and rebound. Fluid movement is shown by arrows. Fluid under high pressure is shown darker than fluid not under pressure. (*Chrysler Corporation*)

(Fig. 2-13). As this happens, the piston moves into the upper part of the cylinder tube, thereby forcing fluid from the upper into the lower part of the tube.

As the fluid is forced in one direction or the other, it must pass through small orifices. This slows the motion of the piston and tends to place restraint on the spring action. In this way, the *shock* of the wheel meeting a bump or hole is *absorbed*. The orifices have spring-loaded valves which open varying amounts to allow varying speeds of fluid movement through the orifices. This permits rapid spring motion while still imposing a restraining action. At the same time, it prevents excessive pressure rise in the fluid that might otherwise occur when large bumps in the road are encountered by the wheels. Also, the restraining action prevents excessive oscillations of the wheel after it passes a bump or hole.

⊘ **2-5 Steering System**   To guide the car, some means of turning the front wheels is necessary so that the car can be pointed in the direction the driver wants to go. The steering wheel in front of the driver is linked by gears and levers to the front wheels for this purpose. A simplified drawing of a steering system is shown in Fig. 2-14. The front wheels are supported on pivots so that they can be swung to the left or right. They are attached by steering-knuckle arms to tie rods. The tie rods are, in turn, attached to a pitman arm. As the steering wheel is turned in one direction or the other, gearing in the steering-gear assembly causes the end of the pitman arm to swing to the left or right. This movement is carried by the tie rods to the steering-knuckle arms, and wheels, causing them to swing to the left or right.

Various arrangements of linkage are used. Although they are considerably different in general arrangement, all operate basically in the same manner. These linkage arrangements will be explained in more detail in the following paragraphs and in Chaps. 5 and 7.

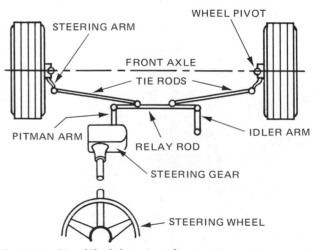

WHEEL PIVOT
STEERING ARM
FRONT AXLE
TIE RODS
PITMAN ARM
IDLER ARM
RELAY ROD
STEERING GEAR
STEERING WHEEL

Fig. 2-14. Simplified drawing of a steering system as seen from above.

Figure 2-15 shows, in cutaway view, a steering-gear assembly. The steering shaft has a special sort of worm gear on its lower end. Meshing with the teeth of this worm gear is a special gear called a *sector*. The sector is attached to one end of a shaft. The other end of the shaft carries the pitman arm. When the steering wheel is turned, the worm on the steering shaft rotates. This causes the sector to move toward one end or the other of the worm. The sector movement causes the sector shaft to rotate, and this rotary motion is carried to the pitman arm, causing it to swing to the left or right, as already described.

Most steering systems use a worm gear on the lower end of the steering shaft. But there are several types of devices on the pitman-arm shaft. Some steering gears use studs that ride between the worm-gear teeth; others use a half nut, a plain gear, ball bearings, and so on. A different arrangement uses a pinion on the end of the steering shaft. The pinion is meshed with a rack which moves to the right or left as the shaft and pinion turn to provide the steering action. In addition, several devices that use hydraulic pressure have been developed to assist in steering. These are called *power-steering* devices, and they take most of the effort out of steering; hydraulic pressure supplies most of the effort. Steering and power-steering mechanisms are discussed in detail in the chapters on steering systems.

2-6 Brakes Brakes are necessary to slow or stop the car. Practically all cars use hydraulic brakes (which operate by applying pressure to a fluid). A typical hydraulic brake system is shown in Fig. 2-16. Most modern brake systems have a fluid-filled cylinder, called the *master cylinder,* containing two sepa-

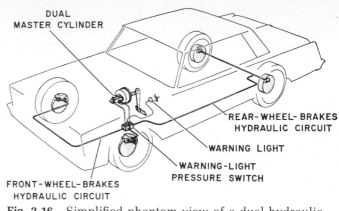

Fig. 2-16. Simplified phantom view of a dual hydraulic-brake system.

rate sections. There is a piston in each section, and both pistons are connected to a brake pedal in the driver's compartment. When the brake pedal is pushed by the driver, the two pistons move in the two sections of the master cylinder. This forces brake fluid out and through the brake lines, or tubes, to the brake mechanisms at the wheels. In a typical system, the brake fluid from one section of the master cylinder goes to the two front-wheel brakes. The brake fluid from the other section goes to the two rear-wheel brakes. The purpose of having two sections is that, if one section fails, the other section will still provide braking.

There are two different types of brake mechanisms at the wheels: the drum-and-shoe type and the disk type. The drum-and-shoe type has a wheel brake cylinder with two pistons. When brake fluid is forced into the brake cylinder by the action at the master cylinder, the two pistons are forced outward. This causes the curved brake shoes to move into contact with the brake drum. The brake shoes apply friction to the brake drum, forcing it, and the wheel, to slow or stop.

In the disk type, a rotating disk attached to the wheel is positioned between flat brake shoes. One or more pistons, actuated by the brake fluid from the master cylinder, force the shoes into contact with the rotating disk, and slow or stop the car.

Many vehicles now use power brakes. In these, vacuum and air pressure supply most of the brake-applying effort. As the driver pushes down on the brake pedal, vacuum is applied on one side of a piston and air pressure is applied on the other. This causes the piston to move in a cylinder. The piston then takes over most of the effort required to build up the hydraulic pressure in the lines to the wheel cylinders. Details of this and other braking mechanisms are discussed in Chap. 14.

2-7 Tires Tires are of the air-filled, or pneumatic, type. Their function is to transmit the driving power of the wheels to the road through frictional contact. They also absorb a considerable part of the road

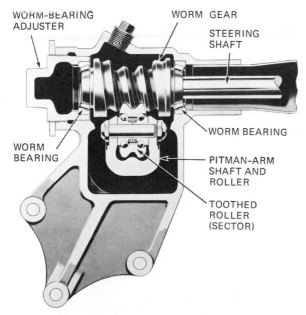

Fig. 2-15. One type of steering gear (in sectional view) using a roller sector with an hourglass worm gear. (*Chevrolet Motor Division of General Motors Corporation*)

shock resulting from small bumps and holes and prevent these shocks from being carried to the frame and the body of the car. As the tires roll over small bumps, they flex; the outer surface, or tread, moves inward against the cushion of air inside the tires.

Tires are of two types: those with inner tubes and those without. Tubeless types are in general use today, although years ago all pneumatic (air) tires had inner tubes. The tubeless tire mounts on the wheel rim in such a way that the tire beads seal airtight against the rim (Fig. 2-17). In tires with inner tubes, the air is held in the inner tube itself.

The tire casing has an outer coating of rubber which is baked, or vulcanized, onto an inner structure of fabric. The fabric is built up in layers, or plies (a four-ply tire has four layers, for example). The tread, which is the thickest part of the rubber coating, is supplied in a number of different patterns which provide good traction under various operating conditions, such as driving on the turnpike, in mud or snow, or off the highway.

Air is introduced into the tire or tube through a valve. The valve closes after the air has entered, sealing against a seat and preventing leakage of air.

⊘ **2-8 Body** Some automobiles have a "unitized" frame-body construction: The body shell and underbody are made as a single unit, and there is no separate frame. On automobiles which have separate frames and bodies, the supporting points, where the body is attached to the frame, are cushioned by rubber insulators (Fig. 2-18). These rubber insulators

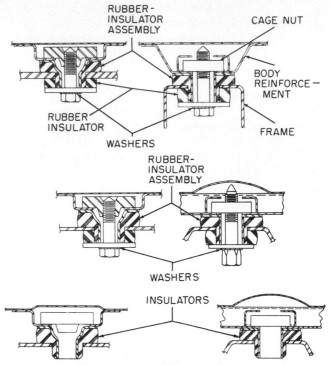

Fig. 2-18. Different types of body-to-frame attachments, showing the use of rubber insulators. (*Pontiac Motor Division of General Motors Corporation*)

absorb noise and vibrations from the frame and prevent them from traveling to the body and from there to the car passengers.

The body (Fig. 2-19) is designed to contain and protect not only the engine and other car components but also the passengers within the car. Much thinking and engineering work have gone into making the body sturdy and thus safe. Also, since the appearance of the body is one of the important factors in sales appeal, an attempt has been made to shape the contours so that the external structure will have a pleasing appearance and at the same time will provide ample room for the driver and passengers. It will be noted that most modern cars have flowing lines, with few noticeable sharp angles. Curves are more pleasing to the human eye than sharp angles.

Not only must the car body be pleasing to the eye, but it must also have the proper aerodynamic properties for easy handling. These properties relate to the way in which the car body passes through air when it is being driven on the highway. For example, some shapes act a little like an airplane wing at high speed; the air flowing over and under the car tends to lift it off the highway. Of course, the car would not actually fly, but the effect does increase handling difficulties. Also, some shapes handle better in crosswinds than others. In order to make sure that a car body is correct, aerodynamically, car makers test scale models of new cars in wind tunnels (Fig. 2-20). This enables the engineers to determine the effect of various shapes on ease of handling.

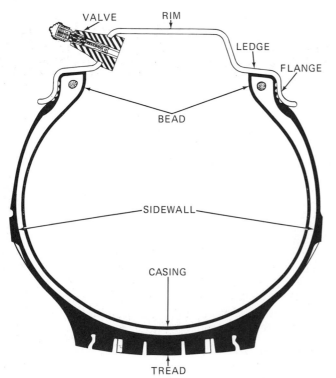

Fig. 2-17. Sectional view of a tubeless tire, showing how the tire bead rests between the ledge and flange of the rim. This arrangement produces a good seal. (*Pontiac Motor Division of General Motors Corporation*)

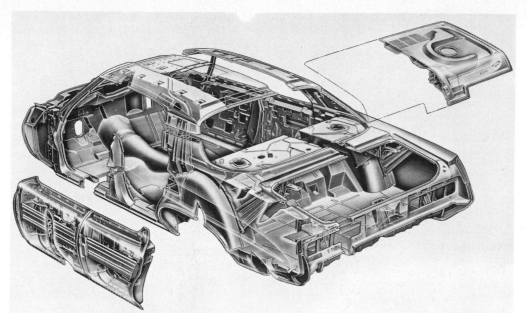

Fig. 2-19. Construction of a typical passenger-car body. (*Fisher Body Division of General Motors Corporation*)

Fig. 2-20. Testing a quarter-scale model of a new car in a wind tunnel. (*Chevrolet Motor Division of General Motors Corporation*)

For some high-speed vehicles, engineers add air foils, sometimes called *spoilers*, to counteract the "airplane-wing" effect. The air foils, slanted forward, cause the air to push the rear of the vehicle downward. Other performance cars have the rear end cut off almost square; this produces a downward dragging effect that improves handling characteristics.

Another matter of great importance is *safety*. Engineers are concentrating on making cars more crashproof in order to give passengers greater protection in the event of an accident. We have already mentioned the collapsing frame (⊘ 2-2), which helps to absorb the crash forces in a front-end collision. Many cars are also being made with reinforcing bars, or plates, in the sides and car doors to provide protection in case of a sideward smashup.

The details of door suspension, latches, locks, window-operating mechanisms, no-draft ventilation, air conditioning, and other devices that add to the comfort of the passengers are covered in later chapters.

CHAPTER 2 CHECKUP

NOTE: Since the following is a chapter review test, you should review the chapter before taking it.

The following questions will help you determine how well you remember what you have been reading. If you have any trouble answering the questions, you should reread the past few pages. Don't be discouraged if questions stump you. That simply means you should review the chapter. Most good students read their "lessons" several times. As you do this, and take the tests in the book, you will gradually find that your mind is becoming keener, more alert. You will be able to pick out the important facts you should remember. This is because you are improving your studying habits and learning what is most important in the material you are reading. Answering the questions helps you by pointing out the important facts to remember.

Write the answers in your notebook. This is an aid to your memory. Also, you build up a valuable compilation of important information in your notebook that you can refer to later.

Correcting Parts Lists The purpose of this exercise is to give you practice in spotting unrelated items in a list. For example, in the list "Parts of the automobile include engine, frame, filling station, brakes, wheels," you can see that "filling station" does not belong because it is the only thing named that is not part of an automobile. In each of the lists, one item is named that does not belong. Write each list in your notebook, *but do not write* the item that does not belong.

1. Parts of the chassis include frame, springs, shock absorbers, windshield, steering system, brakes, engine.

2. Parts of the shock absorber include pistons, valves, coupler, valve springs.

3. Parts of the steering system include worm gear, pitman arm, fan belt, tie rods, steering wheel.

4. Parts of the brake system include brake shoes, master brake cylinder, engine cylinders, wheel cylinders.

5. Parts of the tire include the inner tube, valve, piston, casing.

Picking Out the Right Answer Several answers are given for each question or statement listed below. Read each statement carefully, then decide which of the several answers or phrases is the correct one. Write the statement or question in your notebook, including the correct answer.

1. At how many places is the engine ordinarily attached to the frame? (*a*) one or two, (*b*) two or three, (*c*) three or four, (*d*) four or five.

2. The frame provides support for the engine, body, power-train members, and: (*a*) road, (*b*) tires, (*c*) wheels.

3. What is the purpose of the shock absorbers? (*a*) attach spring to frame, (*b*) dampen spring oscillations, (*c*) tighten the mounting, (*d*) attach frame to wheel.

4. As the steering wheel is turned, a worm gear on the steering shaft causes the end of the (*a*) kingpin, (*b*) steering gear, (*c*) pitman arm to swing toward one side or the other of the car.

5. Movement of the brake pedal forces brake fluid out of the master brake cylinder, through brake lines, and into the: (*a*) brake shoes, (*b*) brake cables, (*c*) wheel cylinders, (*d*) pedal rod.

Listing Parts In the following, you are asked to list parts that go into various automotive components discussed in the chapter. Write these lists in your notebook.

1. List the various parts attached to the frame.

2. List the major parts that make up a typical front-suspension system.

3. List the major parts that make up a shock absorber.

4. List the parts that make up a steering system.

5. List the parts that make up a brake system.

Purpose, Construction, and Operation of Components In the following, you are asked to write the purpose, construction, or operation of certain components of the automobile discussed in the chapter. If you have any difficulty in writing your explanations, turn back to the chapter and reread the pages that will give you the answer. Then write your explanation. Don't copy; try to tell it in your own words. This is a good way to fix the explanation firmly in your mind. Write in your notebook.

1. Describe the construction of an automotive frame.

2. Describe the operation of the coil spring used in a front-suspension system.

3. Describe the operation of a shock absorber.

4. Describe the purpose and operation of a car steering system.

5. Describe the operation of a hydraulic-brake system.

SUGGESTIONS FOR FURTHER STUDY

If you would like to study the engine and power train, there are several things you can do. You can read the other books in the McGraw-Hill Automotive Technology Series (*Automotive Engines, Automotive Transmissions and Power Trains, Automotive Electrical Equipment, Automotive Fuel, Lubricating, and Cooling Systems*). Also, you can inspect your own and your friends' cars as well as cars in the school automotive shop or in any friendly service garage where work on these automotive components is done. Many school automotive shops have cutaway models of the various components that help you to understand their construction and operation. In addition, the manuals issued by automotive manufacturers usually have many illustrations and explanations of how these parts work.

While examining various cars, you should note carefully the manner in which the different parts are attached to the car frame, how the springs and shock absorbers are attached, and so on. Write important facts in your notebook.

chapter 3

SPRINGS AND SUSPENSION SYSTEMS

This chapter describes the various springs and suspension systems used in automotive vehicles, with the exception of shock absorbers. Chapter 4 discusses shock-absorber construction and operation in detail, and Chap. 7 describes the servicing of springs and suspension systems.

⊘ **3-1 Function of Springs** The car frame supports the weight of the engine, power-train components, body, and passengers. The frame, in turn, is supported by the springs. The springs are placed between the frame and the wheel axles. Figure 3-1 shows an automotive chassis using coil springs at both the front and rear. Figure 3-4 shows a car using leaf springs at the rear and coil springs at the front. Regardless of the type of spring, all work in a similar manner. The weight of the frame, body, and so on applies an initial compression to the springs. The springs will further compress, or will expand, as the car wheels encounter irregularities in the road. Thus, the wheels can move up and down somewhat independently of the frame. This allows the springs to absorb a good part of the up-and-down motion of the car wheels. This motion therefore is not transmitted to the car frame and from it to the passengers.

Figure 2-8 and 2-9 show how coil springs compress and expand as the wheels encounter bumps or holes in the road.

⊘ **3-2 Types of Springs** The automobile uses three basic types of springs: coil, leaf, and torsion bar. Air suspension was offered at one time as optional equipment for passenger cars; it is now used on some buses. A modification of the air-suspension system, used on some cars, is called the *automatic level control* (⊘ 3-25). It keeps the car level even though the load changes. Most automobiles use either coil springs or torsion bars at the two front wheels. Some cars use coil springs at the rear wheels (Fig. 2-6 shows coil springs at the rear wheels). Other cars use leaf springs at the rear wheels (Fig. 3-4). A few cars and many heavy-duty vehicles also use leaf

Fig. 3-1. Phantom view of a chassis, showing the location of the coil springs at the front of the car (*left*) and at the rear of the car (*right*). (*Chevrolet Motor Division of General Motors Corporation*)

springs at the front wheels. Cars built by Chrysler Corporation in recent years have been equipped with torsion-bar front-suspension systems (⊘ 3-5). In addition, some General Motors front-drive cars (Cadillac Eldorado and Oldsmobile Toronado), as well as certain foreign cars, use torsion-bar front suspension.

⊘ **3-3 Coil Springs**   The coil spring is made of a length of special spring steel (usually round in cross section) which is wound in the shape of a coil (Fig. 3-2). The spring is formed at high temperature—while the steel is white-hot—and it is then cooled and properly heat-treated so as to give it the

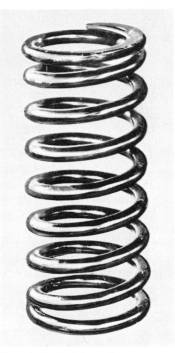

Fig. 3-2.   Coil spring used in a front-suspension system.

proper characteristics of elasticity and "springiness." Spring characteristics are discussed in a later section.

⊘ **3-4 Leaf Springs**   There are two types of leaf spring: the multileaf and the single-leaf. The latter is called a *tapered-plate spring* by the manufacturer.
1. MULTILEAF SPRING   The multileaf spring is made up of a series of flat steel plates of graduated length placed one on top of another, as shown in Fig. 3-3. Figure 3-4 shows a car using leaf springs at the rear. The plates, or leaves, are held together at the center by a center bolt which passes through holes in the leaves. Clips placed at intervals along the spring keep the leaves in alignment. Instead of clips, as shown in Fig. 3-3, some leaf springs are sheathed in a metal cover. The longest, or master, leaf is rolled at both ends to form spring eyes through which bolts are placed to attach the spring ends. On some springs, the ends of the second leaf are also rolled partway around the two spring eyes to reinforce the master leaf.

In operation, the leaf spring acts much like a flexible beam. An ordinary solid beam strong enough to support the car weight would not be very flexible. This is because, as the beam bends (Fig. 3-5), the top edge tries to become longer and the lower edge tries to become shorter. There is a pull-apart effect at the upper, or elongating, edge, and a push-together, or shortening, effect, along the lower edge. The result is that the upper edge pulls apart if the beam is overloaded, and the beam breaks. However, there would be a different action if the beam were made of a series of thin leaves, one on top of another (right in Fig. 3-5). The leaves would slip over each other to take care of the pull-apart and push-together tendencies of the two edges of the beam. You can see how much the leaves will slip over each other if the beam is sharply bent (lower right in Fig. 3-5). All leaves are the same length, and the amount that

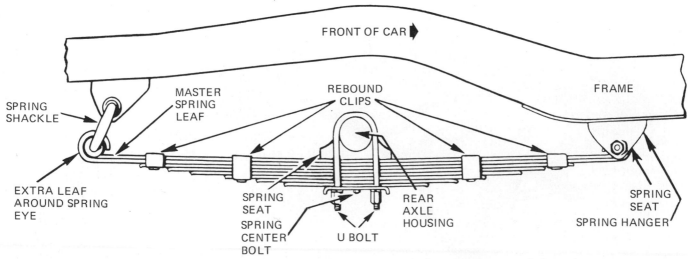

Fig. 3-3.   Typical leaf spring, showing how it is attached to the frame and the axle.

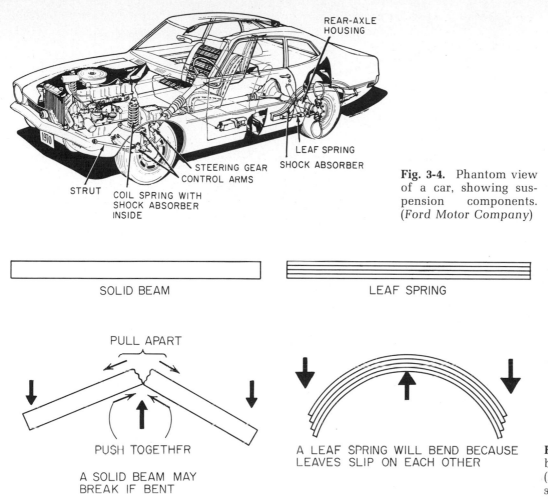

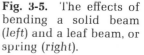

Fig. 3-4. Phantom view of a car, showing suspension components. (*Ford Motor Company*)

SOLID BEAM

LEAF SPRING

PULL APART

PUSH TOGETHER

A SOLID BEAM MAY BREAK IF BENT

A LEAF SPRING WILL BEND BECAUSE LEAVES SLIP ON EACH OTHER

Fig. 3-5. The effects of bending a solid beam (*left*) and a leaf beam, or spring (*right*).

the inner leaves project beyond the outer leaves (when curved) indicates the amount of slippage.

In the actual leaf spring, the leaves are of graduated length. To permit them to slip, various means of applying lubricant between the leaves are used. In addition, some leaf springs have special inserts of various materials placed between the leaves to permit easier slipping. The clips shown on the spring in Fig. 3-3 are called *rebound clips* because they prevent excessive leaf separation during rebound after the wheel has passed over an obstruction in the road. In addition, springs may be covered with a metal sheath to retain lubricant and prevent the entrance of moisture and dirt.

2. SINGLE-LEAF SPRING The single-leaf spring, also called a *tapered-plate spring,* is made of a single steel plate which is thick at the center and tapers to the two ends. Figure 3-6 shows a rear-suspension system using two single-leaf springs. The methods of mounting and operation are generally the same as with the multileaf spring.

⊘ **3-5 Torsion-Bar Suspension** Figures 2-12 and 3-7 to 3-9 show torsion-bar front-suspension systems. Figure 3-9 shows a torsion-bar front-suspension system partly disassembled so the details can be seen.

In the system shown, the rear end of the torsion bar is rigidly attached to a cross member of the car frame so it is held stationary. The front end is attached to the lower control arm at a point halfway between the arm pivots. Thus, as the lower control arm moves up and down, pivoting on the frame, the torsion bar twists more or less. The car weight places an initial twist on the bar, just as it places an initial

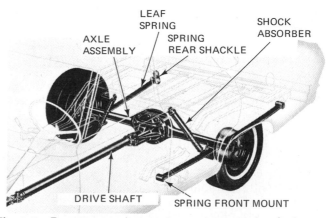

Fig. 3-6. Rear-suspension system using a tapered plate, or single-leaf spring.(*Chevrolet Motor Division of General Motors Corporation*)

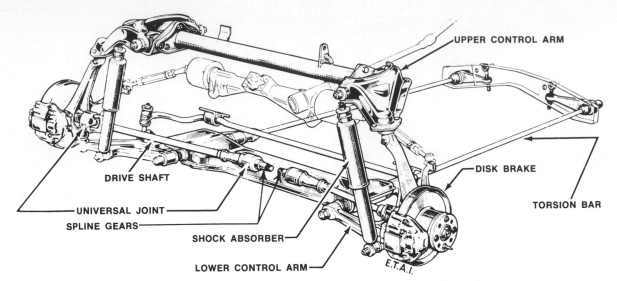

Fig. 3-7. Front suspension and drive shaft for a front-drive car. (*Simca*)

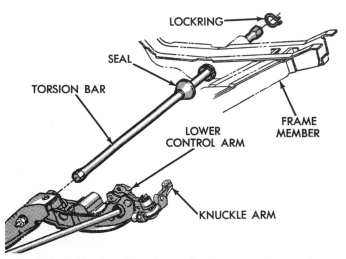

Fig. 3-8. Torsion bar in a front-suspension system. (*Chrysler Corporation*)

compression on the coil springs of the cars with coil-spring suspension. The twisting of the torsion bar provides the springing effect.

As a further comparison, think of this. The torsion bar is simply a coil spring straightened out. When a coil spring is compressed, the bar from which the spring is made twists. It must twist to permit the coils of the spring to move closer together. This twisting provides the springing effect of the coil spring, just as the twisting effect does in the torsion bar.

The torsion-bar suspension system includes a means of height adjustment. Thus if sag has occurred due to a change in the torsion-bar characteristic, correction can be made by turning an adjuster bolt. On some cars, the adjustment is made at the rear of the torsion bar, where the bar is attached to the frame cross member (see Fig. 3-9). On other cars (late-model Plymouth, for example), the

adjustment is made at the lower control arm where the torsion bar is attached to the control arm.

⊘ **3-6 Sprung and Unsprung Weight** In the automobile the terms "sprung weight" and "unsprung weight" refer to the part of the car that is supported on springs and the part that is not. The frame and the parts attached to the frame are sprung; that is, their weight is supported on the car springs. However, the wheels, wheel axles, rear-axle housing, and differential are not supported on springs; they represent unsprung weight.

Generally speaking, unsprung weight should be kept as low as possible because the roughness of the ride increases as unsprung weight increases. For example, consider a single wheel. If it is light, it can move up and down as road irregularities are encountered without causing much reaction to the car frame. But if the weight of the wheel is increased, its movement will become more noticeable to the car occupants. To take a ridiculous example, suppose the unsprung weight at the wheel is equal to the sprung weight above the wheel. In such case, the sprung weight would tend to move almost as much as the unsprung weight. The unsprung weight, which must move up and down as road irregularities are encountered, would tend to cause a like motion of the sprung weight. This is the reason for keeping the unsprung weight as low as possible so that it represents only a small portion of the total weight of the car.

⊘ **3-7 Characteristics of Springs** The ideal spring for automotive suspension would be one that would absorb road shock rapidly and then return to its normal position slowly. Such an ideal is not possible, however. An extremely flexible, or soft, spring would allow too much movement, and a stiff, or

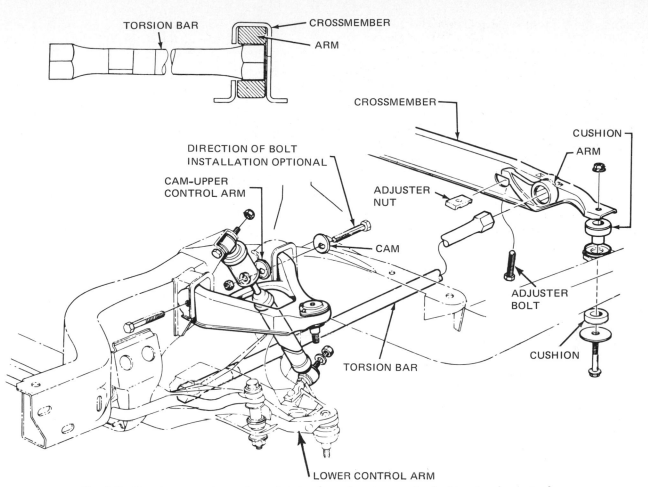

TORSION BAR   CROSSMEMBER
ARM

DIRECTION OF BOLT
INSTALLATION OPTIONAL

CAM–UPPER
CONTROL ARM

CROSSMEMBER

CUSHION
ARM

ADJUSTER
NUT

CAM

ADJUSTER
BOLT

TORSION BAR

CUSHION

LOWER CONTROL ARM

Fig. 3-9. Front suspension using a torsion bar, showing method of torsion-bar attachment. (*Cadillac Motor Car Division of General Motors Corporation*)

hard, spring would give too rough a ride. However, satisfactory riding qualities are attained by using a fairly soft spring combined with a shock absorber (Chap. 4).

Softness or hardness of a spring is referred to as its "rate." The rate of a spring is the weight required to deflect it 1 inch [25.4 mm]. The rates of automotive springs are almost constant throughout their operating range, or deflection, in the car. This is an example of Hooke's law, as applied to coil springs: The spring will compress in direct proportion to the weight applied. Thus, if 600 pounds [272.2 kg] will compress the spring 3 inches [76.2 mm], 1,200 pounds [544.3 kg] will compress the spring 6 inches [152.4 mm].

⊘ **3-8 Hotchkiss and Torque-Tube Drives** Before we discuss rear-suspension systems further, we should note that the rear springs may have an additional job to do besides supporting the car load. This additional job is to absorb a kind of force known as *rear-end torque*. Whenever the rear wheel is being driven through the power train by the engine, it rotates as shown in Fig. 3-10 (for forward car motion). A fundamental law of nature states that for

every action there must be an equal and opposite reaction. Thus, when the wheel rotates in one direction, the wheel-axle housing tries to rotate in the opposite direction, as shown (Fig. 3-10). The twisting motion thus applied to the axle housing is called rear-end torque. Two different rear-end designs are used to combat this twisting motion of the axle

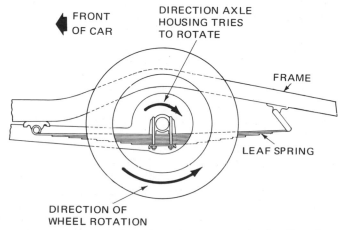

FRONT
OF CAR

DIRECTION AXLE
HOUSING TRIES
TO ROTATE

FRAME

LEAF SPRING

DIRECTION OF
WHEEL ROTATION

Fig. 3-10. The axle housing tries to rotate in the direction opposite to that of wheel rotation.

housing, the Hotchkiss drive and the torque-tube drive (Fig. 3-11).

1. HOTCHKISS DRIVE In the Hotchkiss drive, the twisting effect, or torque, is taken by the springs. Note that the spring (Fig. 3-10) is firmly attached to the axle housing. The torque applied by the housing to the spring tends to lift the front end of the spring (on the left in Fig. 3-10 or on the right in Fig. 3-11). At the same time, it tends to lower the rear end of the spring. The spring does flex a little to permit a slight amount of housing rotation, thus absorbing the rear-end torque, or twisting effort.

2. TORQUE-TUBE DRIVE The torque-tube drive is no longer used on cars. It consists of a rigid tube (Fig. 3-11) that surrounds the propeller shaft. (The propeller shaft carries the power developed by the engine from the transmission to the rear-wheel axles.) The rigid tube is attached to the transmission at the front and to the axle housing—actually the differential housing—at the rear. The axle housing, in attempting to rotate, tries to bend the tube, but the tube resists this effort. The twisting effort of the housing, or rear-end torque, is thus absorbed by the torque tube.

NOTE: Another book in the McGraw-Hill Automotive Technology Series (*Automotive Transmissions and Power Trains*) describes these drives, as well as the operation of the propeller shaft, differential, and other power train components, in detail.

⊘ **3-9 Rear-End Torque and Squat** As we mentioned, when the rear wheels are driving the car, the wheel-axle housing tries to rotate in a direction opposite to wheel rotation (Fig. 3-10), causing a motion called rear-end torque. In a leaf-spring rear suspension, the leaf springs absorb the rear-end torque. On the coil-spring rear suspension, the control arms absorb the rear-end torque. See ⊘ 3-10 and 3-11 for details of these two types of rear-end suspension systems.

One effect of rear-end torque is rear-end "squat" on acceleration (Fig. 3-12). When a car is accelerated from a standing start, the drive pinion in the differential tries to climb the teeth of the differential ring gear. Thus, the drive pinion and differential move upward, and the springs are twisted and compressed by the differential action. In other words, the rear end of the car moves down, or squats, when the car is accelerated. On deceleration, or braking, the rear of the car moves upward, owing to the inertia of the car. (Another book in the McGraw-Hill Automotive Technology Series, *Automotive Transmissions and Power Trains,* describes differentials in detail.)

⊘ **3-10 Coil-Spring Rear Suspension** In some rear-suspension systems using coil springs, the springs are placed between spring housings in the car frame and brackets on the rear-axle housing (Figs. 2-6 and 3-13). Figure 3-14 is a closeup view of

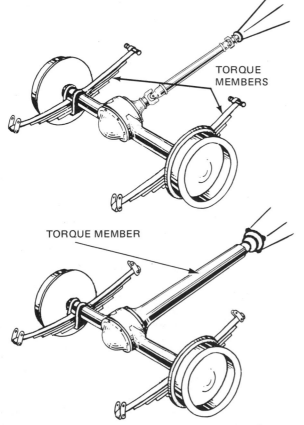

Fig. 3-11. Hotchkiss drive (*top*) compared with torque-tube drive (*bottom*).

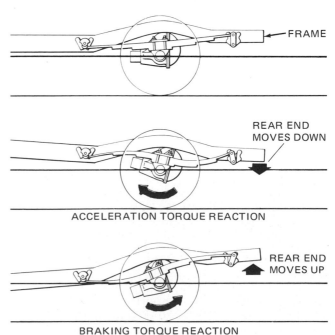

Fig. 3-12. Actions of the spring and rear end when the car is accelerated or braked. (*Ford Motor Company*)

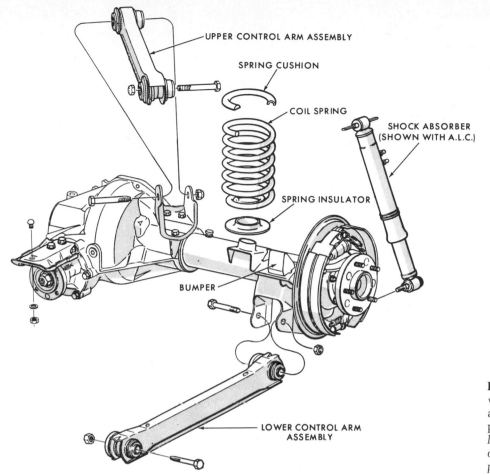

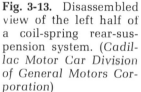

UPPER CONTROL ARM ASSEMBLY

SPRING CUSHION

COIL SPRING

SHOCK ABSORBER
(SHOWN WITH A.L.C.)

SPRING INSULATOR

BUMPER

LOWER CONTROL ARM
ASSEMBLY

Fig. 3-13. Disassembled view of the left half of a coil-spring rear-suspension system. (*Cadillac Motor Car Division of General Motors Corporation*)

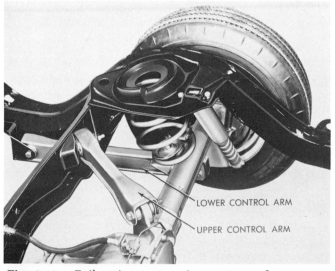

LOWER CONTROL ARM

UPPER CONTROL ARM

Fig. 3-14. Coil-spring suspension system of one rear wheel. (*Pontiac Motor Division of General Motors Corporation*)

one coil spring on a similar suspension design. Note how the spring fits between a circular depression in the frame and a bracket mounted on the axle housing. Somewhat different arrangements are shown in Fig. 3-15. In these designs, the coil springs are installed between the frame and the lower control arms. A disassembled view of a similar design is shown in Fig. 3-16.

The purpose of the control arms or links, the track bar, and the control yoke is to hold the rear-axle housing and assembly, with the wheels in proper alignment with the frame. The axle housing must be permitted to move up and down in relation with the frame, but it must not be allowed to move forward or backward, or sideways, with respect to the car frame. The control arms permit the rear-axle housing to move upward and downward as the springs compress or expand. At the same time, they keep the axle in proper alignment with the frame. On some cars, control arms are also used to prevent sideward movement of the axle housing. In Fig. 2-6,

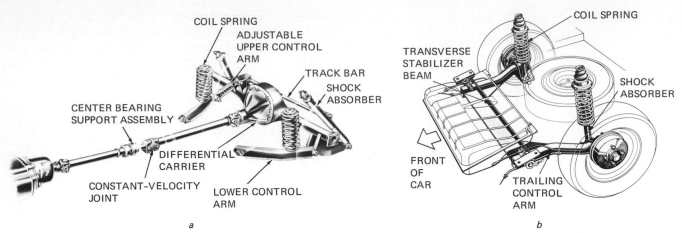

Fig. 3-15. (*a*) Coil-spring rear suspension system in which coil springs are located between the frame and the lower control arms; (*b*) coil-spring rear suspension in which coil springs are connected to the frame through seats on the shock absorbers. (*Buick Motor Division of General Motors Corporation; Volkswagen of America, Inc.*)

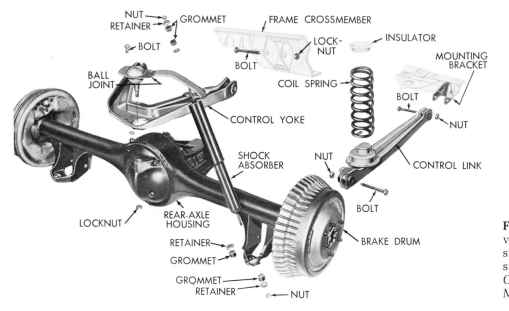

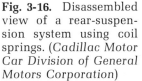

Fig. 3-16. Disassembled view of a rear-suspension system using coil springs. (*Cadillac Motor Car Division of General Motors Corporation*)

for example, the lower control arms prevent backward and forward movement, and the upper control arms prevent sideward movement. Other cars use a track bar (Fig. 3-15) connected between the axle housing and the frame to prevent sideward movement. The design shown disassembled in Fig. 3-16 is still different. It uses a control yoke to prevent sideward movement.

In all these designs, the shock absorbers are connected between the car frame and axle housing. (Shock absorbers are discussed in detail in the following chapter.)

✪ **3-11 Leaf-Spring Rear Suspension** A considerable variety of leaf-spring rear-suspension systems have been used. The leaf spring most commonly used in automotive vehicles is a semielliptical

spring. It has the shape of half an ellipse, and that is the reason for its name. Refer to the different illustrations of rear-suspension systems using leaf springs to see their semielliptical shape.

Note also the methods shown in the illustrations for attaching the spring to the car frame and the rear-axle housing. The usual method is to attach the center of the spring to the axle housing with two U bolts so that the spring is, in effect, hanging from the axle housing. A spring plate or straps are used at the bottom of the spring (Fig. 3-17). Some installations include insulating strips or pads of rubber to reduce noise transfer from the axle housing to the spring.

Note that leaf-spring rear-suspension systems do not require control arms, as do coil-spring rear-suspension systems. The leaf springs absorb rear-

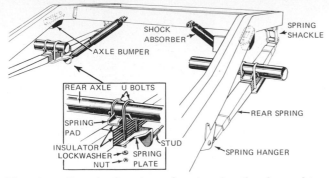

Fig. 3-17. Rear-leaf springs showing details of attaching the spring to the axle housing.

end torque and side thrust (as when rounding a corner). The exception to this is the system using a transverse leaf spring (⊘ 3-12).

On some vehicles, the spring is placed on top of the axle housing, rather than under it. This is a common arrangement in heavy-duty suspension (⊘ 3-13).

The two ends of the spring are attached to the frame by a spring hanger (usually at the front) and by a spring shackle (usually at the rear). Typical modern installations are shown in disassembled view in Figs. 3-18 and 3-19. Note the construction and arrangement of the hanger and shackle as you read the following explanation on the purpose of each. Other types of hanger and shackle are also described in the discussion that follows.

NOTE: In some heavy-duty installations, no shackle or hanger attachment is used. Instead, the two ends of the spring are straight and ride on hangers on the frame. This permits the spring ends to move back and forth as the effective length of the spring changes. See Fig. 3-29.

1. SPRING HANGER One end of the spring is attached to a hanger on the frame by means of a bolt and bushings in the spring eye (lower left in Fig. 3-18). The spring, as it bends, causes the spring eye to turn back and forth with respect to the spring hanger. The attaching bolt and bushing must permit this rotation. Some forms have a hollow spring bolt with a lubrication fitting that permits lubrication of the bushing. Other designs do not require lubrication. Some designs have a bushing made up of an inner and an outer metal shell. Between these two shells is a molded rubber bushing. The weight is carried through the rubber bushing. The rubber also acts to dampen vibration and noise and thus prevents them from entering the car frame. Figure 3-20 shows one type of rubber-bushed mounting. These mountings require no lubrication.

2. SPRING SHACKLE As the spring bends, the distance between the two spring eyes changes. If both ends of the spring were fastened rigidly to the frame, the spring would not be able to bend. To permit bending, the spring is fastened at one end to the frame through a link called a *shackle*. The shackle is a swinging support attached at one end to the spring eye and at the other end to a supporting

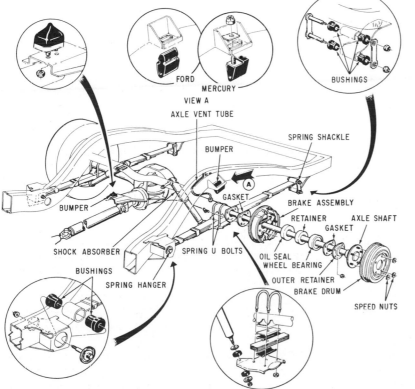

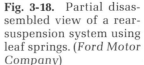

Fig. 3-18. Partial disassembled view of a rear-suspension system using leaf springs. (*Ford Motor Company*)

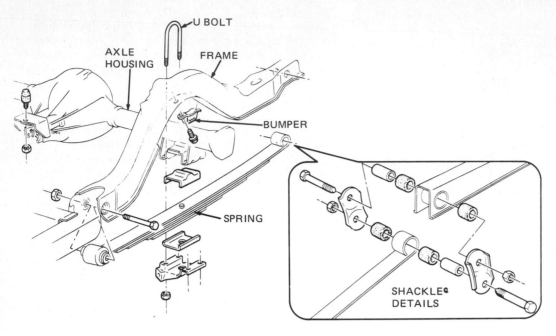

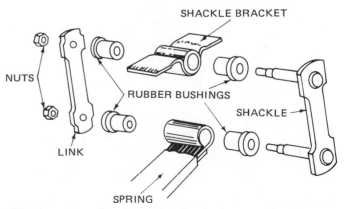

Fig. 3-19. Disassembled view of a leaf-spring rear-suspension system. (*Chevrolet Motor Division of General Motors Corporation*)

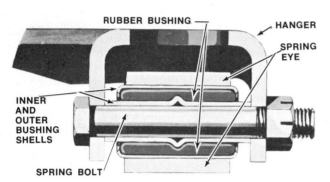

Fig. 3-20. Details of the bushing in a spring eye through which the spring eye is attached to the hanger on the car frame. (*Chevrolet Motor Division of General Motors Corporation*)

bracket on the car frame. Spring shackles can be seen in Figs. 2-11, 3-3, and 3-17. Spring shackles are shown in disassembled view in Figs. 3-18, 3-19, and 3-21. The two links provide the swinging support that the spring requires, and the bolts attach the links to the shackle bracket on the frame and the spring eye. The rubber bushings insulate the spring from the frame to prevent transfer of noise and vibration between the two. A link-type shackle very similar to this unit is shown in sectional view in Fig. 3-22.

Another type of shackle is shown in Fig. 3-23. This shackle is made up of two internally threaded steel bushings, two threaded hollow steel pins, a draw bolt, shackle links, and cork or rubber washers. The steel bushings are installed in the spring eye and the frame bracket, and the threaded steel pins are screwed into them. The shackle links are held on the pins by the draw bolt. The cork and rubber washers protect the threaded pins from dirt and retain the lubricant in the shackle.

A U-type shackle is shown in partial sectional view in Fig. 3-24. The bushings are threaded on the inside and screw onto the threaded legs of the shackle. Lubricant fittings are provided for each bushing.

Shackles with lubrication fittings require periodic lubrication. However, the rubber-bushed shackles, such as those shown in Figs. 3-21 and 3-22, must not be lubricated. Oil or grease on the rubber bushings will cause them to soften and deteriorate.

⊘ **3-12 Transverse-Leaf-Spring Rear Suspension** Some rear-suspension systems use a single multileaf spring mounted transversely so that each rear wheel is independently suspended by one end of the spring (Fig. 3-25). On the system shown, each rear wheel is driven by a separate shaft which includes two universal joints. These universal joints are necessary to permit the power from the engine to be carried through the differential and the shafts to the rear wheels.

Fig. 3-21. Details of a rubber-bushed spring shackle.

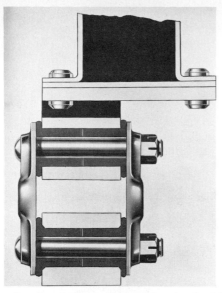

Fig. 3-22. Sectional view of a rubber-bushed link-type spring shackle. (*Chevrolet Motor Division of General Motors Corporation*)

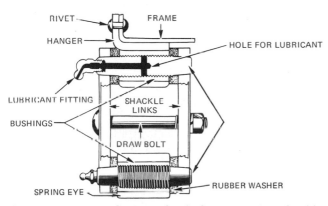

Fig. 3-23. Sectional view of a link-type spring shackle. Note how the bushing is lubricated.

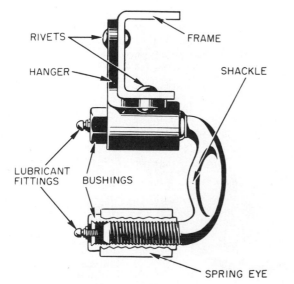

Fig. 3-24. U-type spring shackle. Note how the bushings are lubricated.

NOTE: Another book in the McGraw-Hill Automotive Technology Series (*Automotive Transmissions and Power Trains*) describes differentials and universal joints.

⊘ **3-13 Heavy-Duty Rear Suspension** Figure 3-26 and 3-27 show the spring arrangement used at the rear of heavy-duty trucks. Note that the spring is above the axle housing (not slung below it, as in other suspension systems previously described). Note also that there is an auxiliary, or helper, spring above the main spring (Figs. 3-26 and 3-27). This helper spring comes into action only when the truck is heavily loaded or when the wheel encounters a large road bump. Then, as the main spring goes through a large deflection, the ends of the helper spring encounter the two bumpers on the frame. The auxiliary spring then deflects and adds its tension to the tension of the main spring. Figure 3-28 illustrates a heavy-duty front-suspension system with the spring above the axle.

Some heavy-duty leaf springs are not attached at either end (Fig. 3-29). Instead, the two ends bear on spring hangers attached to the frame. The radius leaf maintains forward-and-back relationship of the axle with the frame.

⊘ **3-14 Front Suspension** The suspension of the front wheels is more complicated than the suspension for the rear wheels. Not only must the front wheels move up and down with respect to the car frame for spring action, but they must also be able to swing at various angles to the car frame for steering. In the pages that follow, we discuss the various types of front-suspension systems used on modern cars. Chapter 5 covers steering systems.

To permit the front wheels to swing to one side or the other for steering, each wheel is supported on a spindle which is part of a steering knuckle. The steering knuckle is supported, through ball joints, by upper and lower control arms which are attached to the car frame.

⊘ **3-15 Independent Front Suspension** Practically all passenger cars now use the independent type of front-suspension system in which each front wheel is independently supported by a coil, torsion bar (⊘ 3-5), or leaf spring. The coil-spring arrangement is the most common. There are three general types of coil-spring front suspension. In one, the coil spring is located between the upper and lower control arms (Figs. 3-30 and 3-31), and the lower control arm has two points of attachment to the car frame. This control arm is called the *A* or *wishbone-type arm* because of its shape. In the second type, the coil spring is located between the upper and lower control arms (Figs. 3-32 and 3-33), and the lower control arm has one point of attachment to the car frame. This is called a *beam-type arm*. In the third type, the coil spring is between the upper control

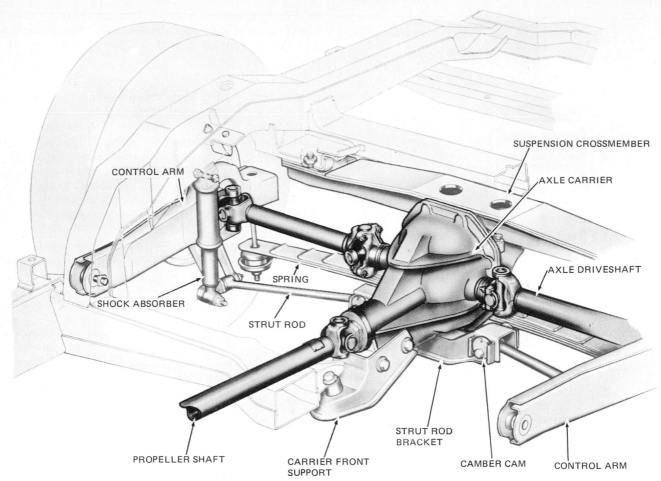

Fig. 3-25. Rear-suspension and drive-line components in the Corvette. Note the transverse leaf spring and the axle driveshafts with their two universal joints each. (*Chevrolet Motor Division of General Motors Corporation*)

Fig. 3-26. How the leaf spring is attached to the frame and axle housing on a heavy-duty truck. Note the upper spring, which is an auxiliary, or helper, spring; it comes into use when heavy loads are applied. (*International Harvester Company*)

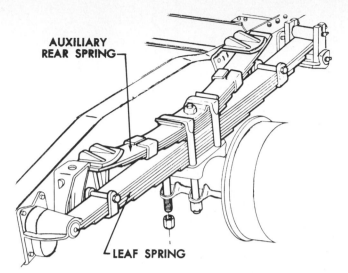

AUXILIARY REAR SPRING

LEAF SPRING

Fig. 3-27. Heavy-duty-truck leaf-spring suspension system using an auxiliary spring. (*Chevrolet Motor Division of General Motors Corporation*)

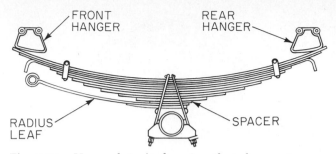

FRONT HANGER **REAR HANGER**

RADIUS LEAF **SPACER**

Fig. 3-29. Heavy-duty leaf spring that does not use a spring bolt or shackle to attach the spring to the frame. Instead, the top leaf rides on hangers at the front and back. (*Chevrolet Motor Division of General Motors Corporation*)

arm and spring tower or housing that is part of the front-end sheet-metal work (Figs. 3-34 and 3-35).

In the beam type with a single point of attachment for the lower control arm (Figs. 3-32 and 3-33), a strut, or brake reaction rod, is used to prevent forward or backward movement of the lower control arm. This strut, or rod, can also be seen in Fig. 3-34.

It is attached between the outer end of the lower control arm and the car frame. This construction prevents forward or backward movement of the outer end of the lower control arm but allows it to move up or down. Note that, in Fig. 3-35, the strut is behind the control arm. In Fig. 3-34, it is in front of the control arm. The A, or wishbone type, with its two points of attachment (Fig. 3-31), does not require this extra bracing. In the designs shown in Figs. 3-30 to 3-35, the shock absorber is the telescoping type and is located inside the coil spring. (Chapter 4 describes shock absorbers.)

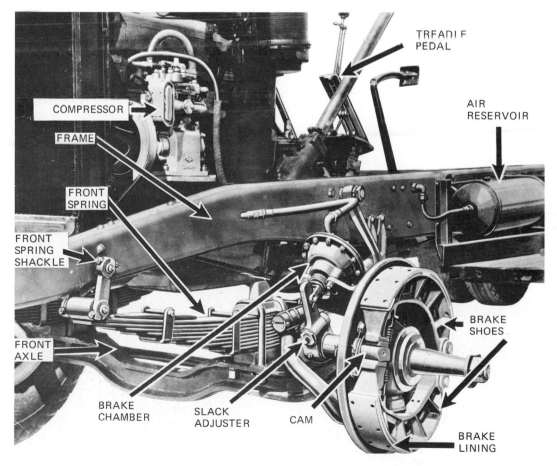

Fig. 3-28. Front end of a heavy-duty truck, showing the suspension and braking system. (*International Harvester Company*)

COMPRESSOR

FRAME

FRONT SPRING

FRONT SPRING SHACKLE

FRONT AXLE

BRAKE CHAMBER

SLACK ADJUSTER

CAM

TREADLE PEDAL

AIR RESERVOIR

BRAKE SHOES

BRAKE LINING

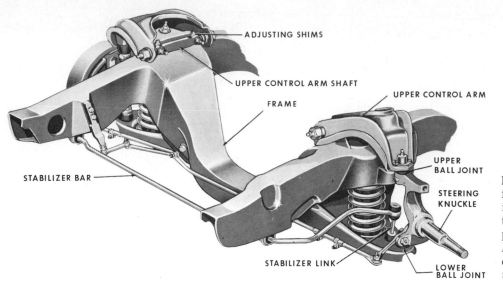

Fig. 3-30. Coil-spring front suspension, showing only the front end of the frame and the suspension parts. (*Buick Motor Division of General Motors Corporation*)

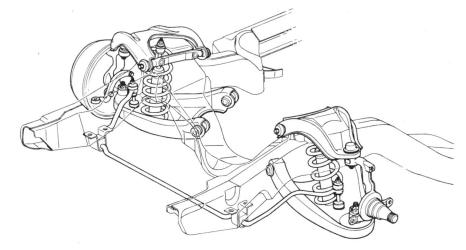

Fig. 3-31. Line drawing of a coil-spring front suspension similar to the one shown in Fig. 3-30. (*Chevrolet Motor Division of General Motors Corporation*)

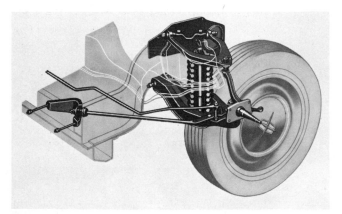

Fig. 3-32. Front-suspension system that uses a narrow lower control arm with a single attachment to the frame. Note the spring is between the lower and upper control arms. (*Ford Motor Company*)

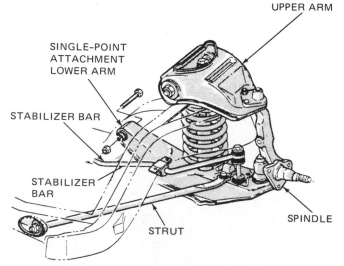

Fig. 3-33. Front-suspension system at the left-front wheel. The lower arm has a single point of attachment to the frame. A strut connects the lower arm to the frame. (*Ford Motor Company*)

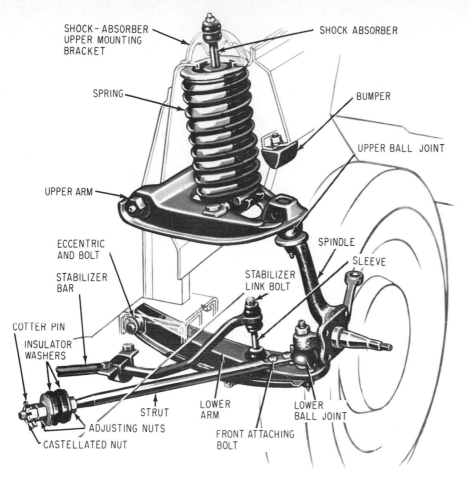

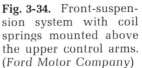

Fig. 3-34. Front-suspension system with coil springs mounted above the upper control arms. (*Ford Motor Company*)

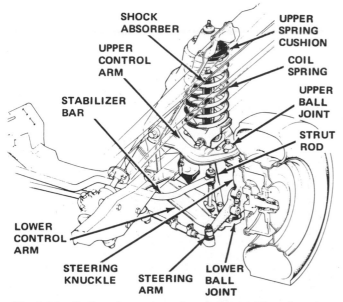

Fig. 3-35. Coil-spring suspension system with coil spring above the upper control arm. The lower control arm has a single point of attachment to the frame. The strut rod is located back of the arm. (*American Motors Corporation*)

The brake assembly is mounted on the spindle, or steering knuckle, as shown in Fig. 3-36. It is attached rigidly to the steering knuckle. The brake drum and wheel are mounted, by bearings, on the tapered spindle shaft. The wheel can turn freely on the bearings. At the same time, the steering knuckle can be swung back and forth on the two ball joints. This turns the attached wheel in or out so the car can be steered (Chap. 5).

⊘ **3-16 Parallelogram vs. SALA Suspension** Early independent front-suspension systems had two control arms of about the same length (Fig. 3-37). They were called *parallelogram systems* because the lines through the four pivot points formed a parallelogram. While this system did permit the two wheels to move up and down independently, as shown in Fig. 3-38, there was a drawback. Whenever a tire encountered a bump in the road, it, and the wheel, moved upward and inward (Fig. 3-38). This inward movement made the tire slide sideways and, naturally, caused excessive tire wear.

To eliminate this sideward movement of the tire tread on the road, the SALA suspension system was

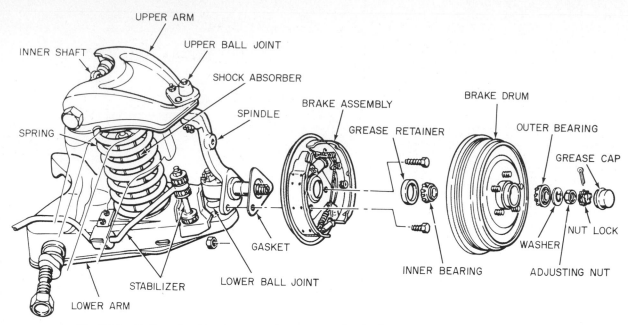

Fig. 3-36. Coil-spring front suspension at one wheel, showing the brake assembly and drum attachment to the spindle (also called the *steering knuckle*). (*Ford Motor Company*)

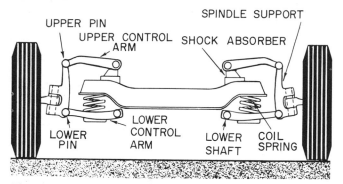

Fig. 3-37. Front-suspension system in which both upper and lower control arms are the same length. (*Ammco Tools, Inc.*)

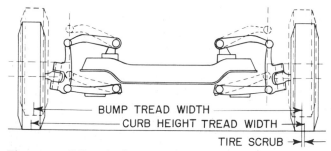

Fig. 3-38. When both control arms are the same length, upward movement of the wheel causes the wheel also to move inward. This forces the tire to slide sideways on the road. (*Ammco Tools, Inc.*)

introduced. "SALA" stands for short arm, long arm (Fig. 3-39). With this system, the centerline of the tread at the road remains the same as the tire moves up and down (Fig. 3-40). Thus, there is no sideward sliding of the tread on the road as the tire meets bumps and holes. Another effect is also important. The top of the tire moves inward whenever the wheel moves up or down (Fig. 3-40); that is, the wheel tips inward. To say it another way, the camber of the wheel changes. *Camber* is the inward or outward tilt of the wheel (viewed from the front of the car). A wheel that is perfectly vertical (not tilted inward or outward) is said to have zero camber. When the wheel tilts inward, it has negative camber. If it tilts outward, it has positive camber. The SALA suspension system shown in Fig. 3-39 gives the wheel negative camber as it moves up or down. There is more on camber in Chap. 5.

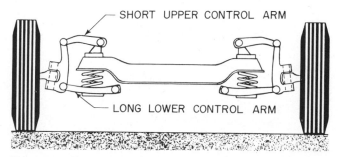

Fig. 3-39. Front-suspension system in which the upper control arm is shorter than the lower control arm. (*Ammco Tools, Inc.*)

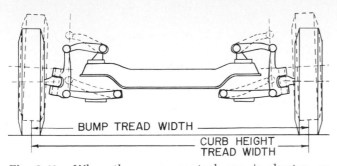

BUMP TREAD WIDTH

CURB HEIGHT
TREAD WIDTH

Fig. 3-40. When the upper control arm is shorter, as shown, the tread width at the road remains the same even though the wheel moves up and down. However, the top of the tire moves inward, as shown. (*Ammco Tools, Inc.*)

⊘ **3-17 Moving Instant Center Outside the Car** The instant center is the point of intersection of lines drawn through the control-arm attachment points for any one position of the wheel. Earlier-model cars were designed so the instant center was inside the car (Fig. 3-41). Note that, in earlier design, the wheel tilted inward as it moved upward—it took on a negative camber. On the later design, with the instant center *outside* the car, the wheel tilts outward as it moves upward—it takes on a positive camber. Now, refer to Fig. 3-42 to see how this affects car stability. When a front wheel encounters a bump, as shown, the later design causes the wheel to tilt outward as

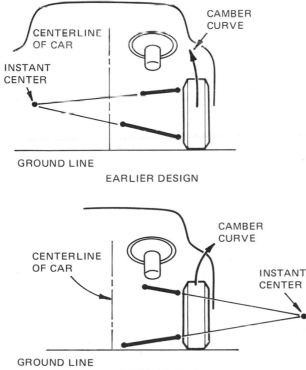

Fig. 3-41. Comparison of earlier and later front-suspension systems. In the later design, the inner attachment points to the control arms have been moved apart so that the instant center is outside the car. (*Buick Motor Division of General Motors Corporation*)

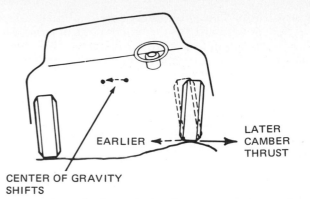

Fig. 3-42. How the later-design front-suspension system causes the center of gravity to shift as the wheel moves up. (*Buick Motor Division of General Motors Corporation*)

it moves up. The effect of this is to impart an outward thrust at the road which reduces the side effect of the bump (which tends to push the car to the left in Fig. 3-42). The stability factor is even more pronounced as the car rounds a curve. Centrifugal force throws more of the weight on the outer wheel, so this wheel moves up. As it does so, it tilts outward as shown in Fig. 3-42, and the tire opposes the centrifugal force that is trying to push the car sideways. In addition, because the contact point of the tire with the road shifts inward as it moves up, the center of gravity of the car shifts also. It shifts into the curve to help counteract the centrifugal force pushing the car outward.

⊘ **3-18 Rubber Bumpers** Rubber bumpers are placed on the frame and lower suspension arm to prevent metal-to-metal contact between frame and arms as limits of spring compression or expansion are reached.

⊘ **3-19 Stabilizer Bar** A stabilizer bar, or sway bar, is used on most cars to interconnect the two lower suspension arms (Figs. 3-30 to 3-36). The bar is a long steel rod. Its purpose is to reduce "lean out," or body roll, when the car goes around a curve. When the car is moving around a curve, centrifugal force tends to keep the car moving in a straight line. The car therefore leans out. With lean out, or body roll, additional weight is thrown on the outer springs on the turn. This puts additional compression on the outer spring, and the lower control arm pivots upward. As the control arm pivots upward, it carries the end of the stabilizer bar with it. At the inner wheel on the turn, the opposite happens. There is less weight on the spring. Weight has shifted to the outer spring because of centrifugal force. Therefore, the inner spring tends to expand and allow the lower control arm to pivot downward, carrying the end of the stabilizer downward.

Now see the condition we have. The outer end of the stabilizer bar is carried upward by the outer control arm. The inner end of the stabilizer bar is carried downward by the inner control arm. This combined action twists the stabilizer bar. The resistance of the bar to twisting combats the tendency of the car to lean out on turns. Thus, there is less body roll, or lean out, than there would be without the stabilizer bar.

⊘ **3-20 Kingpin** Earlier passenger-car front-suspension systems used a kingpin (Fig. 3-43). Notice, in this design, that the knuckle support is attached by pivots, top and bottom, to the two control arms. The knuckle is supported on the knuckle support by means of the kingpin. The knuckle can swing back and forth on the kingpin for steering. In later designs, the support, kingpin, and knuckle have been combined into a single part, the steering knuckle, which is supported at the top and bottom by ball joints (see Figs. 3-30 to 3-36). Note how this reduces the unsprung weight (⊘ 3-6) and thus improves the riding qualities of the car.

Many front-suspension systems, especially the heavy-duty types, still use kingpins, as we shall note when we study leaf-spring front-suspension systems (⊘ 3-22). In front-alignment work, where measuring and changing various angles are important, the inclination, or angle from vertical, of the kingpin (where present) is usually measured. This is the centerline around which the front wheel swings for steering. When the system has no kingpin, the steering-axis inclination is measured. The steering axis is an imaginary line drawn through the centers of the two ball joints; the front wheel swings around this line for steering.

One advantage of the ball-joint type of front suspension is that it is lighter than the type using a kingpin. This means that the unsprung weight at

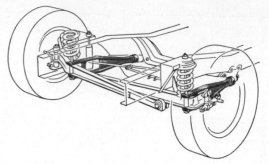

Fig. 3-44. Twin I-beam front suspension using coil springs. (*Ford Motor Company*)

the wheel is less. This helps produce a smoother ride as explained in ⊘ 3-6.

⊘ **3-21 Twin I-Beam Front Suspension** Figure 3-44 illustrates a twin I-beam front suspension with coil springs used on some Ford trucks. Each front wheel is supported at the end of a separate I beam. The opposite ends of the I beams are attached to the frame by pivots. The wheel ends of the two I beams are attached to the frame by radius arms which prevent backward or forward movement of the wheels. The arrangement provides adequate suspension flexibility with the added strength of the I-beam construction.

⊘ **3-22 Leaf-Spring Front Suspension** Most passenger cars today use either coil-spring or torsion-bar front-suspension systems. Some cars manufactured outside the United States use leaf-spring front-suspension systems. Many trucks and other heavy-duty equipment also use leaf springs at the front.

Figure 3-45 shows a front-suspension system using a single transverse leaf spring. Note that this spring is not fastened to the frame at its center point. Instead, it is fastened at two intermediate points. The two ends of the spring support the two front wheels. In effect, each end of the spring becomes the lower control arm of the system, with the lower end of the steering knuckle attached to it.

Many trucks and other heavy-duty equipment use a solid, one-piece axle, or I beam, at the front instead of independent front suspension (Fig. 3-46). As a rule, this arrangement uses two leaf springs, one at each wheel. Figure 3-47 shows the manner in which the steering knuckle is supported on the end of the axle beam. Figure 3-48 is a sectional view of a suspension system of this type. The springs normally rest on top of the axle instead of being suspended from underneath, as in passenger-car rear-suspension systems using leaf springs. The front ends of the leaf springs are attached to the frame hangers. In some designs, the rear end of the spring is attached to the frame by a shackle. In others, the rear end of the spring is straight and rides in a hanger on the frame that permits it to move back

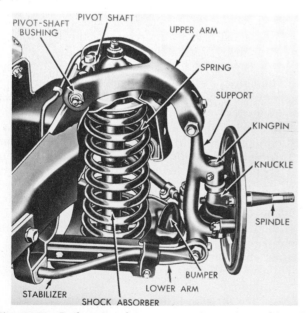

Fig. 3-43. Coil-spring front suspension using a kingpin. (*Ford Motor Company*)

Fig. 3-45. Front-suspension system using a leaf spring, viewed from underneath the car. In this car the engine is located at the rear. (*Fiat*)

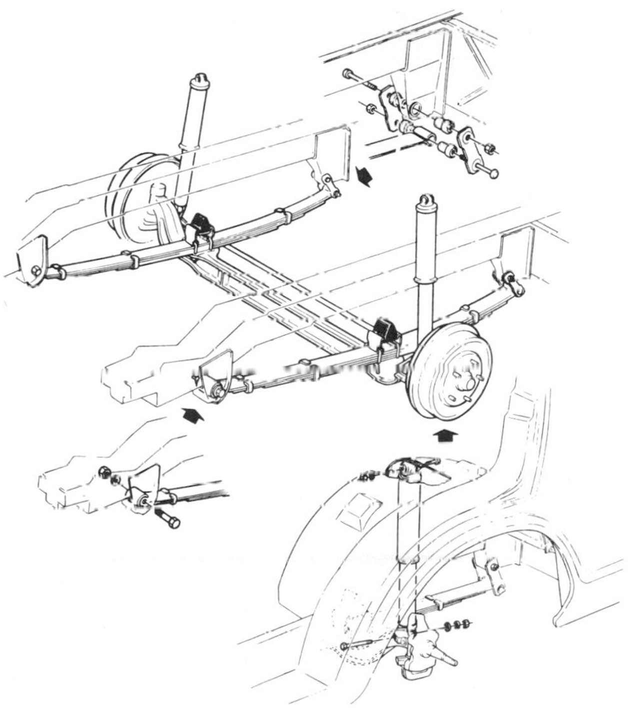

and forth as the effective length of the spring changes. Figure 3-28 illustrates a heavy-duty front-suspension system.

⊘ 3-23 MacPherson Strut-Type Front Suspension
The MacPherson strut-type front suspension (Figs. 3-49 and 3-50), also called a *strut* suspension, is used on many foreign cars (Toyota, Datsun, Porsche, Volkswagen, Plymouth Cricket, Mercury Capri, and others). The struts (shock absorbers) are inside the coil springs. On most cars, the top supporting bearing is an oilless ball bearing. The bottom has a ball joint. The assembly includes a stabilizer, as do other independent front suspensions.

⊘ 3-24 Air Suspension
Air suspension was at one time widely offered by automobile manufacturers as optional equipment, but it was not generally accepted and is no longer available (except on a few foreign cars and some heavy-duty equipment such as trailers and buses). A modification of the system has been adopted on some cars, however, which provides leveling of the car. This system, called *automatic level control,* brings the car back to level as the load changes (⊘ 3-25).

Fig. 3-46. Front-suspension system for a truck using an I-beam front axle and two leaf springs. (*Chevrolet Motor Division of General Motors Corporation*)

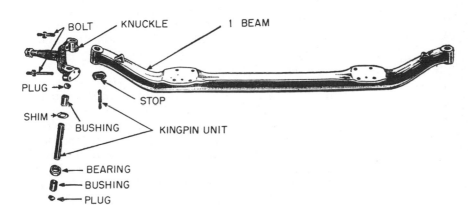

Fig. 3-47. Beam-type front axle, showing the method of supporting the steering knuckle on the end of the beam. (*Chevrolet Motor Division of General Motors Corporation*)

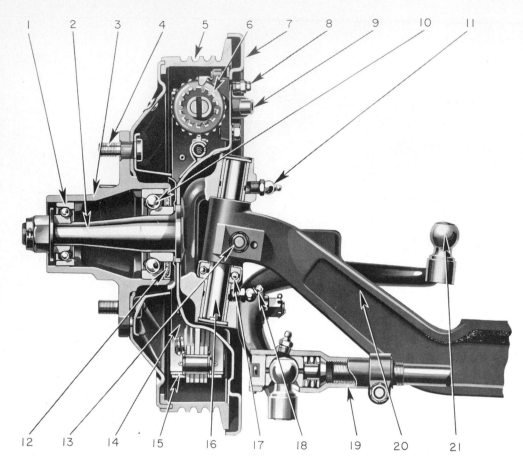

1 2 3 4 5 6 7 8 9 10 11

12 13 14 15 16 17 18 19 20 21

Fig. 3-48. Beam-type front-axle assembly, partly cut away. (*Chevrolet Motor Division of General Motors Corporation*)

1. Outer wheel bearing
2. Wheel spindle
3. Wheel hub
4. Wheel-hub bolt
5. Brake drum
6. Brake-wheel cylinder
7. Brake-flange plate
8. Brake bleeder valve and screw
9. Brake-wheel-cylinder hose connection
10. Inner wheel bearing
11. Lubrication fitting
12. Inner-bearing seal
13. Kingpin lock pin
14. Brake shoe
15. Brake lining
16. Kingpin
17. Kingpin thrust bearing
18. Lubrication fitting
19. Tie-rod end
20. Axle beam
21. Steering and third arm

In air suspension, the four conventional springs are replaced by four air bags or air-spring assemblies. Figure 3-51 is a disassembled view of an air-suspension system at one front wheel. Figure 3-52 is a schematic diagram of a complete system.

Essentially each air-spring assembly is a flexible bag enclosed in a metal dome, or girdle. The bag is filled with compressed air, which supports the car's weight. When a wheel encounters a bump in the road, the air is further compressed and absorbs the shock.

An air compressor, or pump, supplies air to the system (Fig. 3-52). On the system shown, the compressor is driven by a belt from the water-pump pulley. Pressure is maintained in the reservoir at about 300 psi [21.09 kg/cm^2]. The air then passes by two circuits to the four air bags. In one circuit the air pressure is reduced to 160 psi [11.25 kg/cm^2] by a pressure regulator. This pressure is admitted to the four air bags through height-control or leveling valves. When there is insufficient air in an air bag, that side of the car will ride low. This causes the linkage to move the leveling arm so that the valve is opened, admitting more air.

The 300-psi [21.09 kg/cm^2] air supply is used to correct for additional loading of the car. This keeps the car level the same regardless of whether there are passengers or not. The action is as follows: When a car door is opened, the door switch closes, turning

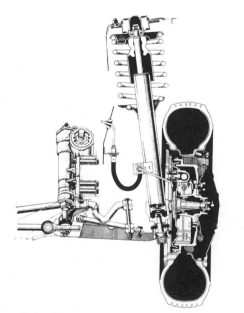

Fig. 3-49. Partial sectional view of a MacPherson front suspension. (*Toyota Motor Sales, Limited*)

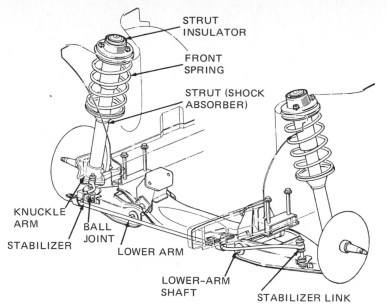

Fig. 3-50. MacPherson, or strut, type of front-suspension system.

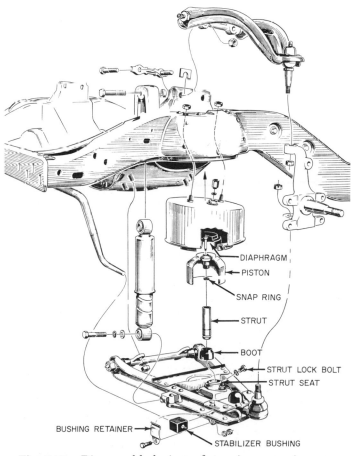

Fig. 3-51. Disassembled view of an air-suspension system on the front of a car. (*Oldsmobile Division of General Motors Corporation*)

on the courtesy light. At the same time, the air-suspension solenoid is connected to the battery through the switch, and the solenoid valve opens. Now air at 300 psi [21.09 kg/cm²] is admitted to the leveling valves. If the air bag has been compressed by added weight, as when a passenger climbs in, the leveling valve quickly feeds additional air pressure to the low air bag and it is brought up to the proper level. On the other hand, if a passenger has gotten out, the air bag is high. Now the leveling valve releases air to lower the bag to the proper level.

⊘ **3-25 Automatic Level Control** Automatic level control, which is standard equipment on some cars and optional equipment on others, compensates for variations in load in the rear of the car. To explain why this is desirable, consider the following. When a heavy load is added to the trunk or rear seat, the springs will give and allow the rear end to settle. This changes the handling characteristics of the car and also causes the headlights to point upward. The automatic level control prevents all this by automatically raising the rear back to level when a load is added, and automatically lowering the rear back to level when the load is removed. The system consists of a compressor (with reservoir and regulator), a height-control valve, two special shock absorbers or two rubber air cylinders, and air-pressure lines connecting the components (Figs. 3-53 and 3-56).

NOTE: The two systems in Figs. 3-53 and 3-56 are essentially the same except that one uses a special shock absorber (termed a Superlift by the manufacturer) while the other uses rubber air cylinders inside the rear coil springs (Fig. 3-56).

1. TYPE WITH SHOCK ABSORBERS The compressor is operated by engine intake-manifold vac-

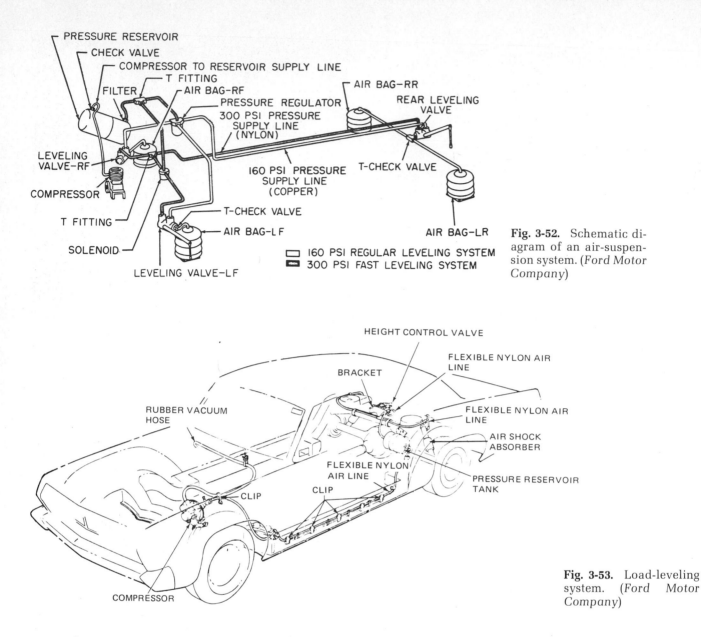

Fig. 3-52. Schematic diagram of an air-suspension system. (*Ford Motor Company*)

PRESSURE RESERVOIR
CHECK VALVE
COMPRESSOR TO RESERVOIR SUPPLY LINE
T FITTING
FILTER
AIR BAG-RF
PRESSURE REGULATOR
AIR BAG-RR
REAR LEVELING VALVE
300 PSI PRESSURE SUPPLY LINE (NYLON)
LEVELING VALVE-RF
160 PSI PRESSURE SUPPLY LINE (COPPER)
T-CHECK VALVE
COMPRESSOR
T FITTING
T-CHECK VALVE
SOLENOID
AIR BAG-LF
AIR BAG-LR
LEVELING VALVE-LF
☐ 160 PSI REGULAR LEVELING SYSTEM
▨ 300 PSI FAST LEVELING SYSTEM

HEIGHT CONTROL VALVE
FLEXIBLE NYLON AIR LINE
BRACKET
RUBBER VACUUM HOSE
FLEXIBLE NYLON AIR LINE
AIR SHOCK ABSORBER
FLEXIBLE NYLON AIR LINE
CLIP
CLIP
PRESSURE RESERVOIR TANK
COMPRESSOR

Fig. 3-53. Load-leveling system. (*Ford Motor Company*)

uum. The vacuum actuates a pump which builds up air pressure in the compressor reservoir. When a load is added to the rear of the car, this air pressure is passed through the height-control valve to the two special rear shock absorbers. Each shock absorber contains an air chamber (Fig. 3-54). The air pressure, entering this chamber, will raise the upper shell of the shock absorber to bring the rear of the car back up to level again.

The height-control valve (Fig. 3-55) has a linkage to the rear suspension. When this linkage is raised by the addition of a load, it opens the intake valve, thus allowing compressed air to flow to the shock absorbers. When the load is removed, and the rear of the car is thus raised, the linkage operates the exhaust valve, allowing air to exit from the shock absorber until the correct level is achieved. The height-control valve has a time-delay mechanism that allows the valve to respond only after several seconds. This eliminates fast valve action, which would tend to cause the system to function every

time a wheel encountered a bump in the road. Thus the system functions on load changes only, and not on road shocks.

The compressor, mounted at the front end of the car, works on the difference in pressure between atmospheric pressure and intake-manifold vacuum. Air pressure is applied to one side of a diaphragm in the compressor; intake-manifold vacuum is applied to the other side of the diaphragm. This difference in pressure moves the diaphragm. A piston attached to the diaphragm is made to move by this action. A pulsating action of the diaphragm is set up by means of a small valve which opens each time the diaphragm has moved to the vacuum side. This valve now admits air to the vacuum side and vacuum to the other side, so the diaphragm moves to the opposite side. The pulsations of the diaphragm move the piston and the piston pumps air into the reservoir, building up a pressure that may go as high as 275 psi [19.33 kg/cm²]. A relief valve prevents excessive pressure.

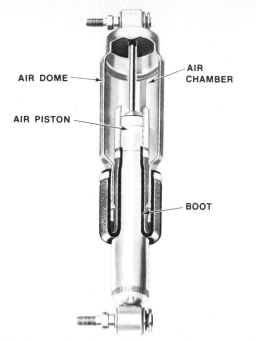

Fig. 3-54. Cutaway view of the special shock absorber with air chamber used in the automatic level control. (*Cadillac Motor Car Division of General Motors Corporation*)

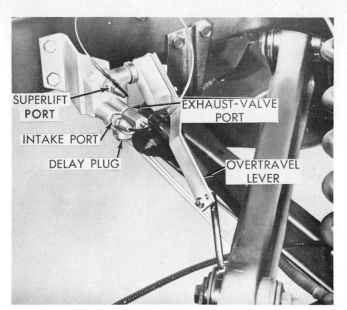

Fig. 3-55. Location of the height-control valve at the rear axle of the car. (*Cadillac Motor Car Division of General Motors Corporation*)

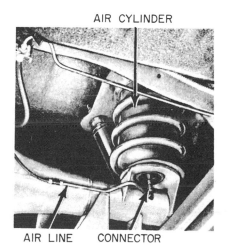

Fig. 3-57. View from under the car of an air-cylinder installation inside the coil spring. (*Ford Motor Company*)

2. TYPE WITH RUBBER AIR CYLINDERS The type shown in Fig. 3-56, no longer in common use for passenger cars, uses rubber air cylinders enclosed within the coil springs, as shown in Fig. 3-57. The height-control valve and compressor work in a manner similar to those already described. When the rear of the car is lowered by the addition of a load, as for instance when someone climbs in, the height-control valve directs air from the compressor to the rubber air cylinders within the rear coil springs. The rubber air cylinders expand and raise the rear of the car back to level again. When the load is removed so the rear of the car goes above level, the height-control valve releases air from the rubber air cylinders to allow the car to settle back down to level.

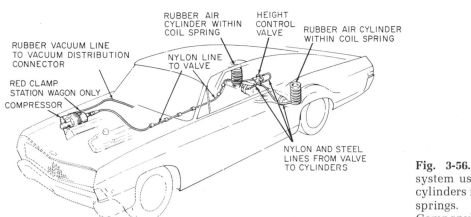

Fig. 3-56. Air-leveling system using rubber air cylinders inside rear coil springs. (*Ford Motor Company*)

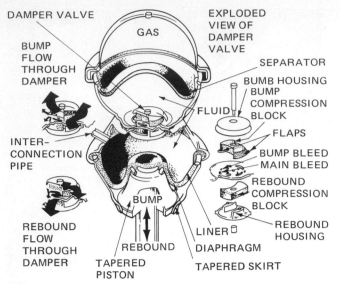

Fig. 3-58. Partial cutaway view of a Hydragas spring. (*British Motor Corporation*)

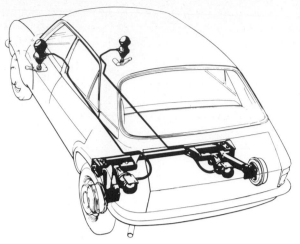

Fig. 3-59. Front-to-rear hydraulic connections of the Hydragas suspension system. (*British Motor Corporation*)

⊘ **3-26 Hydraulic Suspension** The hydraulic suspension system uses gas-filled spring units (called *Hydragas springs*), one at each wheel (Fig. 3-58). Each unit has a sealed chamber containing a quantity of nitrogen gas at high pressure. Below this chamber is a displacement chamber filled with water-based fluid. When the wheel meets a bump, the fluid is pushed upward, compressing the gas. This action provides the springing effect. In addition, the two units on each side of the car are interconnected front to back (Fig. 3-59). Therefore, when the left front wheel meets a bump, for example, part of the fluid from the left front unit is forced through a pipe to the left rear unit. This action raises the left rear wheel also. The shock is thus distributed between the left front and the left rear wheels. This is said to improve the ride.

CHAPTER 3 CHECKUP

NOTE: Since the following is a chapter review test, you should review the chapter before taking it.

Once more, you will want to test your knowledge of the subjects covered in the chapter you have just completed. The questions that follow have two purposes: (1) to test your knowledge and (2) to help you review the chapter and fix the facts discussed firmly in your mind. It may be that you will not be able to answer, offhand, all the questions. If this happens, don't worry. Few people can remember everything they read the first time they read it. Just turn back into the chapter and reread the pages that will give you the answers. The questions require written answers. Write them in your notebook.

Correcting Parts Lists The purpose of this exercise is to give you practice in spotting unrelated parts in a list. In each list below, one item is named that does not belong. Write each list in your notebook, but do not write the item that does not belong.

1. Parts in the leaf spring include master leaf, rebound clips or cover, spring eyes, center bolt, frame.
2. Parts that may be found in a spring shackle include bolts, links, bushings, levers, nuts.
3. Parts that may be found in a front-suspension system include spring, steering knuckle, suspension arms, suspension gears, shock absorber, stabilizer.
4. Parts that may be found in a rear-suspension system include springs, frame, axle housing, shackles, spring hangers, shock absorbers, snugger, rubber bumpers.
5. Parts in the automatic level control include the compressor, Superlift shock absorber or air cylinder, height-control valve, distribution valve, tubing.

Completing the Sentences The sentences below are incomplete. After each sentence there are several words or phrases, only one of which will correctly complete the sentence. Write each sentence in your notebook, selecting the proper word or phrase to complete it correctly.

1. One end of the semielliptical spring is usually attached to the frame through a: (*a*) chain, (*b*) lever, (*c*) shackle, (*d*) brace.
2. The clips placed at intervals along some leaf springs to prevent spring-leaf separation on rebound are called: (*a*) separation clips, (*b*) interval clips, (*c*) relief clips, (*d*) rebound clips.
3. Three types of springs used in automotive suspension systems are: (*a*) coil, leaf, and torsion bar; (*b*) coil, torsion bar, and lever; (*c*) leaf, suspension, and superlift; (*d*) lever, leaf, and coil.

4. The device that permits variation in the distance between the spring eyes of a leaf spring as the spring flexes is called: (*a*) spring hanger, (*b*) spring shackle, (*c*) spring leaf, (*d*) spring U bolt.

5. The weight or pressure required to deflect a spring 1 in [25.4 mm] is called the: (*a*) spring rate, (*b*) spring weight, (*c*) spring deflection, (*d*) spring rebound.

6. The rear-end-suspension arrangement in which rear-end torque is absorbed by the springs is called the: (*a*) torque-tube drive, (*b*) differential drive, (*c*) Hotchkiss drive, (*d*) Hooke's drive.

7. The rear-end-suspension arrangement in which rear-end torque is absorbed by a tube connected between the transmission and the differential housing is called a: (*a*) torque-tube drive, (*b*) differential drive, (*c*) Hotchkiss drive, (*d*) Hooke's drive.

8. In rear-suspension systems using coil springs, the devices connected between the axle housing and frame to prevent forward or backward movement of the housing are called: (*a*) axle arms, (*b*) control arms, (*c*) stabilizers.

9. In the typical front-suspension system, the lower suspension arm is connected between the car frame and the: (*a*) upper suspension arm, (*b*) shock-absorber arm, (*c*) steering knuckle.

10. In the typical front-suspension system, the upper suspension arm is connected between the steering knuckle and the: (*a*) car frame, (*b*) shock-absorber arm, (*c*) lower suspension arm.

Purpose, Construction, and Operation of Components In the following, you are asked to write the purpose, construction, or operation of various suspension components discussed in the chapter. If you have any difficulty in writing your explanations, turn back to the chapter and reread the pages that cover the components you want to write about. Then write your explanation. Don't copy; tell it in your own words. This a good way of fixing the explanation in your mind. Write in your notebook.

1. Describe the construction of a semielliptical spring.

2. Describe the construction of a typical spring shackle.

3. What is the purpose of the shackle?

4. What would happen if no spring shackle were used on a leaf spring?

5. What is the basic difference between the Hotchkiss drive and the torque-tube drive?

6. Describe a typical coil-spring rear-suspension system.

7. Describe a typical coil-spring front-suspension system.

8. Describe the construction and operation of a torsion-bar suspension system.

9. Describe the construction and operation of an air-suspension system.

SUGGESTIONS FOR FURTHER STUDY

Study the various front- and rear-suspension systems on different cars. Try to identify the various parts in them and study their purposes. You can see many different makes and models of cars in any automobile garage or filling station, as well as in your school automotive shop. Many school shops also have cutaway parts and automotive chassis which make it easy to see how the suspension parts are related. In addition, study whatever automotive shop manuals you can find. Notice the illustrations and descriptions of the different suspension systems. Write important facts in your notebook.

chapter 4

SHOCK ABSORBERS

This chapter describes the construction, operation, and servicing of the various types of shock absorbers in use on automotive vehicles.

⊘ **4-1 Purpose of Shock Absorbers** Springs alone are not satisfactory for a car suspension system. As already mentioned (in ⊘ 3-7), the spring must be a compromise between flexibility and stiffness. It must be flexible so that is can absorb road shock. But if it is too flexible, it will flex and rebound excessively and repeatedly, giving a rough ride. A stiff spring will not flex and rebound so much after a bump has been passed. On the other hand, it will also give a hard ride because it will transmit too much of the road shock to the car. By using a relatively flexible, or soft, spring and a shock absorber, a satisfactorily smooth ride will be achieved.

You can demonstrate to yourself why a spring alone would be unsatisfactory for a vehicle suspension. Hang a weight on a coil spring, as shown in Fig. 4-1. Then lift the weight and let it drop. It will expand the spring as it drops. Then it will rebound, or move up. The spring, as it expands and contracts, will keep the weight moving up and down, or oscillating, for some time.

On the car, a very similar action will take place with a flexible spring. The spring is under an initial compression because of the car weight. As the wheel passes over a bump, the spring is further compressed. After the bump is passed, the spring attempts to return to its original position, but it overrides the position and expands too much, causing the car frame to be thrown upward. Now, having overexpanded, the spring compresses. Again it overrides and compresses too much. As this happens, the wheel may be raised clear of the road and the frame may drop. Now the spring expands again, so the oscillations continue, gradually dying out. But every time the wheel encounters a bump or hole in the road, the same series of oscillations will take place.

Such spring action on a vehicle produces a rough and unsatisfactory ride. On a bumpy road, and especially on a curve, the oscillations might become serious enough to cause the driver to lose control of the car. Therefore it is necessary to use some device to quickly dampen out the spring oscillations once the wheel has passed the hole or

bump in the road. The shock absorber is the device universally used today. There have been many types of shock absorber, operating on friction, on compressed air, and hydraulically. The hydraulic shock absorber is the only type in common use at the present. It contains a fluid that is forced through restricting orifices as the shock absorber is operated by spring flexure. The resistance to the movement of the fluid through the restricting orifices imposes a drag on spring movement, thus quickly dampening out spring oscillations.

Several designs of hydraulic shock absorbers have been used, including the parallel-cylinder, opposed-cylinder, and vane types. In the parallel- or opposed-cylinder types, there was one cylinder for compression and another for rebound. Suspension-arm movement, as the wheel moved up and down, caused pistons to be forced into one or the other of these cylinders. The piston movement forced fluid to flow through restricting orifices, thus imposing restraint on the spring, and wheel, movement. The vane-type shock absorber had vanes that rotated in a cylindrical chamber filled with fluid. The most commonly used shock absorber is the direct-acting type, described in the following section, although other types are still in use on some cars, particularly cars manufactured outside the United States.

⊘ **4-2 Direct-acting Shock Absorber** The direct-acting, or telescope, shock absorber is the most widely used shock absorber and is found on both front- and rear-suspension systems. Several of the illustrations in the previous chapter show methods of mounting the shock absorber at front and rear wheels. Figures 4-2 and 4-3 show the details of front- and rear-mounting direct-acting shock absorbers. Notice that in the mounting methods shown, the two ends of the shock absorber, which are the studs or eyes by which they are attached, are encased in rubber grommets or bushings. This provides a rea-

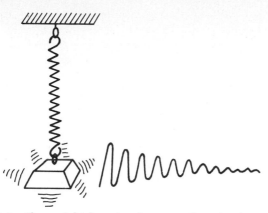

Fig. 4-1. If a weight hanging from a coil spring is set into up-and-down motion, it will oscillate for some time. The distance the weight moves up and down gradually shortens, as indicated by the curve (*to right*). Finally, the motion will die out.

sonably flexible mounting, and at the same time the rubber absorbs vibration and noise.

Regardless of the method of mounting, the shock absorber is attached in such a way that, as the wheel moves up and down, the shock absorber shortens and lengthens, or telescopes and extends. Since the shock absorber imposes a restraint on this movement (in the manner explained below), excessive wheel and spring movements as well as spring oscillations are prevented.

A direct-acting shock absorber is shown in sec-

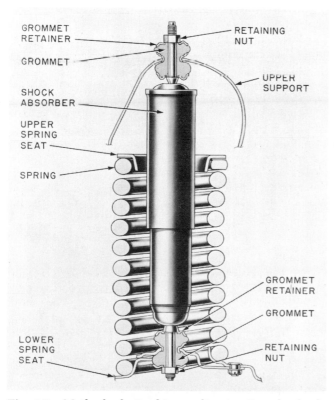

Fig. 4-2. Method of attaching a direct-acting shock absorber in a front-suspension system. (*Chevrolet Motor Division of General Motors Corporation*)

tional view in Fig. 4-4, with internal parts illustrated. Figure 4-5 shows a cutaway view of an assembled shock absorber. Figure 4-6 shows a similar unit disassembled. The shock absorber consists of three concentric tubes and a piston, together with valves, gaskets, and so on, as shown in Fig. 4-4. The outer tube is a dust shield, while the two inner tubes are sealed from each other except for a valve at the bottom of the shock absorber. The space between the two inner tubes is the fluid reservoir. The piston, which is attached through a heavy piston rod to the upper shock-absorber mounting eye, moves up and down as the length of the shock absorber changes. As it does this, the fluid in the shock absorber moves one way or the other through small passages in the piston. Let us see how such action takes place and what effect it has on spring movement.

Figure 4-7 shows the actions taking place in the shock absorber when the wheel is moving up, compressing the spring and shock absorber, and the actions taking place when the wheel is moving down, expanding the spring and shock absorber. When the wheel encounters a bump, causing it to move up toward the frame, the spring compresses. At the same time, the shock absorber is telescoped, or shortened: this causes the piston to move downward in the inside cylinder, or tube. Downward movement of the piston puts pressure on the fluid below the piston. At the same time, it creates a vacuum in the cylinder above the piston. The fluid is forced through the small openings—orifices—in the piston and passes into the upper part of the cylinder. Meanwhile, fluid in the lower end of the cylinder can flow out through the check-valve orifice and into the reservoir that surrounds the inner cylinder.

If the spring movement is very rapid—as it might be if a large bump in the road is encountered—the relief valves flex away from the upper face of the piston, permitting the opening of additional passages. Regardless of this, however, the orifices in the piston tend to restrict the movement of the liquid and thus to slow the movement of the piston. This, in turn, places a restriction on the spring action. In other words, the *shock* of the wheel meeting the bump *is absorbed*.

On rebound, when the wheel moves downward after passing a bump, or when it encounters a hole in the road, the shock absorber is extended (Fig. 4-7). As this happens, the piston moves into the upper part of the cylinder, and the fluid above it is forced to pass to the lower part of the cylinder through the small orifices in the piston. At the same time, the check valve in the bottom of the cylinder is lifted off its seat, permitting fluid to flow from the reservoir into the lower end of the cylinder.

In both compression and rebound, the spring valves open varying amounts, allowing varying speeds of liquid movement through the orifices. This permits rapid spring movements, while still imposing a restraining action, and prevents the excessive pressure rise in the fluid that might otherwise occur when large bumps in the road are encountered.

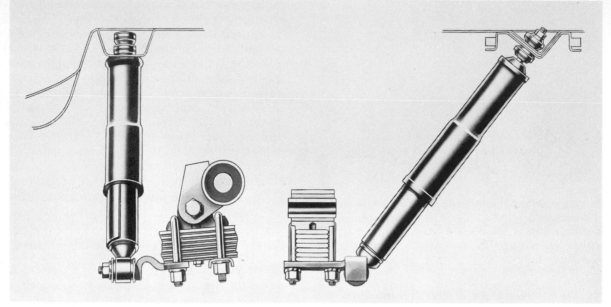

Fig. 4-3. Front and side views showing the method of attaching a direct-acting shock absorber in a rear-suspension system using a leaf spring. (*Chevrolet Motor Division of General Motors Corporation*)

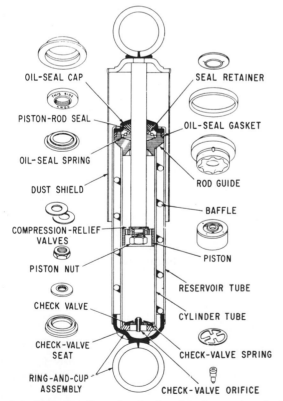

OIL-SEAL CAP

PISTON-ROD SEAL

OIL-SEAL SPRING

DUST SHIELD

COMPRESSION-RELIEF VALVES

PISTON NUT

CHECK VALVE

CHECK-VALVE SEAT

RING-AND-CUP ASSEMBLY

SEAL RETAINER

OIL-SEAL GASKET

ROD GUIDE

BAFFLE

PISTON

RESERVOIR TUBE

CYLINDER TUBE

CHECK-VALVE SPRING

CHECK-VALVE ORIFICE

Fig. 4-4. Direct-acting shock absorber in sectional view. The internal parts are illustrated and their positions in the assembly shown. (*Chrysler Corporation*)

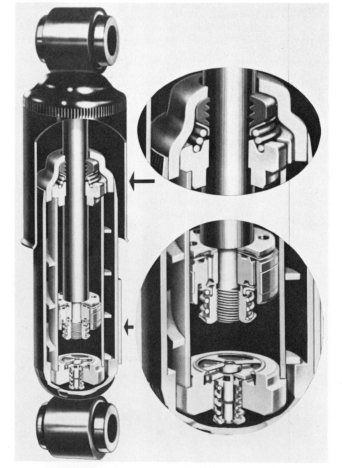

Fig. 4-5. Cutaway view of a direct-acting shock absorber. (*Monroe Auto Equipment Company*)

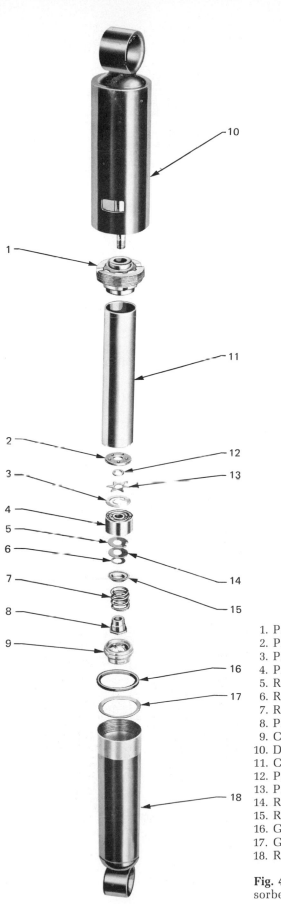

NOTE: Some replacement shock absorbers are adjustable. By turning the upper part (the dust tube) in relation to the lower part (the reservoir tube), the absorber response is changed. Thus, turning the dust tube one way will produce a softer ride. Turning it the other way will produce a harder ride. This arrangement permits the driver to choose the ride best suited to the operating needs. For example, tough going over rough terrain is best handled by a stiffer ride. A soft ride would result in excessive up-and-down motion.

⬦ **4-3 Gas-filled Cell in Shock Absorber** The rapid movement of the fluid between the chambers during rebound and compression can cause foaming (or aeration) of the fluid. That is, free air mixes with the fluid. When this occurs, the shock absorber develops lag. The piston moves through an air pocket which offers little resistance before it hits fluid again. Thus the effectiveness of the shock absorber action is reduced. Two means of eliminating this foaming are used. One uses a spiral groove in the reservoir tube (Fig. 4-8). The groove breaks up the air bubbles in the fluid. The other uses a sealed gas-filled cell (Fig. 4-9). The gas replaces the air in the shock absorber. This cell, in the reservoir, acts the same as an air chamber, expanding and contracting as the piston moves up and down. There is no free air to mix with the fluid; thus aeration and foaming are prevented.

⬦ **4-4 Parallel-Cylinder Shock Absorber** Figure 4-10 shows the front suspension of the British MGB car, which uses parallel-cylinder shock absorbers. Figure 4-11 is a sectional view of the shock absorber. The manufacturer calls these *hydraulic dampers*, which is perhaps a good name because they do hydraulically damp out the extra movements of the wheels. The unit shown has two cylinders, side by side, each with a piston. The shock-absorber arms

1. Piston-rod guide and seal
2. Piston washer
3. Piston-intake-valve plate
4. Piston
5. Rebound-valve orifice plate
6. Rebound-valve back plate
7. Rebound-valve spring
8. Piston-rod nut
9. Compression valve
10. Dust-shield tube and piston rod
11. Cylinder tube
12. Piston-washer spacer
13. Piston-intake-valve-plate spider spring
14. Rebound-valve spring disk
15. Rebound-valve spring seat
16. Gasket-upper (rubber)
17. Gasket retainer
18. Reservoir tube and cylinder-base assembly

Fig. 4-6. Disassembled view of a direct-acting shock absorber. (*Chrysler Corporation*)

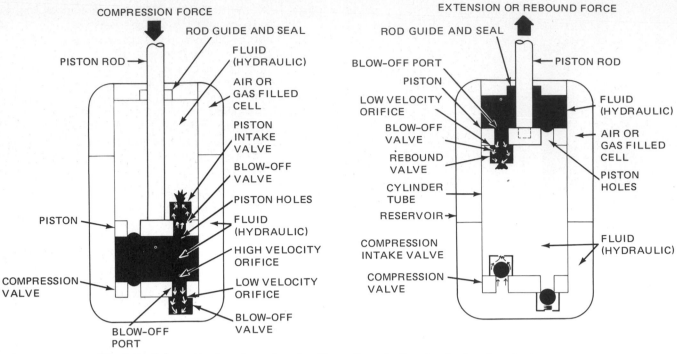

COMPRESSION FORCE

ROD GUIDE AND SEAL

PISTON ROD

FLUID (HYDRAULIC)

AIR OR GAS FILLED CELL

PISTON INTAKE VALVE

BLOW-OFF VALVE

PISTON HOLES

PISTON

FLUID (HYDRAULIC)

HIGH VELOCITY ORIFICE

COMPRESSION VALVE

LOW VELOCITY ORIFICE

BLOW-OFF PORT

BLOW-OFF VALVE

EXTENSION OR REBOUND FORCE

ROD GUIDE AND SEAL

BLOW-OFF PORT

PISTON

LOW VELOCITY ORIFICE

BLOW-OFF VALVE

REBOUND VALVE

CYLINDER TUBE

RESERVOIR

COMPRESSION INTAKE VALVE

COMPRESSION VALVE

PISTON ROD

FLUID (HYDRAULIC)

AIR OR GAS FILLED CELL

PISTON HOLES

FLUID (HYDRAULIC)

Fig. 4-7. Schematic drawings showing the actions in the shock absorber during compression and extension or rebound. (*Chevrolet Motor Division of General Motor Corporation*)

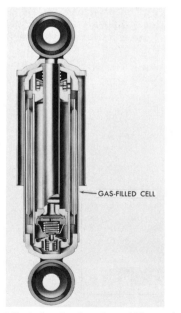

SPIRAL-GROOVE RESERVOIR

Fig. 4-8. Spiral-groove shock absorber. (*Chevrolet Motor Division of General Motors Corporation*)

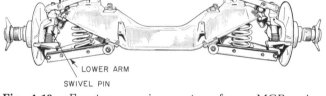

ARM

SHOCK ABSORBER

LOWER ARM

SWIVEL PIN

Fig. 4-10. Front-suspension system for a MGB using parallel-cylinder shock absorbers. (*British Motor Corporation, Limited*)

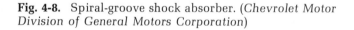

GAS-FILLED CELL

Fig. 4-9. Gas-filled shock absorber. (*Chevrolet Motor Division of General Motors Corporation*)

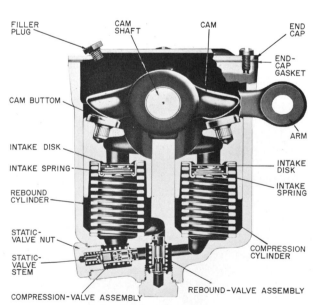

FILLER PLUG

CAM SHAFT

CAM

END CAP

END-CAP GASKET

CAM BUTTOM

INTAKE DISK

INTAKE SPRING

REBOUND CYLINDER

STATIC-VALVE NUT

STATIC-VALVE STEM

COMPRESSION-VALVE ASSEMBLY

ARM

INTAKE DISK

INTAKE SPRING

COMPRESSION CYLINDER

REBOUND-VALVE ASSEMBLY

Fig. 4-11. Parallel-cylinder shock absorber in sectional view. (*General Motors Corporation*)

are attached to the swivel pin (kingpin) as shown in Fig. 4-10. Up-and-down movement of the wheel causes the shock-absorber arms to pivot about the shock absorber. This action moves either one or the other piston in its cylinder. Piston movement is restricted hydraulically, just as in the direct-acting shock absorber.

⊘ **4-5 Shock-Absorber Service** Some of the early-model shock absorbers could be disassembled and reassembled in the shop. However, the direct-acting shock absorbers now in general use are usually serviced by complete replacement, although some of these, too, can be disassembled (as described in ⊘ 4-6).

One off-the-car test of shock absorbers, recommended by Ford, is as follows. Hold the shock absorber upside down and pull it to its full extension. Then push the shock absorber to its shortest length. Repeat this until all air is expelled. Now, clamp the lower end (smaller diameter) in a vise in a vertical position. Extend the shock absorber to its full length, then compress it to its shortest length. There should be a constant drag throughout the complete stroke. Any sudden loss of drag indicates that there is air in the shock absorber or that the valves are faulty. In such a case, discard the shock absorber.

⊘ **4-6 Direct-acting Shock-Absorber Service** On the type of shock absorber that can be disassembled (see Fig. 4-6), service it as follows. Clamp the lower eye on flat sides in a vise. Pull it to its fully extended position, clean it, and insert the special wrench through the holes in the dust sleeve so that the wrench lugs engage in the slots in the top guide. Unscrew the guide and lift off the top of the unit. Remove the compression-valve-and-cage assembly by tapping it lightly. Clamp the top eye in a vise and disassemble the piston and rebound-valve assembly by removing the nut, spring, spring seat, and plates. Note the relationship of parts so that you can reassemble them in the same relative positions. Before removing the piston, mark the rod and piston location with respect to each other so that you can assemble them in the same relationship. Then remove the piston, intake valve, valve-plate spider spring, and spacing and piston washers. Next remove the cylinder from the piston rod.

After disassembly, wash all parts in cleaner. Do not use thinner or paint remover, as either would damage the piston-rod seal. Always install a new rubber gasket and, if necessary, a new gasket retainer. Dip the gasket in shock-absorber fluid before installation. When assembling the top guide and seal assembly, use a shock-absorber rod-guide pilot to avoid damaging the seal when sliding it under the piston-rod shoulder. In reassembly, be sure all parts are replaced in the proper order and in correct relationship to each other. In particular, make sure the piston and rod markings are aligned. Stake the nut in place on the piston rod to prevent loosening in

service. Replace the compression-valve-and-cage assembly and tap it into place. Fill the shock absorber with the exact amount of fluid specified for the type being repaired. Pour fluid into the pressure tube until the tube is filled. Replace the compression valve in the end of the pressure tube, keeping the pressure tube extended. Pour the remaining fluid into the reservoir tube with the tube in the upright position. Place the reservoir tube in a vise, and assemble the dust shield and reservoir tube. Use a new rod-guide retainer gasket. Insert a special wrench through slots in the dust tube, and tighten the rod-guide assembly securely.

CHAPTER 4 CHECKUP

You have been making good progress in the book and have a right to feel that you have made a fine start in your studies of automotive suspension systems and shock absorbers. You may not have much to do with shock absorbers in your automotive work. Nevertheless, you will want to know how they are constructed and how they work so that you can talk intelligently about them to anyone. To check up on yourself and find out how well you remember what you have just read, take the following test. If any of the questions stump you, just reread the chapter. As we have said before, there are few people who can remember everything they read, even though they read it more than once. Write your answers in your notebook. Writing down the answers helps you remember them. Also, you make your notebook a valuable source of information you can refer to whenever some facts become hazy in your mind.

Correcting Parts Lists The purpose of this exercise is to give you practice in spotting unrelated parts in a list. In each of the lists below, one item is named that does not belong. Write each list in your notebook, but do not write the item that does not belong.

1. Parts in the direct-acting shock absorber include piston, check valve, compression relief valve, dust shield, connecting rod, piston rod.
2. Parts in the direct-acting shock absorber that are in contact with fluid include sealing gaskets, valves, piston, dust shield, piston nut, cylinder tube.

Completing the Sentences The sentences below are incomplete. After each sentence there are several words or phrases, only one of which will correctly complete the sentence. Write each sentence in your notebook, selecting the proper word or phrase to complete it correctly.

1. In a coil-spring suspension system, as the wheel passes over a bump the spring is: (a) expanded, (b) extended, (c) compressed.
2. When the direct-acting shock absorber is compressed or telescoped, fluid passes through the piston orifices into the upper part of the cylinder and

also: (*a*) out of the reservoir, (*b*) into the reservoir, (*c*) into the dust shield, (*d*) out of the dust shield.
3. On rebound, in the direct-acting shock absorber, fluid flows out of the upper part of the cylinder and also: (*a*) out of the reservoir, (*b*) into the reservoir, (*c*) into the dust shield, (*d*) out of the dust shield.

Purpose and Operation of Shock Absorbers In the following, you are asked to write the purpose and operation of the various shock absorbers. If you have any difficulty in your explanations, turn back and reread the pages in the chapter that will clarify the matter for you. But don't copy; try to tell it in your own words. This is a good way of fixing the explanation in your mind. Write in your notebook. Number 3 refers to a shock absorber that is no longer in common use, although it may be found on older cars. It is mentioned here in case you want to do a little research on older-model shock absorbers.

1. Explain why shock absorbers are needed.
2. Explain how a direct-acting shock absorber is constructed and how it operates.
3. Explain how a double-acting, parallel-cylinder shock absorber operates.

Servicing Procedures Some of the items below refer to shock absorbers that are no longer widely used. However, they are included here in case you would like to do a little research on some of the older-model shock absorbers. Write the answers to the following in your notebook.

1. What is the basic test of a shock absorber?
2. How can leakage of fluid from the shock absorber be detected?
3. How is the single-acting shock absorber filled?
4. How is the double-acting shock absorber filled?
5. How is the vane type of shock absorber filled?
6. How is the direct-acting shock absorber filled?
7. Describe the procedure for changing relief valves on the single-acting shock absorber. The double-acting, parallel-cylinder shock absorber. The double-acting, opposed-cylinder shock absorber with external valves. The double-acting, opposed-cylinder shock absorber with internal valves.
8. Describe the procedure for disassembling the single-acting shock absorber. The double-acting, parallel-cylinder shock absorber. The double-acting, opposed-cylinder, internal-valve shock absorber. The double-acting, opposed cylinder, external-valve shock absorber. The direct-acting shock absorber.
9. How is the vane type of shock absorber adjusted?

SUGGESTIONS FOR FURTHER STUDY

If you are especially interested in shock absorbers, you might be able to obtain, from a local service shop, discarded and defective shock absorbers which you can disassemble and study in detail. Some automotive shop manuals also cover the operation and servicing of the shock absorbers used on their cars. Study these manuals if you have a chance. Write important facts in your notebook.

chapter 5

STEERING SYSTEMS

This chapter covers the various types of steering systems used in automotive vehicles. The requirements of a steering system, as well as types of steering gears and linkages, are described. The discussion of steering gears takes up most of the chapter, since there are many varieties of steering gears, both manually and hydraulically operated. The latter type is known as power steering. Most cars produced today have power steering.

⊘ **5-1 Function of the Steering System** A simplified drawing of a steering system is shown in Fig. 2-14. We have already described the various methods of supporting the front-wheel spindles (Chap. 3) so that the wheels can be swung to the left or right for steering. This movement is produced by gearing and linkage between the steering wheel in front of the driver and the steering knuckle or wheel. The complete arrangement is called the *steering system*. Actually, the steering system is composed of two elements: a steering gear at the lower end of the steering column and the linkage between the gear and the wheel steering knuckle. Before we discuss linkages and steering gears in detail, let us take a look at the steering system from the standpoint of geometry, or the angles involved.

⊘ **5-2 Front-End Geometry** Front-end geometry is the angular relationship among the front wheels, the front-wheel attaching parts, and the car frame. The angle of the steering axis or kingpin away from vertical, the pointing in (toe-in) of the front wheels, the tilt of the front wheels from vertical—all these are involved in front-end geometry. Every one of them influences the steering ease, steering stability, and the riding qualities of the car and has a direct effect on tire wear. The various factors that enter into front-end geometry are classified under the following terms: *camber, steering-axis inclination (kingpin inclination), caster, toe-in,* and *toe-out on turns.* These are discussed in detail below.

NOTE: Even though most late-model cars do not use kingpins (⊘ 3-14 and Figs. 3-30 to 3-36), they are treated as though they have kingpins during the front-alignment checks and adjustments. On these cars, reference is made to the "apparent," or theoretical, kingpin inclination (actually the steering-axis inclination). This is discussed further in ⊘ 8-11.

⊘ **5-3 Camber** Camber is the tilting of the front wheels from the vertical (Fig. 5-1). When the tilt is outward so that the wheels are farther apart at the top than at the bottom, the camber is positive. Positive camber is shown in Fig. 5-1. When the tilt is inward so that the wheels are closer together at the top than at the bottom, the camber is negative. The amount of tilt is measured in degrees from the vertical, and this measurement is called the *camber angle*. The wheels are given a slight outward tilt to start with so that when the vehicle is loaded and rolling along on the road, the load will just about bring the wheels to a vertical position. If you started with no camber angle—wheels vertical—loading the car might give them a negative camber. Any amount of camber—positive or negative—tends to cause uneven or more rapid tire wear, since the tilt puts more of the load on one side of the tread than on the other.

If the vehicle were rolling on a perfectly level road, the ideal camber would be the same for both front wheels. This ideal camber would be just sufficient to bring the front wheels to the vertical position when the vehicle is loaded and moving. However, roads are seldom perfectly level. Many roads are crowned slightly; that is, they are higher at the center than on the two sides. The result is that when a car is moving along on one side of the road, it tends to lean out slightly. This could ultimately cause the outside of the tread on the right front tire to wear excessively because this part of the tread would be taking most of the action. In passenger cars, this is not particularly important because the vehicle weight is relatively light and the wear relatively small. On the other hand, the tires on heavy-duty vehicles could show this sort of wear at relatively low mileages. For this reason, some heavy-duty vehicles have a front adjustment that gives the right front wheel less positive camber than the left front.

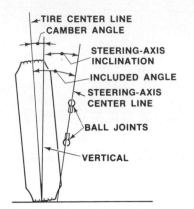

Fig. 5-1. Camber angle and steering-axis inclination. Positive camber is shown.

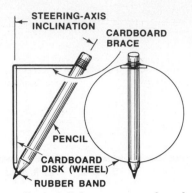

Fig. 5-2. A cardboard disk to serve as the wheel, a rubber band, a pencil, and a cardboard brace demonstrate the effects of steering-axis inclination.

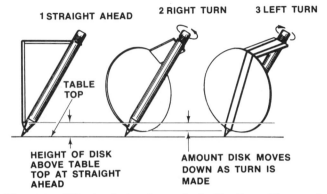

Fig. 5-3. Effect of steering-axis inclination. The cardboard disk represents the left front wheel as viewed from the driver's seat. 1, straight-ahead position; 2, right turn; 3, left turn.

⊘ **5-4 Steering-Axis (or Kingpin) Inclination** At one time, all steering systems had a kingpin which attached the steering knuckle to a support (Fig. 3-43). Later, ball-joint supports were adopted (Figs. 3-30 to 3-36). In this design, the steering knuckle and the steering-knuckle support have, in effect, been combined into a single part, called the *steering knuckle,* or *spindle;* no kingpin is used. The steering knuckle is supported at top and bottom by the control arms and is attached to the arms by ball joints.

The inclination from the vertical of the centerlines of the ball joints, or of the kingpin, is a very important factor in steering action. This is the centerline around which the front wheel swings for steering. This inclination is called the *steering-axis inclination* (on ball joint systems) or *kingpin inclination* (on systems with kingpins). It is also called the *ball-joint angle.* This inclination is the inward tilt of the ball-joint centerline, or kingpin, from the vertical (Fig. 5-1). This inward tilt is desirable for several reasons. First, it helps provide steering stability by tending to return the wheels to the straight-ahead position after any turn. Second, it reduces steering effort, particularly when the car is stationary. Third, it reduces tire wear.

The inward tilt, or inclination, of the steering axis tends to keep the wheels straight ahead. It helps recovery, or the return of the wheels to the straight-ahead position after a turn has been made. You can make a tabletop demonstration of why this is so with a pencil, a rubber band, a cardboard disk, and a piece of cardboard (Fig. 5-2). Put them together as shown in Fig. 5-2. The cardboard disk represents the wheel, the pencil the steering axis (or centerline through the ball joints); the cardboard brace at the top holds the two apart there so as to give "steering-axis inclination." Needless to say, the angle is greatly exaggerated in the illustration. Now, hold the pencil at an angle with the tabletop so the wheel is vertical, as shown in Fig. 5-3. Then rotate the pencil, but do not change its angle with the tabletop. Notice that as you turn the pencil, the wheel is carried around and down toward the tabletop (Fig. 5-3). If the wheel could not move down, what would happen? As you turned the pencil, the pencil would have to be

moved up, always maintaining the same angle with the tabletop.

This last movement is what actually takes place in the automobile. The wheel is in contact with the ground. It cannot move down. Therefore, as it is swung away from straight ahead, the ball joints and supporting parts are moved upward. This means that the car body is actually lifted. In other words, steering-axis inclination causes the car to be raised every time the front wheels are swung away from straight ahead. Then the weight of the car brings the wheels back to straight ahead after the turn is completed and the steering wheel is released.

⊘ **5-5 Included Angle** The included, or combined, angle is the camber angle plus the steering-axis-inclination angle (Fig. 5-1). The included angle is important because it determines the point of intersection of the wheel and the ball-joint centerlines (Fig. 5-4). This in turn, determines whether the wheel will tend to toe out or toe in. "Toe-out" is a term used to describe the tendency for the wheel to point outward. A soldier standing at attention has his feet "toed out." Toe-in is just the opposite; a pigeon-toed person turns the toes of his feet inward. Likewise, a wheel that toes in tries to point inward as it rolls.

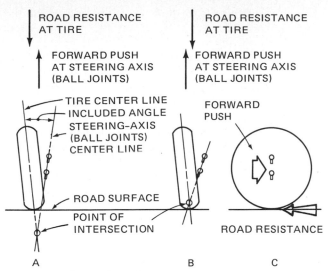

Fig. 5-4. Effect when the point of intersection is below the road surface (A) and above the road surface (B). The left front wheel as viewed from the driver's seat is shown in A and B. C is a side view of the wheel to show two forces acting on the wheel and ball joints.

Figure 5-9 shows what toe-in is on a vehicle. The tire on a wheel that is toed in or toed out will wear more rapidly. The tire has to go in the direction that the car is moving. But, since it is not pointed in that direction—it is toed out or toed in—it is dragged sideways as it rolls forward. The more toe-out or toe-in, the more it is dragged sideways and the faster the tire wears.

When the point of intersection (Fig. 5-4) is below the road surface, the wheel will tend to toe out. This is because the forward push, which is through the centerline of the ball joints, is inside the tire centerline at the road surface. In the right hand picture in Fig. 5-4, the two opposing forces working on the wheel are shown. One is the forward push through the ball joints; the other is the road resistance to the tire. If these two forces are exactly in line, the wheel will have no tendency to toe out or toe in. The two forces will be in line with each other only when the point of intersection is at the road surface. When it is below the road level, as shown at A in Fig. 5-4, the wheel attempts to swing outward, or toe out. When the point of intersection is above the road level, as shown at B in Fig. 5-4, the wheel attempts to swing inward, or toe in.

⊘ **5-6 Caster** In addition to being tilted inward toward the center of the car, the steering axis may also be tilted forward or backward from the vertical (Fig. 5-5). Backward tilt from the vertical is called *positive caster*. Positive caster aids directional stability, since the centerline of the ball joints passes through the road surface ahead of the centerline of the wheel. Thus, the push on the ball joints is ahead of the road resistance to the tire. The tire is trailing behind, just as the caster on a table leg "trails behind" when the table is pushed (Fig. 5-6).

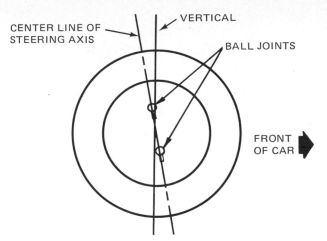

Fig. 5-5. Left front wheel (as viewed from driver's seat). The view is from inside so that the backward tilt of steering axis from the vertical can be seen. This backward tilt is called *positive caster*.

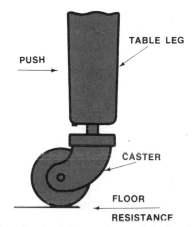

Fig. 5-6. The wheel of the caster trails behind and follows in the direction of the push when the table leg is moved.

Caster has another effect that is important. When both front wheels have positive caster, the car tends to roll out or lean out on turns. But if the front wheels have negative caster, the car tends to bank, or lean in, on turns. Let us use a pencil, a rubber band, and a cardboard disk to demonstrate why this is so (Fig. 5-7). Fasten the cardboard disk and the pencil together as shown. The disk represents the left front wheel. Note that we do not include any steering-axis inclination here; we want to show only the effect of positive caster. Hold the disk vertical with the pencil at an angle so that both the pencil point and the edge of the disk rest on the tabletop. Now, rotate the pencil as shown. Note that the disk is lifted from the tabletop. Actually, in the car, the wheel (the disk) would not be lifted. Instead, the ball joints (the pencil) would move down. In other words, on a right turn, the left side of the car would drop.

Now, let us see what happens at the right front wheel (Fig. 5-8). As the right turn is made, the wheel

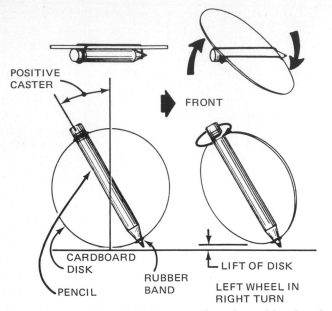

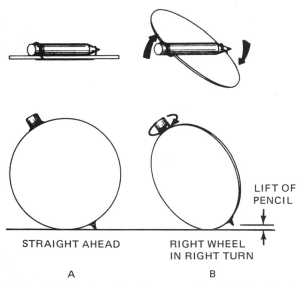

Fig. 5-7. A cardboard disk, a pencil, and a rubber band show the effects of positive caster in a right turn. The disk represents the left front wheel. The pencil represents the centerlines of the ball joints.

Fig. 5-8. Effect of positive caster on the right front wheel during a right turn.

pivots on the road surface, causing the ball joints (the pencil) to be lifted. The right side of the car is lifted.

When the left side of the car is lowered and the right side of the car is lifted as a right turn is made (as described above), the car rolls, or leans out, on the turn. This is just the opposite of what would be most desirable, since it adds to the effect of centrifugal force on the turn. By using negative caster—tilting the centerline of the ball joints forward—the car can be made to lean in on a turn and thus decrease the effect of centrifugal force. For instance, with negative caster the left side of the car would

lift during a right turn, and the right side of the car would drop. This would combat the roll-out effect of centrifugal force.

Caster has another important effect. Positive caster tends to make the front wheels toe in. With positive caster, the car is lowered as the wheel pivots inward. Thus, the weight of the car is always exerting force to make the wheel toe in. With negative caster, the wheels would tend to toe out.

Note that positive caster increases the effort required to steer. Positive caster tries to keep the wheels straight ahead. In order to make a turn, this tendency must be overcome. Note that steering-axis inclination also tries to keep the wheels straight ahead. Thus, to make a turn, the effects of both caster—when positive—and steering-axis inclination must be overcome. Late-model vehicles, particularly heavy-duty trucks, tend to have a negative caster. This makes steering easier, and a sufficient tendency toward recovery, or the return of the wheels to straight ahead, is still provided by steering-axis inclination.

⊘ **5-7 Toe-in** As mentioned, toe-in is the turning in of the front wheels; they attempt to roll inward instead of straight ahead. On a car with toe-in (Fig. 5-9), the distance between the front wheels is less at the front (A) than at the rear (B). The actual amount of toe-in is normally only a fraction of an inch. The purpose of toe-in is to ensure parallel rolling of the front wheels, to stabilize steering, and to prevent sideslipping and excessive wear of tires. The toe-in on the front wheels of a car serves to offset the small deflections in the wheel-support system which come about when the car is moving forward. These deflections are due to the rolling resistance of the tires on the road. In other words, even though the wheels are set to toe in slightly when the car is standing still, they tend to roll parallel on the road when the car is moving forward.

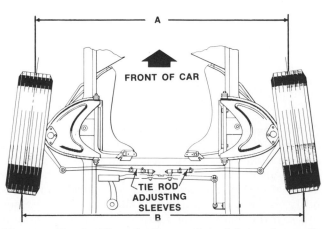

Fig. 5-9. Toe-in. The wheels are viewed from above; the front of the car is at the top of the illustration. A is less than B. Toe-in angles are shown greatly exaggerated. (*Bear Manufacturing Company*)

⊘ **5-8 Toe-out during Turns** Toe-out during turns, also called *steering geometry, front-wheel turning angle,* and *cornering wheel relationship,* refers to the difference in angles between the two front wheels and the car frame during turns. Since the inner wheel is rotating on, or following, a smaller radius than the outer wheel when the car is rounding a curve, its axle must be at a sharper angle with the car frame; that is, it must toe out more. This condition is shown in Fig. 5-10. When the front wheels are steered to make the turn illustrated, the inner wheel turns at an angle of 23 degrees with the car frame, while the outer wheel turns at an angle of only 20 degrees with the car frame. This permits the inner wheel to follow a shorter radius than the outer wheel, and the circles on which the two front wheels turn are concentric: their centers are at the same place (D). Toe-out is secured by providing the proper relationship between the steering knuckle arms, tie rods, and pitman arm. This relationship is such that the inner wheel on a curve always toes out more than the outer wheel. Figure 5-11 illustrates the manner of securing this condition. When the tie rod is moved to the left during a right turn, it pushes at almost a right angle against the left steering-knuckle arm. The right end of the tie rod, however, not only moves to the left but also swings forward (as shown by the dotted line) so that the right wheel is turned an additional amount. When a left turn is made, the left wheel is turned an additional amount over that which the right wheel turns. Figure 5-11 shows a parallelogram type of linkage (see ⊘ 5-9). Other types of linkage give a similar effect and provide a similar toe-out on turns.

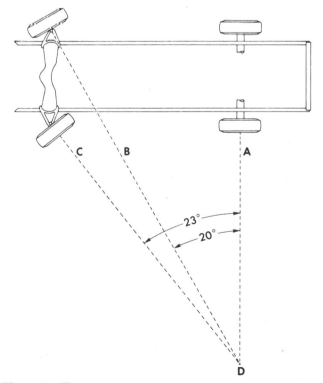

Fig. 5-10. Toe-out on turns.

⊘ **5-9 Steering Linkages** Many types of steering linkages have been made to connect the steering knuckles of the front wheels and the pitman arm of the steering gear. You will recall that the pitman arm swings from one side to the other—or forward and backward, on some cars—as the steering wheel is turned. This movement must be carried to the steering knuckles at the wheels by some form of linkage. Figure 5-12 shows several types of linkages diagrammatically. All these have some means of adjusting the lengths of the tie rods or links so that proper alignment of the front wheels can be established. This alignment gives the front wheels a slight toe-in when the car is at rest. When the car begins to move forward, the toe-in practically disappears as all looseness, or "sloppage," in the steering system is taken up.

The most commonly used type of steering linkage is some form of the parallelogram system. Figure 5-13 is a modified form of the parallelogram type of steering linkage. Points of attachment between the metal parts of the rods, pitman and idler arms, and steering spindles (knuckles) are insulated by bushings. The connecting-rod (or tie-rod) ends are attached to the spindles (knuckles) by ball joints. The sleeves that connect the spindle connecting rods to the connecting-rod ends are threaded, as are the mating ends of the rods, permitting adjustment of the toe-in. The sleeves can be turned one way or the other to change the effective length of the connecting rods, thus altering the toe-in adjustment at the wheels.

Figure 5-14 is a schematic layout of a similar steering linkage. Notice that this steering linkage is the same for both manual and power steering.

⊘ **5-10 Ball Sockets and Ball Joints** The various parts of the steering linkage are connected by ball sockets or ball joints of several kinds (Fig. 5-15). Some have provisions for lubrication; others are prelubricated at the factory and require no lubrication for the life of the car. On many cars, the idler arm is connected through rubber bushings. These bushings twist as the idler arm swings to one side or the other. They then supply some force to help return the wheels to center after a turn is completed.

⊘ **5-11 Steering Gears** The steering gear converts the rotary motion of the steering wheel into straight-line motion of the linkage. Essentially, on most cars, the steering gear consists of two parts: a worm on the end of the steering shaft and a pitman-arm shaft (or cross shaft) on which there is a gear sector, a toothed roller, or a stud.[1] The gear sector, toothed roller, or stud meshes with the worm as shown in Fig. 5-16. In this illustration, the steering gear uses a toothed roller. The roller and worm teeth mesh. When the worm is rotated (by rotation of the steer-

[1] Some foreign and small domestic cars use a rack-and-pinion steering gear, as explained in ⊘ 5-12.

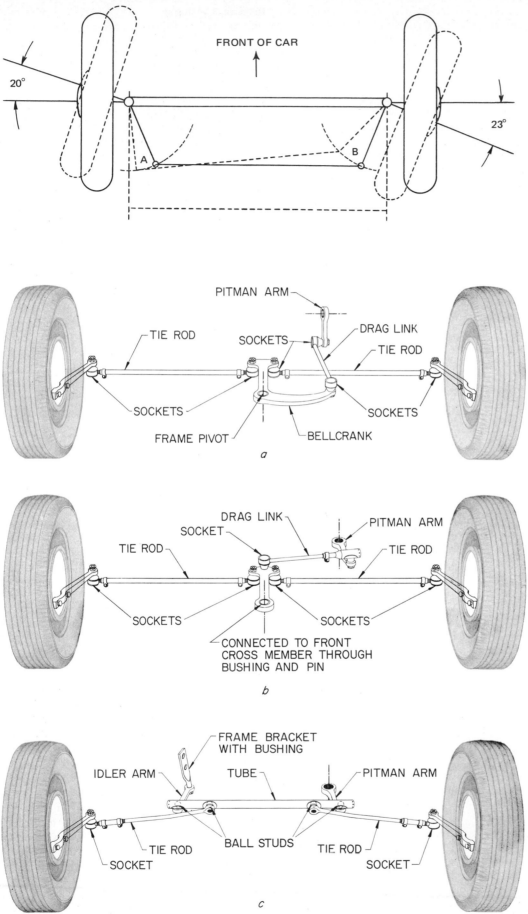

FRONT OF CAR

20°

A

B

23°

Fig. 5-11. How toe-out on turns is obtained. (*Chevrolet Motor Division of General Motors Corporation*)

PITMAN ARM

TIE ROD

SOCKETS

DRAG LINK

TIE ROD

SOCKETS

SOCKETS

FRAME PIVOT

BELLCRANK

a

DRAG LINK

SOCKET

PITMAN ARM

TIE ROD

TIE ROD

SOCKETS

SOCKETS

CONNECTED TO FRONT CROSS MEMBER THROUGH BUSHING AND PIN

b

FRAME BRACKET WITH BUSHING

IDLER ARM

TUBE

PITMAN ARM

TIE ROD

BALL STUDS

TIE ROD

SOCKET

SOCKET

c

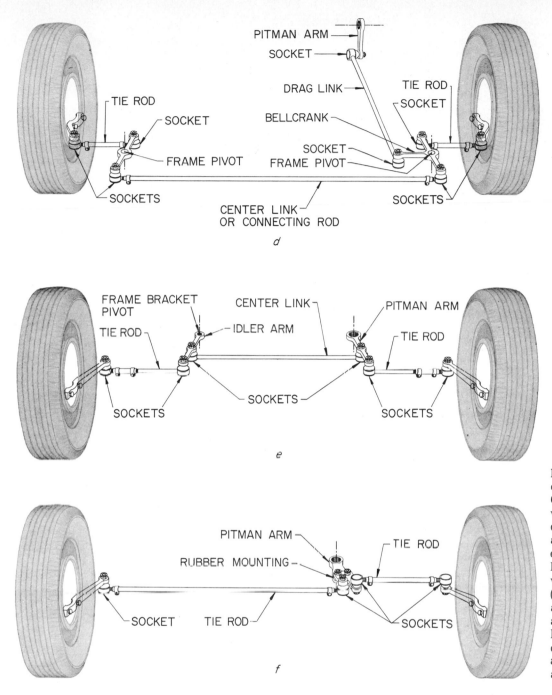

Fig. 5-12. Various types of steering linkages: (*a*) Center-arm steering with bellcrank intermediate arm. (*b*) Center-arm steering with traverse drag link. (*c*) Parallelogram linkage with tubular center link. (*d*) Parallelogram linkage with center link ahead of axle. (*e*) Parallelogram linkage with center link in back of axle. (*f*) Long-arm, short-arm linkage. (*TRW, Inc.*)

ing wheel), the roller teeth must follow along, and this action causes the pitman-arm shaft to rotate. The other end of the pitman-arm shaft carries the pitman arm; rotation of the pitman-arm shaft causes the arm to swing in one direction or the other. This motion is then carried through the linkage to the steering knuckles at the wheels.

NOTE: The pitman-arm shaft is also called the *cross shaft, pitman shaft, roller shaft, steering-arm shaft,* and *sector shaft.*

Two versions of the recirculating-ball steering gear are shown in Figs. 5-17 and 5-18. In these units,

friction is kept exceptionally low by interposing balls between the major moving parts or between the worm teeth and grooves cut in the inner face of a ball nut. The rotation of the worm gear causes the balls to roll in the worm teeth. The balls also roll in grooves cut in the inner face of the nut. Thus as the worm rotates, the balls cause the nut to move up or down along the worm. The up-or-down motion is carried to the gear sector by teeth on the side of the ball nut. This then forces the gear sector to move along with the ball nut so that the pitman-arm shaft rotates.

The balls are called *recirculating* balls because they can continuously recirculate from one end of

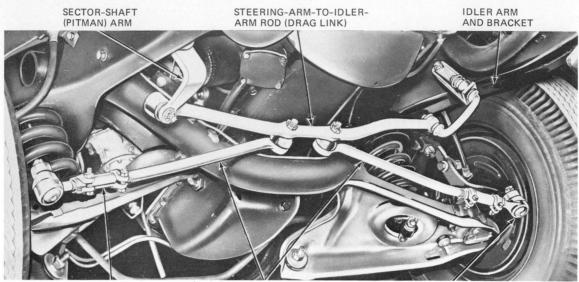

SECTOR-SHAFT (PITMAN) ARM   STEERING-ARM-TO-IDLER-ARM ROD (DRAG LINK)   IDLER ARM AND BRACKET

SLEEVE   SPINDLE CONNECTING RODS   CONNECTING-ROD END

Fig. 5-13. Steering linkage with traverse drag link (relay rod). (*Ford Motor Company*)

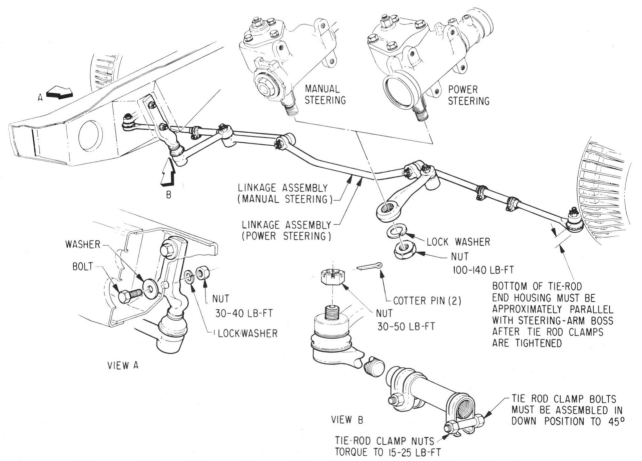

A

MANUAL STEERING

POWER STEERING

B

LINKAGE ASSEMBLY (MANUAL STEERING)

LINKAGE ASSEMBLY (POWER STEERING)

LOCK WASHER

NUT 100-140 LB-FT

WASHER

BOLT

NUT 30-40 LB-FT

LOCKWASHER

VIEW A

COTTER PIN (2)

NUT 30-50 LB-FT

BOTTOM OF TIE-ROD END HOUSING MUST BE APPROXIMATELY PARALLEL WITH STEERING-ARM BOSS AFTER TIE ROD CLAMPS ARE TIGHTENED

TIE ROD CLAMP BOLTS MUST BE ASSEMBLED IN DOWN POSITION TO 45°

VIEW B

TIE-ROD CLAMP NUTS TORQUE TO 15-25 LB-FT

Fig. 5-14. Schematic layout of a parallelogram type of steering linkage. (*Buick Motor Division of General Motors Corporation*)

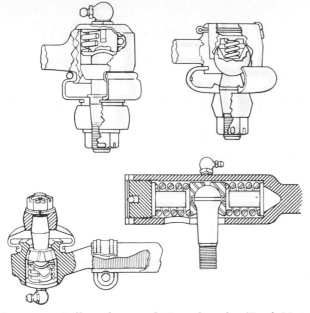

Fig. 5-15. Ball sockets and tie-rod ends. (*Ford Motor Company*)

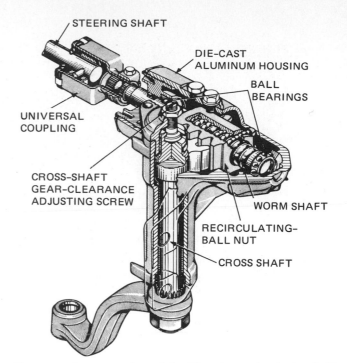

STEERING SHAFT

DIE-CAST ALUMINUM HOUSING

BALL BEARINGS

UNIVERSAL COUPLING

CROSS-SHAFT GEAR-CLEARANCE ADJUSTING SCREW

WORM SHAFT

RECIRCULATING-BALL NUT

CROSS SHAFT

Fig. 5-17. Cutaway view of the Chrysler recirculating-ball steering gear. (*Chrysler Corporation*)

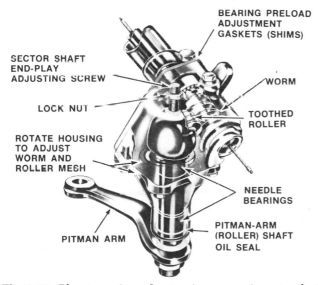

BEARING PRELOAD ADJUSTMENT GASKETS (SHIMS)

SECTOR SHAFT END-PLAY ADJUSTING SCREW

LOCK NUT

WORM

TOOTHED ROLLER

ROTATE HOUSING TO ADJUST WORM AND ROLLER MESH

NEEDLE BEARINGS

PITMAN-ARM (ROLLER) SHAFT OIL SEAL

PITMAN ARM

Fig. 5-16. Phantom view of a steering gear using a toothed roller attached to the pitman-arm shaft. The worm and roller teeth mesh. (*Ford Motor Company*)

the ball nut to the other through a pair of ball return guides. For example, suppose that the driver makes a right turn. The worm gear is rotated in a clockwise direction—viewed from the driver's seat—and this causes the ball nut to move upward. The balls roll between the worm and ball nut, and as they reach the upper end of the nut, they enter the return guide and then roll back to the lower point, where they reenter the groove between the worm and the ball nut.

⊘ 5-12 Rack-and-Pinion Steering Gear The rack-and-pinion steering gear (Figs. 5-19 and 5-20), used on some imported cars and small domestic cars such as the Ford Pinto, has a pinion on the end of the steering shaft. The pinion meshes with a rack which is the major cross member of the steering linkage. When the steering wheel and shaft are turned for steering, the gear causes the rack to move to the left or right in the housing. This motion, carried through the tie rods and ball joint, causes the front wheels to pivot for steering. This is a satisfactory arrangement for small cars where the steering forces are light. For larger cars, a greater mechanical advantage is necessary, and a worm on the end of the steering shaft, engaging a ball nut and gear sector, toothed roller, or stud, is used to gain this mechanical advantage.

Still other types of steering gears are in use. All are very similar in operation. A later chapter describes the servicing procedures required on the most popular makes of steering gear in use today.

Check Your Progress

Progress Quiz 5-1 Here is your chance to check up on yourself again and find out how well you are remembering what you are reading. As we have mentioned before, there are two good reasons for the quizzes. One is to help you review and remember the important points covered in the book. The other is to let you check yourself on the progress you are making.

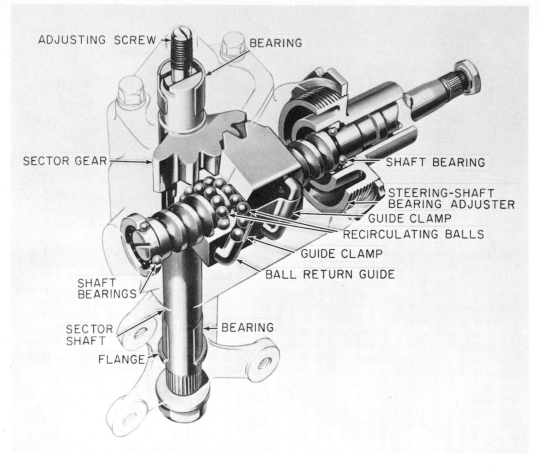

ADJUSTING SCREW
BEARING
SECTOR GEAR
SHAFT BEARING
STEERING-SHAFT BEARING ADJUSTER
GUIDE CLAMP
RECIRCULATING BALLS
GUIDE CLAMP
BALL RETURN GUIDE
SHAFT BEARINGS
SECTOR SHAFT
BEARING
FLANGE

Fig. 5-18. Phantom view of the Ford recirculating-ball steering gear. (*Ford Motor Company*)

Completing the Sentences The sentences below are incomplete. After each sentence there are several words or phrases, only one of which will correctly complete the sentence. Write each sentence in your notebook, selecting the proper word or phrase to complete it correctly.

1. The tilting of the front wheels away from the vertical is called: (*a*) camber, (*b*) caster, (*c*) toe-in, (*d*) toe-out.
2. The inward tilt of the centerline of the ball joints is called: (*a*) caster, (*b*) camber, (*c*) steering-axis inclination, (*d*) included angle.
3. Camber angle plus steering-axis-inclination angle is called the: (*a*) caster, (*b*) included angle, (*c*) point of intersection, (*d*) toe-out.
4. The point at which the centerline of the wheel and the centerline of the ball joints cross is called the: (*a*) included angle, (*b*) point of departure, (*c*) point of intersection, (*d*) point of included angle.
5. When the point of intersection is below the road surface, the front wheel will tend to: (*a*) toe out, (*b*) toe in, (*c*) roll straight.
6. The backward tilt of the centerline of the ball joints from the vertical is called: (*a*) positive caster, (*b*) negative caster, (*c*) positive camber, (*d*) negative camber.
7. Positive caster will tend to cause the car to: (*a*) roll out on turns, (*b*) bank on turns, (*c*) lean on turns.

8. Positive caster tends to make front wheels: (*a*) toe in, (*b*) toe out.
9. Toe-out on turns means that the right wheel, in a right-hand turn, would turn out, or away from straight ahead: (*a*) more than the left wheel, (*b*) less than the left wheel, (*c*) the same as the left wheel.
10. In the steering gear, a gear sector, stud, or toothed roller is meshed with: (*a*) a worm, (*b*) a ball bearing, (*c*) a roller bearing, (*d*) a steering wheel.

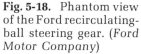 **5-13 Power Steering** Power steering was used for a number of years on heavy-duty applications before it became popular with the passenger-car purchaser. Today, more than half the automobiles made in the United States are equipped with power steering. The principle of power steering is very simple. A booster arrangement is provided which is set into operation when the steering-wheel shaft is turned. The booster then takes over and does most of the work of steering. Power steering has used compressed air, electrical mechanisms, and hydraulic pressure. Hydraulic pressure is used on the vast majority of power-steering mechanisms today. You will recall that we discussed hydraulic pressure in some detail (⊘ 1-12 to 1-15) and learned that pressure and movement can be transferred from one part of a hydraulic system to another.

In the hydraulic power-steering system, a con-

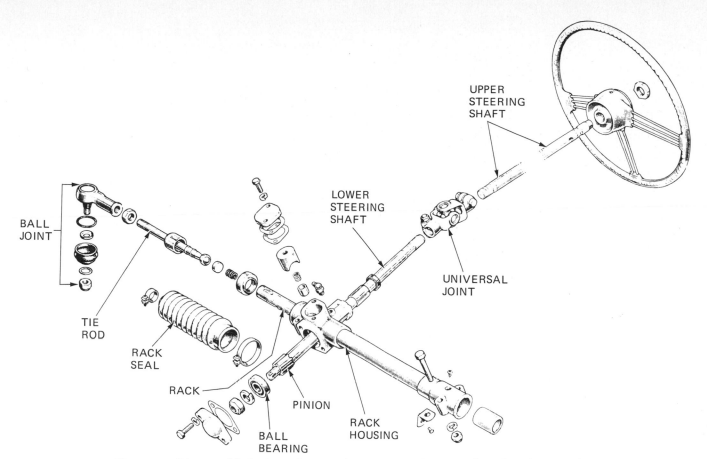

Fig. 5-19. Disassembled view of a steering system using a rack-and-pinion steering gear. (*British Motor Corporation, Ltd.*)

tinuously operating pump provides hydraulic pressure when needed. As the steering wheel is turned, valves are operated that admit this hydraulic pressure to a cylinder. Then the pressure causes a piston to move, and the piston does most of the steering work. Specific power-steering systems are described in the sections that follow. There are actually two general types of power-steering systems. In one, the integral type, the power operating assembly is part of the steering gear. In the other, the linkage type, the power operating assembly is part of the steering linkage. Figure 5-21 shows a power-steering system of the integral type.

Figure 5-22 shows a power-steering system for a front-wheel-drive car. Instead of the power-steering gear being located at the lower end of the steering shaft, it is set forward and is connected to the

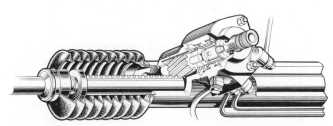

Fig. 5-20. Cutaway view of a rack-and-pinion steering gear. (*Burman & Sons, Ltd.*)

steering shaft by a secondary steering shaft. The two shafts are at an angle and are connected by a universal joint. This arrangement is required by the front-drive design so that there will be ample room above the steering shaft and linkage for the transmission and other power-train components.

⊘ **5-14 Variable Ratio Steering** The ratio of a steering system is the relationship between the steering-wheel movement and the front-wheel movement from straight ahead. In measurement, it is the number of degrees the steering wheel must be turned to move the front wheels from straight ahead 1 degree. A typical steering ratio is 17.5:1. That means the steering wheel must be rotated 17.5 degrees to turn the front wheels 1 degree from straight ahead.

Part of the ratio is developed in the steering linkage, but most of it is developed in the steering gear itself. Actual ratios vary greatly, according to the type of vehicle and type of operation. For example, many cars with manual steering use steering ratios as high as 28:1 to minimize steering effort. On the other hand, some lightweight sports cars have steering ratios as low as 10:1. High steering ratios are often called "slow" steering because the steering wheel has to be turned many degrees to produce a small steering effect. Low steering ratios are called "fast" or "quick" steering because much less

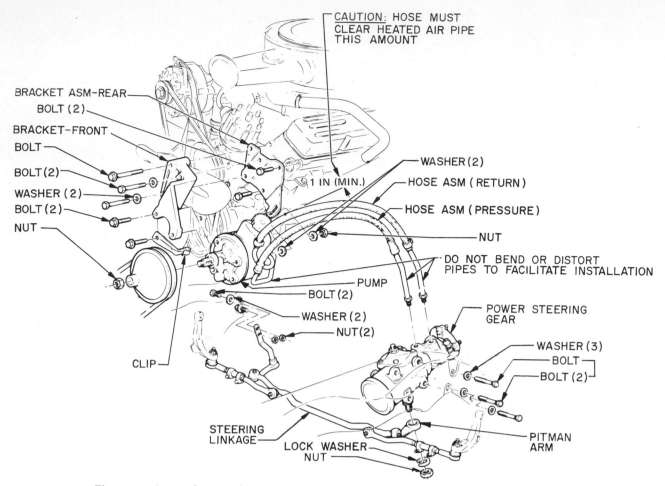

Fig. 5-21. Integral type of power-steering system, partly disassembled to show how steering gear, pump, and steering linkages are mounted on engine and frame. (*Buick Motor Division of General Motors Corporation*)

steering-wheel movement is required to produce the steering effect.

In power steering, the steering ratio is typically 16:1 for straight-ahead driving to as low as 13:1 during full turns. The low ratio is acceptable with power steering because the power-steering gear provides most of the steering effort. Now let us see how the variable steering ratio is achieved, and its purpose.

Fig. 5-22. Power-steering system for a car with front-wheel drive. (*Oldsmobile Division of General Motors Corporation*)

From the straight-ahead position the steering ratio stays constant for the first 40 degrees of steering-wheel movement in either direction. The steering ratio then decreases gradually from 16:1 with further steering-wheel movement. This provides good steering control for highway driving; that is, for normal maneuvering and passing on the highway. Such driving seldom requires more than a quarter turn of the wheel.

In city driving, the steering wheel is turned much more than 40 degrees, as for instance when turning corners or parking. As the steering wheel is turned well past 40 degrees, the steering ratio drops. Typically, it drops to as low as 13:1 (see Fig. 5-23). Note that by the time the steering wheel has been turned a full turn, the steering ratio is 13:1. The advantage of this is that when a short turn must be made, as in going around a corner or backing and parking, the steering-wheel movement has a greater effect. That is, as the need increases, the response increases.

The variable ratio is achieved by the shape of the teeth in the piston rack and the pitman-shaft sector (Fig. 5-24). In a constant-ratio arrangement,

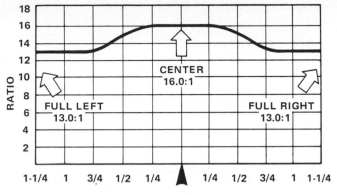

Fig. 5-23. Graph showing the relationship, or ratio, between steering-wheel turns and movement of the front wheels in right and left turns. (*American Motors Corporation*)

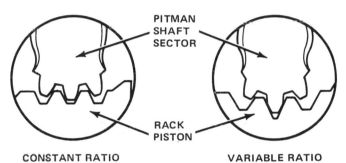

Fig. 5-24. *Left,* shape of teeth on piston rack and pitman-shaft sector for constant steering ratio; *right,* shape of teeth for variable ratio. (*American Motors Corporation*)

the teeth are the same size. But in the variable-ratio arrangement, the center teeth are larger. Therefore, when the piston rack has moved enough to bring one of the outer teeth into action, the effective leverage is changed. This means that the movement of the piston rack produces a greater movement of the pitman-shaft sector.

⊘ **5-15 Hydraulic Pump** All power-steering systems require hydraulic pumps that will produce pressures of several hundred pounds per square inch. A variety of designs and different mounting and driving arrangements have been used. Typical arrangements are shown in Fig. 5-25. The pump mounts on a bracket at the front of the engine and is driven by a belt from the crankshaft pulley.

Three types of hydraulic oil pumps are shown in Figs. 5-26 to 5-29. All operate on a similar principle. A rotor turns in an oval body. The rotor has a series of vanes, slippers, or rollers set in slots in the rotor, as shown in the illustrations. As the rotor turns, the pockets formed between the rotor, the body, and the vanes, slippers, or rollers increase and then decrease in size. As the pockets increase, they

draw hydraulic fluid (a special oil) into the pockets. Then, as they decrease, the fluid is forced out through the exit ports.

⊘ **5-16 Power-Steering Idle-Speed Control** With a low hot-idle setting, it is possible to stall the engine during parking. This is how it could happen. When the steering wheel is turned to its limit in one direction or the other, the steering linkage stops further movement. However, high hydraulic pressure can develop in the system as the pump builds up pressure in trying to force further movement. As the pump works harder, it requires more power. This increasing power demand imposes an added load on the idling engine; the added load may slow down the engine so much that it stalls.

To prevent stalling from this cause, some systems are equipped with an idle speedup control (Fig. 5-30). When pump pressure reaches its maximum, the pressure causes the speedup control to move the throttle valve slightly toward the open position so that idle speed is temporarily increased. This prevents stalling. When the steering wheel is backed off from the limiting stop position, pump pressure falls and the engine idle drops off to its normal hot-idle speed.

⊘ **5-17 General Motors Power Steering** Since 1959, General Motors cars have used a Saginaw in-line power-steering gear of the rotary-valve or torsion-bar type. This is an integral unit and mounts on the lower end of the steering shaft as shown in Fig. 5-21. The power-steering gear itself consists of a recirculating-ball steering gear to which has been added a hydraulic booster actuated by the pressure from the hydraulic pump. In operation, movement of the steering wheel by the driver, and the resulting twisting action on the steering shaft, actuates a valve that directs oil pressure to the booster. Booster action then supplies most of the steering effort. This greatly reduces the amount of twisting effort the driver must apply to the steering wheel.

The recirculating-ball steering gear in the power-steering unit is very similar to the manual type. Compare Figs. 5-17 and 5-18 with Figs. 5-31 to 5-35. In both types, manual and power, there is a ball nut surrounding the worm gear. Balls circulate between grooves in the worm gear and in the ball nut when the steering wheel is turned. This moves the ball nut up or down on the worm gear. The nut movement causes the pitman-shaft gear to turn so the pitman arm swings to one side or the other. Linkages from the pitman arm to the front wheels then cause the wheels to pivot to one side or the other for steering.

The ball nut in the power-steering gear has an additional job to do, however. It also serves as a piston to provide an assisting force which does most of the work of steering. Whenever more than about 3 pounds [1.4 kg] of effort is required to turn the

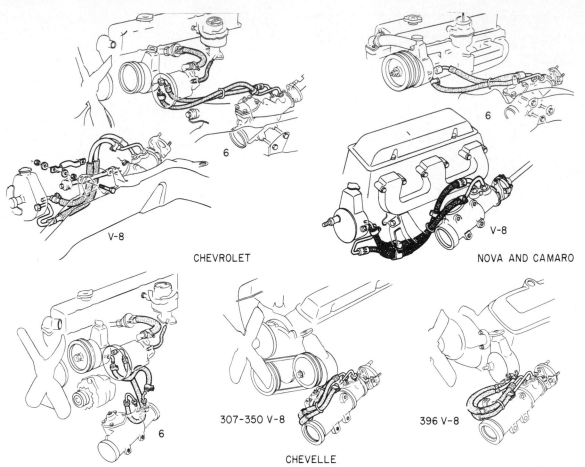

Fig. 5-25. Various pump and power-steering-gear locations on different models of Chevrolet automobiles. (*Chevrolet Motor Division of General Motors Corporation*)

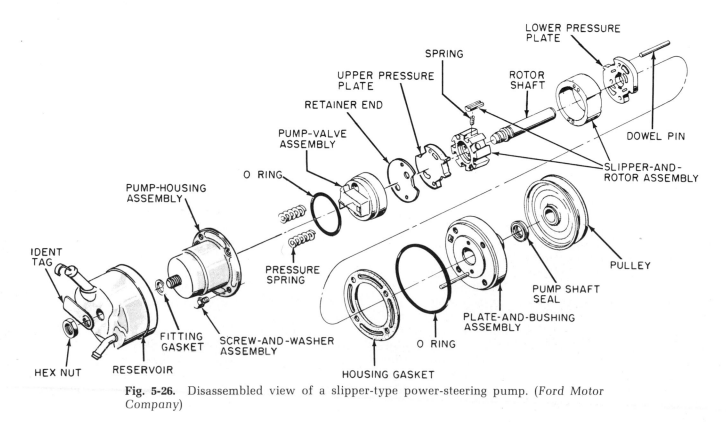

Fig. 5-26. Disassembled view of a slipper-type power-steering pump. (*Ford Motor Company*)

Fig. 5-27. Roller type of power-steering pump. The pressure plate and cover are removed to show how the rollers are installed in the rotor. (*Chrysler Corporation*)

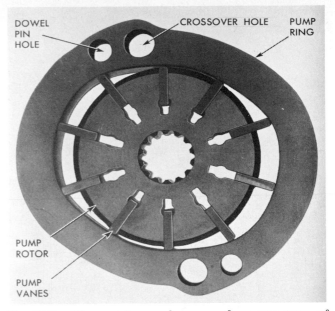

Fig. 5-29. Rings, rotor, and vanes of a vane type of power-steering pump. Note how the vanes fit into the pump rotor. (*Chevrolet Motor Division of General Motors Corporation*)

steering wheel, hydraulic fluid from the pump is introduced to one or the other end of the piston. This provides assistance to the piston so that most of the effort required to move the piston is provided by hydraulic pressure. As a result, steering is easier.

Control of the hydraulic fluid is by a rotary valve that is connected through a torsion bar to the steering-wheel shaft. When the steering wheel is turned, steering resistance at the car wheels causes the torsion bar to twist. This, in turn, causes the rotary valve to turn slightly so that oil flow under high pressure is directed to one or the other end of the piston to produce steering assistance.

In the straight-ahead position (Fig. 5-33), the rotary-valve spool is positioned in the neutral position. Oil from the oil pump flows equally through the various ports in the valve, and no pressure builds up on the piston.

When the steering wheel is rotated for a right

turn (Fig. 5-34), the movement encounters resistance at the car wheels in the normal manner. This means that some turning effort must be applied to the steering wheel. The turning effort twists the torsion bar, causing the valve spool to rotate slightly in the valve housing. Now the ports are partly shut off so that oil pressure builds up and oil must flow to the piston (left end in Fig. 5-34), as shown by the arrows. Oil pressure applied to the end of the piston helps to move the piston rack, and this action takes over most of the steering effort. The more steering resistance the front wheels of the car offer, the harder the driver must twist the steering wheel. As a result, the torsion bar is twisted more and the rotary valve is

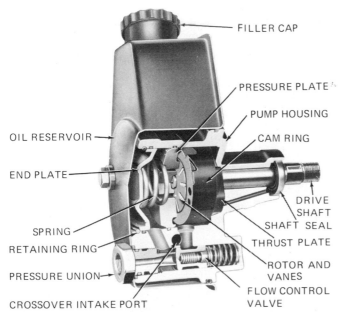

Fig. 5-28. Pump for power-steering system cut away. (*Cadillac Motor Car Division of General Motors Corporation*)

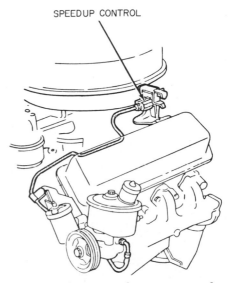

Fig. 5-30. Idle speedup control arrangement for a power-steering system. (*Ford Motor Company*)

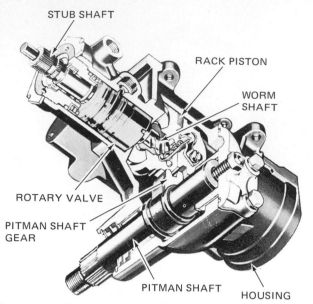

STUB SHAFT

RACK PISTON

WORM SHAFT

ROTARY VALVE

PITMAN SHAFT GEAR

PITMAN SHAFT

HOUSING

Fig. 5-31. Cutaway view of a Saginaw rotary-valve power-steering unit. (*Cadillac Motor Car Division of General Motors Corporation*)

further rotated. This action causes the valve ports to be more nearly shut, so a higher oil pressure is built up and directed to the piston. Thus, there is a proportional effect at work, and most of the steering effort is produced by the oil pressure.

When the driver returns the steering wheel to straight ahead, the rotary valve centers itself as the

torsion bar resumes the neutral position. Now the front-end steering geometry returns the car wheels to straight ahead.

Figure 5-35 shows the oil flow through the steering unit when a left turn is made. Note that the rotary valve is turned in the opposite direction from that shown in Fig. 5-34 and that the oil pressure is directed to the opposite end of the rack piston.

⊘ **5-18 Chrysler Power Steering** Since 1958, Chrysler Corporation cars have used what they term a *constant-control power-steering gear*. This unit (Fig. 5-36) is similar in many ways to the Saginaw unit covered in the previous section. However, instead of using a rotary valve, it uses a spool valve which is actuated by a pivot lever. The spool valve looks a little like the wooden spools on which sewing thread comes (Fig. 5-37). However, it has holes and grooves in it through which oil can circulate. In addition, it has a hole in which the end of the pivot lever rides. The lower end of the pivot lever is held in a reaction member which is positioned between two flat springs. The springs, shaped like washers, are slightly bowed to provide tension. During straight-ahead driving, the springs keep the reaction member centered so that the spool valve is centered, as shown in Fig. 5-38. In this position, the oil circulates as shown by the dashed arrows, and the same pressure is applied to both sides of the piston. Note that the piston is part of the ball-nut assembly, just as in the Saginaw unit. However, the piston

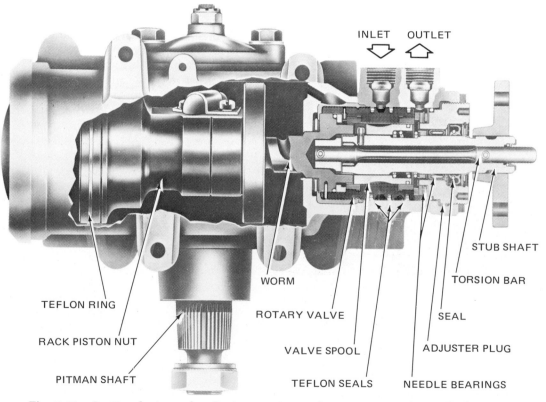

INLET   OUTLET

STUB SHAFT

TORSION BAR

SEAL

ADJUSTER PLUG

NEEDLE BEARINGS

TEFLON SEALS

VALVE SPOOL

ROTARY VALVE

WORM

TEFLON RING

RACK PISTON NUT

PITMAN SHAFT

Fig. 5-32. Sectional view of a Saginaw rotary-valve power steering unit. (*Pontiac Motor Division of General Motors Corporation*)

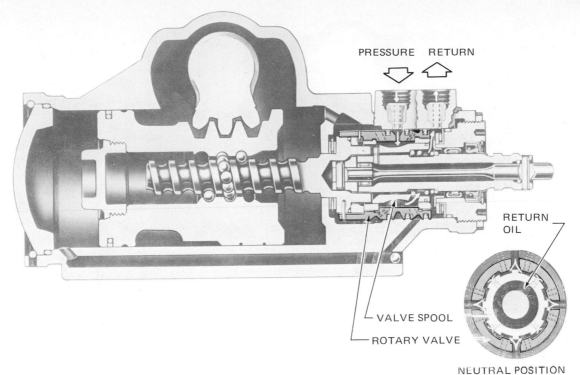

PRESSURE   RETURN

RETURN OIL

VALVE SPOOL

ROTARY VALVE

NEUTRAL POSITION

Fig. 5-33. Rotary-valve power-steering unit in the straight-ahead position. (*Pontiac Motor Division of General Motors Corporation*)

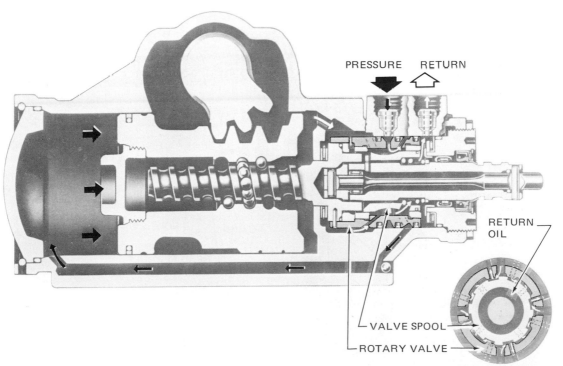

PRESSURE   RETURN

RETURN OIL

VALVE SPOOL

ROTARY VALVE

RIGHT-TURN POSITION

Fig. 5-34. Oil flow in a rotary-valve power steering unit during a right turn. Arrows show the oil flow and the direction of oil pressure on the piston. (*Pontiac Motor Division of General Motors Corporation*)

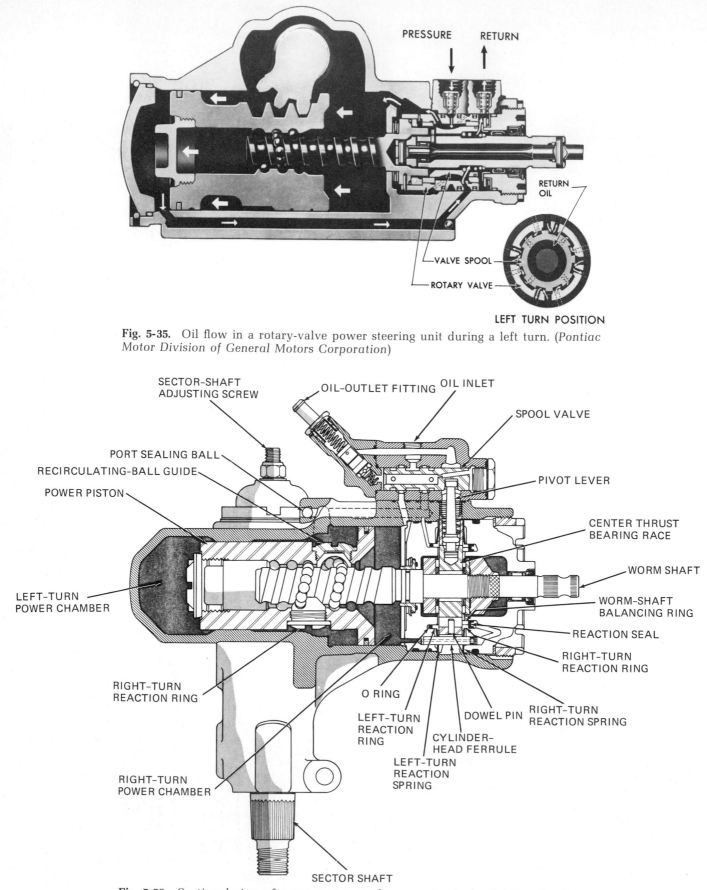

PRESSURE   RETURN

RETURN
OIL

VALVE SPOOL

ROTARY VALVE

LEFT TURN POSITION

Fig. 5-35. Oil flow in a rotary-valve power steering unit during a left turn. (*Pontiac Motor Division of General Motors Corporation*)

SECTOR-SHAFT
ADJUSTING SCREW

OIL-OUTLET FITTING   OIL INLET

SPOOL VALVE

PORT SEALING BALL

RECIRCULATING-BALL GUIDE

POWER PISTON

PIVOT LEVER

CENTER THRUST
BEARING RACE

WORM SHAFT

LEFT-TURN
POWER CHAMBER

WORM-SHAFT
BALANCING RING

REACTION SEAL

RIGHT-TURN
REACTION RING

RIGHT-TURN
REACTION RING

O RING

LEFT-TURN
REACTION
RING

DOWEL PIN

RIGHT-TURN
REACTION SPRING

CYLINDER-
HEAD FERRULE

LEFT-TURN
REACTION
SPRING

RIGHT-TURN
POWER CHAMBER

SECTOR SHAFT

Fig. 5-36. Sectional view of a constant-control power-steering unit. (*Chrysler Corporation*)

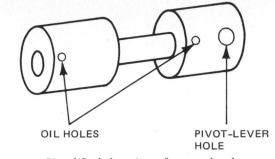

OIL HOLES   PIVOT-LEVER
HOLE

Fig. 5-37. Simplified drawing of a spool valve.

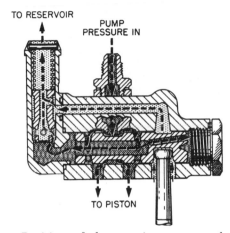

TO RESERVOIR   PUMP
PRESSURE IN

TO PISTON

Fig. 5-38. Position of the steering-gear spool valve in straight-ahead driving. (*Chrysler Corporation*)

itself is somewhat differently arranged, as you will note if you compare Figs. 5-31 to 5-35 with Fig. 5-36.

Now, let us see how the power-steering unit works when a turn is made. On a turn that requires more than a few pounds pull on the steering wheel, a considerable end thrust develops on the worm and steering shaft. This is the same effect you would get if you backed a screw out of a nut and at the same time held the nut stationary. The screw would rise up out of the nut as it is backed out. In the steering gear, there is resistance to any movement of the ball nut because the front wheels have a natural resistance to turning away from the straight-ahead position. This means that, in making a right turn, the worm will tend to move up in the ball nut. The upward movement carries the reaction member upward with it. The reaction member includes a bearing race in which the lower end of the pivot lever rides. Thus, the endwise movement of the bearing race causes the pivot lever to pivot as shown in Fig. 5-39. This moves the spool valve down (to the left in the illustration). As the spool valve moves into this position, it directs high-pressure oil to one side of the piston and opens the circuit from the other side of the piston to the reservoir. The resulting differential oil pressure, applied to the two sides of the piston, provides most of the effort needed to turn the front wheels from straight-ahead position.

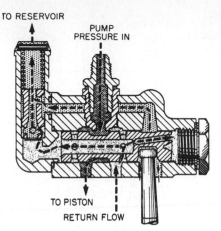

TO RESERVOIR   PUMP
PRESSURE IN

TO PISTON

RETURN FLOW

Fig. 5-39. Position of the steering-gear spool valve during a left turn. (*Chrysler Corporation*)

As soon as the turning pressure on the steering wheel is relieved and the wheel is returned to the straight-ahead position, the end thrust on the worm is relieved. Now, the pivot lever and spool valve return to the centered position, as shown in Fig. 5-38.

⊘ **5-19 Ford Power Steering** In recent years, automobiles manufactured by the Ford Motor Company have used three types of integral power-steering gears as well as linkage-type systems. One of the integral power-steering gears is the Saginaw unit, discussed in ⊘ 5-17. A second type is the double-sector unit, which is a torsion-bar unit using parallel worm shaft and rack-and-piston assemblies (Fig. 5-40). This unit has not been used for several years. The third type is a Ford-designed unit somewhat similar to the Saginaw power-steering gear (Fig. 5-43). The last two are discussed below. Linkage-type power-steering gears are described in ⊘ 5-20.

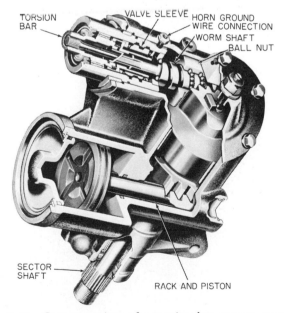

TORSION   VALVE SLEEVE   HORN GROUND
BAR   WIRE CONNECTION
            WORM SHAFT
            BALL NUT

SECTOR
SHAFT   RACK AND PISTON

Fig. 5-40. Cutaway view of a torsion-bar power-steering unit. (*Ford Motor Company*)

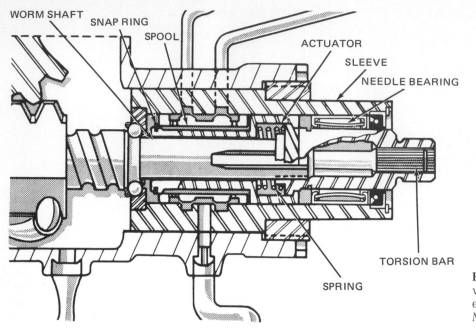

WORM SHAFT SNAP RING SPOOL ACTUATOR SLEEVE NEEDLE BEARING TORSION BAR SPRING

Fig. 5-41. Details of the valve in torsion-bar power-steering unit. (*Ford Motor Company*)

1. DOUBLE-SECTOR TYPE Figure 5-40 is a cutaway view of the torsion-bar power-steering gear using parallel worm shaft and rack-and-piston assemblies. The sector shaft (pitman-arm shaft) has two sectors, one meshed with a rack on the piston and the other meshed with the ball nut on the worm shaft. The worm shaft is connected through the torsion bar to the steering-wheel shaft in a manner similar to that used in the rotary-valve power-steering unit (⊘ 5-17). Steering effort applied at the steering wheel causes the torsion bar to twist. This twisting motion, applied through an actuator with coarse threads, causes the spool valve to move endwise (and not rotate, as does the rotary-valve type).

Figure 5-41 shows details of the actuator and the valve spool (which fits around the outside of it).

Figure 5-42 shows the hydraulic circuits through the system during a left turn, straight-ahead driving, and a right turn. When a turn is made, the valve spool moves endwise, as already mentioned, directing oil at high pressure to one or the other end of the piston. This high-pressure oil then provides the steering assistance, acting through the piston and rack on the sector shaft.

2. FORD-DESIGN POWER-STEERING GEAR An external view of the Ford power-steering gear is shown in Fig. 5-43. This unit uses a torsion bar and a valve spool much like the bar and valve in the double-sector type. The basic difference is that the worm shaft and rack-and-piston sectors have been arranged in a single line in the Ford-designed unit. In the straight-ahead situation, the valve spool is

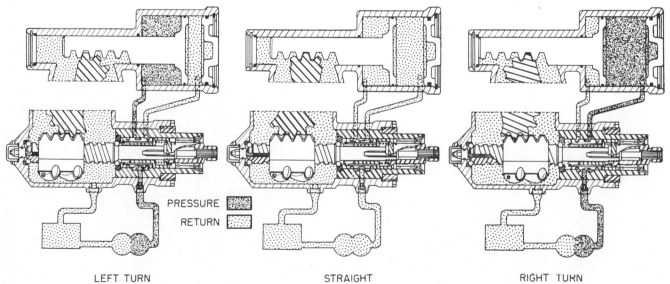

PRESSURE
RETURN

LEFT TURN   STRAIGHT   RIGHT TURN

Fig. 5-42. Hydraulic circuits in the torsion-bar power-steering unit during a left turn, straight-ahead driving, and a right turn. (*Ford Motor Company*)

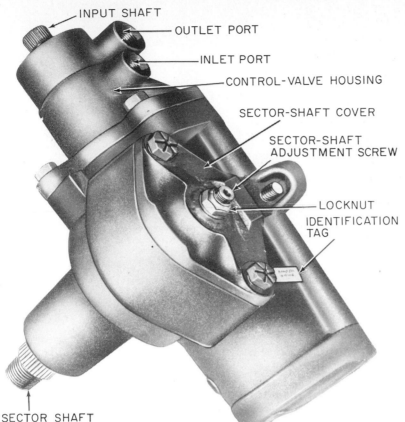

INPUT SHAFT
OUTLET PORT
INLET PORT
CONTROL-VALVE HOUSING
SECTOR-SHAFT COVER
SECTOR-SHAFT ADJUSTMENT SCREW
LOCKNUT
IDENTIFICATION TAG
SECTOR SHAFT

Fig. 5-43. Ford-design integral power-steering gear. (*Ford Motor Company*)

centered so that no oil pressure builds up on either side of the piston. The piston therefore maintains its centered position.

The piston is part of the ball-nut assembly, which also carries the rack to which the sector is meshed. This is similar to the arrangements used in the other integral power-steering gears previously described.

When a left turn is made, the torsion bar twists to the left, causing the valve spool to move downward. This directs oil under pressure to the upper side of the power piston. The oil on the lower side of the power piston is free to return to the pump. The pressure differential provides an assist by moving the piston downward. The instant the driver stops applying effort to the steering wheel, the valve spool is returned to the neutral position by the unwinding of the torsion bar.

When a right turn is made, the torsion bar twists to the right, causing the valve spool to move upward. This directs oil under pressure to the lower side of the power piston. The oil on the upper side of the power piston is free to return to the pump. The pressure differential provides an assist by moving the piston upward.

⊘ **5-20 Linkage-Type Power Steering** In the linkage-type power-steering system, the power cylinder is not part of the steering gear. Instead, the power cylinder, or *booster cylinder,* as it is also called, is connected into the steering linkage. In ad-

dition, the valve assembly is included in the steering linkage, either as a separate assembly or united with the power cylinder. Figure 5-44 shows one linkage-type power-steering system in which the booster cylinder and valve assembly are separate units. In operation, the steering gear works in exactly the same way as the mechanical types described in ⊘ 5-11. However, the swinging end of the pitman arm is not directly connected to the steering linkage; instead, it is connected to a valve assembly. As the end of the pitman arm swings when a turn is made, it actuates the valve assembly. The valve assembly then directs hydraulic oil pressure from the oil pump to the booster cylinder. Inside the booster cylinder, pressure is applied to one or the other end of a piston. Movement then takes place—actually, in this unit the cylinder moves instead of the piston—and this movement is transferred to the connecting rod in the steering linkage. Thus, most of the effort required to move the connecting rod and steer the car is furnished by the booster cylinder. Figure 5-45 is a cutaway view of the valve assembly, and Fig. 5-46 is a cutaway of the booster, or power, cylinder.

1. VALVE AND POWER-CYLINDER OPERATION In many ways, the valve assembly is very similar to that used in the Chrysler power-steering unit (Figs. 5-38 and 5-39). The operating part consists of a valve spool that looks much like the valve spool shown in Fig. 5-37. The valve spool is assembled into the valve body as shown in Fig. 5-45. The ball on the end of the pitman arm fits a socket in the stem of the valve spool. During neutral, or straight-ahead,

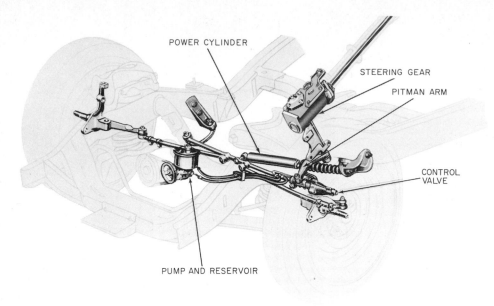

POWER CYLINDER

STEERING GEAR

PITMAN ARM

CONTROL VALVE

PUMP AND RESERVOIR

Fig. 5-44. Arrangement of the power cylinder, pump, and control valve in a linkage-type power-steering system. (*Ford Motor Company*)

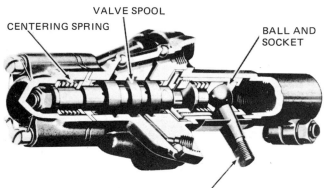

CENTERING SPRING

VALVE SPOOL

BALL AND SOCKET

BALL STUD ON PITMAN ARM

Fig. 5-45. Cutaway view of a valve assembly showing the valve spool, the centering spring, and ball-and-socket attachment of the pitman arm to the valve-spool stem. (*Ford Motor Company*)

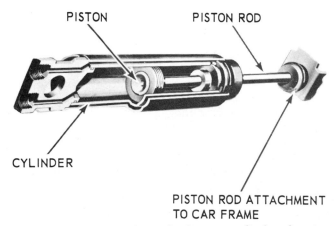

PISTON

PISTON ROD

CYLINDER

PISTON ROD ATTACHMENT TO CAR FRAME

Fig. 5-46. Cutaway view of a booster cylinder showing the relationship of the piston, rod, cylinder, and rod attachment. (*Ford Motor Company*)

operation, the valve spool is centered in the valve assembly by centering springs. In this position, the oil circuits through the valve body will impose equal pressure on both sides of the piston in the booster cylinder. Thus, there is no tendency for the booster cylinder to exercise any action (Fig. 5-47).

When a turn is made, the pitman arm swings in one direction or the other, causing valve action (as already mentioned). Figure 5-48 shows what happens when a left turn is made. Turning the steering wheel to the left (as shown) makes the pitman arm swing to the right. The ball on the end of the pitman arm moves the valve spool to the right. Now, oil under pressure from the pump can flow through the valve body only to one side of the piston in the booster cylinder. In the illustration, oil flows into the cylinder on the right-hand side of the piston, as shown by the arrows. Since the piston is fastened to the car frame by the piston rod, it cannot move. Therefore, the hydraulic pressure in the cylinder causes the cylinder itself to move. The cylinder is fastened to the connecting rod. Thus, the major effort of steering is supplied by the booster cylinder. As the cylinder moves to the right (in the illustration), the oil in the left-hand side flows back to the reservoir through the valve body (as shown by the arrows). Note that movement of the valve spool to the right has connected the left-hand side of the cylinder to the reservoir. Figure 5-49 shows the hydraulic circuits and the valve and power-cylinder actions during a right turn.

2. *INTEGRAL VALVE AND POWER-CYLINDER ACTIONS* Some linkage-type power-steering systems use a power-cylinder-and-valve assembly. Both units are placed in a single assembly, as shown in Fig. 5-50.

Figure 5-51 shows the actions in the valve and power cylinder during a left turn. When the steering wheel is turned, the ball on the end of the pitman

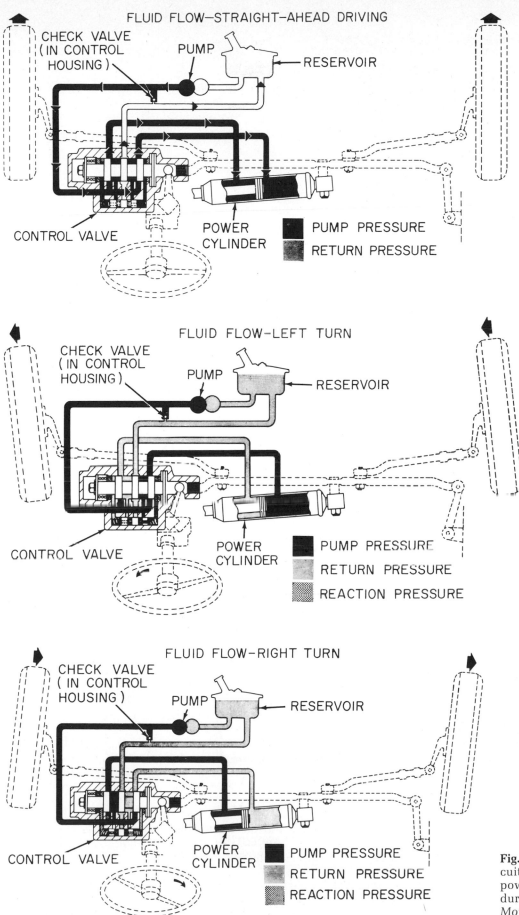

FLUID FLOW—STRAIGHT-AHEAD DRIVING

CHECK VALVE (IN CONTROL HOUSING)

PUMP

RESERVOIR

CONTROL VALVE

POWER CYLINDER

■ PUMP PRESSURE

▓ RETURN PRESSURE

Fig. 5-47. Hydraulic circuits in a linkage-type power-steering system during straight-ahead driving. (*Ford Motor Company*)

FLUID FLOW—LEFT TURN

CHECK VALVE (IN CONTROL HOUSING)

PUMP

RESERVOIR

CONTROL VALVE

POWER CYLINDER

■ PUMP PRESSURE

░ RETURN PRESSURE

▓ REACTION PRESSURE

Fig. 5-48. Hydraulic circuits in a linkage-type power-steering system during a left turn. (*Ford Motor Company*)

FLUID FLOW—RIGHT TURN

CHECK VALVE (IN CONTROL HOUSING)

PUMP

RESERVOIR

CONTROL VALVE

POWER CYLINDER

■ PUMP PRESSURE

▓ RETURN PRESSURE

▓ REACTION PRESSURE

Fig. 5-49. Hydraulic circuits in a linkage-type power-steering system during a right turn. (*Ford Motor Company*)

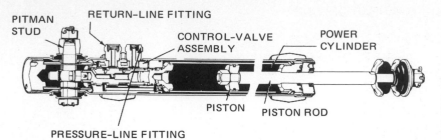

Fig. 5-50. Cutaway view of a one-unit type of linkage power-steering assembly. (*Monroe Auto Equipment Company*)

arm shifts the valve spool to the right. This permits oil to flow from the pump under pressure, through the ports in the valve section of the assembly, and into the right-hand side of the power cylinder. The high-pressure oil then forces the cylinder to move to the right, and the movement of the cylinder provides the major steering effort.

⊘ **5-21 Other Steering Systems** In addition to hydraulic pressure, other systems use mechanical assistance from the engine or air pressure to help in steering. To increase maneuverability, some applications use four-wheel steering (with or without power steering). Also, new steering systems for passenger cars are being developed which eliminate the traditional steering wheel. For example, Fig. 5-52 shows one experimental steering system which uses two small plastic rings in place of the steering wheel. In Fig. 5-52, the shroud has been removed so that

the chain-and-sprocket arrangement can be seen. Either plastic ring can be turned to steer the car, and thus either hand can be used for steering control. As a ring is turned, it rotates the steering shaft in the center. The power-steering unit is modified to be sensitive to the small steering torque delivered to the steering shaft by the small plastic rings and the chain-and-sprocket arrangement.

The system illustrated has an electrically driven backup system that goes into operation automatically in case there is loss of power in the regular steering system. The system shown is one of several that have been proposed.

1. FULL MECHANICAL POWER STEERING One power-steering system, tried some years ago, uses mechanical power directly from the engine. It does not use hydraulic pressure, as in the power-steering systems previously described. Power is supplied by an input shaft driven from the engine-crankshaft

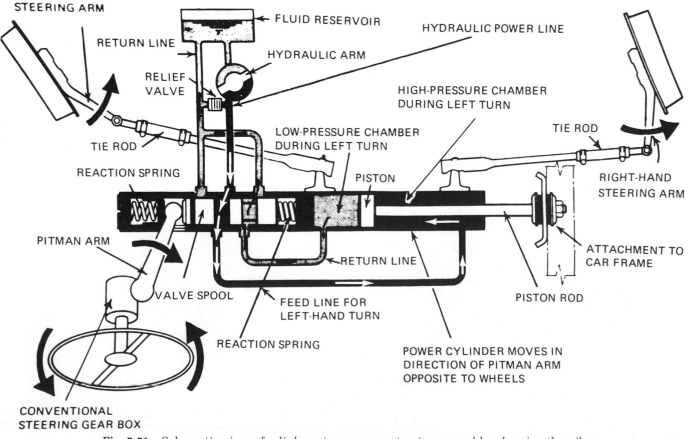

Fig. 5-51. Schematic view of a linkage-type power-steering assembly, showing the oil flow and movement of parts during a left turn. (*Monroe Auto Equipment Company*)

Fig. 5-52. Experimental steering system using two small plastic rings instead of the traditional steering wheel. The shroud has been removed so that the chain-and-sprocket arrangement can be seen. (*Ford Motor Company*)

pulley through a V belt. The input shaft, through a ratchet arrangement, drives a pinion gear in the steering assembly. Rotary motion from this pinion is carried through a pair of pinion gears to a pair of ring gears. Each ring gear carries within it a multiple-disk clutch. The upper clutch assists in a left turn, and the lower clutch assists in a right turn. Their respective ring gears are turning in opposite directions; the upper ring gear turns to the left, the lower to the right.

In operation, when the steering wheel is turned and a pull of more than 2 pounds [0.9 kg] is required at the wheel rim, the clutch-actuating plate moves up or down to actuate one clutch or the other. For example, when a left turn is made, the actuating plate moves upward. This compresses the upper clutch; that is, the disks in the clutch are moved together so that power is transmitted through the clutch. This power is applied, through the clutch hub, to the steering shaft so that the driver is assisted in the steering effort. When the driver makes a right turn, the lower clutch—which applies turning effort in the opposite direction to the upper clutch—acts to assist.

2. *AIR POWER-STEERING SYSTEM* Figure 5-53 is a schematic diagram of a power-steering system that uses compressed air. An engine-driven air compressor supplies the compressed air. Note that the system is of the linkage type, with a control-valve assembly actuated by the pitman arm. The control valve is moved one way or the other by the pitman arm as the steering wheel is turned. This causes compressed air to be admitted to one or the other end of the power cylinder. The compressed air then forces a piston to move in the cylinder. This movement is carried by the piston rod to the steering linkage, and major steering assistance is thereby furnished. The system is balanced to provide steering feel.

3. *FOUR-WHEEL STEERING* On some vehicles, all

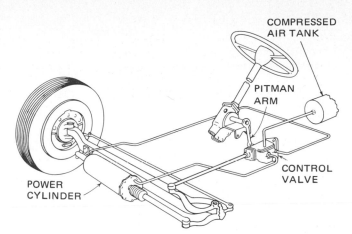

Fig. 5-53. Schematic layout of an air power-steering system. (*Bendix-Westinghouse Automotive Air Brake Company*)

four wheels are steered as the steering wheel is turned. This makes for greater maneuverability of the vehicle. The rear, or driving, axles have universal joints that permit the rear wheels to turn at various angles to the frame of the vehicle. The driving axles continue to deliver power to the wheel through the universal joints, regardless of the angle at which the wheels are turned. The steering-knuckle arms on the rear wheels are linked by tie rods to the same pitman arm to which the front-wheel steering-knuckle arms are linked. Quite often, a vehicle with four-wheel steering also has provision for four-wheel driving. In this arrangement all four wheels are linked by propeller shafts or driving shafts to the engine.

⊘ **5-22 Tilt Steering Wheel and Column** A number of automobiles have steering wheels that tilt up or down and also can be moved out of or into the steering column (Figs. 5-54 and 5-55). This makes it easier for the driver to get into or out of the car. The driver can also vary the position of the wheel to suit his or her build and can also change the position during a long drive to vary driving posture.

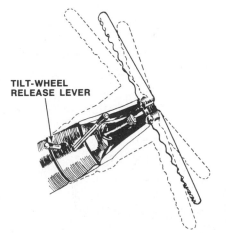

Fig. 5-54. Tilt steering wheel. Lifting the release lever permits the steering wheel to be tilted to various positions, as shown. (*Buick Motor Division of General Motors Corporation*)

Steering Systems 79

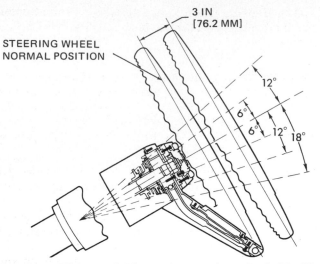

Fig. 5-55. Tilting and telescoping steering wheel. (*Cadillac Motor Car Division of General Motors Corporation*)

Some Ford automobiles have, as optional equipment, a steering column that can be moved inward toward the center of the car to make it easier for the driver to get in and out of the car. The pivot point on this arrangement is just above the steering gear, at the lower end of the steering column. At that point there is a flex joint that connects between the upper steering shaft and the worm shaft in the steering gear. This permits the steering shaft and steering column to be pivoted toward the center of the car. A locking mechanism is connected to the transmission selector lever. The steering column is locked in the DRIVE position and in all selector lever positions except PARK. To unlock the steering column, the selector must be moved to PARK. Also, if the steering column is moved out of the driving position, the selector lever is locked in the PARK position. This interlocking is a safety feature which prevents the steering column from being accidentally moved while the car is in operation.

⊘ **5-23 Collapsible Steering Column** The collapsible steering column (Figs. 5-56 and 5-57), used on modern cars as a protective device, will collapse on impact. Then, if the car should become involved in a front-end collision that throws the driver forward, the steering column will absorb the energy of this forward movement and greatly reduce the possibility of injury. The steering shaft is made in two parts which are fitted together so they can telescope as the steering column collapses.

The steering column shown in Fig. 5-56 is called the "Japanese lantern" design because, on impact, it folds up like a Japanese lantern. The type shown in Fig. 5-57 is of the tube-and-ball design and is more recent than the other. In the tube-and-ball design, two tubes are placed, one inside the other, with tight-fitting ball bearings between. On impact, the tubes are forced together as shown, and the balls must plow furrows in the tubes to permit the relative motion. This design is said to give a more uniform collapse rate than the earlier design.

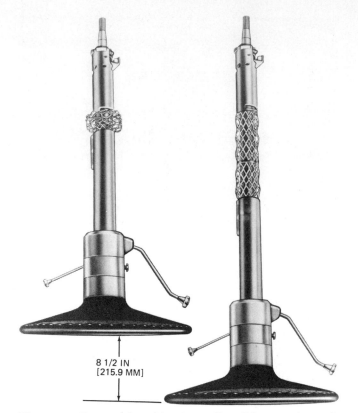

Fig. 5-56. Energy-absorbing, or collapsible, steering column of the "Japanese lantern" design. The column can collapse, as shown at the left, during impact. (*Cadillac Motor Car Division of General Motors Corporation*)

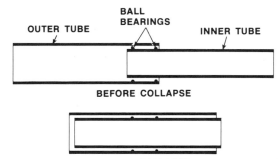

Fig. 5-57. Energy-absorbing, or collapsible, steering column of the tube-and-ball design. (*General Motors Corporation*)

⊘ **5-24 Steering and Ignition Lock** In 1969, automotive manufacturers began to equip their cars with a combination ignition switch and steering-wheel lock (Fig. 5-58). The ignition switch is mounted on the steering column, as shown, and it has a gear attached to the cylinder in the lock. When the ignition key is inserted and the ignition switch is turned to ON, the gear rotates and pulls the rack and plunger out of the notch in the disk. The disk is mounted on the steering shaft. This frees the steering shaft and wheel so the car can be steered. When the ignition switch is turned to OFF, the rotation of the gear moves the rack and plunger toward the locked position. If the plunger is lined up with a notch in the disk, it will enter the notch and lock the steering

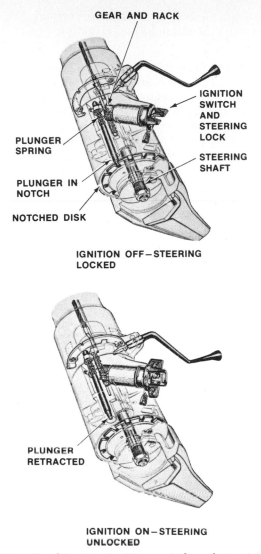

GEAR AND RACK

IGNITION SWITCH AND STEERING LOCK

PLUNGER SPRING

STEERING SHAFT

PLUNGER IN NOTCH

NOTCHED DISK

IGNITION OFF—STEERING LOCKED

PLUNGER RETRACTED

IGNITION ON—STEERING UNLOCKED

Fig. 5-58. Combination ignition switch and steering lock in phantom view, showing the two positions of the lock. (*General Motors Corporation*)

wheel. However, if the wheel and disk happen to be in a position where the plunger cannot enter a notch in the disk, the plunger will be spring-loaded against the side of the disk. Now, a slight turn of the wheel will turn the disk enough that the plunger will enter a notch and thereby lock the steering wheel.

Check Your Progress

Progress Quiz 5-2 Once more we pause to give you a chance to check up on yourself and find out what progress you are making in your studies of automotive steering systems. Remember that these quizzes are included for your benefit; they are designed to help you. They not only let you review the material you have just covered, but they also help your memory by laying out before you the important points that you should remember. The more times you think of a fact, the easier it will be for you to remember it. Then too, if you write down the an-

swers to the questions, your memory will be further fortified. Writing down a fact is a fine way to remember it.

Completing the Sentences The sentences below are incomplete. After each sentence there are several words or phrases, only one of which will correctly complete the sentence. Write each sentence in your notebook, selecting the proper word or phrase to complete it correctly.

1. Two basic types of power-steering systems are the: (*a*) integral and valve, (*b*) booster and power, (*c*) integral and linkage.
2. The maker of the power-steering system (used in General Motors cars) that has a rotary valve is: (*a*) linkage, (*b*) Saginaw, (*c*) Monroe.
3. The valve spool in the Saginaw in-line power-steering unit is centered, in neutral, by: (*a*) the torsion bar, (*b*) oil pressure, (*c*) two disk clutches.
4. In the double-sector power-steering gear, one sector meshes with a rack on the piston and the other meshes with the: (*a*) ball nut, (*b*) pitman-arm gear, (*c*) rotary valve, (*d*) steering shaft.
5. In the Saginaw rotary-valve unit, rotation of the valve spool from the neutral position results in application of hydraulic oil pressure from the oil pump to one or the other end of the: (*a*) pitman arm, (*b*) connecting rod, (*c*) piston, (*d*) disk clutch.
6. Three types of oil pumps used in power-steering systems are vane, roller, and: (*a*) shoe, (*b*) slipper, (*c*) gear.
7. In the Ford-design power-steering gear, the valve spool is moved by: (*a*) coil springs, (*b*) a torsion bar, (*c*) the ball nut.
8. In the constant-control power-steering unit, the spool valve is moved by: (*a*) a pivot lever, (*b*) a valve rotor, (*c*) high oil pressure.
9. In the linkage type of power-steering system, the swinging end of the pitman arm actuates: (*a*) a spool valve, (*b*) a tie rod, (*c*) an oil pump, (*d*) an idler lever.
10. In the linkage type of power-steering system, the piston rod is attached at one end to: (*a*) a tie rod, (*b*) a connecting rod, (*c*) the car frame.

CHAPTER 5 CHECKUP

NOTE: Since the following is a chapter review test, you should review the chapter before taking it.

You have now completed your studies of the construction and operation of automotive suspension and steering systems. The next few chapters describe trouble-diagnosis, maintenance, and repair procedures on these systems. Before you start on them, you should have a good understanding of how the units operate. The checkup that follows tests your knowledge of steering systems as discussed in the chapter you have just finished. If you have any trouble answering the questions, it means you should reread the chapter. If that happens, don't worry; most good students reread their lessons several times. Few people can remember everything they read, especially when they read it only once or twice. Write your answers to the test below in your notebook. Writing down the answers helps you remember them. Also, it makes your notebook an increasingly valuable reference you can go to when you need information in a hurry.

Correcting Parts Lists The purpose of this exercise is to give you practice in spotting unrelated parts in a list. In each list below, there is one item that does not belong. Write each list in your notebook, but do not write the item that does not belong.

1. In front-end geometry, factors that are involved include camber, caster, steering-axis inclination, toe-in, toe-up, toe-out on turns.
2. The included angle, in front-end geometry, includes camber angle, caster angle, and steering-axis-inclination angle.
3. Included in the various types of steering linkage are pitman arm, tie rods, drag link, idler arm, connecting rod, steering-knuckle arms, propeller shaft.
4. Parts to be found in all the steering gears described in the chapter include worm, pitman-arm shaft, oil pump, housing.
5. Parts included in the Saginaw power-steering gear include pitman-shaft gear, ball nut and piston, rotary valve, worm, valve-centering block, pitman shaft.
6. Parts to be found in the constant-control power-steering unit include pivot lever, thrust bearing, rotary valve, power piston, worm shaft, and spool valve.
7. Parts included in the linkage-type power-steering system include valve spool, power cylinder, centering spring, piston, friction clutch.
8. Parts included in the fully mechanical power-steering system are input shaft, multiple-disk clutches, pinion gears, ring gears, valve spool.

Unscrambling the Lists (Front-End Geometry) When the two lists below are unscrambled and combined, they will form a list of the factors involved in front-end geometry and the conditions that produce them. To unscramble the lists, take one item at a time from the factors list, and then find the item from the conditions list that goes with it. Write the results in your notebook.

FACTORS:
camber
steering-axis inclination
included angle
caster
toe-in

CONDITIONS:
turning in of front wheels
forward or backward tilt of steering axis
tilting of wheels from vertical

inward tilt of steering axis from vertical
camber plus steering-axis inclination

Purpose and Operation of Components In the following, you are asked to write the purpose of certain factors or the operation of various components in the steering systems described in the chapter. If you have any difficulty in writing your explanations, turn back to the chapter and reread the pages that will give you the answer. Don't copy; try to tell it in your own words. This is an excellent way to fix the explanation firmly in your mind. Write in your notebook.

1. What is the purpose of camber?
2. How does steering-axis inclination tend to return the front wheels to straight ahead when the steering wheel is released?
3. What is the point of intersection?
4. Which will the wheel attempt to do, toe in or toe out, when the point of intersection is below the road surface? Why?
5. What is the relation between caster and the tendency for the car to roll out, or bank, on turns?
6. Does positive caster make the car tend to roll out on turns?
7. What is toe-in?
8. Describe the action of a typical steering gear when the steering wheel is turned.
9. Describe the action of the Saginaw in-line power-steering unit when a right turn is made.
10. Describe the action in the Saginaw rotary-valve power-steering unit when a right turn is made.
11. Describe the action of the constant-control power-steering unit when a right turn is made.
12. Describe the action of the linkage-type power-steering system when a right turn is made.

SUGGESTIONS FOR FURTHER STUDY

You will have a good chance to study various types of steering linkages at any service station where automobiles are raised on lifts for chassis lubrication. Note the different ways in which the pitman arm is linked to the steering knuckles at the front wheels. Automotive repair shops that handle steering-gear servicing will usually have steering-gear parts that you may be able to examine. Note especially the different methods employed in the various steering gears for changing the rotary motion of the steering wheel into a swinging motion of the pitman arm. If you have a chance, examine the internal mechanisms in power-steering units. The automotive manufacturers describe these mechanisms in their shop manuals. If you can study these manuals, you will learn a great deal about how such units are constructed and serviced. Be sure you write important facts in your notebook. This helps you remember them and also gives you a permanent record.

chapter 6

DIAGNOSING STEERING AND SUSPENSION TROUBLES

This chapter discusses various steering and suspension troubles and relates them to possible causes and corrections; that is, it describes trouble-diagnosis procedures on steering and suspension systems. It is not an easy chapter to study, but at the same time it is an important chapter. It gives you the information you need to understand the various effects produced by different kinds of trouble in the steering and suspension. In addition, it tells you what corrections should be made. Later chapters explain how these corrections are made.

⊘ **6-1 How to Study This Chapter** There are various ways to study this chapter. One way is to go through it page by page, just as you have studied the previous chapters. Perhaps a better way is to take one complaint at a time (as listed in the trouble-diagnosis chart), read through the possible causes and checks or corrections, and then study the section later in the chapter that discusses the complaint. For example, you could take Complaint 1, "Excessive play in steering system," and after reading the causes and checks or corrections listed in the second and third columns in the chart, you could turn to ⊘ 6-3 referred to under the complaint and study it.

Since a knowledge of trouble causes and corrections is so helpful, you will probably be referring to the trouble-diagnosis chart many times. One way to help yourself remember the complaints, causes, and corrections is to write each complaint, with its list of causes and corrections, on a separate 3- by 5-inch card. Then carry the cards around with you. Every time you get a chance—for instance, when you are riding a bus, eating your lunch, or getting ready for bed—take out a card and read it over. Soon you will know the complaints, and their causes and corrections, from "A to Z."

⊘ **6-2 Steering and Suspension Trouble-Diagnosis Chart** If you are able to relate various complaints with the conditions that cause them, you are much better off than the person who seeks blindly to find what is causing a trouble. You will know what items to check and correct to eliminate the trouble. You can save a great deal of time and effort when you know where to look.

The chart that follows tells you where to look when various complaints are made regarding the steering or suspension. Following the chart are detailed explanations of the checking procedures to use with each trouble complaint. Then, the next few chapters describe the servicing or repair procedures required to correct the trouble.

A variety of steering and suspension troubles will bring the driver to the mechanic, but it is rare that the driver will have a clear idea of what causes the trouble. The driver can detect an increase in steering difficulty, hard steering, or excessive play in the steering system, but probably does not have a very good idea of what would cause those conditions. The chart that follows lists possible causes of these, as well as other steering and suspension troubles, and then refers to numbered sections after the chart for fuller explanations of the way to locate and eliminate the troubles.

NOTE: The troubles and possible causes are not listed in the chart in the order of frequency of occurrence; that is, item 1 does not necessarily occur more frequently than item 2, nor does item a under Possible Cause necessarily occur more frequently than item b.

STEERING AND SUSPENSION TROUBLE-DIAGNOSIS CHART

(See ⊘ 6-3 to 6-17 for detailed explanations of trouble causes and corrections listed below.)

COMPLAINT	POSSIBLE CAUSE	CHECK OR CORRECTION
1. Excessive play in steering system (⊘ 6-3)	a. Looseness in steering gear	Readjust, replace worn parts
	b. Looseness in linkage	Readjust, replace worn parts
	c. Worn ball joints or steering-knuckle parts	Replace worn parts
	d. Loose wheel bearing	Readjust

(See ⊘ 6-3 to 6-17 for detailed explanations of trouble causes and corrections listed below.)

COMPLAINT	POSSIBLE CAUSE	CHECK OR CORRECTION
2. Hard steering (⊘ 6-4)	a. Power steering inoperative	See Chaps. 10 to 13
	b. Low or uneven tire pressure	Inflate to correct pressure
	c. Friction in steering gear	Lubricate, readjust, replace worn parts
	d. Friction in linkage	Lubricate, readjust, replace worn parts
	e. Friction in ball joints	Lubricate, replace worn parts
	f. Alignment off (caster, camber, toe-in, steering-axis inclination)	Check alignment and readjust as necessary
	g. Frame misaligned	Straighten
	h. Front spring sagging	Replace or adjust
3. Car wander (⊘ 6-5)	a. Low or uneven tire pressure	Inflate to correct pressure
	b. Linkage binding	Readjust, lubricate, replace worn parts
	c. Steering gear binding	Readjust, lubricate, replace worn parts
	d. Front alignment off (caster, camber, toe-in, steering-axis inclination)	Check alignment and readjust as necessary
	e. Looseness in linkage	Readjust, replace worn parts
	f. Looseness in steering gear	Readjust, replace worn parts
	g. Looseness in ball joints	Replace worn parts
	h. Loose rear springs	Tighten
	i. Unequal load in car	Readjust load
	j. Stabilizer bar ineffective	Tighten attachment, replace if damaged
4. Car pulls to one side during normal driving (⊘ 6-6)	a. Uneven tire pressure	Inflate to correct pressure
	b. Uneven caster or camber	Check alignment, adjust as necessary
	c. Tight wheel bearing	Readjust, replace parts if damaged
	d. Uneven springs (sagging, broken, loose attachment)	Tighten, replace defective parts
	e. Wheels not tracking	Check tracking, straighten frame, tighten loose parts, replace defective parts
	f. Uneven torsion-bar adjustment	Adjust
5. Car pulls to one side when braking (⊘ 6-7)	a. Brakes grab	Readjust, replace brake lining, etc. (see Chap. 15)
	b. Uneven tire inflation	Inflate to correct pressure
	c. Incorrect or uneven caster	Readjust
	d. Causes listed under item 4	
6. Front-wheel shimmy at low speeds (⊘ 6-8)	a. Uneven or low tire pressure	Inflate to correct pressure
	b. Loose linkage	Readjust, replace worn parts
	c. Loose ball joints	Replace worn parts
	d. Looseness in steering gear	Readjust, replace worn parts
	e. Front springs too flexible	Replace, tighten attachment
	f. Incorrect or unequal camber	Readjust
	g. Irregular tire tread	Replace worn tires, match treads
	h. Dynamic imbalance	Balance wheels
7. Front-wheel tramp (high-speed shimmy) (⊘ 6-9)	a. Wheels out of balance	Rebalance
	b. Too much wheel runout	Balance, remount tire, straighten or replace wheel
	c. Defective shock absorbers	Repair or replace
	d. Causes listed under item 6	
8. Steering kickback (⊘ 6-10)	a. Tire pressure low or uneven	Inflate to correct pressure
	b. Springs sagging	Tighten attachment, replace
	c. Shock absorbers defective	Repair or replace
	d. Looseness in linkage	Readjust, replace worn parts
	e. Looseness in steering gear	Readjust, replace worn parts
9. Tires squeal on turns (⊘ 6-11)	a. Excessive speed	Take curves at slower speed
	b. Low or uneven tire pressure	Inflate to correct pressure
	c. Front alignment incorrect	Check and adjust
	d. Worn tires	Replace

(See ⊘ 6-3 to 6-17 for detailed explanations of trouble causes and corrections listed below.)

COMPLAINT	POSSIBLE CAUSE	CHECK OR CORRECTION
10. Improper tire wear (⊘ 6-12)	a. Wear at tread sides from underinflation	Inflate to correct pressure
	b. Wear at tread center from overinflation	Inflate to correct pressure
	c. Wear at one tread side from excessive camber	Adjust camber
	d. Featheredge wear from excessive toe-in or toe-out on turns	Correct toe-in or toe-out on turns
	e. Cornering wear from excessive speeds on turns	Take turns at slower speed
	f. Uneven or spotty wear from mechanical causes	Adjust brakes, align wheels, balance wheels, adjust linkage, etc.
	g. Rapid wear from speed	Drive more slowly for longer tire life
11. Hard or rough ride (⊘ 6-13)	a. Excessive tire pressure	Reduce to correct pressure
	b. Defective shock absorbers	Repair or replace
	c. Excessive friction in spring suspension	Lubricate, realign parts
12. Sway on turns (⊘ 6-14)	a. Loose stabilizer bar	Tighten
	b. Weak or sagging springs	Repair or replace
	c. Caster incorrect	Adjust
	d. Defective shock absorbers	Replace
13. Spring breakage (⊘ 6-15)	a. Overloading	Avoid overloading
	b. Loose center or U bolts	Keep bolts tight
	c. Defective shock absorber	Repair or replace
	d. Tight spring shackle	Loosen, replace
14. Sagging springs (⊘ 6-16)	a. Broken leaf	Replace
	b. Spring weak	Replace
	c. Coil spring short	Install shim
	d. Defective shock absorber	Repair or replace
15. Noises (⊘ 6-17)	Could come from any loose, worn, or unlubricated part in the suspension or steering system.	

⊘ 6-3 Excessive Play in Steering System Excessive play or looseness in the steering system means that there will be excessive free movement of the steering wheel without corresponding movement of the front wheels. A small amount of steering-wheel play is desirable in order to provide easy steering. But when the play becomes excessive, it is considered objectionable by most drivers. Excessive play can be due to wear or improper adjustment of the steering gear, to wear or improper adjustments in the steering linkage, to worn ball joints or steering-knuckle parts, or to loose wheel bearings.

The tie rods and linkage may be checked for looseness by jacking up the front end of the car, grasping both front wheels, pushing out on both at the same time, and then pulling in on both at the same time (Fig. 6-1). Excessive relative movement between the two wheels means that the linkage connections are worn or out of adjustment. Other steering and suspension check points are shown in Figs. 6-2 to 6-5. Service on these items is covered in Chap. 7.

Worn steering-knuckle parts and loose wheel bearings can be detected by jacking up the front end

of the car, grasping the wheel top and bottom, and checking it for side play (Fig. 6-5). Try to see how much you can wobble the wheel. Excessive looseness indicates worn or loose parts, either in the steering knuckle or in the wheel bearing. The bearing should be readjusted (⊘ 7-5, item 3, and ⊘ 7-7,

Fig. 6-1. Checking tie rods and linkage for looseness. (*Bear Manufacturing Company*)

Fig. 6-2. Check arrowed items—tie-rod ends, idler arm, and control-arm shaft mounting bolts—for looseness. (*Bear Manufacturing Company*)

Fig. 6-4. Pry up on the tire with a bar to check for loose ball joints. (*Bear Manufacturing Company*)

Fig. 6-3. Check arrowed items—pitman arm and steering-gear mounting bolts—for looseness. (*Bear Manufacturing Company*)

Fig. 6-5. Checking for wear in the steering knuckle and wheel bearing. (*Bear Manufacturing Company*)

item *1*) to see whether the looseness is in the bearing or in the knuckle.

Ball joints can be checked for wear by supporting the wheel as shown in Figs. 6-6 and 6-7. Axial play is checked by moving the wheel up and down. Radial play is measured by rocking the wheel back and forth.

On the suspension with the spring on the lower arm (Fig. 6-6), the upper ball joint should be replaced

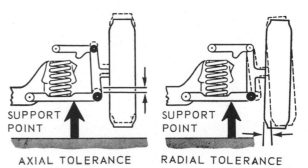

Fig. 6-6. To check the ball joints for wear on a suspension system with the spring on the lower arm, support the wheel under the arm as shown.

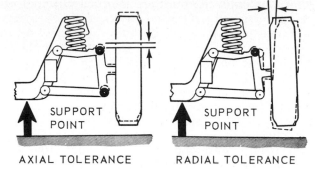

SUPPORT POINT   SUPPORT POINT

AXIAL TOLERANCE   RADIAL TOLERANCE

Fig. 6-7. To check the ball joints for wear on a suspension system with the spring on the upper arm, support the front end of the frame, as shown.

if there is any noticeable looseness at the joint.[1] The lower ball joint should be replaced if radial play exceeds 0.250 inch [6.35 mm]. The lower ball joint should be replaced if axial play between the lower control arm and the spindle exceeds the tolerance specified by the vehicle manufacturer. This specification may vary from zero to 0.200 inch [5.08 mm], so always refer to the manufacturer's shop manual.

Many ball joints have wear indicators (Fig. 6-8). On these, the lower ball joints can be checked by visual inspection alone. Wear is indicated by the recession of the grease-fitting nipple into the ball-joint socket, as shown. The nipple protrudes from the socket 0.050 inch [1.27 mm] when new. As the ball joint wears, the nipple recedes into the socket. If the wear has caused the nipple to recede as much as 0.050 inch [1.27 mm], it will be level with the

---

[1] Some manufacturers (Chevrolet, for example) specify replacement of the lower ball joint, also, when the upper ball joint is replaced.

socket, and the ball joint should be replaced. Figure 6-8 shows the nipple being checked with a steel scale, but it can be checked with a screwdriver or even a fingernail. Replacement procedures are covered in Chap. 7.

On the suspension with the spring on the upper arm (Fig. 6-7), the *lower* ball joint should be replaced if there is any noticeable looseness at the joint. The *upper* ball joint should be replaced if radial play exceeds 0.250 inch [6.35 mm]. The *upper* ball joint should be replaced if axial play between the upper control arm and spindle exceeds the tolerances specified by the vehicle manufacturer. This specification may vary from zero to 0.200 inch [5.08 mm], so always refer to the manufacturer's shop manual.

NOTE: Some lower ball joints are not internally preloaded. When the car weight is removed from these, they will exhibit some looseness due to normal operating clearance. But such looseness does not necessarily mean the ball joint should be replaced. A method of checking these non-preloaded ball joints is described in ⊘ 7-5.

A rough check for looseness in the steering gear can be made by watching the pitman arm while an assistant turns the steering wheel one way and then the other with the front wheels on the floor. If, after reversal of steering-wheel rotation, considerable initial movement of the steering wheel is required to set the pitman arm in motion, the steering gear is worn or in need of adjustment (Chap. 9).

⊘ **6-4 Hard Steering** If hard steering occurs just after the steering system has been worked on, chances are it is due to excessively tight adjustments in the steering gear or linkages. If hard steering de-

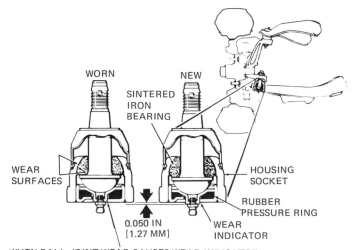

Fig. 6-8. Wear-indicating ball joint. *Left,* sectional views showing a ball joint in good condition and a ball joint worn to the point where it requires replacement. *Right,* checking with a scale to see how much the nipple protrudes. (*Chevrolet Motor Division of General Motors Corporation*)

velops at other times, it could be due to low or uneven tire pressure, abnormal friction in the steering gear, in the linkage, or at the kingpin or ball joints, or to improper wheel or frame alignment.

On a car equipped with power steering, failure of the power-steering mechanism will cause the steering system to revert to straight mechanical operation and a considerably greater steering effort. In such a case, the power-steering unit and the hydraulic pump should be checked as outlined in Chaps. 10 to 13.

The steering system may be checked for excessive friction by jacking up the front end of the car, turning the steering wheel, and observing the steering-system components to locate the source of excessive friction. Disconnect the linkage at the pitman arm. If this eliminates the frictional drag that makes it hard to turn the steering wheel, the friction is either in the linkage itself or at the steering knuckles. If the friction is not eliminated when the linkage is disconnected at the pitman arm, the steering gear is probably at fault. Steering-gear service is discussed in Chap. 9, and linkage service is described in Chap. 7.

If the trouble does not seem to be due to excessive friction in the steering system, chances are it is due to incorrect front-wheel alignment or to a misaligned frame or sagging springs. Excessive caster especially causes hard steering (see Chap. 8, "Front-End Alignment").

⊘ **6-5 Car Wander** Car wander is experienced as difficulty in keeping the car moving straight ahead; frequent steering-wheel movements are necessary to prevent the car from wandering from one side of the road to the other. Inexperienced drivers may sometimes complain of car wander because they tend to oversteer. They keep moving the wheel back and forth unnecessarily to stay on their side of the road.

A variety of conditions can cause car wander. Low or uneven tire pressure, binding or excessive play in the linkage or steering gear, or improper front-wheel alignment will cause car wander. Any condition that causes tightness in the steering system will keep the wheels from automatically seeking the straight-ahead position. The driver has to correct the wheels constantly. This condition would probably also cause hard steering (⊘ 6-4). Looseness or excessive play in the steering system might cause car wander, too, since this would tend to allow the wheels to waver somewhat and would permit the car to wander.

Excessively low caster, uneven caster, or a point of intersection too far above or below the road surface (due to the wrong camber angle) will tend to cause the wheels to swing away from straight ahead so that the driver must steer continually. Excessive toe-in will cause the same condition. Front-end alignment is covered in Chap. 8.

⊘ **6-6 Car Pulls to One Side (Normal Driving)** If the car persistently pulls to one side so that pressure must constantly be applied to the steering wheel to maintain forward movement, the trouble could be due to uneven tire pressure, uneven caster or camber, a tight wheel bearing, uneven springs, uneven torsion-bar adjustment, or to the wheels not tracking (rear wheels not following in the tracks of the front wheels). Anything that would tend to make one wheel drag or toe in or toe out more than the other would make the car pull to that side. The methods used to check tracking and front-wheel alignment are covered in Chap. 8.

⊘ **6-7 Car Pulls to One Side (When Braking)** The most likely cause of pulling to one side when braking is grabbing brakes. Such brake action could be due to the brake linings' becoming soaked with oil or brake fluid, to brake shoes that are unevenly or improperly adjusted, to a brake backing plate that is loose or out of line, or to other causes that would cause the brake at one wheel to apply harder than the brake at the corresponding wheel on the other side. Chapter 15 covers brake service. The other conditions listed in ⊘ 6-6 could also cause pulling to one side when braking, since the condition, from whatever cause, tends to become more noticeable when the car is braked.

⊘ **6-8 Front-Wheel Shimmy (Low Speed)** Front-wheel shimmy and front-wheel tramp (⊘ 6-9) are sometimes confused. Low-speed shimmy is the rapid oscillation of the wheel on the steering-knuckle support. The wheel tries to turn in and out alternately. This action causes the front end of the car to shake from side to side. On the other hand, front-wheel tramp, or high-speed shimmy, is the tendency for the wheel-and-tire assembly to hop up and down and, under severe conditions, actually to leave the pavement. Even when the tire does not leave the pavement, tramp can be observed as a rapid flexing-unflexing action of the part of the tire in contact with the pavement. That is, the bottom of the tire first appears deflated (as the wheel moves down) and then inflated (as the wheel moves up).

Low-speed shimmy can result from low or uneven tire pressure, loose linkage, excessively soft springs, incorrect or uneven wheel camber, dynamic imbalance of the wheels, or from irregularities in the tire treads.

⊘ **6-9 Front-Wheel Tramp** As explained in the previous section, front-wheel tramp is often called *high-speed shimmy*. This condition causes the front wheels to move up and down alternately. One of the most common causes of front-wheel tramp is unbalanced wheels, or wheels that have too much runout. An unbalanced wheel is heavy at one part; as it rotates, the heavy part sets up a circulating outward thrust that tends to make the wheel hop up and down. A similar action occurs if the wheel has too much runout. Runout is the amount the wheel is out of line with the axle so that one part of the wheel "runs out," or moves to the side more than other parts of the wheel. Defective shock absorbers, which fail to control natural spring oscillations, also cause wheel tramp. Any of the causes described in the previous section may also cause wheel tramp. Later sections describe the servicing of the wheel and tire so that they can be restored to proper balance and alignment.

⊘ **6-10 Steering Kickback** Steering shock, or kickback, consists of sharp and rapid movements of the steering wheel that occur when the front wheels encounter obstructions in the road. Normally, some kickback to the steering wheel will always occur; when it becomes excessive, an investigation should be made. This condition could result from incorrect or uneven tire inflation, sagging springs, defective shock absorbers, or looseness in the linkage or steering gear. Any of these defects could permit road shock to carry back excessively to the steering wheel.

⊘ **6-11 Tires Squeal on Turns** If the tires skid or squeal on turns, the cause may be excessive speed on the turns. If this is not the cause, it is probably low or uneven tire pressure, worn tires, or misalignment of the front wheels—particularly camber and toe-in.

⊘ **6-12 Improper Tire Wear** Various types of abnormal tire wear can be experienced. The type of tire wear found is often a good indication of a particular defect in the suspension or steering system, or improper operation or abuse. For example, if the tire is operated with insufficient air pressure—underinflated—the sides will bulge over and the center of the tread will be lifted clear of the road. The sides of the tread will take all the wear; the center will barely be worn (Fig. 6-9). The uneven tread wear shortens tire life. But even more damaging is the excessive flexing of the tire sidewalls that takes place as the underinflated tire rolls on the pavement. The repeated flexing causes the fabric in the sidewalls to crack or break and the plies to separate (Fig. 6-10). Naturally, this seriously weakens the sidewalls and may soon lead to complete tire failure. Aside from all this, the underinflated tire is unprotected against rim bruises. Thus if the tire should strike a rut or stone on the road, or if it should bump a curb a little too hard, the tire will flex so much under the blow that it will actually be pinched on the rim. This causes plies to break and leads to early tire failure.

NOTE: The belted radial tire applies a much larger area of tread to the pavement, as explained in Chap.

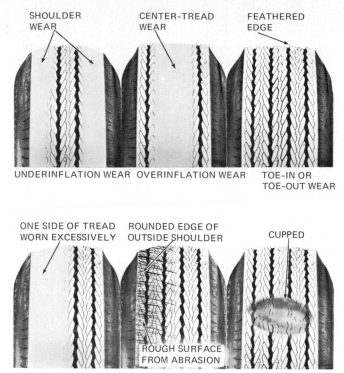

Fig. 6-9. Patterns of abnormal tire-tread wear. (*Buick Motor Division of General Motors Corporation*)

17. These tires therefore appear to be running underinflated, when compared with the bias-ply tire used on cars for many years. The information in the previous paragraph applies more to bias-ply tires than to radial-ply tires.

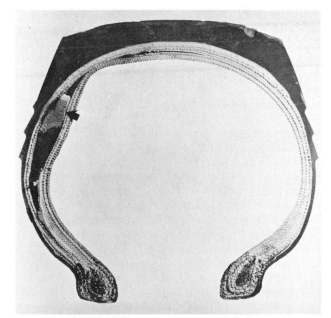

Fig. 6-10. The separation of plies in the sidewall of this tire has resulted from driving with the tire in an underinflated condition. A piece of wood (at arrow) has been inserted between the plies to show where the separation has occurred.

Continuous high-speed driving on curves, both right and left, can produce tread wear that looks almost like underinflation wear. The side thrust on the tires as they round the curves causes the sides of the tread to be worn. The only remedy here is to reduce car speed on turns.

Overinflation causes the tire to ride on the center of its tread so that only the center of the tread wears (Fig. 6-9). The uneven tread wear shortens tire life. But equally damaging is the fact that the over-inflated tire does not have normal "give" when it meets a rut or bump in the road. Instead of giving normally, the tire fabric takes the major shock of the encounter. As a result, the fabric may crack or break so that the tire quickly fails.

Excessive toe-in or toe-out on turns causes the tire to be dragged sideways while it is moving forward. The tire on a front wheel that toes in 1 inch [25.4 mm] from straight ahead will be dragged sideways about 150 feet [45.7 m] every mile [1.6 km]. This sideward drag scrapes off rubber as shown in Fig. 6-9. Characteristic of this type of wear are the feather-edges of rubber that appear on one side of the tread design. If both front tires show this type of wear, the front system is misaligned. But if only one tire shows this type of wear—and if both tires have been on the car for some time—a bent steering arm is indicated. This causes one wheel to toe in more than the other.

Excessive camber of a wheel causes one side of the tread to wear more rapidly than the other (Fig. 6-9). If the camber is positive, the tires will tilt outward and the heavy tread wear will be on the outside. If the camber is negative, the tires will tilt inward and the heavy tread wear will be on the inside.

Cornering wear, caused by taking curves at excessively high speeds, may be mistaken for camber wear or toe-in or toe-out wear (Fig. 6-9). Cornering wear is due to centrifugal force acting on the car and causing the tires to roll, as well as skid, on the road. This produces a diagonal type of wear, which rounds the outside shoulder of the tire and roughens the tread surface near the outside shoulder. In severe cornering wear, fins or sharp edges will be found along the inner edges of the tire treads. There is no adjustment that can be made to correct the steering system for this type of wear. The only preventive is for the driver to slow down on curves.

Uneven tire wear (such as shown in Fig. 6-9), with the tread unevenly or spottily worn, can result from a number of mechanical conditions. These include misaligned wheels, unequal or improperly adjusted brakes, unbalanced wheels, overinflated tires, out-of-round brake drums, and incorrect linkage adjustments.

High-speed operation causes much more rapid tire wear because of the high temperature and greater amount of scuffing and rapid flexing to which the tires are subjected. The chart (Fig. 6-11) shows just how much tire wear increases with car speed. According to the chart, tires wear more than

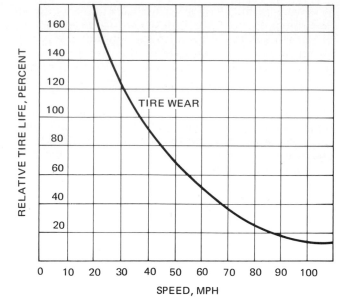

Fig. 6-11. Graph showing how tire wear increases with speed.

three times faster at 70 mph (miles per hour) [112.6 km/h (kilometers per hour)] than they do at 30 mph [48.3 km/h]. More careful, slower driving and correct tire inflation will increase tire life greatly.

⊘ **6-13 Hard or Rough Ride** A hard or rough ride could be due to excessive tire pressure, improperly operating shock absorbers, or excessive friction in the spring suspension. The spring suspension can be checked easily for excessive friction in leaf-spring-suspension systems. Place strips of adhesive tape at the lower edges of the car body, front and back. Lift the front end of the car as high as possible by hand, and very slowly let it down. Carefully measure from the floor to the tape and note the distance. Then push down on the car bumper at the front end, and again slowly release the car. Remeasure the distance from the floor to the tape, and note the difference in measurements. Repeat this action several times to obtain accurate measurements. The difference is caused by the friction in the suspension system and is called *friction lag*. After determining friction lag at the front end, check it at the back end of the car. Make correction by lubricating the springs, shackles, and bushings (on types where lubrication is specified) and by loosening the shock-absorber arm linkages, shackle bolts, and U bolts. Then retighten the U bolts, shackle bolts, and shock-absorber linkages, in that order. Such a procedure permits realignment of parts that might have slipped and caused excessive friction.

Shock-absorber action on cars giving a hard or uneven ride may be roughly checked by bouncing each corner of the car in turn. This is done by seizing the bumper, pulling up and pushing down on it several times so that the car bounces, and then re-

releasing the bumper.[2] If the shock absorber is operating normally, the car will come to rest immediately. If the car continues to bounce after the bumper is released, the shock absorber is probably defective. A more accurate check can be made by disconnecting the shock absorber at one end and then noting its resistance to shortening and lengthening. If the resistance is small or is not uniform through the full stroke, or if the movement is very stiff, the shock absorber will require additional attention (⊘ 4-5 and 4-6).

⊘ **6-14 Sway on Turns** Sway of the car body on turns or on rough roads may be due to a loose stabilizer bar or shaft. Their attachments to the frame, axle housing, or suspension arms should be checked. Weak or sagging springs could also cause excessive sway. If the shock absorbers are ineffective, they may permit excessive spring movement, which could cause strong body pitching and sway, particularly on rough roads. If the caster is excessively positive, it will cause the car to roll out, or lean out, on turns (see ⊘ 5-6). This requires front-wheel realignment.

⊘ **6-15 Spring Breakage** Breakage of leaf springs can result from (1) excessive overloading; (2) loose U bolts, which cause breakage near the center bolt; (3) loose center bolt, which causes breakage at the center-bolt holes; (4) improperly operating shock absorber, which causes breakage of the master leaf; or (5) tight spring shackle, which causes breakage of the master leaf near or at the spring eye. Determining the point at which breakage has occurred will make the cause obvious.

⊘ **6-16 Sagging Springs** Springs will sag if they have become weak—as they might, for example, from habitual overloading. Loss of the shim from the coil-spring seat on coil-spring suspension—due to failure to return it during overhaul—will also cause the spring to sag and to seem shorter. Not all coil springs require or use shims (see the discussion on shims in the following chapter). If a torsion-bar suspension system sags, the torsion bars can be adjusted to restore normal car height. Defective shock absorbers may tend to restrict spring action and thus make them appear to sag more than normal.

⊘ **6-17 Noises** The noises produced by spring or shock-absorber difficulties will usually be either rattles or squeaks. Rattling noises can be produced by looseness of such parts as spring U bolts, metal spring covers, rebound clips, spring shackles, or shock-absorber linkages or springs. These can generally be located by a careful examination of the

[2] Some direct-acting shock absorbers cannot be tested in this way, since they are valved to permit slow spring oscillations in the interest of smoother riding.

various suspension parts. Spring squeaks can result from lack of lubrication in the spring shackles, at spring bushings (on the type requiring lubrication), or in the spring itself (leaf type requiring lubrication). Shock-absorber squeak could result from tight or dry bushings. Steering-linkage rattles may develop if linkage components become loose. Under exceptional circumstances, squeaks during turns could develop because of lack of lubrication in steering-linkage joints or bearings. This would, of course, also produce hard steering.

Some of the connections between steering-linkage parts are with ball joints that can be lubricated. Others are permanently lubricated on original assembly and have no provision for further lubrication. If the latter develop squeaks or excessive friction, they must be replaced. Lubricating and replacing steering-linkage ball joints are covered in the following chapter.

CHAPTER 6 CHECKUP

The chapter you have just completed is a hard one. But it is very important to anyone who wants real insight into various kinds of trouble—and their causes—that might occur in steering and suspension systems. The fact that you have come this far in the book shows that you have made a determined start toward becoming an automotive expert. As you increase your fund of knowledge of the automobile, you become better equipped for the future that lies ahead of you. The checkup below will help you check yourself on how well you remember the material you have just completed. If any of the questions seem hard to answer, just review the chapter again. Technical material, such as you are reading, will not "stick with you" the first time you read it. You may have to go over it several times before all the facts will stay in your mind.

Correcting Trouble Lists The purpose of this exercise is to help you spot related and unrelated troubles on a list. For example, in the list "Hard steering: low tire pressure, friction in linkage, friction in steering gear, front alignment off, power-steering unit operating, frame misaligned," you can see that the term "power-steering unit operating" does not belong because that would *not* make steering hard. Any of the other conditions in the list could.

In each list, you will find one item that does not belong. Write each list in your notebook, but *do not write* the item that does not belong.

1. Excessive play in steering system: looseness in steering gear, looseness in linkage, excessive caster, worn steering-knuckle parts, loose wheel bearing.
2. Hard steering: low tire pressure, friction in steering system, front-wheel alignment off, tight U bolt, frame misaligned, front spring sagging.
3. Car wander: low or uneven tire pressure, binding in linkage or steering gear, front-wheel alignment

off, looseness in linkage or steering gear, engine mounting tight, loose rear springs, unequal load in car, stabilizer bar ineffective.

4. Car pulls to one side during normal driving: uneven tire pressure, uneven caster or camber, tight wheel bearing, wheels out of balance, uneven springs, wheels not tracking.

5. Car pulls to one side when braking: brakes grab, uneven tire inflation, incorrect or uneven caster, defective shock absorbers.

6. Front-wheel shimmy at low speeds: uneven or low tire pressure, looseness in linkage or steering gear, springs too flexible, steering gear binding, incorrect or unequal camber.

7. Front-wheel tramp: wheels out of balance, grabbing brakes, too much wheel runout, defective shock absorbers.

8. Steering kickback: low or uneven tire pressure, sagging springs, defective shock absorbers, caster too low, looseness in linkage or steering gear.

9. Tires squeal on turns: excessive speed, power steering inoperative, low tire pressure, wheel alignment incorrect.

10. Improper tire wear: underinflation, overinflation, wheel aligned with axle, excessive camber, excessive toe-in or toe-out on turns, excessive speed.

11. Hard or rough ride: excessive tire pressure, underinflation, defective shock absorbers, excessive friction in spring suspension.

12. Sway on turns: loose stabilizer bar, weak or sagging springs, caster incorrect, binding in steering linkage.

13. Spring breakage: overloading, loose center or U bolts, defective shock absorber, underinflation, tight spring shackle.

14. Sagging spring: broken leaf, spring weak, tight wheel bearing, coil spring short, defective shock absorber.

15. Noises in suspension or steering system: caster too low, loose bolts, lack of lubrication, loose rebound clips or spring shackles.

SUGGESTIONS FOR FURTHER STUDY

Careful observation of steering and front-alignment checking procedures in the automotive shop will be of great value to you. If you can watch a good front-alignment technician at work, you will be able to learn a great deal about the various factors that make up proper wheel alignment. Knowledge of the different troubles that can occur if any of the factors are out of line will help you when you go into the automotive shop or office and have to deal with such matters.

You will want to remember the important trouble-diagnosis covered in this chapter. To help you do this, write each trouble and its related causes on a 3- by 5-inch card, and carry the cards around with you. You can study the cards every chance you get. For example, just before you go to bed, read over one of the cards several times. Or pick up the cards while listening to the radio, and study them. If you do this earnestly, it won't be long before you know the troubles and their causes thoroughly.

chapter 7

SERVICING STEERING LINKAGE AND FRONT AND REAR SUSPENSION

This chapter introduces the servicing procedures required for various types of steering linkages and front- and rear-suspension systems. Later chapters describe front-wheel alignment service and steering-gear service (manual and power). It is extremely important always to check and correct front-wheel alignment whenever any work has been done on the front suspension that might disturb alignment. In the pages that follow, typical steering-linkage and suspension servicing procedures for Chevrolet, Ford, and Plymouth are described in detail. Servicing procedures for other cars usually will be found to be similar to one of these three procedures, although there may be some variations in individual details. Always refer to the shop manual covering the specific car model you are working on when servicing steering linkage and front- and rear-suspension systems.

⊘ **7-1 Steering Linkage Service** The only service that steering linkages normally require is periodic lubrication of the connecting joints between the links. The connecting joints are ball joints (⊘ 5-10). Figure 7-1 shows a typical arrangement. The joints arrowed are ball joints and have a means of lubrication. Note that the joints at the pitman arm and the idler arm are not arrowed. These joints are permanently lubricated on assembly and do not require lubrication. The arrangement shown in Fig. 7-1 is for a specific model of car. Other cars may have different arrangements.

The lubricating procedure varies slightly, according to whether the ball joints have plugs to be removed (Fig. 7-2) or regular grease fittings (Fig. 7-3). Typical recommendations (Ford and Chrysler) are that the seals at the ball joints should be inspected at least every 6 months and lubricated every 3 years. Chevrolet recommends lubricating the linkage every 6,000 miles [9,656 km] or 4 months with water-resistant chassis lubricant.

1. BALL JOINT WITH PLUG (FIG. 7-2) First, wipe the plug and area around the plug so no dirt will get into the ball joint. Then use a rubber-tipped, hand-operated grease gun, filled with the proper lubricant. Apply the tip to the plug hole and operate the grease gun at low pressure. This forces lubricant into the joint. When the joint boot (dust cover) begins to swell, stop. Do not overlubricate or you will destroy the weathertight seal.

2. BALL JOINT WITH GREASE FITTING (FIG. 7-3) First, wipe the grease fitting so no dirt will get into the ball joint. Then take a hand-operated grease gun with the proper applicator for the fitting, and fill it with the proper lubricant. Operate the grease gun at low pressure. Chrysler says to "fill and flush" the joint with lubricant. Stop filling when the grease begins to flow freely from the bleed area at the base of the seal or if the seal begins to balloon.

If ball joints or other parts are worn or have been bent or damaged, they should be replaced. Never try to straighten and reuse bent steering-linkage parts. This is a dangerous practice that could lead to a fatal accident.

If the linkage is disassembled, check the front alignment after all parts have been put back together again (Chap. 8). Following pages describe the servicing of steering linkages and front- and rear-suspension systems, including wheel-bearing inspection, lubrication, and adjustment.

NOTE: A good service mechanic always inspects the steering linkage and suspension when working on a car on the lift for whatever purpose. It takes only a moment to check seals and note the conditions of the ball joints and links. A steering-linkage system in good condition is necessary to the safe operation of the car. Therefore you should make sure that the steering linkage of every car you service is in good shape.

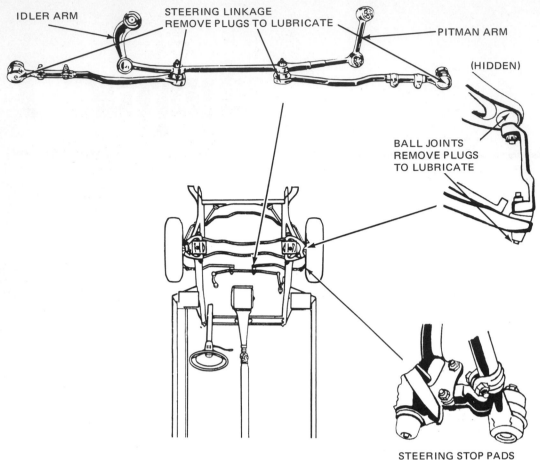

Fig. 7-1. Lubrication points in a steering-linkage and front suspension system. (*Ford Motor Company*)

CAUTION: When assembling automotive components, you must always use the proper attaching parts—bolts, nuts, cotter pins, etc. This means using parts of the same manufacturer, or their equivalent. Never use a replacement part of lesser quality or different design. To do so is to risk a failure that could result in a fatal accident. Also, always torque all nuts and bolts to specifications.

⊘ **7-2 Chevrolet Steering-Linkage Service** Figure 7-4 shows steering linkages described in this section. Removal and installation of the tie rods, relay rod, idler arm, and steering arms are covered in following paragraphs.

1. TIE-ROD REMOVAL Remove the cotter pins from the ball studs and take off the castellated nuts.

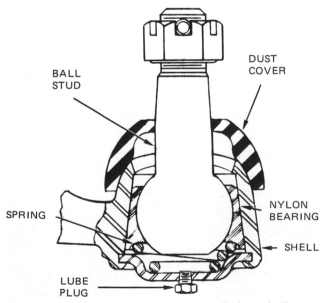

Fig. 7-2. Sectional view of a steering-linkage ball joint. (*American Motors Corporation*)

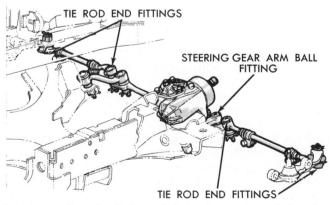

Fig. 7-3. Steering-linkage lubrication points. (*Chrysler Corporation*)

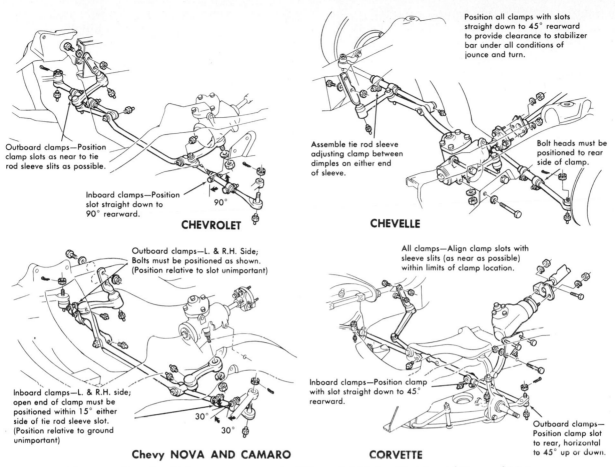

Fig. 7-4. Steering-linkage arrangements. (*Chevrolet Motor Division of General Motors Corporation*)

To disconnect the outer ball stud, tap on the steering arm at the tie-rod end with a hammer, using a heavy hammer as a backing (Fig. 7-5). Pull down on the tie rod if necessary to free it from the steering arm. Disconnect the other end of the tie rod from the relay rod in the same manner. If necessary, take the tie-rod end off by loosening the clamp bolts and screwing it off.

2. *TIE-ROD INSTALLATION* When replacing the tie-rod ends, lubricate the threads with EP chassis lubricant. Make sure both ends are threaded an equal distance on the tie rod. Be sure that the threads on the ball-stud nuts are clean and smooth. If they bind, they may turn the ball studs in the tie-rod ends when the nuts are tightened. Install neoprene seals, and place the ball studs in the steering arm and relay rod. Put the nut on, tighten it securely, and install the cotter pin. Lubricate the tie-rod ends and adjust the toe-in.

NOTE: Before locking the clamp bolts, be sure the tie-rod ends are aligned with their ball studs with each ball joint in the center of its travel. Otherwise, binding will result. The bolts must be installed facing forward as shown in Fig. 7-6 with the centerlines of the bolts within the angles shown. The slot of the adjusting sleeve may be in any position but

not closer than 0.010 inch [0.254 mm] to the edge of the clamp jaw, or between the clamp jaws. These angles are for the Chevrolet models shown in Fig. 7-6. Other models require somewhat different arrangements. Refer to the Chevrolet shop manual.

Fig. 7-5. Freeing the ball stud from the tie rod. (*Chevrolet Motor Division of General Motors Corporation*)

3. *RELAY-ROD REMOVAL* Remove the inner ends of the tie rods from the relay rod as noted in the previous paragraphs. Remove damper from relay rod, where present (on Monte Carlo and Chevelle with manual steering). Remove the cotter pin and nut from the relay-rod ball-stud attachment at the pitman arm. Detach the relay rod from the pitman arm. Move the steering linkage as necessary to free the pitman arm from the relay rod. Remove the cotter pin and nut from the idler arm and take the relay rod from the idler arm.

4. *RELAY-ROD INSTALLATION* Install the relay rod on the idler arm, making sure the stud seal is in place, and then install and tighten the nut. Advance the nut just enough beyond the specified torque to align the castellated nut with the cotter-pin hole and install the pin. Raise the end of the rod and install it on the pitman arm. Secure with the nut and cotter pin. Install the tie-rod ends on the relay rod as noted above in item 2. Install damper, if used. Adjust the toe-in and center the steering wheel (see Chap. 8).

5. *IDLER-ARM REMOVAL* The idler-arm assembly should be replaced if an up-and-down push of 25 pounds [11.3 kg], applied at the relay-rod end, produces a vertical movement of more than 0.125 inch [3.175 mm]. Such movement means a worn ball stud. To remove the idler-arm assembly, raise the car on a hoist. Remove the nut, washer, and bolt attaching the idler arm to the frame. Remove the cotter pin and nut from the ball stud attaching the idler arm to the relay rod. Detach the relay rod from the idler arm by tapping the relay rod with a hammer. Use a heavy hammer as a backing in the manner shown in Fig. 7-5. Remove the idler arm.

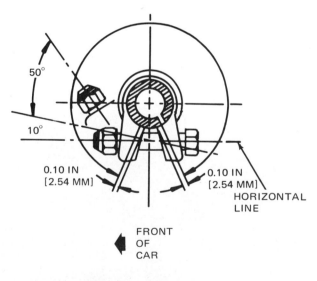

Fig. 7-6. Proper installation of bolts and tie-rod clamps. (*Chevrolet Motor Division of General Motors Corporation*)

6. *IDLER-ARM INSTALLATION* The installation procedure differs somewhat with the various models shown in Fig. 7-4. On Chevrolet, put the seal in position on the idler-arm stud, position the stud up through the frame, and secure with lock washer and nut. On Monte Carlo, Nova, and Corvette, position the idler arm on the frame and install the mounting bolts, washers, and nuts (no washer is used on Corvette). Install the relay rod on the idler arm, making sure the seal is on the stud. Install and tighten the nut to the specified torque and install the cotter pin.

7. *PITMAN-ARM REMOVAL* Remove the cotter pin and nut from the pitman-arm ball stud. Remove the relay rod from the pitman arm by tapping with a hammer on the side of the rod or arm in which the stud mounts. Use a heavy hammer as a backing in the manner shown in Fig. 7-5. Pull down on the relay rod to remove it from the stud. Remove the pitman-arm nut. Mark the relationship of the pitman arm to the shaft. Then use a special puller to pull the arm off the shaft.

8. *PITMAN-ARM INSTALLATION* Install the pitman arm on the sector shaft, aligning marks. Install the sector-shaft nut. Position the relay rod on the pitman arm and install the nut and cotter pin.

9. *STEERING-ARM REMOVAL* The only time a steering arm requires replacement is after an accident. To remove an arm, first detach the tie rod as explained in item 1. Then remove the front wheel, hub, and brake drum as a unit by taking off the hubcap, dust cap, cotter pin, and spindle nut. Pull the assembly outward. If the assembly is hard to remove, back off the brake adjustment to increase the shoe-to-drum clearance. On models with disk brakes, remove the caliper and disk. Now, steering-arm retainer nuts and bolts can be removed so the steering arm can be taken off.

10. *STEERING-ARM INSTALLATION* Put the steering arm in place and install the retaining bolts. Secure with special locknuts. Pack the wheel bearings with the specified lubricant. Install the bearings and wheel-hub-brake assembly. Or, on disk-brake models, install the disk and caliper. Install the keyed washer and spindle nut and adjust the front-wheel bearing as outlined in ⊘ 7-5. Install the tie-rod ball stud in the steering arm. Make sure the dust cover is in place on the ball stud. Install the castellated nut and cotter pin. Check the toe-in and steering-wheel centering (Chap. 8).

⊘ **7-3 Ford Steering-Linkage Service** Different models require different service procedures. Figures 7-7 to 7-9 show the different linkage arrangements used on the various Ford models.

1. *CONNECTING-ROD ASSEMBLY (TYPE IN FIG. 7-7)* The ball studs in the connecting-rod ends are nonadjustable and cannot be lubricated. The rod-end assembly must be replaced if the ball studs become loose.

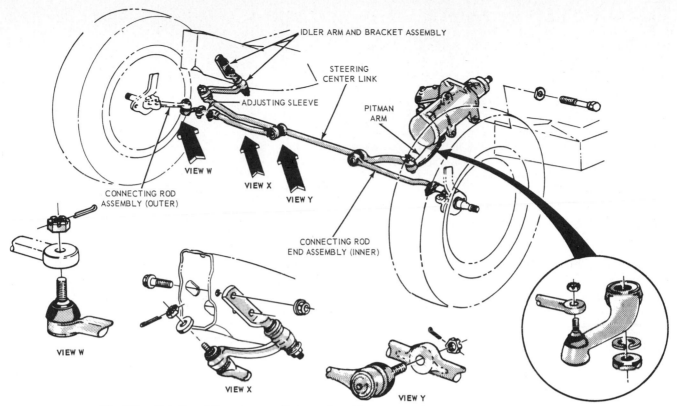

Fig. 7-7. Details of the steering linkage for cither manual or integral power steering. (*Ford Motor Company*)

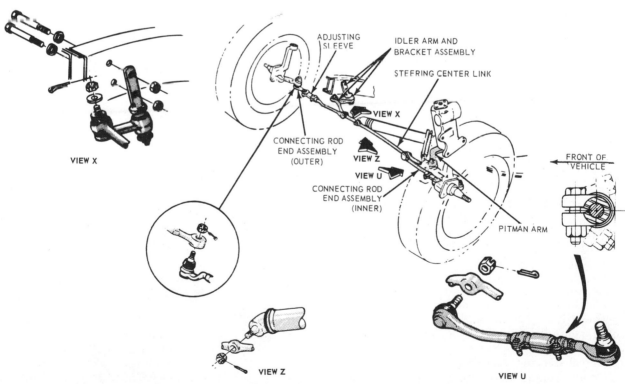

Fig. 7-8. Details of the steering linkage for a system using linkage-type power steering. (*Ford Motor Company*)

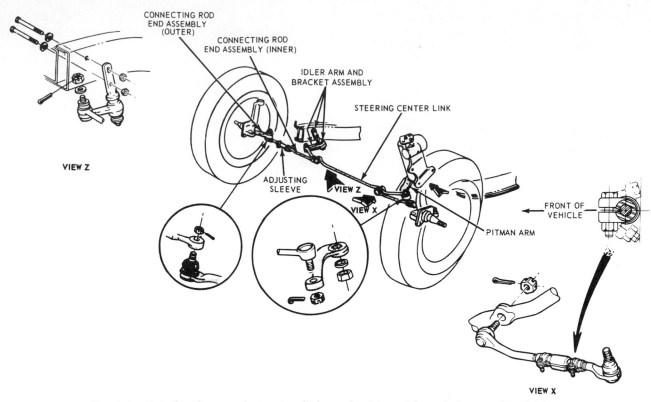

Fig. 7-9. Details of manual steering linkage for Maverick and Comet. (*Ford Motor Company*)

a. Removal Remove the cotter pin and nut from the ball stud. Disconnect the end from the spindle arm or center link. Loosen the connecting-rod-sleeve clamp bolt and count the number of turns needed to remove the rod end from the sleeve. Discard all rod-end parts that have been removed. Always use all new parts when replacing a connecting rod.

b. Replacement Thread the new rod end into the sleeve, but do not tighten the clamp bolt. Insert the stud into the spindle arm or center link and install the stud nut, torquing it to the specified tightness. Check and adjust the toe-in (Chap. 8). After this, loosen the adjusting-sleeve clamps; oil the sleeve, clamps, and bolts; torque the nuts to the correct specifications. Make sure the sleeve clamps are installed as shown in Fig. 8-54 to avoid interference with the side rail.

2. *CONNECTING-ROD ASSEMBLY (TYPE IN FIG. 7-7)* In this linkage, the rod-end assembly must be replaced if the ball stud becomes loose.

a. Removal Raise the front end and install safety stands. Remove the cotter pin and nut from the worn rod-end ball stud. Loosen the connecting-rod-sleeve clamp bolts, and remove the rod end from the spindle arm or center link, using the tool shown in Fig. 7-10. Remove the end assembly from the sleeve and discard it. Always use all new parts when replacing a connecting rod.

b. Replacement Thread the new end into the adjusting sleeve, but do not tighten the clamp bolt at this time. Install the seal on the rod-end ball

stud and insert the stud into the hole in the center link or spindle arm. Install and torque the nut to specifications and install the cotter pin. Check and adjust the toe-in. Loosen the clamp bolts; oil the sleeve, clamps, bolts, and nuts; position the clamp openings over the slots in the sleeve. Tighten the clamp nuts after the toe-in is adjusted.

3. *REPLACEMENT OF ADJUSTING SLEEVE (TYPES IN FIGS. 7-7 TO 7-9)* A damaged sleeve should be replaced. To remove it, first remove the spindle connecting-rod assembly as already explained. Screw the spindle connecting-rod end as-

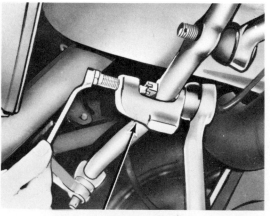

SPECIAL TOOL

Fig. 7-10. Removing the ball stud from the rod. (*Ford Motor Company*)

sembly into the new sleeve the same number of turns as required to remove the old assembly. Do not tighten the clamp bolt. Position the sleeve and end assembly on the center link and spindle arm. Install the attaching nut and torque it to specifications; install the cotter pin. Check and adjust the toe-in as necessary. Then oil the sleeve clamp bolts and torque them to specifications. The clamps must be in the position shown in Fig. 8-54.

4. *CENTER LINK (FIGS. 7-7 TO 7-9)* The center link connects the pitman arm and idler arm. It is nonadjustable and must be replaced if damaged or bent.

a. *Removal* Raise the front end and install safety stands. Remove the cotter pins and nuts that attach both inner connecting-rod ends to the center link. Remove the cotter pin and nut attaching the link to the idler arm. Disconnect the idler arm. Remove the cotter pin and nut attaching the pitman arm to the center link. Use a special tool (shown in Fig. 7-10) to disconnect the pitman arm from the link. Remove the center link. On models with the linkage-type power steering (Fig. 7-8), remove the center link from the power cylinder.

b. *Replacement* Replace the rubber seals on the spindle connecting-rod ends if required. Position the center link on the pitman arm and idler arm, and install nuts loosely. Put the idler arm and front wheels in the straight-ahead position. This will ensure proper steering-wheel alignment and prevent bushing damage as the attaching nuts are torqued. Tighten the nuts and install the cotter pins. Position the spindle connecting-rod ends to the center link and install the attaching nuts. Torque to specifications and install the cotter pins. Remove safety standards, lower the car, and check the toe-in.

5. *STEERING-IDLER-ARM-AND-BRACKET ASSEMBLY (FIGS. 7-7 TO 7-9)* If the idler-arm bushings are worn, the complete assembly must be replaced.

a. *Removal* Remove the cotter pin and nut attaching the center link. Disconnect the center link from the idler arm. Remove the two bolts that attach the idler-arm-and-bracket assembly to the frame and remove the assembly.

b. *Replacement* Secure the new idler-arm-and-bracket assembly to the frame with two attaching bolts, nuts, and washers. Place the idler arm and front wheels in the straight-ahead position so the steering wheel will be aligned and to prevent bushing damage as the nuts are torqued. Insert the center-link stud through the hole in the idler arm and install the nut and washer. Torque to specifications and install the cotter pin.

6. *PITMAN ARM* If the pitman arm is damaged, it must be replaced.

a. *Removal* Position the front wheels to straight ahead. Remove the cotter pin and the castellated nut that attaches the center link to the pitman arm. Disconnect the pitman center link from the pitman arm, using the tool shown in Fig. 7-10.

Remove the pitman-arm attaching nut and lock washer. Remove the pitman arm with a special puller.

b. *Replacement* With wheels straight ahead, put the pitman arm on the sector shaft with it pointing straight forward. Install the nut and lock washer, and torque the nut to specifications. Secure the center link to the pitman arm with the castellated nut, torquing it to specifications, and then install the cotter pin.

⊘ **7-4 Plymouth Steering-Linkage Service** Figures 7-11 to 7-13 show various linkage arrangements used on late-model Plymouth, Dodge, and Chrysler cars.

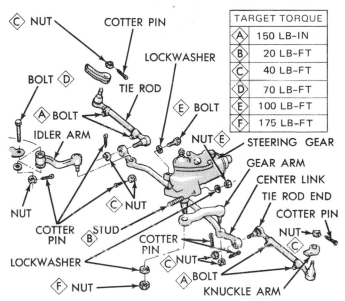

TARGET TORQUE	
Ⓐ	150 LB-IN
Ⓑ	20 LB-FT
Ⓒ	40 LB-FT
Ⓓ	70 LB-FT
Ⓔ	100 LB-FT
Ⓕ	175 LB-FT

Fig. 7-11. Steering linkage for carlines P, D, C, and Y. (*Chrysler Corporation*)

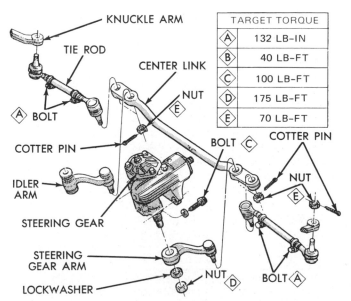

TARGET TORQUE	
Ⓐ	132 LB-IN
Ⓑ	40 LB-FT
Ⓒ	100 LB-FT
Ⓓ	175 LB-FT
Ⓔ	70 LB-FT

Fig. 7-12. Steering linkage for carlines V and L. (*Chrysler Corporation*)

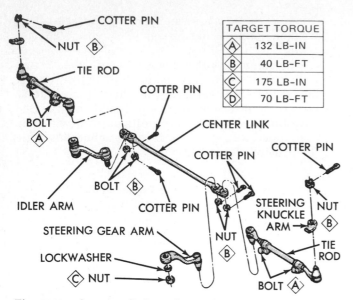

TARGET TORQUE	
A	132 LB-IN
B	40 LB-FT
C	175 LB-IN
D	70 LB-FT

Fig. 7-13. Steering linkage for carlines B, J, R, and W. (*Chrysler Corporation*)

Fig. 7-14. Using the special tool to remove the ball stud in a steering linkage. (*Chrysler Corporation*)

Tie-rod-end seals should be inspected for damage at all oil-change periods. About the only time steering-linkage service is required is when seals require replacement or parts are damaged or worn. If seals are damaged, remove them and check the parts for loss of lubricant, wear, or rust. If adequate lubricant is still present and parts are in good condition, simply replace the seals. Otherwise, replace parts.

CAUTION: Use only the recommended tools and procedures to avoid damaging the seals.

1. REMOVAL Remove the tie-rod ends from the steering-knuckle arms, using the special puller as shown in Fig. 7-14. Do not damage the seals. Remove the inner tie-rod ends from the center link. Remove

the idler-arm stud from the center link. Remove the idler-arm bolt from the cross-member bracket. Remove the steering-gear-arm stud from the center link. Remove the steering-gear arm from the gear.

2. REPLACEMENT Position the idler-arm assembly in the bracket and install the bolt. Tighten the nut to 65 pound-feet [8.98 kg-m] and install the cotter pin. Put the center link over the idler arm and steering-gear-arm studs and tighten the nuts to 40 pound-feet [5.53 kg-m]. Install the cotter pins. Connect the tie-rod ends to the steering-knuckle arms and center link. Tighten the nuts to 40 pounds-feet [5.53 kg-m] and install the cotter pins. Check and adjust the toe-in.

⬡ **7-5 Chevrolet Front-Suspension Service** Figures 7-15 to 7-17 show a front-suspension system of the type described in following paragraphs. Servicing procedures are outlined below for front-wheel bear-

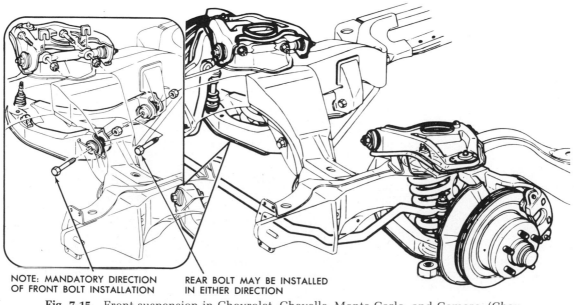

NOTE: MANDATORY DIRECTION OF FRONT BOLT INSTALLATION

REAR BOLT MAY BE INSTALLED IN EITHER DIRECTION

Fig. 7-15. Front suspension in Chevrolet, Chevelle, Monte Carlo, and Camaro. (*Chevrolet Motor Division of General Motors Corporation*)

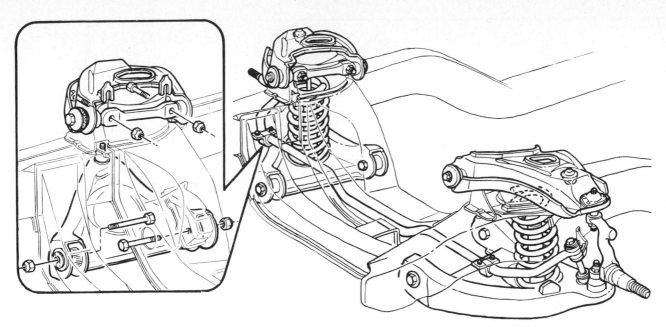

Fig. 7-16. Front suspension in Nova. (*Chevrolet Motor Division of General Motors Corporation*)

ings, hubs, shock absorbers, coil springs, and upper and lower control arms.

1. BRAKE-DRUM REMOVAL To remove the brake drum, take off the wheel and, with the vehicle jacked up, pull off the brake drum. It may be necessary to back off the brake adjustment. Check and service the drum (⊘ 15-36). On reinstallation, make sure the alignment dowel pin on the drum web indexes with the hole in the wheel hub. The brakes may require readjustment after the installation is completed (Chap. 15).

2. BRAKE-DISK REMOVAL Removal requires detaching of the disk caliper so that the disk (or rotor as Ford calls it) can be removed. See Chap. 15.

3. FRONT-WHEEL-BEARING ADJUSTMENT The bearings should be lubricated and adjusted every 24 months or 24,000 miles [38,624 km]. Proper adjustment is extremely important. Improper adjustment can cause poor steering stability, wander or shimmy, and excessive tire wear. Tapered roller bearings are used on all late models. These bearings must never be preloaded. Cones must be a slip fit on the spindle, and the inside diameters of the cones should be lubricated so that the cones can creep. The spindle nut must be a free-running fit on the threads.

To check the adjustment, raise the car and support it at the front lower control arm. Spin the wheel to check for unusual noise or roughness. If bearings

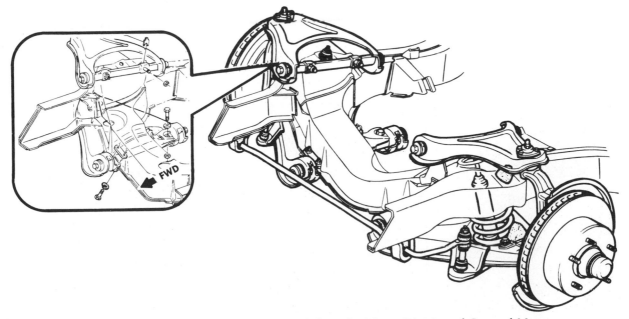

Fig. 7-17. Front suspension in Corvette. (*Chevrolet Motor Division of General Motors Corporation*)

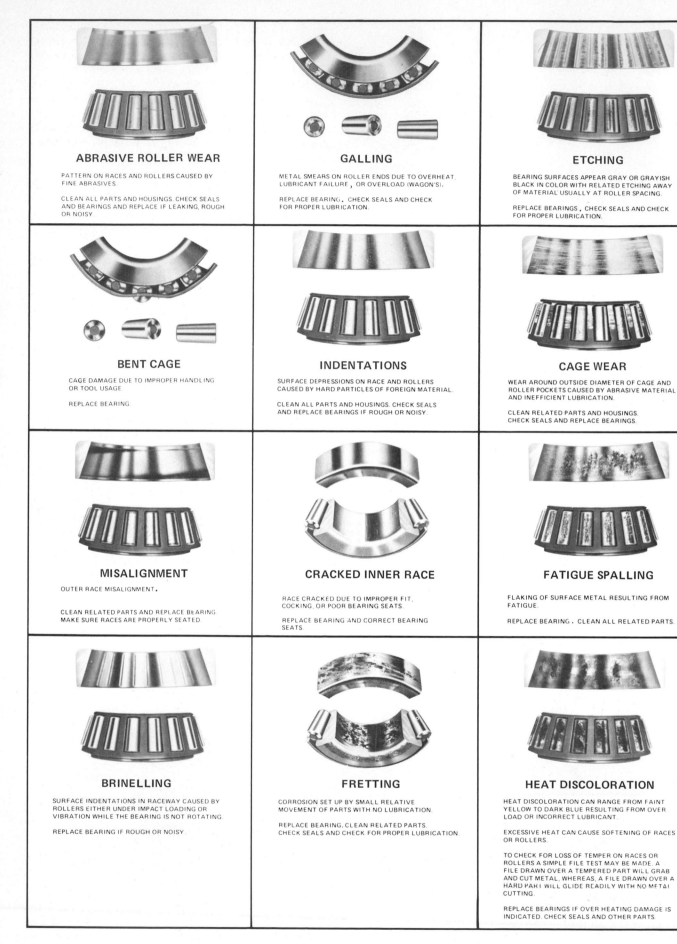

ABRASIVE ROLLER WEAR

PATTERN ON RACES AND ROLLERS CAUSED BY FINE ABRASIVES.

CLEAN ALL PARTS AND HOUSINGS. CHECK SEALS AND BEARINGS AND REPLACE IF LEAKING, ROUGH OR NOISY.

GALLING

METAL SMEARS ON ROLLER ENDS DUE TO OVERHEAT, LUBRICANT FAILURE, OR OVERLOAD (WAGON'S).

REPLACE BEARING, CHECK SEALS AND CHECK FOR PROPER LUBRICATION.

ETCHING

BEARING SURFACES APPEAR GRAY OR GRAYISH BLACK IN COLOR WITH RELATED ETCHING AWAY OF MATERIAL USUALLY AT ROLLER SPACING.

REPLACE BEARINGS, CHECK SEALS AND CHECK FOR PROPER LUBRICATION.

BENT CAGE

CAGE DAMAGE DUE TO IMPROPER HANDLING OR TOOL USAGE

REPLACE BEARING.

INDENTATIONS

SURFACE DEPRESSIONS ON RACE AND ROLLERS CAUSED BY HARD PARTICLES OF FOREIGN MATERIAL.

CLEAN ALL PARTS AND HOUSINGS. CHECK SEALS AND REPLACE BEARINGS IF ROUGH OR NOISY.

CAGE WEAR

WEAR AROUND OUTSIDE DIAMETER OF CAGE AND ROLLER POCKETS CAUSED BY ABRASIVE MATERIAL AND INEFFICIENT LUBRICATION.

CLEAN RELATED PARTS AND HOUSINGS. CHECK SEALS AND REPLACE BEARINGS.

MISALIGNMENT

OUTER RACE MISALIGNMENT.

CLEAN RELATED PARTS AND REPLACE BEARING. MAKE SURE RACES ARE PROPERLY SEATED.

CRACKED INNER RACE

RACE CRACKED DUE TO IMPROPER FIT, COCKING, OR POOR BEARING SEATS.

REPLACE BEARING AND CORRECT BEARING SEATS.

FATIGUE SPALLING

FLAKING OF SURFACE METAL RESULTING FROM FATIGUE.

REPLACE BEARING, CLEAN ALL RELATED PARTS.

BRINELLING

SURFACE INDENTATIONS IN RACEWAY CAUSED BY ROLLERS EITHER UNDER IMPACT LOADING OR VIBRATION WHILE THE BEARING IS NOT ROTATING.

REPLACE BEARING IF ROUGH OR NOISY.

FRETTING

CORROSION SET UP BY SMALL RELATIVE MOVEMENT OF PARTS WITH NO LUBRICATION.

REPLACE BEARING, CLEAN RELATED PARTS. CHECK SEALS AND CHECK FOR PROPER LUBRICATION.

HEAT DISCOLORATION

HEAT DISCOLORATION CAN RANGE FROM FAINT YELLOW TO DARK BLUE RESULTING FROM OVER LOAD OR INCORRECT LUBRICANT.

EXCESSIVE HEAT CAN CAUSE SOFTENING OF RACES OR ROLLERS.

TO CHECK FOR LOSS OF TEMPER ON RACES OR ROLLERS A SIMPLE FILE TEST MAY BE MADE. A FILE DRAWN OVER A TEMPERED PART WILL GRAB AND CUT METAL, WHEREAS, A FILE DRAWN OVER A HARD PART WILL GLIDE READILY WITH NO METAL CUTTING.

REPLACE BEARINGS IF OVER HEATING DAMAGE IS INDICATED. CHECK SEALS AND OTHER PARTS.

Fig. 7-18. Front-wheel-bearing trouble diagnosis. When diagnosing bearing condition:

1. Check the general condition of all parts during disassembly and inspection
2. Classify the failure with the aid of the illustrations
3. Determine the cause
4. Make all repairs following recommended procedures (*Chevrolet Motor Division of General Motors Corporation*)

are noisy, tight, or too loose, they should be cleaned, inspected, and, if okay, relubricated. To check for looseness, grip the tire at top and bottom. Push and pull with both hands to see if you can move the hub on the spindle. If you cannot move it 0.001 inch [0.025 mm], or if it moves more than 0.005 inch [0.127 mm], adjust the bearings.

To adjust, jack up the front end and remove the hubcap or wheel disk and the dust cap. Take out the cotter pin. Tighten the spindle nut to 12 pound-feet [1.66 kg-m] torque while rotating the wheel. Back off the adjustment nut one flat or to the "just loose" position. Insert the cotter pin. If the slot and the cotter pin do not align, back off the adjustment nut just barely enough to get alignment. When bending back ends of the cotter pin, bend them inboard or cut ends off to avoid the possibility of their damaging the static collector in the dust cap. Reinstall the dust cap and the hubcap.

4. FRONT-WHEEL-BEARING REPLACEMENT Remove the wheel, brake drum, dust cap, cotter pin, spindle nut, and washer. Discard the old cotter pin. With your fingers, remove the outer bearing assembly. Pry out the lip-seal assembly and remove the inner bearing assembly from the hub. Discard the seal. Wash the bearings in cleaning solvent and inspect them for damaged roller separators, worn or cracked rollers, and pitted or cracked races (see Fig. 7-18). Races can be removed and replaced with a special tool (Fig. 7-19). After reassembly of the bearings, adjust them (see item 3, above).

CAUTION: You *must* have clean hands, clean tools, and a clean work area when you work on bearings. Hands must be not only clean but dry. Chevrolet recommends wearing clean canvas gloves. Remember that the slightest trace of dirt in a bearing can quickly ruin it. As soon as you wash a bearing, oil it lightly and wrap it in clean oilproof paper to protect it from dirt or rusting. Never spin a bearing with compressed air and do not spin an uncleaned bearing even by hand.

5. FRONT-WHEEL HUB If the hub bore is out of round or the flange is distorted, the hub must be replaced. If the trouble is due only to bent hub bolts, they can be pressed out and new bolts pressed in (see Fig. 7-20).

6. SHOCK ABSORBERS (FIG. 7-21) Hold the upper stem with an open-end wrench to keep it from turn-

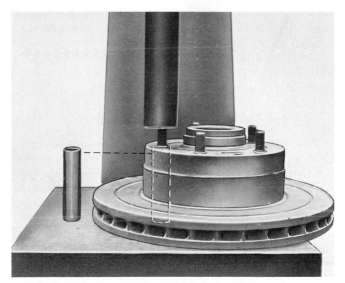

Fig. 7-20. Pressing out front-hub bolts. (*Chevrolet Motor Division of General Motors Corporation*)

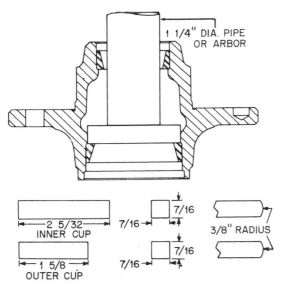

Fig. 7-19. Front-wheel-bearing-race removers. (*Chevrolet Motor Division of General Motors Corporation*)

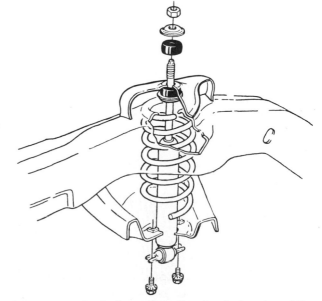

Fig. 7-21. Method of attaching the shock absorber. (*Chevrolet Motor Division of General Motors Corporation*)

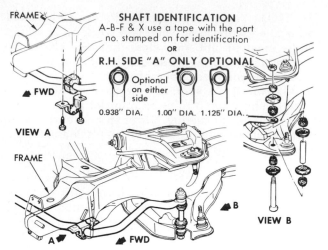

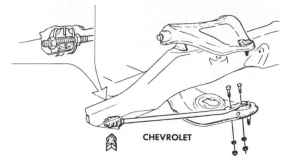

Fig. 7-23. Location of the strut rod on Chevrolet. (*Chevrolet Motor Division of General Motors Corporation*)

Fig. 7-22. Details of stabilizer-bar attachments. (*Chevrolet Motor Division of General Motors Corporation*)

ing, and remove the retaining nut, retainer, and rubber grommet. Remove the two bolts at the lower end which attach the pivot to the lower control arm, and pull the shock absorber down and out. During reinstallation, tighten the upper stem nut to the specified torque.

7. FRONT STABILIZER BAR The front stabilizer bar (Fig. 7-22) is attached at four places: at the two frame side rails and to the two lower control arms. Detaching it from these four points will permit its removal. Reach through the hole in the frame side rail to hold the bolt heads while unscrewing the nuts attaching the stabilizer support.

If new insulators are necessary, coat the stabilizer with the recommended rubber lubricant, and slide the bushings into position. Never get lubricant on the outside of the frame-stabilizer-bar bushings, or they may slip out of the brackets. Connect the brackets to the frame and attach the stabilizer ends to the lower control arms. Torque the bracket bolts and link nuts to specifications.

8. STRUT ROD (FIG. 7-23) Put the car on the hoist and remove the nut, retainer, and rubber bushing from the front end of the strut rod. Remove the two bolts attaching the rear end of the strut rod to the lower control arm. Pull the strut rod from the bracket.

If the rear nut on the front end of the strut rod has been removed, turn it on until it is about $\frac{3}{4}$ inch

[19.05 mm] from the end of the threads. Install the rear retainer, sleeve, and bushing on the rod so the pilot diameter faces forward. Insert the rod into the bracket and install the front bushing on the sleeve so the raised pilot diameter faces the rear to enter the hole in the bracket and rear bushing. Install the forward retainer and nut on the rod. Attach the strut rod to the top of the lower control arm with two bolts, washers, and nuts. Torque to specifications. Check the caster, camber, and toe-in.

9. FRONT-COIL-SPRING CHECK To check for spring sag, position the car on a smooth, level surface, bounce the front end several times, raise up on the front end, and allow it to settle. Then take the measurements as shown in Fig. 7-24. The differences should be as noted in the specifications for the car being checked. Next, take the measurements on the other side. The difference between the two sides should be no greater than $\frac{1}{2}$ inch [12.7 mm]. To make a correction, the springs must be replaced. Shimming up under a spring is *not recommended*.

a. Removal Raise the car on a hoist. Remove the two shock-absorber attaching screws and push the shock up through the control arm and into the spring. The car should be supported so the control arms hang free. Put the special tool shown in Fig. 7-25 into position so it cradles the inner bushings. Note that the special tool must be attached to a suitable jack.

Detach the stabilizer bar from the lower control arm. Raise the jack to remove the tension on the lower-control-arm pivot bolts. Install a chain around the spring and through the control arm so the spring cannot jump out as the tension is released. Remove the rear bolt and nut, and then

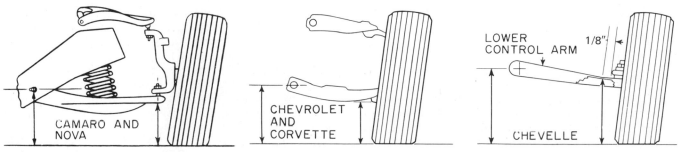

Fig. 7-24. Measurements to check for front-spring sag. (*Chevrolet Motor Division of General Motors Corporation*)

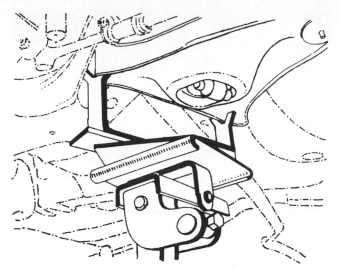

Fig. 7-25. Removing the front coil spring with a special adaptor.

the front bolt and nut. Lower the jack to lower the control arm. When all spring compression is removed, take off safety chain and spring.

CAUTION: Do not apply pressure on the lower control arm and ball joint as you remove the spring. Maneuver the spring so it will come out easily.

b. Replacement Position the spring properly on the control arm (see Fig. 7-26) and lift the control arm with the special tool shown in Fig. 7-25. Position the control arm into the frame and install the pivot bolts (front bolt first) and nuts. See Figs. 7-15 to 7-17 for mandatory bolt directions. Torque to specifications and lower the jack. Reattach the stabilizer bar and shock absorber.

10. *UPPER-CONTROL-ARM BALL-JOINT CHECK* Figures 6-4, 6-6, and 6-7 illustrate methods of checking ball joints for wear. A second method which requires partial disassembly follows. Raise the car to take weight off the control arms. Remove the tire and wheel assembly. Remove the upper ball-stud cotter pin and loosen the nut one turn. Install the special tool between ball studs as shown in Fig. 7-27. Turn the threaded end of the tool until the stud is free of the steering knuckle.

Remove the upper ball-joint-stud nut and allow the steering knuckle to swing out of the way. Lift the upper arm and put a block of wood between the frame and arm to act as a support.

Check the ball joint for wear and looseness. If the stud has any preceptible lateral shake, or if it can be twisted in its socket with the fingers, replace the ball joint.

a. Replacement Use a grinding wheel to grind off the rivet heads. Do not damage the control arm or ball-joint seat. Then install the new ball joint in the arm and attach it with the bolts and nuts supplied with the replacement ball joint. Install the bolts pointing up. Torque to specifications. Turn the ball-stud cotter-pin hole fore and aft (pointing toward front of car).

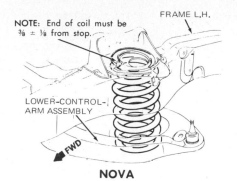

NOTE: End of coil must be ⅜ ± ⅛ from stop. FRAME L.H.

LOWER-CONTROL-ARM ASSEMBLY

FWD

NOVA

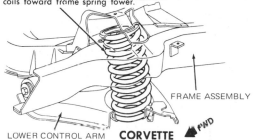

NOTE: Install spring with close spaced coils toward frame spring tower.

FRAME ASSEMBLY

LOWER CONTROL ARM **CORVETTE** FWD

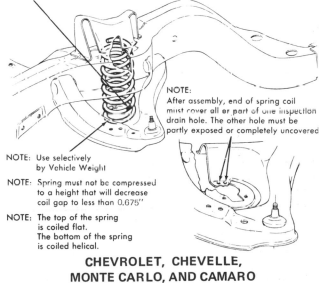

NOTE: Spring to be installed with tape at lowest position. Bottom of spring is coiled helical, and top is coiled flat with a gripper notch near end of wire.

NOTE: After assembly, end of spring coil must cover all or part of one inspection drain hole. The other hole must be partly exposed or completely uncovered

NOTE: Use selectively by Vehicle Weight

NOTE: Spring must not be compressed to a height that will decrease coil gap to less than 0.675″

NOTE: The top of the spring is coiled flat. The bottom of the spring is coiled helical.

CHEVROLET, CHEVELLE, MONTE CARLO, AND CAMARO

Fig. 7-26. Positioning the coil spring on different models. (*Chevrolet Motor Division of General Motors Corporation*)

Remove the block of wood. Inspect the steering-knuckle tapered hole into which the stud fits. It must be clean and round. If it is not round, or if you note other wear or damage, install a new knuckle.

b. Attachment to Steering Knuckle Mate the ball stud with the steering-knuckle hole and install the stud nut. Torque the nut and install a new cotter pin.

CAUTION: Never back off the nut to align it with the cotter-pin hole. Instead, tighten it to the next slot that lines up with the hole. Install a lubrication

Fig. 7-27. Removing the ball stud from the upper and lower ends of the steering knuckle with a special tool. (*Chevrolet Motor Division of General Motors Corporation*)

fitting and lubricate the joint. Install the tire and wheel.

11. LOWER-CONTROL-ARM BALL-JOINT CHECK Late model cars are equipped with lower-control-arm ball joints with wear indicators as explained in ⬡ 6-3 and illustrated in Fig. 6-8. On earlier models, the lower ball joint can be checked for wear by measuring from the top of the lubrication fitting to the bottom of the ball stud with a micrometer. Take the measurement with the car supported on its wheels. Then support the car on the outer ends of the lower control arms and remeasure. If the difference is greater than $\frac{1}{16}$ inch [1.59 mm], the joint is worn and must be replaced.

a. *Removal* Raise the car on a hoist. Remove the lower ball-stud cotter pin. Loosen the stud nut one turn. Install the special tool as shown in Fig. 7-27 between the ball studs and turn the threaded end of the tool until the stud is free of the steering knuckle. Remove the stud nut. Pull outward on the bottom of the tire and at the same time push the tire upward to free the knuckle from the ball stud. Remove the wheel and tire.

Lift the upper control arm, with the knuckle and hub assembly attached, and put a block of wood between the frame and the upper control arm.

CAUTION: Do not pull on the brake hose when lifting the assembly!

If the tie-rod end of the steering knuckle is in the way, detach it. If it is not in the way, leave it attached.

Put the tools shown in Fig. 7-28 in position. Turn the bolt until the lower ball joint is pushed out of the control arm.

b. *Inspection* On most late-model Chevrolet cars,

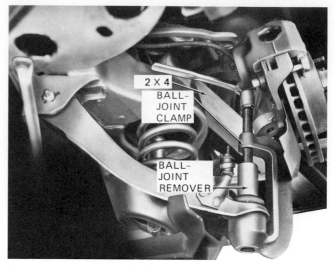

Fig. 7-28. Removing ball joints from a car. (*Chevrolet Motor Division of General Motors Corporation*)

a look at the wear indicators (Fig. 6-8) tells you whether the ball joint is worn. The ball-stud tightness in the knuckle can be checked by shaking the wheel and noting if there is any movement of the stud or nut in the knuckle. It can also be checked by removing the cotter pin and checking torque.

c. *Replacement* Position the ball joint in the lower control arm with the special tools as shown in Fig. 7-29. Position the bleed vent of the new ball joint facing inward. Turn down the bolt until the new ball joint is seated in the control arm. Remove the tools. Turn the stud cotter-pin hole fore and aft. Remove the block of wood holding the upper control arm out of the way.

Inspect the tapered hole in the steering knuckle. If it is out of round or otherwise damaged, replace the steering knuckle. Mate the stud with the hole and install the stud nut. Torque the nut and install the cotter pin.

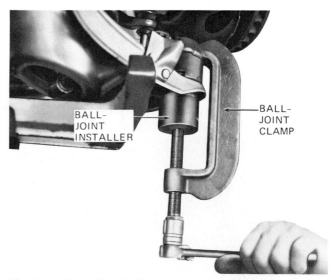

Fig. 7-29. Installing ball joints on a car. (*Chevrolet Motor Division of General Motors Corporation*)

CAUTION: Never back off the nut to align it with the cotter-pin hole. Instead, tighten the nut to the next slot that lines up with the stud hole.

Install a lubrication fitting and lubricate the joint. Then install the wheel and tire, if they have been removed from the steering knuckle.

12. *CONTROL-ARM BUSHINGS* The upper-control-arm bushings are removed and replaced with the special tools shown in Figs. 7-30 and 7-31. Note that when the second bushing is installed, the cross shaft must be in place.

The lower-control-arm bushings are removed and replaced with the tools shown in Figs. 7-32 and 7-33. Note that the metal collars on the bushings are flared on the inner ends after installation (Figs. 7-34 and 7-35). This flare must be removed by tapping on the edge with a hammer before the bushing is pressed out. Then, when the new bushing is in place, flare it with the special tools shown in Fig. 7-34.

NOTE: When reattaching the lower control arm to the frame, observe the mandatory bolt directions (Figs. 7-15 to 7-17).

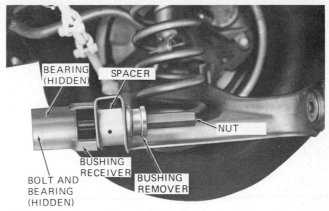

Fig. 7-32. Removing the lower control-arm bushing. (*Chevrolet Motor Division of General Motors Corporation*)

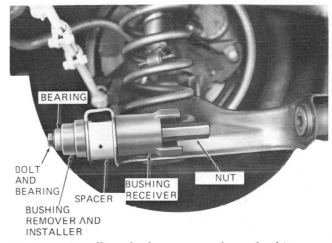

Fig. 7-33. Installing the lower control-arm bushing on a car. (*Chevrolet Motor Division of General Motors Corporation*)

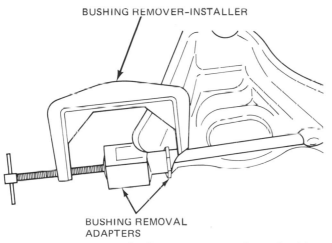

Fig. 7-30. Removing the first upper control-arm bushing. (*Chevrolet Motor Division of General Motors Corporation*)

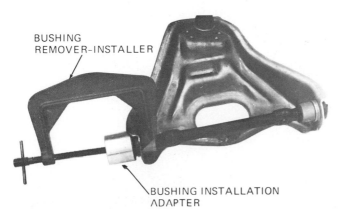

Fig. 7-31. Installing the upper control-arm bushing. (*Chevrolet Motor Division of General Motors Corporation*)

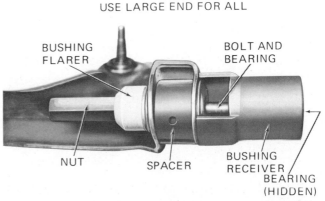

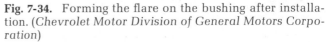

Fig. 7-34. Forming the flare on the bushing after installation. (*Chevrolet Motor Division of General Motors Corporation*)

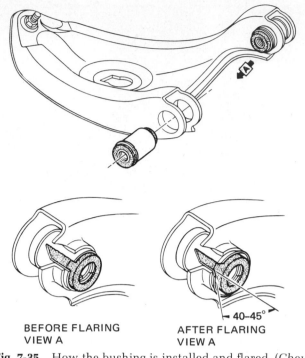

BEFORE FLARING
VIEW A

AFTER FLARING
VIEW A

← 40–45°

Fig. 7-35. How the bushing is installed and flared. (*Chevrolet Motor Division of General Motors Corporation*)

⊘ **7-6 Ford Front-Suspension Service** The first thing to remember about servicing Ford front-suspension systems is that the upper or lower suspension (control) arm must be serviced as a unit. You do not install new ball joints or other components in used suspension arms. Figures 7-36 and 7-37 show various views of front-suspension systems used in Ford cars. The following two sections describe servicing procedures for front-suspension systems with the spring between the two suspension arms (⊘ 7-7) and the procedures for systems with the spring above the upper suspension arms (⊘ 7-8).

⊘ **7-7 Ford Front-Suspension Service—Spring between Arms** The eight necessary procedures are detailed below.

1. FRONT-WHEEL-BEARING ADJUSTMENT AND LUBRICATION Bearings should be lubricated and adjusted every 24 months or 24,000 miles [38,624 km]. Figure 7-38 shows a front-wheel bearing and related parts. Procedures are different for drum and disk brakes.

a. Adjustment (Drum Brakes) Hoist the car and remove the wheel cover and grease cap. Wipe away excess grease and remove the cotter pin and locknut. Rotate the wheel and at the same time torque the adjusting nut to 17 to 25 pound-feet

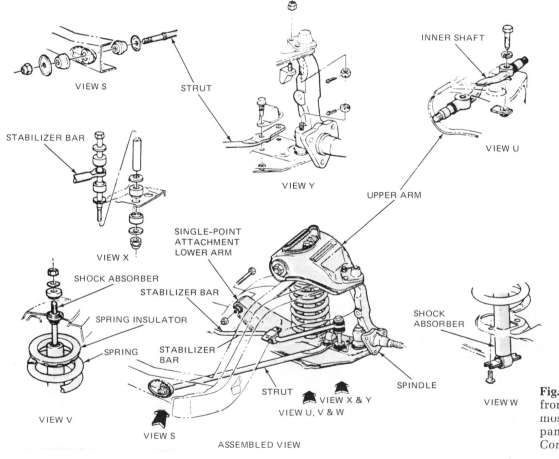

Fig. 7-36. Details of the front suspension for most Ford Motor Company cars. (*Ford Motor Company*)

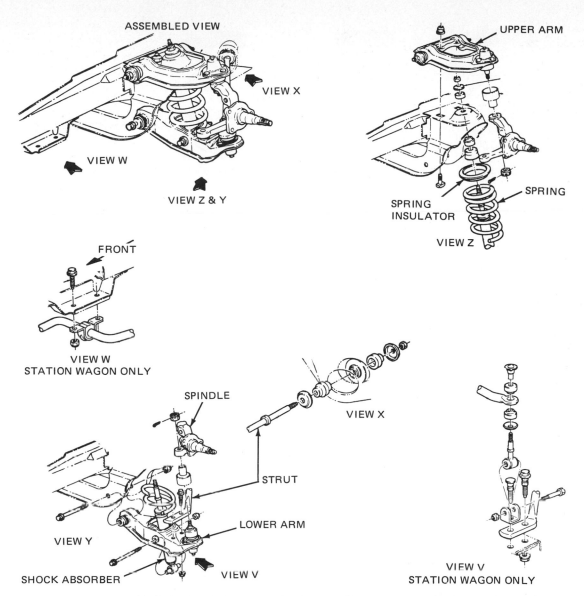

Fig. 7-37. Details of the front suspension for Pinto and Mustang. (*Ford Motor Company*)

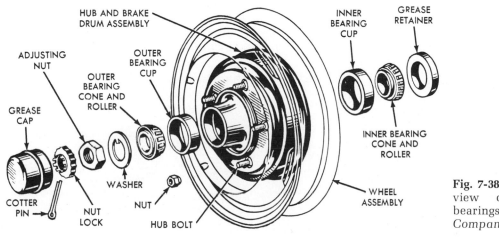

Fig. 7-38. Disassembled view of front-wheel bearings. (*Ford Motor Company*)

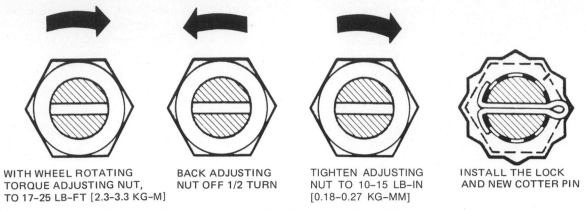

| WITH WHEEL ROTATING TORQUE ADJUSTING NUT, TO 17–25 LB–FT [2.3–3.3 KG–M] | BACK ADJUSTING NUT OFF 1/2 TURN | TIGHTEN ADJUSTING NUT TO 10–15 LB–IN [0.18–0.27 KG–MM] | INSTALL THE LOCK AND NEW COTTER PIN |

Fig. 7-39. Front-wheel bearing adjustment. (*Ford Motor Company*)

[2.3 to 3.5 kg-m] (see Fig. 7-39). Loosen the adjusting nut $\frac{1}{2}$ turn. Then retighten it to 10 to 15 pound-inches [0.18 to 0.27 kg-mm], all the time rotating the wheel. Install the locknut with a new cotter pin. Recheck wheel rotation. If it is rough and noisy, disassemble for inspection and lubrication.

b. *Bearing Service* (*Drum Brakes*) Hoist the car and remove the wheel cover, grease cap, cotter pin, locknut, adjusting nut, flat washer, and outer bearing cone and roller assembly (Fig. 7-38). Pull the wheel, hub, and drum assembly off the spindle. Use the special tool to remove the grease retainer. Discard it. Clean the bearing cups and inspect them (see Fig. 7-18). If cups are worn or damaged, remove them (Fig. 7-40). Install new cups with special tools (Fig. 7-41) after cleaning all lubricant from inside the hub.

Thoroughly clean and inspect the rollers (Fig. 7-18), observing the cautions about handling bearings as detailed in ⊘ 7-5, item 4. Brush all loose dirt from the brake assembly. Clean the spindle. Pack the inside of the hub with the specified wheel grease. Do not overlubricate. Add grease until it is flush with the inside diameters of the bearing cups (Fig. 7-42).

Pack the bearings with the specified grease, using a bearing packer. Grease the cone surfaces. Install a new grease retainer. Then install other parts and adjust the bearings as previously noted.

c. *Adjustment* (*Disk Brakes*) Disk-brake adjustment is similar to that of drum brakes with these exceptions. Loosen the adjusting nut 3 turns (not $\frac{1}{2}$ turn), and rock the wheel and rotor assembly several times to push the shoes and linings away from the rotor. Then tighten the adjusting nut while rotating the wheel (Fig. 7-39). Finish the adjustment as previously explained. Before driving the car, pump the brake pedal several times to restore braking.

d. *Bearing Service* (*Disk Brakes*) Disk-brake service is similar to that of drum brakes except that the caliper must be detached and wired up out of the way. On reassembly, after lubrication and bearing adjustment, install the caliper to the anchor plate. Finally, pump the brake pedal several times before driving the car to restore braking.

2. *STABILIZER-BAR ATTACHMENTS* The stabilizer bar is attached at its two ends to the lower suspension arms through bushings (see view X in Fig. 7-36). It is attached at two points to the frame through insulators. Bushings can be replaced by removing the attaching nut and bolt. Observe carefully the relationship of the washers, insulators, and

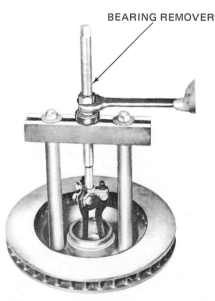

Fig. 7-40. Using a bearing remover to pull the front-wheel-bearing cups. (*Ford Motor Company*)

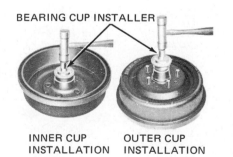

Fig. 7-41. Installing front-wheel-bearing cups. (*Ford Motor Company*)

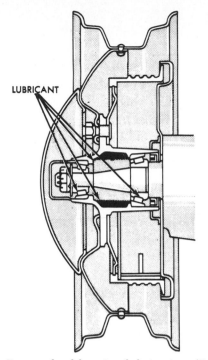

LUBRICANT

Fig. 7-42. Front-wheel-bearing lubrication. (*Ford Motor Company*)

spacers so all parts can be returned in their correct positions. Use a new nut and bolt.

To replace insulators, remove the stabilizer bar from the car. Coat the ends of the bar with Ruglyde or similar lubricant and slide the new insulators into place. Use new bolts to attach the ends of the bar to the suspension arms. Attach the insulators to the frame.

3. LOWER-ARM-STRUT BUSHING See Figs. 7-36 and 7-37. The strut must be removed from the car to replace the bushing. After reinstalling the strut, check caster, camber, and toe-in (Chap. 8).

4. FRONT-SPRING REMOVAL AND REPLACEMENT With the car on a hoist, disconnect the lower end of the shock absorber from the suspension arm. You may need a pry bar to free the shock absorber from the arm. (On some models—Pinto and Mustang—you must remove the shock absorber.) Put a jack under the lower arm. Remove the bolts at-

taching the strut and stabilizer bar to the control arm (Fig. 7-43). Disconnect the inner end of the lower arm from the frame. Then slowly and carefully lower the jack to relieve the spring pressure (Fig. 7-43). You may need to use a pry bar to free the spring.

To replace the spring, tape the insulator to the spring and position the spring on the lower arm. The end of the spring must be no more than $\frac{1}{2}$ inch [12.7 mm] from the end of the depression in the arm. Raise the lower arm carefully to compress the spring and attach the inner end to the frame with nut and bolt. Reattach the shock absorber, strut, and stabilizer bar to the lower control arm. Remove the jack stands and lower the car.

5. LOWER-SUSPENSION-ARM REMOVAL AND REPLACEMENT Raise the front of the car and support it with safety stands under both sides of the frame just behind the lower arms. Remove the wheel-and-tire assembly, caliper and brake hose, and hub-and-rotor assembly. Disconnect the lower end of the shock absorber and push it up out of the way. Disconnect the stabilizer bar and strut. Remove the cotter pins from the ball joints. Loosen the lower ball-joint-stud nut 1 or 2 turns. Install the special tool between the upper and lower ball-joint studs (Fig. 7-44). Make sure the tool is seated on the studs and not on the nuts. Turn the adapter screw to place the stud under pressure. Tap the spindle near the lower stud with a hammer to loosen the stud in the spindle. *Do not loosen the stud with tool pressure alone.* Position a jack under the lower arm (Fig. 7-45). Remove the stud nut, then lower the arm, as shown, and detach it from the frame.

To replace the arm, loosely attach it to the spindle. Do not tighten the stud nut. Position the spring and insulator to the upper spring pad and lower arm. Use a floor jack and raise the control arm to align with the frame connection for the inner end of the arm. Attach the arm with through-bolt and nut. Remove the jack. Tighten the ball-joint attaching nut to specifications. Secure with the cotter pin. Attach the shock absorber, strut, and stabilizer bar. Install the hub and rotor, caliper, and wheel and tire, then adjust wheel bearing. Install the grease cap and wheel cover. If necessary, check caster, camber, and toe-in.

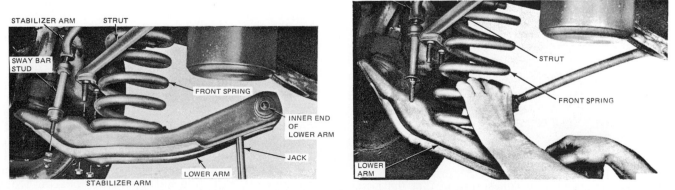

STABILIZER ARM STRUT
SWAY BAR STUD
FRONT SPRING
INNER END OF LOWER ARM
JACK
LOWER ARM
STABILIZER ARM

STRUT
FRONT SPRING
LOWER ARM

Fig. 7-43. Removing or installing a front spring. (*Ford Motor Company*)

Servicing Steering Linkage and Front and Rear Suspension 111

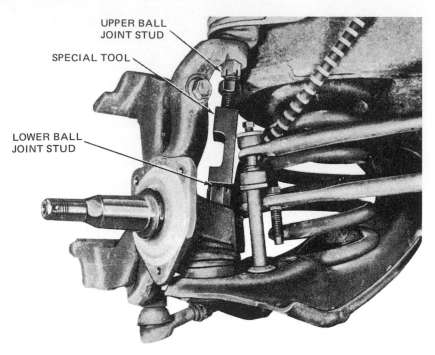

UPPER BALL
JOINT STUD

SPECIAL TOOL

LOWER BALL
JOINT STUD

Fig. 7-44. Using the special tool to loosen a lower ball-joint stud. (*Ford Motor Company*)

6. UPPER-ARM REMOVAL AND REPLACEMENT
Raise the car and support it with jack stands under both sides of the frame just in back of the lower arm. Remove the wheel cover, wheel and tire, and cotter pin from the upper ball-joint-stud nut. Loosen the nut 1 or 2 turns. Use the special tool as shown in Fig. 7-44 to loosen the upper ball-joint stud from the spindle. Do not loosen the stud by tool pressure alone. Tap the spindle near the stud with a hammer while the stud is under pressure from the tool. Put a floor jack under the lower arm and raise it to relieve the pressure from the upper ball joint. Remove the nut, then remove the attaching bolts of the

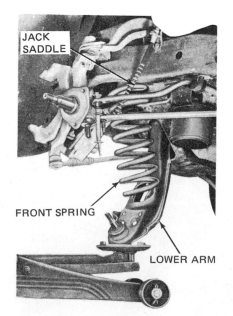

JACK
SADDLE

FRONT SPRING

LOWER ARM

Fig. 7-45. Removing the coil spring so that the lower control arm can be removed. (*Ford Motor Company*)

upper arm inner shaft. Now take off the arm as an assembly.

To replace the arm, attach the inner end to the frame bracket and the ball-joint stud at the outer end to the spindle. Tighten the nut to specifications and tighten further to align the cotter-pin hole in the stud with the nut slots. Install the cotter pin. Then install the wheel and tire and adjust the wheel bearings. Install the wheel cover. Remove the jack stands and lower the car. Adjust caster, camber, and toe-in.
7. SHOCK ABSORBER Remove the shock absorber through the lower suspension arm after removing the attaching nuts and screws. Install it with the new nuts and screws supplied with the replacement shock-absorber kit.
8. UPPER-ARM BUSHING SERVICE If the bushings require replacement, remove the nuts and washers from both ends of the upper-arm shaft. Then use the special tool to press the bushings out (Fig. 7-46). Force the lower bushing out by putting pressure on the tool from above with an arbor press. Then install new bushings with the special tool shown in Fig. 7-47.

⊘ **7-8 Ford Front Suspension Service—Spring above Upper Arm** An upper or lower suspension arm must be installed as a unit. Replace the stabilizer-bar bushings and insulators, and the strut-rod bushing, as for the suspension system with the spring between the arms (⊘ 7-7). Figure 7-48 shows the assembly in exploded view.
1. UPPER-ARM BUSHING SERVICE Remove the shock absorber. Raise and support the car on jack stands. Remove the wheel cover, grease cap, cotter pin, locknut, adjusting nut, and outer bearing from the hub. Pull the wheel, tire, hub, and drum from

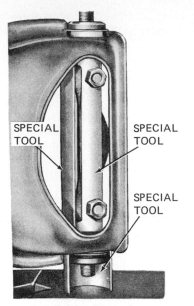

Fig. 7-46. Removing the bushings from an upper control arm. (*Ford Motor Company*)

Fig. 7-47. Installing a bushing in an upper control arm. (*Ford Motor Company*)

the spindle. On disk brakes, detach the caliper before removing the disk assembly.

Compress the spring with the special tool (Fig. 7-49). Remove the two upper arm-to-spring-tower attaching nuts and swing the upper arm out. Rotate the shaft and remove the studs by tapping them out with a soft mallet. Unscrew the bushings from the shaft and suspension arm. Remove the shaft.

To replace the bushings, position the shaft, grease the new bushings and O rings, and install the bushings loosely on the shaft and arm. Turn the bushings in so the shaft is exactly centered (Fig. 7-50). Make a spacer of $\frac{3}{4}$-inch pipe $8\frac{1}{16}$ inches long and position it parallel to the shaft as shown in Fig. 7-51. If it will not fit, the arm is distorted and must be discarded.

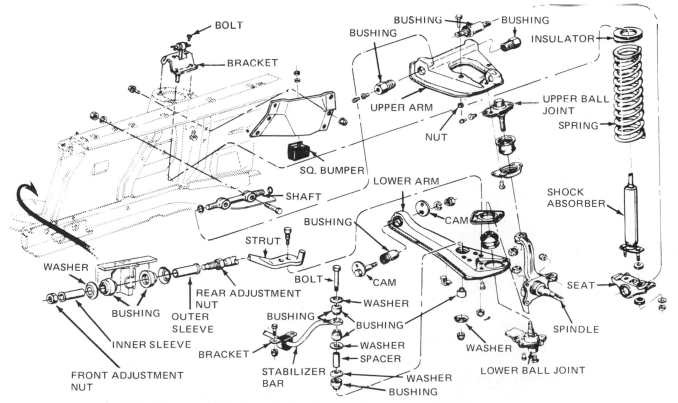

Fig. 7-48. Disassembled view of a front-suspension system which has the spring above the upper control arm. (*Ford Motor Company*)

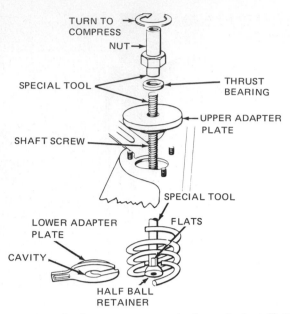

Fig. 7-49. Spring-compressor tool and installation method. (*Ford Motor Company*)

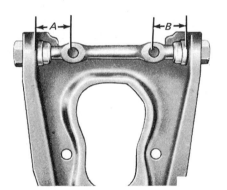

Fig. 7-50. When new bushings are installed, they must be turned in so that the shaft is exactly centered in the control arm. (*Ford Motor Company*)

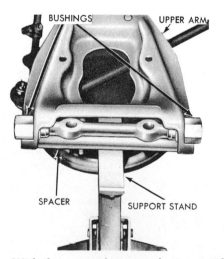

Fig. 7-51. With the spacer between the inner sides of the control arm, torque the bushings to specifications. (*Ford Motor Company*)

With the spacer positioned as shown, torque the bushings to specifications. Make sure the arm can move on the shaft. Then remove the spacer. Attach the upper suspension arm to the underbody. Release the spring. Install the parts removed and adjust the wheel bearing. Lower the vehicle, install the shock absorber, and adjust caster, camber, and toe-in.

2. *FRONT SPRING REMOVAL AND REPLACEMENT* Proceed as for replacement of upper-arm bushings, detailed above, to get the upper arm out of the way. Then replace the spring-compressor tool and remove the spring. Installation is the reverse of removal.

3. *LOWER-ARM REMOVAL AND REPLACEMENT* With the car raised and supported on car stands, remove the wheel and tire. Disconnect the stabilizer bar and strut. Remove the cotter pin from the nut on the lower ball-joint stud and loosen the nut 1 or 2 turns. Use the ball-joint-stud loosening tool (Fig. 7-44) to put pressure on the lower stud. Tap the spindle to loosen the stud from the spindle. Remove the nut from the stud and lower the arm. Detach the arm from the underbody by removing the cam bolt, nut, and washer.

To replace the arm, reattach the arm to the underbody and spindle.

4. *UPPER-ARM REMOVAL AND REPLACEMENT* With the car raised and supported on car stands, remove the wheel and tire. Remove the shock-absorber-attaching nuts and lift the shock absorber out (Fig. 7-52). On eight-cylinder cars, remove the air cleaner. Install the compressor tool and compress the spring (Fig. 7-49). Disconnect the upper ball-joint stud from the spindle using the special tool (Fig. 7-44) and a hammer as already explained. Now detach the upper-arm-shaft nuts and remove the arm.

Installation is just the reverse of removal. Be sure to use the specified keystone-type lock washers to attach the shaft-bolt nuts.

5. *FRONT-WHEEL SPINDLE REMOVAL AND REPLACEMENT* Removal and replacement procedures vary a little because of the different steps required for drum and disk brakes. Basically, the procedure is to detach the wheel-and-tire assembly and the brake assembly from the spindle and move them out of the way. Then loosen the upper and lower ball-joint studs with the special tool (Fig. 7-44) and a hammer. With the studs detached from the spindle, the spindle is free for removal. Replacement is the reverse of removal.

⊘ **7-9 Plymouth Front-Suspension Service** The Plymouth front-suspension system uses torsion bars (Fig. 7-53) instead of coil springs. Service operations include height adjustment, torsion-bar replacement, upper- and lower-control-arm replacement, and ball-joint and sway-bar replacement.

1. *HEIGHT ADJUSTMENT* With the vehicle on a level floor, the tires at the proper pressure, a full tank of gas, and no passengers, jounce the car a few times to settle the suspension. Release the car on the downward motion.

UPPER MOUNTING BRACKET—
MAVERICK, COMET

LOWER RETAINING BOLTS

Fig. 7-52. Removing a front shock absorber from the suspension system having the spring above the upper control arm. (*Ford Motor Company*)

Measure the distance between the adjustment blade to the floor and the lowest point of the steering knuckle to the floor (A and B in Fig. 7-54). The difference varies with different models, but a late-model Plymouth specification is $1\frac{5}{8}$ to $1\frac{7}{8}$ inches [41.28 to 47.63 mm]. Also, the difference between the two sides of the car should be no more than $\frac{1}{8}$ inch [3.17 mm]. To correct, turn the torsion-bar adjustment bolt. After each adjustment, jounce the car before rechecking the measurement.

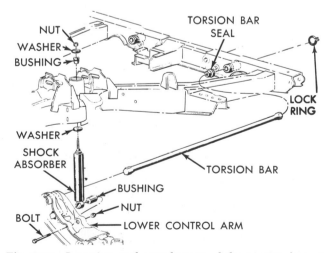

Fig. 7-53. Location and attachment of the torsion bar on a Plymouth. (*Chrysler Corporation*)

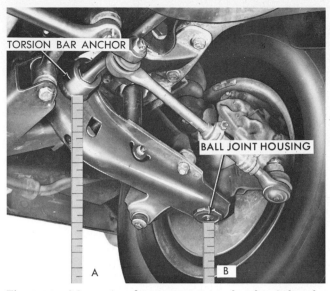

TORSION BAR ANCHOR

BALL JOINT HOUSING

A   B

Fig. 7-54. Measuring front-suspension height. (*Chrysler Corporation*)

2. *TORSION-BAR REPLACEMENT* The torsion bars are not interchangeable between left and right. They are marked either right or left by an R or L stamped on one end of the bar. To remove a torsion bar, raise the front of the car. If you use a hoist, it should be on the body so that the front suspension is under no load. If you use jacks, you must place a support under the frame cross member first to avoid damaging the cross member.

Release the load from the torsion bar (Fig. 7-53) by backing off the adjustment bolt (Fig. 7-55). Remove the lock ring from the rear end of the torsion bar. Attach the special striking tool to the torsion bar as shown in Fig. 7-55 and knock the bar loose. Then remove the tool, slide the rear-anchor balloon seal off the anchor, and slide the bar out through the rear of the anchor. Try not to damage the balloon seal.

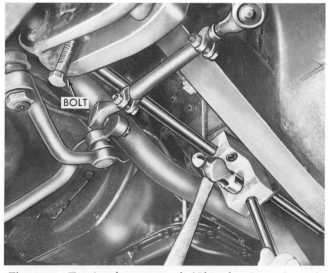

BOLT

Fig. 7-55. Torsion-bar removal. (*Chrysler Corporation*)

Check the torsion bar for scratches or nicks. Dress them down and paint the repaired area with rustproof paint. Check the bar attachments (anchors) and replace any damaged parts. Clean all parts.

Install the torsion bar by sliding it forward through the rear anchor. Slip the balloon seal over the front of the torsion bar (cupped end toward the rear). Coat both ends of the bar with special lubricant and slide the bar forward so that the hex head enters the opening in the lower control arm. Install the lock ring at the rear. Pack the annular opening in the rear anchor completely full of multipurpose grease. Position the balloon seal on the rear anchor so that the lip engages in the groove of the anchor. Tighten the adjustment bolt to place a load on the torsion bar. Lower the vehicle to the floor and adjust its height (item 1, above). Replace the upper bumper.

3. STEERING-KNUCKLE REMOVAL Figures 7-56 to 7-58 show, in disassembled views, various arrangements used. To replace a steering knuckle, turn the ignition switch to OFF or UNLOCKED. Remove the rebound bumper. Raise the vehicle to remove all load from the front suspension. Place jack stands under the frame. Remove the wheel cover, wheel, and tire assembly. On cars with disk brakes, remove the brake caliper and support it with a piece of wire so it does not hang from the brake hose. Remove the hub and disk or drum assembly and brake splash shield. Remove all load from the torsion bar by backing off the adjusting bolt.

Remove the upper ball joint from the steering knuckle by removing the cotter pin and nut from the upper ball joint. Force out the ball joint with the special tool (Fig. 7-59). Remove bolts attaching the steering arm to the steering knuckle. Take the steering knuckle off. Note that the lower ball joint is in the steering arm.

4. STEERING-KNUCKLE REPLACEMENT Attach the steering knuckle to the steering arm, then install the upper ball-joint stud in the steering knuckle and secure with the nut properly tightened. Install the cotter pin. Put the load on the torsion bar by turning

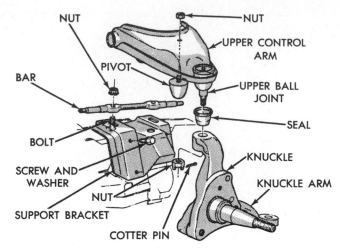

Fig. 7-57. Steering knuckle and upper control arm on carlines R and W. (*Chrysler Corporation*)

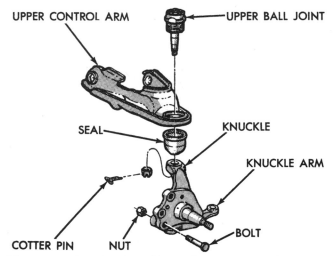

Fig. 7-58. Steering knuckle and upper control arm on carlines B and J. (*Chrysler Corporation*)

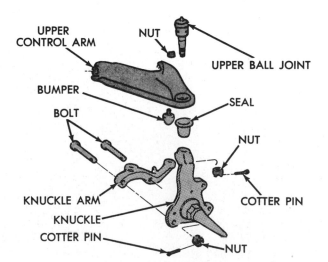

Fig. 7-56. Steering knuckle and upper control arm on carlines P, D, C, and Y. (*Chrysler Corporation*)

Fig. 7-59. Using the special tool to loosen the ball-joint stud. (*Chrysler Corporation*)

the adjusting bolt. Replace parts removed (splash shield, hub and disk or drum, and caliper if so equipped). Adjust wheel bearings. Install the wheel and cover, then lower the car to the floor. Install the rebound bumper. Adjust front-suspension height and wheel alignment.

5. *STEERING-KNUCKLE-ARM REMOVAL* Turn the ignition switch to OFF or UNLOCKED. Remove the rebound bumper. Raise the vehicle so that the front suspension is unloaded. Put jack stands under the frame. Remove the wheel cover, wheel, and tire. Remove the brake caliper (where present) and hang it by a wire to prevent damage to the brake hose. Remove the hub and brake disk or drum assembly. Remove the brake splash shield. Unload the torsion bar. Disconnect the tie rod from the steering-knuckle arm by removing the cotter pin and nut. Remove the lower ball-joint stud from the knuckle arm (Fig. 7-59) and detach the arm from the knuckle.

6. *STEERING-KNUCKLE-ARM REPLACEMENT* Install the ball-joint stud and attach it with nut and cotter pin. Attach the tie rod. Load the torsion bar. Install the brake splash shield, hub and brake disk or drum assembly. Install the caliper (if present). Adjust wheel bearings, install the wheel and cover, then lower the car. Install the rebound bumper and adjust height and alignment.

7. *LOWER-CONTROL-ARM AND SHAFT REMOVAL (FIG. 7-60)* With ignition switch at OFF or UNLOCKED and car supported as previously explained, remove the rebound bumper, wheel cover, wheel, brake caliper, hub-and-rotor assembly (or brake drum), and splash shield.

Disconnect the lower end of the shock absorber. Disconnect the strut and sway (stabilizer) bar. On some models, as shown in Fig. 7-61, the strut is removed with the control arm as an assembly. On some models, the automatic-transmission gearshift torque-shaft assembly must be removed. Measure the depth of the torsion-bar anchor bolt in the lower control arm, then unwind the torsion bar. Remove the torsion bar as explained above.

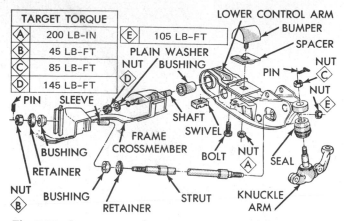

TARGET TORQUE	
A	200 LB-IN
B	45 LB-FT
C	85 LB-FT
D	145 LB-FT
E	105 LB-FT

Fig. 7-61. Lower control arm arrangement of the type that is removed from the car with the strut still attached. (*Chrysler Corporation*)

Separate the lower ball joint from the knuckle arm (Fig. 7-59). Remove the nut from the lower-control-arm shaft and push the shaft out of the frame cross member. Tap the threaded end of the shaft with a soft hammer if necessary to loosen it. Remove the lower control arm and shaft as an assembly. If the shaft bushing is worn, replace it.

8. *LOWER-CONTROL-ARM AND SHAFT REPLACEMENT* Position the lower control arm with the shaft in the frame cross member. Install and tighten the nut finger-tight. Attach the lower ball-joint stud to the knuckle arm with the nut properly tightened. Install the torsion bar and load it by returning the adjusting bolt to its original position. Replace the transmission torque shaft if it was removed. Reattach the strut and sway bar. Reinstall other parts that were removed. Adjust the wheel bearing and check height and front alignment.

9. *LOWER-BALL-JOINT REMOVAL* Figure 7-62

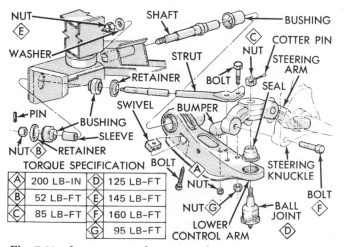

TORQUE SPECIFICATION			
A	200 LB-IN	D	125 LB-FT
B	52 LB-FT	E	145 LB-FT
C	85 LB-FT	F	160 LB-FT
		G	95 LB-FT

Fig. 7-60. Lower control arm attachment arrangement in carlines R and W. (*Chrysler Corporation*)

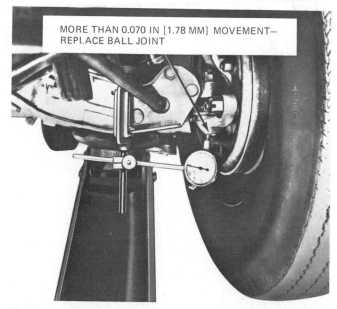

MORE THAN 0.070 IN [1.78 MM] MOVEMENT—REPLACE BALL JOINT

Fig. 7-62. Measuring lower ball-joint axial travel. (*Chrysler Corporation*)

shows the procedure of measuring the lower-ball-joint axial travel. With the weight of the car on the lower control arm, as shown, raise and lower the wheel with a pry bar under the center of the tire. The removal of the ball joint requires all the preliminary steps already outlined up to the point of installing the removal tool (Fig. 7-59) with the cotter pins and nuts removed from both the upper and lower ball-joint studs. The removal tool now will rest on the lower stud. Tighten tool enough to put pressure on the stud, but do not try to remove the ball joint by pressure alone. Strike the knuckle arm with a hammer to loosen the ball joint stud. The ball joint can then be pressed out of the lower control arm with a special tool (Fig. 7-63).

10. LOWER-BALL-JOINT REPLACEMENT Press the new ball joint in the lower control arm with the special tool (Fig. 7-63). Install a new seal over the ball joint, if necessary, using the special tool which is essentially a collar of the proper size. Insert the stud into the hole in the knuckle arm. Install the retainer nut and tighten as specified. Secure with the cotter pin. Lubricate the new ball joint (⊘ 7-1). Load the torsion bar and install the parts you removed. Lower vehicle to floor and adjust height and front alignment as needed.

11. UPPER-CONTROL-ARM AND BALL-JOINT REMOVAL Figure 7-64 shows one arrangement. To remove the upper control arm, position ignition switch at OFF or UNLOCKED. Raise the front of the car with a hand jack and remove the wheel cover and wheel. Position a short jack stand under the lower control arm near the splash shield, and lower the hand jack. Make sure the jack stand does not touch the shield and that the rebound bumpers are under no load. Remove the cotter pin and nut from both ball joints. Slide the special tool in place with the lower end resting on the steering-knuckle arm and the upper end on the upper ball-joint stud. Tighten the tool enough to put pressure on the stud. Then strike the steering knuckle with a hammer to loosen the stud. Do not loosen the stud with tool pressure alone.

Remove the tool and disengage the ball joint from the steering knuckle. Remove the rubber engine splash shield and pivot-shaft-bolt nuts or bolts. Lift the upper control arm with the ball joint and pivot bar as an assembly from the bracket. Remove the pivot bar nuts, retainers, and bushings. Install new bushings if the old ones are worn. Unscrew the ball joint from the upper arm with the special tool.

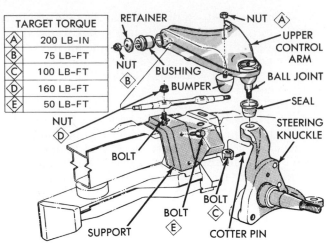

TARGET TORQUE	
Ⓐ	200 LB-IN
Ⓑ	75 LB-FT
Ⓒ	100 LB-FT
Ⓓ	160 LB-FT
Ⓔ	50 LB-FT

Fig. 7-64. Upper control arm arrangement in carlines R and W. (*Chrysler Corporation*)

12. UPPER-CONTROL-ARM AND BALL-JOINT REPLACEMENT Install the new ball joint with the special tool. The new ball joint will cut threads into a new arm. Install new bushings into the control arm. Press the old bushings out from inside out. Press new bushings from outside in until the tapered part seats on the arm. Install new ball-joint seal with the special collar tool. Put the control arm in the support bracket and install cams, cam bolts, lock washers, and nuts. Position the stud in the steering knuckle and install the nut. Tighten end nut and install the cotter pin. Lubricate the ball joint (⊘ 7-1). Reinstall nut and cotter pin on the lower ball-joint stud. Install the wheel and wheel cover. Lower the vehicle and adjust height and front alignment.

13. SHOCK ABSORBERS The front shock absorbers can be taken out by removing the upper nut and washer (accessible from the engine compartment) and then raising the front end of the car and removing the pivot bolt and nut from the lower shock-absorber eye. Compress the shock absorber to take it off the vehicle. Install new upper and lower bushings if necessary. A special tool is required to press out the lower bushing and install a new one. Replace the shock absorber by attaching the two ends with the pivot bolt and nuts and washers.

14. FRONT-WHEEL BEARINGS Figure 7-65 is a sectional view of the front-wheel bearings. They are very similar to those in Ford cars, shown in Fig. 7-38. They are checked, removed, cleaned, replaced, and adjusted in a similar manner.

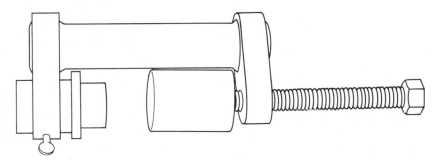

Fig. 7-63. Special tool used to press the ball joint out of the control arm. (*Chrysler Corporation*)

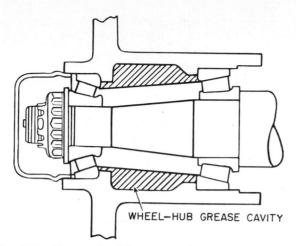

Fig. 7-65. Front-wheel bearing. (*Chrysler Corporation*)

⊘ **7-10 Rear-Suspension Service** As a rule, rear suspensions require no special service. If parts are worn or broken, they must be replaced. Sections that follow describe specific replacement procedures for Chevrolet, Ford, and Plymouth cars; these are typical for all cars. Possibly the parts that most often require replacement are the rubber grommets in spring eyes, control arms, and track bars. In addition, cars using independent rear suspension, such as the Corvette (Fig. 3-25), require periodic rear-end alignment as explained in Chap. 8.

⊘ **7-11 Chevrolet Rear-Suspension Service** Chevrolet models use two general types of rear suspension: coil and leaf (Fig. 7-66; see also Fig. 3-19).

1. COIL-SPRING REPLACEMENT (FIG. 7-66) Raise the rear of the car with a hoist under the axle housing, and put jack stands under the frame. Remove both rear wheels. Disconnect the lower ends of the shock absorbers. Loosen the upper-control-arm pivot bolt and both the left and right lower-control-arm rear attachments (loosen only, do not disconnect).

Remove the rear-suspension tie rod from the stud on the axle housing. At the lower seat of both rear coil springs, slightly loosen the nut on the retaining bolt.

CAUTION: Do not remove nuts!

Slowly lower the hoist so as to allow the axle housing to swing down. Springs and insulators can now be removed by removing the lower seat-attaching parts.

To replace, position the springs and upper insulators in the upper seats. Install the lower seat parts on the control arm, and tighten the nuts finger-tight.

NOTE: Omit lock washers so sufficient bolt thread will be available to start the nuts.

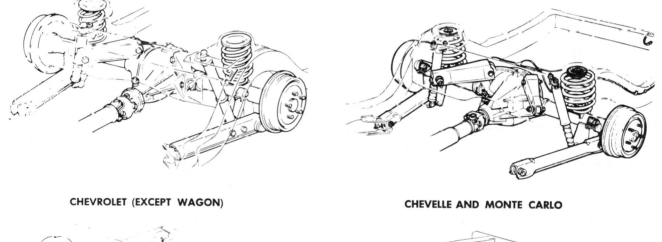

CHEVROLET (EXCEPT WAGON)

CHEVELLE AND MONTE CARLO

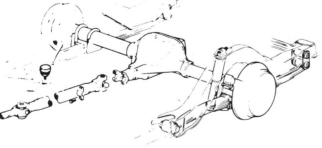

CHEVROLET WAGON

NOVA AND CAMARO (TYPICAL)

Fig. 7-66. Types of rear-suspension systems. (*Chevrolet Motor Division of General Motors Corporation*)

Alternately raise the axle slightly and resnug the bolt until the vehicle is fully supported on the hoist. Then, torque the nuts to specifications. Reconnect the shock absorbers, torque the upper- and lower-control-arm attachments, and reconnect the axle tie rod.

Finally, install the lock washers by removing the nuts (one at a time), putting the lock washers on, and torquing the nuts to specifications. Install the rear wheels and lower the car to the floor. Check riding height between the top of the axle tube and the frame.

2. *LEAF-SPRING REPLACEMENT (FIG. 7-67)* Raise the rear of the car so the axle assembly hangs free. Then support the car at both frame side rails near the front eye of the spring. Lift the axle housing so all tension is removed from the spring. Detach the lower end of the shock absorber.

Loosen the spring-eye-to-bracket retaining bolt and remove the screws attaching the bracket to the underbody of the car. Lower the axle assembly enough to allow you to remove the bracket from the spring.

Pry the parking-brake cable from the retainer bracket mounted on the spring plate. Remove the nuts from under the car that attach the spring to the axle housing (Fig. 7-67).

Support the spring and remove the lower bolt from the spring rear shackle. Now, the spring can be removed from the car.

If a spring leaf requires replacement, both it and any damaged spring-leaf insert can be replaced by removing the center-bolt nut.

To install the leaf spring, loosely attach the bracket to the spring eye. Put the spring in place and attach the rear of the spring to the shackle. Then loosely attach the front bracket to the underbody. Loosely attach the spring to the mounting pad on the axle housing.

NOTE: Be sure all insulators and cushions are in place.

Attach the parking-brake cable. Remove the jack stands and lower the car to the floor. Torque all parts to specifications.

3. *SHOCK-ABSORBER REPLACEMENT* Refer to Fig. 7-68, which shows a typical mounting arrangement. The only special point to watch when removing a shock absorber is to make sure that the stud on the shock absorber is prevented from turning when the nut is loosened. The hex on the thread end of the stud will enable you to hold the stud stationary when the nut is loosened or tightened. If the stud

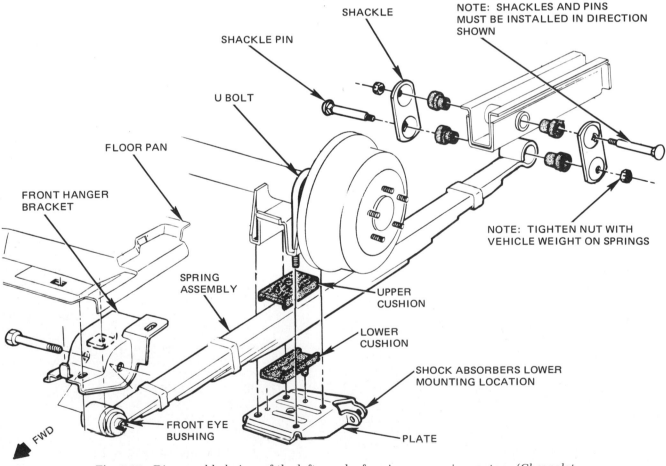

Fig. 7-67. Disassembled view of the left rear leaf-spring suspension system. (*Chevrolet Motor Division of General Motors Corporation*)

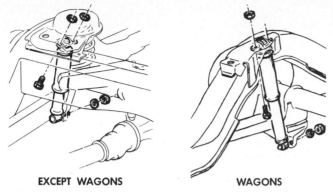

EXCEPT WAGONS   **WAGONS**

Fig. 7-68. Shock-absorber mounting arrangements. (*Chevrolet Motor Division of General Motors Corporation*)

turns, it will damage the rubber grommet in which the stud is mounted.

4. *CONTROL ARM* Figure 7-69 shows the control-arm attaching points. One point must be watched: The rear axle must be supported in such a way as to prevent the housing from rotating when the control arm is detached.

5. *STABILIZER BAR* Figure 7-70 shows the stabilizer bar attaching points. Removing and replacing the bar is a simple job. To provide sufficient working space, raise the car on a hoist.

6. *CORVETTE REAR SUSPENSION* The Corvette rear suspension is independent with a transverse leaf spring (Fig. 7-71). There is nothing very complicated about removing and replacing the parts in it. However, the rear wheels must be checked for alignment. Camber and toe-in can be adjusted (Chap. 8).

⊘ **7-12 Ford Rear-Suspension Service** Ford has two general types of rear-suspension systems: coil (Fig. 7-72) and leaf-spring (Fig. 7-73). The procedures for replacing shock absorbers, springs, control arms, tracking bars, and other parts are very similar to

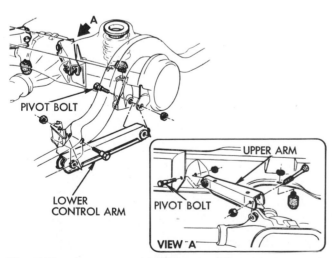

PIVOT BOLT

LOWER CONTROL ARM

UPPER ARM

PIVOT BOLT

VIEW A

Fig. 7-69. Arrangement of the control arms in a coil-spring rear-suspension system. (*Chevrolet Motor Division of General Motors Corporation*)

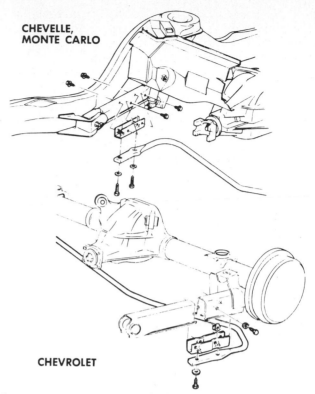

CHEVELLE, MONTE CARLO

CHEVROLET

Fig. 7-70. Arrangement of the stabilizer bar on rear-suspension systems. (*Chevrolet Motor Division of General Motors Corporation*)

those on the Chevrolet cars, discussed in ⊘ 7-11. Special points to watch include:

1. In some models, it is necessary to remove an access cover in the luggage compartment in order to get at the shock-absorber upper attaching nut.

2. The rear-suspension lower arms on the coil-spring suspension are not interchangeable. The lower arm on the left side is identified by the notches in the bushing flange (Fig. 7-72).

3. One check that can be made on the leaf-spring suspension pertains to tracking. This determines whether the rear wheels are following, or tracking, properly. To make the check, drive straight ahead on pavement, part of which is wet, and stop about 10 feet [3.05 m] beyond the wet area. Check the wet tracks of the tires. Rear-wheel tracks should be an equal distance inside the front tracks (Fig. 7-74). If they are not, the spring tie-bolt head possibly is not centered in the locating hole on the spring mounting pad of the axle housing. This may be checked by measuring A in Fig. 7-75 at both springs. The measurement is taken from the locating hole in the side frame member and the forward edge of the axle housing. If the measurements differ more than $\frac{1}{8}$ inch [3.17 mm], it will be necessary to reposition the tie bolt, as follows.

Loosen the four spring-clip nuts and use a jack to push the axle housing into position. Then move the spring clip into line and tighten the clip nuts to the specified torque. If this does not correct the

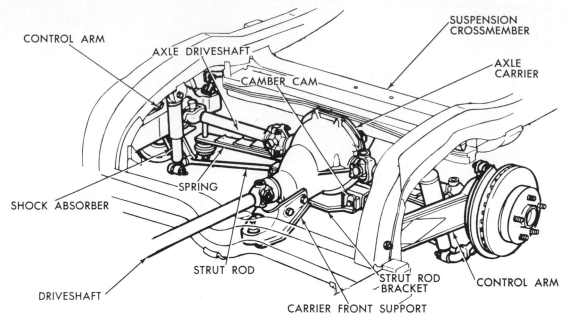

Fig. 7-71. Independent rear-suspension system used on the Corvette. (*Chevrolet Motor Division of General Motors Corporation*)

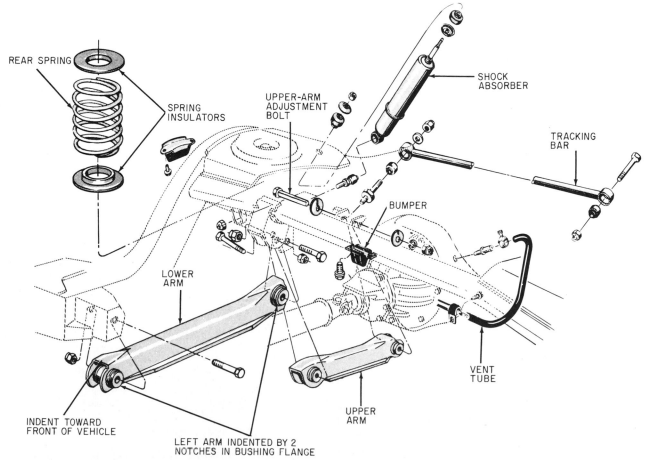

Fig. 7-72. Disassembled view of the rear suspension for Ford, Mercury, Thunderbird, and Continental Mark III. (*Ford Motor Company*)

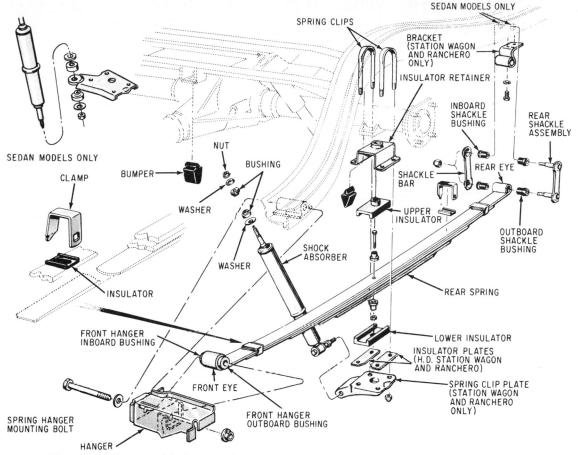

Fig. 7-73. Disassembled view of a rear suspension using a leaf spring. (*Ford Motor Company*)

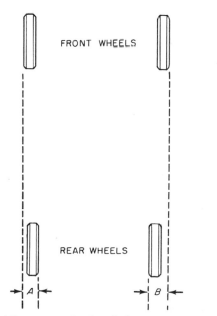

Fig. 7-74. Alignment check of the rear suspension. *A* should equal *B*. (*Ford Motor Company*)

tracking, consider the possibility that the frame may be out of line because of an accident (see ⊘ 19-3).

The dimension B in Fig. 7-75 is a measurement to be taken to determine whether the front hanger should be replaced. If this dimension is not correct, cut off the old hanger with a welding torch and weld a new hanger to the frame. (Some hangers are attached with nuts and bolts.)

⊘ **7-13 Plymouth Rear-Suspension Service** Figure 7-76 shows disassembled views of typical Plymouth rear-suspension systems. Following paragraphs describe the various service operations on this suspension system.

1. MEASURING SPRING HEIGHT Jounce the car several times, first at the front and then at the back,

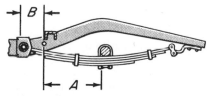

Fig. 7-75. Alignment check of the rear suspension. *A* should be the same (or within ⅛ inch [3.18 mm]) at both springs. (*Ford Motor Company*)

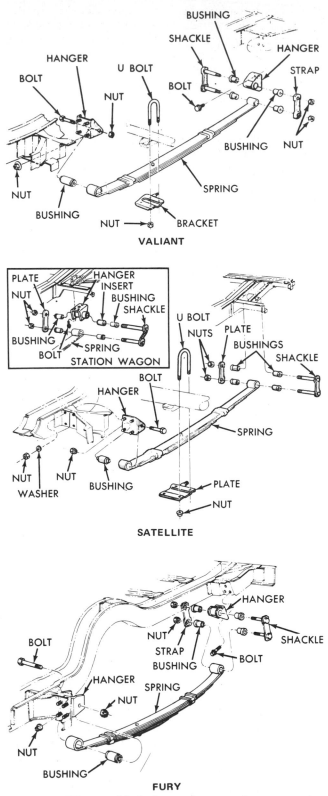

Fig. 7-76. Disassembled views of rear-spring suspension systems. (*Chrysler Corporation*)

the distance is more than ¾ inch, one of the rear springs needs replacement.

2. REAR-SPRING REMOVAL Disconnect the rear shock absorbers at the lower mounting studs. Raise the vehicle at the lifting points so that the rear springs hang free, and use a jack to support the axle housing in this position. Remove the nuts that attach the spring front hanger to the frame. Remove the U-bolt nuts and the spring plate. Remove the rear hanger bolts and take the spring off the car. Take out the front pivot bolt to remove the front hanger from the spring. Remove the rear shackle and bushings from the spring.

3. REAR-SPRING INSTALLATION If the front-pivot-bolt bushing needs replacement in the spring, use a special tool to remove the old bushing and install a new one.

Attach the front hanger with the front pivot bolt and run on the nut, but do not tighten it. Assemble the rear shackle and bushings (Fig. 7-76). *Do not lubricate the rubber bushings.* Start the shackle-bolt nuts, but do not tighten them.

Now, put the spring in place on the car and attach the hangers to the car frame, tightening the bolts and nuts to the proper tension. Remove the axle support and put the center hole of the axle-spring seat over the head of the spring center bolt. Put the spring plate under the spring and install the U bolts, tightening the nuts to the specified tension. Lower the vehicle and reconnect the shock absorbers.

Jounce the car several times and recheck the spring height. Tighten the front pivot bolt and the shackle nuts to the proper tension.

4. REAR-SPRING FRONT-PIVOT-BUSHING RE-PLACEMENT This bushing may be replaced without removing the spring from the car. The vehicle should be raised just enough so that the spring is relaxed and the rear wheels are just touching the floor. Never allow the weight of the rear axle to be suspended on the fully extended shock absorbers. This would damage them. Now the front hanger can be detached from the car frame and taken off the spring so that the new bushing can be installed. A special tool is needed to remove the old and install the new bushing.

5. INTERLEAVES Zinc interleaves (Fig. 7-77) are used between the spring leaves to reduce corrosion and improve spring life. When the interleaves are replaced, the spring must be removed from the car and disassembled.

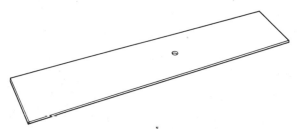

Fig. 7-77. Zinc interleaf used between the spring leaves. (*Chrysler Corporation*)

releasing the bumpers at the same point in each cycle. Locate the highest point on the underside of the rear-axle bumper strap (at the rear of the bumper), and measure from here to the top of the axle housing. Take measurements on both sides. If

CHAPTER 7 CHECKUP

You have now finished the first of several chapters in the book that cover the servicing of various chassis components. It is important for you to have a good understanding of how the steering linkage and the front and rear suspension on cars are serviced; thus the information in the chapter you have just completed is of value to you. Here is your chance to check up on how well you remember the important points covered in the chapter. If any of the questions stump you, do not be discouraged. Just reread the chapter so that you can get the material in it "down pat." These periodic checkups are included in the book to help you. They tell you whether you are ready to go on to the next chapter. When you do well in answering the questions, you know you are ready to go on. In this way, you get the most out of the book, and you are doing a better job for yourself.

Completing the Sentences   The sentences below are incomplete. After each sentence there are several words or phrases, only one of which will correctly complete the sentence. Write each sentence in your notebook, selecting the proper word or phrase to complete it correctly.

1. The only service that the steering linkage normally requires is periodic: (*a*) tie-rod adjustment, (*b*) lubrication, (*c*) ball-joint replacement.
2. If a steering-linkage part is bent, it should be: (*a*) heated and straightened, (*b*) cold-straightened, (*c*) discarded.
3. The only time the steering arm would require replacement would be after: (*a*) wheel-bearing replacement, (*b*) an accident, (*c*) wheel replacement.
4. If the ball stud in the Ford spindle-connecting-rod end shows excessive looseness: (*a*) it should be adjusted, (*b*) the ball stud should be replaced, (*c*) the rod-end assembly should be replaced.
5. Chevrolet recommends that the front-wheel bearings be: (*a*) lubricated and adjusted every 24,000 mi [38,624 km], (*b*) replaced every 24,000 mi [38,624 km], (*c*) lubricated and adjusted every 1,000 mi [1,609 km].
6. The Chevrolet recommendation is that if a front coil spring has been found to sag: (*a*) shims should be installed, (*b*) the shock absorber should be replaced, (*c*) the spring should be replaced.
7. On the typical front suspension, the shims between the frame and the upper-control-arm shaft provide adjustments of the front-wheel: (*a*) caster and camber, (*b*) toe-in and toe-out, (*c*) included angle and toe-in.
8. On the Plymouth front suspension, if there is spring sag, it can be corrected by: (*a*) adding shims, (*b*) replacing springs, (*c*) adjusting torsion bar.
9. One of the basic cautions to observe when removing the ball joints from the steering knuckle is: (*a*) do not loosen by tool pressure alone, (*b*) tighten tool until ball joints pop loose, (*c*) drive ball joints out with a soft hammer.

10. A basic part of the front-wheel-bearing adjustment procedure is to always: (*a*) tighten adjustment or spindle nut with wheel stationary, (*b*) tighten adjustment or spindle nut with wheel rotating, (*c*) tighten adjustment or spindle nut until wheel stops rotating.

Servicing Procedures   In the following, you should write down in your notebook the procedures asked for. Do not copy from the book; try to write in your own words, the way you would explain it to another person. Give a step-by-step story. This will help you to remember the procedure later, when you go into the shop.

1. List the service procedures for Chevrolet front suspension and steering linkage.
2. Describe, step by step, how to perform the service procedures listed in the previous question. (If you do not have time to write out all the procedures, select one or two of them.)
3. List the service procedures for Ford front suspension and steering linkage.
4. Describe, step by step, how to perform the service procedures listed in the previous question. (If you do not have time to write out all of them, select one or two.)
5. List the service procedures for Plymouth front suspension and steering linkage.
6. Describe, step by step, how to perform the service procedures listed in the previous question. (If you do not have time to write out all of them, select one or two.)
7. Describe the procedure for removing, servicing, and replacing a rear leaf spring.
8. Describe the procedure for removing and replacing a rear coil spring.

SUGGESTIONS FOR FURTHER STUDY

When you are in the service shop or a service station, you can learn a great deal about different suspension and steering-linkage systems by studying the various cars as they are put on the lift or jacked up. Study car shop manuals whenever you can get your hands on them. If possible, watch automotive mechanics at work servicing front suspensions and steering linkages. Keep writing important facts in your notebook. This methodical recording of facts will not only give you a valuable reference notebook, it will also help train you in the good habit of noticing and remembering important facts. And writing down these facts will teach you, above all, how to express yourself. In this way, you will learn to think more clearly, to talk more easily, to "get your point across" to others. All this, of course, equips you for the bigger job ahead of you.

chapter 8

FRONT-END ALIGNMENT

This chapter discusses the various procedures required to check and adjust front-end alignment. It explains how caster, camber, toe-in, toe-out on turns, and steering-axis inclinations are checked. It also explains how to adjust caster, camber, and toe-in, where possible. On some cars, caster and camber are preset at the factory and no adjustment is possible. The chapter also discusses the preliminary checks and adjustments that precede a front-end alignment job. In addition, it tells how to adjust the rear-wheel alignment of independent rear-suspension systems (Fig. 7-71).

⊘ **8-1 Front-Wheel Alignment—Preliminary** Numerous devices have been used to check front-wheel alignment, varying from lines marked on the floor to complete wheel-alignment machines using light beams and electronic vibration detectors. Different alignment-checking devices vary in complexity and construction, but they all check the same fundamental factors on the front end of the car.

Several interrelated factors besides wheel alignment influence steering control. Before caster, camber, toe-in, toe-out on turns, and steering-axis (or kingpin) inclination are checked, these other factors should be investigated. They include tire pressure, wheel-bearing condition, wheel balance, wheel runout, shock-absorber action, frame alignment, and steering-knuckle and ball-joint condition. Remember that if any of these factors is off, the wheel-alignment checks and adjustments will mean little; they may actually make conditions worse. Even though you adjusted caster and camber exactly "on the nose" in a car with loose wheel bearings or worn ball joints, it would mean little. As soon as the car went out on the road, the looseness or wear would probably throw the adjustments off.

⊘ **8-2 Preliminary Checks** The first step in wheel alignment is to make sure that all tires are inflated to the proper air pressure. Next, jack up the front end of the car and check the tie rods and linkages for looseness and the ball joints or kingpin and wheel bearings for wear and adjustment, as already outlined (⊘ 6-3). Correct wheel alignment cannot be maintained if steering-system parts are worn or out of adjustment. A worn wheel bearing can often be detected by spinning the wheel and placing a finger on the car bumper. If the wheel bearing is worn, a slight vibration or grinding may be felt as the wheel is spun. Front-wheel-bearing adjustment is described in ⊘ 7-5, item 3, and ⊘ 7-7, item 1.

Wobble, or runout, of the tire should be checked to determine whether the tire wobbles sideways (has lateral runout) or whether it is out of round (has radial runout). Spin the wheel and slowly bring a piece of chalk to the sidewall of the tire. If the tire is wobbling (or has lateral runout), the chalk mark will not be uniform around the sidewall. It will be wide where the side of the tire is out from the center, and will be narrow or miss where the side is in from the center.

Out-of-roundness (radial runout) can be checked by spinning the tire slowly and bringing a pointer or piece of chalk toward the center of the tread until it touches. If it touches uniformly all around, the tire tread is centered. If the tread is off-center, or out of round (radial runout), the pointer will touch some places and miss others.

If wobble or out-of-roundness exceeds $\frac{1}{16}$ to $\frac{1}{4}$ inch [1.58 to 6.35 mm] (specifications vary), correction must be made.

The setup shown in Fig. 8-1 can be used to make accurate measurements of both the tire and the wheel rim. Although the setup is shown with a wheel off the car, it can also be used for mounted wheels.

To correct excessive tire runout, it may be necessary only to deflate the tire and work it around to another position on the rim. In some cases of excessive radial runout, it may be necessary to remove some of the rubber from the tread by the use of a special machine that trims off the excess. This trues up the tread.

If the excessive runout is due to a bent wheel rim, the rim must be replaced or straightened.

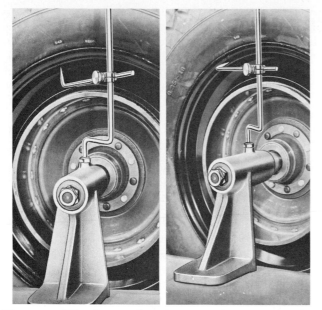

Fig. 8-1. Wheel-mounting device and pointer used to check wheel runout. (*Chrysler Corporation*)

Wheel balance should be checked and corrected if necessary (see (⊘ 8-3). Condition of the shock absorbers should be checked (⊘ 6-13). Another factor that should be considered is alignment, or tracking. Tracking is the following of the rear wheels directly behind, or in the tracks of, the front wheels. Failure to track usually means that the frame or rear springs are out of alignment; this causes rapid tire wear and poor steering control. If tracking is bad, it can be readily detected by following the car on the highway and observing the tracks. A check of alignment, or tracking, is described in ⊘ 7-12, item 3, along with the procedure for realigning the rear leaf springs. Checking and restoring frame alignment are covered in Chap. 19.

CAUTION: Never attempt to straighten any suspension part by heating or bending it. Either of these procedures could so weaken the part that it could fail on the highway and cause a fatal accident.

⊘ 8-3 Wheel Balance If a wheel-and-tire assembly is out of balance, the car will be hard to steer, riding will be rough, and tire wear will be rapid. Wheel balance can be checked in several ways. One method is to use a so-called shimmy detector, which drives the wheel after the car has been jacked up (Fig. 8-2). The shimmy detector, consisting of an electric motor and a driving wheel, is placed in contact with the jacked-up car wheel and drives the wheel at high speed. If the car wheel is out of balance, the end of the car will shake, or shimmy, as the wheel is spun (Fig. 8-2). The shimmy detector is a demonstrator and does not indicate what must be done to balance the wheel. The device is seldom used by itself except as a demonstration unit. Instead, it is used with an auxiliary mechanism that

determines how much and where weight must be installed on the wheel to achieve balance. One mechanism is installed directly on the wheel and has a means of adding and positioning weight while the wheel is being spun. There is also an electronic signaler attached to the car suspension which indicates the amount that the wheel is out of balance.

NOTE: Wheels with disk brakes are harder to spin than wheels with drum brakes. The reason is that the disk-brake shoes are nearly in contact with the disk. Therefore, wheel spinners with greater power are required for wheels with disk brakes. Earlier spinners, designed for wheels with drum brakes, may burn out if they are used on wheels with disk brakes.

Both front and back wheels can be checked for balance, and balanced, either on or off the car, depending on the type of checking equipment available. Correction is made by fastening weights to the wheel rim to balance heavy spots in the tire or wheel.

Wheels can be checked for balance in two ways, statically and dynamically. A wheel that is statically out of balance is heavier in one section than in another. When it is suspended on a spindle in a vertical plane (as on the car), it will rotate until the heaviest section is at the bottom. A dynamically out-of-balance wheel does not have an even distribution of weight in a plane vertical to the wheel axle. A wheel that is statically in balance can be dynamically out of balance. For example, a wheel with a heavy spot on one side can be balanced, statically, by a heavy spot 180 degrees from it (Fig. 8-3). When this wheel starts to rotate, it will try to

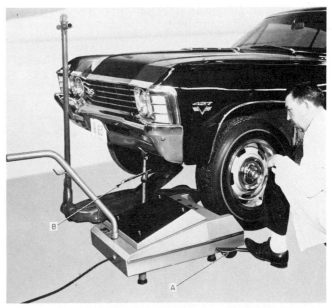

Fig. 8-2. Wheel spinner in position to spin the front wheel and check its balance. A, electric-motor-control pedal; B, jiggler to indicate out-of-balance condition. (*Bear Manufacturing Company*)

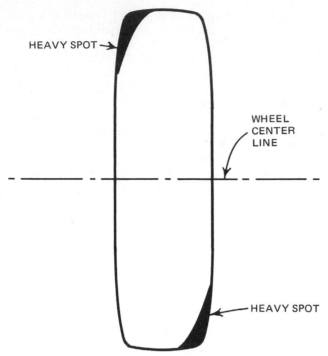

HEAVY SPOT →

WHEEL
CENTER
LINE

← HEAVY SPOT

Fig. 8-3. A wheel may be statically in balance but dynamically out of balance. For example, a heavy spot on a tire might be statically balanced by another heavy spot, or a weight, placed on the other side of the tire and 180 degrees around the tire. But such a wheel would be dynamically out of balance and would wobble, or run out, as it rotates.

wobble, or run out, because the heavy spots have a greater centrifugal force working on them.

⊘ **8-4 Wheel Balancing off the Car** There are two general types of off-the-car wheel balancers: one that balances statically only and one that balances both statically and dynamically.

1. STATIC BALANCER Figure 8-4 shows one type of static balancer. It has a bubble under a convex glass that will center under the crossmarks when the floating wheel support is balanced (Fig. 8-5). To use the balancer, the wheel-and-tire assembly is placed on the support. Any lack of balance of the assembly will show up by causing the bubble to move off center. The amount and direction of displacement indicate how much and where weight must be added to the rim, as explained below.

NOTE: This wheel balancer is less accurate than other types described below, particularly in the hands of inexperienced operators.

2. STATIC-AND-DYNAMIC BALANCER This balancer (Fig. 8-6) can be used to check both static and dynamic balance and is preferred by many operators. As previously noted, a wheel that is statically balanced may be dynamically out of balance. Thus, many operators prefer to check both items.

a. Checking Static Balance First, remove all weights and make sure that all stones have been removed from the tire tread. Then mount the wheel on the balancer in a vertical position and spin it. Allow it to come to rest. The heaviest part of the tire will come to rest at the bottom. Make a chalk mark at the top of the tire to indicate the point opposite the heaviest part (Fig. 8-7).

Static balance is corrected by placing weights on the wheel rim. Figure 8-8 shows how a weight is attached to the rim to balance a wheel. Figure 8-9 shows weights of various sizes. Add sufficient weight at the chalk mark to balance the wheel. Balance is good if the wheel will not turn from any position at which it is stopped. If more than 2 ounces [56.70 g (grams)] is required, put the additional weight on the other side of the tire rim. If two 2-ounce [56.70 g] weights are not enough, increase both weights an equal amount.

Fig. 8-4. *Left,* bubble type of static wheel balancer; *right,* tire and wheel on balancer in readiness for balance check. (*John Bean Division of FMC Corporation*)

Fig. 8-5. Close-up view of bubble and cross marks on the bubble type of static wheel balancer. (*John Bean Division of FMC Corporation*)

Fig. 8-7. Chalk mark (A) at the top of the tire opposite the heavy part. (*Bear Manufacturing Company*)

Fig. 8-6. Wheel balancer in operation. The balancer is spinning the wheel to check it for dynamic balance. A device in the balancer indicates where and how much the wheel is out of dynamic balance. (*Bear Manufacturing Company*)

Fig. 8-8. Balancing a wheel by placing a weight on the wheel rim. (*Bear Manufacturing Company*)

NOTE: Tap lightly on weights during the location tests so they can be removed or slid along the rim.

If you cannot achieve exact static balance with weights placed exactly opposite the heavy spot (at the chalk mark), then use two weights which total slightly more than the amount needed to achieve balance. Put one weight inside the wheel, the other one outside the wheel, both at the chalk mark. Then move them slightly apart, equal amounts, and recheck static balance (Fig. 8-10). Repeat this until balance is achieved. Tap weights firmly into position.

NOTE: It has occasionally been found that soapstone, spikes, nails, or other loose objects have been

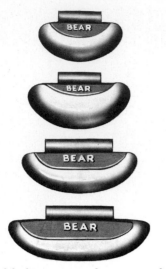

Fig. 8-9. Wheel-balancing weights are available in different sizes. (*Bear Manufacturing Company*)

left in the tire. This creates an unbalance that cannot be cured by attaching weights because the loose objects would continue to shift. Therefore, make a check for loose objects by allowing the wheel to come to rest with the heavy spot at the bottom, chalk the light spot (at the top), turn the wheel a quarter turn, and strike the tire several times with a hammer. Then spin the wheel again and allow it to come to rest. If it comes to rest in a different position, there is loose material in the tire that must be removed.

b. *Dynamic Balance* To check dynamic balance, spin the wheel and read the indicating device in the wheel balancer to learn the place and approx-

imate amount the wheel is dynamically out of balance. Balance is then achieved by putting additional weights on the indicated spots on the rim.

CAUTION: Make sure all stones are removed from the tire tread before spinning the tire!

It may happen that a weight will be required, for dynamic balance, on a spot on a rim that is near a weight installed for static balance. For example, suppose a weight A is added (as shown in Fig. 8-11) to achieve static balance. For dynamic balance, another weight B is required on the other side of the rim, as shown. Adding the second weight throws the wheel out of static balance. But static balance can be restored by a weight at C (Fig. 8-11). The weight at C does not throw dynamic balance off, since it is on the same side as weight B. A better way to take care of the balance is to combine the effect of weights A and B. For instance, if weight A is 4 ounces [113.40 g] and weight B is 2 ounces [56.70 g], approximately correct static *and* dynamic balance can be achieved by using only one weight, at B, of 2 ounces [56.70 g]. In such case, no weight would be needed at C. Other combining arrangements are possible. The reason they are desirable is that they keep the total amount of weight added to the rim to a minimum. The less weight added the better, so long as static and dynamic balance are achieved. In any event, *no more than 8 ounces [226.80 g] should be added to a rim,* according to authorities.

NOTE: After each readjustment of weights for dynamic balance, recheck the static balance, as previously explained.

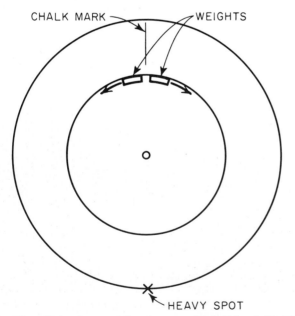

Fig. 8-10. Using two weights—one on each side of wheel—to achieve static balance. Move the weights apart equal amounts until static balance is attained.

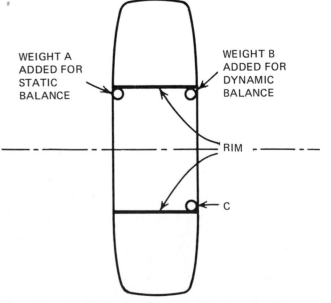

Fig. 8-11. Method of adding weights to wheel rim to achieve static and dynamic balance.

⊘ 8-5 Wheel Balancing on the Car A variety of dynamic wheel-balancing devices are available for checking wheel balance on the car. One of the simplest consists of a wheel spinner and a vibration indicator, or jiggler (Fig. 8-2). The wheel spinner contains an electric motor and a driving wheel which is held against the tire to cause the car wheel to spin. The jiggler is installed under the bumper or bumper bracket and adjusted so that the pointer is in a horizontal position. The pointer is connected through a lever to the vertical shaft so that a slight up-and-down motion of the shaft, due to car vibration, will cause the pointer to jiggle. The operator watches the pointer as he or she spins the wheel to note how much it moves and thus how much out of balance the wheel is.

Instead of a jiggler, some systems use an electronic device that sends out a signal with each movement of the suspension system. Both systems are discussed below.

NOTE: Some successful alignment experts merely open the car door nearest the wheel being checked and watch it while the wheel is spun. Door movement then takes the place of the jiggler or electronic device.

1. BALANCING FRONT WHEELS WITH JIGGLER
The wheel is spun with the spinner, and the operator turns it with increasing speed while watching the jiggler, as already noted. If jiggling is noticeable, a special adapter and detecting device are mounted on the wheel. First, remove all weights. Then install the adapter as shown in Fig. 8-12.

CAUTION: Adapters and installation procedures vary with different makes and models of balancers. Carefully follow the detailed instructions for the balancer you are using. Above all, make sure the adapter is securely in place.

Put the balancer unit on the adapter (Fig. 8-13), making sure it is securely in place. There are two knobs on the balancer shown. The outer knob (WC) controls the amount of unbalanced weight that is added to the wheel, and the inner knob (PC) controls the position around the wheel rim where the unbalanced weight is applied. Thus, with the wheel spinning, unbalanced weight can be added or subtracted, and moved around the rim, until the exact amount of weight, and its proper location to produce balance, can be determined. When the pointer on the vibration indicator is quiet, the wheel is in balance. Then, with the wheel stopped, the amount and position of the weight required are shown on the indicator scale (P and R in Fig. 8-13). Figure 8-14 shows the operator performing a wheel-balance test.
2. BALANCING REAR WHEELS WITH JIGGLER
Figure 8-15 shows an operator checking the balance of a rear wheel. The adapter, balancer, and jiggler

Fig. 8-12. Installation of adapter on wheel in preparation for checking dynamic wheel balance. A, wing nut; B, locating stop. (*Bear Manufacturing Company*)

Fig. 8-13. Balance unit in place on adapter. G, hand nut; P, weight indicator; R, spot where weight should be added; PC, position control knob; WC, weight control knob. (*Bear Manufacturing Company*)

Fig. 8-14. Operator making a wheel-balance check on the left front wheel of a car. (*Bear Manufacturing Company*)

are installed in the same manner as for a front wheel. However, for checking rear wheels, the engine drives the wheels with transmission in high, or drive. With the standard differential, only one wheel is raised from the floor at a time and balanced. Then the other wheel is raised for the balance check, and the first wheel is lowered to the floor.

CAUTION: Never exceed 35 mph [56.33 km/h] on the speedometer. This is equivalent to 70 mph [112.65 km/h] at the wheel due to the differential action. Do the job fast—never spin the wheel more than 2 minutes or you may damage the differential!

3. BALANCING REAR WHEELS WITH NO-SLIP DIFFERENTIAL On these wheels, a different procedure is required. Raise both wheels, remove one wheel-and-tire assembly, and then replace the wheel nuts to hold the brake drum in place. Reverse the

nuts so the flat face contacts the brake drum. Do not use an impact wrench!

Then balance the wheel remaining on the car. Do not exceed 70 mph [112.65 km/h] on the speedometer! When the first wheel is balanced, reinstall the other wheel and balance it. The first wheel can be left in place because it has been balanced and will not disturb the balancing check of the second wheel.

CAUTION: Never take longer than 2 minutes to make a balance check!

4. BALANCING WITH ELECTRONIC DETECTOR The equipment required for an electronic-detector test is shown in Fig. 8-16. The signal-pickup unit is placed under the car, as near the wheel as possible. The magnet is placed on a flat surface such as the underside of the lower control arm. This pickup will

Fig. 8-15. Making a wheel-balance check on the rear wheel of a car. A jiggler is used to indicate vibration. (*Bear Manufacturing Company*)

Fig. 8-16. Checking wheel balance with an electronic signal pickup and a stroboscope. (*Alemite Division of Stewart-Warner Corporation*)

detect suspension movement caused by an out-of-balance condition in the wheel and tire. Every movement will cause the pickup to send out a signal. The signal will activate the strobe (stroboscopic light), which is a flasher that produces a powerful flash of light on signal. (A strobe is used for timing the ignition on engines.) The system works like this:

An unbalanced wheel will tend to move up and down as it is spun. This causes the pickup to send out a signal every time the wheel moves up. The signal causes the strobe to flash. When the strobe is pointed at the wheel, it will strongly illuminate the wheel in the position at which the upward motion occurs. Since the strong light is on only a fraction of a second, the wheel will appear to stand still.

Now, you see how the system works. To begin, you make a mark on the tire sidewall with a piece of chalk. (Also, remove all weights from the rim and stones from the tread.) Then you spin the tire and point the strobe light at the sidewall. The chalk mark will appear to stand still. Note its position. An easy way is to think of the hour hand of a clock. Suppose the mark is at 5 o'clock. Stop the wheel and position the mark at 5. Then put a weight at the 12 o'clock position. The size of weight will be indicated by a meter on the top of the strobe. The meter needle moves more or less, depending on how much the wheel is unbalanced. Recheck balance after adding weight.

The above procedure corrects for up-and-down movement. To check for lateral runout, place the pickup so that the magnet will be in contact with the backing plate at the front edge, as close to the horizontal centerline as possible (Fig. 8-17). Spin the wheel and point the strobe at the tire. Note the location of the chalk mark when the light flashes. Stop the wheel and position it so the mark is in the same location (same o'clock). Add weights *inside* and *outside* to correct lack of balance. The inside weight should go as close to the pickup as possible, the outside weight 180 degrees away (Fig. 8-18). Recheck balance.

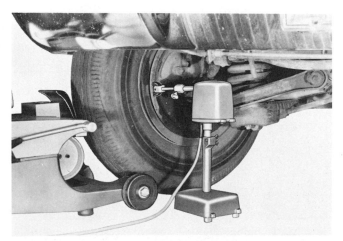

Fig. 8-17. Electronic signal pickup in place to detect lateral runout. (*Alemite Division of Stewart-Warner Corporation*)

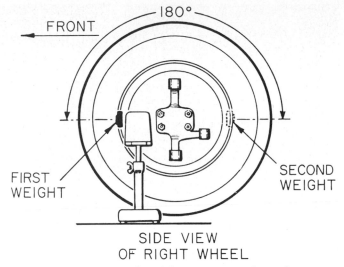

Fig. 8-18. Location of weights to correct lateral runout. (*Alemite Division of Stewart-Warner Corporation*)

NOTE: This system balances front wheels for both radial and lateral runout but balances rear wheels for radial runout only. Note procedures and cautions given in the description of balancing rear wheels with the jiggler, above.

5. BALANCING WHEELS ON ALEMITE VIBRA-TEC ANALYZER This analyzer, shown in Fig. 8-19, is a fully automated electronic balance analyzer and represents the latest type of balancing equipment. The analyzer includes a hydraulic jacking system to lift the front or rear of the car, as required, for spinning the wheels. It has wheel spinners built into the floor, as shown. Pendant controls, hanging from the ceiling, enable the operator, while seated at the car wheel, to drive onto the analyzer and then make the complete test without leaving the seat (Fig. 8-20). The meters record the condition of balance at the wheels so that corrections can be quickly made.

⊘ **8-6 Dynamic-Alignment Indicators** A number of dynamic-alignment indicators are available that give evidence of any out-of-line conditions when the car is driven over them. The Weaver Sign-Align (Fig. 8-21) has a pair of test plates over which the car front wheels are driven. If the wheels are out of line, they will exert a sideward push on the plates, and this sideward push registers on the dial. Further, it actuates the display-board lights to show either green (for okay), yellow (for caution, which means that alignment is required to reduce excessive tire wear), or red (which means the misalignment is so bad that immediate service is required). Further, a record of the findings can be punched out on a card by pressing a button.

Figure 8-22 shows another dynamic-alignment tester, this one using indicating blades instead of test plates. With either tester, the procedure is simple. After a 20-foot [6.10 m] or more straight-ahead approach, drive the front wheels, in the straight-ahead

Fig. 8-19. Wheel-balance analyzer of the type with floor-mounted rollers and electronic pickup devices to detect balance conditions as wheels are spun. (*Alemite Division of Stewart-Warner Corporation*)

Fig. 8-20. You can make wheel-balance checks without leaving the driver's seat when using the analyzer shown in Fig. 8-19. (*Alemite Division of Stewart-Warner Corporation*)

position, over the tester blades or plates. Stop before the rear wheels cross the tester platform. Record the misalignment reading. Back the car so that the front wheels roll back over the platform for a few inches. Then drive the car forward again. Record the misalignment reading once again. The first reading indicates the amount of misalignment. The difference between the first and the second reading indicates the amount of looseness in the suspension and steering system. If the difference is excessive, the car will require a complete front-end analysis so that the cause of the excessive looseness can be found and eliminated.

NOTE: The rear wheels can also be checked for misalignment with the dynamic-alignment tester. Excessive misalignment would indicate a bent rear axle or housing, a misaligned spring, or worn or bent attachment parts or control arms.

Although these dynamic-alignment testers do give an indication of front-end or rear-end misalignment, they do not accurately measure the amount

Fig. 8-21. Dynamic-alignment tester in use. When the wheels roll over the tester plates, the machine registers the amount of misalignment. (*Weaver Manufacturing Division of Dura Corporation*)

Fig. 8-22. Dynamic-alignment tester in use. As the wheels roll across the indicating blades, the tester dial registers the amount of misalignment. (*Bear Manufacturing Company*)

of misalignment or pinpoint the cause. They simply indicate that something is wrong and that further analysis is required to find and correct the trouble.

⊘ **8-7 Front-Alignment Testers** There are several alignment testers that will show the type and amount of front-end misalignment. They vary from relatively simple spirit-level (or bubble) devices that are mounted on the wheel hub or rim, to more complex instruments that use beams of light or that report the alignment conditions directly on recording meters. With the spirit-level devices, the position of the bubble in the level indicates the alignment condition being checked. With the beam-of-light instruments, the position of the beam on a wall chart or similar scale indicates the alignment condition. The tester that reports alignment conditions on recording meters picks up the alignment angles through two sets of rollers in the floor. Regardless of type, the alignment testers check caster, camber, and steering-axis inclination (or kingpin angle). In addition, toe-in is checked with a gauge that measures the amount that the tires point inward at the front of the car. Toe-out on turns is measured with turntables or turning-radius gauges placed under the front wheels to measure the degrees of turn at each front wheel as the steering wheel is rotated in one direction and the other.

CAUTION: All the preliminary checks and adjustments to the tires, wheel bearings, wheels (for run-out and balance), and suspension and steering linkages must be made, as already described, before wheel alignment is checked.

NOTE: The instructions for the operation of the tester being used, as well as the special instructions and specifications for the model of car being checked, must be carefully followed.

⊘ **8-8 Camber-Caster Testers** Some camber-caster testers mount on the wheel hub; others mount on the wheel rim. Some use a beam of light that spotlights a viewing screen. Others use a spirit level. These are described below.

1. HUB-MOUNTED SPIRIT-LEVEL TYPE This type is shown in Fig. 8-23. It contains three curved spirit levels and a magnetic attachment to hold it in place on the wheel hub. It also has a series of templates, each of which is calibrated to apply to certain models of automobile. Figure 8-23 shows the tester attached to the wheel hub with a template in position above the tester, ready to be placed down over the four screw studs. Figure 8-24 shows how the tester looks when held in the hand ready for installation on a wheel hub.

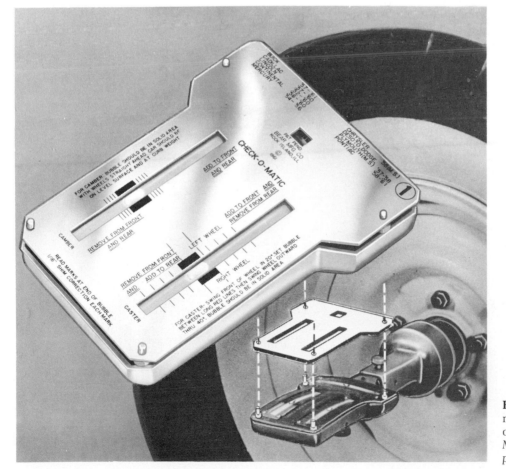

Fig. 8-23. Wheel-alignment tester used to check camber and caster. (*Bear Manufacturing Company*)

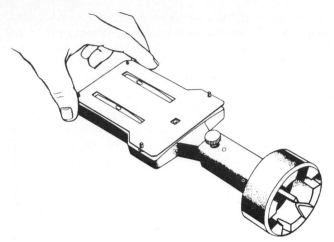

Fig. 8-24. Wheel-alignment tester used to check camber and caster. The tester is shown ready for installation on the wheel hub. (*Bear Manufacturing Company*)

To use the tester, roll the car forward until the front wheels are centered on the turning-radius gauges (Fig. 8-25). Turning-radius gauges are a part of wheel-alignment racks and are also available separtely. Their purpose is to measure the number of degrees that a front wheel is turned in or out as the steering wheel is turned.

With the front wheels straight ahead, remove the hub and the dust cap, wipe off excess grease from the end of the spindle, and clean the face of the wheel hub. Install the brake-pedal depressor so that the brake pedal is held down to lock all four wheels. Make sure all tires are inflated to the proper pressure.

Select the template for the make and model of car being checked. Put it on the four stud screws (Fig. 8-23). Install the tester on the wheel hub (Fig.

8-25), centering it on the spindle with the centering pin so that it is horizontal, as shown by the bubble being centered in the small window closest to the wheel hub.

a. Checking Camber Camber can now be checked by noting the location of the camber bubble. It should lie entirely within the solid area of the camber scale (Fig. 8-26). If the bubble is not entirely within the solid area, the amount that lies outside will determine the amount and direction of adjustment required. For example, if the end of the bubble lies two graduations, or marks, outside the solid area, this means that, on cars adjusted by shims, the camber adjustment must be changed by two $\frac{1}{16}$-inch [1.59 mm] shims. If the bubble is on one side, the shims must be added; if on the other, they must be removed. ⊘ 8-9 describes camber adjustments.

b. Checking Caster With the tester in place and the wheel straight ahead, set the turning-radius gauge to zero. Turn the wheel in (front of wheel moving in) until the turning-radius gauge reads 20 degrees. With the thumbscrew, adjust the caster level until the bubble lies squarely between the two long red crosslines on the caster scale. Now turn the wheel back in the opposite direction, stopping it when the turning-radius gauge reads 20 degrees (this is a 40-degree total swing). Now the entire bubble should lie in the solid area on the left side of the caster scale when the left wheel is being checked (Fig. 8-27). It should lie entirely in the solid area at the right side of the caster side when the right wheel is being checked (Fig. 8-28).

If the bubble is not properly located, the amount and direction that it is off indicate the amount and direction of correction that need to be made. ⊘ 8-9 describes caster adjustment.

2. *RIM-MOUNTED SPIRIT-LEVEL TYPE* This

Fig. 8-25. Front wheel on a turning-radius gauge with the alignment tester attached to the wheel hub. (*Bear Manufacturing Company*)

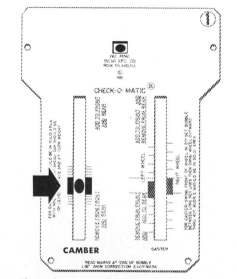

Fig. 8-26. If camber is correct, the bubble will lie entirely within the solid area of the camber scale. (*Bear Manufacturing Company*)

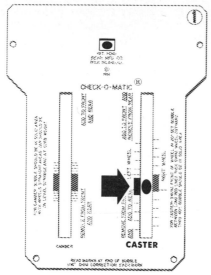

Fig. 8-27. If caster is correct at the left wheel, the bubble will lie entirely within the solid area of the left caster scale. (*Bear Manufacturing Company*)

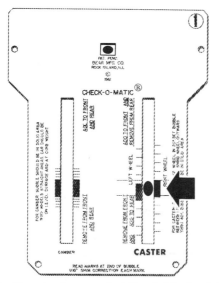

Fig. 8-28. If caster is correct at the right wheel, the bubble will lie entirely within the solid area of the right caster scale. (*Bear Manufacturing Company*)

alignment gauge mounts on the wheel rim, as shown in Fig. 8-29. After being mounted, the spirit level and attached pointer are adjusted until the bubble is centered. The pointer then indicates on the scale the number of camber or caster degrees. The checking procedures are similar to those outlined above for the hub-mounted alignment gauge.

3. LIGHT-BEAM TYPE There are several variations of the light-beam type of alignment checker. Figure 8-30 shows one of these, the ramp type. It has a ramp on which the car must be driven for checking. (There are also the pit type and the lift type.) The system includes two light projectors, one on each side, plus screens straight ahead hung in shadow boxes for easier viewing. In addition, there

are two turntables, or turning-radius gauges, on which the front wheels rest, as well as gauges to mount on the wheel rims. Figure 8-31 shows the system in operation, checking the right front wheel. The principle of the system is this: A light inside the projector is directed to a mirror on the wheel-mounted gauge. It passes through aiming lenses and then strikes the screen ahead of the car. The position of the spot or lines of light indicates the camber and caster angles. Checking procedures are similar to those outlined above for the hub-mounted alignment gauge.

4. FLOOR-ROLLER TYPE The floor-roller alignment tester, one of the newer devices for checking front-end alignment, is shown in Figs. 8-32 to 8-34. Figure 8-32 shows a car on the aligner, being tested. Figure 8-33 shows the rollers on which the wheels ride. There is a pair of rollers for each wheel. Each roller pair is free to tilt sideways and also swing through the horizontal plane. In operation, the rollers are driven so the wheel spins. As it spins, it assumes normal operating position. The rollers align with the wheel, and their position is sensed and reported to the console (Fig. 8-34). The console contains solid-state circuits with computerized read-out meters, as shown. These meters report camber and caster of both wheels. Note that pushing the control buttons and turning the steering wheel are the only operations required (see Fig. 8-32). The tester checks not only caster and camber, but also toe-in.

Fig. 8-29. Camber-caster gauge mounted on a right front wheel. (*Ammco Tools, Inc.*)

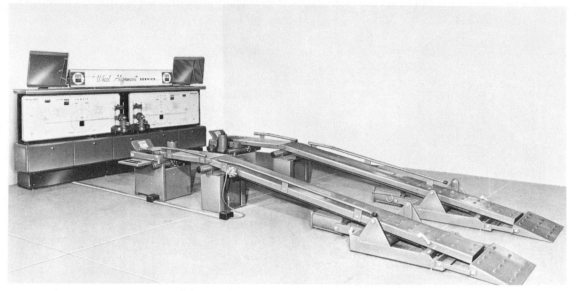

Fig. 8-30. Ramp type of front-alignment checker which uses beams of light. (*Hunter Engineering Company*)

⊘ **8-9 Caster and Camber Adjustments** Some cars have eccentric pins, or bushings, which are rotated to move the upper or lower control arm and thus change caster and camber. Other cars have shim-type adjustments of caster and camber. The locations of the shims on one car are shown in Fig. 3-30. The shims are located between the upper-control-arm shaft (or pivot shaft) and the frame bracket. When shims are added or removed from between the shaft and the frame bracket, the upper control arm is moved in relation to the frame. This changes the position of the upper ball joint and thus the caster and camber. Another adjustment method requires changing the effective length of the strut rod

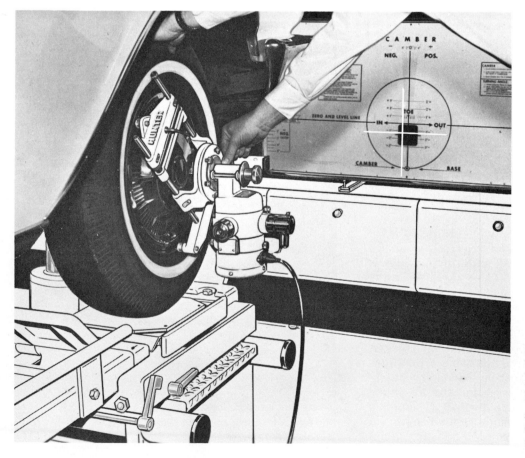

Fig. 8-31. Adjusting the wheel gauge to make a wheel-alignment check. Note the horizontal and vertical lines of light shining on the screen. (*Hunter Engineering Company*)

Fig. 8-32. Dynamic wheel-alignment tester. With this tester, you can check camber, caster, and toe-in in 1 minute. (*Hunter Engineering Company*)

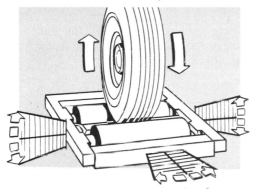

Fig. 8-33. The principle of the dynamic wheel-alignment tester shown in Fig. 8-32. The spinning rollers are free to move up, down, or sideways, as shown by the arrows. (*Hunter Engineering Company*)

Fig. 8-34. The console for the dynamic wheel-alignment tester. The meters report the alignment conditions at the wheels. (*Hunter Engineering Company*)

attached to the lower arm, thus moving the end of the arm back or forward. Also, some cars have an eccentric bushing in which the upper ball stud mounts. This bushing can be turned in its upper-arm mounting to move the ball joint in or out to change the camber. In addition, many cars have elongated bolt holes for attaching the upper-arm inner shaft to the frame. The bolts are loosened so the upper-arm shaft can be moved to change camber and caster. These various adjustment methods are described below.

1. SHIM ADJUSTMENTS Figures 8-35 and 8-36 show the locations of the shims on many makes of car. Note that on some cars, the shims are inside the frame bracket (Fig. 8-35). On others, the shims are outside the frame bracket (Fig. 8-36). When the shims and shaft are *inside* the frame bracket (Fig. 8-35), adding shims will move the upper control arm inward and thus bring the top of the wheel inward. This *decreases* positive camber. On the other hand, when the shims and upper-control-arm shaft are *outside* the frame bracket (Fig. 8-36), adding shims will move the upper control arm outward and thus tilt the wheel outward more to *increase* the positive camber.

Caster is changed by adding shims at one of the upper-control-arm attachment bolts and removing shims from the other. Refer again to Fig. 8-35. If a shim is taken away at the front attachment bolt (the upper bolt in the picture) and added at the rear bolt, the outer end of the upper control arm will be shifted forward. Thus, positive caster will be decreased. Remember that positive caster is the *backward* tilt of the steering axis (ball-joint center lines) from the vertical.

To sum it all up, caster and camber adjustments are made by loosening the shaft attachment bolts and installing or removing the correct number of shims. The alignment tester will indicate how far off the camber and caster angles are and thus the

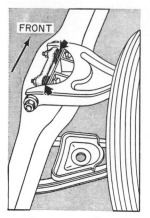

Fig. 8-35. Location of caster- and camber-adjusting shims (indicated by heavy arrows). Note that the shims and upper-control-arm shaft are inside the frame bracket. (*Bear Manufacturing Company*)

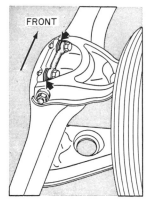

Fig. 8-36. Location of caster- and camber-adjusting shims (indicated by heavy arrows). Note that the shims and upper-control-arm shaft are outside the frame bracket. (*Bear Manufacturing Company*)

amount of correction (number of shims) to add or subtract.

2. ADJUSTMENTS WITH CAMS A variety of eccentric bushing, or pin, arrangements have been used to provide camber and caster adjustment of the front wheels. One widely used method, found on many late-model Chrysler Corporation cars, is illustrated in Fig. 8-37. The two bushings at the inner end of the upper control arm are attached to the frame brackets by two attachment bolt and cam assemblies. When these cam assemblies are turned, the camber and caster are changed.

If both cam assemblies are turned the same amount and in the same direction, the control arm is moved in or out to change the camber. If only one cam is turned, or if the two are turned in opposite directions, the outer end of the control arm is shifted back or forward to change the caster.

To make the adjustments, after the direction and type of correction needed are determined, the bolt nuts are loosened and the cam bolts are turned. Caster should be adjusted first. Then, camber is

adjusted by turning both cam bolts the same amount.

NOTE: One complete rotation of a cam bolt represents the full amount of possible adjustment.

CAUTION: Always recheck the final caster and camber settings after retightening the cam-bolt nuts.

3. ADJUSTMENT BY SHIFTING INNER SHAFT
This system uses elongated holes in the frame at the two points where the inner shaft is attached (Fig. 8-38). Thus, if the attaching bolts are loosened and the inner shaft shifted inward or outward, the caster and camber are changed because this movement will move the upper arm. First, however, special alignment spacers must be installed at both front wheels, as shown in Fig. 8-39. To do this, lift the car enough to allow the spacers to be placed between the lower arms and the frame spring pocket, as shown. Then, when the car is lowered so it rests on the wheels, the proper curb height is established by the spacers. Adjust caster and camber by shifting the inner shaft with a special tool after loosening the shaft attaching bolts. For some cars, the tool shown in Fig. 8-40 is used. For others, the tool shown in Fig. 8-41 is used. If both ends of the inner shaft are moved in or out together, the camber is changed. But if only one end is moved, the caster is changed. You can see that this is very similar to installing or removing shims as in the type adjusted with shims. After making the adjustment tighten the attaching bolts and check the adjustment again. Then, if it is okay, remove the spacers (Fig. 8-39).

4. ADJUSTMENT WITH STRUT ROD AND CAM
This arrangement (Fig. 8-42) shortens or lengthens the strut rod to change the caster angle. When the strut rod is shortened, for example (by turning the nuts at the front of the rod), the outer end of the

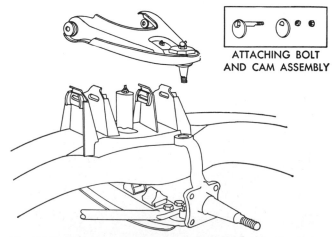

Fig. 8-37. The upper control arm is attached to the frame brackets by two bolt and cam assemblies so that the two attachment bushings can be shifted back and forth for caster and camber adjustments. (*Bear Manufacturing Company*)

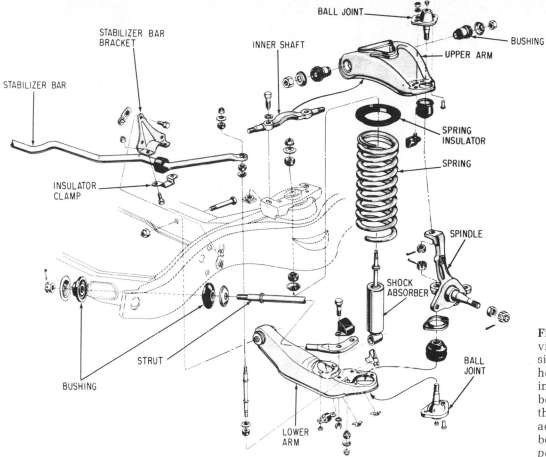

Fig. 8-38. Disassembled view of a front suspension having elongated holes in the frame. The inner-shaft attaching bolts can be shifted in the elongated holes to adjust caster and camber. (*Ford Motor Company*)

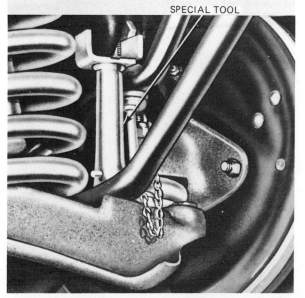

Fig. 8-39. Alignment spacer (special tool) installed at the front. (*Ford Motor Company*)

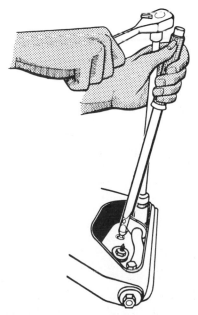

Fig. 8-40. Adjusting caster and camber with the special tool that shifts the inner shaft in or out. (*Ammco Tools, Inc.*)

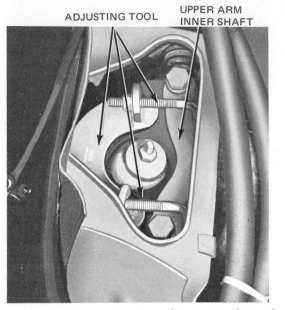

ADJUSTING TOOL   UPPER ARM INNER SHAFT

Fig. 8-41. Camber and caster adjusting tool in place. Tightening or loosening the hooks moves the inner shaft to make the adjustment. (*Ford Motor Company*)

lower control arm is pulled forward, thus increasing the caster.

Camber is adjusted by turning the cams on which the inner end of the lower control arm is mounted (Fig. 8-42). This action moves the lower control arm in or out to change the camber.

5. ADJUSTMENT WITH ECCENTRIC PIVOT PIN
On this older system, the upper control arm is attached to the upper end of the steering-knuckle support by an eccentric pivot pin. Caster and camber are adjusted together by turning the upper-control-arm pivot pin with an allen wrench (Fig. 8-43). The pivot pin changes both the caster and the camber of the wheel when it is turned. Both ends of the pivot pin are threaded in the front and rear bushings in the upper control arm. Thus, when the pivot pin is turned with an allen wrench, the pin and upper end of the steering-knuckle support are shifted backward or forward with respect to the upper control arm. This causes the kingpin to tilt backward or forward to change the caster angle. Change of the camber is effected by an eccentric section of the pivot pin on which the upper end of the steering-knuckle support pivots. As the pivot pin is turned with an allen wrench, this eccentric center section rotates, moving the upper end of the steering-knuckle support in toward, or out away from, the car. This moves the top of the wheel in to decrease,

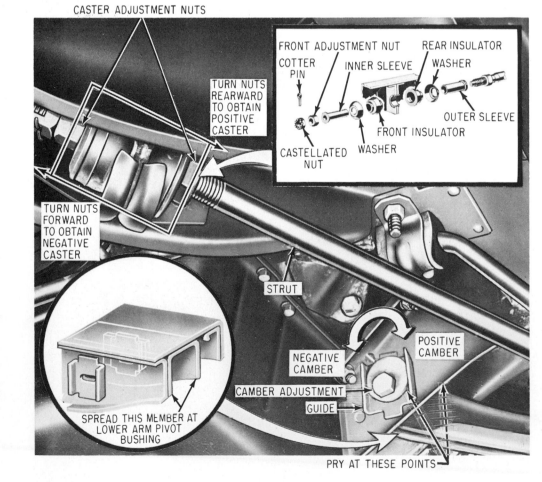

Fig. 8-42. Caster and camber adjustments on the Cougar, Fairlane, Falcon, Montego, and Mustang. (*Ford Motor Company*)

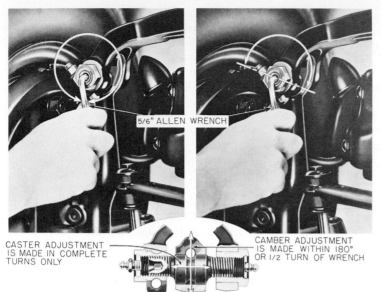

CASTER ADJUSTMENT IS MADE IN COMPLETE TURNS ONLY

5/6" ALLEN WRENCH

CAMBER ADJUSTMENT IS MADE WITHIN 180° OR 1/2 TURN OF WRENCH

Fig. 8-43. Adjusting caster and camber by turning the pivot pin. (*Cadillac Motor Car Division of General Motors Corporation*)

or out to increase, the camber. One rotation of the pivot pin represents the full range of camber adjustment. The adjustment procedure, in detail, follows:

1. Loosen the clamp bolt at the top of the steering-knuckle support (Fig. 8-43).
2. Remove the lubrication fitting from the upper front pivot-pin bushing.
3. Use an allen wrench and turn the pivot pin clockwise to increase the caster or counterclockwise to decrease the caster. If the pin is turned one or more full turns, the eccentric will always be brought back to the same position to provide the same camber angle.
4. To change camber, turn the pivot pin only part of a turn. If the caster angle has been adjusted to the approximately correct value, adjusting the camber by turning the pivot pin a part turn will change the caster angle slightly but not enough to throw the caster angle out of specifications.
5. Recheck caster and camber adjustments and, if they are correct, tighten the clamp bolt and install the lubrication fitting.
6. *ADJUSTMENT BY STRUT ROD AND STEERING-KNUCKLE ECCENTRIC* With this system, caster is adjusted by shortening or lengthening the strut rod that is attached between the frame and the outer end of the lower control arm. Camber is adjusted by turning an eccentric bushing in the upper end of the steering knuckle. The ball joint mounts in this steering knuckle, and it can be shifted back and forth by turning the eccentric bushing to change the camber.
7. *OTHER ADJUSTMENT METHODS* Several other adjustment methods have been used. Essentially, all are similar in that the adjustments move the control-arm attachments in such a way as to alter the caster and camber angles.

On the solid, or I-beam, front axle, camber and kingpin-inclination-angle adjustment must be made by bending the axle with special correction tools.

Caster adjustments can be made by inserting wedge-shaped shims between the spring seat on the axle and the spring or by use of correction tools that bend the axle. Figure 8-44 illustrates the use of a correction tool to decrease the caster on the right side. This tool merely twists the axle slightly to correct the caster. Figure 8-45 illustrates the use of a correction tool to correct the camber and kingpin-inclination angles. This tool slightly bends the axle

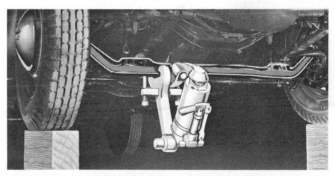

Fig. 8-44. Correcting tool being used to decrease caster on the right side. (*Chevrolet Motor Division of General Motors Corporation*)

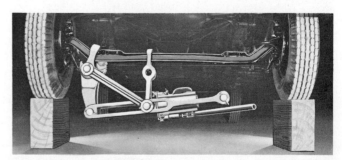

Fig. 8-45. Correcting tool being used to adjust camber and kingpin inclination. (*Chevrolet Motor Division of General Motors Corporation*)

to make the correction. Correction can be made by this method only when both camber and kingpin inclination are off the same amount. When one is off more than the other, the wheel spindle is bent and should be replaced; in addition, the axle may require bending to bring the two angles within specifications.

CAUTION: The I beam should be replaced if any amount of bending is required, because the chances are that a significant distortion of the I beam has caused invisible cracks or weakening of the beam. Such an I beam is unsafe to use.

⊘ 8-10 Toe-in Toe-in is the amount, in fractions of an inch, that the front wheels point inward. It is measured in various ways, but the adjustment procedure is similar on all cars. One method of measurement, recommended by the Bear Manufacturing Company, uses the dynamic-alignment tester (Fig. 8-22). After the camber and caster have been checked and adjusted, the front wheels are driven slowly across the tester in the straight-ahead position (hands off steering wheel). Because other factors have already been adjusted, the only factor that affects the tester reading is the amount of toe-in of the front wheels.

Figure 8-46 shows a typical steering linkage. To adjust the toe-in, change the effective lengths of the two tie rods by loosening the clamp bolts on the adjustment sleeves and turning the sleeves as required. The sleeves and the matching ends of the rod and tie-rod end have right-hand and left-hand threads. Thus, turning the sleeve one direction increases the effective length of a tie rod, and turning the sleeve the other direction shortens the length.

Adjustment of the sleeves can also affect the steering-wheel position in straight-ahead driving.

For example, if both sleeves are turned in the same direction and the same amount, the toe-in will remain unchanged but the steering-wheel position will be changed (see ⊘ 8-12).

A very accurate method of checking toe-in makes use of gauge bars that measure the distance between the backs and fronts of the tires. The difference between the two is due to toe-in. A tester of this type is shown in Fig. 8-47. To use the tester, drive the front wheels onto turning-radius gauges, and attach the parallel bars to the front-wheel spindles (Fig. 8-48). Level the parallel bars (with the use of their built-in spirit levels). Then attach the gauge bar to the parallel bars at the back, behind the wheels (Fig. 8-49). Set the reading on the scale to zero, as shown. Next, transfer the gauge bar to the front of the parallel bars and note the reading on the scale (Fig. 8-50).

A somewhat simpler toe-in gauge is shown in Fig. 8-51. To use this gauge, mark the centerlines of the tires with chalk and roll the car ahead to settle the linkage in the running position. Then measure the distance between the two centerlines accurately with the gauge at the back of the tires, hub high. Next, roll the car forward until the two points that have been measured come around to the front, hub high. Now measure them with the gauge at the front of the tires. The difference between the two measurements is the toe-in.

The floor-roller type of alignment tester (Figs. 8-32 to 8-34) reads off the toe-in along with caster and camber. No separate check is required to measure toe-in when this tester is used.

⊘ 8-11 Steering-Axis Inclination and Toe-out on Turns These two factors, described in ⊘ 5-4 and 5-8, are not adjustable. They are, however, factors to be checked during an alignment job. If they are not within specifications after the camber and caster

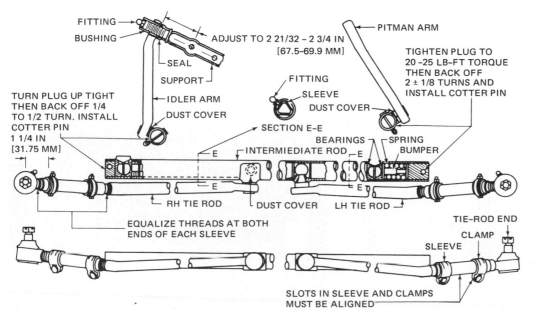

Fig. 8-46. Typical steering linkage, showing attaching arrangements for linkage and adjusting points. (*Bear Manufacturing Company*)

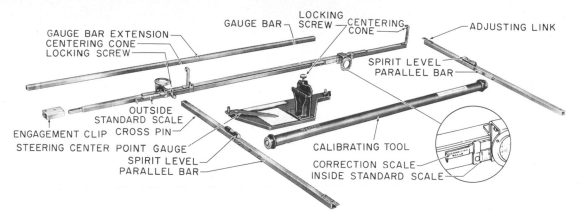

GAUGE BAR EXTENSION
CENTERING CONE
LOCKING SCREW
GAUGE BAR
LOCKING SCREW
CENTERING CONE
CENTERING CONE
ADJUSTING LINK
SPIRIT LEVEL
PARALLEL BAR
OUTSIDE STANDARD SCALE
ENGAGEMENT CLIP
CROSS PIN
STEERING CENTER POINT GAUGE
SPIRIT LEVEL
PARALLEL BAR
CALIBRATING TOOL
CORRECTION SCALE
INSIDE STANDARD SCALE

Fig. 8-47. Toe-in gauge parts, placed in the approximate positions in which they are used on the car. (*Weaver Manufacturing Division of Dura Corporation*)

Fig. 8-48. Attaching the parallel bar to the left front-wheel spindle. (*Weaver Manufacturing Division of Dura Corporation*)

Fig. 8-50. Attaching the gauge bar to the parallel bars in front of the wheels. (*Weaver Manufacturing Division of Dura Corporation*)

Fig. 8-49. Attaching the gauge bar to the parallel bars behind the wheels. (*Weaver Manufacturing Division of Dura Corporation*)

Fig. 8-51. Toe-in gauge for measuring the toe-in of front wheels. (*Bear Manufacturing Company*)

Front-End Alignment 145

are adjusted to specifications, then wheel-supporting parts or steering arm is bent.

Toe-out on turns is easily checked by rolling the front wheels onto turning-radius gauges (Fig. 8-25). Then turn the steering wheel until one front wheel is angled at 20 degrees, and measure the amount of turning of the other wheel on the other turning-radius gauge. A typical specification, for late-model Fords, is that with power steering, when the inside wheel (the left wheel in a left turn, for example) is turned 20 degrees, the outside wheel should be turned 17° (degrees) 30′ (minutes) (17°21′ with manual steering).

If the toe-out is not correct, it means that a steering arm is bent and must be replaced. Then, front alignment must be rechecked.

CAUTION: Never attempt to straighten a bent steering or suspension part! This could weaken the part to the point where it might break in operation and cause a serious accident.

Steering-axis (or kingpin) inclination is checked with a tester attached to the wheel spindle as shown in Fig. 8-52. It is leveled until the bubble in the steering-axis-inclination scale is at zero. Then, camber and caster should be checked as already explained for another tester (⊘ 8-8). Camber is read directly from the camber scale on the face plate. Caster is checked by turning the wheel 20 degrees in (as measured on the turning-radius gauge). Then the caster spirit level should be set to zero and the wheels turned 40 degrees so that it is pointed out at a 20-degree angle. Caster can now be read directly from the caster scale.

At the same time that caster is checked, the steering-axis inclination can also be checked. This is done by adjusting the steering-axis-inclination scale so that the bubble is at zero when the wheel is turned in 20 degrees. Then when the wheel is turned out 20 degrees (a total of 40 degrees of turn), the steering-axis-inclination scale will indicate the inclination angle.

If the steering-axis inclination is incorrect but other factors check out okay, the chances are that the spindle is bent and must be replaced.

CAUTION: Never attempt to straighten a bent steering or suspension part! This could so weaken the part that it might fail in service, causing a serious accident.

⊘ **8-12 A Typical Alignment Procedure** Let us review the alignment procedure and at the same time outline the steps required to check and adjust alignment on a typical application.

All the preliminary steps must be taken before the alignment checks start. These include checking tire inflation, wheel bearings, wheel runout, wheel balance, linkages and ball joints for looseness, suspension for height and looseness, shock absorbers, and tracking.

Drive the car forward far enough to establish the straight-ahead position of the front wheels, and then mark the steering-wheel hub and column (Fig. 8-53). This establishes the position that the steering wheel actually takes when the front wheels are pointed straight ahead. If the wheel spokes are not in a balanced position, adjustment will have to be made when the toe-in is adjusted.

Adjust caster and camber as shown in Figs. 8-40 to 8-42. After completing adjustment, tighten the nuts to the proper torque.

Figure 8-54 shows the location and arrangement of one of the two spindle-connecting-rod (tie-rod) sleeves. Figure 8-55 shows how to adjust the sleeves to increase or decrease the rods' effective length.

Figure 8-56 shows the adjustments to be made to get the steering-wheel spokes centered. It is important to center the spokes because this means that the steering gear will then also be centered.

⊘ **8-13 Rear Suspension Alignment** On cars with independent rear suspension such as the Corvette (Fig. 7-71), the wheel alignment should be checked periodically. To do this, back the car onto the ma-

Fig. 8-52. *Left,* alignment gauge attached to the wheel spindle; *right;* leveling the face plate. (*Weaver Manufacturing Division of Dura Corporation*)

ALIGNMENT MARKS

Fig. 8-53. Straight-ahead-position marks. (*Ford Motor Company*)

SPINDLE ARM   SPINDLE CONNECTING ROD

SLEEVE   CLAMP BOLT

Fig. 8-54. Spindle-connecting-rod (tie-rod) sleeve. (*Ford Motor Company*)

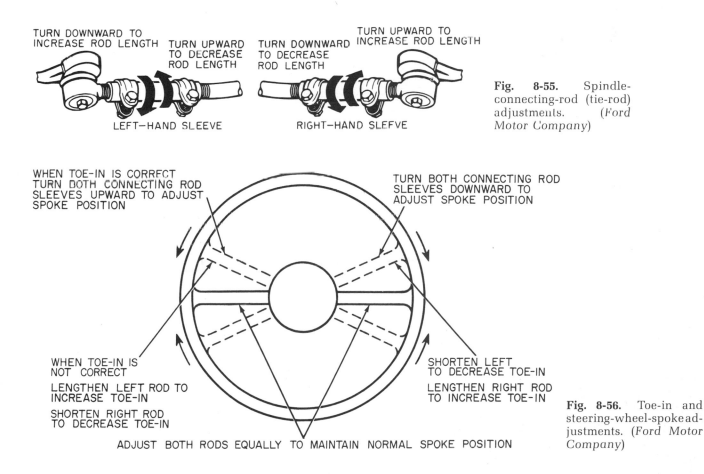

TURN DOWNWARD TO INCREASE ROD LENGTH   TURN UPWARD TO DECREASE ROD LENGTH

LEFT—HAND SLEEVE

TURN DOWNWARD TO DECREASE ROD LENGTH   TURN UPWARD TO INCREASE ROD LENGTH

RIGHT—HAND SLEEVE

Fig. 8-55. Spindle-connecting-rod (tie-rod) adjustments. (*Ford Motor Company*)

WHEN TOE-IN IS CORRECT TURN BOTH CONNECTING ROD SLEEVES UPWARD TO ADJUST SPOKE POSITION

TURN BOTH CONNECTING ROD SLEEVES DOWNWARD TO ADJUST SPOKE POSITION

WHEN TOE-IN IS NOT CORRECT
LENGTHEN LEFT ROD TO INCREASE TOE-IN
SHORTEN RIGHT ROD TO DECREASE TOE-IN

SHORTEN LEFT TO DECREASE TOE-IN
LENGTHEN RIGHT ROD TO INCREASE TOE-IN

ADJUST BOTH RODS EQUALLY TO MAINTAIN NORMAL SPOKE POSITION

Fig. 8-56. Toe-in and steering-wheel-spoke adjustments. (*Ford Motor Company*)

chine that is normally used to align front suspension. Camber will read in the normal manner. But toe-in will now read as toe-out, while toe-out will read as toe-in.

Make sure the strut rods are straight. If they are bent, they should be replaced.

1. CAMBER ADJUSTMENT Adjust camber by turning the eccentric cam and bolt (Fig. 8-57). Loosen the cam-bolt nut and turn the cam-and-bolt assembly to get the correct camber. The location of the cam can be seen in Figs. 3-25 and 7-71. It is shown to the lower right of the differential in these two pictures. Tighten the locknut after making the adjustment.

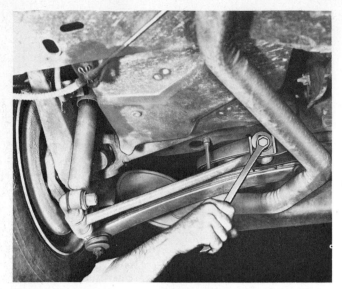

Fig. 8-57. Adjusting rear-wheel camber. (*Chevrolet Motor Division of General Motors Corporation*)

2. TOE-IN ADJUSTMENT Adjust toe-in by inserting shims inside the frame side member on both sides of the torque-control-arm pivot bushing as shown in Fig. 8-58.

CHAPTER 8 CHECKUP

Because automobiles are bigger, heavier, and faster than they used to be, proper front-end alignment is more important than ever. Proper front-end alignment assures maximum steering stability and maneuverability. Thus, you should have a good understanding of the factors involved in front-end alignment and how each of these factors is adjusted. The chapter you have just completed covers the use of three types of alignment-checking devices. The questions in the checkup that follows give you a

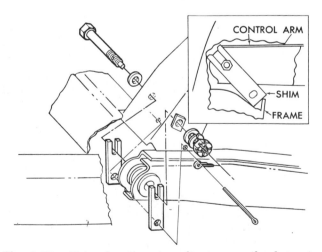

Fig. 8-58. Shim location to adjust rear-wheel toe-in. (*Chevrolet Motor Division of General Motors Corporation*)

chance to check yourself and find out whether you remember the details of how these various devices are used and how alignment adjustments are made. Don't worry if you have trouble with some of the questions. That simply means that you should review the chapter again. Rereading and reviewing the material and then answering the questions will really fix the important facts in your mind so that you won't forget them.

Completing the Sentences The sentences below are incomplete. After each sentence there are several words or phrases, only one of which will correctly complete the sentence. Write each sentence in your notebook, selecting the proper word or phrase to complete it correctly.

1. Before front-wheel alignment is checked, several items should be checked, including tire inflation, bearing condition, and: (*a*) wheel runin, (*b*) wheel runout and balance, (*c*) steering-axis runout, (*d*) toe-in on turns.
2. Weights can be attached to the wheel rim to correct: (*a*) wheel runout, (*b*) wheel turnout, (*c*) wheel balance, (*d*) wheel alignment.
3. Wheels should be checked for balance in two ways: (*a*) statically and at rest, (*b*) statically and dynamically, (*c*) at high speed and at low speed.
4. Wheels must be balanced: (*a*) on the car only, (*b*) either on or off the car, (*c*) off the car only.
5. The dynamic-alignment testers: (*a*) pinpoint the cause of misalignment, (*b*) can be used to check front-end alignment only, (*c*) give an indication of misalignment but do not pinpoint causes.
6. To check caster, camber, and steering-axis inclination, some alignment testers use: (*a*) turning-radius gauges, (*b*) level-measuring devices, (*c*) tester plates.
7. One device which measures camber and caster is: (*a*) attached to the front-wheel spindle, (*b*) attached to the rear-wheel spindle, (*c*) hung between the two front wheels.
8. When caster is checked, the front wheels: (*a*) must not be moved, (*b*) must be turned a total of 20 degrees, (*c*) must be turned a total of 40 degrees.
9. With shim-type adjustment, camber is adjusted by adding or removing the same number of shims at: (*a*) both shim locations, (*b*) only one shim location, (*c*) the lower-control-arm shaft.
10. Removing shims at one of the control-arm attachment bolts and adding shims at the other adjusts: (*a*) caster, (*b*) camber, (*c*) toe-in.
11. On the type of suspension system with a single inner support for the lower control arm, changing the length of the strut rod between the lower control arm and the frame: (*a*) changes camber, (*b*) adjusts toe-in, (*c*) changes caster.
12. Toe-in is adjusted by: (*a*) adding or removing shims, (*b*) changing the effective length of the tie rods, (*c*) changing the effective length of the strut rods.
13. Toe-out on turns: (*a*) is adjusted by shims, (*b*) is

adjusted by changing the effective length of the tie rods, (c) cannot be adjusted.

14. If one of the steering arms is found to be bent, (a) straighten it, (b) discard both steering arms, (c) discard it.

15. If all other factors in the suspension and steering system check out okay but the toe-out on turns is incorrect, chances are that: (a) a steering arm is bent, (b) the tie rods are bent, (c) the toe-in needs readjustment.

Servicing Procedures In taking the following test, write in your notebook the procedures asked for. Do not copy from the book; write in your own words, the way you would explain it to another person. Thinking out and then writing down the procedure is a fine way to fix the procedure in your mind.

1. List the preliminary checks and corrections to be made before the front wheels are aligned.

2. How are wheels checked for balance, and how are corrections made?

3. Explain how to check and adjust caster and camber on cars with shim-type adjustments.

4. Explain how to check steering-axis inclination. What should be done if steering-axis inclination is incorrect?

5. Explain how to check and adjust toe-in.

6. Explain how the location of the shims and the upper-control-arm shaft affects the caster and camber adjustments.

7. Explain how to check and adjust camber and caster on cars with eccentric bushings or cams.

8. Explain how to check and adjust caster on cars with a strut rod between the lower control arm and the frame.

9. Explain how to adjust caster and camber on the solid, or I-beam, axle.

10. What should be done if toe-out on turns is incorrect?

SUGGESTIONS FOR FURTHER STUDY

Because of the increasing importance of proper front-end alignment—due to heavier cars and higher speeds—a variety of alignment-checking devices have become available in recent years. Only three types of devices were covered in the chapter; there are other types. It may be that you can find other alignment-checking devices in your school shop or in an automotive service shop. If you can, see how they are used. If possible, study the instruction manual issued by the equipment manufacturer. Notice how the various factors in front-end alignment are checked and adjusted on different automobiles. Be sure to write important facts in your notebook.

chapter 9

MANUAL-STEERING-GEAR SERVICE

This chapter explains how to check, adjust, and repair various types of manually operated steering gears used on passenger cars. Chapter 6 describes trouble-diagnosis methods for determining the causes of different steering and suspension troubles. Following sections discuss the adjustments and repairs required to eliminate causes of trouble in manually operated steering gears. Following chapters describe power-steering checks, adjustments, and repairs.

⊘ **9-1 Steering-Gear Adjustments** As noted in Chap. 5, a variety of manual steering-gear designs have been used on automobiles. All have two basic adjustments: one for taking up the worm-gear and steering-shaft end play and the other for removing backlash between the worm and the sector (or roller or lever studs). In addition, some designs have a means of adjusting the sector-shaft (pitman-arm-shaft) end play.

Before attempting to adjust a steering gear to take up excessive end play or to relieve binding, make sure the condition is not the result of faulty alignment or of wear in some other component of the linkage or front suspension. Adjustment and repair procedures on various manual-steering gears follow.

⊘ **9-2 Saginaw (General Motors) Steering-Gear Service** The Saginaw manual steering gear, used on General Motor cars since 1961, is shown in sectional view in Fig. 9-1 and exterior view in Fig. 9-2. This steering gear is filled at the factory with steering-gear lubricant. No lubrication is required for the life of the steering gear. This means that it should never be drained and refilled with lubricant if it continues to operate normally. However, the gear should be inspected every 36,000 miles [57,936 km] for leakage (actual solid grease, not just oily film). If a seal is replaced or the gear is overhauled, the housing should be filled with the specific lubricant called for by General Motors. *Do not overfill!*

Adjustment will be required if the steering is too loose (too much lash) or too tight (requiring too much turning effort). Before any adjustment is made, however, be sure that all other front-end factors are up to specifications. Check tires, wheel balance, front-end-alignment, steering linkage, and shock absorbers, and make any corrections that are required. Then steering-gear adjustments can be made.

⊘ **9-3 Saginaw Steering Gear Adjustments** Two adjustments can be made: pitman-shaft lash and worm-shaft bearing end play (see Fig. 9-2). Follow this sequence.

1. Disconnect the battery ground cable. Raise the car. Remove the pitman-arm nut and mark the relationship of the pitman arm to the pitman shaft.
2. Remove the pitman arm with the special tool as shown in Fig. 9-3.
3. Loosen the lash-adjuster-screw locknut and back off the screw ¼ turn.
4. Measure the worm-shaft-bearing drag with a spring scale. On earlier models, the procedure was to hook the spring scale to the steering wheel as shown in Fig. 9-4. On later models, the instructions are to remove the horn button or shroud and use a ¾-inch [19 mm] socket on a torque wrench, as shown in Fig. 9-5, to measure the torque required.

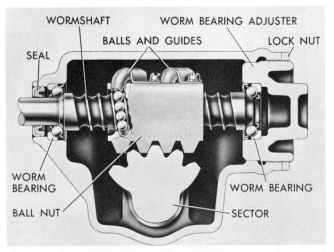

Fig. 9-1. Sectional view of the Saginaw (General Motors) recirculating-ball-and-nut manual-steering gear. (*Chevrolet Motor Division of General Motors Corporation*)

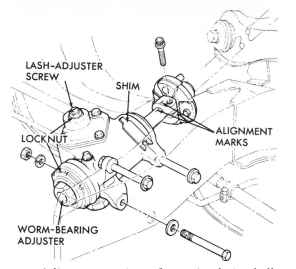

Fig. 9-2. Adjustment points of a recirculating-ball-and-nut manual-steering gear. (*Chevrolet Motor Division of General Motors Corporation*)

In either case, take the measurement with the steering gear centered. Do this by turning the steering wheel *gently* in one direction until it is stopped by the gear. Turn it all the way to the other extreme, counting the turns. Then turn the wheel back exactly one-half of the total turns.

CAUTION: Do not turn the steering wheel hard against the stops. This could damage the steering gear.

5. If the pull or torque is not correct, adjust the worm bearings. Loosen the worm-bearing-adjuster locknut and turn the worm-bearing adjuster to ob-

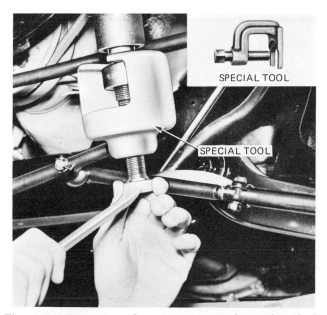

Fig. 9-3. Removing the pitman arm from the shaft. (*Chevrolet Motor Division of General Motors Corporation*)

Fig. 9-4. Measuring the pull at the steering wheel required to keep the wheel in motion. (*Chevrolet Motor Division of General Motors Corporation*)

tain the proper bearing preload (pull or torque on wheel). Then tighten the locknut and recheck the pull or torque.

NOTE: If the gear feels "lumpy" or rough after adjustment, chances are that there is damage in the bearings which will require disassembly of the gear for replacement of the defective parts.

6. Check the pitman-shaft lash, also called the *over-center preload*, with the steering wheel centered, as

Fig. 9-5. Using a torque wrench to measure the turning effort of the steering wheel. (*Chevrolet Motor Division of General Motors Corporation*)

explained above. Then, turn in the lash-adjuster screw to take up all lash between the ball nut and pitman-shaft sector gear. Next tighten the locknut. Now check the pull on the steering wheel, or torque (Figs. 9-4 and 9-5) as the wheel is turned through the center position. Adjust, if necessary, by loosening the locknut and readjusting the lash-adjuster screw.

NOTE: If you go above the maximum specification, back off the screw and then come back up on adjustment by turning the adjuster locknut in.

7. Reassemble the pitman arm to the pitman shaft, lining up the marks made during disassembly. Tighten the pitman shaft nut to specifications. If you removed the horn button cap or shroud, replace it.

⊘ **9-4 Saginaw Steering-Gear Overhaul** Figure 9-1 is a sectional view of the Saginaw steering gear discussed in this section. Figure 9-6 is a disassembled view of the steering gear.

1. REMOVAL Raise the car so that you can get under it conveniently. Disconnect the pitman arm from the shaft as already described (⊘ 9-3 and Fig. 9-3). Remove the splash-pan attachment bolts and the pan. Remove the nuts and lock washers from the steering-gear attachment bolts and take out the bolts (and shims, where present). The steering gear is now loose from the frame and can be taken off the car as soon as the gear is detached from the intermediate shaft. This is done by loosening the bolt on the lower universal-joint clamp.

2. DISASSEMBLY Clamp one of the steering-gear mounting tabs in a vise with the worm shaft hori-

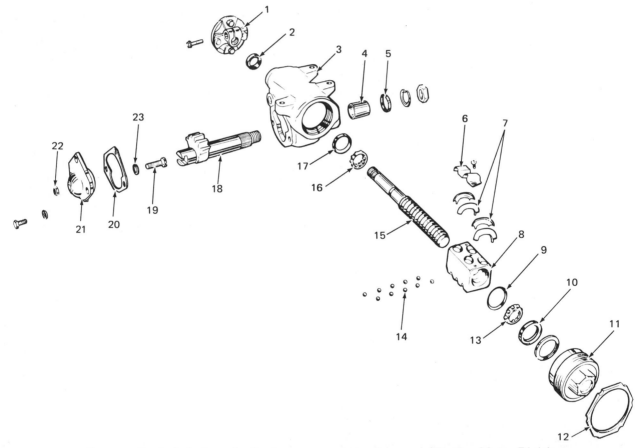

Fig. 9-6. Exploded view of a Saginaw manual-steering gear. (*Pontiac Motor Division of General Motors Corporation*)

1. Coupling and lower flange
2. Seal
3. Housing
4. Bushing
5. Seal
6. Clamp
7. Guide
8. Ball nut
9. Retainer
10. Bearing race
11. Adjuster
12. Locknut
13. Bearing
14. Balls
15. Worm shaft
16. Bearing
17. Bearing race
18. Shaft and sector
19. Screw, lash adjuster
20. Gasket
21. Cover
22. Locknut
23. Shims, lash adjuster

zontal. Rotate the worm shaft from one extreme to the other and then turn it back exactly halfway so the gear is centered. Now, loosen the locknut and back off the lash-adjuster screw (Fig. 9-2) several turns. Then loosen the locknut and back off the worm-bearing adjuster a few turns.

Put a pan under the unit to catch the lubricant. Remove the three bolts and washers attaching the side cover to the housing (Fig. 9-7). Pull the side cover with the pitman (sector) shaft from the housing. If the sector does not clear the housing opening, turn the worm shaft by hand until it does.

Remove the worm-bearing adjuster, locknut, and lower ball bearing from the housing. Then draw the worm shaft and nut from the housing (Fig. 9-8). Remove the upper ball bearing.

CAUTION: Do not allow the ball nut to run down to either end of the worm. This could damage the ends of the ball guides.

Unscrew the lash-adjuster locknut and adjuster from the side cover and slide the adjuster and its shim from the slot in the end of the sector shaft. Pry out and discard the pitman shaft and worn shaft seals from the housing.

Do not disassemble the ball nut unless it is tight, binds, or runs roughly up and down the worm. In such cases, disassemble it by removing the screw and clamp-retaining ball guides in the nut and pull the guides from the nut. Turn the nut upside down and rotate the worm shaft back and forth until all the balls have fallen out of the nut. Have a clean pan handy in which to catch the balls. Now, the nut can be slid off the worm.

3. INSPECTION Carefully inspect the ball bearings, balls, bearing cups, worm, and nut for signs of wear, dents, cracks, chipping, etc. Replace any part that shows signs of wear or damage. Check the fit

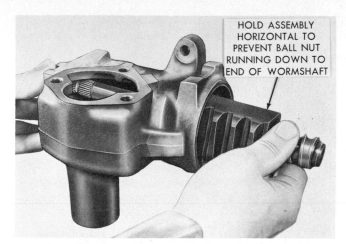

Fig. 9-8. Removing the worm shaft and ball nut. (*Chevrolet Motor Division of General Motors Corporation*)

of the sector shaft in the bushing. Examine the bushing in the side cover; if this bushing is worn, replace the side cover and bushing as an assembly. Examine the ends of the ball guides; if they are bent or damaged, replace the guides.

4. REPAIRS Replace the sector-shaft bushing in the housing by pressing out the old bushing with an arbor press and a special tool and pressing in the new bushing. New bushings are already bored to size and need no reaming.

Replace the worm-shaft seal if necessary. Always replace the sector-shaft packing whenever the steering gear is torn down. If the worm-shaft bearing cup in the bearing adjuster requires replacement, remove it with a special tool (Fig. 9-9) and press a new cup into place.

5. REASSEMBLY Adjustment procedures are as follows:

a. *Ball Nut* The model of steering gear used on most General Motors cars has ball guides with holes in the top through which all balls can be installed (Fig. 9-10). Twenty balls go into each guide. The worm must be turned back and forth to get the balls to run down into the circuits and fill them. Before assembly, the worm and the inside of the nut should be coated with steering-

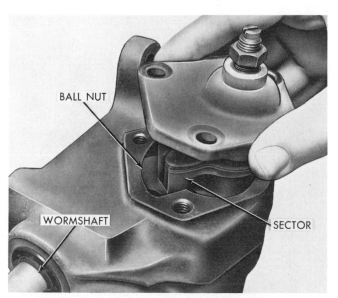

Fig. 9-7. Removing the pitman-shaft assembly. (*Chevrolet Motor Division of General Motors Corporation*)

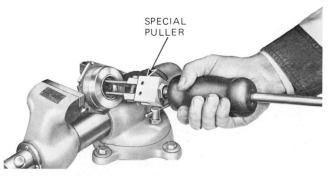

Fig. 9-9. Using a special puller to remove the bearing cup from the adjuster. (*Chevrolet Motor Division of General Motors Corporation*)

Fig. 9-10. Installing balls in the ball nut through holes in the ball guides. (*Chevrolet Motor Division of General Motors Corporation*)

gear lubrication. When the balls are all in place, the guide clamp should be attached with screws.

On some Saginaw steering gears, there are no holes in the ball guides, and a different method of installing the balls is required. On these, some of the balls must be installed in the nut circuits before the guides are put into place. This is done by slipping the nut over the worm with the ball holes up and the shallow end of the rack teeth to the left (from the steering-wheel position). Align the worm and nut grooves by looking into a ball hole. Count out 27 balls. Start feeding balls into one of the guide holes and turning the worm away from this hole at the same time. Continue until the circuit is filled in the nut. Then lay one-half of the ball guide down, groove up, and put the rest of the 27 balls into it. Put the other half of the guide on top and plug the two ends with petroleum jelly so that the balls will not fall out. Push the guide into place in the ball holes. Tap it down if necessary with the wooden handle of a screwdriver. Fill the other ball circuit in the nut the same way. Install the guide clamp. Check the assembly by rotating the worm to make sure that the nut can move freely from one end of the worm to the other.

b. *Steering Gear* Cleaning the parts will remove the sealing compound from the screw threads. Thus, the threads on the adjuster, side-cover bolts, and lash adjuster should be coated with a sealing compound, such as Permatex #2. Do not get compound on the worm-shaft bearing in the adjuster. Apply grease to the worm bearings, sector-shaft bushings, and ball-nut teeth.

With the worm-shaft seal, bushings, and bearing cups installed, slip the upper ball bearing over the worm shaft and insert the worm-shaft-and-nut assembly into the housing. Put the ball bearing in the adjuster cup, press the retainer into place, and install the adjuster and locknut in the lower end of the housing.

Assemble the lash adjuster with a shim in the slot in the end of the sector shaft. End clearance between the bottom of the slot and the head of the lash adjuster should be no greater than 0.002 inch [0.051 mm]. If it is greater, install another shim.

Start the end of the sector shaft into the side-cover bushing, and pull the shaft into place by turning the lash adjuster. Rotate the worm shaft to put the nut in the center of its travel. This is to make sure that the rack and sector will mesh properly with the center tooth of the sector entering the center-tooth space in the rack on the nut.

Put a new gasket on the side cover and push the cover-and-sector-shaft assembly into the housing, making sure that the teeth mesh properly. Make sure that there is some lash between the sector and the rack, and then secure the side cover with screws.

c. *Adjustment on Bench* The steering gear can be adjusted on the bench by tightening the worm-bearing adjuster to remove all shaft end play, tightening the locknut, and then installing the steering wheel on the worm shaft.

CAUTION: Do not force the steering wheel on the shaft, but tap it into place lightly. Forcing the wheel on would damage the bearings.

The adjustment procedure is the same as that already described (⊘ 9-3).

⊘ **9-5 Ford Steering-Gear Adjustments** Figure 5-18 is a phantom view of the recirculating-ball-and-nut steering gear described in this section. Figure 9-11

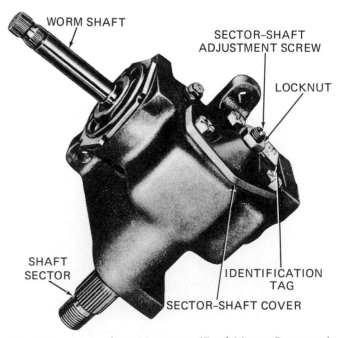

Fig. 9-11. Manual-steering gear. (*Ford Motor Company*)

is an exterior view. Two adjustments are required to provide minimum worm-shaft end play (also called *steering-shaft end play*) and minimum backlash between the sector and the ball nut. Adjustments are to be made in the following order.

1. Disconnect the pitman arm from the steering-arm-to-idler-arm rod (see Fig. 5-13). On cars with power steering, disconnect the arm from the valve ball stud.

2. Loosen the locknut on the sector-shaft adjustment screw (Fig. 9-12). Turn the adjustment screw counterclockwise. This relieves the load on the teeth.

3. Use a torque wrench on the steering-wheel nut (Fig. 9-13) to measure the worm-bearing preload. With the steering wheel off center, read the pull required to move the shaft at points about $1\frac{1}{2}$ turns to either side of center. If it is not within specifications, adjust by loosening the bearing-adjuster locknut and tightening or backing off the adjuster. Tighten the locknut and recheck the pull.

4. Adjust the backlash next. Turn the steering wheel slowly to either stop. *Do not bump it against the stop because this could damage the ball guides.* Then rotate the wheel to center the ball nut. Turn the sector-shaft adjustment screw clockwise, repeatedly checking the pull required to pull the steering wheel through center (Fig. 9-13). When the correct pull is attained, hold the adjustment screw and tighten the locknut. Recheck the pull.

CAUTION: There should be no perceptible backlash at 30 degrees on either side of center.

5. Connect the pitman arm to the steering-arm-to-idler-arm rod (or control-valve ball stud, on power steering).

Fig. 9-13. Checking steering-gear preload with a torque wrench. (*Ford Motor Company*)

⊘ **9-6 Ford Steering-Gear Service** Figure 5-18 is a phantom view of the steering gear described in this section.

1. REMOVAL If the steering column is of the movable type, remove the three steering-column pivot-plate bolts.

Then, on all types, remove the bolt that attaches the flex coupling to the worm shaft of the steering gear. Raise the front end of the car, disconnect the pitman arm from the sector shaft (Fig. 9-14). Remove the bolts that attach the steering gear to the frame. It may be necessary on some cars to disconnect the muffler inlet pipe. It may also be necessary to disconnect the clutch linkage (on cars so equipped).

2. DISASSEMBLY Rotate the worm shaft to the center position. Remove the locknut from the sector-shaft adjustment screw and the three cover bolts. Now the cover and sector shaft can be taken from the housing (Fig. 9-15).

Loosen the locknut and back off the worm-shaft-bearing-adjuster nut so that the shaft and ball nut can be withdrawn from the housing (Fig. 9-16).

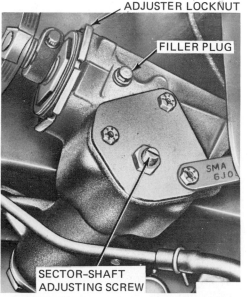

Fig. 9-12. Adjustment points of a recirculating-ball-and-nut steering gear. (*Ford Motor Company*)

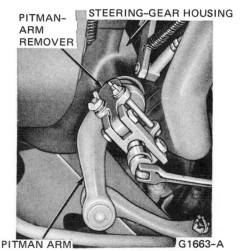

Fig. 9-14. Removing the pitman arm. (*Ford Motor Company*)

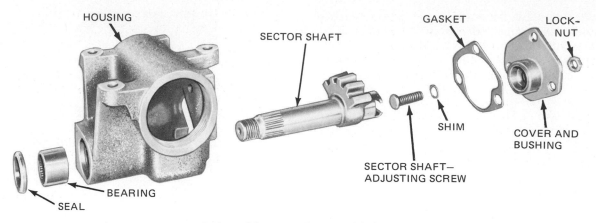

Fig. 9-15. Sector shaft and housing disassembled. (*Ford Motor Company*)

CAUTION: Do not let the nut run down to the end of the worm. This could damage the ball guides.

Remove the ball-guide clamp, turn the nut upside down over a clean pan, and rotate the worm shaft back and forth until all 50 balls fall out. The nut will now slide off the shaft.

Remove the needle bearings only if they require replacement. They can be pressed out with an arbor press and special tools. The bearing cups can be removed from the housing and adjuster by tapping the housing or adjuster on a wooden block to jar them loose.

3. REASSEMBLY Install new needle bearings and oil seal if the old ones have been removed. Apply steering-gear lubricant to the bearings. Install sector-shaft bearing cups in the housing and adjuster. Install a new seal in the adjuster.

Insert the ball guides into the holes in the ball nut, tapping them lightly with the wood handle of a screwdriver if necessary to seat them. Put the ball nut into position on the steering shaft and drop 25 balls into the hole in the top of each ball guide. Rotate the shaft slightly back and forth to distribute the balls.

Install ball-guide clamps. Check the steering shaft to make sure it is free to turn in the ball nut.

Coat the threads of the steering-shaft bearing adjuster, the housing-cover bolts, and the sector adjustment screw with oil-resistant sealing compound. *Do not get sealer on the internal threads or on the bearings.* Coat the worm bearings, sector-shaft bearings, and gear teeth with steering-gear lubricant.

Clamp the housing in a vise, sector-shaft axis horizontal, and position the worm-shaft lower bearing in its cup. Install the worm shaft, with its nut, in the housing. Put the upper bearing in place on the worm, and then run the bearing adjuster (with cup in place) down. Adjust the worm-bearing preload as already described (⊘ 9-5).

Put the sector-shaft adjustment screw, with a shim, in the slot in the end of the sector shaft. Clearance should be less than 0.002 inch [0.051 mm] between the end of the screw and the bottom of the slot in the shaft. If it is greater, add shims.

Install a new gasket on the housing cover. Start the adjustment screw into the cover. Apply enough lubricant to fill the pocket in the housing between the sector-shaft bearings (about 30 percent full). Rotate the worm shaft so that the ball nut will mesh properly with the sector teeth.

Put the sector shaft, with its cover, into place, turn the cover out of the way, and pack about 0.7

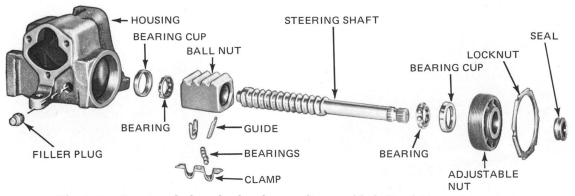

Fig. 9-16. Steering shaft and related parts disassembled. (*Ford Motor Company*)

pound [0.32 kg] of lubricant into the gear. Push the sector shaft and cover into place and install the *top two* cover bolts, but do not tighten them until you are sure that there is some lash between the teeth. Then tighten the top two cover bolts and adjust the lash as already explained (⊘ 9-5). The lower bolt goes in after final lubrication of the steering gear.

4. INSTALLATION With the steering wheel and the sector shaft in their center, or stright-ahead, positions, attach the steering gear to the frame and tighten the attachment bolts to the specified torque. Connect the pitman arm to the sector shaft (the front wheels must be straight ahead). Reconnect the muffler inlet pipe (if it was disconnected).

Reinstall the flex-coupling bolt (and pivot-plate bolts on the movable-column type).

Turn the steering wheel to the left to move the ball nut away from the filler hole. Now fill the steering gear with lubricant until it comes out the lower cover-bolt hole. Then install this lower bolt and tighten it to the specified tension.

⊘ 9-7 Plymouth Steering-Gear Adjustments The steering gear described in this section is illustrated in Fig. 5-17. There are two adjustments: for worm-shaft-bearing preload and for ball-nut-rack and sector-shaft-teeth mesh (Fig. 9-17). These are the same as required on the two steering gears previously discussed (⊘ 9-3 and 9-5). The adjustments are checked and corrected, if necessary, in the manner already described.

⊘ 9-8 Plymouth Steering-Gear Service Figure 5-17 illustrates the steering gear described in this section. Figure 9-18 shows the relationship of the steering gear to the steering column.

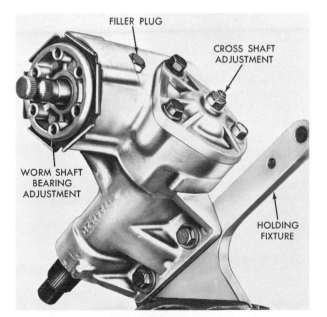

Fig. 9-17. Steering-gear adjustments. (*Chrysler Corporation*)

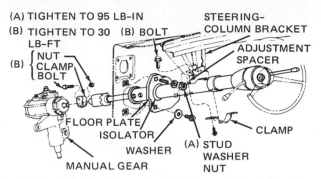

Fig. 9-18. Relationship and attaching points of the steering column and steering gear. (*Chrysler Corporation*)

1. REMOVAL To remove the steering gear, first remove the pitman-arm nut and pull the arm from the sector shaft (or cross shaft) with a special tool. Remove the coupling-clamp bolt from the upper end of the worm shaft.

To get enough room to remove the steering gear, loosen the column-jacket clamp bolts (Fig 9-18) and slide the column assembly up far enough to disengage the coupling from the worm shaft.

CAUTION: Do not scratch the steering column on the clamps!

Remove the three mounting bolts and take off the steering gear. On cars with six-cylinder engines, the steering gear can be removed from the engine compartment. On eight-cylinder models, the steering gear must be removed from underneath. On some models (Valiant, for example), the left-front engine mount must be detached and the engine raised $1\frac{1}{2}$ inches [38.1 mm]. Also, the starting motor may require removal.

2. DISASSEMBLY AND REASSEMBLY The disassembly and reassembly procedures for this steering gear are about the same as for the steering gears previously described. Special tools are required to remove and replace oil seals, bearings, and bearing cups.

3. INSTALLATION The steering wheel, steering gear, and front wheels must all be in the straight-ahead position when the steering gear is reinstalled on the car. First, attach the steering gear to the frame. Then, slide the steering column down far enough to permit the worm shaft to enter the flexible coupling. The master serration must be aligned with the notch mark on the coupling housing. When the grooves in the coupling and worm shaft are aligned, install and tighten the coupling bolt and nut.

Position the column assembly so that the steering-shaft coupling is centered at the midpoint of its travel, as determined by the $\frac{3}{16}$-inch [4.76 mm] gauge hole in the steering shaft (Fig. 9-19). Then tighten the column clamp bolts.

With the steering gear, wheel, and front wheels in the straight-ahead position, install the pitman arm on the sector shaft.

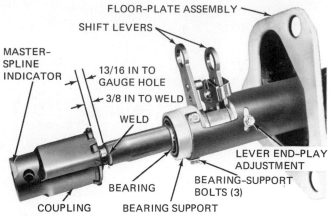

FLOOR-PLATE ASSEMBLY

SHIFT LEVERS

MASTER-SPLINE INDICATOR

13/16 IN TO GAUGE HOLE

3/8 IN TO WELD

WELD

LEVER END-PLAY ADJUSTMENT

BEARING-SUPPORT BOLTS (3)

BEARING

COUPLING

BEARING SUPPORT

Fig. 9-19. Steering-column adjustments. (*Chrysler Corporation*)

CHAPTER 9 CHECKUP

As a rule, steering gears give little trouble and, aside from lubrication, require attention only when wear of parts has progressed to such an extent that readjustment or replacement of parts is required. Nevertheless, for a well-rounded education in automobiles, you should know how various steering gears are adjusted and repaired. The information in the chapter covers this subject; the questions that follow will help you to review the information and find out how well it has stayed with you.

Completing the Sentences   The sentences below are incomplete. After each sentence there are several words or phrases, only one of which will correctly complete the sentence. Write each sentence in your notebook, selecting the proper word or phrase to complete it correctly.

1. There are two basic adjustments on steering gears, one for taking up worm-gear and steering-shaft end play, the other for removing steering-gear: (a) front-lash, (b) side play, (c) backlash.
2. Two types of ball guides have been used in recirculating-ball-and-nut steering gears, the split type and the type with: (a) screw threads, (b) a hole in the top, (c) four bends.
3. One of the most important precautions to observe in turning the steering wheel with the linkage dis-

connected from the pitman arm is to avoid: (a) bumping at the ends of turns, (b) bumping at the center of turns, (c) spinning the wheel slowly.
4. On some models, worm-bearing adjustment, or preloading, is made by turning a bearing adjuster; on other models, it is made by means of: (a) adjustment nuts, (b) roller bearings, (c) shims, (d) bushings.
5. Generally speaking, the steering-gear backlash is adjusted by moving the sector in relation to the: (a) pitman shaft, (b) worm, (c) steering wheel, (d) pitman arm.

Servicing Procedures   Write the procedures asked for in the following questions in your notebook. Do not copy from the book; write the procedures in your own words, just as though you were explaining to a friend how to do the jobs.

1. How is a late-type Chevrolet steering gear adjusted?
2. Explain how to remove, repair, and replace a Chevrolet steering gear.
3. How is the Ford steering gear adjusted?
4. Describe the procedure for removing, disassembling, assembling, and reinstalling a Ford steering gear.
5. Explain how to adjust a Plymouth steering gear.
6. Describe how to remove the sector shaft from a Plymouth steering gear.
7. Explain how to adjust a recirculating-ball-and-nut steering gear.
8. Explain how to remove, disassemble, assemble, and reinstall a recirculating-ball-and-nut steering gear.

SUGGESTIONS FOR FURTHER STUDY

When you are in your school or local automotive service shop, examine various steering gears that are available. Note how the automotive mechanic makes adjustments to steering gears and, if possible, how the mechanic removes and tears one down for complete service. If you have a chance to study automotive shop manuals, be sure to note the details of servicing the steering gear. Write important facts in your notebook.

chapter 10

SAGINAW ROTARY-VALVE POWER-STEERING SERVICE

This chapter describes the trouble-diagnosis adjustment, removal, repair, and reinstallation of the Saginaw rotary-valve power-steering units used on late-model General Motors cars. ⊘ 5-17 describes the operation of these units. Chapter 6 discusses trouble-diagnosis procedures on steering and suspension generally. The material that follows carries this a step further into power steering and includes complete repair procedures on the rotary valve units.

⊘ 10-1 In-Line and Rotary-Valve Power Steering Trouble-Diagnosis Chart These units were described in detail in ⊘ 5-17. The list, below, of trouble symptoms, causes, and checks or corrections is provided to give you a means of logically analyzing trouble and quickly locating the cause. Once the cause is known, the trouble is usually easy to cure. Following the trouble chart are several sections that describe the repair procedures on the Saginaw power-steering units.

NOTE: The troubles and possible causes are not listed in the chart in the order of frequency of occurrence. That is, item 1 does not necessarily occur more often than item 2, nor does item a under Possible Cause necessarily occur more often than item b.

IN-LINE AND ROTARY-VALVE POWER-STEERING TROUBLE-DIAGNOSIS CHART

(See ⊘ 10-2 to 10-12 for details of checks and corrections listed.)

COMPLAINT	POSSIBLE CAUSE	CHECK OR CORRECTION
1. Hard steering	a. Tight steering-gear adjustment	Readjust
	b. Pump drive belt loose	Tighten
	c. Low oil pressure	Check (see item 3, below)
	d. Air in hydraulic system	Bleed system
	e. Low oil level	Add oil
	f. Lower coupling flange rubbing on adjuster plug	Loosen flange bolt and adjust to $\frac{1}{16}$-in [1.59 mm] clearance
	g. Internal leakage	Check pump pressure (see item 3, below)
	h. Tire pressure low	Inflate to correct pressure
	i. Frame bent	Repair
	j. Front springs weak	Check standing height; replace springs
2. Poor centering (or recovery from turns)	a. Valve sticky	Free up
	b. Steering shaft binding	Align, replace bushings
	c. Incorrect steering-gear adjustments	Readjust
	d. Lower coupling flange rubbing on adjuster plug	Loosen flange bolt, adjust to $\frac{1}{16}$-in [1.59 mm] clearance
	e. Front end needs alignment	Align
	f. Steering gear out of adjustment	Adjust
	g. Steering linkage or ball joints binding	Replace affected parts

(See ⊘ 10-2 to 10-12 for details of checks and corrections listed.)

COMPLAINT	POSSIBLE CAUSE	CHECK OR CORRECTION
3. Low oil pressure	a. Loose pump belt	Tighten
	b. Low oil level	Add oil
	c. Mechanical trouble in pump	Check relief valve, rotor parts
	d. Oil leaks, external	Check hose connections, O sealing rings at cover, etc.
	e. Oil leaks, internal	Replace cylinder adapter, valve cover, or upper housing seal
	f. Engine idling too slowly	Set idle speed to specifications, check speedup control
4. Excessive wheel kickback or loose steering	a. Steering-linkage ball joints loose	Replace
	b. Steering-gear adjustments loose	Adjust
	c. Front-wheel bearings out of adjustment or worn	Adjust or replace
	d. Air in system	Fill, bleed
	e. Steering gear loose on frame	Tighten attaching bolts
	f. Flexible coupling loose	Tighten pinch bolts
5. Pump noise	a. Oil cold	Oil will warm up in a few minutes
	b. Air in system	Bleed
	c. Oil level low	Add oil
	d. Air vent plugged	Open
	e. Dirt in pump	Clean
	f. Mechanical damage	Disassemble pump, replace defective parts
6. Gear noise	a. Loose over-center adjustment	Adjust
	b. Loose thrust-bearing adjustment	Adjust
	c. Air in system	Bleed
	d. Oil level low	Add oil
	e. Hose rubbing body or chassis part	Relocate hose

⊘ **10-2 Trouble Diagnosis (Rotary-Valve Power Steering)** The chart above lists possible troubles, causes, and corrections. When trouble is reported on the steering system, the following checks should be made in an attempt to pinpoint the trouble. Often, it may be some such simple thing as a loose belt that can be corrected without difficulty.

1. CHECK BELT TENSION As noted in the chart, low belt tension can cause low oil pressure and hard steering. A quick check of belt tension can be made—while the engine and pump are warm—by turning the steering wheel with the front wheels on a dry floor. As the wheel is turned, maximum pressure is built up, and this imposes a full load on the belt. If the belt now slips, the tension is too low. To check tension more accurately, turn the engine off and push in on the belt midway between the pulleys. The specifications for one car state that the belt should deflect ½ to ¾ inch [12.7 to 19.05 mm] with a push of 15 pounds [6.81 kg] halfway between the fan and pump pulleys. Loosen the mounting bolts and move the pump out to increase tension. Then tighten the bolts.

Some adjustment procedures call for the use of a special belt-adjustment tool (Fig. 10-1). The tool fits on the belt as shown and measures the pull required to deflect the belt a standard distance.

Fig. 10-1. Checking pump-belt tension with the special tool. (*Chevrolet Motor Division of General Motors Corporation*)

2. CHECK OIL LEVEL If the oil level is low, add oil to bring the level up to the marking on the side of the reservoir. Use only the special oil recommended. If the oil level is low, the possibility exists that there is an oil leak; check all hose and power-steering connections for signs of a leak. Leakage may occur at various points in the power-steering unit if the seals are defective. Check around the piston and valve housings for leakage signs. Replace the seals or tighten the connections to eliminate leaks.

3. CHECK STEERING ACTION A check of the power-steering action can be made with a pull scale hooked to the wheel rim (Fig. 9-4). Oil in the system must be warm before the test is made, and the front wheels must be resting on a level, dry floor. If the oil is cold, set the hand brake, start the engine, and allow it to idle for several minutes. While the engine is idling, turn the steering wheel back and forth so as to build up pressure in the system; this hastens the warming of the oil. With the oil warm, hook the pull scale on the steering-wheel rim, and see how much pull is required to turn the front wheels first in one direction and then in the other. The amount of pull specified varies with different models (because of tire and wheel size, linkage design, and so on); in general, if the pull exceeds about 10 pounds [4.54 kg], the unit is not working properly and the oil pressure should be checked.

NOTE: Be sure the engine is idling at the specified speed. If it is idling too slowly, it may not be driving the pump fast enough to build up normal pressure.

4. CHECK OIL PRESSURE A special hydraulic pressure gauge is required to check oil pressure from the pump. To use the gauge, disconnect the pressure hose from the pump and connect the gauge between the pressure fitting on the pump and the pressure hose (Fig. 10-2). To make the test, the pump reservoir must be filled, the tires inflated to the correct pressure, and the engine idling at specified speed. Hold the steering wheel against one stop and check connections at the gauge you just installed for leaks. Bleed the system (⊘ 10-3). Insert a thermometer in the pump reservoir. Move the steering wheel from one stop to the other several times until the thermometer registers 150 to 170 degrees Fahrenheit [65.6 to 76.7°C].

CAUTION: To prevent scrubbing wear and flat spots on tires, move the car if you have to turn the steering wheel more than five times.

Hold the wheel against the stop and read the pressure. If it is below specifications, check further to find the trouble, as follows.

Slowly turn the shutoff valve to the closed position and read the pressure. Quickly reopen the valve to prevent damage to the pump. If the pressure is low, the pump is at fault. If the pressure comes up to normal, the trouble is in the hoses, connections, valve, or steering gear.

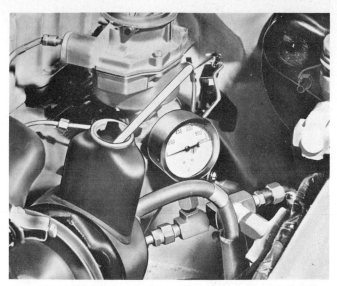

Fig. 10-2. The pressure gauge is connected into the line from the pump to check maximum pump pressure. (*Chevrolet Motor Division of General Motors Corporation*)

⊘ **10-3 Bleeding Hydraulic System** Air will enter the hydraulic system while oil lines are being disconnected and reconnected, after the pump or steering gear has been removed and replaced, or possibly because of a low oil level in the reservoir. The air must be removed; otherwise the unit will operate noisily and unsatisfactorily. To bleed the system, fill the oil reservoir to the proper level and allow the car to sit for at least 2 minutes. Start the engine and let it run for about 2 seconds. Add oil if necessary. Repeat until the oil level remains constant.

Raise the car so the front wheels are off the ground. Start the engine and run it at about 1,500 rpm. Turn the steering wheel right and left. Turn to stops, but avoid banging them hard. Add more oil if necessary. Lower the car to the ground and turn the wheel right and left. Add more oil if necessary.

If the oil is foamy, wait for a few minutes and repeat the procedure. Then check the pulley for wobble, and hoses and connections to make sure they are tight and not leaking. Foamy oil may indicate air leakage into the system, so check all points at which this could occur.

⊘ **10-4 Adjusting Steering Gear on Car** At one time, an overcenter adjustment could be made on the car (Fig. 10-3). Today, however, the manufacturers discourage adjustment of the steering gear in the car. Getting to the steering gear is difficult, and the hydraulic fluid tends to confuse the adjustment. It is therefore recommended that the steering gear be removed from the vehicle before any adjustments are attempted.

⊘ **10-5 Adjusting Steering Gear off Car** With the steering gear off the car (⊘ 10-6) and drained of

Fig. 10-3. Making the overcenter adjustment. (*Chevrolet Motor Division of General Motors Corporation*)

fluid, clamp it in a vise (Fig. 10-4). Make adjustments as follows.

1. Adjust worm thrust-bearing preload by backing off the locknut and pitman-shaft adjuster screw 1½ turns. Then loosen the adjuster-plug locknut. Use the special spanner tool (Fig. 10-4) to bottom the adjuster plug by turning it clockwise. *Avoid excessive torque!* Then back off the adjuster plug 5 to 10 degrees, or about ³⁄₁₆ inch [4.76 mm] at the outside diameter of the adjuster plug. Use the torque wrench as shown in Fig. 10-4 to make sure the torque required to turn the worm shaft is within specifica-

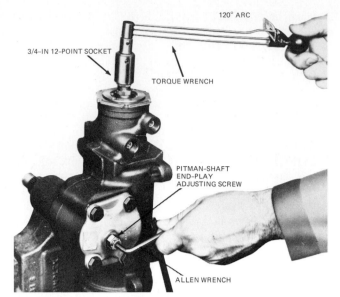

Fig. 10-5. Adjusting the overcenter preload. (*Chevrolet Motor Division of General Motors Corporation*)

tions. Then hold the adjuster plug with the spanner and tighten the locknut.

2. Overcenter preload is adjusted by turning the pitman-shaft adjusting screw as shown in Fig. 10-5 while turning the worm shaft through its center position with a torque wrench. First, check the torque with the adjusting screw backed out all the way. Then turn the adjusting screw in slowly, all the time swinging the torque wrench through center. Adjustment is correct when the torque wrench reads 4 to 8 pound-inches [4 to 8 kg-cm] more than the torque with the adjusting screw backed out. When adjustment is correct, tighten the locknut.

NOTE: The permissible additional torque for a used gear (400 miles [643.7 km] or more) is 4 to 5 pound-

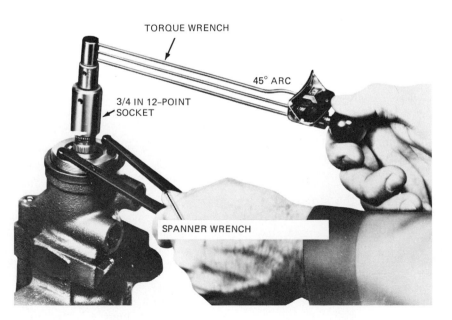

Fig. 10-4. Adjusting the thrust-bearing preload. (*Chevrolet Motor Division of General Motors Corporation*)

inches [4 to 5 kg-cm]. But the total torque should not exceed 14 pound-inches [14 kg-cm].

⊘ **10-6 Removing Steering Gear from Car** The removal procedure varies somewhat from car to car because of individual variations in the installations. Figure 10-6 illustrates one installation. A typical removal procedure follows.

Disconnect the pressure and return hoses and elevate the ends of the hoses so that the oil will not run out. Cap both the hoses and the steering gear outlets to keep dirt from getting in. Remove the two nuts that attach the coupling lower flange to the steering-shaft coupling (Fig. 10-6). Jack up the car and remove the pitman arm from the pitman shaft. Loosen the three bolts that attach the steering gear to the frame and remove the steering gear.

⊘ **10-7 Disassembly** Figure 10-7 is a disassembled view of the steering gear. It is preferable to mount the steering gear on a holding fixture which can be clamped in a vise (Fig. 10-8). Never clamp the housing in a vise; this could distort it. Clean the steering gear and drain out all lubricant, turning the worm shaft through its entire range several times to assist drainage.

NOTE: It is not always necessary to completely disassemble the steering gear to find and fix a trouble. Most of the components can be removed from the housing without complete disassembly. However, the complete procedure follows.

CAUTION: When disassembling a steering gear, the work area, tools, and parts must be kept absolutely clean. Even a trace of dirt can cause malfunctioning of the steering gear. Note also that if a broken component or dirt is found in either the steering gear or pump, the entire hydraulic system must be disassembled and cleaned. Then the system must be flushed out and fresh oil added after everything is back together again.

1. Use a punch and a screwdriver as shown in Fig. 10-9 to remove the end-plug retaining ring. Turn the worm shaft to push the end plug out. Discard the O ring. Do not turn the shaft farther than necessary; this could allow the balls to drop out of the ball nut. Remove the rack-piston end plug with a drive that is ½-inch [12.7 mm] square (Fig. 10-10).
2. Remove the side-cover screws and washers. Move the cover around so that you can see the location of the sector. Turn the worm shaft until the sector is centered so that the pitman shaft and cover can be removed. Discard the side-cover O ring.
3. Remove the rack piston by using a special arbor held in the end of the piston while turning the worm shaft (Fig. 10-11). The tool prevents the balls from falling out while the worm is threaded out of the rack nut.
4. Take the coupling flange off the worm shaft by removing the locking bolt. Remove the adjuster-plug locknut with a punch or a spanner wrench and then remove the adjuster plug. Push on the end of the worm with a hammer handle while turning the shaft to slip the assembly (Fig. 10-12) out of the housing.

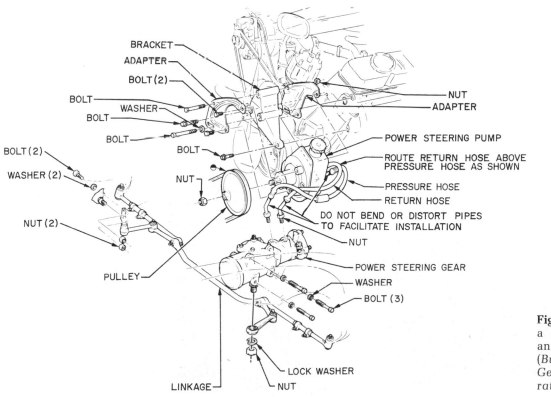

Fig. 10-6. Installation of a power-steering gear and pump on an engine. (*Buick Motor Division of General Motors Corporation*)

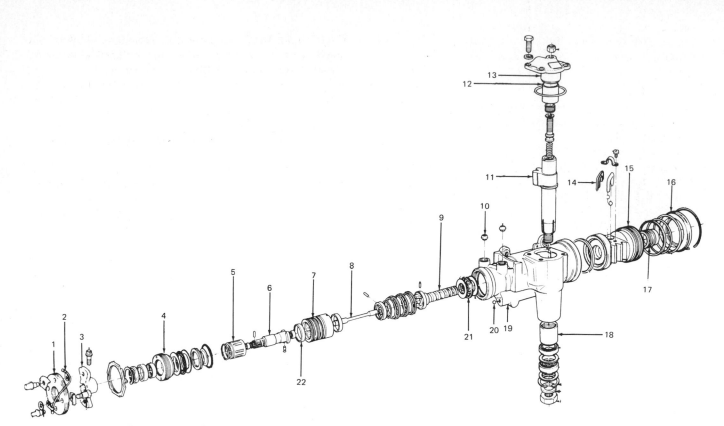

Fig. 10-7. Exploded view of a power-steering gear. (*Pontiac Motor Division of General Motors Corporation*)

1. Flange coupling
2. Horn ground strip
3. Lower flange
4. Adjuster plug
5. Spool valve
6. Stub shaft
7. Valve body
8. Torsion bar
9. Steering worm
10. Hose connector
11. Pitman-shaft gear
12. Housing-side-cover bushing
13. Housing side cover
14. Ball-return guide
15. Piston rack
16. End cover
17. Piston end plug
18. Bearing, needle bearing
19. Steering-gear housing
20. Ball, oil-passage plug ball
21. Thrust bearing
22. Valve-body sleeve

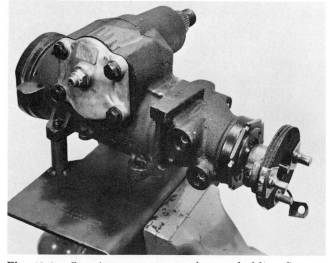

Fig. 10-8. Steering gear mounted on a holding fixture. (*Pontiac Motor Division of General Motors Corporation*)

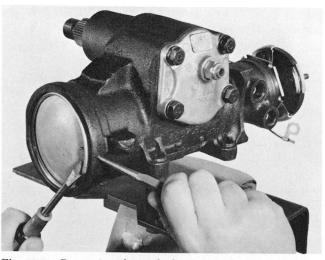

Fig. 10-9. Removing the end-plug retaining ring. (*Pontiac Motor Division of General Motors Corporation*)

Fig. 10-10. Removing the end plug. (*Chevrolet Motor Division of General Motors Corporation*)

SPECIAL TOOL

Fig. 10-11. Holding the special tool against the end of the rack piston to keep the balls from falling out. (*Pontiac Motor Division of General Motors Corporation*)

Pull the adjuster plug off the shaft. Pull the worm shaft from the rotary valve and discard the O ring. Discard the O ring from the adjuster plug.

5. If necessary, separate the side cover from the pitman shaft by removing and discarding the locknut and backing out the lash adjuster from the cover. Do not disassemble the lash adjuster from the pitman shaft; these parts are serviced as a single assembly.

6. The rotary valve should be disassembled only if necessary. If a "squawk" has developed in the steering gear, the valve-spool-dampener O ring probably needs replacement (Fig. 10-13). This can be done by working the spool spring onto the bearing diameter of the shaft so that the spring can be removed. Tap the end of the shaft gently down against the workbench so that the spool comes off.

CAUTION: Use great care because the clearance is small and the spool could cock and jam in the valve body.

Remove and discard the O ring. Put a new O ring in the spool groove, lubricate with type A hydraulic fluid, and install the spool in the valve body. Do not allow the O ring to twist in the groove. Extreme care is required to prevent damage to the O ring! The notch in the spool must align with the pin in the stub shaft.

7. On the housing, the pitman-shaft lower seal and bearing can be replaced, if necessary, by using special tools to drive out the old and drive in the new bearing.

⊘ **10-8 Inspection** If the pitman-shaft bearing in the side cover is worn, replace the side-cover assembly. Likewise, replace the pitman-shaft-and-lash-adjuster assembly if the sector teeth or bearing surfaces are worn or damaged or if the lash adjuster has end play in the shaft.

The worm groove and rack-piston interior grooves and balls should be checked for wear. If replacement is required, both the worm and rack piston must be replaced as a matched assembly.

Check the ball-return guides, making sure the ends, where the balls enter and leave, are not dam-

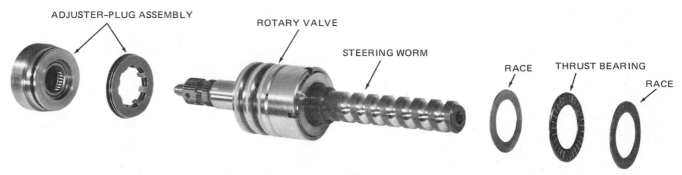

ADJUSTER-PLUG ASSEMBLY   ROTARY VALVE   STEERING WORM   RACE   THRUST BEARING   RACE

Fig. 10-12. Rotary valve and worm assembly. (*Pontiac Motor Division of General Motors Corporation*)

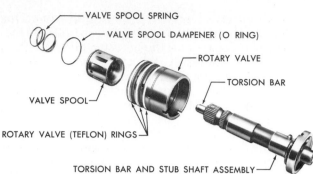

VALVE SPOOL SPRING

VALVE SPOOL DAMPENER (O RING)

ROTARY VALVE

TORSION BAR

VALVE SPOOL

ROTARY VALVE (TEFLON) RINGS

TORSION BAR AND STUB SHAFT ASSEMBLY

Fig. 10-13. Disassembled view of the rotary valve. (*Pontiac Motor Division of General Motors Corporation*)

aged. Replace the lower thrust bearing and races if they are worn or otherwise damaged.

If the rotary valve is damaged, the valve must be replaced as an assembly. The valve parts are matched and are not serviced separately.

The housing will require replacement if there are defects in the piston bore or rotary-valve bore. A slight polishing of the bores is normal.

⊘ **10-9 Reassembly** Lubricate all parts as they are assembled.

1. Screw the lash adjuster through the side cover until the cover bottoms on the shaft. Install but do not tighten the locknut.
2. Use great care when assembling the rotary valve (Fig. 10-13), making sure the valve spool does not cock and jam in the valve body. The notch in the spool must line up with the pin in the shaft.
3. Figure 10-14 shows the proper relationship of the pitman-shaft seals and washers. These can be installed, if the old ones were removed, by using special driving tools.
4. Working on the rack piston, lubricate and install the O and piston rings. Insert the worm into the rack piston all the way. Align the ball-return guide holes with the worm groove. Load 15 balls into the guide

hole nearest the piston ring while slowly rotating the worm to the left. Alternate black and silver balls. Fill one half of a ball-return guide with 7 balls. Place the other guide over the balls and plug the ends with grease. Insert the guide into the guide holes. Secure with a guide clamp and screws.

5. Check the worm preload. The worm has a high point at the center which should cause a small increase in torque when the rack piston passes over this point. If this torque is not as specified in the manufacturer's instructions, it may be necessary to fit smaller or larger balls. Note, however, that this is not necessary unless a complaint of loose steering has been received. Normally, a thrust and overcenter adjustment will correct the problem (see ⊘ 10-5). Put a special arbor into the end of the rack piston and turn the worm out of the rack piston. Keep the arbor in contact with the worm so that the balls do not fall out.
6. Install the lower thrust bearing and races on the worm and assemble the valve assembly to the worm, making sure the slot aligns with the pin on the worm head. Make sure the O ring is between the valve body and the worm head. Install a new O ring on the adjuster plug and put the plug on the shaft.
7. Put the worm-valve assembly into the housing and turn the adjuster plug into the housing until it is snug. Back it off about $\frac{1}{8}$ turn. Use a torque wrench to check the torque required to turn the worm shaft. Tighten the adjuster plug to obtain the correct reading. Install and tighten the locknut and recheck the torque.
8. Put the coupling flange on the worm shaft. Use a special piston-ring compressor so that the ring will go into the housing, and push the rack piston into the housing until the special arbor contacts the end of the worm (Fig. 10-15). Hold the arbor tightly against the end of the worm and turn the coupling flange to draw the rack piston onto the worm and

SINGLE-LIP OIL SEAL

INNER BACKUP WASHER

DOUBLE-LIP OIL SEAL

OUTER DUST SEAL

RETAINING RING

Fig. 10-14. Pitman-shaft seals and washers. (*Pontiac Motor Division of General Motors Corporation*)

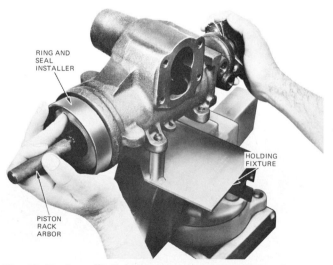

RING AND SEAL INSTALLER

HOLDING FIXTURE

PISTON RACK ARBOR

Fig. 10-15. Installing the rack-piston assembly with a ring compressor and special arbor. (*Pontiac Motor Division of General Motors Corporation*)

into the housing. Do not drop the balls out of the rack piston!

9. Replace the pitman shaft and the side cover. Make sure the center tooth of the shaft sector aligns with the center groove of the rack piston. Use a new O ring on the side cover and make sure it is in place before pushing the cover against the housing. Install and tighten the side-cover screws.

Install the end plug in the rack piston with a drive that is ½ inch [12.7 mm] square and tighten to the proper torque.

10. Replace the housing lower end plug with a new O ring and secure with a retainer ring.

11. Adjust the pitman-shaft preload at the center point. Remove the coupling flange and use a torque wrench to check the preload at the center point. Adjust the lash adjuster to increase the torque to the specified reading. Tighten the locknut and recheck it.

12. Replace the coupling flange and secure it with a clamp bolt.

⊘ **10-10 Installation** Figure 10-16 illustrates the details of installation of the power-steering gear on one vehicle. Details may vary in some installations, so always check the shop manual of the specific car being worked on before attempting installation. Be sure to replace the shims between the steering-gear housing and the car frame in the original positions.

The steering gear should align properly with the steering shaft. Tighten the attachment bolts.

After installation is complete, check the fluid level in the pump reservoir. Add fluid as necessary to bring it up to the mark. With the car wheels off the floor, start the engine and turn the steering wheel back and forth to the limit several times to bleed out all air.

Make a final check of the through-center pull after the installation is complete to make sure there is no misalignment.

⊘ **10-11 Oil-Pump Removal** To remove the pump from the engine, disconnect the hoses from the pump and fasten them in an elevated position so they will not drain. Put caps on all pump connections. Take off the pump-mounting bolts. Then remove the pump. Drain all oil from the reservoir after removing the cover.

⊘ **10-12 Vane-Type Pump Service (See Fig. 10-17.)** The vane-type pump, widely used in power-steering systems, has a series of vanes assembled in slots in a rotor (see Fig. 5-29). A typical overhaul procedure follows.

1. DISASSEMBLY Clean the outside of the pump with a nontoxic solvent. Remove the pulley retaining nut with a special tool. Clamp the pump in the soft jaws of a vise (lightly to avoid distortion) and re-

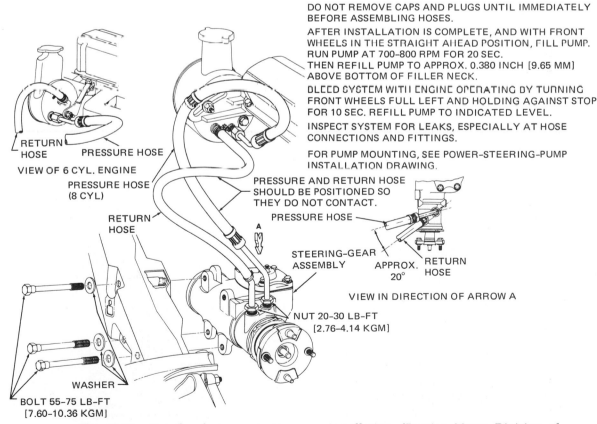

Fig. 10-16. Details of power-steering-gear installation. (*Pontiac Motor Division of General Motors Corporation*)

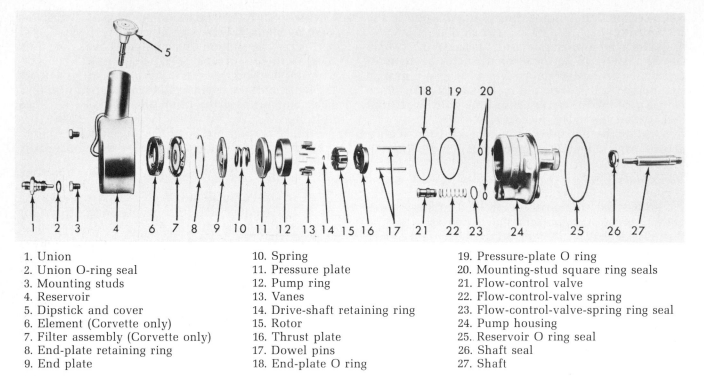

1. Union
2. Union O-ring seal
3. Mounting studs
4. Reservoir
5. Dipstick and cover
6. Element (Corvette only)
7. Filter assembly (Corvette only)
8. End-plate retaining ring
9. End plate
10. Spring
11. Pressure plate
12. Pump ring
13. Vanes
14. Drive-shaft retaining ring
15. Rotor
16. Thrust plate
17. Dowel pins
18. End-plate O ring
19. Pressure-plate O ring
20. Mounting-stud square ring seals
21. Flow-control valve
22. Flow-control-valve spring
23. Flow-control-valve-spring ring seal
24. Pump housing
25. Reservoir O ring seal
26. Shaft seal
27. Shaft

Fig. 10-17. Exploded view of a power-steering pump. (*Chevrolet Motor Division of General Motors Corporation*)

move: Union (1 in Fig. 10-17), O-ring seal (2), mounting studs (3), and reservoir (4). Tap lightly on the outer edge of the reservoir to break it loose. Remove the reservoir O ring seal (25) and discard it.

Remove the stud square ring seals (20) and discard them. On the Corvette, remove the filter assembly (7) and discard it.

Remove the end-plate ring (8), using a small punch to compress the ring and a screwdriver to pry it out (Fig. 10-18). Remove the end plate (9). The end plate is spring-loaded and will usually rise above the housing when the ring is removed. If it sticks, tap it lightly with a soft hammer or rock it.

With the end plate off, remove the spring (10) and shaft woodruff key. Then take out the impeller unit as an assembly. This includes parts numbered 11 through 16 plus the shaft (27) in Fig. 10-17. These parts can then be separated. Discard old O rings and seals, including the shaft seal (26), which must be pried out of the housing.

2. *INSPECTION OF PARTS* After cleaning all parts in a nontoxic solvent, check the following.

The flow-control valve must slide freely in the housing bore. The cap screw in the end of the flow-control valve must be tight. The pressure-plate and pump-plate surfaces must be flat and free of cracks and scoring. The vanes must be installed with rounded edges toward the pump ring, and they must move freely in the rotor slots. Check the drive shaft for worn splines and cracks.

3. *REASSEMBLY* Make sure all parts are clean during reassembly. Install a new shaft seal in the pump housing with a special tool. Put dowel pins in the pump housing and install a new pressure-plate O ring lubricated with transmission fluid. In-

stall the thrust plate (16 in Fig. 10-17) on the shaft with ports facing toward the splined end of the shaft.

Install the rotor on the shaft with the countersunk side toward the thrust plate. Install the new shaft retaining ring, tapping it onto the shaft with a drift and then tapping it into place with a ⅜-inch [9.53 mm] socket. Put the housing in the vise and install the shaft, thrust plate, and rotor assembly. Align the holes in the thrust plate with the dowels in the housing. Install the pump ring on the dowels with the arrow showing the direction of rotation to the rear of the housing. Install the vanes in the rotor slots with rounded edges out. Lubricate the pressure plate with transmission fluid and install it with ports toward the pump ring. Seat the plate by pressing

Fig. 10-18. Removing the end-plate ring with a punch and screwdriver. (*Chevrolet Motor Division of General Motors Corporation*)

down with a large socket on top of the plate. Put the pressure-plate spring in place.

Lubricate a new end-plate O ring with transmission fluid and install it in the housing groove. Lubricate the outer diameter of the end plate with transmission fluid and install it in the housing, using an arbor press to hold it down while the retaining ring is installed. The end of the ring should be near the hole in the housing.

Install the flow-control spring and valve. The hex-head screw goes into the bore first. On the Corvette, install the cage and new filter. Install new square ring seals and a new reservoir O-ring seal. Lubricate the sealing edge of the reservoir with transmission fluid and put the reservoir on the housing. Install the new union O ring, union, and studs.

Support the drive shaft on the opposite side and tap the woodruff key into place. Slide the pulley onto the shaft, install the pulley nut, and tighten it to 60 pound-feet [8.29 kg-m].

CHAPTER 10 CHECKUP

With the widespread adoption of power steering, it becomes increasingly important for everyone in the automotive field to know how these units operate, what can go wrong with them, and how they are repaired. Thus, the chapter just finished, on one make of power steering, is of special importance to you. Now that you have completed the chapter, let's find out how well you remember the important points covered in the chapter. If you have any trouble answering the questions, reread the chapter.

Correcting Troubles Lists The purpose of this exercise is to help you spot related and unrelated troubles in a list. For example, in the list "Hard steering: tight steering-gear adjustment, pump drive belt loose, low oil pressure, full oil reservoir, air in hydraulic system," you can see that the term "full oil reservoir" is the only item that does not belong because it will not cause hard steering. Any of the other conditions in the list could.

In each list, you will find one item that does not belong. Write each list in your notebook, but *do not write* the item that does not belong.

1. Poor centering: valve sticky, steering shaft binding, pump pressure above 700 psi [49.216 kg/cm²], incorrect steering-gear adjustments.
2. Low oil pressure: loose pump belt, low oil level, mechanical trouble in pump, excessive caster, oil leaks, engine idling too slowly.
3. Hard steering: tight steering-gear adjustment, pump drive belt loose, low oil pressure, air in hydraulic system, low oil level, engine idles too fast.
4. Pump noise: oil cold, air in system, oil level low, air vent plugged, tires overinflated, dirt in pump, mechanical damage.
5. Gear noise: loose overcenter adjustment, loose thrust-bearing adjustment, air in system, oil level low, steering gear tight on car frame, hose rubbing.

Completing the Sentences The sentences below are incomplete. After each sentence there are several words or phrases, only one of which will correctly complete the sentence. Write down each sentence in your notebook, selecting the proper word or phrase to complete it correctly.

1. The only adjustment to the Saginaw steering gear that can be made with the unit in the car is adjustment of the: (*a*) thrust-bearing preload, (*b*) overcenter pull, (*c*) oil pressure.
2. Turning the adjustment screw to make the overcenter adjustment causes: (*a*) endwise movement of the ball nut, (*b*) endwise movement of the pitman shaft, (*c*) endwise movement of the worm shaft, (*d*) endwise movement of the steering shaft.
3. In the Saginaw steering gear, the thrust-bearing preload is adjusted by: (*a*) turning an adjustment screw, (*b*) adding or removing shims, (*c*) turning an adjustment plug.
4. In disassembling the steering gear, the pitman-shaft assembly must be removed: (*a*) after the rack piston is removed, (*b*) before the rack piston is removed, (*c*) after the rotary valve is removed.
5. In removing the rack piston from the steering gear, an arbor must be held in the end of the piston to: (*a*) keep the worm from turning, (*b*) protect the O ring, (*c*) keep the balls from falling out.

Servicing Procedures Write down the procedures asked for in your notebook. Do not copy from the book; write the procedures in your own words. This will help you to remember them.

1. Pick a car equipped with a rotary-valve power-steering unit and describe in detail the procedure for removing the steering gear.
2. Explain how to test the steering gear (belt tension, oil level, steering action, oil pressure).
3. Describe the procedure in bleeding the hydraulic system.
4. Explain how to make the steering-gear adjustments.
5. List the main steps in disassembling the Saginaw power-steering unit.
6. List the main steps in inspecting steering-unit parts.
7. List the main steps in assembling the steering unit.
8. List the main steps in oil-pump service, including removal, disassembly, inspection, and reassembly.

SUGGESTIONS FOR FURTHER STUDY

When in your local school or automotive service shop, examine power-steering components that are available. If possible, be on hand when a power-steering gear is being disassembled. Note how the job is done. If you can, study the shop manual issued by the manufacturer, which gives detailed instructions on the repair procedure. Be sure to write important facts in your notebook.

chapter 11

CHRYSLER CONSTANT-CONTROL POWER-STEERING SERVICE

This chapter describes the trouble-diagnosis, adjusting, removal, repair, and reinstallation of the constant-control power-steering units used on Chrysler Corporation cars. ⊘ 5-18 describes the operation of this unit. Chapter 6 discusses trouble-diagnosis procedures on steering and suspension systems generally. The material that follows carries this a step further into the power-steering unit and includes complete repair procedures on this equipment.

⊘ **11-1 Constant-Control Power-Steering Trouble-Diagnosis Chart** The list, below, of trouble symptoms, causes, and checks or corrections will help you to analyze troubles and locate their causes in the power-steering unit. Later sections describe procedures required to eliminate the troubles when servicing or repairing the unit.

NOTE: Troubles and possible causes are not listed in the chart in the order of frequency of occurrence. That is, item 1 does not necessarily occur more often than item 2, nor does item a under Possible Cause necessarily occur more often than item b.

CONSTANT-CONTROL POWER-STEERING TROUBLE-DIAGNOSIS CHART

COMPLAINT	POSSIBLE CAUSE	CHECK OR CORRECTION
1. Hard steering in both directions	a. Leak in hydraulic system b. Fluid level low c. Pump belt slipping or broken d. Linkage not lubricated e. Tire pressure low f. Oil pressure low g. Bind in steering column or gear h. Front alignment off	Correct leak, refill Check for and correct leak, refill reservoir Tighten, install new belt Lubricate Inflate tires properly See item 2, below Align or adjust Align front end
2. Low oil pressure	a. Belt loose b. Pump valve stuck c. Mechanical trouble in pump d. Pressure loss in steering gear	Tighten, replace if necessary Free, clean if necessary Repair or replace pump* Repair, adjust steering gear
3. Oil leaks	a. Hose adapters b. At pump c. Between gear and worm housings d. Gear-shaft oil seal	Tighten or replace adapters or gaskets Repair or replace pump* Tighten attaching screws, replace O ring Replace oil seal
4. Smaller turning radius in one direction	Wheel stops out of adjustment	Readjust wheel stops
5. Hard steering in one direction	a. Low tire pressure b. Internal troubles, oil leak past seal ring, piston end plug loose, etc. c. Bind in steering column or gear d. Front alignment off	Inflate tires properly Recondition steering gear Align or readjust Realign front end

COMPLAINT	POSSIBLE CAUSE	CHECK OR CORRECTION
6. Car attempts to turn unless pressure is maintained on steering wheel	a. Tire pressure uneven b. Control valve out of adjustment	Inflate tires properly Readjust
7. Poor centering, or recovery from turns	a. Low tire pressure b. Balls in worm connector are binding c. Bind in steering column or gear d. Bind in steering knuckles e. Worm bearing adjustment too tight f. Front alignment off g. Gear-shaft adjustment too tight	Inflate tires properly Disassemble unit to clear or replace balls and connector Align or readjust Check kingpin and bushings, shim properly Readjust Align front end Adjust
8. Noises	a. Belt tension incorrect b. Fluid level low c. Worm pump bearings d. Dirt or sludge in pump e. Noise in power unit	Adjust Check for leaks, fill oil reservoir Repair or replace pump* Disassemble and clean pump,* drain system, refill, change filter element Check for air in system, hose clearance, gear-shaft adjustment

*For pump service, see ⊘ 11-8.

⊘ **11-2 In-vehicle Service** The gear shaft can be adjusted, the valve body reconditioned, and the gear-shaft oil seal replaced without removing the steering gear from the vehicle.

1. GEAR-SHAFT ADJUSTMENT Disconnect the center link from the steering-gear arm. Start the engine and run at idle speed. Turn the steering wheel gently from one stop to the other, counting the number of turns. Then turn the wheel exactly halfway, to centered position. Loosen the adjusting screw until backlash is evident in the steering-gear arm. You can feel the backlash by holding the end of the arm with a very light grip and attempting to move it. Tighten the adjusting screw until backlash just disappears. Continue to tighten beyond this point $\frac{3}{8}$ to $\frac{1}{2}$ turn. Tighten the lock nut to 50 pound-feet [6.91 kg-m].

2. VALVE-BODY RECONDITIONING Figure 11-1 is a disassembled view of the valve body. To recondition it on the vehicle, disconnect the hoses and tie the ends up to avoid loss of fluid. Remove two screws and lift the valve body up and off. Separate the control-valve body from the steering-valve body by removing the screws. Then, from the control-valve body, remove the fitting, gasket, spring, piston, and spring. Carefully shake out the spool valve from the steering-valve body. Do not remove the end plug unless the gasket is leaking so that it must be replaced.

Clean the parts with solvent and blow out the passages with compressed air. Examine the spool valve for burrs and nicks. These may be removed with fine crocus cloth provided you do not round off the sharp edges. If the valve or body is damaged, replace as an assembly.

Lubricate parts with power-steering fluid. Install the spool valve in the body so the valve-lever hole aligns with the lever opening in the valve body. Use new O rings during the reassembly described below.

Put the cushion (inner) spring in counterbore in the bottom of the control-valve body. Lubricate the piston and insert the nose end into bore. Make sure the cushion spring is not cocked, and that the piston slides easily in bore. Install the other spring, brass washer, and fitting. Tighten to 25 pound-feet [3.45 kg-m].

Using new O rings, attach the control-valve body to the steering-valve body. Tighten the attaching screws to 95 pound-inches [95 kg-cm]. Install the assembly on the steering gear with new O rings, making sure that the valve lever enters the hole in the valve spool. Also, the key section on the bottom

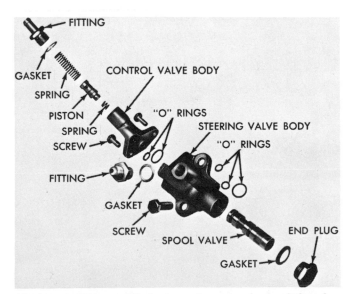

Fig. 11-1. Disassembled view of a valve body. (*Chrysler Corporation*)

of the valve body must nest with the keyway in the gear housing.

Secure the assembly with attaching screws tightened to only 7 pound-inches [7 kg-cm], or just enough to hold the assembly in place during the adjusting procedure.

Connect the hoses to the valve body and start the engine. If the assembly tries to steer itself, the valve body is not in correct position. Tap it up or down to move the valve body and stop the steering effect. When tapping down, tap on the end plug. When tapping up, tap on the head of the screw attaching the control-valve body to the steering-valve body. Do not hit the control-valve body.

Turn the steering wheel gently from one stop to the other to eliminate air from the system. Refill the reservoir as necessary.

With the steering wheel straight ahead, start and stop the engine several times, tapping the valve body up or down as necessary to eliminate any steering-wheel movement when the engine is started or stopped. Tighten the two attaching screws to 200 pound-inches [200 kg-cm].

3. PITMAN-ARM-SHAFT OIL-SEAL REPLACEMENT This seal is located at the outer end of the pitman-arm shaft. It can be replaced by removing the pitman-arm nut and pulling the pitman arm off with a special puller. Then, pull out the grease retainer with a special tool. Next, remove the oil-seal snap ring and oil seal, again with special tools. Then install the new seal and secure it with the snap ring and new grease retainer. Finally, replace the pitman arm on the shaft in its original position and tighten the pitman-arm nut to 175 pound-feet [24.185 kg-m].

⊘ 11-3 Steering-Gear Removal To avoid damaging the energy-absorbing steering column, the column should be completely detached from the floor and instrument panel. Then, disconnect the power steering pressure and return hoses from the gear. Tie the free ends of the hoses above the pump level and cap them to prevent loss or contamination of fluid.

Lift the vehicle and remove the pitman steering arm retaining nut and lock washer. Use the special puller to pull the pitman steering arm from the gear worm shaft.

Remove the three gear-to-frame retaining bolts or nuts. Then remove the gear. It may be necessary to raise the engine by removing mounting stud nuts and washers to provide sufficient clearance.

⊘ 11-4 Disassembly Figure 11-2 is a completely disassembled view of the unit. To disassemble, drain

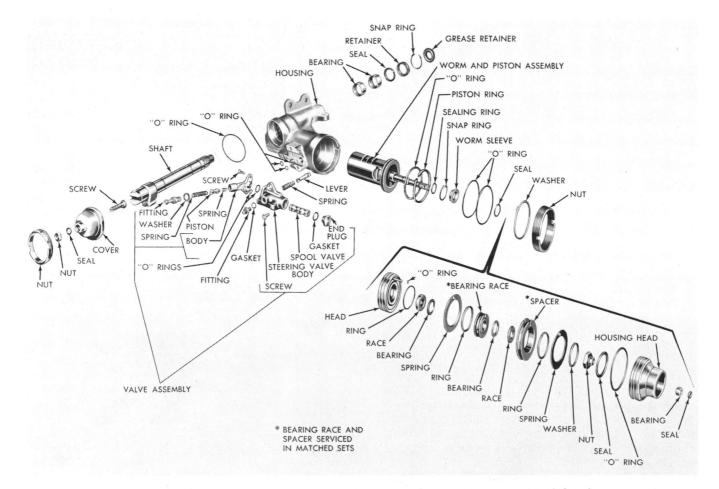

Fig. 11-2. Disassembled view of a constant-control power-steering unit. (*Chrysler Corporation*)

the oil by turning the steering worm shaft from one extreme to the other. Remove the coupling pin and the coupling, the valve body (and the three O rings), and the valve pivot lever (pry under the spherical head, but do not use pliers). Remove the gear-shaft inner and outer oil seals with special tools. Loosen the gear-shaft adjustment-screw locknut, and remove the cover nut with a special spanner tool.

Rotate the worm shaft to position the gear-shaft sector teeth at the center of piston travel. Loosen the steering-gear power-train retaining nut with a special spanner tool. Turn the steering gear so the sector shaft is in a horizontal position (Fig. 11-3). Put the arbor on the threaded end of the sector shaft and slide the arbor into the housing until both tool and shaft are engaged with bearings. Turn the worm shaft by hand to full left position to compress the power-train parts. Remove the power-train retaining nut with a special tool (Fig. 11-4). Remove the housing tang washer. Hold the power-train parts fully compressed and pry on the piston teeth with a screwdriver, using the sector shaft as a fulcrum. This will push the power train up so it can be removed.

CAUTION: Be sure to keep the power train compressed. Otherwise the reaction rings (springs) may slip out of their grooves, or the center spacer may become cocked in the housing, thus making it impossible to remove the power train without ruining some parts.

1. POWER-TRAIN DISASSEMBLY Put the power train in the soft jaws of a vise. (Never turn the worm shaft more than ½ turn during disassembly.) Remove the worm-shaft-support tang washer and use a special arbor tool to hold the support-bearing rollers in place. Lift off the support. Remove the large O ring from the shaft support.

Use air pressure (Fig. 11-5) to remove the reaction seal from the groove in the face of the worm-shaft support. Now the reaction spring, ring, balanc-

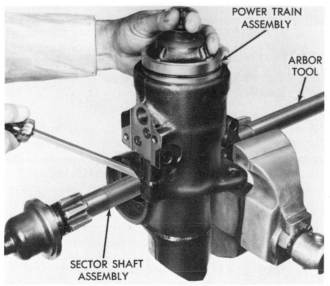

Fig. 11-3. Removing the power-train assembly. (*Chrysler Corporation*)

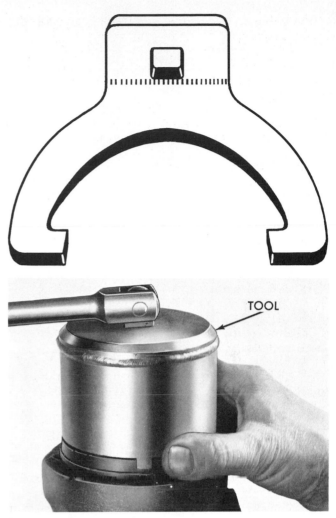

Fig. 11-4. Removing the power-train retaining nut. Two types of tools are shown. The one in use has two lugs that fit into two slots in the nut. The other one is used in a similar manner. (*Chrysler Corporation*)

ing ring and spacer, O ring, and center-bearing spacer can be removed.

Hold the worm and turn the nut to break the staked parts and remove the nut. Wire-brush the knurled section to remove chips and blow out the nut and worm.

Remove the upper and lower bearings and races, the reaction ring and spring, and the cylinder-head assembly. Remove the O rings from the cylinder head. Use air pressure in the oilhole between the two O-ring grooves to blow the reaction O ring in the cylinder face loose.

Remove the retainer, backup ring, and oil seal from the cylinder-head counterbore. Test the operation of the worm shaft to measure the torque required to turn the shaft in the piston. If it is not correct, or if there is other damage, discard the assembly. The worm and piston are serviced as a unit and must not be disassembled.

2. CONTROL-VALVE DISASSEMBLY Figure 11-1 is a disassembled view of the control valve. Follow this illustration when disassembling the valve (⊘ 11-2). Seals can be replaced in the steering-gear housing by use of special tools.

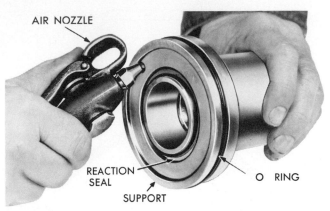

Fig. 11-5. Removing the reaction seal from the worm-shaft support with air pressure. (*Chrysler Corporation*)

⊘ **11-5 Reassembly**   Reassembly procedures on most components have already been indicated or are obvious. All new O rings and seals must be used on reassembly, and all parts should be lubricated with petroleum jelly during reassembly.

To reassemble the power train, first put the piston assembly on the bench, worm shaft up. Put the cylinder head, ferrule up, on the worm shaft and against the piston flange. Make sure the gap on the worm-shaft ring is closed to avoid breaking the shaft seal ring.

Note that on late-model units, the ends of the ring lock together, and a special tool is required to compress and lock the ring in the piston groove.

Install the lower bearing race (thick), bearing, reaction spring and ring (flange up), and center bearing race (index lever holes). Install the outer spacer, upper thrust bearing, race (thin), and a new worm-shaft thrust-bearing nut. Tighten the nut by turning the worm shaft counterclockwise ½ turn, hold the shaft, and tighten the nut to the specified torque. (Do not turn the worm shaft more than ½ turn!) Rotate the worm center bearing race several turns to position the parts, loosen the adjustment nut, and re-tighten it to give the specified bearing torque. Check this by wrapping a cord around the center bearing race, and measure the pull required to turn the race with a spring scale. Stake the nut into the slot in the worm shaft.

Install the center bearing spacer, engaging the dowel pin with the slot. Put the reaction rings over the center spacer and install the upper reaction spring with the cylinder-head ferrule through the hole in the spring. Install a new O ring in the ferrule groove. Install the jacket support, engaging the cylinder-head ferrule and O rings, making sure the reaction rings enter the groove in the jacket support. Align the parts so that the valve-lever hole in the center bearing spacer is 90 degrees from the piston-rack teeth. Lock the parts to the worm shaft with a drill rod through the jacket support and the worm-shaft holes.

Install the power train in the housing with the center-bearing-spacer valve-lever hole up. Align the hole with the clearance hole in the housing with an alignment tool. Install the column-support spanner nut and tighten to the specified torque. Set the piston at its center of travel and install the gear shaft and cover. Install the cover spanner nut and tighten it to the specified torque. Install the valve lever and valve body. Be sure the three O rings are in place.

⊘ **11-6 Adjustments**   Back off the gear-shaft adjustment screw. With the steering unit in the test fixture, connect the test hoses to the hydraulic pump on the car with a pressure gauge to check pressures. With pressure applied, position the steering valve by tapping lightly on one of the pressure-control valve screws or on the valve end plug. This should give equal gear-shaft torque (within 5 pound-feet [0.691 kg-m] and not to exceed 20 pound-feet [2.764 kg-m] in either direction) when the shaft is slowly turned.

With the gear shaft on center, tighten the adjustment screw until the backlash just disappears. Tighten the screw 1¼ turns; then hold it and tighten the locknut. Check the operation and oil pressure.

Readjust the gear-shaft backlash by loosening the adjustment screw until backlash is evident. Re-tighten it until the backlash disappears and then tighten it further ⅜ to ½ turn. Tighten the locknut to 28 pound-feet [3.869 kg-m].

The steering valve must be positioned to give equal torque. Test the torque by turning the worm shaft 1 turn to either side of center and checking the torque required to turn the shaft through center. If it varies more than 5 pound-feet [0.691 kg-m] from left to right, shift the steering valve to get equal torque and tighten the attachment screws to 15 pound-feet [2.073 kg-m].

Note that while the valve body can be centered as explained above, the latest recommendation from Chrysler is to make the final centering adjustment after the steering gear is reinstalled on the car. This procedure is explained in ⊘ 11-2.

⊘ **11-7 Installation**   Installation of the unit is essentially the reverse of removal. After installation, fill the oil reservoir in the pump, start the engine, and let it idle until the steering gear is up to operating temperature. Turn the steering wheel to the right and left to expel air. Refill the reservoir.

⊘ **11-8 Pump Service**   Recent Chrysler-built cars have used two types of power-steering pumps: the vane type and the roller type. The vane type is similar to the unit previously described (⊘ 10-12). The roller type (Fig. 11-6) has rollers fitted into grooves in the rotor (Fig. 5-27). The disassembly-reassembly procedure is much like that for the vane-type pump. Refer to Fig. 11-6 for relationship of parts.

CHAPTER 11 CHECKUP

The chapter you have just finished discusses another one of the power-steering systems used on modern

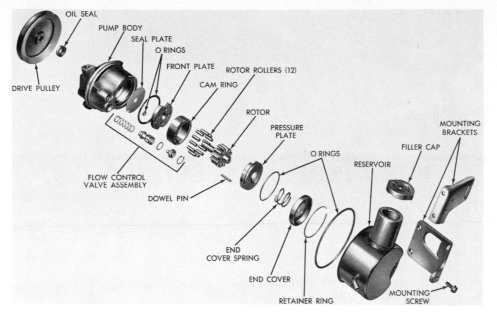

Fig. 11-6. Disassembled view of a roller-type power-steering pump. (*Chrysler Corporation*)

automobiles. No doubt still different power-steering mechanisms will be brought out on future cars. However, if you know the fundamentals discussed in the last few chapters, you will have no difficulty in understanding how the new steering gears operate and how they are to be serviced.

Correcting Troubles Lists The purpose of this exercise is to help you spot related and unrelated troubles on a list. Refer to the test instructions at the end of Chap. 10 for an explanation of how to take this test.

Write the lists in your notebook, but do not write the item that does not belong.

1. Hard steering in both directions: front alignment off, bind in steering column or gear, oil pressure low, tire pressure low, fluid level high.
2. Low oil pressure: belt loose, pump valve stuck, mechanical trouble in pump, engine idle excessive, pressure loss in steering gear.
3. Hard steering in one direction: low tire pressure, oil leaks past seal ring, bind in steering column or gear, front alignment off, excessive oil pressure
4. Poor centering or recovery from turns: low tire pressure, balls in worm connector binding, bind in steering column or gear, bind in steering knuckles, worm-bearing adjustment too tight, front alignment off, pump valve stuck, gear-shaft adjustment too tight.
5. Car attempts to turn unless pressure is maintained on steering wheel: uneven tire pressure, control valve out of adjustment, gear-shaft adjustment too tight.

Completing the Sentences The sentences below are incomplete. Write each sentence in your notebook, selecting the proper word or phrase to complete it correctly.

1. During disassembly of the steering gear, the old O rings and seals should be: (*a*) cleaned and reused, (*b*) greased and reused, (*c*) thrown away.

2. If the steering gear tries to steer itself: (*a*) the valve body is incorrectly positioned, (*b*) the idle speed is too high, (*c*) the steering linkage needs adjustment.
3. To remove the reaction seal from the groove in the face of the worm-shaft support, use: (*a*) a screwdriver, (*b*) a special puller tool, (*c*) air pressure.
4. The steering valve must be positioned to give: (*a*) equal torque in each direction, (*b*) quick recovery, (*c*) 30 lb-ft [4.146 kg-m] torque.

Servicing Procedures Write in your notebook the procedures that are asked for. Do not copy from the book; write the procedures in your own words just as you might explain them to a friend.

1. Describe the procedure for removing the power-steering unit from a car.
2. Explain how to drain and refill the hydraulic system.
3. Explain how to lubricate the worm housing.
4. List the main steps in disassembling the power-steering unit.
5. List the main steps in assembling the unit.
6. Explain how to center the steering gear (that is, center the valve).
7. Explain how to adjust the gear backlash.
8. List the major steps in installing the steering gear.

SUGGESTIONS FOR FURTHER STUDY

If you can, examine the complete assembly and the parts that go into it. Your local school or automotive service shop may have an assembly, or parts of one, that you can examine. If possible, be on hand when the unit is being serviced. Notice carefully how the job is done. Study the repair manual issued by the manufacturer if you can locate one. Be sure to write important facts in your notebook.

chapter 12

FORD POWER-STEERING SERVICE

This chapter describes the adjustment, removal, repair, and reinstallation of the double-sector torsion bar and the Ford designed power-steering gears used in automobiles manufactured by the Ford Motor Company. Some of these cars also use the Saginaw power-steering gear, described in Chap. 10. ⊘ 5-19 describes the operation of these steering gears. Chapter 6 discusses trouble-diagnosis procedures on steering and suspension systems generally. The material that follows carries this a step further into the adjustment and repair of steering gears.

⊘ **12-1 Torsion-Bar Steering-Gear Adjustments** The steering gear discussed in this and the following several sections is the double-sector type illustrated in Fig. 5-40. It has not been installed on new cars as original equipment for a number of years. However, there are still many in operation, and so we discuss the adjustments and services required on this unit.

The two adjustments to be made are worm-bearing preload and sector mesh (Fig. 12-1). To make the adjustments, the fluid must be discharged from the steering gear and the pitman arm must be disconnected from the sector shaft of the gear. To discharge the fluid, remove the fluid from the reservoir with a suction gun and then disconnect the fluid-return line from the reservoir. Put the end of the line in a container and turn the steering wheel back and forth to discharge the fluid from the gear.

Remove the hubcap from the steering wheel and use a torque wrench on the wheel attachment nut to measure the torque required to turn the steering shaft at points 20 degrees from either stop. If it is not correct, loosen the worm-bearing-preload-adjuster locknut and turn the adjuster to get the correct worm-bearing preload. Tighten the locknut and recheck.

Locate the center position by turning the steering wheel to one stop and then back 1¾ turns. Measure the torque required to move the steering wheel through center, first in one direction and then in the other. The larger is the total on-center mesh load. If it is incorrect, loosen the sector-adjuster-screw locknut and turn the adjuster screw to get the proper sector-mesh load. Tighten the locknut and recheck.

⊘ **12-2 Steering-Gear Removal** Disconnect the pressure and return lines from the steering gear, plug the openings, and cap the lines. Disconnect the horn ground wire from the sleeve-alignment bolt. Remove the clamp bolt that attaches the flex joint to the worm shaft (Fig. 12-2). Raise the car and disconnect the pitman arm from the sector shaft. Remove the mounting bolts that attach the steering gear to the frame and take off the steering gear (Fig. 12-3). Save the insulators.

⊘ **12-3 Disassembly** Figure 12-4 is a disassembled view of the steering gear. Drain the fluid and clean

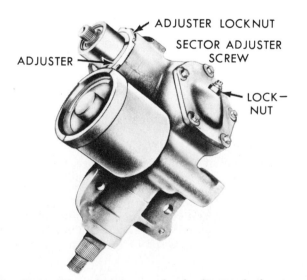

Fig. 12-1. Worm-bearing preload-adjuster locknut and sector adjusting screw. (*Ford Motor Company*)

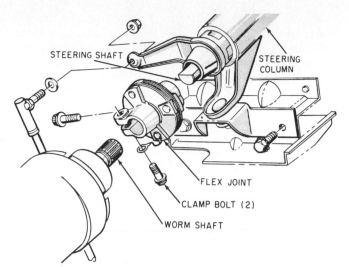

Fig. 12-2. Attachment of the steering-gear worm shaft to the steering shaft. (*Ford Motor Company*)

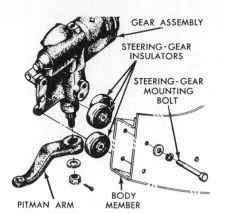

Fig. 12-3. Steering-gear mounting. (*Ford Motor Company*)

the exterior of the steering gear with a suitable solvent. Mount the unit on a disassembly stand, or holder. Remove the cylinder-plug snap ring and blow out the plug with compressed air.

Remove the cylinder cap and the O ring after taking out the snap ring.

Check the backlash between the sector gear and the piston rack by positioning a dial indicator against the piston (Fig. 12-5). Hold the sector shaft firmly and then push the piston by hand in one direction and the other to check the movement. If it is excessive, a new piston will be required on reassembly.

Loosen the sector-shaft-adjustment-screw locknut, remove the cover-attaching screws, and, with the worm turned so that the sector shaft is in the center position, remove the sector shaft and cover. It may be necessary to tap on the lower end of the shaft with a soft-faced hammer to loosen it. Discard

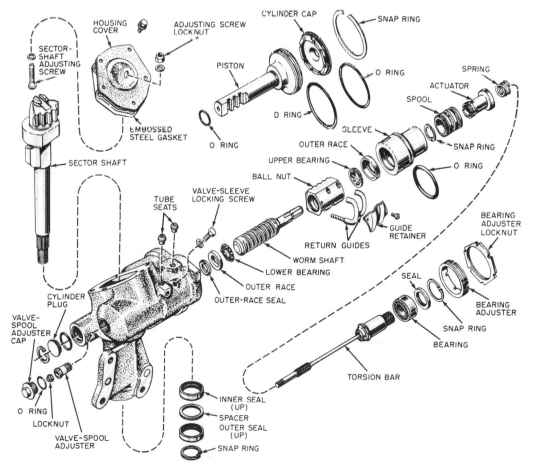

Fig. 12-4. Disassembled view of a torsion-bar steering gear. (*Ford Motor Company*)

Ford Power-Steering Service 177

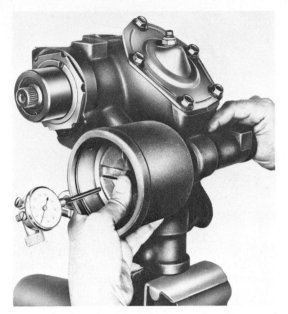

Fig. 12-5. Checking backlash between the piston rack and sector gear with a dial indicator. (*Ford Motor Company*)

the cover gasket and screws. Remove the piston and take the small O ring out of the housing bore (Fig. 12-6).

Loosen the valve-sleeve locking screw. Remove the valve-spool adjustment cap and O ring. From the opposite end, remove the locknut and the bearing adjuster. Now the torsion-bar-and-sleeve assembly can be removed. Tap on the torsion-bar end if necessary.

The snap ring and the sector-shaft oil seals can now be removed from the housing.

1. TORSION-BAR-AND-SLEEVE DISASSEMBLY Use a clean cloth to protect the ball nut from the vise jaws, and clamp the nut in a vise. Remove the

Fig. 12-6. Removing the piston-shaft O ring from the housing. (*Ford Motor Company*)

valve-spool sleeve (and the O ring from the sleeve), take off the valve-spool-adjuster locknut and the adjuster from the torsion bar, and remove the torsion bar, valve spool, actuator, seal, bearing, and race from the worm shaft. Discard the lower-bearing-race seal. Separate the valve spool and the actuator by turning the actuator and the torsion bar. Remove the valve-spool snap ring and the valve spool from the actuator.

Check the ball-nut assembly for binding and rough spots on the worm. Do not disassemble unless there is binding or rough spots.

CAUTION: Do not rotate the nut to the end of the worm; this could damage the ball guides.

If ball-nut disassembly is required, remove the ball-guide retainer and guides. Rotate the worm shaft back and forth so that the balls fall out of the nut. Catch them in a clean pan. With the balls out, the nut can be slipped off the worm.

⊘ **12-4 Inspecting Parts** All old seals and O rings should be discarded. Check the balls, nut, and worm for wear or scoring. If defects are found, replace all parts as a matched set.

Check valve parts for scores or wear, and replace any parts found defective. Check the housing for cracks, stripped threads, clogged fluid passages, and piston-bore wear. If the sector-shaft bushings are worn, replace the housing assembly. Put a new O ring in the housing inlet port.

Replace the torsion-bar assembly if the splines are damaged or if the blind spline does not line up with the dot on the upper end of the assembly.

⊘ **12-5 Reassembly** Refer to Fig. 12-4 for relationship of parts during reassembly.

1. TORSION-BAR-AND-SLEEVE REASSEMBLY Slide the ball nut over the worm in the correct position, as shown in Fig. 12-7. Align the ball-guide holes with the worm groove and feed 21 balls into one guide hole to fill one circuit. Turn the shaft back and forth to fill the circuit. Coat half a guide with grease and lay 10 balls in the half. Put the other half on, and push the guide into the two guide holes in the ball nut. Tap it down lightly with a soft hammer if it does not go down easily. Repeat the procedure for the second circuit. Secure the guides with the guide retainer.

Check the fit of the actuator on the torsion bar with the spring in place. If the actuator does not pop off the threads when released as it is turned, replace the spring and check for burred threads.

Install the bearing and seal in the valve sleeve with the special tools and secure with a snap ring. Install the upper bearing race and bearing on the worm shaft. Put the valve spool on the actuator and retain it with a snap ring. Install the spring and the actuator on the torsion bar. Turn the lower end of the shaft so that the two identifying punch marks

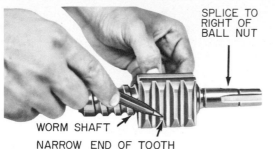

Fig. 12-7. Correct ball-nut position on the worm. (*Ford Motor Company*)

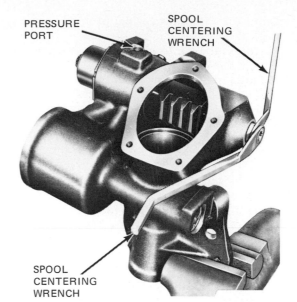

Fig. 12-9. Using a spool-centering wrench to center the spool. (*Ford Motor Company*)

are aligned (Fig. 12-8). Hold the assembly together and insert the torsion bar into the worm shaft, aligning the blind spline with the end of the spiral groove of the worm. The valve spool should bottom against the upper bearing and the race.

Hold the lower bearing, race, and seal in position on the worm shaft and install the valve-spool adjuster on the torsion bar, but do not tighten it. Install the locknut. Lubricate the lip of the input-shaft seal with fluid. Install the valve sleeve over the spool so that the upper-bearing outer race seats in the sleeve recess. Install a new O ring on the sleeve.
2. *STEERING-GEAR ASSEMBLY* Align the slot in the sleeve with the locking screw in the housing, and put the torsion-bar-and-sleeve assembly in the housing. Make sure the seal and the lower-bearing outer race seat against the housing. Install the bearing adjuster and locknut.

Use a special spool-centering wrench (Fig. 12-9) on the valve-spool adjuster and locate the valve spool so that the valley between the lands can be seen through the pressure port. Lock the adjuster with the locknut. This is only a preliminary adjustment.

Center the ball nut with the centerline of the sector-shaft opening. Install a new O ring in the piston-shaft bore of the housing (Fig. 12-6). If the

rack teeth are sharp, hone them so that they will not cut the O ring. Clean away all filings. Install a new O ring on the piston, lubricate the parts, and carefully install the piston. Align the center tooth with the sector bore in the housing.

Lubricate the sector-shaft spines and install the shaft. Make sure the shaft is centered by rotating the worm shaft. It should turn at least $3\frac{1}{2}$ turns. If it does not, the sector-rack worm teeth are not properly aligned. Install the sector-shaft lower inner and outer seals and spacer (Fig. 12-4) with the special tools. Secure them with a snap ring.

Install the sector-shaft adjustment screw, with the proper shim in the slot in the end of the shaft. Put the cover in place and turn the screw to bring the cover down on the housing. Use a new gasket and new attachment screws to secure the cover to the housing.

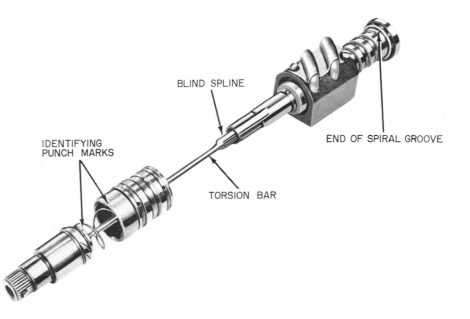

Fig. 12-8. Relationship of the torsion bar to other parts. (*Ford Motor Company*)

Adjust the worm-bearing preload and sector mesh (⊘ 12-1).

To adjust the centering of the valve spool, connect a high-pressure gauge (2,000 psi) [140.62 kg/cm²] into the high-pressure line from the car steering-gear pump (Fig. 12-10). Connect the return line to the pump, as shown. Fill the pump reservoir with the specified fluid, start the engine, and turn the steering gear from stop to stop several times to fill the gear and heat the fluid. Recheck the pump reservoir and add fluid if necessary.

Turn the input shaft with a torque wrench (Fig. 12-11) to one stop, applying sufficient torque to cause the pressure gauge to go up to 300 psi [21.092 kg/cm²]. Repeat at the opposite stop. If the torque readings for the two stops (with 300 psi [21.092 kg/cm²]) vary more than 3 pound-inches [3 kg-cm], loosen the valve-spool adjuster and turn the adjuster in the direction of the low reading (Fig. 12-11). Only a slight movement of the adjuster will be required. Tighten the locknut and recheck.

When the adjustment is correct, stop the engine and disconnect the hoses. Install a new cylinder-plug O ring and cylinder plug in the piston-shaft bore. Secure them with a snap ring.

⊘ 12-6 Installation Attach the steering gear, with insulators, to the car frame (Fig. 12-3). As you do this, center the gear and steering wheel and insert the input shaft into the flexible coupling. Position the pitman arm on the shaft and secure it with a lock washer and a nut. Connect the pressure and return lines and the horn ground wire. Install the flex-joint clamp bolt (Fig. 12-2). Fill the pump reservoir with fluid and cycle the steering gear by turning the wheel from one stop to the other. Do not hold the wheel against the stops long enough to overheat the fluid.

⊘ 12-7 Roller-Type Oil-Pump Service Figure 12-12 illustrates the roller-type pump used in a power-steering system. It is serviced as follows.

1 REMOVAL Remove all fluid from the pump reservoir with a suction gun. Disconnect the hoses and fasten them in a raised position so that the fluid will not run out. Loosen and remove the pump belt. Re-

11/16-IN 12-POINT SOCKET

Fig. 12-11. Adjusting the centering of the valve spool. (*Ford Motor Company*)

move the pivot and adjustment bolt and lift the pump off the engine.

2. DISASSEMBLY Handle all parts carefully to avoid nicks or scratches which would ruin them. Detach the reservoir by removing the retaining nut from inside the reservoir. Remove the two orifice O rings from the pump. Take off the pulley and the key. Remove all the bolts so that the bracket, pump housing, and cover can be separated. Lift the cover vertically so that the rollers will not fall out. Tap the cover loose (do not pry) if it sticks.

Use a straightedge and a feeler gauge to check the end clearance of the carrier and rollers (Fig. 12-12). If the clearance is excessive, or if parts are damaged, replace all rollers and the carrier (these parts come in a service kit).

Check the valve in the cover by removing the plug retainer and O ring. It should be free of nicks or scratches and slide easily in the valve bore.

3. REASSEMBLY Coat all parts with steering-gear fluid on reassembly. The carrier teeth should point in a counterclockwise direction when the carrier is installed in the housing. Do not damage the seal when installing the shaft in the housing. After replacing the valve in the cover, tightening the plug retainer, and replacing the O rings, put the cover in place and attach it with bolts. Attach the adjustment bracket to the housing. Put the pulley and its key on and secure them with a bolt. Put new O rings on the grooves on top of the housing and install the housing. Cement a new gasket around the inside of the reservoir cover.

4. INSTALLATION On installation, make the attachment bolts finger-tight. Check the alignment of the crankshaft and pump pulleys, install the belt,

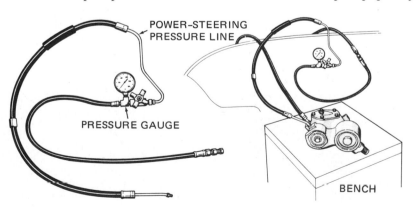

POWER-STEERING PRESSURE LINE

PRESSURE GAUGE

BENCH

Fig. 12-10. Installing a pressure gauge in the high-pressure line from the car steering-gear pump. (*Ford Motor Company*)

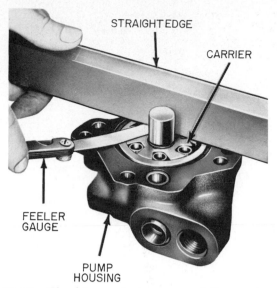

Fig. 12-12. Checking end clearance of the carrier and rollers in the pump. (*Ford Motor Company*)

and adjust tension to the proper specification. Tighten the attachment bolts. Connect the two hoses. Position the filter seat in the reservoir, put the filter on, and secure with a washer and a spring. Fill the reservoir with fluid. Start the engine and allow it to run while cycling the steering gear to eliminate air from the system. Check all connections for fluid leaks. Check the fluid level in the reservoir and add fluid if necessary.

⊘ **12-8 Ford Design In-vehicle Service** This steering gear is illustrated in Fig. 5-43. One check and one adjustment can be made with the power-steering unit in the car.

1. VALVE-SPOOL CENTERING CHECK Install a 2,000 psi [140.62 kg/cm²] pressure gauge between the power-steering pump outlet port and the steering-gear inlet port. The valve must be open in the gauge! Check fluid level in the reservoir and fill it to proper level. Start the engine and turn the steering wheel gently from stop to stop to bring the steering lubricant up to operating temperature. Recheck the reservoir and add more fluid if necessary. Remove the ornamental cover from the steering wheel.

Run the engine at 1,000 rpm and, with the steering wheel centered, use a torque wrench to apply enough torque to the steering-wheel nut to bring the pressure up to 250 psi [17.577 kg/cm²]. Apply torque first in one direction and then in the other. If the difference in readings in the two directions is more than 4 pound-inches [4 kg-cm], a correction must be made.

To correct, remove the steering gear. Then remove the valve housing and substitute either a thicker or a thinner valve-centering shim (see ⊘ 12-10). Use only one shim. If steering effort is heavy, substitute a thicker shim.

2. STEERING-GEAR ADJUSTMENT Only the

mesh load can be adjusted on the car (Fig. 12-13). To do this, disconnect the pitman arm from the shaft. Disconnect the fluid return line at the reservoir. Put the end of the return line in a clean container. Start the engine and turn the steering wheel from stop to stop to discharge the fluid from the steering gear. Remove the ornamental cover from the steering wheel and turn the steering wheel to 45 degrees from the left stop.

With a torque wrench on the steering-wheel nut, check the torque required to turn the steering wheel through ⅛ turn from the 45-degree position.

Center the steering wheel and check the torque required to turn the wheel back and forth across the center position. Loosen the locknut and turn the adjustment screw (Fig. 12-13) in until the reading is 8 to 9 pound-inches [8 to 9 kg-cm] greater at the center position than at the 45-degree position. Tighten the locknut while holding the adjustment screw stationary. Recheck the readings. Replace the steering-wheel hub cover and pitman arm. Refill the reservoir after reconnecting the return line.

⊘ **12-9 Steering-Gear Removal** Disconnect the fluid lines from the steering gear, and plug the lines and ports to prevent the entrance of dirt. Remove the two bolts connecting the flex coupling to the steering gear.

Raise the vehicle and remove the pitman-arm attaching nut and the pitman arm, using a special puller. If the car has a standard transmission, remove the clutch-release-lever retracting spring to provide clearance. Then support the steering gear and remove the three attaching bolts. Work the steering gear free of the flex coupling and remove it from the car. If the flex coupling stays on the steering gear, remove it.

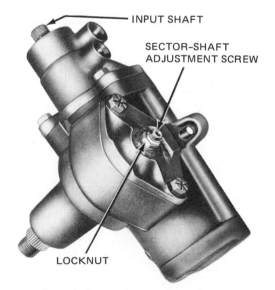

Fig. 12-13. Sector-shaft adjustment screw to adjust mesh load. (*Ford Motor Company*)

⊘ 12-10 Repair The steering gear will rarely require complete disassembly. Instead, only those subassemblies which are faulty will require repair, as follows.

1. VALVE CENTERING-SHIM REPLACEMENT Hold the steering gear upside-down over a drain pan and cycle the input shaft several times to drain the remaining fluid. Turn the input shaft to either stop and then back 1¾ turns to center it.

Remove the two sector-shaft-cover screws and identification tag. Tap the lower end of the sector shaft with a soft hammer to loosen it, and then lift the cover and shaft from the housing. Discard the O ring.

Remove the four valve-housing bolts and lift the housing off. The worm shaft and piston will come off with it. Hold the piston to prevent it from rotating off the worm shaft. Remove O rings and discard them.

Put the assembly in a holding fixture, as shown in Fig. 12-14, with the piston up. Rotate the piston up 3½ turns and insert the piston-holding tool into the bolt hole to hold the piston up, as shown in Fig. 12-14. Use the worm-bearing locknut tool as shown to loosen the worm-bearing locknut. Hold the locknut up out of the way and loosen the attaching nut (Fig. 12-15).

Now, lift the piston-worm assembly off, holding the piston to prevent it from spinning off the worm.

Change the centering shim, as noted (⊘ 12-8).

Put the piston-worm assembly on the valve housing, holding the piston to prevent it from spinning off the worm. Install the attaching nut, and torque to specifications (Fig. 12-16). Install the locknut, and torque to specifications. Rotate the piston

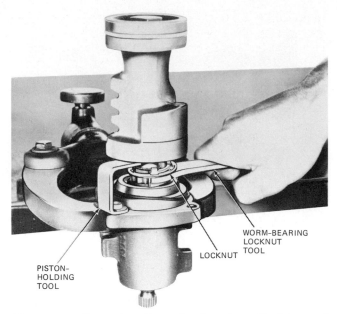

Fig. 12-15. Removing the valve-housing attaching nut. (*Ford Motor Company*)

up ½ turn and remove the piston-holding tool (Fig. 12-14). Take the assembly off the holding fixture. Position a new O ring in the counterbore of the gear housing. Apply petroleum jelly to the piston seal. Put a new O ring on the valve housing. Slide the piston and valve into the gear housing carefully to avoid damaging the piston seal.

Align the fluid passages in the valve and gear housings, and install but do not tighten the attaching bolts. Rotate the piston so the teeth align with the

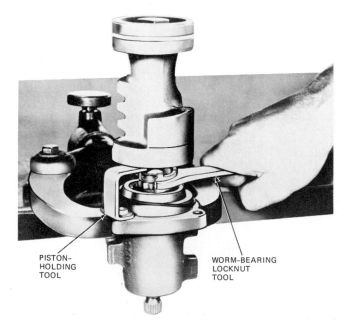

Fig. 12-14. Removing the worm-bearing locknut. (*Ford Motor Company*)

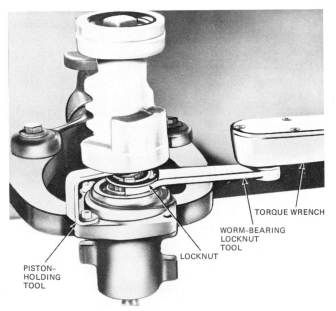

Fig. 12-16. Installing the valve-housing attaching nut. (*Ford Motor Company*)

sector-shaft teeth. Tighten the four valve-housing attaching bolts to specifications.

Put the sector-shaft O ring in the steering-gear housing. Turn the input shaft as required to center the piston. Slide the sector-shaft-and-cover assembly into position and secure with two bolts. Put the identification tag under one bolt head.

Adjust the mesh load to about 4 pound-inches [4 kg-cm] and then torque the cover bolts to specifications. Finally, readjust the mesh load to specifications (⊘ 12-8).

2. STEERING-GEAR DISASSEMBLY (FIG. 12-17) If the steering gear requires repair, remove the worm-shaft-and-piston assembly, as previously noted. Stand the assembly on end, piston down, and rotate the input shaft counterclockwise out of the piston, allowing the balls to drop into the piston. Put a cloth over the open end of the piston and turn it upside down to catch the balls.

To remove the worm-and-valve assembly from the housing, install the housing in a holding fixture and use a special tool to remove the lock and attaching nuts (Fig. 12-18). Then slide the assembly from the housing, using extreme care not to cock it. This could cause it to jam and ruin the housing and valve.

3. VALVE HOUSING Figure 12-19 shows the housing parts. Special tools are required to remove and replace the bearing and oil seal.

4. STEERING-GEAR HOUSING Figure 12-20 shows how the seals line up in the steering-gear housing. They must be removed and replaced with special tools.

5. STEERING-GEAR ASSEMBLY Never wash, clean, or soak seals in cleaning solvent. This would ruin them. To start the assembly, mount the valve housing in the holding fixture, flanged end up. Put the valve-spool centering shim (Fig. 12-17) in the housing and install the worm and valve. Install attaching and locknuts and torque them to specifications.

Fig. 12-18. Removing the locknut. *(Ford Motor Company)*

Put the piston on the bench with the ball-guide holes facing up. Insert the worm shaft into the piston so the first groove is in alignment with the hole nearest to the center of the piston (Fig. 12-21). Put the ball guide in the piston and drop 27 balls into the ball-guide hole. Turn the worm in a clockwise direction so the balls will feed in. Install the ball-guide clamp. Reattach the valve-housing-and-piston assembly to the steering-gear housing as already explained (in ⊘ 12-10, item 1) and adjust the mesh load (⊘ 12-8).

⊘ **12-11 Installation** On installation slide the flex coupling into place on the steering shaft. Turn the steering wheel to the middle. Center the steering-gear input shaft. Slide the input shaft into the flex coupling and attach the gear to the frame with three bolts. Torque to specifications. With wheels straight ahead, install the pitman arm on the sector shaft. Secure with attaching nut. Position the flex coupling and install attaching bolts to specifications. Connect fluid lines to the steering gear. Fill the pump reservoir, start the engine, and turn the steering wheel from stop to stop. Check for leaks and refill the reservoir to the proper level.

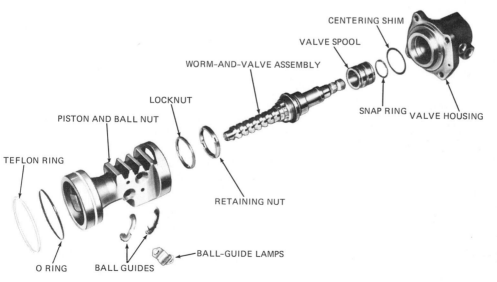

Fig. 12-17. Disassembled view of the ball nut and housing. *(Ford Motor Company)*

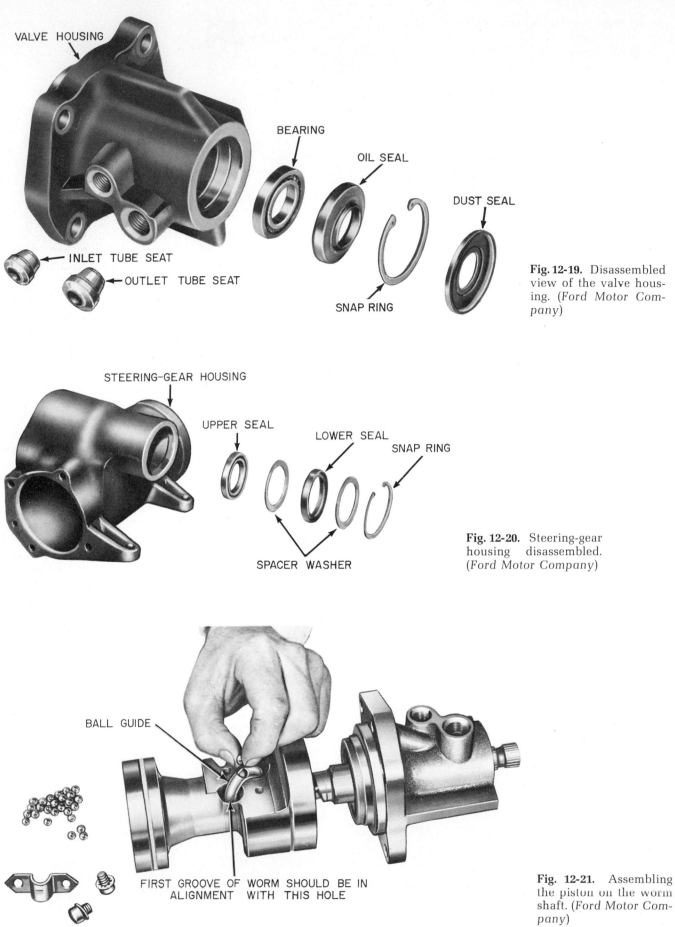

VALVE HOUSING

BEARING

OIL SEAL

DUST SEAL

INLET TUBE SEAT

OUTLET TUBE SEAT

SNAP RING

Fig. 12-19. Disassembled view of the valve housing. (*Ford Motor Company*)

STEERING-GEAR HOUSING

UPPER SEAL

LOWER SEAL

SNAP RING

SPACER WASHER

Fig. 12-20. Steering-gear housing disassembled. (*Ford Motor Company*)

BALL GUIDE

FIRST GROOVE OF WORM SHOULD BE IN ALIGNMENT WITH THIS HOLE

Fig. 12-21. Assembling the piston on the worm shaft. (*Ford Motor Company*)

CHAPTER 12 CHECKUP

You may or may not plan to specialize in, or work on, power-steering equipment. But in any event, you will want to know how these units work and the general servicing program they require. Thus, you will want to remember the high points of the chapter you have just finished. The checkup that follows will tell you how well you do remember what you have just studied. Don't be discouraged if you cannot answer, offhand, all the questions. Most good students reread their lessons several times. When you can't answer all the questions, it just means that you should reread the chapter once more.

Completing the Sentences   The sentences below are incomplete. After each sentence there are several words or phrases, only one of which will correctly complete the sentence. Write each sentence in your notebook, selecting the proper word or phrase to complete it correctly.

1. Two adjustments to be made on the torsion-bar steering gear are worm-bearing preload and: (*a*) oil pressure, (*b*) pullthrough at 20 degrees from stop, (*c*) sector mesh.
2. The worm-bearing preload is adjusted by: (*a*) turning a bearing adjuster, (*b*) turning an adjustment screw, (*c*) adding or removing shims.
3. To adjust the sector-mesh load: (*a*) add or remove shims, (*b*) turn adjustment screw, (*c*) turn adjuster nut.
4. If the backlash between the sector gear and the rack on the piston assembly is excessive: (*a*) lash must be adjusted, (*b*) a new sector is required, (*c*) a new piston assembly is required.
5. The sector shaft and housing cover are removed from the housing: (*a*) separately, (*b*) together, (*c*) side and end, respectively.
6. On reassembly, as a rule the old O rings and seals should be: (*a*) thrown away; (*b*) relubricated and reused; (*c*) washed carefully and, if not cut, reused.
7. To adjust the centering of the valve spool, the steering gear must be: (*a*) installed in the car, (*b*)

connected to the steering-gear pump, (*c*) disconnected from the steering-gear pump.
8. If the centering of the valve spool is not correct, it can be adjusted by: (*a*) changing the oil pressure, (*b*) adding or removing shims, (*c*) turning the valve-spool adjuster.
9. One of the main checks to be made on the roller-type pump during disassembly is to measure the: (*a*) clearance between the carrier and the housing, (*b*) end clearance of the carrier and rollers, (*c*) side clearance between the carrier and rollers.
10. On reassembly of the roller-type pump, make sure the carrier teeth: (*a*) point in a clockwise direction, (*b*) are firmly in place against the shaft, (*c*) point in a counterclockwise direction.

Servicing Procedures   Write in your notebook the procedures that are asked for. Do not copy from the book; write the procedures in your own words. This will help you to remember them.

1. Pick a car equipped with a torsion-bar power-steering unit and describe in detail the procedure for removing a steering gear.
2. List the main steps in disassembling the steering gear.
3. List the main steps in assembling the steering gear.
4. List and describe the adjustment procedures required on the steering gear.
5. List the main steps in installing the steering gear on a car.
6. List the main steps in disassembling and reassembling a roller-type pump.

SUGGESTIONS FOR FURTHER STUDY

When you are in your school or local automotive service shop, examine power-steering equipment that is available. If possible, watch an expert mechanic remove, disassemble, and service a power-steering gear. If you can, study the shop manual describing the steering gear discussed in this chapter. Write important facts in your notebook.

chapter 13

LINKAGE-TYPE POWER-STEERING SERVICE

This chapter describes the trouble diagnosis, adjustment, removal, repair, and reinstallation of the linkage-type power-steering units. You will recall that there are two general types of linkage power-steering units, the integral type in which the valve and power cylinders are combined, and the type in which the two are separate. Both work in the same general manner (⊘ 5-20). Chapter 6 describes trouble-diagnosis procedures on steering and suspension generally. The material that follows carries this a step further into linkage-type power steering and includes complete repair procedures on this equipment.

⊘ **13-1 Linkage-Type Power-Steering Trouble-Diagnosis Chart** Refer to ⊘ 5-20 for descriptions of this unit. The list, below, of trouble symptoms, causes, and checks or corrections will give you a means of logically analyzing troubles so that their causes can be quickly located and eliminated. Not all the troubles, causes, and corrections listed apply to all models of linkage power-steering units, since there are

some variations in design and operation from model to model.

NOTE: The troubles and possible causes are not listed in the chart in the order of frequency of occurrence. That is, item 1 does not necessarily occur more often than item 2, nor does item a under "Possible Cause" necessarily occur more often than item b.

LINKAGE-TYPE POWER-STEERING TROUBLE-DIAGNOSIS CHART

(See ⊘ 13-2 to 13-4 for details of checks and corrections listed.)

COMPLAINT	POSSIBLE CAUSE	CHECK OR CORRECTION
1. Hard steering	a. Low oil or leaks	Check for leaks, add oil
	b. Low oil pressure	See item 2, below
	c. Binding in steering linkage	Check, adjust linkage as needed
	d. Power-cylinder piston rod bent	Replace rod or cylinder
	e. Low tire pressure	Inflate to proper pressure
	f. Incorrect front alignment	Align front end
	g. Binding in steering column	Align steering column
	h. Valve stuck or out of adjustment	Adjust. Remove valve and check for cause. Replace valve if it is damaged.
2. Low oil pressure	a. Pump belt slipping	Tighten to proper tension
	b. Relief and flow-control valve stuck	Remove and clean
	c. Valve spring weak or broken	Replace
	d. Drive coupling broken	Replace
	e. Pump rotors, body, or cover worn or broken	Replace rotors or pump
	f. Leaks past piston in power cylinder	Replace piston rings or cylinder
	g. Leaks past valve	Replace seal rings
3. Hard steering—one direction only	This could be caused by d, e, f, or g, listed under item 1, or by a misadjusted or sticky valve in the power cylinder or valve body.	

(See ⊘ 13-2 to 13-4 for details of checks and corrections listed.)

COMPLAINT	POSSIBLE CAUSE	CHECK OR CORRECTION
4. Poor centering or recovery from turns	a. Pitman arm and stud binding on power cylinder	Adjust to proper tension
	b. Bind in steering column or gear	Align column, adjust gear
	c. Bind in steering linkage	Check, adjust linkage as needed
	d. Bent power-cylinder piston rod	Replace piston rod or cylinder
	e. Incorrect front alignment	Align front end
	f. Valve misadjusted or stuck	Free up, adjust
	g. Antiroll pin and bracket binding (on some models)	Align pin with bracket
5. Car wander	a. Uneven tire pressure	Inflate correctly
	b. Pitman arm and stud binding on power cylinder	Adjust to proper torque
	c. Valve stuck or misadjusted	Clean, replace
	d. Incorrect front alignment	Align front end
6. Noises	a. Low oil level	Replace oil, check for leaks
	b. Pump bushing worn	Replace bushing
	c. Dirty pump	Clean after disassembly, drain system, and refill with clean oil
	d. Looseness in steering linkage	Check, adjust, and tighten
	e. Tie rods improperly attached	Loosen clamps and retighten with bolts in proper position

⊘ **13-2 Trouble Diagnosis** The chart above lists possible troubles, causes, and corrections. When trouble is reported in the steering system, make the following checks to pinpoint the cause accurately:

1. Check belt tension. A quick check of belt tension can be made by turning the steering wheel to the extreme position while watching the belt (with engine operating). If the belt slips, the tension is too low. On the type of pump which is mounted on the generator, the belt is adjusted by loosening the adjustment-bracket bolt and pivoting the generator out as necessary to correct the tension. Then tighten the bolt. On the type of pump that is driven by a separate belt, the pump-mounting bracket has slotted holes that permit the pump to be shifted outward to increase the tension as necessary (see ⊘ 10-2, item 1).

2. Check the oil level in the pump reservoir. If it is low, add oil to bring it up to the proper level. Also, check the pump, power-cylinder, and valve connections for signs of leakage.

3. Two additional tests, for steering effort required and for oil pressure developed, should be made. First, however, make sure that the wheel alignment, tire pressure, suspension, and shock absorbers are in normal condition. Then, to make the steering-effort check, use a pull scale hooked to the wheel rim (Fig. 9-4) and see what effort is required to pull the wheel through center, first in one direction, then in the other. Specifications vary, so refer to the shop manual on the car being checked.

CAUTION: Do not turn and hold the wheel at the extreme left or right position.

4. To check the oil pressure, install a special gauge in the pressure line from the pump. With the engine idling and the oil in the steering system warmed up, turn the steering wheel a full turn either to the left or the right. The gauge should read high pressure (specifications vary on different units: refer to the shop manual on the car being checked). If pressure is too low, close the shutoff valve, quickly read the pump pressure, and open the valve again. (Do not leave the valve closed more than a few seconds, since this might damage the pump.) If the pump pressure goes up to the specified value as the valve is closed, it indicates that the pump is all right and that the loss of pressure is due to leakage at the power cylinder or valves. If the pump pressure stays low as the valve is closed, the loss of pressure is due to a defect in the pump—relief or flow-control valve stuck or damaged, rotors worn or broken, and so on.

5. Bleed the system, if necessary, by adding oil to the reservoir and turning the steering wheel to the left and right several times (do not bump the wheel at the extreme positions). Add more oil if the level in the reservoir falls too low.

⊘ **13-3 Servicing Power Cylinder and Valve (Separately Mounted Type)** (See Figs. 5-44 to 5-49.)
1. POWER-CYLINDER SERVICE The power cylinder is so constructed that repair of the unit in the

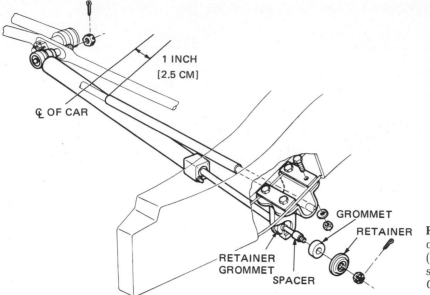

Fig. 13-1. Power-cylinder attachment. (*Chevrolet Motor Division of General Motors Corporation*)

field is not feasible if internal damage has occurred. Removal and installation of the power cylinder and replacement of piston-rod seals are covered in following paragraphs.

1. To remove the power cylinder, first raise the car on a hoist, wipe the hose fittings at the power cylinder so that they are really clean, detach the hoses, and let the system drain. For complete drainage, move the wheels back and forth several times. Do not reuse the old fluid.

Several methods of attaching the piston rod to the frame bracket are used. Figure 13-1 shows one method of attachment. On this model, the cotter pins and nuts at the piston-rod end and the ball-stud end are removed so that the power cylinder can be taken off. Figure 13-2 shows the method of attaching the ball stud to the piston body.

Figure 13-3 illustrates a typical arrangement for sealing the piston-rod end. The seals can be

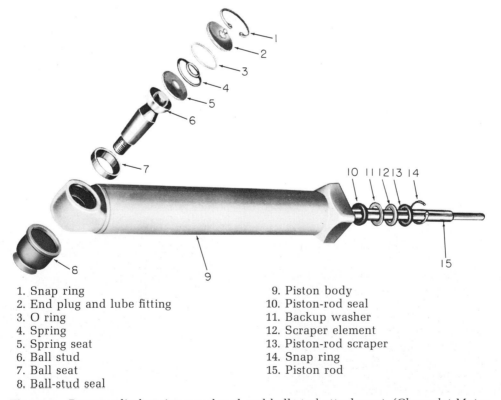

1. Snap ring
2. End plug and lube fitting
3. O ring
4. Spring
5. Spring seat
6. Ball stud
7. Ball seat
8. Ball-stud seal
9. Piston body
10. Piston-rod seal
11. Backup washer
12. Scraper element
13. Piston-rod scraper
14. Snap ring
15. Piston rod

Fig. 13-2. Power-cylinder piston-rod seal and ball-stud attachment. (*Chevrolet Motor Division of General Motors Corporation*)

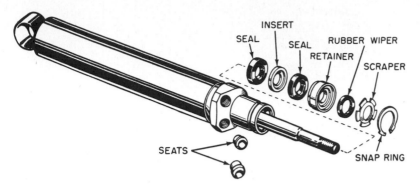

Fig. 13-3. Power-cylinder sealing arrangement at the piston-rod end. (*Ford Motor Company*)

replaced by removing the snap ring. New seals should be lubricated and pressed into place over the piston rod with a deep socket.

2. To install the power cylinder, reverse the removal procedure. If the grommet at the piston-rod end is worn, replace it. Grease the ball joint after the attachment is complete. Fill the pump reservoir, start the engine, and turn the steering wheel right and left to bleed the system. Refill the reservoir.

2. VALVE REMOVAL Attachments on different cars may require slightly different removal procedures; one procedure follows. Disconnect the four fluid lines from the control valve. Drain the fluid, turning the steering wheel to the right and left several times to force the fluid out. Loosen the clamping nut and bolt at the right end of the sleeve. Locate the roll pin in the steering-arm-to-idler-arm rod and remove it through the slot in the sleeve. Remove the control-valve ball-stud nut. Use the tool as shown in Fig. 13-4 to remove the ball stud from the control valve. Turn the front wheels to the left and unthread the control valve from the rod.

3. VALVE DISASSEMBLY Be very clean when working on the valve. Make sure your hands, the workbench, and the tools you use are clean. Even small traces of dirt are liable to cause damage to, and malfunctioning of, the valve assembly.

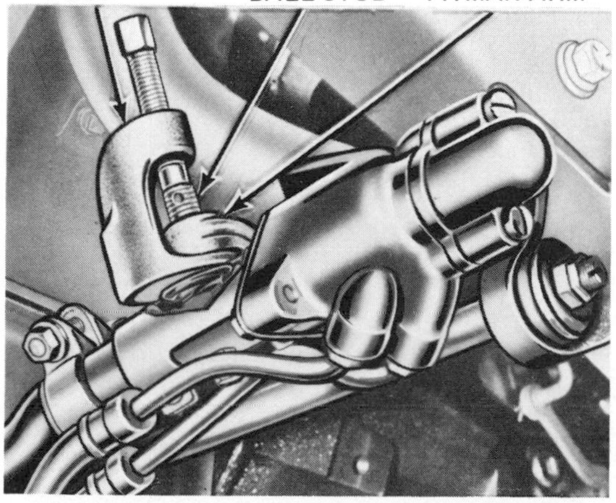

Put the valve assembly (Fig. 13-5) in the soft jaws of the vise, but do not tighten the vise more than necessary, since this could distort the valve. Clamp the vise around the sleeve flange.

Figure 13-6 is a disassembled view of one model of control valve. It is disassembled by removing the centering-spring cap from the valve housing and then removing the nut from the end of the valve-spool bolt. Now, the washers, spacer, centering spring, adapter, and bushing can be removed from the bolt and the valve housing.

Remove the two bolts and separate the valve sleeve from the housing. Remove the plug from the sleeve. Push the valve spool out of the centering-spring end of the valve housing and take the seal from the spool. Remove the spacer, bushing, and seal from the sleeve end of the housing.

Pull the head of the valve-spool bolt tightly against the travel-regulator stop and drive the stop pin out of the regulator stop with a punch (Fig. 13-7). Turn the travel regulator counterclockwise to remove it from the valve sleeve. Remove the spool bolt, spacer, and rubber washer from the travel-regulator stop. Other parts (dust shield, clamp, and ball stud) can now be removed from the valve sleeve.

If necessary, the plug, reaction spring, and reaction valve can be removed from the valve housing.

4. VALVE-PART INSPECTION Clean all parts in solvent and inspect them for wear, cracks, scores,

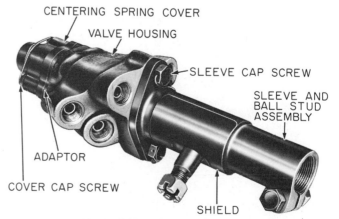

Fig. 13-4. Removing the control-valve ball stud. (*Ford Motor Company*)

Fig. 13-5. Valve-and-sleeve assembly. (*Ford Motor Company*)

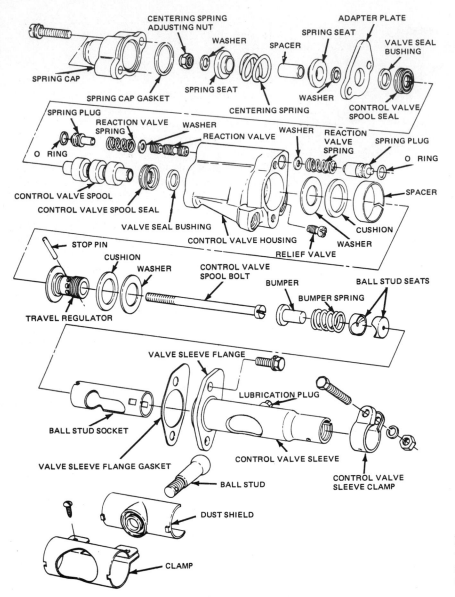

Fig. 13-6. Disassembled view of the control-valve assembly. (*Ford Motor Company*)

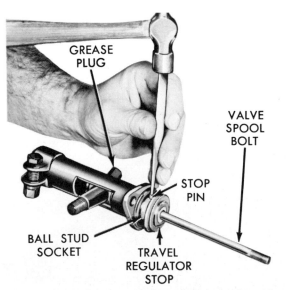

Fig. 13-7. Driving the stop pin out of the travel regulator. (*Ford Motor Company*)

or other damage that would require replacement. If the valve spool has small burrs, they can be removed with very fine crocus cloth provided the sharp edges of the spool *are not rounded off*.

5. *CONTROL-VALVE ASSEMBLY* Coat all parts with specified lubricants. Install the reaction valve, spring, and plug in housing. Install the return-port relief valve and the hose seat if they have been removed.

Insert one ball-stud seat, flat end first, into the ball-stud socket, and insert the threaded end of the ball stud into the socket. Put the socket into the control-valve sleeve so that the threaded end can be pulled out through the sleeve slot (Fig. 13-8). Put the other ball-stud seat, spring, and bumper into the socket and install and tighten the travel-regulator stop.

Loosen the stop just enough to align the nearest hole in the stop with the slot in the ball-stud socket, and install the stop pin in the socket, travel-regulator stop, and valve-spool bolt. Install the rubber boot,

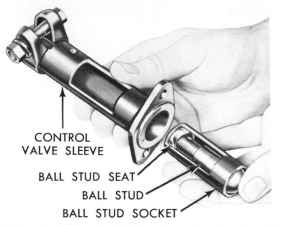

CONTROL
VALVE SLEEVE

BALL STUD SEAT

BALL STUD

BALL STUD SOCKET

Fig. 13-8. Installing the ball-stud seal and socket. (*Ford Motor Company*)

clamp, and plug on the sleeve. Make sure the lubrication fitting is tight but does not bind on the ball-stud socket.

Insert the valve spool in the housing, rotating it carefully while installing it. Move the spool toward the centering-spring end of the housing and put the small seal, bushing, and spacer in the sleeve end of the housing.

Press the valve spool against the inner lip of the seal and guide the lip of the seal over the spool with a small screwdriver. Do not nick or scratch the seal or spool!

Put the sleeve end of the housing on a flat surface so that the seal, bushing, and spacer are at the bottom, and push down on the valve spool until it stops. Carefully install the spool seal and bushing in the centering-spring end of the housing around the large end of the spool. Guide the seal over the spool with a small screwdriver. Do not nick or scratch the seal or spool!

Pick up the housing and move the spool back and forth to make sure it moves freely. Attach sleeve

assembly to housing, making sure the ball stud is on the same side of the housing as the ports for the power-cylinder lines.

Put the adapter on the housing and install the bushings, washers, spacers, and centering spring on the valve-spool bolt. Compress the centering spring and install the nut on the bolt, tightening it securely. (But not excessively tight, as this could break the travel-regulator stop pin.) Back the nut off not more than $\frac{1}{4}$ turn.

Move the ball stud back and forth in the sleeve slot to check the spool for free movement. Install the centering-spring cap on the housing. Put the nut on the ball stud temporarily so that the nut can be clamped in a vise and the control valve pushed back and forth to check for free movement of the valve spool.

6. VALVE INSTALLATION As a first step in installing the valve on the car, screw it onto the steering-arm rod until about four threads are showing on the rod. Then put the ball stud in the pitman arm and check the distance between the center of the grease plug in the sleeve and the center of the stud at the inner end of the left-steering-spindle-arm connecting rod (Fig. 13-9). This distance should be $11\frac{15}{16}$ inches [303.2 mm] on the installation shown. To adjust, turn the valve in or out on the rod. Then line the slot in the sleeve with the hole in the rod and lock the valve in this position with a roll pin. Tighten the sleeve-clamp bolt to specifications.

Install the ball-stud nut and tighten it to the specified torque. Lock it with a cotter pin. Install the pressure and return lines.

Lower the car on the hoist and make any adjustments necessary at the tie-rod ends to secure straight-ahead position of the steering wheel and the front wheels. Check and correct the toe-in, if necessary.

Fill the pump reservoir and start the engine. Bleed the system by idling for 2 minutes, adding

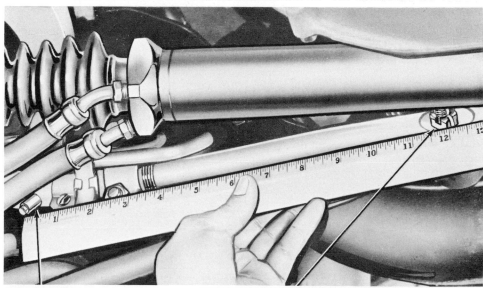

GREASE PLUG   SPINDLE CONNECTING ROD BALL STUD

Fig. 13-9. Measuring control-valve length on the installation. (*Ford Motor Company*)

more oil if necessary, and then increasing engine speed to 1,000 rpm and turning the wheels back and forth several times. Do not hit the stops at the extreme positions! Check the connections for leaks and add more oil if necessary. Finally, check the steering effort with a pull scale as already explained (⊘ 13-2, item 3).

⊘ **13-4 Pump Service** The pumps used with the linkage-type power-steering units are similar to those used with the integral-type systems (Chaps. 10 and 12). Servicing procedures for these other systems that have already been discussed will, in general, cover servicing of the pumps used with the linkage-type systems.

CHAPTER 13 CHECKUP

Here is your chance to check up on yourself and find out how well you remember the important points in testing and servicing linkage-type power-steering units described in the chapter. Now that more and more cars are being supplied with power steering, it is important for you to know how all types are serviced. This chapter describes servicing procedures on one type of power-steering equipment. Preceding chapters describe other types. Thus, if you remember the procedures outlined in these chapters, you will have the basic knowledge that will assist you in working on power steering.

Correcting Troubles Lists The purpose of this exercise is to help you spot related and unrelated troubles on a list. Refer to the test instructions at the end of Chap. 10 for an explanation of how to take this test.

Write the lists in your notebook, but do not write the item that does not belong.

1. Hard steering: low oil or leaks, low oil pressure, binding in steering linkage, piston rod bent, tight pump drive belt, valve stuck or out of adjustment.
2. Low oil pressure: pump belt slipping, valve stuck, drive coupling broken, pump defective, low tire pressure, leaks past piston or valve.
3. Poor centering or recovery from turns: pitman arm and stud binding on power cylinder, bind in steering column or gear, bind in steering linkage, bent piston rod, excessive oil in cylinder, incorrect front alignment, valve misadjusted or stuck.
4. Car wander: uneven tire pressure, pitman arm and stud binding on power cylinder, valve stuck or

misadjusted, oil pressure low, front alignment incorrect.
5. Noises: low oil level, pump bushing worn, dirty pump, looseness in steering linkage, tie rods improperly attached, high oil level.

Completing the Sentences The sentences below are incomplete. After each sentence there are several words or phrases, only one of which will correctly complete the sentence. Write each sentence in your notebook, selecting the proper word or phrase to complete it correctly.

1. A quick check of belt tension can be made by turning the wheel to the extreme position; if the belt slips, it is: (a) too tight, (b) too loose, (c) undersized, (d) worn and should be replaced.
2. If the oil pressure goes up to specifications when the shutoff valve on the gauge is turned off, it is likely that the oil pump: (a) is all right, (b) is worn, (c) needs a new belt, (d) requires replacement.
3. If the separately mounted power cylinder is internally damaged, it must: (a) be disassembled for adjustment, (b) have internal parts replaced, (c) be replaced as a unit.
4. If right turn is too hard and left turn too easy on the integral type of power-steering unit, the valve plug should be: (a) removed, (b) replaced, (c) turned in, (d) turned out.

Servicing Procedures Write in your notebook the procedures that are asked for. Do not copy from the book; write the procedures in your own words just as you might tell a friend. This will help you remember them.

1. Pick a car equipped with separately mounted linkage-type equipment and describe in detail how to remove and replace the power cylinder and valve.
2. Describe how to disassemble and reassemble the valve.

SUGGESTIONS FOR FURTHER STUDY

When you are in your school or local automotive service shop, examine various linkage types of power-steering equipment. If you have a chance, watch an expert disassemble or service this equipment. Study car manuals which explain how the units are serviced. Be sure to write important facts in your notebook.

chapter 14

AUTOMOTIVE BRAKES

This chapter describes the construction and operation of the various types of brakes used on automobiles. The chapters that follow explain how to service brakes. Since the great majority of brakes in use today are hydraulically actuated, the chapter reviews hydraulic principles and explains their application to brakes. There are two general types of hydraulic brakes: drum and disk (also spelled "disc"). In the drum type, curved brake shoes move out against the inner surfaces of brake drums. In the disk type, flat brake pads or shoes move in against a flat disk.

⊘ **14-1 Function and Types of Brakes**   Brakes slow and stop the car. They may be operated by mechanical, hydraulic, air-pressure, or electrical devices. Essentially, however, all function in the same manner. The operating device forces brake shoes or pads against the rotating brake drums or disks at the wheels when the driver operates the brake pedal. Friction between the brake shoes or pads and the brake drums or disks then slows or stops the wheels so that the car is braked. You should reread ⊘ 1-16 to 1-21 on friction if you do not remember the details of frictional action.

Figure 14-1 shows a front-wheel brake mechanism of the drum type in disassembled view so that the relationship of the parts can be seen. When the

mechanism is assembled, the brake drum fits around the brake shoes as shown in Fig. 14-2. Figure 14-3 shows a rear-wheel brake mechanism in disassembled view.

The brake shoes are lined with an asbestos material that can withstand the heat and dragging effect imposed when the shoes are forced against the brake drum or disk. During hard braking, the shoe may be pressed against the drum or disk with a pressure of as much as 1,000 psi [70.31 kg/cm^2]. Since friction increases as the load, or pressure, increases (⊘ 1-17), a strong frictional drag is produced on the brake drum or disk and a strong braking effect results on the wheel.

A great deal of heat is produced, also, by the

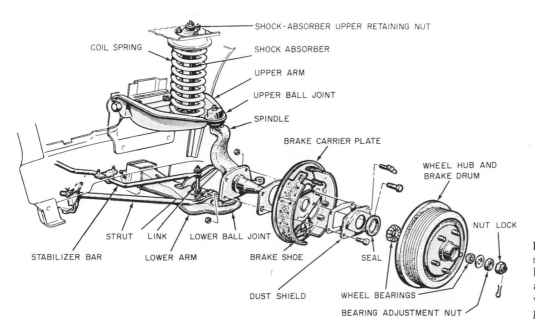

Fig. 14-1. Front-suspension and drum-type brake mechanism in a partly disassembled view. (*Ford Motor Company*)

SHOCK-ABSORBER UPPER RETAINING NUT
COIL SPRING
SHOCK ABSORBER
UPPER ARM
UPPER BALL JOINT
SPINDLE
BRAKE CARRIER PLATE
WHEEL HUB AND BRAKE DRUM
NUT LOCK
STRUT   LINK   LOWER BALL JOINT
STABILIZER BAR
LOWER ARM
BRAKE SHOE
SEAL
DUST SHIELD
WHEEL BEARINGS
BEARING ADJUSTMENT NUT

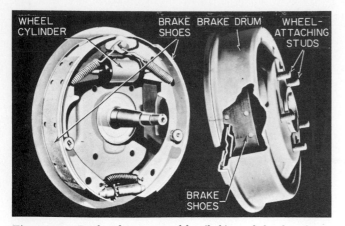

Fig. 14-2. Brake-shoe assembly (*left*) and brake drum in place on the assembly (*right*). The drum is partly cut away to show a shoe. The studs are for attaching the wheel to the drum. (*Oldsmobile Division of General Motors Corporation*)

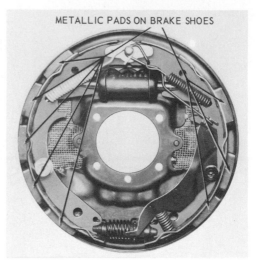

Fig. 14-4. Details of the brake assembly using metallic pads instead of brake lining. (*Chevrolet Motor Division of General Motors Corporation*)

frictional effect between the brake shoes and the drum or disk. When you rub your hands together vigorously, they become warm. In a similar manner, when the drum or disk rubs against the shoe, the drum or disk and shoe get warm. In fact, under extreme braking conditions, temperatures may reach 500 degrees Fahrenheit [260°C]. The heat is disposed of in different ways in drum and disk brakes. In the drum type, some of the heat goes through the brake linings to the shoes and backing plate, where it is radiated to the surrounding air. But most of it is absorbed by the brake drum. Some brake drums have cooling fins that provide additional radiating surface for dispelling the heat more readily. Excessive temperature is not good for brakes, since it may char the brake lining; also, with the lining and shoes hot, less effective braking action results. This is the reason that brakes "fade" when they are used continuously for relatively long periods, as they are, for instance, when the car is coming down a mountain or long slope.

Some special-performance vehicles, such as racing cars, are equipped with metallic brakes. Instead of linings of asbestos material, these brakes have a series of metallic pads attached to the brake shoes (Fig. 14-4). These brakes can withstand more

severe braking and higher temperatures and have less tendency to fade.

The disks in disk brakes are ventilated to improve cooling and reduce fade. For example, the disk shown in Fig. 14-5 has cooling louvers or fins to aid in the dissipation of heat. Also, note that only a small part of the disk is in contact with the brake shoes or pads during braking. The rest of the disk is dissipating heat. Disk brakes are described in detail in ⊘ 14-12.

⊘ **14-2 Mechanical Brakes** Mechanical brakes are no longer widely used for braking or stopping the car, although almost all cars have a mechanically operated parking brake. Mechanical brakes incorporate cables that link the brake pedal with the brake-shoe operating devices. Figure 14-6 illustrates a mechanically operated four-wheel brake system. Pressing down on the brake pedal pulls against cables attached to the brake-shoe expanding devices. The brake-shoe expanding device consists of a lever or cam that is actuated or rotated to push one end of the brake shoe out. The other end of the brake shoe is attached to the brake backing plate by an anchor pin. Figure 14-7 illustrates one type of cam-operated brake shoe.

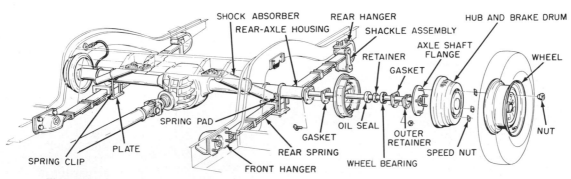

Fig. 14-3. Rear-suspension and drum-type brake mechanism in partly disassembled view. (*Ford Motor Company*)

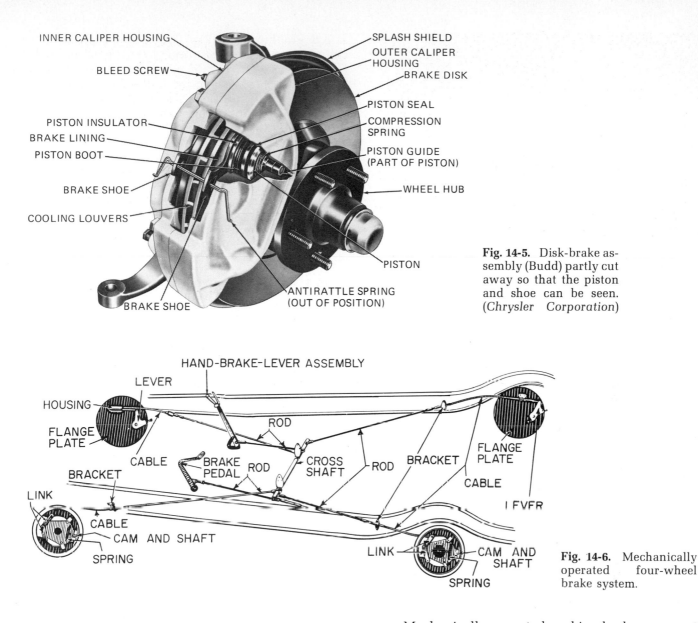

INNER CALIPER HOUSING

BLEED SCREW

PISTON INSULATOR

BRAKE LINING

PISTON BOOT

BRAKE SHOE

COOLING LOUVERS

BRAKE SHOE

SPLASH SHIELD

OUTER CALIPER HOUSING

BRAKE DISK

PISTON SEAL

COMPRESSION SPRING

PISTON GUIDE (PART OF PISTON)

WHEEL HUB

PISTON

ANTIRATTLE SPRING (OUT OF POSITION)

Fig. 14-5. Disk-brake assembly (Budd) partly cut away so that the piston and shoe can be seen. (*Chrysler Corporation*)

HAND-BRAKE-LEVER ASSEMBLY

LEVER

HOUSING

FLANGE PLATE

CABLE

BRAKE PEDAL

ROD

ROD

CROSS SHAFT

ROD

BRACKET

FLANGE PLATE

CABLE

LEVER

BRACKET

LINK

CABLE

CAM AND SHAFT

SPRING

LINK

CAM AND SHAFT

SPRING

Fig. 14-6. Mechanically operated four-wheel brake system.

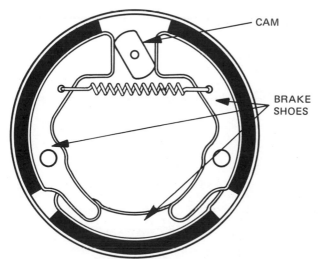

CAM

BRAKE SHOES

Fig. 14-7. Brake-shoe actuating device. The pull of a cable from the brake pedal rotates the cam. The cam, as it rotates, forces the ends of the shoes outward and into contact with the brake drum.

Mechanically operated parking brakes on most cars make use of a foot or hand brake connected by cables to the rear-wheel brake shoes or to a separate brake that is part of the transmission shaft. Figure 14-8 illustrates the layout of a parking brake that makes use of the two rear-wheel brakes. The hand lever, when pulled, pulls cables that operate levers in the two rear-wheel brake mechanisms. The levers, as they operate, force the brake shoes apart and into contact with the brake drum. In many cars, the parking brake is released by a vacuum cylinder when the engine is started and the transmission selector lever is moved out of PARK.

⊘ **14-3 Hydraulic Principles** Since most brakes are hydraulically operated, we might review briefly the hydraulic principles that cause them to operate. ⊘ 1-12 to 1-15 describe the manner in which motion and pressure can be transmitted by a fluid. Since fluid is not compressible, pressure on a fluid will force it through a tube and into chambers or cylinders, where it can force pistons to move. This is

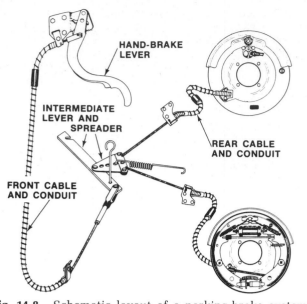

Fig. 14-8. Schematic layout of a parking-brake system. Operation of the hand-brake lever causes the intermediate lever to pivot forward. This pulls on the two rear cables so that the rear brakes are mechanically applied. (*Pontiac Motor Division of General Motors Corporation*)

shown graphically in Fig. 1-12, where a piston in a cylinder applies a pressure of 100 psi [7.03 kg/cm²]. In the illustration, fluid is shown being forced through lines or tubes to three other cylinders. The force the fluid applies to the pistons in the three cylinders is proportional to the size of the pistons. When the piston has an area of 1 square inch [6.5 cm²], there will be a force of 100 pounds [45.3 kg] on it (100 psi, in other words). If the piston has an area of 0.5 square inch [3.3 cm²] the force on it will be 50 pounds [22.7 kg] (100 psi × 0.5 square inch). If the piston has an area of 2 square inches, the force on it will be 200 pounds [90.6 kg] (100 psi × 2 square inches). You should review ⊘ 1-12 to 1-15 if these fundamentals are not clear in your mind.

⊘ **14-4 Hydraulic-Braking Action** Hydraulic-type brakes use the pressure of a fluid (hydraulic pressure) to force the brake shoes outward and against the brake drums or disk. Figure 14-9 illustrates schematically a typical hydraulic-brake system. The system consists essentially of two components: the brake pedal with master cylinder, and the wheel brake mechanisms, together with the connecting tubing or brake fluid lines and the supporting arrangements.

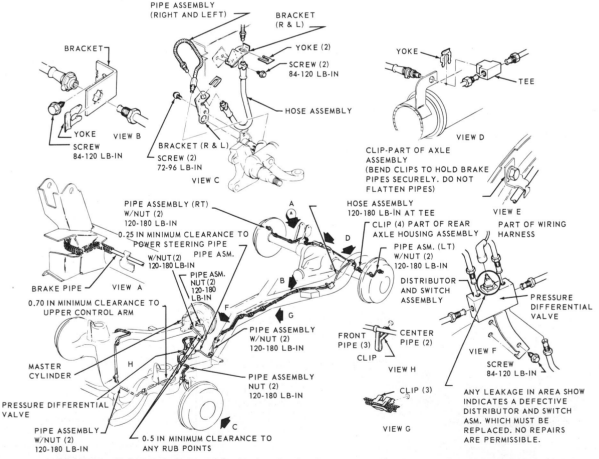

Fig. 14-9. Schematic layout of a hydraulic-brake system. This is one of several layouts shown in a recent shop manual. The illustration supplies details on how all components of the system are arranged. (*Buick Motor Division of General Motors Corporation*)

In operation, movement of the brake pedal forces a piston to move in the master cylinder. This applies pressure to fluid ahead of the piston, forcing the fluid—under pressure—through the brake lines to the wheel cylinders (Fig. 14-10). On the drum type,[1] each wheel cylinder has two pistons, as shown. Each piston is linked to one of the brake shoes by an actuating pin. Thus, when the fluid is forced into the wheel cylinders, the two wheel-cylinder pistons are pushed outward. This outward movement forces the brake shoes outward and into contact with the brake drum.

Note that in Fig. 14-10, piston sizes and hydraulic pressures are given as examples of the pressures involved. The piston in the master cylinder has an area of 0.8 square inch [5.2 cm^2]. A push of 800 pounds [362.9 kg] is being applied to the piston. This gives a pressure of 1,000 psi [70.31 kg/cm^2] in the system. This pressure at the rear wheels gives an outward force of 700 pounds [317.5 kg] on each piston. The pistons are 0.7 square inch [4.5 cm^2] in area. At the front wheels, the piston area is shown to be 0.9 square inch, so that a pressure of 900 pounds [408.2 kg] is applied by the pistons to the front brake shoes.

The pistons are usually larger at the front wheels because when the brakes are applied, the forward momentum of the car throws more of the weight on the front wheels. A stronger braking effort at the front wheels is therefore necessary to achieve balanced braking effort.

⊘ **14-5 Dual-Brake System**   In older-model cars, the master cylinder contained only one piston, and its movement forced brake fluid to all four wheel cylinders. In recent years, however, the hydraulic system has been split into two sections, a front section and a rear section (Fig. 14-11). With this arrangement, if

[1]Disk brakes are described in ⊘ 14-12.

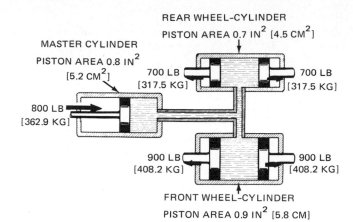

Fig. 14-10.   As the brake pedal is moved, the piston in the master cylinder applies pressure to the liquid. This pressure forces the liquid into the wheel cylinders. (*Pontiac Motor Division of General Motors Corporation*)

one section fails due to damage or leakage, the other section will still provide braking. This system also includes a warning light that comes on when one section has failed.

⊘ **14-6 Master Cylinder**   In the older braking system, the master cylinder had but one piston. The dual-brake system has a master cylinder with two pistons, set in tandem. Figures 14-12 to 14-15 illustrate the two types. The operation is similar in both systems, except that in the dual system there are two separate sections functioning independently. The master-cylinder pistons are linked to the brake pedal through a lever arrangement that provides a considerable mechanical advantage. That is, the push on the brake pedal is multiplied several times by the lever arrangement. For example, in the arrangement shown in Fig. 14-12, a push of 100 pounds [45.4 kg] on the brake pedal will produce a push of 750 pounds [340.2 kg] at the piston.

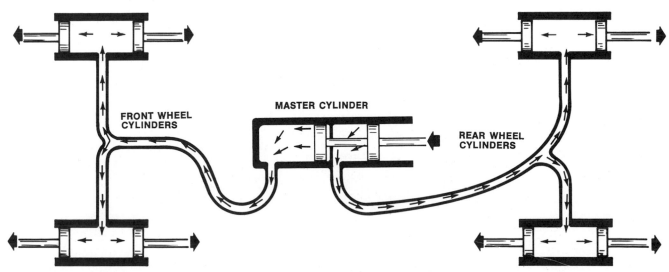

Fig. 14-11.   Flow of brake fluid to the four wheel cylinders when the pistons are pushed into the master cylinders.

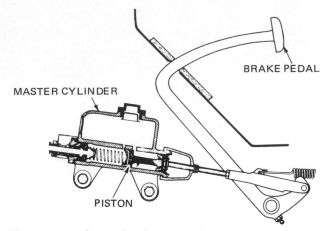

MASTER CYLINDER

BRAKE PEDAL

PISTON

Fig. 14-12. Relationship between the brake pedal and the single-piston master cylinder. (*Pontiac Motor Division of General Motors Corporation*)

As the piston in the master cylinder moves in (from the position shown in Fig. 14-12 to the position shown in Fig. 14-15), it moves past the compensating port. This traps the fluid in the cylinder that is ahead of the piston. Pressure rises rapidly, and fluid is forced through the brake lines to the wheel cylinders. This action is shown in Fig. 14-15.

⊘ **14-7 Wheel Cylinders** Figure 14-16 shows the construction of a wheel cylinder for a drum-type brake. Hydraulic pressure applied between the two piston cups forces the pistons out. Thus, the brake-shoe actuating pins force the brake shoes into contact with the brake drums. The piston cups are so

formed that the hydraulic pressure forces them tightly against the cylinder wall of the wheel cylinder. This produces a good sealing action that holds the fluid in the cylinder. For a description of the arrangement used at the wheels in the disk-type brake, see ⊘ 14-12.

⊘ **14-8 Self-energizing Action** When the brakes are applied, as shown in Fig. 14-15, the wheel cylinder pushes the brake shoes toward the rotating drum. The primary shoe—the shoe toward the front of the car—comes into contact with the drum first. The friction between the primary shoe and the drum forces the brake assembly to shift in the direction of drum rotation. It can shift only a little, because the anchor pin permits only limited movement (Fig. 14-17). This movement forces the primary shoe more tightly against the revolving drum, greatly increasing the braking action (Fig. 14-18).

At the same time, the adjusting screw and pin are forced to move as the primary shoe moves. In Fig. 14-19 we see how this shifts the adjusting screw in the direction of drum movement. Thus, the secondary shoe is forced against the drum by the wheel cylinder and the shifting of the adjusting screw. As a result, the secondary shoe provides about twice as much braking effect as the primary shoe. For this reason, the lining in the secondary shoe is larger (Fig. 14-20).

Always remember, when doing a brake job, that the primary shoe with the smaller lining, is toward the front of the car. The secondary shoe, with the larger lining, is toward the rear.

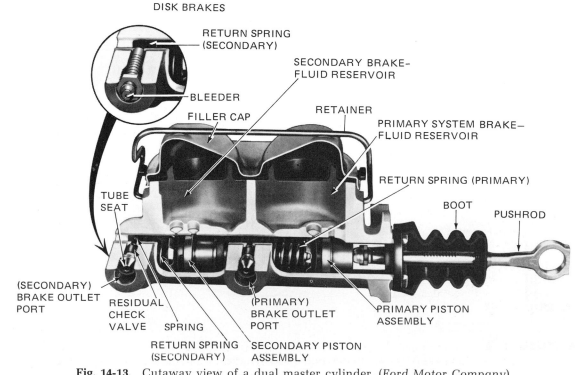

DISK BRAKES

RETURN SPRING (SECONDARY)

SECONDARY BRAKE-FLUID RESERVOIR

BLEEDER

FILLER CAP

RETAINER

PRIMARY SYSTEM BRAKE-FLUID RESERVOIR

RETURN SPRING (PRIMARY)

BOOT

PUSHROD

TUBE SEAT

(SECONDARY) BRAKE OUTLET PORT

RESIDUAL CHECK VALVE

SPRING

RETURN SPRING (SECONDARY)

(PRIMARY) BRAKE OUTLET PORT

SECONDARY PISTON ASSEMBLY

PRIMARY PISTON ASSEMBLY

Fig. 14-13. Cutaway view of a dual master cylinder. (*Ford Motor Company*)

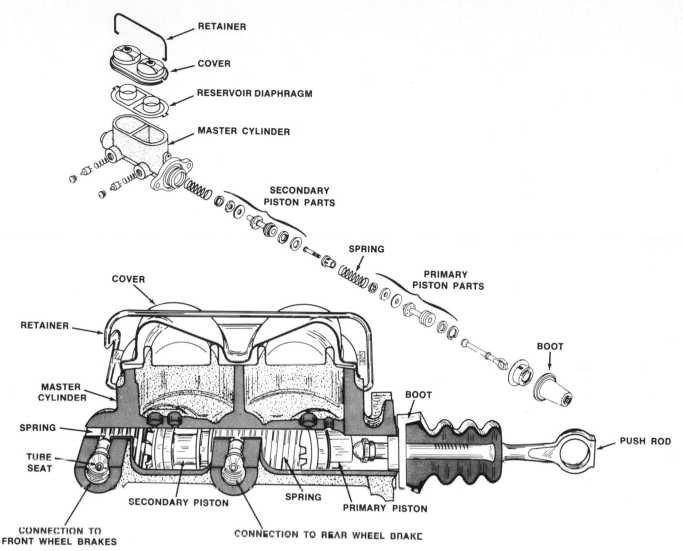

Fig. 14-14. Disassembled and cutaway assembled views of a master cylinder.

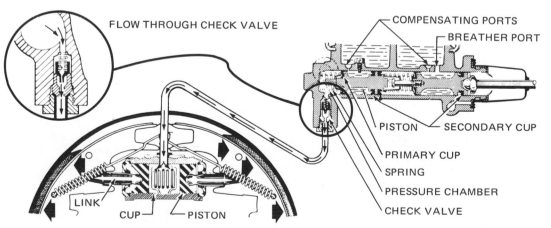

BRAKES BEING APPLIED

Fig. 14-15. Conditions in a drum-type brake system with the brakes applied. Brake fluid flows from the master cylinder to the wheel cylinder, as shown. There the fluid causes the wheel-cylinder pistons to move outward and thereby apply the brakes.

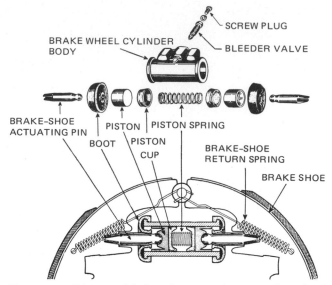

Fig. 14-16. Disassembled and sectional views of a wheel cylinder. (*Pontiac Motor Division of General Motors Corporation*)

⊘ **14-9 Return Stroke** On the return stroke, spring tension on the brake linkage and spring pressure against the master-cylinder piston force the piston to move back in its cylinder. Fluid now flows from the wheel cylinders to the master cylinder, as shown in Fig. 14-21. The tension of the brake-shoe springs forces the brake shoes away from the brake drums and thus pushes the wheel-cylinder pistons inward. Fluid is thus returned from the wheel cylinders to the master cylinder, as shown by the arrows. However, some pressure is trapped in the lines by the check valve at the end of the master cylinder (see

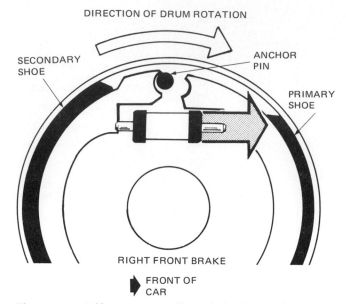

Fig. 14-17. Self-energizing effect of the brake shoes. The top of the primary shoe is forced against the rotating drum as the first effect. (*Ford Motor Company*)

Fig. 14-15). As the pressure drops, the check valve closes, trapping a few pounds of pressure in the lines and wheel cylinders. This pressure serves the purpose of keeping the wheel cylinders from leaking and also of reducing the chances of air leaking into the system.

⊘ **14-10 Warning Light** In the dual-brake system, a pressure differential valve is used to operate a warning-light switch. Figure 14-22 is a schematic view of the system. The valve (Fig. 14-23*a*) has a

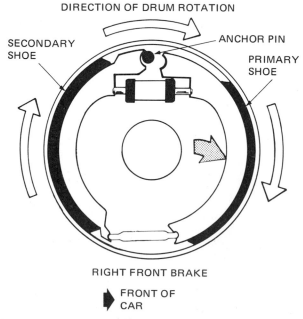

Fig. 14-18. Friction of the rotating drum against the top of the primary shoe forces the shoe to shift downward, as shown. This forces the whole shoe against the drum. (*Ford Motor Company*)

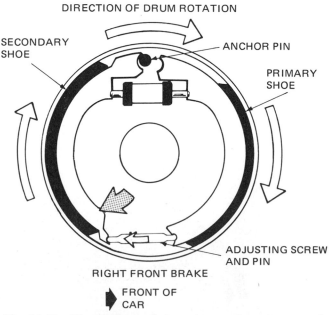

Fig. 14-19. The shifting of the primary shoe downward pushes the adjusting screw and pin to the left so that the bottom of the secondary shoe is forced against the drum. (*Ford Motor Company*)

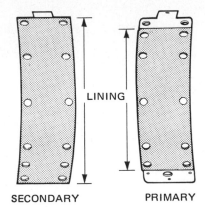

Fig. 14-20. The primary shoe lining is smaller, and the primary shoe is installed toward the front of the car. The secondary shoe lining is larger, and the secondary shoe is installed toward the rear of the car. (*Ford Motor Company*)

piston that is centered when both front and rear brakes are operating normally. However, if one section should fail, there will be low pressure on one side of the piston. The high pressure, from the normally operating section, will then move the piston and cause it to push the switch plunger upward (Fig. 14-23b). This closes contacts, which turns on the warning light on the instrument panel. The driver is thus warned that either the rear-wheel or the front-wheel brakes have failed.

Some switches have a tripping arrangement that causes the light to remain on, even though the brakes are not used again, until the trouble is fixed and the switch is reset.

⊘ **14-11 Self-adjusting Brakes (Drum Type)** Most automotive brakes now have a self-adjusting mechanism that automatically adjusts the brakes when they need it as a result of brake-lining wear. Figures 14-24 and 14-25 illustrate typical arrangements. The adjustment takes place only when the brakes are

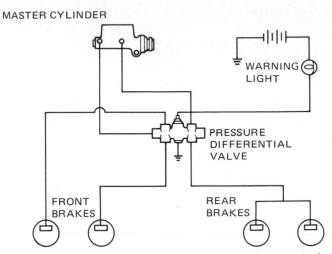

Fig. 14-22. Schematic drawing of dual-brake system with a pressure-differential valve. (*Chevrolet Motor Division of General Motors Corporation*)

applied as the car is moving rearward. When this happens, an adjustment is made only when the brake linings have worn enough to make adjustment necessary.

As the brakes are applied with the car moving backward, friction between the primary shoe and the brake drum forces the primary shoe against the anchor pin. Then hydraulic pressure from the wheel cylinder forces the upper end of the secondary shoe away from the anchor pin and downward (Fig. 14-26). This causes the adjuster lever to pivot on the secondary shoe so that the lower end of the lever is forced against the sprocket on the adjuster screw. If the brake linings have worn enough, the adjuster screw will be turned a full tooth. This spreads the lower ends of the brake shoes a few thousandths of an inch—enough to compensate for lining wear.

On some cars, the self-adjustment mechanism operates with the car moving forward when the brakes are applied.

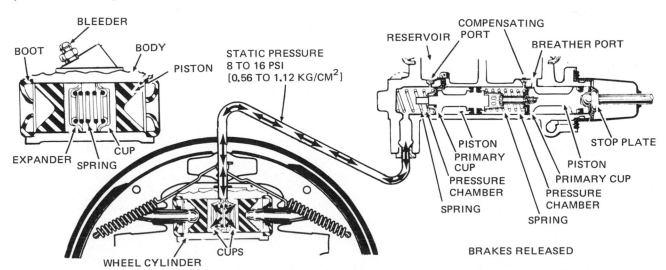

Fig. 14-21. Conditions in a drum-brake system when the brakes are released. Brake fluid flows back to the master cylinder, as shown. (*Buick Motor Division of General Motors Corporation*)

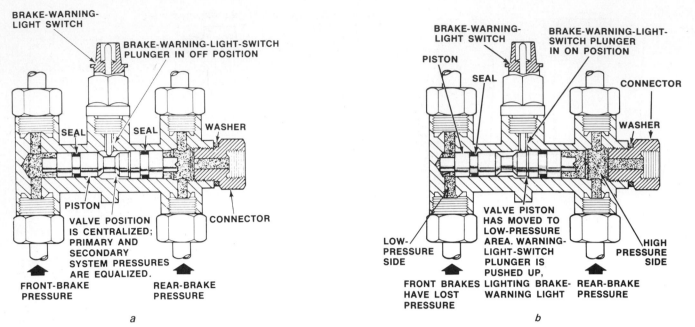

Fig. 14-23. The two positions of the pressure-differential valve: (*a*) normal operation; (*b*) with front brake system failed. (*Ford Motor Company*)

⊘ **14-12 Disk Brakes** The disk, or caliper, brake has a metal disk instead of a drum, and a pair of pads, or flat shoes, instead of the curved shoes used with the drum brakes. There are three general types, fixed-caliper, sliding-caliper, and floating-caliper. The caliper is the assembly in which the brake shoes are held. It contains the flat shoes or pads, which are positioned on the two sides of the disk (Figs. 14-27 and 14-28). In operation, the shoes are forced inward against the two sides of the disks by the movement of pistons in the caliper assembly (Fig. 14-29). These pistons are actuated by the hydraulic pressure developed in the master cylinder as the brake pedal is pushed down by the driver. The effect is to clamp the disk between the shoes. This is the same action you get when you pick up a piece of

paper; your fingers and thumb clamp on both sides of the paper to hold it. In the same way, the shoes apply friction to the disk and attempt to stop its rotation. This provides the braking action.

1. FIXED CALIPER The fixed-caliper disk brake (Figs. 14-27 and 14-30) has pistons on both sides of the disk (two on each side). The caliper is rigidly attached to a stationary car part. With front disk brakes, for example, the caliper is attached to the steering knuckle (or spindle), as shown in Fig. 14-30. On rear disk brakes, the caliper is attached to the rear-axle-housing flange. In operation, all four pistons are forced inward by hydraulic pressure, thus causing the two shoes to move in against the rotating disk.

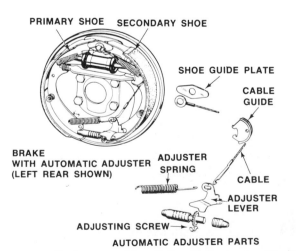

Fig. 14-24. Brake assembly of the drum type with the automatic self-adjuster and adjuster parts disassembled. (*Bendix-Westinghouse Automotive Air Brake Company*)

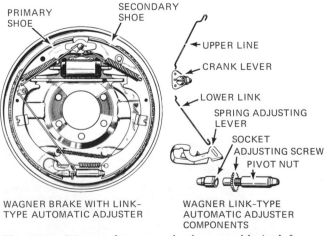

Fig. 14-25. Wagner drum-type brake assembly (at left rear wheel) with the link-type automatic self-adjuster and adjuster components disassembled. (*Bendix-Westinghouse Automotive Air Brake Company*)

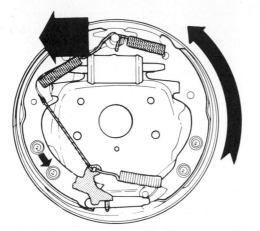

Fig. 14-26. Illustrating the self-adjustment of brakes. When the brakes are applied as the car is being backed, the shifting of the brake shoes actuates the adjusting lever. (*Ford Motor Company*)

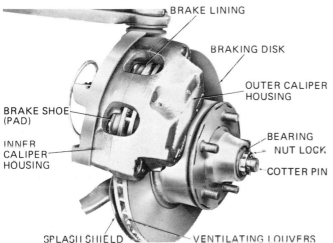

Fig. 14-27. Disk-brake assembly of the fixed-caliper type. (*Chrysler Corporation*)

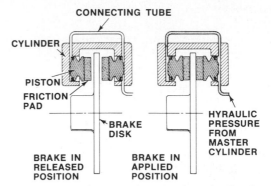

Fig. 14-29. Sectional views showing how hydraulic pressure forces friction pads inward against the brake disk to produce braking action.

2. FLOATING CALIPER The floating, or swinging, caliper (Fig. 14-31) can pivot, or swing in or out. It is mounted through rubber bushings which give enough to permit this movement. The caliper has only one piston. In operation, hydraulic pressure forces the piston to move toward the disk, thus forcing the inner brake shoe against the disk. At the same time, the pressure of the shoe against the disk causes the caliper to swing inward slightly so that the fixed brake shoe on the opposite side is brought into contact with the other side of the disk. Now, braking action is the same as with the fixed-caliper type.

3. SLIDING CALIPER The sliding caliper is similar to the floating caliper. The difference is that the sliding caliper is suspended from rubber bushings on bolts (Fig. 14-32). When hydraulic pressure is applied back of the piston, the piston pushes the inboard shoe into hard contact with the rotating brake disk. At the same time, the hydraulic pressure on the bottom end of the piston cylinder forces the caliper to slide inward. This brings the outboard shoe into hard contact with the outer surface of the rotating disk. The pressure of the shoes on the two sides of the disk provide the braking effect.

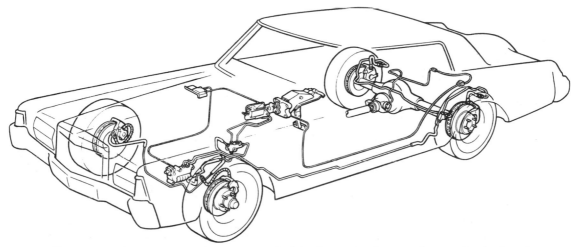

Fig. 14-28. Phantom view of a car using disk brakes at the front and rear wheels. (*Ford Motor Company*)

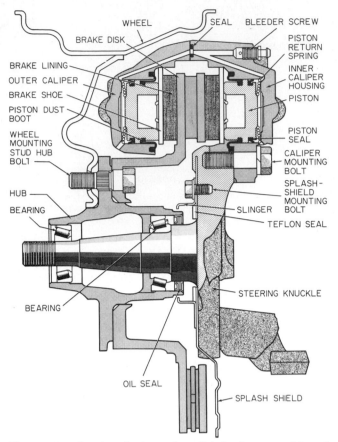

Fig. 14-30. Sectional view of a disk-brake assembly of the fixed-caliper type. (*Chrysler Corporation*)

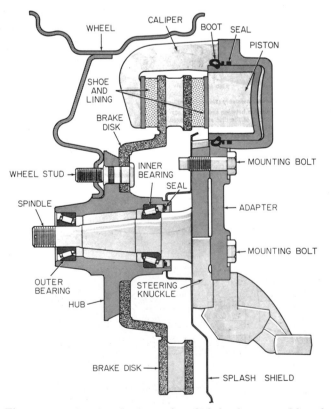

Fig. 14-31. Sectional view of a disk-brake assembly of the floating-caliper type. (*Chrysler Corporation*)

It is important to remember that the brake lining on the shoes is actually in contact with the brake disk at all times. This is not heavy contact (except when braking). It is a light sliding contact that keeps the disk wiped clean of foreign matter. Because of this "zero" clearance, relatively little brake pedal movement is required to produce braking action.

4. *TELLTALE TABS* Some brake shoes have telltale tabs (Fig. 14-33) which come into action when the brake linings are worn down to where they must be replaced. When this happens, the tabs rub against the disk and give off a scraping noise. This noise warns the driver that the brake shoes must be replaced.

⊘ **14-13 Self Adjustment of Disk Brakes** Disk brakes are self-adjusting. On some types, there is a piston-return spring back of each piston. This is a light spring that keeps the piston in the forward position and holds the brake lining lightly against the disk when the brakes are released. In this position, only a small additional movement of the pistons will bring the lining up hard against the disk for quick braking. Another system provides automatic self-adjustment by means of the piston seals. When the brakes are applied, the piston slides toward the disk, distorting the piston seal as shown in Fig. 14-34. Then, when the brakes are released, relaxation of the seal draws the piston slightly away from the disk, as shown. As the brake linings wear, piston travel tends to exceed the limit of deflection of the seal. The piston therefore slides outward through the seal to the precise extent necessary to compensate for lining wear.

⊘ **14-14 Metering Valve** Disk-brake systems have a metering valve. This valve keeps the front brakes from applying until the rear brakes apply. If the front brakes were applied first, the car could be thrown into a rear-end skid.

⊘ **14-15 Proportioning Valve** The proportioning valve improves braking action during hard braking, when more of the car weight is transferred to the front wheels. As a result, more braking is needed at the front wheels and less at the rear wheels. If normal braking continued, the rear wheels could skid and could throw the entire car into a rear-end skid. The proportioning valve reduces the pressure to the rear wheel brakes when hard braking and high fluid pressures develop. Figure 14-35 is a schematic view of the system and a sectional view of the proportioning valve.

⊘ **14-16 Combination Valve** In many cars the warning-light valve (⊘ 14-10), the metering valve, and the proportioning valve are combined into a single unit. Figure 14-36 is a sectional view of this combination valve.

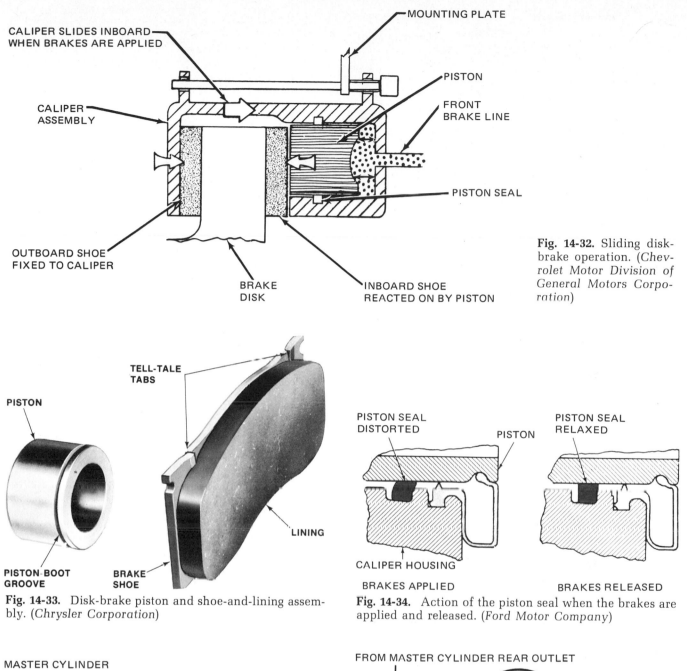

CALIPER SLIDES INBOARD
WHEN BRAKES ARE APPLIED

MOUNTING PLATE

CALIPER
ASSEMBLY

PISTON

FRONT
BRAKE LINE

OUTBOARD SHOE
FIXED TO CALIPER

PISTON SEAL

BRAKE
DISK

INBOARD SHOE
REACTED ON BY PISTON

Fig. 14-32. Sliding disk-brake operation. (*Chevrolet Motor Division of General Motors Corporation*)

PISTON

TELL-TALE
TABS

PISTON-BOOT
GROOVE

BRAKE
SHOE

LINING

PISTON SEAL
DISTORTED

PISTON

PISTON SEAL
RELAXED

CALIPER HOUSING

BRAKES APPLIED

BRAKES RELEASED

Fig. 14-33. Disk-brake piston and shoe-and-lining assembly. (*Chrysler Corporation*)

Fig. 14-34. Action of the piston seal when the brakes are applied and released. (*Ford Motor Company*)

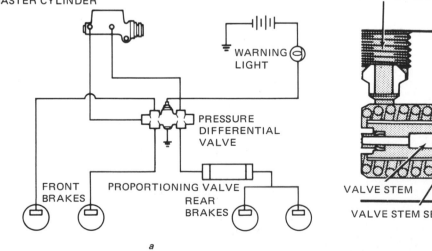

MASTER CYLINDER

WARNING
LIGHT

PRESSURE
DIFFERENTIAL
VALVE

FRONT
BRAKES

PROPORTIONING VALVE

REAR
BRAKES

a

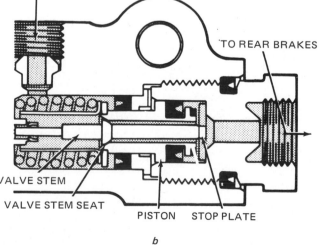

FROM MASTER CYLINDER REAR OUTLET

TO REAR BRAKES

VALVE STEM

VALVE STEM SEAT

PISTON   STOP PLATE

b

Fig. 14-35. Schematic drawing of a brake system with proportioning valve, and sectional view of the valve. (*Chevrolet Motor Division of General Motors Corporation*)

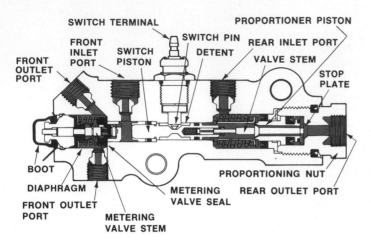

Fig. 14-36. Combination valve with warning-light, metering, and proportioning valves all in the same assembly. (*Chevrolet Motor Division of General Motors Corporation*)

⊘ 14-17 Parking Brake for Rear Disk Brakes

As explained in ⊘ 14-2, the drum brake shoes at the rear wheels can be actuated by a mechanical pull from a hand-brake lever in the driver's compartment. This arrangement provides sufficient braking to hold the car stationary when it is parked. However, the disk brakes cannot be directly actuated by a mechanical pull. The disk brakes at the rear wheels, therefore, must have a separate parking-brake arrangement. This arrangement consists of a brake drum and pair of brake shoes. The assembly is much like that used with the regular drum brakes described in ⊘ 14-1. The major difference is that the parking brakes are actuated by a mechanical pull whereas the hydraulic brakes are actuated by hydraulic pressure.

Figure 14-37 is a disassembled view of a rear disk-brake assembly, showing the shoes. The brake drum for these shoes is inside the disk-drum brake rotor. A cam or lever is located between the tops of the two brake shoes. When the cable from the parking-brake system is pulled, it rotates the cam or moves the lever to force the brake shoes tightly against the drum on the inside of the disk-drum rotor. With the brake shoes tightly applied, the rotor and wheel are held stationary for parking. Figure 14-38 is a sectional view of the assembly, showing how a parking-brake-shoe adjusting tool is used to get to the star (adjusting) wheel and turn it. This action moves the brake shoes closer to, or farther away from, the drum, thus establishing the proper parking-brake adjustment.

⊘ 14-18 Antiskid Devices

As mentioned (⊘ 1-21), the most efficient braking takes place when the wheels are still revolving. If the brakes lock the wheels so that the tires skid, kinetic friction results and braking is much less effective. To prevent skidding and thus provide maximum effective braking, several antiskid devices have been proposed. Some provide skid control of the rear wheels only. Others provide control at all four wheels. The meaning of "control" is this: As long as the wheels are rotating, the antiskid device permits normal application of the brakes. But if the brakes are applied so hard that the wheels tend to stop turning, and thus a skid starts to develop, the device comes into operation

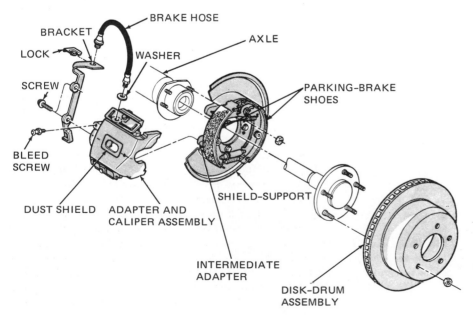

Fig. 14-37. Disassembled view of a sliding-caliper disk brake for a rear wheel. Note the parking-brake shoes. (*Chrysler Corporation*)

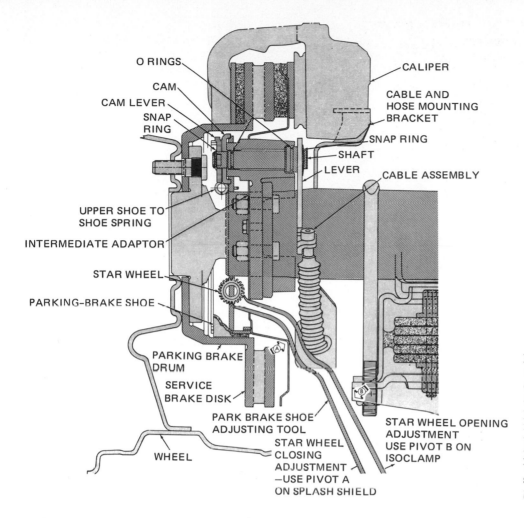

O RINGS
CAM
CAM LEVER
SNAP RING
CALIPER
CABLE AND HOSE MOUNTING BRACKET
SNAP RING
SHAFT
LEVER
CABLE ASSEMBLY
UPPER SHOE TO SHOE SPRING
INTERMEDIATE ADAPTOR
STAR WHEEL
PARKING-BRAKE SHOE
PARKING BRAKE DRUM
SERVICE BRAKE DISK
PARK BRAKE SHOE ADJUSTING TOOL
WHEEL
STAR WHEEL CLOSING ADJUSTMENT —USE PIVOT A ON SPLASH SHIELD
STAR WHEEL OPENING ADJUSTMENT USE PIVOT B ON ISOCLAMP

Fig. 14-38. Sectional view of a sliding-caliper disk brake assembly for a rear wheel. The two positions of the parking-brake-shoe adjusting tool for turning the adjusting star wheel one way or the other are shown. (*Chrysler Corporation*)

and partly releases the brakes so the wheels continue to rotate. However, braking continues. But it is held to just below the point where a skid would start. The result is maximum braking effect.

⊘ **14-19 Buick Max Trac** The Buick antiskid device is called *Max Trac*. It uses two sensing devices, one for the rear wheels and one for the left front wheel. The rear-wheel sensing device is actually located at the transmission output shaft. The two sensing devices feed data to a solid-state computer located under the instrument panel. The computer is constantly comparing wheel speeds. If at any time the rear-wheel speed gets to be 10 percent greater than the front wheel speed—which indicates a skid is starting—the computer repeatedly interrupts the ignition-system action for a brief moment ($\frac{1}{100}$ second). This of course slows the rear wheels. Depending on the severity of the rear-wheel spin, or skid, the interruptions take place up to 50 times a second. They continue until there is less than 10 percent difference between the rear- and front-wheel speeds. There is no risk of stalling the engine with such short interruptions of the ignition-system actions.

With less than 10 percent difference, the rear wheels are assumed to have adequate traction to stop the skid, or wheel spin.

The rear-wheel speed sensor, located in the speedometer drive opening in the transmission housing, has a gear which spins when the transmission output shaft, and the rear wheels, are turning. Surrounding the gear is a housing with internal splines, and a coil. A magnet is located within the coil. The rotating gear causes the magnetic lines of forces to change, or weave, as it were, as the gear teeth pass the splines in the housing. This moving magnetic field creates an alternating current (ac) in the coil. This ac flows to the computer. The higher the speed, the higher the frequency of the ac.

At the same time, the left front wheel is sending ac to the computer. This ac originates from a round metal plate with 30 elongated holes in it that rotates with the wheel. A magnetic pickup is mounted directly opposite the holes. As the wheel turns, the holes alternately allow and prevent the magnetic field from acting on a coil. This produces ac which is fed to the computer. The faster the wheel turns, the higher the frequency of the ac.

Actually, the computer is comparing the frequencies of the ac from the two sensors, and it acts when the frequency of the rear-wheel sensor ac shows the rear wheels are turning 10 percent or more faster than the front wheels. Not only does this inhibit rear-wheel skid or spin, it also prevents wheel spin when accelerating on dry pavement.

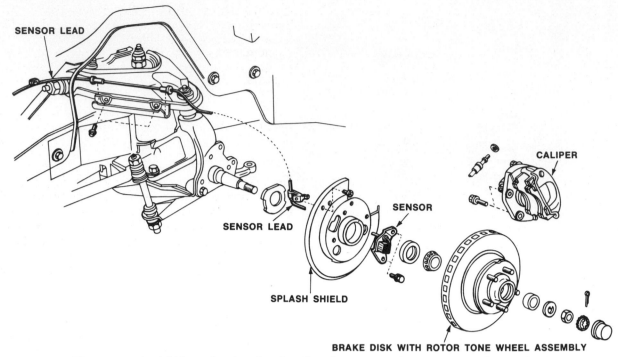

Fig. 14-39. Antiskid mechanism for the Chrysler Sure-Brake system at a front wheel. (*Chrysler Corporation*)

⊘ **14-20 Chrysler Sure-Brake** The antiskid system used on cars manufactured by Chrysler Corporation is called the *Sure-Brake system.* Figure 14-39 shows the antiskid mechanism at a front wheel. Figure 14-40 shows the mechanism at a rear wheel. The action is the same at both wheels. At the front wheel there is a magnetic wheel attached to the brake disk. As the wheel and disk revolve, the magnetic wheel produces alternating current (ac) in the sensor. The

sensor is a coil of wire, or a winding. A similar action takes place at the other wheels. These ac signals from the car wheels are fed into a logic control unit, located in the trunk, as shown in Fig. 14-41.

When the brakes are applied, the logic control compares the ac signals from the wheels. The frequency of the ac increases with speed. As long as the frequency of the ac from all wheels is about the same, normal braking will take place. However, if

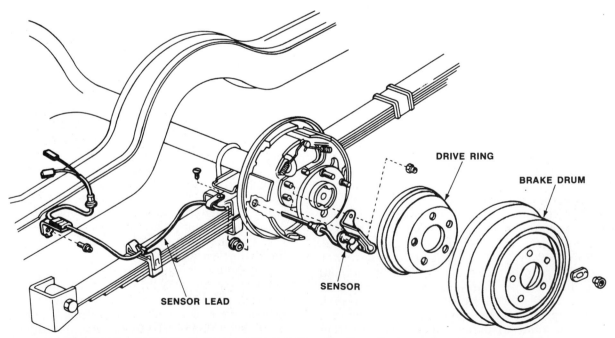

Fig. 14-40. Antiskid mechanism for the Chrysler Sure-Brake system at a rear wheel. (*Chrysler Corporation*)

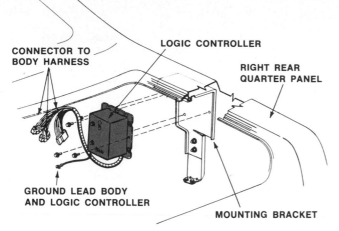

Fig. 14-41. Location of the logic control unit. (*Chrysler Corporation*)

the ac from any wheel is slowing down too rapidly, it means that the wheel is also slowing down too rapidly. It is beginning to skid.

When the logic control unit senses a rapid drop in the frequency of the ac, it signals modulators at the front of the car. Figure 14-42 shows the locations of the front-wheel and rear-wheel modulators. The hydraulic pressure from the master cylinder to the wheel cylinder or calipers passes through these modulators. When the logic control unit senses that a wheel is about to skid, it signals the modulator for that wheel to "ease up." It "tells" the modulator to reduce the hydraulic pressure to the brake for that wheel. When the pressure is reduced, the braking effect at that wheel is reduced, so the skid is prevented.

⊘ 14-21 Brake Fluid The liquid used in the hydraulic-brake system is called *brake fluid*. Brake fluid must have very definite characteristics. It must be chemically inert, it must be little affected by high or low temperatures, it must provide lubrication for the master-cylinder and wheel-cylinder pistons, and it must not attack the metallic and rubber parts in the braking system. Therefore, only the brake fluid recommended by the car manufacturer must be used when the addition of brake fluid becomes necessary.

CAUTION: **Mineral oil must never be put into the brake system. Mineral oil will cause the rubber parts in the system, including the piston cups, to swell and disintegrate. This would, of course, cause faulty braking action and possibly complete brake failure. Nothing except the fluid recommended by the manufacturer must be put into the hydraulic-brake system.**

⊘ 14-22 Brake Lines Steel pipe is used between the master cylinder and the frame connections, and between the rear-axle T (or "tee") fitting and the rear-wheel cylinders. Flexible hose connects the brake pipe to the front-wheel cylinders and to the rear-axle fitting. These various hoses and pipes can be seen in Fig. 14-9. If a section of pipe or a hose becomes damaged, be sure to replace it with the proper pipe or hose specified by the manufacturer. Since these lines are required to withstand considerable pressure, they are special. Ordinary copper tubing, for example, would not be satisfactory. The steel pipe, or tubing, must be double-flared (as explained in Chap. 15) when it is installed.

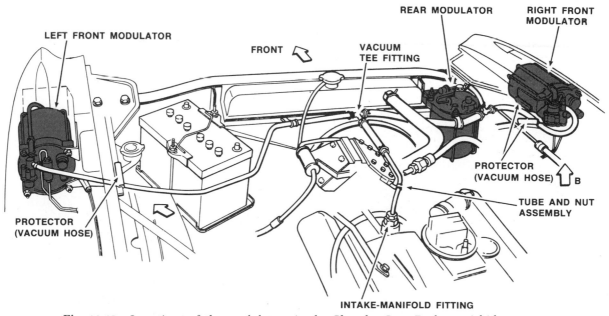

Fig. 14-42. Locations of the modulators in the Chrysler Sure-Brake antiskid system. (*Chrysler Corporation*)

⊘ **14-23 Stoplight Switch** Until the introduction of the dual-brake system, most stoplight switches were hydraulic. They contained a small diaphragm that was moved by hydraulic pressure when the brakes were applied. This action closed a switch which connected the stoplights to the battery.

When the dual-brake system came on the scene, however, the hydraulic switch could no longer be used. With this system, there are two separate hydraulic systems: one for the front wheels and one for the rear wheels. If the hydraulic switch were connected into one system, and if that system failed, the car would have no stoplights even though the other system was still working and stopping the car.

Thus, the mechanical switch came into use. Figures 14-43 and 14-44 illustrate one design. When the pedal is pushed for braking, it carries the switch contacts with it (to left in Fig. 14-44). This brings the switch contacts together so the stoplights come on.

Check Your Progress

Progress Quiz 14-1 Before you continue your study of automotive brake systems and start reading about power brakes, let us stop here and check up on the progress you have been making. There are two good reasons for the quizzes and the chapter checkups, as we have mentioned. First, they help you to review and thus to remember important points discussed in the book. Second, they give you a chance to check yourself on the progress you have been making. If you don't do as well as you would like, you can reread the previous pages and take the quiz again. This helps you to remember the important details you have been studying.

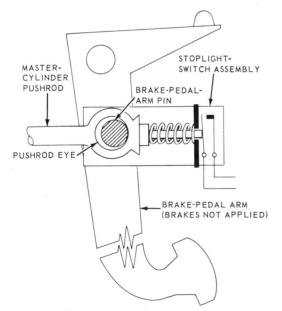

Fig. 14-43. Mechanical stoplight switch shown open, with brakes not applied. (*Ford Motor Company*)

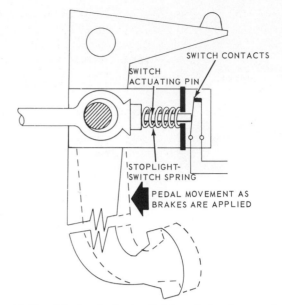

Fig. 14-44. Mechanical stoplight switch shown closed, with brakes applied. (*Ford Motor Company*)

Completing the Sentences The sentences below are incomplete. After each sentence there are several words or phrases, only one of which will correctly complete the sentence. Write each sentence in your notebook, selecting the proper word or phrase to complete it correctly.

1. The most widely used brakes are operated: (*a*) electrically, (*b*) hydraulically, (*c*) by air pressure, (*d*) by vacuum.
2. During braking, the brake shoe is moved outward to press against the: (*a*) wheel piston or cylinder, (*b*) brake lining, (*c*) brake drum or disk, (*d*) wheel rim or axle.
3. A piston with an area of 2.5 in^2 is forced into a liquid-filled cylinder with a push of 500 lb. The pressure on the liquid is: (*a*) 200 psi, (*b*) 500 psi, (*c*) 1,250 psi, (*d*) 5,000 psi.
4. With a pressure of 800 psi acting on it, the push on a piston with an area of 0.4 in^2 would be: (*a*) 200 lb, (*b*) 320 lb, (*c*) 500 lb, (*d*) 5,000 lb.
5. If the piston in the master cylinder has an area of 0.8 in^2 and the push applied on it is 800 lb, the hydraulic pressure in the brake fluid is: (*a*) 100 psi, (*b*) 640 psi, (*c*) 1,000 psi.
6. In most models of drum-type brakes, each wheel cylinder contains: (*a*) one piston, (*b*) two pistons, (*c*) three pistons.
7. As a rule, when comparing the front and rear wheel-cylinder pistons, it will be found that the pistons in the front wheel cylinders are: (*a*) larger in diameter, (*b*) smaller in diameter, (*c*) the same size.
8. In the dual-brake system, the master cylinder has: (*a*) one piston, (*b*) two pistons, (*c*) three pistons, (*d*) four pistons.
9. There are three general types of disk brake: (*a*) fixed-caliper, tab-action and two-piston, (*b*) fixed-

caliper, sliding-caliper, and floating-caliper, (c) float-ing-caliper, swinging-caliper, and proportioning. 10. The antiskid control system called Sure-Track uses a vacuum-powered actuator, an electronic control module, and: (a) wheel sensors, (b) a load-sensing valve, (c) a governor.

⊘ 14-24 Power Brakes

For hard braking and fast stops, a considerable pressure must be exerted on the brake pedal with the brake system described above. Also, the heavier the vehicle, the greater the braking effort required. For many years, buses and trucks have used special equipment that assists the driver to brake the vehicle. This equipment may use either compressed air or vacuum. When the driver applies the brake, the compressed air or vacuum supplies most of the effort required for braking. There is another system that uses an electrical means of braking.

In recent years, passenger cars have been supplied with vacuum-assisted braking systems, called *power brakes*. Essentially, they all operate in a similar manner. When the brake pedal is moved to apply the brakes, a valving arrangement is actuated. The valves admit atmospheric pressure on one side of a piston or diaphragm and apply vacuum to the other side. The piston or diaphragm then moves toward the vacuum side; this movement transmits most of the hydraulic pressure, through the brake fluid, to the wheel cylinders.

⊘ 14-25 Atmospheric Pressure and Vacuum

You will recall that, as noted in ⊘ 1-4 to 1-7, the atmospheric pressure is about 15 psi [1.05 kg/cm^2] at sea level. Vacuum is an absence of air. If we arranged a simple cylinder and piston (as shown in Fig. 14-45) and then applied atmospheric pressure to one side and vacuum to the other, the piston would move toward the vacuum side, as shown. If we held the piston stationary, we could calculate the pressure, or push, being exerted on it, provided we knew the area of the piston, the atmospheric pressure, and amount of vacuum. Suppose the piston had an area of 50 square inches (about 8 inches in diameter). We'll assume also that the atmospheric pressure is 15 psi [1.05 kg/cm^2] and the vacuum is great enough to have brought the pressure down to only 5 psi [0.35 kg/cm^2]. With 15 psi [1.05 kg/cm^2] on one side, and only 5 psi [0.35 kg/cm^2] on the other, the difference in pressure is 10 psi [0.70 kg/cm^2]; that is, there is an effective pressure of 10 pounds on every square inch of the piston area. Since there are 50 square inches of piston area, the push on the piston, urging it to the vacuum side, is 500 pounds (50 × 10). It is this effective pressure, or push, that is utilized in power brakes. The vacuum is supplied by the automobile engine. We learned, in ⊘ 1-7, that the engine is a vacuum pump in one sense of the word. With every intake stroke, the downward-moving piston produces a partial vacuum in the cylinder and thus

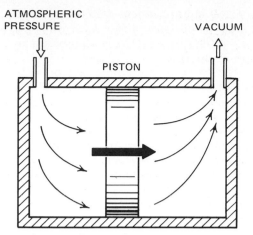

Fig. 14-45. If atmospheric pressure is applied on one side of a piston and vacuum on the other side, the piston will move toward the vacuum side, as shown.

in the intake manifold. The vacuum side of the power-brake cylinder (Fig. 14-45) is connected to the intake manifold so that it can utilize intake-manifold vacuum.

⊘ 14-26 Putting the Vacuum to Work

If we add a hydraulic cylinder to the cylinder and piston of Fig. 14-45 as shown in Fig. 14-46, we can utilize the push on the piston to produce hydraulic pressure. All the pressure on the piston is carried through the piston rod and into the hydraulic cylinder. Thus, in the example described above, the piston rod would push into the hydraulic cylinder with a 500 pound force. If the end of the piston rod had an area of 0.5 square inch, the pressure in the hydraulic fluid would be 1,000 psi [70.31 kg/cm^2] (or 500 pounds divided by the area, 0.5 square inch). The hydraulic pressure can be altered by changing the size of either the piston or the rod (with the same pressure differential acting on the piston). For instance, a piston with an

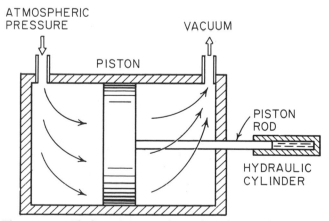

Fig. 14-46. If the piston rod is placed in a hydraulic cylinder, the pressure on the piston in the atmospheric-pressure cylinder will be translated into hydraulic pressure.

area of 100 square inches and a rod of 0.2 square inch area would produce a hydraulic pressure of 5,000 psi [351.54 kg/cm²] (or 1,000 pounds divided by 0.2 square inch).

If the hydraulic cylinder is connected to the wheel cylinders (as shown in Fig. 14-47), the hydraulic pressure produced will result in braking action. Note that even though the hydraulic cylinder has been increased in diameter, the piston rod entering it (Fig. 14-47) still displaces liquid; and it still produces the same pressure increase as it would if the cylinder were the same size as the rod (as shown in Fig. 14-46).

⊘ **14-27 Types of Vacuum-Assisted Power Brakes** Vacuum-assisted power brakes can be divided into two general catagories: vacuum-suspended and atmospheric-suspended. In the vacuum-suspended type, intake-manifold vacuum is applied to both sides of a piston or diaphragm in the power assembly when no braking action is taking place. To produce braking, atmospheric pressure is admitted to one side of the piston or diaphragm; the difference in pressures causes the piston or diaphragm to move, producing the braking action. Most automotive power-brake systems are of this type.

In the atmospheric-suspended type, atmospheric pressure is applied to both sides of the diaphragm or piston. To produce braking action, one side must be connected to a source of vacuum such as the intake manifold. This type of power brake will not operate, however, if the engine is not running, unless there is a reserve vacuum supply. In some applications of this type of power brake, a small vacuum tank is included to provide enough vacuum for several brake applications after the engine has stopped.

Of course, both of these types of brake can be operated even though the power assistance is not operating. In other words, even though the power diaphragm or piston does not operate, braking can still be achieved. However, a much heavier brake-pedal application is necessary.

The vacuum-assisted power brakes can be classified in another way, as the integral type, the multiplier type, and the assist type.
1. INTEGRAL TYPE The integral-type power-brake system (Fig. 14-48) has the brake master cylin-

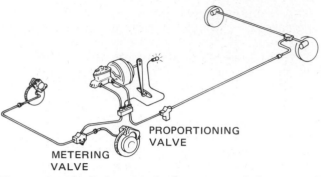

Fig. 14-48. Typical power-brake system of the integral type. (*Wagner Lockheed*)

der as an integral part of the power-brake assembly. When the brake pedal is operated, it actuates a valve in the power-brake assembly that applies atmospheric pressure to one side of a piston or diaphragm and vacuum to the other side. This causes the piston or diaphragm to move, and the movement forces a piston to move into the master cylinder and thus apply the brakes. An integral-type system is described in ⊘ 14-29. Most passenger cars and light trucks use this type of system.
2. MULTIPLIER TYPE The multiplier-type power-brake system (Fig. 14-49) multiplies the pressure produced by the master cylinder. The pressure from the master cylinder is directed to the multiplier unit through a brake tube. In the multiplier unit, the pressure of the brake fluid actuates a valve. The valve causes atmospheric pressure to be directed to one side of a piston or diaphragm and vacuum to the other side. The piston or diaphragm thus is forced to move, and the movement causes a piston to move in a hydraulic cylinder that is part of the multiplier unit. This produces a high hydraulic pressure which is carried by brake lines to the wheel cylinders. To sum up, the relatively low pressure from the master cylinder, produced by brake-pedal movement, is multiplied to a high pressure by the multiplier unit. Thus, a relatively light brake-pedal pressure produces heavy braking action. A multiplier-type power-brake system is described in ⊘ 14-31.
3. ASSIST TYPE The assist-type power-brake system (Fig. 14-50) has a power-cylinder assembly that assists in applying the brakes through a mechanical

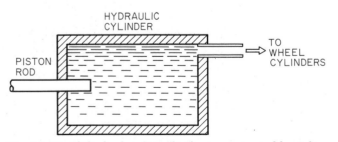

Fig. 14-47. If the hydraulic cylinder is connected by tubes to the wheel cylinders, movement of the piston rod into the hydraulic cylinder will produce braking action.

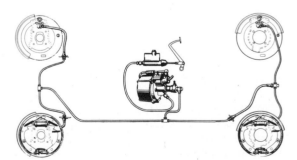

Fig. 14-49. Typical power-brake system of the multiplier type. (*Bendix-Westinghouse Automotive Air Brake Company*)

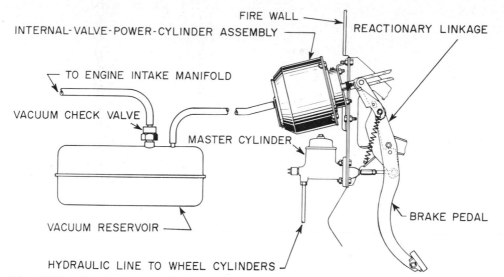

Fig. 14-50. Typical power-brake system of the assist type. (*Bendix-Westinghouse Automotive Air Brake Company*)

linkage. When the brake pedal is moved, linkage to the power cylinder is actuated, causing valve action and thus movement of a diaphragm or bellows within the cylinder. This movement is carried through linkage to the master cylinder, thereby increasing the total force being applied, which in turn increases the braking action. A power-brake system of this type is described in ⊘ 14-32.

⊘ 14-28 Hydraulic-Assisted Brake Booster The hydraulic-assisted brake booster (Fig. 14-51) uses hydraulic pressure supplied by the power-steering pump to assist in applying the brakes. Figure 14-52 is a disassembled view of the booster unit. Figure 14-53 is a sectional view. The four ports (pressure, accumulator, return, and gear) are connected to the power-steering system. When the power-steering pump is running, there is always pressure in the smaller cylinder of the assembly. As the brakes are applied, the pressure through the input rod moves the lever. This forces the spool assembly to move off center. The spool assembly now admits hydraulic pressure back of the large piston in the large cylinder. This pressure is applied to the output pushrod, which is pressing against the pistons in the master cylinder. Then the master-cylinder pistons move to send brake fluid to the wheel cylinders or calipers, thus producing braking.

⊘ 14-29 Integral-Type Power Brake Figure 14-48 illustrates the integral-type power-brake system schematically. A sectional view of one model is shown in Fig. 14-54. A disassembled view of the unit is shown in Fig. 14-55. This unit has a tandem master cylinder for a dual-brake system.

Let us examine the operation of a typical integral-power-brake assembly. Figure 14-56 shows the assembly in the released position, that is, with the brakes not applied. In this position, there is intake-manifold vacuum on both sides of the diaphragm. Spring action has moved the piston in the master cylinder and the diaphragm all the way to the right. The atmospheric valve is closed.

When the brake pedal is depressed for braking action (Fig. 14-57), the brake-pedal pushrod is moved forward (to the left in Fig. 14-57). This action causes the valve to close the vacuum port and open the atmospheric port. Now atmospheric pressure can enter on the right side of the diaphragm and exert a pressure on the diaphragm. The diaphragm is forced to move to the left, and this causes the pushrod to push the master-cylinder piston to the left. Hydraulic pressure now develops in the master cylinder, forcing brake fluid through the brake lines to the wheel cylinders. The brakes are therefore applied. The harder the driver presses on the brake pedal, the wider the atmospheric port is opened and the harder the diaphragm presses on the pushrod to produce braking.

As hydraulic pressure develops in the hydraulic

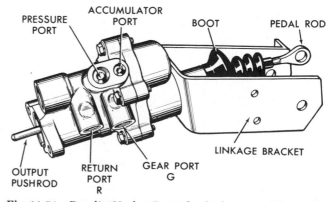

Fig. 14-51. Bendix Hydro-Boost brake booster. (*Chevrolet Motor Division of General Motors Corporation*)

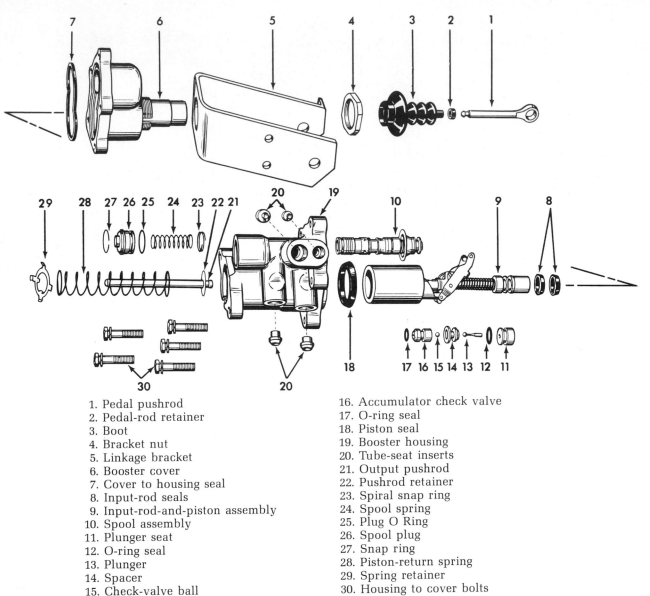

1. Pedal pushrod
2. Pedal-rod retainer
3. Boot
4. Bracket nut
5. Linkage bracket
6. Booster cover
7. Cover to housing seal
8. Input-rod seals
9. Input-rod-and-piston assembly
10. Spool assembly
11. Plunger seat
12. O-ring seal
13. Plunger
14. Spacer
15. Check-valve ball
16. Accumulator check valve
17. O-ring seal
18. Piston seal
19. Booster housing
20. Tube-seat inserts
21. Output pushrod
22. Pushrod retainer
23. Spiral snap ring
24. Spool spring
25. Plug O Ring
26. Spool plug
27. Snap ring
28. Piston-return spring
29. Spring retainer
30. Housing to cover bolts

Fig. 14-52. Disassembled view of a Bendix Hydro-Boost brake booster. (*Chevrolet Motor Division of General Motors Corporation*)

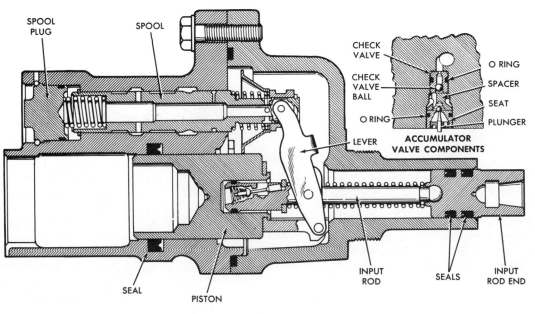

Fig. 14-53. Sectional view of a Bendix Hydro-Boost brake booster. (*Chevrolet Motor Division of General Motors Corporation*)

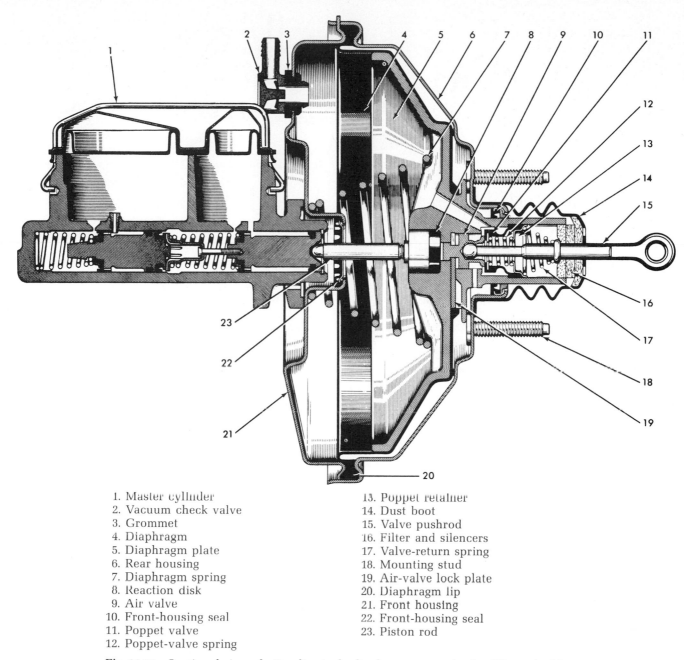

1. Master cylinder
2. Vacuum check valve
3. Grommet
4. Diaphragm
5. Diaphragm plate
6. Rear housing
7. Diaphragm spring
8. Reaction disk
9. Air valve
10. Front-housing seal
11. Poppet valve
12. Poppet-valve spring
13. Poppet retainer
14. Dust boot
15. Valve pushrod
16. Filter and silencers
17. Valve-return spring
18. Mounting stud
19. Air-valve lock plate
20. Diaphragm lip
21. Front housing
22. Front-housing seal
23. Piston rod

Fig. 14-54. Sectional view of a Bendix single-diaphragm power brake. (*Chevrolet Motor Division of General Motors Corporation*)

system, a reaction counterforce acts against the reaction disk (see Fig. 14-55). This disk then transmits the reaction force back through the valve pushrod and the brake pedal. The reaction, or "push-back," force is proportional to the hydraulic pressure and thus to the actual braking taking place. The reaction therefore gives the driver a feel of the braking action. The higher the hydraulic pressure and thus the harder the brakes are applied, the stronger will be the reaction on the brake pedal.

When the brake-pedal movement is stopped and the driver holds the pedal in the braking position (Fig. 14-58), the valve pushrod stops its movement of the control-valve plunger. However, the unbalanced pressures on the two sides of the diaphragm will continue to move the outer sleeve of the control-valve plunger forward, keeping the vacuum port closed. At the same time, the reaction force acting on the reaction disk will tend to move the atmospheric valve to the closed position. When these forces reach a balance, the vacuum port will remain closed and the atmospheric valve will cut off any further passage of atmospheric pressure to the right-hand side of the diaphragm. Thus, the hydraulic pressure will be maintained at a constant value so that the braking effect continues.

When the brake pedal is released (Fig. 14-56), the spring action closes the atmospheric port and

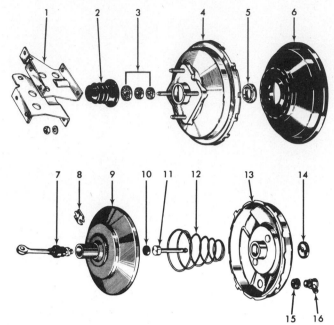

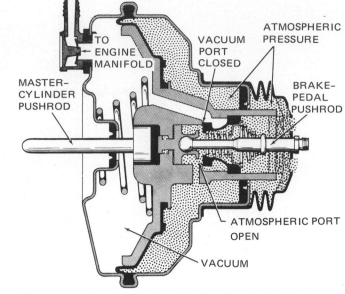

Fig. 14-57. Sectional view of a Bendix single-diaphragm power brake in the applying position. (*Chevrolet Motor Division of General Motors Corporation*)

1. Rear-housing mounting brackets (truck)
2. Pushrod boot
3. Foam and felt air-filter silencers
4. Rear housing
5. Rear-housing seal
6. Diaphragm
7. Air-valve pushrod assembly
8. Air-valve lock
9. Diaphragm plate
10. Reaction disk
11. Piston rod
12. Diaphragm return spring
13. Front housing
14. Front-housing seal
15. Grommet
16. Check valve

Fig. 14-55. Disassembled view of a Bendix single-diaphragm power brake. (*Chevrolet Motor Division of General Motors Corporation*)

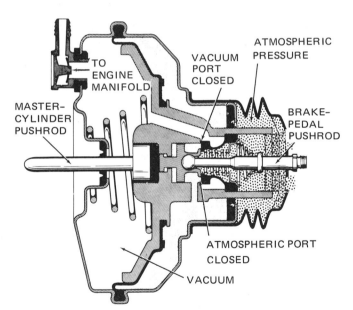

Fig. 14-58. Sectional view of a Bendix single-diaphragm power brake in the holding position. (*Chevrolet Motor Division of General Motors Corporation*)

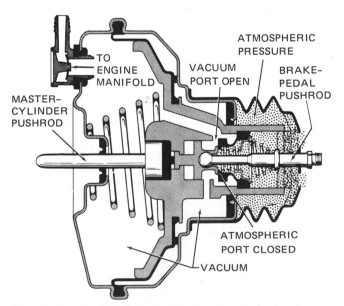

Fig. 14-56. Sectional view of a Bendix single-diaphragm power brake in the released position. (*Chevrolet Motor Division of General Motors Corporation*)

opens the vacuum port so that vacuum is applied to both sides of the diaphragm. The brakes therefore are released.

⊘ **14-30 Bendix Dual-Diaphragm Power Brake** The Bendix dual-diaphragm assembly, shown in Fig. 14-59, is similar to the unit previously discussed. However, it has a second diaphragm and plate. A disassembled view of a very similar construction is shown in Fig. 14-60. The purpose of the secondary diaphragm is to provide additional braking power.

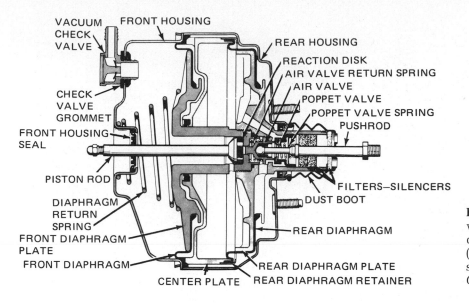

VACUUM CHECK VALVE
FRONT HOUSING
REAR HOUSING
REACTION DISK
AIR VALVE RETURN SPRING
AIR VALVE
POPPET VALVE
POPPET VALVE SPRING
PUSHROD
CHECK VALVE GROMMET
FRONT HOUSING SEAL
PISTON ROD
FILTERS—SILENCERS
DUST BOOT
DIAPHRAGM RETURN SPRING
FRONT DIAPHRAGM PLATE
FRONT DIAPHRAGM
REAR DIAPHRAGM
REAR DIAPHRAGM PLATE
REAR DIAPHRAGM RETAINER
CENTER PLATE

Fig. 14-59. Sectional view of a Bendix dual-diaphragm power brake. (*Chevrolet Motor Division of General Motors Corporation*)

The unit works in the same manner as the power-brake assembly described in ⊘ 14-29.

⊘ **14-31 Multiplier-Type Power Brake** Figure 14-49 shows a multiplier-type brake system schematically. Figures 14-61 to 14-63 show a brake assembly of this type. In operation, when the brakes are applied, the hydraulic pressure from the master cylinder is applied to the control valve. This action causes the valve to admit atmospheric pressure to one side of the power diaphragm. With intake-manifold vacuum on the other side of the power diaphragm, the diaphragm is forced to move. This motion forces the piston into the hydraulic cylinder so that brake fluid is forced from the hydraulic cylinder to the wheel

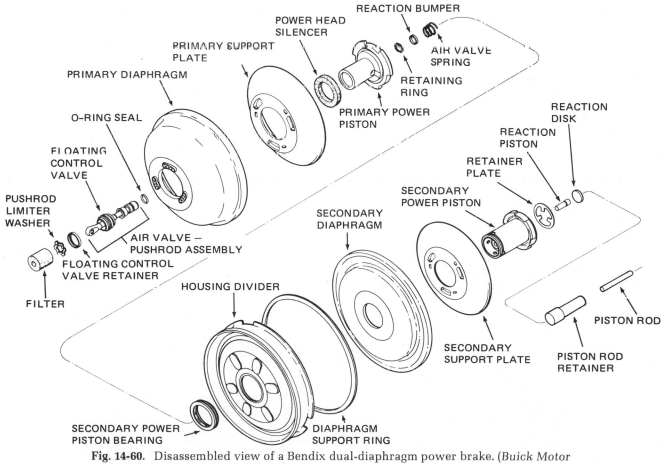

REACTION BUMPER
POWER HEAD SILENCER
PRIMARY SUPPORT PLATE
PRIMARY DIAPHRAGM
AIR VALVE SPRING
RETAINING RING
PRIMARY POWER PISTON
O-RING SEAL
REACTION DISK
REACTION PISTON
RETAINER PLATE
FLOATING CONTROL VALVE
SECONDARY POWER PISTON
PUSHROD LIMITER WASHER
SECONDARY DIAPHRAGM
AIR VALVE—PUSHROD ASSEMBLY
FLOATING CONTROL VALVE RETAINER
FILTER
HOUSING DIVIDER
SECONDARY SUPPORT PLATE
PISTON ROD
PISTON ROD RETAINER
SECONDARY POWER PISTON BEARING
DIAPHRAGM SUPPORT RING

Fig. 14-60. Disassembled view of a Bendix dual-diaphragm power brake. (*Buick Motor Division of General Motors Corporation*)

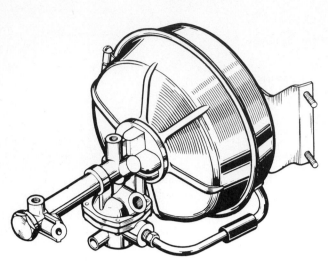

Fig. 14-61. Power-brake assembly of the multiplier type. (*Chrysler Corporation*)

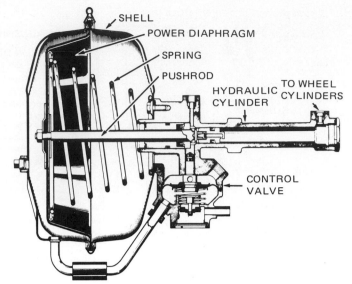

Fig. 14-62. Sectional view of a power-brake assembly of the multiplier type. (*Chevrolet Motor Division of General Motors Corporation*)

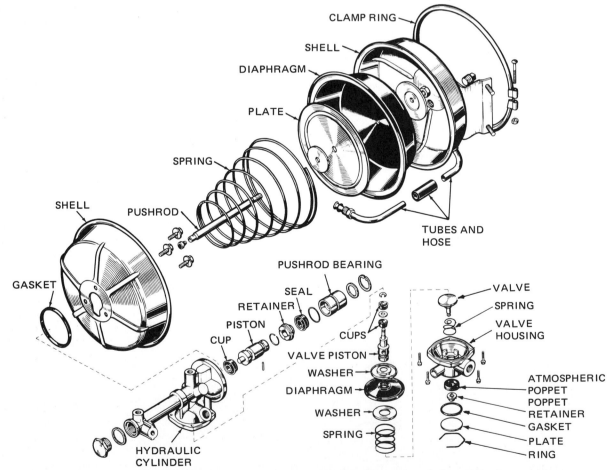

Fig. 14-63. Disassembled view of a power-brake assembly of the multiplier type. (*Chevrolet Motor Division of General Motors Corporation*)

cylinders. Thus, braking takes place. The relatively light brake-pedal pressure and the hydraulic pressure in the master cylinder are multiplied several times by the power brake.

⊘ **14-32 Assist-Type Power Brake** Figure 14-50 shows a typical installation of an assist-type power brake. Figures 14-64 and 14-65 show sectional views of a specific model. This type of power brake uses a bellows which is mechanically linked to the brake pedal and the master cylinder. When the brake is applied, a valve in the power-brake assembly admits vacuum into the bellows. This collapses the bellows and causes the upper end of the power lever to move (to the left, in Fig. 14-64). The brake-pedal pushrod is also pushing on the power lever. This combined push is applied to the master-cylinder pushrod, forcing it to push the master-cylinder piston into the master cylinder so that the brakes are applied.

Figure 14-64 shows the assembly in the unapplied position. The vacuum valve is closed and the air valve is open. The bellows is fully extended because it is filled with atmospheric pressure.

When the brake pedal is moved, applying the brakes (Fig. 14-65), the linkage to the bellows assembly causes the vacuum valve to open and the air valve to close. Now the vacuum applied in the bellows causes it to collapse, or shorten, and this motion is carried through the power lever to the master-cylinder pushrod. Thus, both the brake-pedal pushrod and the bellows work together to move the master-cylinder pushrod and to apply the brakes. However, most of the braking effort comes from the bellows.

This power-brake system includes a brake "feel" arrangement similar to those described previously for other power-brake systems. The increasing hydraulic pressure in the master cylinder, resulting from increased application of the brakes, causes a reaction through the reaction disk and the piston. This reaction is carried through a secondary lever

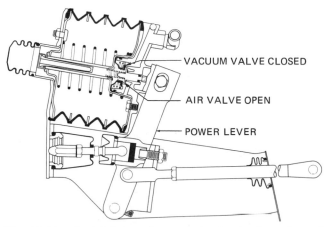

Fig. 14-64. Assist type of power brake in the released position. (*Buick Motor Division of General Motors Corporation*)

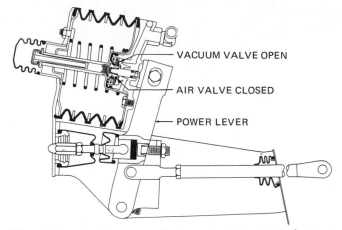

Fig. 14-65. Assist type of power brake in the applied position. (*Buick Motor Division of General Motors Corporation*)

(the reaction or actuating lever) to the valves in the bellows. The reaction causes a small movement of the vacuum valve, which shuts it. The reaction force, which is proportional to the hydraulic pressure in the master cylinder (and therefore braking effort), thus provides the driver with brake "feel."

Note that this system includes a vacuum reserve tank to ensure that vacuum will be available for braking when the engine is not running. Vacuum is built up in the tank from the intake manifold when the engine is running. The reserve thus stored permits the power brakes to be applied several times after the engine has stopped. Even though the vacuum is exhausted, however, the brakes can still be applied, but there will be no power assist, so the brake-pedal pressure must be considerably greater to achieve braking.

⊘ **14-33 Air Brake** The air brake uses compressed air to apply the braking force to the brake shoes. A typical air-brake-system layout is illustrated in Fig. 14-66; the compressor unit, air-reservoir tank, brake chamber, and wheel mechanism are shown in Fig. 14-67. Air-reservoir tanks are necessary in order to maintain adequate braking power at all times, even when the engine is not running. The air compressor, which is a small air pump, maintains air pressure in the tanks. When the air pressure is applied to the brake chambers by operation of the treadle pedal, the brake chamber rotates the cam and causes the brake shoes to push outward against the brake drum.

⊘ **14-34 Electric Brakes** Electric brakes use electromagnets to provide the braking force against the brake shoes. Each wheel contains a semistationary circular electromagnet and an armature disk that revolves with the wheel (Fig. 14-68). The electromagnet operates from battery current. A controller in the driver's compartment enables the driver to connect

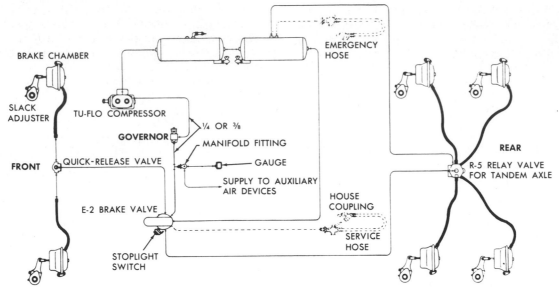

Fig. 14-66. Schematic layout of a typical air-brake system. (*Chevrolet Motor Division of General Motors Corporation*)

the electromagnets to the battery and to vary the amount of current flowing from the battery to the electromagnets in order to vary the amount of braking action. When the brakes are not applied, there is no magnetic attraction between the electromagnet and the armature disk in the wheel. When the driver applies the brakes, current begins to flow through the electromagnets. This builds up a magnetic field, causing magnetic attraction between the semistationary electromagnet and the rotating armature disk. The electromagnet is thus forced to shift through a limited arc in the direction of the wheel rotation. A lug on the electromagnet is connected to a cam; movement of the electromagnet and the lug causes the cam to press against the end of the brake shoes and forces the brake shoes outward against the brake drum. The greater the current flowing through the electromagnet, the greater the braking effect.

Check Your Progress

Progress Quiz 14-2 Here is your progress quiz on the last half of the chapter on power brakes. In recent years, power brakes have increased in importance, since many cars have been supplied with them. Thus, you will want to know all you can about them. The quiz that follows will help you to remember the explanations of the power brakes given in the past few pages. It will also check your memory on the facts about this subject. If your memory does not "check out" very well, it simply means that you should review the material again.

Fig. 14-67. Installation of an air-brake system on a heavy-duty truck. (*International Harvester Company*)

Fig. 14-68. Construction of an electric-brake mechanism. *Left*, controller; *right*, wheel-braking mechanism. (*Warner Electric Brake Manufacturing Company*)

Completing the Sentences The sentences below are incomplete. After each sentence there are several words or phrases, only one of which will correctly complete the sentence. Write each sentence in your notebook, selecting the proper word or phrase to complete it correctly.

1. The type of brake system referred to as power brakes uses: (*a*) compressed air, (*b*) vacuum, (*c*) electromagnets.

2. With a pressure differential of 9 psi between the two sides of the piston in a power-brake assembly and a piston area of 45 in^2, the effective push on the piston is: (*a*) 50 lb, (*b*) 405 lb, (*c*) 455 lb.

3. Two general types of vacuum-assisted power brakes are: (*a*) vacuum-suspended and pressure-suspended, (*b*) integral and pressure-suspended, (*c*) atmospheric-suspended and vacuum-suspended.

4. Another way of classifying vacuum-assisted power brakes is as integral, (*a*) hydraulic, and multiplier; (*b*) multiplier, and assist; (*c*) vacuum, and compressed air.

5. In the multiplier type of power brake, the diaphragm acts directly on the hydraulic piston in the: (*a*) master cylinder, (*b*) wheel cylinder, (*c*) multiplier unit.

6. In the integral type of power brake, the diaphragm acts directly on the hydraulic piston in the: (*a*) master cylinder, (*b*) wheel cylinder, (*c*) multiplier unit.

7. In the assist type of power brake, the bellows applies force to the master-cylinder piston: (*a*) through diaphragm linkage, (*b*) through mechanical linkage, (*c*) directly.

8. In the vacuum-suspended system, the brakes are applied when: (*a*) vacuum is applied to both sides of diaphragm, (*b*) atmospheric pressure is applied to both sides of diaphragm, (*c*) atmospheric pressure is applied to one side of diaphragm.

9. In the atmospheric-suspended system, the brakes are applied when: (*a*) vacuum is applied to one side of diaphragm, (*b*) atmospheric pressure is applied to both sides of diaphragm, (*c*) vacuum is applied to both sides of diaphragm.

10. In the air brake, air pressure is supplied by: (*a*) engine intake manifold, (*b*) a compressor, (*c*) the diaphragm valve.

CHAPTER 14 CHECKUP

NOTE: Since the following is a chapter review test, you should review the chapter before taking it.

You have been moving along very well in your studies of the automobile chassis and have completed most of the book. This book may be somewhat more difficult to study than other books in the McGraw-Hill Automotive Technology Series, since it discusses several more or less independent mechanisms. These mechanisms have little in common except that they are all used on the automobile. Thus, the steering system has a different purpose and different operating principles from the brake system, for example. Yet all the mechanisms are important to the automobile, and it is important for you to understand them all—and understand them well. The chapter checkup that follows gives you the chance to review the important details of brake systems covered in the chapter. Be sure to write the answers to the questions in your notebook. You'll be glad you've kept a notebook when you have finished the book: you can go to the notebook to refresh your memory whenever you are hazy about some point. Further, writing the facts in your notebook helps you remember them.

Correcting Parts Lists The purpose of this exercise is to give you practice in spotting unrelated parts in a list. In each list below, there is one item that does not belong. Write each list in your notebook, but do not write the item that does not belong.

1. Hydraulic-brake system: master cylinder, brake pedal, brake fluid, brake lines, cable linkage, wheel cylinders.

2. Master cylinder: body, check-valve assembly, activating pin, piston return spring, piston, pushrod, fluid reservoir.

3. Wheel cylinder: body, piston spring, pushrod, piston, piston cup, actuating pin.

4. Integral-power-brake assembly: diaphragm, plunger, pushrod, master cylinder, atmospheric valve, rocker plate.

5. Disk brakes: disk, caliper, flat shoes, piston, drum, piston seal.

Completing the Sentences The sentences below are incomplete. After each sentence there are several words or phrases, only one of which will correctly complete the sentence. Write each sentence in your notebook, selecting the proper word or phrase to complete it correctly.

1. In the hydraulic-brake system, movement of a piston in the master cylinder produces hydraulic pressure which causes movement of the: (*a*) brake shoes, (*b*) brake pedal, (*c*) brake cam.

2. Braking is produced by the frictional effect between the brake drum and the: (*a*) wheel-cylinder pistons, (*b*) brake shoes, (*c*) wheel studs, (*d*) wheel rim.

3. Rubber parts in the hydraulic-brake system will swell and disintegrate from the effects, in the system, of: (*a*) brake fluid, (*b*) low pressure, (*c*) mineral oil.

4. To operate, power brakes make use of the pressure differential between vacuum from the intake manifold and: (*a*) venturi vacuum, (*b*) compressed air, (*c*) atmospheric pressure.

5. In the vacuum-suspended power brake of the integral type, movement of the brake pedal: (*a*) increases the hydraulic pressure which actuates the control valve, (*b*) actuates the valve in the bellows through linkage, (*c*) actuates the valve to admit atmospheric pressure to one side of the diaphragm.

6. In the multiplier power-brake system, movement of the brake pedal: (*a*) increases the hydraulic pressure which actuates the control valve, (*b*) actuates the valve in the bellows through linkage, (*c*) actuates the valve to admit atmospheric pressure to one side of the diaphragm.

7. In the assist power-brake system, movement of the brake pedal: (*a*) increases the hydraulic pressure which actuates the control valve, (*b*) actuates the valve in the bellows through linkage, (*c*) actuates the valve to admit atmospheric pressure to one side of the diaphragm.

8. In a vacuum-suspended unit, when the brakes are off, the piston or diaphragm has, on both sides of it: (*a*) atmospheric pressure, (*b*) a vacuum, (*c*) hydraulic pressure.

Purpose and Operation of Components   In the following, you are asked to write down the purpose of certain parts, or the operation of various components, in the brake systems described in the chapter. If you have any difficulty in writing your explanations, turn back to the chapter and reread the pages that will make the explanations clear. Don't copy; try to tell it in your own words, just as you would explain it to a friend. Write in your notebook.

1. Describe the operation of a mechanical braking system.
2. Describe the operation of a hydraulic-brake system.
3. Why are the wheel-cylinder pistons usually larger in the front-wheel cylinders?

4. Describe the construction of a master cylinder.
5. Describe the construction of a wheel cylinder.
6. Describe the construction of a typical vacuum-suspended power-brake assembly.
7. Describe the operation of a typical vacuum-suspended power-brake assembly when the brakes are applied. When they are held, or poised. When they are released.
8. Describe the operation of the multiplier-type power brake when the brakes are applied. When they are held. When they are released.
9. Describe the operation of the assist-type power brake when the brakes are applied. When they are held. When they are released.
10. Explain the way in which brake "feel" is achieved in the brake units mentioned in the three previous questions.

SUGGESTIONS FOR FURTHER STUDY

If you can obtain shop manuals issued by the car or equipment manufacturers which describe the various power-brake or booster-brake systems, be sure to study them very carefully. Also, if you can examine these units, assembled or disassembled, in your school or local service shop, it will help you to understand how these units operate. Be sure to write in your notebook everything important that you learn. Later, you will be glad that you did this because your notebook will become a valuable reference source.

chapter 15

BRAKE SERVICE

This chapter discusses trouble diagnosis, adjustments, and servicing of the various components in automotive hydraulic-brake systems.

⊘ **15-1 Brake Trouble Diagnosis** The charts and the sections that follow them give you a means of tracing troubles in the brakes to their causes. This permits quick location of causes and, thus, quick correction of troubles. If the cause is known, the trouble is usually easy to correct. Following the trouble-diagnosis sections are several sections that cover the adjustment and repair procedures on different types of automotive brakes.

⊘ **15-2 Drum-Brake Trouble-Diagnosis Chart** A variety of braking problems bring the driver to the mechanic. It is a rare driver who will know exactly what is causing a trouble. The chart that follows lists possible troubles in drum-brake systems, their possible causes, and checks or corrections to be made. Following sections describe the troubles and causes or corrections in detail. The chart in ⊘ 15-15 covers possible disk-brake troubles.

NOTE: The troubles and possible causes are not listed according to how often they occur. That is, item 1 (or item a under "Possible Cause") does not necessarily occur more often than item 2 (or item b).

DRUM-BRAKE TROUBLE-DIAGNOSIS CHART

(See ⊘ 15-3 to 15-14 for detailed explanations of the trouble causes and corrections listed in the chart.)

COMPLAINT	POSSIBLE CAUSE	CHECK OR CORRECTION
1. Brake pedal goes to floorboard (⊘ 15-3)	a. Linkage or shoes out of adjustment	Adjust
	b. Brake linings worn	Replace
	c. Lack of brake fluid	Add fluid; bleed system (see item 10 below)
	d. Air in system	Add fluid; bleed system (see item 9 below)
	e. Worn master cylinder	Repair
2. One brake drags (⊘ 15-4)	a. Shoes out of adjustment	Adjust
	b. Clogged brake line	Clear or replace line
	c. Wheel cylinder defective	Repair or replace
	d. Weak or broken return spring	Replace
	e. Loose wheel bearing	Adjust bearing
3. All brakes drag (⊘ 15-5)	a. Incorrect linkage adjustment	Adjust
	b. Trouble in master cylinder	Repair or replace
	c. Mineral oil in system	Replace damaged rubber parts; use only recommended brake fluid
4. Car pulls to one side when braking (⊘ 15-6)	a. Brake linings soaked with oil	Replace linings and oil seals; avoid overlubrication
	b. Brake linings soaked with brake fluid	Replace linings; repair or replace wheel cylinder
	c. Brake shoes out of adjustment	Adjust
	d. Tires not uniformly inflated	Inflate correctly
	e. Brake line clogged	Clear or replace line
	f. Defective wheel cylinder	Repair or replace
	g. Brake backing plate loose	Tighten
	h. Mismatched linings	Use same linings all around

(See ⊘ 15-3 to 15-14 for detailed explanations of the trouble causes
and corrections listed in the chart.)

COMPLAINT	POSSIBLE CAUSE	CHECK OR CORRECTION
5. Soft, or spongy, pedal (⊘ 15-7)	a. Air in system	Add brake fluid; bleed system (see item 9 below)
	b. Brake shoes out of adjustment	Adjust
6. Poor braking action requiring excessive pedal pressure (⊘ 15-8)	a. Brake linings soaked with water	Will be all right when dried out
	b. Shoes out of adjustment	Adjust
	c. Brake linings hot	Allow to cool
	d. Brake linings burned	Replace
	e. Brake drum glazed	Turn or grind drum
	f. Power-brake assembly not operating	Overhaul or replace
7. Brakes too sensitive or grab (⊘ 15-9)	a. Shoes out of adjustment	Adjust
	b. Wrong linings	Install correct linings
	c. Brake linings greasy	Replace; check oil seals; avoid overlubrication
	d. Drums scored	Turn or grind drums
	e. Backing plates loose	Tighten
	f. Power-brake assembly malfunctioning	Overhaul or replace
	g. Brake linings soaked with oil	Replace linings and oil seals; avoid over-lubrication
	h. Brake linings soaked with brake fluid	Replace linings; repair or replace wheel cylinders
8. Noisy brakes (⊘ 15-10)	a. Linings worn	Replace
	b. Shoes warped	Replace
	c. Shoe rivets loose	Replace shoe or lining
	d. Drums worn or rough	Turn or grind drums
	e. Loose parts	Tighten
9. Air in system (⊘ 15-11)	a. Defective master cylinder	Repair or replace
	b. Loose connections, damaged tube	Tighten connections; replace tube
	c. Brake fluid lost	See item 10 below
10. Loss of brake fluid (⊘ 15-12)	a. Master cylinder leaks	Repair or replace
	b. Wheel cylinder leaks	Repair or replace
	c. Loose connections, damaged tube	Tighten connections; replace tube

Note: After repair, add brake fluid and bleed system.

COMPLAINT	POSSIBLE CAUSE	CHECK OR CORRECTION
11. Brakes do not self-adjust (⊘ 15-13)	a. Adjustment screw stuck	Free and clean up
	b. Adjustment lever does not engage star wheel	Repair; free up or replace adjuster
	c. Adjuster incorrectly installed	Install correctly
12. Warning light comes on when braking (dual system) (⊘ 15-14)	a. One section (front or back) has failed	Check both sections for braking action; repair defective section
	b. Pressure-differential valve defective	Replace

⊘ 15-3 Brake Pedal Goes to Floorboard When the brake pedal goes to the floorboard, there is no pedal reserve. Full pedal movement does not produce adequate braking. This would be a very unlikely situation with a dual-brake system. One section (front or rear) might fail, but it would be rare for both to fail at the same time. It is possible that the driver has continued to operate the car with one section out. (Either the driver ignores the warning light or the light or pressure-differential valve has failed.) Causes of failure could be linkage or brake shoes out of adjustment, linings worn, air in the system, lack of brake fluid, or a worn master cylinder.

⊘ 15-4 One Brake Drags If one brake drags, this means that the brake shoes are not moving away from the brake drum when the brakes are released. This trouble could be due to a number of problems. It could be caused by incorrect shoe adjustment or a clogged brake line which does not release pressure from the wheel cylinder. It could also be due to sticking pistons in the wheel cylinder, to weak or broken brake-shoe return springs, or to a loose wheel bearing which permits the wheel to wobble so that the brake drum comes in contact with the brake shoes even though they are retracted.

15-5 All Brakes Drag When all brakes drag, it may be that the brake pedal does not have sufficient play. In that case, the pistons in the master cylinder do not fully retract. This would prevent the lip of the piston cup from clearing the compensating port, and hydraulic pressure would not be relieved as it should be. As a result, the wheel cylinders would not release the brake shoes. A similar condition could result if mineral oil had been added to the system. Mineral oil is likely to cause the piston cup to swell. If it swelled enough, it would not clear the compensating port even with the piston in the "fully retracted" position. A clogged compensating port would have the same result. Do not use a wire or drill to clear the port—you might produce a burr that would cut the piston cup. Instead, clear it with alcohol and compressed air. Clogging of the reservoir vent might also cause dragging brakes by trapping pressure in the reservoir which would prevent release of pressure. But this would be just as likely to cause leakage of air into the system (see ⊘ 15-11 below).

15-6 Car Pulls to One Side If the car pulls to one side when the brakes are applied, more braking pressure is being applied to one side than to the other. This happens if some of the brake linings have become soaked in oil or brake fluid, if brake shoes are unevenly or improperly adjusted, if tires are not evenly inflated, or if defective wheel cylinders or clogged brake lines are preventing uniform braking action at all wheels. A loose brake-backing plate or the use of two different types of brake lining will cause the car to pull to one side when the brakes are applied. A misaligned front end or a broken spring could also cause this problem.

Linings will become soaked with oil if the lubricant level in the differential and rear axle is too high. This usually causes leakage past the oil seal (Fig. 15-1). At the front wheel, brake linings may become oil soaked if the front-wheel bearings are improperly lubricated or if the oil seal is defective or not properly installed. Wheel cylinders will leak brake fluid onto the brake linings if they are defective or if an actuating pin has been improperly installed (see ⊘ 15-12). If the linings at a left wheel become soaked with brake fluid or oil, for example, the car pulls to the left because the brakes are more effective on the left side.

15-7 Soft, or Spongy, Pedal If the pedal action is soft, or spongy, the chances are that there is air in the system. Out-of-adjustment brake shoes could also cause this. Refer to ⊘ 15-11 below for conditions that could allow air to get into the system.

15-8 Poor Braking Action Requiring Excessive Pedal Pressure Excessive pedal pressure could be caused by improper brake-shoe adjustment. The use

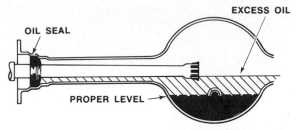

Fig. 15-1. A high lubricant level in the differential and rear-axle housing may cause leakage past the oil seal. This would result in oil-soaked brake linings. (*Pontiac Motor Division of General Motors Corporation*)

of the wrong brake lining could cause the same trouble. Sometimes, brake linings that have become wet after a hard rain or after driving through puddles will not hold well. Normal braking action is usually restored after the brake linings have dried out.

Another possible cause of poor braking action is excessive temperature. After the brakes have been applied for long periods, as in coming down a long hill, they begin to overheat. This overheating reduces braking effectiveness so that the brakes "fade." Often, if brakes are allowed to cool, braking efficiency is restored. However, excessively long periods of braking at high temperature may char the brake linings so that they must be replaced. Further, this overheating may glaze the brake drum so that it becomes too smooth for effective braking action. In this case, the drum must be ground or turned to remove the glaze. Glazing can also take place even though the brakes are not overheated. Failure of the power-brake assembly will considerably increase the amount of pedal pressure required to produce braking.

15-9 Brakes Too Sensitive or Grab If linings are greasy, or soaked with oil or brake fluid, the brakes tend to grab with slight pedal pressure. In any case, the linings must be replaced. If the brake shoes are out of adjustment, if the wrong linings are used, or if drums are scored or rough (Fig. 15-2), grabbing may result. A loose backing plate may cause the same condition. As the linings come into contact with the drum, the backing plate shifts to give hard braking. A defective power-brake assembly can also cause grabbing.

15-10 Noisy Brakes Brakes become noisy if the brake linings wear so much that the rivets come into contact with the brake drum (see Fig. 15-2); if the shoes become warped so that pressure on the drum is not uniform; if shoe rivets become loose so that they contact the drum; or if the drum becomes rough or worn. Any of these conditions is likely to cause a squeak or squeal when the brakes are applied. Loose parts, such as the brake backing plate, also may rattle.

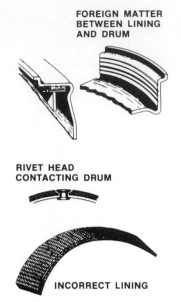

Fig. 15-2. Brake drums can be scored by foreign matter, such as dirt particles, between the lining and drum; by worn linings that permit the rivet head to contact the drum; or by very harsh linings (especially on steel drums). (*Pontiac Motor Division of General Motors Corporation*)

⊘ **15-11 Air in System** If air gets into the hydraulic system, poor braking and a spongy pedal will result. Air can get into the system if the filler vent becomes plugged (Fig. 15-3), since this may tend to create a partial vacuum in the system on the return stroke of the piston. Air could then bypass the rear piston cup, as shown by the arrows, and enter the system. It is possible accidentally to plug the vent when the filler plug or cover is removed. Always check the vent and clean it when the plug or cover is removed. Air can also get into the hydraulic system if the master-cylinder valve is leaky and does not hold pressure in the system. A leak could allow air to seep in around the wheel-cylinder piston cups, since there would be no pressure holding the cups tight against the cylinder walls. Probably the most common cause of air in the brake system is insufficient brake fluid in the master cylinder. If the brake fluid

drops below the compensating port, the hydraulic system will draw air in as the piston moves forward on the braking stroke. Air in the system must be removed by adding brake fluid and bleeding the system, as described in ⊘ 15-40.

⊘ **15-12 Loss of Brake Fluid** Brake fluid can be lost if the master cylinder leaks, if the wheel cylinder leaks, if the line connections are loose, or if the line is damaged. One possible cause of wheel-cylinder leakage is incorrect installation of the actuating pin (Fig. 15-4). If the pin is cocked, as shown, the side thrust on the piston may permit leakage past the piston. Leakage from other causes at the master cylinder or wheel cylinder requires removal and repair, or replacement, of the defective parts.

⊘ **15-13 Brakes Do Not Self-adjust** Brakes do not self-adjust if the adjustment screw is stuck, the adjustment lever does not engage the star wheel, or the adjuster was incorrectly installed. It is necessary to get into the brake to find and correct the trouble.

⊘ **15-14 Warning Light Comes On when Braking (Dual System)** If the warning light comes on when braking, it means that one of the two braking sections has failed. Both sections (front and rear) should be checked so that the trouble can be found and eliminated. It is dangerous to drive with this condition, even though the car brakes, because only half the wheels are being braked.

⊘ **15-15 Disk-Brake Trouble-Diagnosis Chart** The chart that follows lists disk-brake troubles, their possible causes, and checks or corrections to be made. Following sections describe the troubles and causes or corrections in detail.

NOTE: The troubles and possible causes are not listed according to how often they occur; item 1 (or item a under "Possible Cause") does not necessarily occur more often than item 2 (or item b).

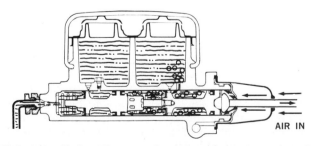

Fig. 15-3. If the filler vent becomes plugged, air may be drawn into the system on the return stroke of the piston, past the rear piston cup. This is shown by the small arrows and bubbles. (*Pontiac Motor Division of General Motors Corporation*)

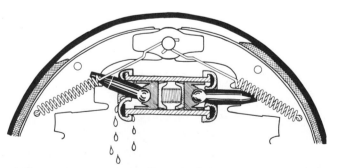

Fig. 15-4. Incorrect installation of the actuating pin will cause a side thrust on the piston which will permit leakage of brake fluid from the wheel cylinder. The pin must always align with the notch in the brake shoe. (*Pontiac Motor Division of General Motors Corporation*)

DISK-BRAKE TROUBLE-DIAGNOSIS CHART

(See ⊘ 15-16 to 15-24 for detailed explanations of the trouble causes
and corrections listed in the chart.)

COMPLAINT	POSSIBLE CAUSE	CHECK OR CORRECTION
1. Excessive pedal travel (⊘ 15-16)	a. Excessive disk runout	Check runout; if excessive, install new disk
	b. Air leak, or insufficient fluid	Check system for leaks
	c. Improper brake fluid (boil)	Drain and install correct fluid
	d. Warped or tapered shoe	Install new shoe
	e. Loose wheel-bearing adjustment	Readjust
	f. Damaged piston seal	Install new seal
	g. Power-brake malfunction	Check power unit
2. Brake roughness or chatter (pedal pulsation) (⊘ 15-17)	a. Excessive disk runout	Check runout; if excessive, install new disk
	b. Disk out of parallel	Check runout; if excessive, install new disk
	c. Loose wheel bearing	Readjust
3. Excessive pedal effort, grabbing, or uneven braking action (⊘ 15-18)	a. Power-brake malfunction	Check power unit
	b. Brake fluid or grease on linings	Install new linings
	c. Lining worn	Install new shoe and linings
	d. Incorrect lining	Install correct lining
	e. Frozen or seized pistons	Disassemble caliper and free-up pistons; install new caliper and pistons, if necessary
4. Car pulls to one side (⊘ 15-19)	a. Brake fluid or grease on linings	Install new linings
	b. Frozen or seized pistons	Disassemble caliper and free pistons
	c. Incorrect tire pressure	Inflate tires to recommended pressures
	d. Distorted brake shoes	Install new brake shoes
	e. Front end out of alignment	Check and align front end
	f. Broken rear spring	Install new rear spring
	g. Restricted hose or line	Check hoses and lines and correct as necessary
	h. Unmatched linings	Install correct lining
5. Noise (⊘ 15-20): Groan	Brake noise when slowly releasing brakes (creep-groan). Not detrimental to function of disk brakes— no corrective action required. This noise may be eliminated by slightly increasing or decreasing brake-pedal efforts.	
Rattle	Brake noise or rattle at low speeds on rough roads may be due to excessive clearance between the shoe and the caliper. Install new shoe and lining assemblies to correct.	
Scraping	a. Mounting bolts too long	Install mounting bolts of correct length
	b. Disk rubbing housing	Check for rust or mud buildup on caliper housing; check caliper mounting and bridge bolt tightness
	c. Loose wheel bearings	Readjust
	d. Linings worn, allowing telltale tabs to scrape on disk	Replace linings
6. Brakes heat up during driving and fail to release (⊘ 15-21)	a. Power-brake malfunction	Check and correct power unit
	b. Sticking pedal linkage	Free sticking pedal linkage
	c. Operator riding brake pedal	Instruct operator how to drive with disk brakes
	d. Frozen or seized piston	Disassemble caliper, clean cylinder bore, clean seal groove and install new pistons, seals, and boots
	e. Residual pressure valve in master cylinder	Remove valve from cylinder
7. Leaky caliper cylinder (⊘ 15-22)	a. Damaged or worn piston seal	Install new seal
	b. Scores or corrosion on surface of piston	Disassemble caliper, clean cylinder bore; if necessary, install new pistons or replace caliper
8. Brake pedal can be depressed without braking effect (⊘ 15-23)	a. Piston pushed back in cylinder bores during servicing of caliper (and lining not properly positioned)	Reposition brake shoe and lining assemblies. Depress pedal a second time and if condition persists, look for the following causes:
	b. Leak in system or caliper	Check for leak, repair as required
	c. Damaged piston seal in one or more cylinders	Disassemble caliper and replace piston seals as required
	d. Air in hydraulic system, or improper bleeding procedure	Bleed system
	e. Bleeder screw opens	Close bleeder screw and bleed entire system
	f. Leak past primary cup in master cylinder	Recondition master cylinder

(See ⊘ 15-16 to 15-24 for detailed explanations of the trouble causes
and corrections listed in the chart.)

COMPLAINT	POSSIBLE CAUSE	CHECK OR CORRECTION
9. Fluid level low in master cylinder (⊘ 15-24)	a. Leaks in system or caliper b. Worn brake-shoe linings	Check for leak, repair as required Replace shoes
10. Warning light comes on when braking (dual system) (⊘ 15-14)	a. One section (front or back) has failed b. Pressure-differential valve defective	Check both sections for braking action; repair defective section Replace

⊘ **15-16 Excessive Pedal Travel** Anything that requires excessive movement of the caliper pistons will require excessive pedal travel. For example, if the disk has excessive runout, it will force the pistons farther back in their bores when the brakes are released. Thus additional pedal travel is required when the brakes are applied. Of course, warped or tapered shoes, a damaged piston seal, or a loose wheel bearing could cause the same problem. In addition, air in the lines, insufficient fluid in the system, or incorrect fluid, which boils, will cause a spongy pedal and excessive pedal travel. If the power brake is malfunctioning, it also could produce excessive pedal travel.

⊘ **15-17 Brake-Pedal Pulsation** Brake-pedal pulsation is probably due to a disk with excessive runout or to a loose wheel bearing.

⊘ **15-18 Excessive Pedal Effort** The first cause you might think of for excessive pedal effort is that the power brake is not operating properly. In addition, if the linings are worn or have brake fluid on them, they will not produce normal braking, so that high pedal pressure is required. Also, if the pistons are jammed in the calipers, high pedal effort will be required.

⊘ **15-19 Car Pulls to One Side or the Other** Pulling to one side is due to uneven braking action. It could be caused by incorrect front-end alignment, uneven tire inflation, or a broken or weak suspension spring. Within the braking system itself, such things as brake fluid on the linings, unmatched linings, warped brake shoes, jammed pistons, or restrictions in the brake lines could cause the car to pull to one side when braking.

⊘ **15-20 Noise** The chart covers various noises and their causes. Refer to it for details.

⊘ **15-21 Brakes Fail to Release** Brake-release failure could result from anything from a sticking pedal linkage or malfunctioning power brake to pistons stuck in the calipers. It could also be due to the driver's riding the brake pedal or to failure of the master cylinder to release the pressure when the brakes are released.

⊘ **15-22 Leaky Caliper Cylinder** A leaky caliper cylinder could be due to a damaged or worn piston seal or to roughness on the surface of the piston as a result of scores, scratches, or corrosion.

⊘ **15-23 Brake Pedal Can Be Depressed without Braking Effect** If the brake calipers have been serviced, the pistons may be pushed back so far in their bores that a single full movement of the brake pedal will not produce braking. Thus, after any service on disk brakes, the brake pedal should be pumped many times, and the master-cylinder reservoir properly filled, before the car is moved. Pumping the pedal several times gradually moves the pistons into normal position so that normal brake-pedal application causes braking.

Of course, other conditions can prevent braking action when the pedal is depressed, among them leaks or air in the system. Leaks can occur at the piston seals, bleeder screws, brake-line connections, or in the master cylinder.

Consider the possibility that the pressure-differential valve is stuck, or that the warning light may be burned out if both the front and rear sections have failed. The driver might have been driving for some time with one section defective and the warning system might not have worked to warn of the trouble.

⊘ **15-24 Fluid Level Low in Master Cylinder** Low fluid level in the master cylinder could be due to leaks in the system or caliper (see ⊘ 15-23). Worn disk-brake shoe linings also can cause this problem. As the linings wear, the fluid drops in the master cylinder.

⊘ **15-25 Drum-Brake Service** Any complaint of faulty brake action should always be analyzed to determine its cause, as noted in previous sections. Sometimes, all that is required (on earlier drum-type brakes) is a minor brake adjustment to compensate for lining wear. On later brakes with the self-adjuster (Figs. 14-24 and 14-25), the brakes automatically adjust themselves to compensate for lining wear. Other brake services include addition of brake fluid, bleeding the hydraulic system to remove air, repair or replacement of master cylinder and wheel cylinders, replacement of brake linings, and refinishing of brake drums or disks.

Many automotive shops have automatic brake testers which check brake action and efficiency in a few moments. Visual inspection may reveal some troubles, but the only way to really check brake action is to operate the brakes and see how they perform.

One automatic brake tester is shown in Fig. 15-5. With this tester, you simply drive the car onto the four tread plates at about 5 miles per hour [8 km/h] and then apply the brakes hard. The braking effort at each wheel is registered on four dials or in four glass columns (in which colored liquid rises in proportion to the braking effort). The four tread plates are supported on rollers and are spring-loaded in a horizontal direction. When a rolling wheel on a tread is suddenly stopped by brake application, the tread is moved forward against the spring tension. This movement causes the needle on a dial to turn or the liquid in a glass column to rise to register the amount of braking action. The use of this type of brake tester gives graphic proof to the operator of the amount of braking at each wheel. If it is inadequate, of course the brakes should be checked and serviced as necessary to restore braking to a safe level.

A dynamic brake analyzer using two pairs of motor-driven rollers is shown in Fig. 15-6. The principle of this analyzer is simple: Either the front or the rear wheels of the car are placed on the rollers, as shown. Then, the operator turns on the electric motors which drive the rollers (see Fig. 15-7). Now, with the wheels being turned by the rollers at medium to high speed, the operator applies the car brakes. The braking effort at each wheel is registered on a dial (Fig. 15-8) so that there is no question as to how well the brakes are operating. Note that there are two hands on the meter dial (Fig. 15-8). One, which is the color red, is for the right wheel; the black is for the left wheel. Not only does the analyzer indicate brake efficiency, but it also shows up imbalance between the left and right brakes. This is important because if one brake takes hold well and the other doesn't, the car will tend to be thrown sideways. This could be fatal at highway speed because it could send the car into another lane of traffic.

Note that, while the brake tester shown in Fig. 15-5 will test brake stopping power at only low speed, the brake analyzer shown in Fig. 15-6 will test the brakes at all speeds.

If the brake test shows low braking efficiency, or braking imbalance between wheels, the brakes should be checked further, as explained in later sections of this chapter.

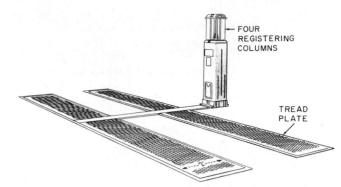

Fig. 15-5. Automatic brake tester. (*Weaver Manufacturing Company*)

NOTE: The analyzer shown in Fig. 15-6 is also supplied with a dynamometer as an integral part of the assembly. Figure 15-9 shows the dynamometer arrangement at one wheel. The dynamometer measures speed and power output. This gives a good indication of the condition of the engine and the power train. To use the dynamometer, place the drive wheels on the rollers and operate the engine to drive the rollers. Water is then introduced into the power absorption unit. The rotor blades pass through this water, absorbing power. The more water in the absorption unit, the greater the power absorption. The power output of the engine can thus be checked at various engine speeds.

NOTE: This type of tester gives only an indication of braking efficiency and does not pinpoint causes of low efficiency. For an accurate analysis of the braking system, checking procedures outlined later in the chapter should be followed.

⊘ **15-26 Adjustment of Brakes** On the early models of brakes without the self-adjustment feature, two types of adjustment are required: minor and major. Minor adjustments are required to compensate for brake-lining wear and are made without removing the car wheels. Major adjustments require removal of the brake drums or shoes for service. With the self-adjusting brakes, however, no adjustment is normally required except after such brake services as brake-shoe replacement or brake-drum grinding or replacement. Adjustments on different types of brakes are described in following sections. Recall that disk-type brakes are self-adjusting.

Before any adjustment is attempted, the fluid level in the master cylinder, the brake-pedal toe-board clearance, and brake-lining and brake-drum conditions should be checked. Fluid should be added and the brake-pedal linkage adjusted, as needed. It is usually not necessary to remove all four wheels to check the brake-lining condition, since similar conditions should be found at each wheel. Thus, as a rule, only one drum and wheel need be removed. Remove a front wheel, since front-wheel linings wear faster than rear-wheel linings. However, for a thorough inspection all four wheels are

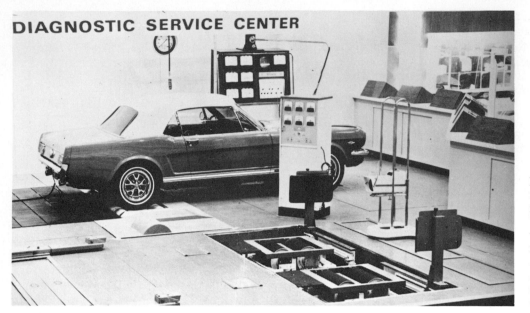

DIAGNOSTIC SERVICE CENTER

Fig. 15-6. Car in dynamic brake tester, ready for a test of the brakes at the rear wheels. The two sets of rollers in the foreground are for testing front alignment dynamically. (*Clayton Manufacturing Company*)

removed so that all brake linings and drums can be checked. Linings should be inspected for wear or contamination with grease or oil. Drums should be inspected for roughness or scoring. See ⊘ 15-35 and 15-36 for lining and drum service.

CAUTION: Handle brake linings with care to avoid getting grease on them. Even slight amounts of grease—from greasy fingers—may cause uneven brake action.

Check Your Progress

Progress Quiz 15-1 Here is another progress quiz—another chance for you to check yourself on the progress you are making in the book. The quiz

below covers the first half of the chapter. As you take the quiz, you will find it helps you to review what you have learned. It will also give you a tip-off if you haven't learned the important details well enough. This gives you a chance to review the important points so that you will remember them.

Correcting Troubles Lists This exercise helps you spot related and unrelated troubles on a list. For example, in the list "All brakes drag: incorrect brake-pedal adjustment, reservoir filler vent clogged, air in lines, mineral oil in system," you can see that "air in lines" does not belong because that condition could hardly cause all brakes to drag. Any of the other conditions in the list could. In each list, you will find one item that does not belong. Write each

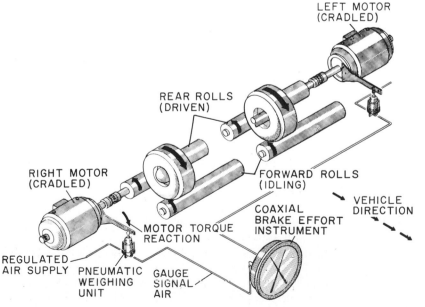

Fig. 15-7. Schematic view of the operating parts of the dynamic brake analyzer. The rollers are driven by the motors, thus driving the wheels. When brakes are applied, the wheels attempt to stop the rollers. This effect causes the motors to swing, thus changing the air pressure through the pneumatic weighing units. This moves the positions of the needles on the dial. (*Clayton Manufacturing Company*)

In the first, or rolling resistance test, the technician does not touch the brake pedal. The solid hand records action of left brake, while the dash indicates operation of right. A wide spread of the hands indicates presence of a dragging brake or uneven tire pressures.

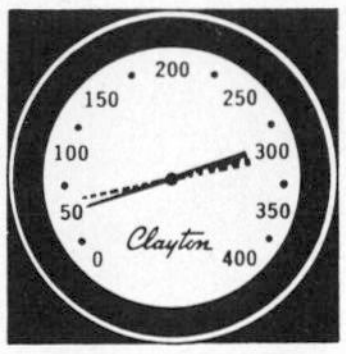

This test determines mechanical application of the brakes. A light application is made to observe first contact of brake shoes with the drums. Often revealed are such things as sticking wheel cylinders, corrosion or ledges between shoes and mounting plates, and/or unhooked or broken return springs.

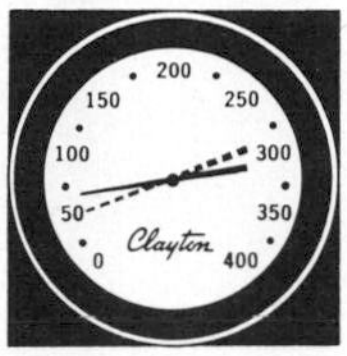

Hydraulic application (the difference in braking power between the two wheels under test) is found by making two short applications of the brakes. Slow application—shown here—reveals brake balance at moderate pressures.

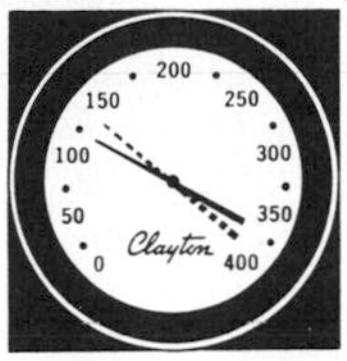

A rapid application is shown here. Any hydraulic restrictions are indicated by a lag in one hand or the other. Hydraulic lag creates momentary imbalance that may cause a car to react wildly during an emergency stop at freeway speeds.

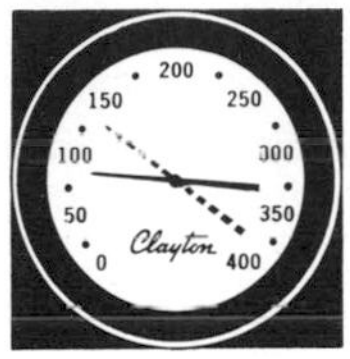

A high effort application on very good brakes. Note closeness of hands.

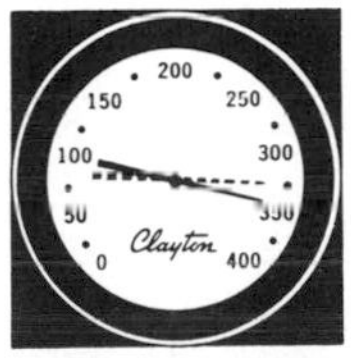

The same hydraulic test on brakes with modest imbalance, but within acceptable limits.

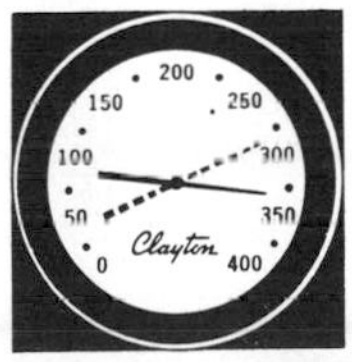

A high effort application or simulated stop from high speeds. These brakes are marginal and can be dangerous in a panic stop. Condition could be improved by repair.

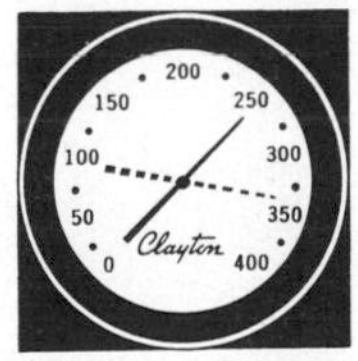

These brakes could cause a fatal accident if not repaired. Note wide spread of the hands. With hydraulic imbalance like this, a car could be literally jerked into another lane of traffic . . . a divider . . . or into a head-on collision. This car is unsafe in any driving situation.

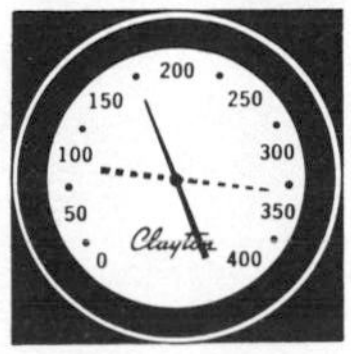

Fig. 15-8. Various readings of the two needles on the dial and their meanings. (*Clayton Manufacturing Company*)

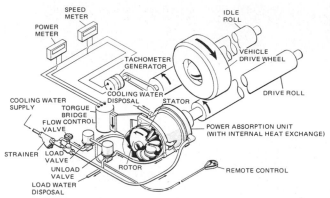

Fig. 15-9. Dynamometer section of the combined dynamic brake analyzer and dynamometer. Note that both units use the same rollers. (*Clayton Manufacturing Company*)

list in your notebook, but *do not write* the item that does not belong.

1. Brake pedal goes to floorboard: brake shoes out of adjustment, brake pedal out of adjustment, brake linings worn, lack of brake fluid, brake line clogged, air in system, worn master cylinder.

2. One brake drags: brake shoes out of adjustment, clogged brake line, wheel cylinder defective, master cylinder defective, weak return spring.

3. All brakes drag: incorrect brake-pedal adjustment, filler vent clogged, mineral oil in system, brake lining soaked with oil.

4. Car pulls to one side when braking: brake linings soaked with oil or brake fluid, shoes out of adjustment, tires not uniformly inflated, brake line clogged, master cylinder defective, defective wheel cylinder, backing plate loose, mismatched linings.

5. Soft or spongy pedal: air in system, brake lining water-soaked, shoes out of adjustment.

6. Poor braking action requiring excessive pedal pressure: brake linings hot, brake linings wet, brake linings soaked with oil or brake fluid, shoes out of adjustment, glazed brake drums, brake drums scored.

7. Brakes too sensitive or brakes grab; shoes out of adjustment, backing plates loose, linings greasy, drums scored, linings soaked with oil, wrong linings.

8. Brakes noisy: linings worn, shoes warped, shoe rivets loose, brake drum rough or worn, air in lines, loose parts.

9. Air in system: plugged filler vent, leaky valve in master cylinder, high fluid level in reservoir, low fluid level in reservoir.

10. Loss of brake fluid: master cylinder leaks, wheel cylinder leaks, mismatched linings, loose line connections, damaged brake tube.

⊘ **15-27 Self-adjusting-Brake Adjustments (Drum Type)** As mentioned, the drum-type self-adjusting brakes require adjustment only after replacement of brake shoes, grinding of brake drums, or other service in which disassembly of the brakes was performed. (Disk-type brakes require no adjust-

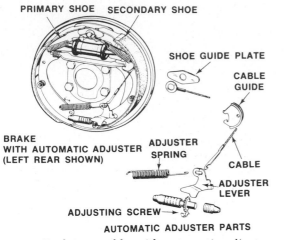

Fig. 15-10. Brake assembly with automatic adjuster and adjuster parts disassembled. (*Bendix-Westinghouse Automotive Air Brake Company*)

ment.) Two typical procedures for drum-type brakes follow.

1. BENDIX BRAKE WITH AUTOMATIC AD-JUSTER The Bendix brake and its automatic adjuster parts are illustrated in Fig. 15-10. To adjust, remove the adjustment-hole cover from the brake backing plate and expand the brake shoes by moving the outer end of the tool downward until the wheel drags heavily when it is turned. Then insert an ice pick or a thin-blade screwdriver into the adjustment hole as shown (Fig. 15-11) to hold the lever away from the adjustment screw. Back off the adjustment screw until the wheel and the drum turn freely. Replace the adjustment-hole cover.

CAUTION: On this type of brake, do not attempt to back off the adjustment screw without holding the adjuster lever away from the screw. To do this would damage the adjuster.

An alternative initial adjustment procedure, described below, is recommended by some service

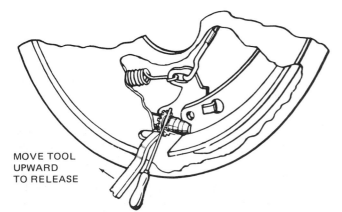

Fig. 15-11. Holding the adjusting lever off the adjusting screw with a screwdriver while turning the screw. (*Bendix-Westinghouse Automotive Air Brake Company*)

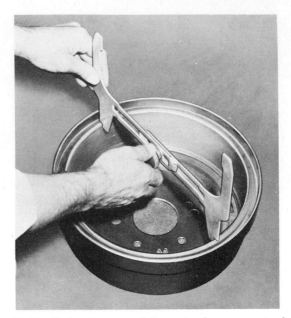

Fig. 15-12. Using the special drum-to-shoe gauge to check brake-drum diameter. (*Chevrolet Motor Division of General Motors Corporation*)

people as being somewhat quicker. It requires a special gauge. With the drum off, use the gauge to check the drum braking-surface diameter (Fig. 15-12). Set the gauge at this diameter and lock with the screw. Then fit it over the brake-shoe linings (Fig. 15-13) to check their diameter. If this is incorrect, turn the adjustment screw. When the gauge will just fit over the linings at all points, the clearance between the linings and the drum will be approximately correct.

Complete the adjustment, after the drum and wheel have been installed, by driving the car back and forth and firmly applying the brakes. Repeat this several times until the brake-pedal height at which braking takes place is correct.

Fig. 15-13. Using the special drum-to-shoe gauge to check the diameter of the brake-shoe linings. (*Chevrolet Motor Division of General Motors Corporation*)

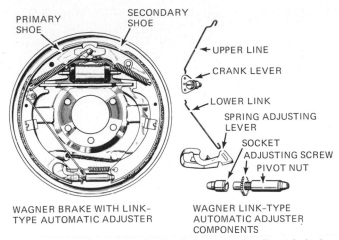

Fig. 15-14. Wagner brake (at left rear wheel) with link-type automatic adjuster and adjuster components. (*Bendix-Westinghouse Automotive Air Brake Company*)

2. WAGNER BRAKE WITH LINK-TYPE AUTO-MATIC ADJUSTER The Wagner brake (Fig. 15-14) can be adjusted by turning the adjustment screw without using an ice pick or screwdriver to hold the adjustment lever off the screw (Fig. 15-15). In fact, you are cautioned not to use a tool to force the adjustment lever off the adjustment screw because this would damage the lever.

⊘ **15-28 Drum-Type Minor Brake Adjustments (Non-self-adjusting)** The brake shown in Fig. 15-16 does not have the self-adjustment feature. It was widely used until supplanted by the later type with the self-adjuster. In this assembly, the brake shoes are held in position by hold-down cups and springs. An expanding adjustment screw (star-shaped) at the bottom (see Fig. 15-16) can be turned to move the

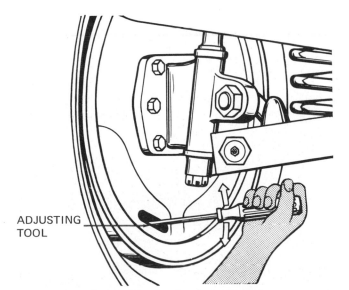

Fig. 15-15. Adjusting brakes having a link-type automatic adjuster. (*Bendix-Westinghouse Automotive Air Brake Company*)

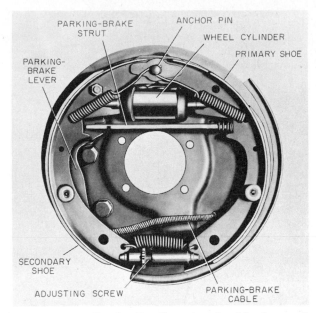

Fig. 15-16. Details of a Bendix rear-wheel brake mechanism. (*Oldsmobile Division of General Motors Corporation*)

brake shoes outward toward the brake drum and thus compensate for brake-lining wear. In addition, the anchor pin is either eccentric or assembled in a slotted hole. This arrangement makes it possible to shift the upper ends of the brake shoes to the front or back, or up or down, so that the clearances between the linings and the drum will be equalized when the brakes are released. Normally, the anchor pin will not require adjustment unless parts have been replaced or repaired.

To make a minor adjustment, jack up the car until all four wheels clear the floor. Loosen or disconnect the parking-brake cables at the parking-brake equalizer, and remove the adjustment-hole covers at all wheels. Expand the brake shoes by turning the star adjustment screw (Fig. 15-17). Do this by moving the outer end of the tool upward (as shown) repeatedly until you feel a heavy drag on the wheel as it is turned. Then back off the adjustment screw approximately 14 to 16 notches. Brake adjustment should then be correct. If a heavy drag is still felt at the wheel, it will be necessary to readjust the anchor pin as explained in ⊘ 15-30 below. If this is not necessary, replace the adjustment-hole covers and then adjust the parking-brake cables.

⊘ **15-29 Parking-Brake Adjustments** In adjusting the parking brakes, the objective is to tighten them sufficiently to ensure adequate braking when the brake handle is pulled most of the way out. There should be some reserve; that is, it should not be necessary to pull the handle all the way out to secure full braking. On the other hand, the adjustment should not be so tight as to cause the brake shoes to be shifted toward the brake drum with the brake handle all the way in (retracted). Parking brakes are

Fig. 15-17. Adjusting brakes with a brake-adjusting tool inserted through the adjusting-hole cover. (*Buick Motor Division of General Motors Corporation*)

adjusted in different ways, depending on the type of linkage used between the brake handle and the cables leading to the parking-brake levers at the wheels. One specification, for example, is that first the parking-brake handle should be pulled out for seven clicks of the pawl (not seven notches). Then, the check nuts at the cable ends should be loosened, the forward check nuts should be turned against the clevis plates to draw each brake cable up until a moderate drag is felt when the wheel is rotated, and the check nuts should be tightened securely. To check, set the parking-brake handle back two clicks from full release; no brake-shoe drag should be felt.

On another make of car, the parking brake is adjusted by first checking the position of the equalizer lever pin with the handle in the released position. The lever pin should align horizontally with the frame cross member. If it does not, adjust the equalizer lever nut until it is correctly positioned. Then remove the slack from the brake cables by turning the adjustment nuts on the equalizer rod. But do not tighten the cables too much; the shoes will be pulled off their anchors.

On disk brakes, the parking-brake shoes themselves may also require adjustment. Figure 14-38 shows the procedure. The adjusting tool is inserted through the backing plate, as shown. It is pivoted on either the splash shield or on the clamp to turn the adjusting star wheel one way or the other.

⊘ 15-30 Drum-Type Major Brake Adjustments (Non-self-adjusting) There are still some non-self-adjusting drum brakes in operation although the self-adjusting feature (Figs. 15-10 and 15-14) has been incorporated in automotive brakes for many years. To make a major adjustment, jack up the car and remove the wheels, wheel hubs, and brake drums. Check the brake linings for wear and the brake-

drum braking surfaces for smoothness. Worn brake linings should be replaced (⊘ 15-35), and excessively rough drums should be turned or ground (⊘ 15-36). Disconnect the brake-shoe return springs, and remove the brake-shoe hold-down cups, springs, and brake shoes. Examine the shoes for defects as noted in ⊘ 15-35. Clean all parts that are dirty or rusty, taking extreme care to avoid getting grease on the brake linings. Even slight traces of grease—from greasy fingers—might be sufficient to cause eccentric braking action and might require brake-lining replacement. If wheel cylinders give any indication of leakage or other defect, they should be removed for servicing or replacement (⊘ 15-37).

Lubricate all metal contact points with special lubricant (Fig. 15-18). Reinstall the brake shoes and the brake-drum assemblies. Adjust the front-wheel bearings as required. Add brake fluid to the master cylinder and adjust the brake-pedal toeboard clearance as already noted (⊘ 15-26). With these preliminaries out of the way, adjust the anchor pin as necessary. The procedure for making these adjustments varies to some extent. Typical procedures follow.

1. SLOTTED-ANCHOR-PIN-HOLE TYPE Loosen the anchor-pin nut (Fig. 15-19) just enough to permit the pin to shift in the slotted hole—but no more than this or the pin will tilt. Turn the brake adjustment screw (star screw) to expand the shoes so that a heavy drag is felt as the drum is turned (Fig. 15-17). Tap the pin and the backing plate lightly to center the shoes in the drum. If the drag on the drum is reduced, tighten the star screw a few notches to restore the drag. Again tap the pin and the backing plate. Repeat if necessary until the drag remains constant. This means the shoes are now centered. Tighten the anchor nut just enough to hold it without shifting.

Back off the adjustment screw 10 notches and

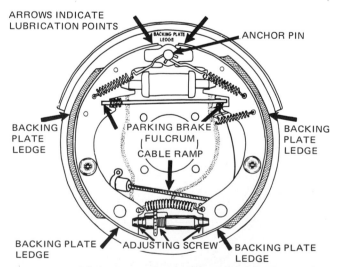

Fig. 15-18. Lubrication points in the wheel-brake mechanism are indicated by arrows. The backing-plate ledges are areas on which the brake shoes ride as they move toward or away from the brake drum. (*Pontiac Motor Division of General Motors Corporation*)

Fig. 15-19. Loosening the anchor-pin nut in preparation for pin adjustment. (*Buick Motor Division of General Motors Corporation*)

Fig. 15-20. Checking the clearance between the shoe and the brake drum by inserting a feeler gauge through the checking slot in the drum. (*Buick Motor Division of General Motors Corporation*)

check the clearance at the toe and heel of the secondary (rear) shoe with a 0.010-inch [0.254 mm] feeler (Fig. 15-20). If the clearances at the ends of the shoe are not equal, tap the anchor pin up or down to equalize the clearance. Then tighten the nut to 60 to 80 pound-feet [8.29 to 11.06 kg-m] torque. Finally, replace the wheels and then make the minor adjustment, as above (⊘ 15-28), backing off each star adjustment screw 14 notches from the light-drag position. Replace the hole covers, adjust the parking brakes, and road-test the brakes.

2. *ECCENTRIC-ANCHOR-PIN TYPE* Loosen the hand-brake cable so that the levers are free at the rear wheels. Then insert a 0.015-inch [0.381 mm] feeler gauge at the lower end of the secondary (rear shoe) and wedge the shoe forward by moving the gauge up. Expand the shoes by turning the star adjustment screw until the primary shoe is tight against the drum and the secondary shoe is snug on the feeler. Back it off just enough to establish a 0.015-inch [0.381 mm] clearance 1½ inches [38.1 mm] from each end of the secondary shoe. If a 0.015-inch [0.381 mm] clearance cannot be obtained, loosen the anchor-pin locknut and turn the eccentric anchor pin as required to equalize clearances. For instance, if clearance is excessive at the top, turn the anchor pin in the direction that the wheel rotates as the car moves forward. Tighten the locknut, recheck the clearances, and road-test the brakes.

⊘ 15-31 Disk-Brake Service (Fixed-Caliper Type)
The chart in ⊘ 15-15 lists troubles and possible causes in disk-brake systems. Although all disk brakes work in much the same manner, their design and construction vary with different manufacturers.

There are three general types, as described in ⊘ 14-12: fixed caliper, floating caliper, and sliding caliper. In this section, we describe the servicing of the fixed-caliper disk brake. Following sections discuss the servicing of the other two types.

1. *REMOVING THE BRAKE SHOES* Raise the vehicle on a hoist or jack stand. Remove wheel covers and the wheel-and-tire assembly. Remove bolts holding the splash shield, and remove the shield and antirattle spring (Fig. 15-21). Now, use two pliers to grip the tabs on the shoe and pull the shoe out (Fig. 15-22). If the shoe hangs up on the pistons, push the pistons in with slip-joint pliers as shown in Fig. 15-22. Watch for master-cylinder reservoir overflow when pushing the pistons in. Mark the shoes so you can return them to the same side of the caliper from which you removed them.

On disk brakes that have spring-loaded pistons, a special piston compressing tool is used to push the pistons back into their bores and hold them in that position during the time that the brake shoe is out.

With the brake shoes out, check the caliper and pistons for possible leaks and wipe all parts clean. If brake fluid is present, remove the caliper as explained below for replacement of piston seals.

2. *REPLACING THE BRAKE SHOES* Push pistons back into their bores to allow room for installation of new thicker shoes and linings. Then slide the new shoe into the caliper with the ears of the shoe resting on the bridges of the caliper. Be sure the shoe is fully seated with lining facing the disk. Install the other shoe. Replace the caliper splash shield and antirattle spring assembly. Pump the brake several times until a firm pedal is obtained. This ensures proper seating of the shoes. Install the wheel and tire. Check and refill the master cylinder if necessary.

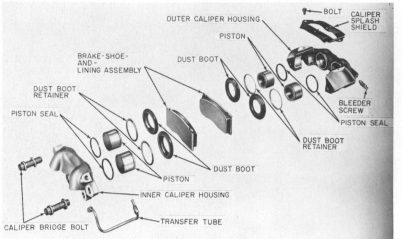

Fig. 15-21. Disassembled view of a caliper assembly. (*Chrysler Corporation*)

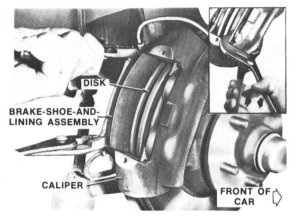

Fig. 15-22. Removing the brake shoe and lining from a disk-brake assembly. *Upper right,* forcing the piston into the bore with slip-joint pliers. (*Chrysler Corporation*)

SPECIAL NOTE: Road-test the car and make several heavy braking stops from about 40 mph [64.37 km/h] to ensure good seating of the brake lining on the disk. Unless this is done, initial braking may cause the car to pull to one side or the other.

3. *REMOVING THE CALIPER* Refer to Fig. 15-23 and proceed as follows. Raise the car on a hoist or jack stand and remove the wheel cover and wheel-and-tire assembly. Disconnect the brake flexible hose from the brake tube at the frame mounting bracket and plug the brake tube to prevent loss of fluid. Remove attaching bolts and lift the caliper assembly up and out (Fig. 15-24).

4. *DISASSEMBLING THE CALIPER* Refer to Fig. 15-21 and proceed as follows. Remove the splash shield and antirattle spring assembly. Clamp caliper mounting lugs in the soft jaws of a vise and remove the transfer tube and jumper tube (armored). Remove shoes. Separate the two halves of the caliper by removing two bolts. Peel dust boots off the caliper and pistons. Use a special tool (Fig. 15-25) to remove pistons, being very careful to avoid scratching the pistons and bores. Then use a small pointed

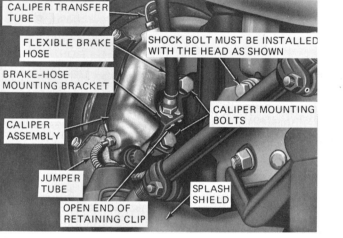

Fig. 15-23. Mounting of the disk-brake caliper at a front wheel. (*Chrysler Corporation*)

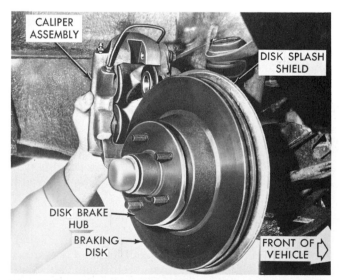

Fig. 15-24. Removing the disk-brake caliper. (*Chrysler Corporation*)

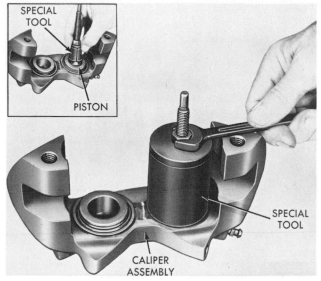

Fig. 15-25. Removing pistons from the caliper. (*Chrysler Corporation*)

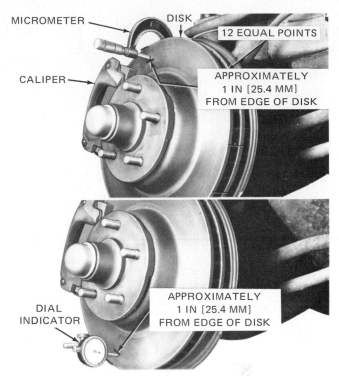

Fig. 15-26. Checking brake-disk thickness and runout. (*Chrysler Corporation*)

wood or plastic stick to remove piston seals from grooves in the piston bores. Do not scratch bores!

5. *CLEANING CALIPER PARTS* Clean all parts, except shoes and linings, in brake fluid and wipe dry with lint-free towels. Blow out drilled passages and bores with compressed air. Discard old piston seals. Also, discard dust boots and pistons that appear damaged in any way. If piston bores are scratched, clean them up with crocus cloth or a special hone. However, if more than about 0.002 inch [0.051 mm] must be removed to clean up deep scratches, discard the old caliper. Carefully clean the caliper to remove all traces of dust or dirt.

6. *REASSEMBLING THE CALIPER* Clamp the inner half, by the mounting lugs, in the soft jaws of a vise. If a new dust-boot retainer ring is necessary, clean the boot-retainer groove in the caliper, apply a special sealing compound to the retainer groove in the caliper, and apply a special sealing compound to the retainer ring where it will seat in the housing. Then install the ring. Dip new piston seals in brake fluid and install them in the grooves in the piston bores. Be sure the seals are not twisted or rolled. Coat outside of pistons with brake fluid and slide them into the bores, using slow, steady pressure. Install new dust boots, making sure they seat over the retaining rings and in piston grooves. Reattach the two halves of the caliper with special bolts, tightened to 70 to 80 pound-feet [9.67 to 11.06 kg-m] torque. Install transfer and jumper tubes. Install the bleeder screw (but do not tighten).

7. *CHECKING DISK FOR THICKNESS AND RUNOUT* Before reinstalling the caliper, check the disk for runout and thickness, as follows. Use a micrometer (Fig. 15-26 top) and measure thickness at 12 equal points about 1 inch [25.4 mm] from the edge. If thickness varies excessively (Plymouth says more than 0.0005 inch [0.0127 mm]), discard the disk and install a new one. Measure runout by first ad-

justing the wheel bearing to zero end play and then mounting a dial indicator as shown in Fig. 15-26, bottom. Rotate the disk and check runout. If it is excessive (Plymouth says more than 0.0025 inch [0.0635 mm]), discard the disk and install a new one.

CAUTION: Readjust wheel bearings after the check!

Light scores and wear of the disk are okay, but if the scores are fairly deep, the disk should be refinished (Fig. 15-27). For rust spots or lining deposits, the grinder may be used. But if the scores or wear marks are deep, the disk must first be refaced with a cutting tool, then given a final grinding with the grinder to remove tool marks.

NOTE: Machining disks produces considerable noise. Several different kinds of silencers are available. One is shown attached to the disk in Fig. 15-27. Another view of this damper, or silencer, is shown in Fig. 15-28. In this figure you can see how it is held in place by magnets. Another silencer is also shown in Fig. 15-28. This one is a heavy rubber band that is wrapped around the disk before it is machined.

CAUTION: Disks usually have a dimension (a number) cast into them. This dimension is the minimum to which the disk can be finished. If it is necessary to refinish the disk to a smaller dimension, discard it, because the disk would be too thin to use safely.

8. *INSTALLING THE CALIPER* After the disk has been reinstalled (if it had been removed for service)

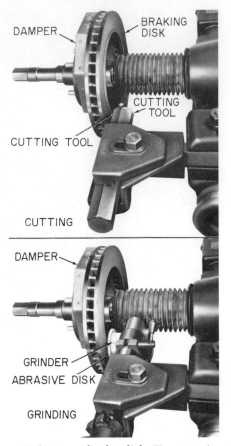

DAMPER   BRAKING
          DISK

CUTTING
TOOL

CUTTING TOOL

CUTTING

DAMPER

GRINDER
ABRASIVE DISK

GRINDING

Fig. 15-27. Refacing a brake disk. *Top,* turning the disk with a cutting tool. *Bottom,* using a grinder on the disk. (*Chrysler Corporation*)

and the wheel bearings adjusted, install the caliper assembly and tighten mounting bolts to 45 to 60 pound-feet [6.22 to 8.29 kg-m] torque. Make sure the disk runs square with the caliper opening. Install the shoes and splash shield. Open the bleeder screw and reconnect the brake line. Allow fluid to flow until all air is pushed out of the caliper (until air bubbles

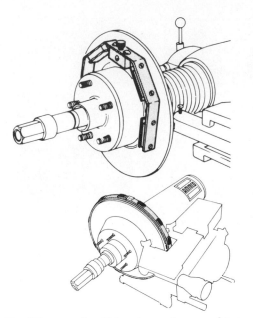

Fig. 15-28. Silencers for disk rotors when machining rotor faces. (*Ammo Tools, Inc.*)

stop flowing out of bleeder). Tighten the bleeder screw. Replenish the reservoir in the master cylinder.

⊘ 15-32 Disk-Brake Service (Floating-Caliper Type)

The chart in ⊘ 15-15 lists troubles and possible causes in disk-brake systems. Although all disk brakes work in the same manner, their design and construction vary with different manufacturers. There are three general types, as already described in ⊘ 14-12: fixed-caliper, sliding-caliper, and floating-caliper. In this section, we describe the servicing of the floating-caliper disk brake. (Fig. 15-29 is a disassembled view of this type of unit.) The preceding section described the servicing of the fixed-caliper disk brake.

1. REMOVING THE BRAKE SHOES Raise the car on a hoist or jack stand and remove the front-wheel

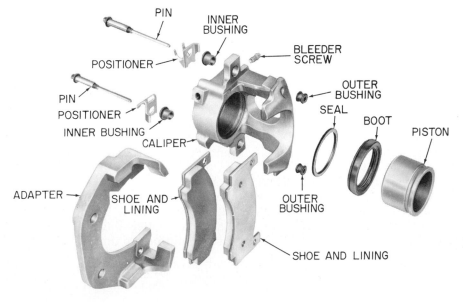

PIN   INNER
       BUSHING

POSITIONER   BLEEDER
                        SCREW

PIN   OUTER
POSITIONER   BUSHING

INNER BUSHING   SEAL   BOOT

CALIPER   PISTON

ADAPTER

SHOE AND
LINING   OUTER
                BUSHING

SHOE AND LINING

Fig. 15-29. Disassembled view of a floating caliper assembly. (*Chrysler Corporation*)

covers and the wheel-and-tire assemblies. Remove the caliper guide pins and positioners that attach the caliper to the adapter. Now, you can slide the caliper up and away from the disk (Fig. 15-30). Support the caliper firmly so you don't damage the brake hose.

Slide outboard and inboard shoe-and-lining assemblies out (Fig. 15-31). Mark shoes so you can put them back in the same places in the caliper. Push outer bushings from the caliper with a wooden or plastic stick (Fig. 15-32). Throw the bushings away. Slide the inner bushings off the guide pins and discard them.

2. INSPECTING CALIPER PARTS Check for piston-seal leaks (brake fluid in or around boot area and inboard lining). If the boot is damaged or fluid has leaked, disassemble the caliper to install new parts as explained in item 5, below. Inspect the brake disk and service it if necessary (⊘ 15-31, item 7).

3. INSTALLING BRAKE SHOES New positioners and inner and outer bushings will be required (see Fig. 15-29). Slowly and carefully push the piston back into the bore until it bottoms. Watch for possible reservoir overflow at the brake master cylinder. Install new bushings, noting their proper relationship as shown in Fig. 15-29. Slide new shoe-and-lining assemblies into position (Fig. 15-31). Make sure the metal part of the shoe is fully in the recess

Fig. 15-31. Removing or installing brake shoes and linings. (*Chrysler Corporation*)

of the caliper and adapter. Hold the outboard lining in position and slide the caliper down into place over the disk (Fig. 15-30). Align guide-pin holes of the adapter, and inboard and outboard shoes (see Fig. 15-33).

Install new positioners over guide pins with the open ends toward the outside and the stamped arrows pointing upward. Install each guide pin through the bushing, caliper, adapter, inboard shoe, outboard shoe, and outer bushing (Fig. 15-33). Press in on the end of the guide pin and thread the pin into the adapter. *Use great care to avoid cross-threading.* Tighten to specifications. Make sure tabs of positioners are over the machined surfaces of the caliper.

Pump the brake pedal several times until a firm pedal has been obtained. Check and refill the master-cylinder reservoir if necessary. If you cannot get a firm pedal, you may have to bleed the brake system and add brake fluid to the reservoir (⊘ 15-40).

Install the wheel-and-tire assemblies and wheel covers. Remove the car from the hoist or jack stands.

4. REMOVING THE CALIPER If a new piston seal or boot is required, the caliper must be removed. Proceed as already outlined in item 1 above, with the additional step that the flexible hose must be

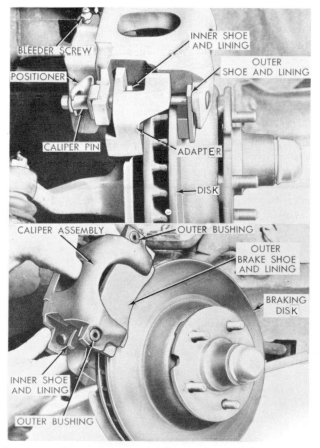

Fig. 15-30. Removing or installing calipers (*Chrysler Corporation*)

Fig. 15-32. Removing outer bushings. (*Chrysler Corporation*)

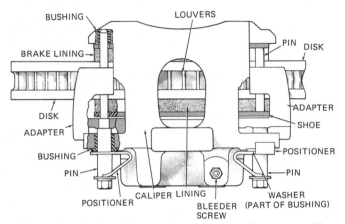

Fig. 15-33. Sectional view of a floating-caliper assembly, showing the positions of the adapter, pins, bushings, and positioners. (*Chrysler Corporation*)

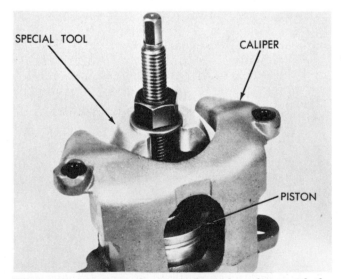

Fig. 15-34. Removing the piston from the caliper with the special tool. (*Chrysler Corporation*)

disconnected from the tube at the frame (tube must then be plugged to prevent loss of fluid).

5. DISASSEMBLING THE CALIPER Clamp the caliper lightly in the soft jaws of a vise, and remove the dust boot. Use a special tool (Fig. 15-34) to remove the piston from the caliper.

Use a pointed wood stick to work the seal out of its groove in the piston bore. *Never use a screwdriver or metal tool; it could scratch the bore or burr the edge of the seal groove, thus ruining the caliper.*

6. CLEANING AND INSPECTING CALIPER PARTS Clean parts with alcohol or other solvent and blow dry with compressed air. Inspect the bore for pits or scoring. Install a new piston if the old one is pitted or scored or if the plating is worn off. Light score marks in the bore can be cleaned off with crocus cloth. Deeper scores require honing (Fig. 15-35), provided no more than 0.002 inch [0.051 mm] is removed. If the bore does not clean up, discard the old caliper.

CAUTION: After using crocus cloth or honing, clean the caliper *thoroughly* with brake fluid, including drilled passages. Wipe the bore with a clean, lintless cloth. Continue wiping until the cloth shows no sign of dirt.

7. ASSEMBLING THE CALIPER Clamp the caliper in the soft jaws of a vise and install the new piston seal in the groove in the bore. (Never reuse the old seal!) Lubricate the seal in special lubricant supplied in the service kit. Position the seal in one area and carefully work it into the groove, *using clean fingers.* Make sure the seal is not twisted or rolled.

Coat the new piston boot with lubricant, leaving plenty on the inside circumference. Install it in the caliper (Fig. 15-36), working it into place with the fingers (clean) only. Temporarily plug the fluid inlet to the caliper and bleeder-screw hole. Coat the piston with a generous amount of lubricant. Spread the boot with the fingers of one hand and push the piston straight down into the bore. The trapped air under the piston will force the boot around the piston and into its groove as the piston is pushed down. Remove the plug and push the piston down until it bottoms. Apply force uniformly all around the piston to keep it from cocking.

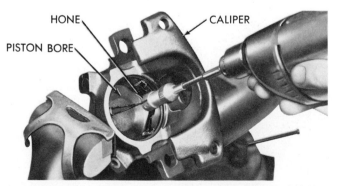

Fig. 15-35. Honing the piston bore in the caliper. (*Chrysler Corporation*)

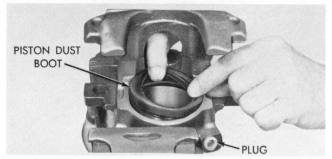

Fig. 15-36. Installing the piston dust boot in the piston bore in the caliper. (*Chrysler Corporation*)

Reinstall the caliper as described, with the additional step of reconnecting the flexible brake hose.

8. CHECKING THE DISK FOR THICKNESS AND RUNOUT This has already been covered in ⊘ 15-31, item 7.

⊘ 15-33 Disk-Brake Service (Sliding-Caliper Type)
The chart in ⊘ 15-15 lists troubles and possible causes in disk-brake systems. Although all disk brakes work in the same general manner, their design and construction vary from one model to another. In this section, we describe servicing of the sliding-caliper disk brake. Figure 14-32 shows how this brake works, and Fig. 15-37 gives a disassembled

view. Note that it is somewhat simpler in construction than the other disk brakes previously described.

1. INSPECTING SHOES AND LININGS Linings should be inspected for wear every 6,000 miles [9,656 km] and also whenever a wheel is removed. The outboard shoe should be checked at both ends as shown by the two arrows in Fig. 15-38. The inboard lining can be checked through the inspection hole as shown by the single arrow. If a lining is worn down to within 0.020 inch [0.508 mm] of the rivet at either end, all shoe-and-lining assemblies should be replaced.

2. REMOVING SHOES AND LININGS Remove two-thirds of the brake fluid from the master cylinder section feeding the disk brakes. Discard, do not reuse, the fluid.

Raise the car and remove the wheel covers and wheels. Use a 7-inch [177.8 mm] C clamp as shown in Fig. 15-39. The solid end of the clamp rests against the inside of the caliper and the screw end rests against the metal part of the outboard shoe. Tighten the C clamp to move the caliper out far enough to push the piston to the bottom of the piston bore. This produces clearance between the disk and shoes.

Remove the two mounting bolts (Fig. 15-40). Lift the caliper off the disk. Support it with a wire hook so it does not hang from the brake hose. Remove the shoes. Mark the shoes so you can return them

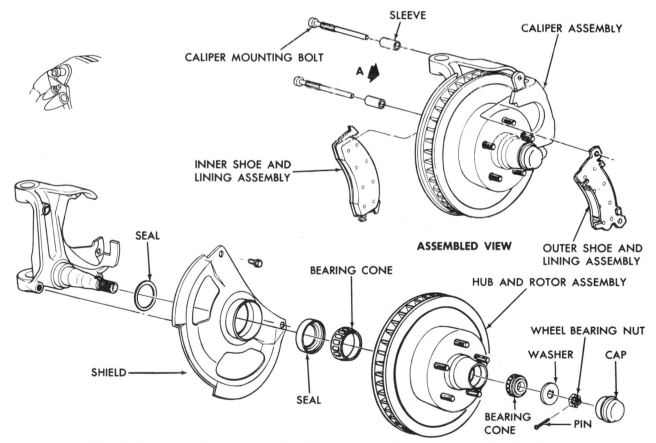

Fig. 15-37. Disassembled view of a sliding-caliper disk-brake assembly. (*Chevrolet Motor Division of General Motors Corporation*)

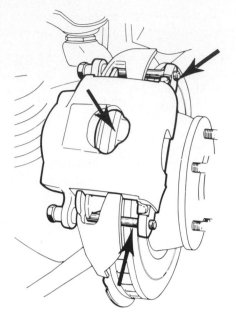

Fig. 15-38. Shoe-lining inspection points (indicated by arrows). (*Buick Motor Division of General Motors Corporation*)

Fig. 15-40. Using a ratchet wrench to remove the mounting bolts. (*Buick Motor Division of General Motors Corporation*)

on the same side of the caliper from which they were removed. Next, remove the sleeves and bushings from the four caliper ears (Fig. 15-41). A special tool is used to remove the sleeves. The bushings fit into grooves in the ears.

3. *CLEANING AND INSPECTION* Clean the holes and grooves in the caliper ears and wipe dirt from the mounting bolts. Replace the bolts if they are corroded or damaged. Wipe the inside of the caliper clean while inspecting it for brake-fluid leakage. If leakage is noted, remove the caliper for overhaul (see below). Make sure the dust boot is in good

condition and is properly installed in the piston and caliper (Fig. 15-42). Check the rotor for wear and runout (⊘ 15-31, item 7). If it needs service, remove it.

4. *INSTALLING SHOES AND CALIPER* Use special silicone lubricant on the new sleeves and bushings, the bolts, and the bushing holes and grooves in the caliper ears (Fig. 15-41).

CAUTION: Always use new sleeves and bushings, properly lubricated, to ensure easy sliding of the caliper.

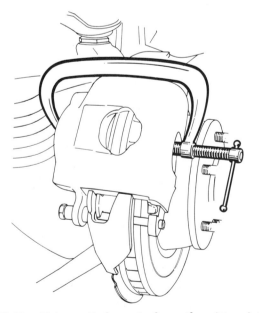

Fig. 15-39. Using a C clamp to force the piston into the bore. (*Buick Motor Division of General Motors Corporation*)

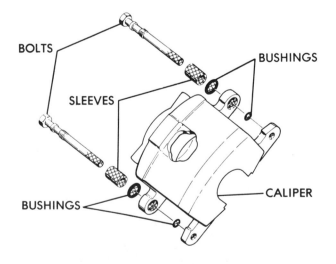

▨ **LUBRICATE AREAS INDICATED**

Fig. 15-41. Relationship of the mounting bolts to the sleeves and bushings. The areas to be lubricated with silicone lubricant are indicated. (*Buick Motor Division of General Motors Corporation*)

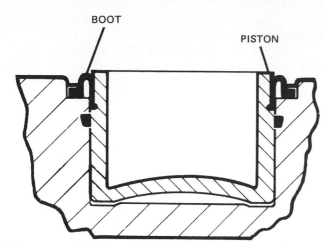

Fig. 15-42. Installation of the piston boot. (*Buick Motor Division of General Motors Corporation*)

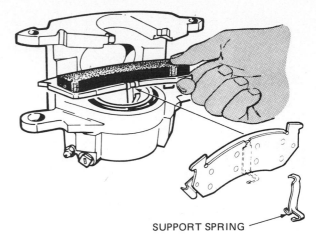

Fig. 15-44. Installing the inboard shoe. Note the location of the support spring. (*Chevrolet Motor Division of General Motors Corporation*)

Install the four bushings in the caliper ears. Use the special tool as shown in Fig. 15-43 to install the sleeves. The outer ends of the sleeves should be flush with the surface of the ears.

Install the shoe support spring and the inboard shoe in the center of the piston cavity as shown in Fig. 15-44. Install the outboard shoe as shown in Fig. 15-45.

Now position the caliper over the disk, making sure the brake hose is not twisted or kinked. Start the bolts through the sleeves, making sure the bolts pass under the retaining ears on the inboard shoes (Fig. 15-46). Push the bolts on through, making sure they go through the holes in the outboard shoe and the ears in the caliper. Screw the bolts into the mounting holes and tighten them to the proper tension.

Add fresh brake fluid to the reservoir and pump the brake pedal to seat the linings against the disk. Now clinch the upper ears of the outboard shoe with Channellock pliers as shown in Fig. 15-47. After clinching, the ears should be flat against the caliper.
5. *OVERHAULING CALIPER* To remove the caliper, first detach the caliper and remove the shoes as previously noted. Then disconnect the hose from the steel brake line and cap the fittings to keep dirt

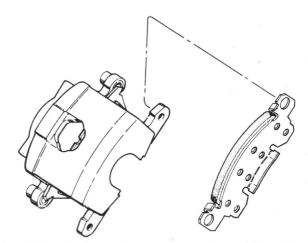

Fig. 15-45. Position of the outboard shoe in the caliper. (*Buick Motor Division of General Motors Corporation*)

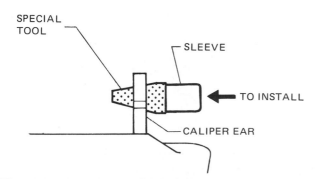

Fig. 15-43. Using the special tool to install the sleeve in the caliper ear. (*Buick Motor Division of General Motors Corporation*)

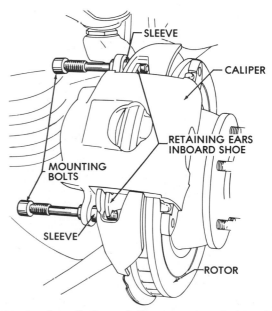

Fig. 15-46. Installation of the mounting bolts. (*Buick Motor Division of General Motors Corporation*)

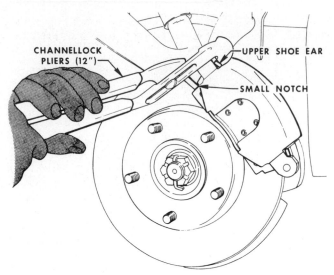

Fig. 15-47. Clinching ears on the outboard shoe. (*Buick Motor Division of General Motors Corporation*)

out. Detach the hose from the frame support bracket and take the caliper to the workbench.

CAUTION: Bench, tools, and hands must be clean!

Disconnect hose from the caliper, discarding the copper gasket; discard the hose, too, if it appears damaged. Drain fluid from caliper. Use a clean shop towel to pad the inside of the caliper as shown in Fig. 15-48. Apply air pressure to force the piston out.

CAUTION: Use only enough pressure to force the piston out! Excessive pressure may drive the piston out so hard that it will be ruined. Also, *never* use your fingers to catch the piston. It can fly out with enough speed to mash your fingers!

Use a screwdriver to pry the boot out of the caliper. Do not scratch the bore! Use a plastic toothpick to remove the seal from the groove in the bore.

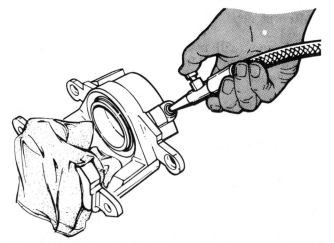

Fig. 15-48. Removing the piston with air pressure. (*Buick Motor Division of General Motors Corporation*)

Do not use a metal tool! It could ruin the bore. Remove the bleeder valve.

Discard the boot, piston seal, rubber bushings, and sleeves. Use new parts on reassembly. Clean piston and caliper with brake cleaner. Blow out all passages with compressed air.

NOTE: Lubricated shop air can leave a film of oil on the metal parts. This oil will damage the rubber parts.

Discard the piston if it has any nicks, scratches, or worn spots. Examine the bore. Minor corrosion or stains can be polished away with crocus cloth (*not* emery cloth!). If the bore cannot be cleaned up, discard it.

To install the piston, first lubricate the bore and new piston seal with brake fluid. Install the seal in the groove. Lubricate the piston and assemble a new boot into the piston groove. Install the piston in the bore, being careful not to unseat the seal. Push the piston to the bottom of the bore. This will require a push of 50 to 100 pounds [22.68 to 45.40 kg]. Put the outside of the boot into the caliper counterbore and seat it with the special tool as shown in Fig. 15-49.

Now reconnect the brake hose using a new copper gasket. Install the caliper, attach the hose to the frame bracket, and reconnect it to the steel tube.

Finish installation as already noted above (in item 4). Bleed the system (see ⊘ 15-40).

⊘ **15-34 Other Brake Services** Disk-brake services have been covered in previous sections, so far as the wheel mechanisms are concerned (calipers, shoes, and disks). In addition, brake lines and the master cylinder may require service. With drum-type

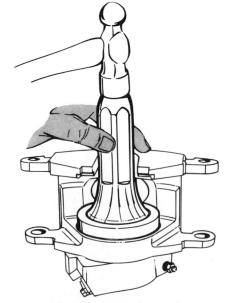

Fig. 15-49. Seating the boot in the caliper. (*Buick Motor Division of General Motors Corporation*)

brakes, the procedures include servicing the brake lines and master cylinder. In addition the brake linings may require replacement and the brake drums may need reboring or grinding. All systems may require flushing and bleeding if other services have been performed. All these servicing procedures are covered in following sections.

⊘ **15-35 Brake Linings (Drum-Type)** As a first step in replacing brake linings, the brake shoes must be removed (as already explained). Brake linings can be checked by removing the right front wheel and noting their condition (the brake drum can be checked at the same time). It can normally be assumed that the brake linings at the other three wheels are in about the same condition. If the linings are oil- or brake-fluid-soaked, or if they are worn down to the replacement point, the linings at all wheels should be replaced.

NOTE: If the drums are in good condition, standard-size linings may be installed. But if the drums require grinding to a larger inside diameter (⊘ 15-36), oversize linings should be installed.

1. *INSPECTING SHOES* When the shoes have been removed, they should be cleaned and checked for distortion, cracks, or other defects (Fig. 15-50). You can check a shoe for distortion or warping by laying the web on a flat surface plate. Put it on the corner of the surface plate so that you can see how snugly the web lies on the surface. If the web is twisted, the shoe is bent. It is somewhat difficult to straighten accurately a bent or warped shoe. Such conditions, and other shoe defects, require installation of new shoes. Shoes may become distorted from high temperatures due to excessive braking or from improper lining installation.

CAUTION: If some shoes and linings require replacement, be sure to replace all shoes on an axle with the same type of lining. For example, don't have riveted linings on the left rear and bonded linings on the right rear.

2. *REPLACING LININGS* Brake linings are either riveted or cemented (bonded) to the brake shoes. Manufacturers recommend that on the bonded type no attempt should be made to install new linings on the shoes. The shoes should be replaced when the linings have become worn.

On the riveted type, drill out the rivets to remove the old lining. Do not punch them out, since this may distort the shoe. Avoid using too large a drill because this would enlarge the rivet holes in the shoe and make it hard to do a good reinstallation job. Clean the shoe surfaces and file off any burrs or rough spots. Wash the shoe in degreasing compound and wipe it dry. Then put the new lining in place and attach it with the two center rivets. Use a roll type of set to set the rivets. A pointed punch might split the rivets. Figure 15-51 shows the right way contrasted with several wrong ways of installing rivets.

CAUTION: Be sure your hands are dry and free of grease or oil. Remember, even a slight trace of grease on a brake lining may cause erratic braking action that would require installation of another lining.

3. *GRINDING BRAKE-LINING RADIUS* To ensure more nearly perfect brake operation when new linings are installed, many manufacturers recommend the use of a brake-lining-radius grinder (Fig. 15-52). With this device, the shoe is swung in an arc in front of a grinding wheel which levels off lining irregularities and gives the lining the same radius, or contour, as the brake drum. This avoids poor contact (see Fig. 15-53), which could result in brake squeal, fade, and

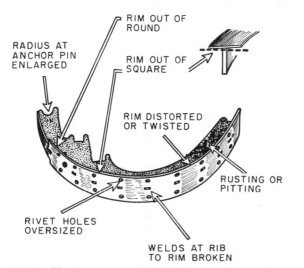

Fig. 15-50. Various types of brake-shoe defects. (*Pontiac Motor Division of General Motors Corporation*)

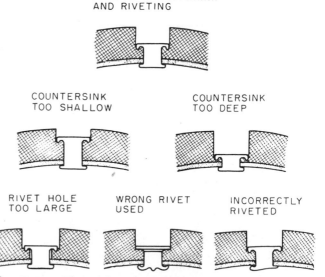

Fig. 15-51. The right method contrasted with several wrong methods of installing brake-shoe rivets. (*Pontiac Motor Division of General Motors Corporation*)

Fig. 15-52. Brake-shoe grinder. (*Ammco Tools, Inc.*)

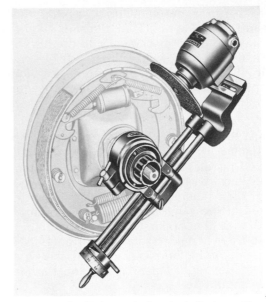

Fig. 15-54. Brake-lining grinder installed on the wheel spindle. (*Barrett Equipment Company*)

drum hot spots. These, in turn, would produce hard or glazed spots on the drum.

Another type of grinder, shown in Fig. 15-54, is used after the brake shoes are installed on the car and brake adjustment has been completed. It is mounted on the wheel spindle or axle and is moved around the brake linings as the grinding wheel spins.

CAUTION: Some automotive manufacturers supply preground linings which require no further grinding. On these, they recommend that the linings be installed without grinding. One preground type of lining has a slight crown (Fig. 15-55). During initial operation, this slight crown wears flat to assure good shoe seating against the drum.

⊘ **15-36 Brake Drums** Brake drums should be inspected for distortion, cracks, scores, roughness, or excessive glaze, or smoothness (glaze lowers friction and therefore braking efficiency). Figure 15-56 shows various drum conditions that can be corrected by the drum grinder. Drums that are distorted or cracked should be discarded and new drums installed. Light score marks can be removed with fine

emery cloth. All traces of emery must be removed after smoothing the drum. Deeper scores and roughness, as well as glaze, can be removed by turning or grinding the drum.

CAUTION: After grinding or turning a drum, be sure all traces of cuttings or abrasives are removed. Do not touch the finished surface or get any oil or grease on it. This would prevent normal braking action.

Cast-iron drums can be either turned or ground, but steel drums, because of their hardness, usually require grinding. Many automobile manufacturers recommend turning in preference to grinding, since a ground drum does not wear in so readily as a turned drum and is more liable to cause uneven

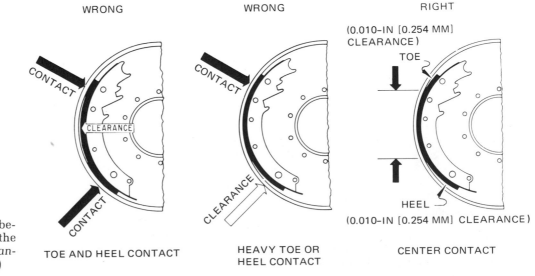

Fig. 15-53. Contact between the lining and the brake drum. (*Bear Manufacturing Company*)

WRONG — TOE AND HEEL CONTACT

WRONG — HEAVY TOE OR HEEL CONTACT

RIGHT — CENTER CONTACT
(0.010-IN [0.254 MM] CLEARANCE)
TOE
HEEL
(0.010-IN [0.254 MM] CLEARANCE)

CROWN GROUND

Fig. 15-55. Some replacement shoes are slightly crowned and do not need to be ground before installation. (*AC Delco Division of General Motors Corporation*)

braking when new. Figure 15-57 illustrates a typical drum lathe. Figure 15-58 shows a portable brake-service table with a lining-radius grinder and a drum grinder.

In servicing drums, only enough material should be removed to smooth up the braking surface. However, if it is necessary to take off considerable material, the drum should be turned oversize, and oversize brake linings should be installed. For instance, one car manufacturer recommends that, if the drum has to be turned to more than 0.010 inch [0.254 mm] oversize, it be turned to 0.030 inch [0.762 mm] oversize so that the regularly supplied linings that are 0.030 inch [0.762 mm] oversize can be installed.

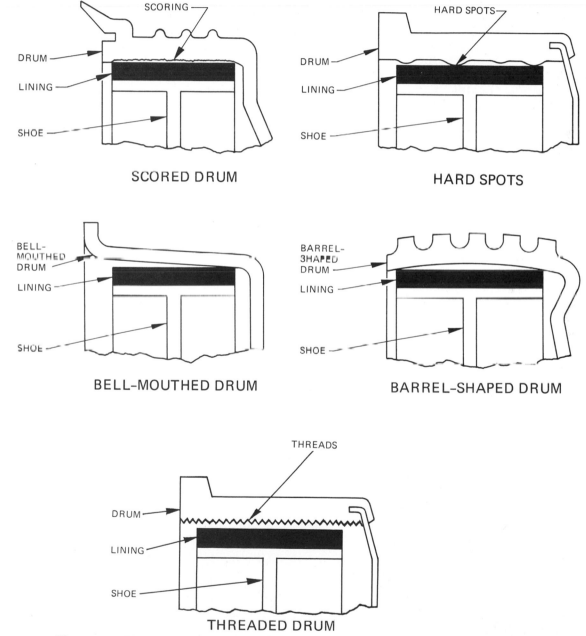

Fig. 15-56. Various types of brake-drum defects that require drum service. (*Bear Manufacturing Company*)

Fig. 15-57. Brake-drum lathe for reconditioning brake drums. (*Barrett Equipment Company*)

CAUTION: Removing excessive amounts of material will result in overheating of the drum during braking action, possible warping, and faulty brake action. Not more than about 25 percent of the total thickness of the drum should be removed. If more than this amount must be removed to take out deep scores or roughness, new drums should be installed. Many brake drums have a dimension (a number) cast into them. This dimension is the maximum allowable diameter. If it is necessary to turn or grind

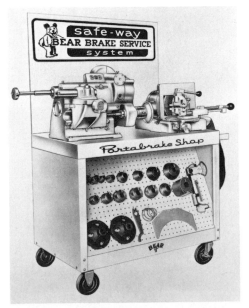

Fig. 15-58. Portable brake-service stand with brake-lining radius grinder and drum grinder. (*Bear Manufacturing Company*)

the drum to a larger diameter, discard it. The drum would be too thin to use safely. It would probably warp or crack when heated up and produce faulty braking.

NOTE: The diameters of the left and right drums on the same axle should be within 0.010 inch [0.254 mm] of each other. When the drum diameters on the same axle differ more than this, replace both drums.

⊘ **15-37 Wheel Cylinders (Drum-Type Brakes)** Wheel cylinders must be disassembled and assembled with extreme care in order to avoid getting the slightest trace of grease or dirt in them. Hands must be clean—washed with soap and water, not gasoline, since any trace of oil or gasoline on the cylinder parts may ruin them. Naturally, the bench and the tools must be clean.

To remove a wheel cylinder from the car, first remove the wheel and the drum, then block up the brake pedal to prevent its operation. Next, disconnect the tube or hose from the cylinder and remove the cylinder by taking out the attachment bolts. The tube end at the wheel should be taped closed to prevent the entrance of dirt. The cylinder can be disassembled by rolling off the rubber boots or taking off the covers (see Fig. 15-59). All parts should be washed in brake-system cleaning fluid. Old boots and piston cups should be discarded if they are not in excellent condition. Some manufacturers recommend replacement of these parts every time the cylinder is disassembled. If the cylinder is scored, polish it with crocus cloth (not sandpaper or emery cloth). Some manufacturers permit the use of a hone if the diameter of the cylinder is not increased more than a few thousandths of an inch. If scores do not come out, replace the cylinder. Cylinder and pistons should also be replaced if the clearance between them is excessive. When reassembling the cylinder, lubricate all parts with brake fluid.

CAUTION: Never allow any grease or oil to come in contact with rubber parts of the brake system, since this would cause them to swell and might destroy braking action.

⊘ **15-38 Master-Cylinder Service** The service procedures for master cylinders used with disk brakes and drum brakes are very similar. The major difference is that, with the disk-brake system, a larger brake-fluid reservoir is required. That is, disk brakes require more brake fluid than drum brakes. Refer to Fig. 15-60, which is a disassembled view of a master cylinder used with a braking system that has drum brakes at the rear and disk brakes at the front. Note that one of the reservoirs is larger than the other. A typical servicing procedure follows.
1. DISASSEMBLY (FIG. 15-60) Clean the outside of the master cylinder and remove the filler cover and gasket. Pour out any remaining brake fluid. Remove

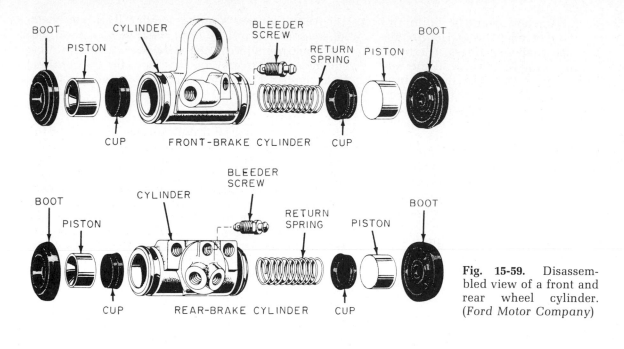

BOOT   PISTON   CYLINDER   BLEEDER SCREW   RETURN SPRING   PISTON   BOOT

CUP   FRONT-BRAKE CYLINDER   CUP

BOOT   PISTON   CYLINDER   BLEEDER SCREW   RETURN SPRING   PISTON   BOOT

CUP   REAR-BRAKE CYLINDER   CUP

Fig. 15-59. Disassembled view of a front and rear wheel cylinder. (*Ford Motor Company*)

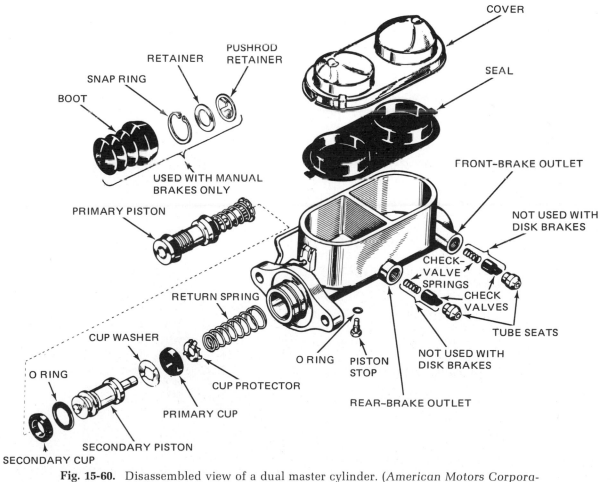

COVER

SEAL

BOOT   SNAP RING   RETAINER   PUSHROD RETAINER

USED WITH MANUAL BRAKES ONLY

PRIMARY PISTON

FRONT-BRAKE OUTLET

NOT USED WITH DISK BRAKES

CHECK-VALVE SPRINGS

CHECK VALVES

RETURN SPRING

TUBE SEATS

O RING   PISTON STOP

NOT USED WITH DISK BRAKES

CUP WASHER

O RING

CUP PROTECTOR

PRIMARY CUP

REAR-BRAKE OUTLET

SECONDARY PISTON

SECONDARY CUP

Fig. 15-60. Disassembled view of a dual master cylinder. (*American Motors Corporation*)

the secondary-piston stop bolt from the bottom of the cylinder. Remove the bleeder screw. Depress the primary piston and use snap-ring pliers to remove the snap ring from the retaining groove at the rear of the master-cylinder bore. Remove the pushrod and primary piston assembly from the master-cylinder bore. Do not remove the screw that retains the primary-return-spring retainer, return spring, primary cup, and protector on the primary piston. This assembly is factory preadjusted and must not be disassembled. Remove the secondary piston assembly. For some models, the service instructions state that you *must not* remove the outlet tube seats, check valves, and springs because they are permanent parts of the master cylinder. The service instructions for other models of master cylinders tell you to remove these parts if they need service.

NOTE: Disk brakes do not use check valves. See Fig. 15-60.

2. INSPECTION AND REPAIR Clean all parts in alcohol and inspect parts for chipping, scores, or wear. When using a master-cylinder repair kit, *install all parts supplied.* Make sure all passages are clean. Blow them out with compressed air. If the master cylinder is scored, rusted, or pitted, it may be necessary to hone the cylinder. This is permissible if only a couple of thousandths of an inch are removed. If the scoring or wear is deep, a new master cylinder will be required.

3. REASSEMBLY Dip all parts into brake fluid (except the master cylinder itself). Insert the complete secondary piston assembly, with return spring, into the master-cylinder bore. Put the primary piston assembly into the bore. Depress the primary piston and install the snap ring in the bore groove. Install the pushrod, boot, and retainer on the pushrod, if so equipped. Install the pushrod assembly into the primary piston. Make sure the retainer is properly seated and holding the pushrod securely.

Position the inner end of the pushrod boot (if so equipped) in the retaining groove in the master cylinder. Install the secondary-piston-stop bolt and the O ring in the bottom of the master cylinder. Install the bleeder screw. Put the gasket into the cover and install the cover on the master cylinder, securing it with the retainer.

NOTE: The master cylinder must be bled before it is installed on the car. Install plastic plugs at both outlet ports. Clamp the cylinder in a vise with the front end tilted slightly downward. Avoid excessive pressure as this could damage the cylinder. Fill both reservoirs with clean brake fluid. Slowly push the piston assemblies in with a wood dowel or smooth rod. Release the pressure and watch for bubbles. Repeat as long as bubbles appear. Then tilt the master cylinder so the front end is slightly raised. Repeat the push on the pistons, release the pistons, and watch for bubbles. Continue until no bubbles appear. Then install the seal and cover.

An alternative bleeding method uses two bleed tubes as shown in Fig. 15-61. With this method, install a master-cylinder check valve on the bleed tube connected to the reservoir that feeds the disk brakes. Note that, in Fig. 15-60, check valves are not used with disk brakes.

⊘ **15-39 Preparing Hydraulic-Brake Tubing for Installation** Special steel tubing must be used for hydraulic brakes, since it is best able to withstand the high pressures developed in the system. Tubing must be cut off square with a special tube cutter. Tubing must not be cut with a jaw-type cutter or with a hacksaw. Either of these methods may distort the tube and leave heavy burrs that would prevent normal flaring of the tube. After the tube has been cut off, a special flaring tool must be used to flare the tube. This is a three-step operation (Fig. 15-62): (1) Install the tubing in the flaring fixtures after the new coupling nuts have been installed on the tubing and the end of the tubing has been dipped into brake fluid (for lubrication during flaring). Then tighten the clamping nut or handle to hold the tubing at the proper depth in the fixture. (2) Insert a forming tool and drive it down with a few light hammer blows. This bows out the end of the tubing as shown at the center in Fig. 15-62. (3) Insert the second forming tool and drive it down with light hammer blows. This laps over the flare as the flare is final-formed (as shown to the right in Fig. 15-62).

⊘ **15-40 Flushing, Filling, and Bleeding the Hydraulic System**
1. FLUSHING If dirt or damaging liquid has been introduced into the hydraulic system, the system must be flushed out. Remember that mineral oil should never be put into the system. It will cause the rubber parts to swell and deteriorate; braking action may be completely lost. When flushing the

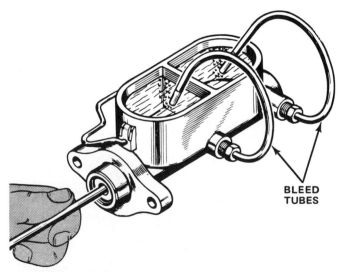

Fig. 15-61. Bleeding the master cylinder with bleed tubes. (*American Motors Corporation*)

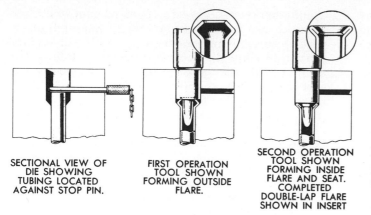

SECTIONAL VIEW OF DIE SHOWING TUBING LOCATED AGAINST STOP PIN.

FIRST OPERATION TOOL SHOWN FORMING OUTSIDE FLARE.

SECOND OPERATION TOOL SHOWN FORMING INSIDE FLARE AND SEAT. COMPLETED DOUBLE-LAP FLARE SHOWN IN INSERT

Fig. 15-62. The three steps required in double-lap flaring hydraulic-brake tubing. (*Ford Motor Company*)

system, use only the special flushing compound recommended by the car manufacturer or new brake fluid. Anything else is apt to cause damage to the rubber, fabric, or metal parts in the system.

To flush the system, remove the cover from the bleeder valve and install a bleeder hose over the bleeder valve.

CAUTION: Clean away dirt and grease from around the valves so as to avoid getting any dirt into the cylinders. Any dirt at a valve or in a bleeder hose may get sucked into the cylinder on the brake-pedal return stroke. This could cause subsequent failure of the wheel cylinder and brakes at the wheel.

Put the lower end of the bleeder hose into a clear plastic container (a hose in a container is shown in Fig. 15-63). Unscrew the bleeder valve about ¾ turn. If the system is being bled manually, operate the brake pedal with full strokes to force all fluid from the system. Close the valve before allowing the pedal to return after each stroke. When

all fluid is out, fill the master cylinder with new brake fluid. Again, operate the brake pedal with full strokes until all the brake fluid draining from the valve appears clean and clear.

Then use dry, clean air—applied through the master cylinder—to blow out all the fluid from the system. Do not apply too much air pressure. Finally, add new brake fluid and bleed the system as outlined in the following paragraphs.

CAUTION: Do not use the power brakes when flushing or bleeding the hydraulic system. Stop the engine and reduce the vacuum reserve to zero by applying the brakes several times before starting to flush or bleed the system. If the vehicle is equipped with disk brakes, the metering valve must be held in the open position while the hydraulic system is bled.

2. FILLING AND BLEEDING Whenever a brake system has been flushed, when the fluid has become low, or when air has leaked into the system, the

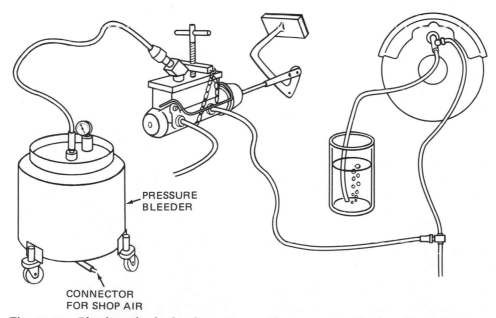

PRESSURE BLEEDER

CONNECTOR FOR SHOP AIR

Fig. 15-63. Bleeding the hydraulic system with a pressure bleeder. (*Pontiac Motor Division of General Motors Corporation*)

system must be bled to eliminate the air. Air in the system will cause a soft or spongy brake-pedal action. The air will compress when the brakes are applied, and poor braking action will result. Air is eliminated by adding brake fluid and bleeding off a little of the fluid from each wheel cylinder. To add brake fluid, first make sure that the bleeder valves are closed at all cylinders. Then, either fill the master-cylinder reservoir manually or use a pressure tank as shown in Fig. 15-63. In either case, use only approved brake fluid.

When the reservoir is filled, install a bleeder hose and container at one wheel cylinder. Make sure all dirt is cleaned from around the connection so that dirt will not get into the wheel cylinder. Open the bleeder valve. When not using the pressure bleeder, have an assistant get into the car and pump the brake pedal with full strokes, allowing it to return slowly only after the bleeder valve has been closed. Continue until the fluid flows from the bleeder hose into the container in a solid stream that is free of air bubbles. Make sure the end of the hose is below the liquid level in the container to prevent air from being sucked into the system on the brake-pedal return strokes. Tighten the bleeder valve, remove the hose, and replace the cover on the valve. Repeat the operation at the other wheel cylinders. Be sure to maintain the proper fluid level in the master-cylinder reservoir. When the bleeding operation is complete, make sure the fluid level in the reservoir is correct, and then install the master-cylinder cover and gasket.

When the pressure tank is used (Fig. 15-63), no assistant is needed. First, partly fill the pressure tank with brake fluid. Then, add compressed air to the tank with the tire-inflating equipment. The brake fluid is therefore under pressure in the tank. When the tank is connected to the master cylinder as shown in Fig. 15-63 and the valve is turned on, brake fluid flows from the tank, under pressure, to the master-cylinder reservoir. When the bleeder valve is opened, brake fluid is forced through the brake line and wheel cylinder. Brake fluid is allowed to flow until it runs from the bleeder hose in a solid stream without air bubbles. Then, the bleeder valve is tightened, the hose removed, and the valve cover replaced. The operation is repeated at each wheel cylinder.

Do not attempt to reuse the brake fluid that drains into the container during bleeding. It is likely to be contaminated or dirty.

CHAPTER 15 CHECKUP

NOTE: The following is a chapter test, and you should review the chapter before taking it.

You are making fine progress in your study of the automotive chassis; a few more chapters and you will have completed the book. The test that follows covers the diagnosis and correction of various hydraulic-brake troubles as well as normal brake servicing. Brake adjustment and repair is an important part of automotive service, so it will be important for you to know about such things. If you have any trouble with the questions below, it means you should reread the chapter so as to fix the facts firmly in your mind. Don't be discouraged if you have to reread the chapter several times. Most good students reread their lessons several times, since this is the best way to remember the facts. Write the answers in your notebook; this is a good aid to your memory.

Diagnosing Brake Complaints Let's see how good a troubleshooter you are. In the following, you assume that a customer has brought a car in with a complaint of improper braking action. After each complaint several brake defects are listed. Pick the defect that would be *most likely* to cause the complaint. Write the complaint and the most likely cause in your notebook.

1. A customer complains that the pedal goes to the floorboard with little or no braking action (drum brakes). This could be due to: (*a*) a clogged brake line, (*b*) worn brake linings, (*c*) a clogged reservoir vent, (*d*) a broken shoe-return spring.
2. The dynamic brake tester can be used to test brakes at various speeds. This tester uses: (*a*) two blades, (*b*) two flat plates, (*c*) two pairs of rollers.
3. The complaint is that all brakes drag. This could be due to: (*a*) lack of brake fluid, (*b*) air in system, (*c*) incorrect pedal adjustment.
4. You are road-testing a car and find, when braking, that the car pulls sharply to the right. This could be due to: (*a*) linings soaked with oil or brake fluid, (*b*) high fluid level in reservoir, (*c*) brake pedal out of adjustment, (*d*) defective master cylinder.
5. You find, when testing the brakes on a car, that the brake pedal feels spongy or soft. You know that this is most likely to be due to: (*a*) tires not uniformly inflated, (*b*) brake linings soaked with oil, (*c*) brake fluid in system, (*d*) air in system.
6. You find, when testing the brakes on a car, that you have to exert a very heavy pedal pressure to get any braking action. Pedal travel seems normal. It is likely that the trouble is due to: (*a*) linings soaked with oil or brake fluid, (*b*) air in system, (*c*) scored brake drums, (*d*) loose backing plates.
7. On disk brakes, excessive pedal travel caused by excessive disk runout may require: (*a*) shoe replacement, (*b*) wheel-bearing replacement, (*c*) disk replacement.
8. You notice, when testing the brakes on the road, that every time you apply the brakes they squeal. The most probable cause is: (*a*) low pedal pressure, (*b*) low brake-fluid level, (*c*) worn brake linings, (*d*) plugged filler vent.

Completing the Sentences The sentences below are incomplete. After each sentence there are several words or phrases, only one of which will correctly complete the sentence. Write down each sentence in your notebook, selecting the proper word or phrase to complete it correctly.

1. Excessive pedal travel on disk brakes could be caused by: (*a*) weak wheel cylinders, (*b*) excessive disk runout, (*c*) weak piston spring.
2. In the dynamic brake tester, the rollers are driven by the: (*a*) engine, (*b*) dynamometer, (*c*) electric motors.
3. To check the condition of the brake linings and drums, it is usually necessary to remove: (*a*) all four wheels, (*b*) one front wheel, (*c*) both rear wheels.
4. The disk, in disk brakes, should be checked for: (*a*) run-in and runout, (*b*) runout and thickness, (*c*) diameter and thickness.
5. In the floating-caliper disk brake, the piston is located: (*a*) outside the disk, (*b*) above the disk, (*c*) inside the disk.
6. On the Bendix brake with automatic adjuster, if manual adjustment is required: (*a*) turn adjustment cam, (*b*) hold lever off screw while turning screw, (*c*) hold lever against screw while turning screw.
7. Brake linings are attached to the brake shoes by either: (*a*) rivets or screws, (*b*) rivets or bonding, (*c*) retainer springs or bolts.
8. Serious damage to rubber parts in the hydraulic-brake system can result from the presence in the system of: (*a*) air, (*b*) brake fluid, (*c*) mineral oil.

Servicing Procedures Write in your notebook the servicing procedures that are asked for. Don't copy from the book; try to explain the procedure in your own words, just as you would tell it to a friend.

1. What steps should be taken before any adjustment to the brake shoes is made?

2. Explain how to adjust the self-adjusting Bendix brake.
3. Explain how to adjust the Wagner brake with the link-type automatic adjuster.
4. Explain how to make a minor brake adjustment (type without self-adjustment feature).
5. Explain how to make a major brake adjustment (type without self-adjustment feature).
6. Explain how to adjust an external-contracting transmission-shaft hand brake.
7. Explain how to adjust an internal-expanding transmission-shaft hand brake.
8. Explain how to replace a riveted brake lining. A bonded brake lining.
9. Explain how to service a brake drum.
10. Explain how to service wheel and master cylinders.
11. Explain how to flush, fill, and bleed a hydraulic system.

SUGGESTIONS FOR FURTHER STUDY

Your local school automotive shop or friendly automotive repair shop probably has some discarded brake components, such as wheel and master cylinder, that you can examine. Possibly you will be able to disassemble and reassemble these units. Further, if you can watch an expert make brake adjustments, replace brake linings, and perform the other services described in the chapter, you will have a much clearer idea of how these jobs are done. Study every shop repair manual that you can. Be sure to write down in your notebook any interesting and important facts you learn in the shop or by studying the manuals.

chapter 16

POWER-BRAKE SERVICE

This chapter discusses the trouble diagnosis, adjustment, removal, repair, and installation of power brakes. The previous chapter describes the servicing procedures on all hydraulic-brake components except the power unit, and so this chapter completes the story on hydraulic brakes by covering power units. Note that this chapter includes overhaul instructions on the Bendix dual-diaphragm power-brake unit (illustrated in Fig. 14-59). This is the unit used on many General Motors cars, and the service manuals for these cars carry overhaul instructions. However, the service manuals for American Motors Corporation, Chrysler Corporation, and Ford Motor Company cars do not carry overhaul instructions. They simply state that, if the power-brake unit is defective, it should be replaced with a new assembly.

⊘ **16-1 Power-Brake Trouble-Diagnosis Chart** The chart below relates various power-brake troubles to their possible causes and corrections. This chart gives you a means of logically tracing troubles to their actual causes and permits quick location of causes and their rapid correction. The chart and the sections that follow pertain to power-brake units only. Generally speaking, the trouble-diagnosis charts in ⊘ 15-2 and 15-15, which cover hydraulic brakes, also apply to power-brake systems. Thus, the

troubles listed in the charts, as well as the trouble corrections described in Chap. 15, also apply to power brakes.

NOTE: The troubles and possible causes are not listed in the chart in the order of frequency of occurrence. That is, item 1 does not necessarily occur more often than item 2, nor does item a under "Possible Cause" necessarily occur more often than item b.

POWER-BRAKE TROUBLE-DIAGNOSIS CHART

(See ⊘ 16-2 and 16-3 for details of checks and corrections listed. Not all the possible causes and checks or corrections listed apply to all models of power brakes described in the chapter; this is because of individual variations among models.)

COMPLAINT	POSSIBLE CAUSE	CHECK OR CORRECTION
1. Excessive brake pedal pressure required	a. Defective vacuum check valve	Free or replace
	b. Hose collapsed	Replace
	c. Vacuum fitting plugged	Clear, replace
	d. Binding pedal linkage	Free
	e. Air inlet clogged	Clear
	f. Faulty piston seal	Replace
	g. Stuck piston	Clear, replace damaged parts
	h. Faulty diaphragm	Replace (applies to diaphragm type only)
	i. Causes listed under item 6 in chart in ⊘ 15-2 or under item 3 in chart in ⊘ 15-15	
2. Brakes grab	a. Reaction, or "brake-feel," mechanism damaged	Replace damaged parts
	b. Air-vacuum valve sticking	Free, replace damaged parts
	c. Causes listed under item 7 in chart in ⊘ 15-2 or item 3 in chart in ⊘ 15-15	

(See ⊘ 16-2 and 16-3 for details of checks and corrections listed. Not all the possible causes and checks or corrections listed apply to all models of power brakes described in the chapter; this is because of individual variations among models.)

COMPLAINT	POSSIBLE CAUSE	CHECK OR CORRECTION
3. Pedal goes to floorboard	a. Hydraulic-plunger seal leaking	Replace
	b. Compensating valve not closing	Replace valve
	c. Causes listed under item 1 in chart in ⊘ 15-2 or item 8 in chart in ⊘ 15-15	
4. Brakes fail to release	a. Pedal linkage binding	Free up
	b. Faulty check-valve action	Free, replace damaged parts
	c. Compensator port plugged	Clean port
	d. Hydraulic-plunger seal sticking	Replace seal
	e. Piston sticking	Lubricate, replace damaged parts as necessary
	f. Broken return spring	Replace
	g. Causes listed under item 3 in ⊘ 15-2 or item 6 in chart in ⊘ 15-15	
5. Loss of brake fluid	a. Worn or damaged seals in hydraulic section	Replace, fill and bleed system
	b. Loose line connections	Tighten, replace seals
	c. Causes listed under item 10 in ⊘ 15-2 or items 7 and 9 in chart in ⊘ 15-15	

⊘ **16-2 Servicing Power-Brake Units** Even though the different types of power-brake units operate in a similar manner and have a similar exterior appearance, each model requires a special disassembly and reassembly procedure. Thus, before you make any attempt to service a specific model, you should refer to the shop manual covering that model.

Be sure to keep the workbench and tools clean. Small particles of dirt in the valves could cause malfunctioning of the power brakes. Examine the rubber parts as the unit is disassembled and discard any part that appears cracked, cut, or worn. The rubber seals and other parts must be in good condition for normal valve and power-brake action. Replace those that you have the slightest doubt about. As a rule, the manufacturer's instructions call for replacement of all old seals during an overhaul.

As an example of disassembly and reassembly procedures, one model of power brakes is described in the following section.

⊘ **16-3 Chevrolet Power Brakes** Chevrolet has used a variety of power brakes in recent years. One that has been very popular is the Bendix unit (Fig. 16-1). 1. *REMOVAL* To remove the unit, disconnect the pushrod clevis from the brake-pedal arm. If the clevis will not pass through the hole in the fire wall, take the clevis off the rod, first noting its approximate location. Disconnect the vacuum hose from the power unit and the hydraulic lines from the master cylinder. Cap the lines to keep dirt out. Remove the nuts and the lock washers that attach the power-brake assembly to the fire wall and take the assembly out of the engine compartment. 2. *DISASSEMBLY* Take the master cylinder off the power unit and lay it aside. The master cylinder is serviced as already described (⊘ 15-38).

Scribe lines across the flanges of the front and rear housings, in line with the master-cylinder cover, to provide guidelines for reassembly. Pull the piston rod from the front housing. (See Figs. 14-59 and 16-1 for the locations and appearance of the parts described.) The seal will come off with the piston rod. Pull the vacuum check valve out. Discard the valve and rubber grommet.

If the pushrod has a clevis, remove the clevis. Unseat the dust boot from the housing and remove it and the silencer. Use a thin-bladed screwdriver to pry the silencer retainer off the end of the hub of the rear diaphragm plate. Do not chip the plastic. Squirt denatured alcohol down the pushrod to lubricate the rubber grommet in the air valve.

Clamp the end of the pushrod in a vise, leaving enough room to position two open-end wrenches between the vise and the retainer on the hub of the rear plate (Fig. 16-2). Using the wrench nearest the vise as a pry, force the air valve off the ball end of the pushrod. Do not damage the plastic hub or allow the power unit to fall to the floor.

Slide the air filter and air silencer from the pushrod. Remove the poppet spring, retainer, and poppet (Fig. 16-3).

Figure 16-4 shows the two types of lances on the edge of the rear housing. Four are the deep type. The metal that forms these must be partly straightened out so the lances will clear the cutouts on the front housing. If the metal tabs break, the housing must be replaced. After straightening the lances, attach a holding fixture to the front housing with nuts and washers drawn tight to eliminate bending of studs. Put the holding fixture in an arbor press (Fig. 16-5) with rear housing up. Use a 1½-inch wrench, as shown, to keep the lower unit from turning. It will turn a little, but when the wrench comes

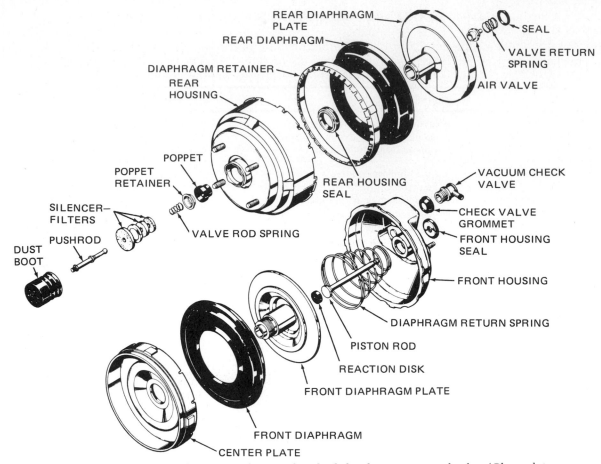

Fig. 16-1. Disassembled view of a Bendix dual-diaphragm power brake. (*Chevrolet Motor Division of General Motors Corporation*)

up tight against the arbor press, the unit cannot turn further.

Fasten the special spanner to studs on the rear shell with nuts and lock washers. Place a piece of 2-inch pipe about 3 inches long over the plastic hub of the diaphragm. Put a piece of flat steel stock over the end of the pipe and press the housing down with the arbor press to relieve the spring pressure. Rotate

the spanner counterclockwise to unlock the shells.

Release the arbor press and remove the diaphragm return spring. Detach the spanner and the holding fixture. Work the edges of the front diaphragm from under the lances of the rear housing and remove the complete vacuum assembly. Bosses

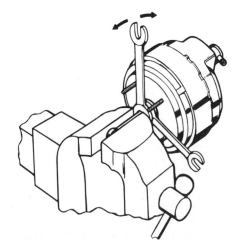

Fig. 16-2. Removing the pushrod. (*Chevrolet Motor Division of General Motors Corporation*)

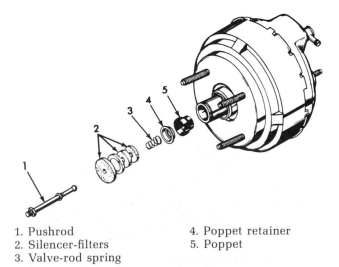

1. Pushrod
2. Silencer-filters
3. Valve-rod spring
4. Poppet retainer
5. Poppet

Fig. 16-3. Locations of the pushrod, silencer-filters, and poppet parts. (*Chevrolet Motor Division of General Motors Corporation*)

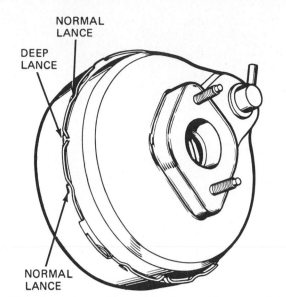

Fig. 16-4. Locations of lances in the rear housing. (*Chevrolet Motor Division of General Motors Corporation*)

on the center plate (Fig. 16-1) must align with cutouts in the rear housing to permit removal.

Wet the rear diaphragm retainer with denatured alcohol and remove it with your fingers only. Do not use any tool.

Clamp the special tool (Fig. 16-6) in a vise, hex head up. Put the diaphragm-and-plate assembly on the tool with the tool seated in the hex opening in the front plate. Twist the rear diaphragm plate counterclockwise, using hand leverage on the outer edge of the plate. Remove the plates from the tool and place them, front plate down, on a bench. Unscrew the rear plate completely and lift it off, catching the air valve and return spring as the parts are separated.

Remove the square ring seal from the shoulder

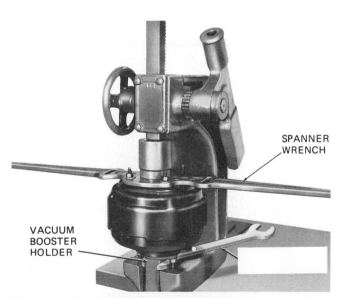

Fig. 16-5. Using special fixtures to hold and separate the housings in an arbor press. (*Chevrolet Motor Division of General Motors Corporation*)

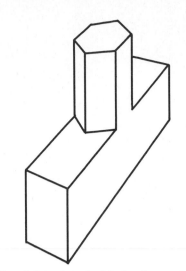

Fig. 16-6. Special tool to hold the front plate. The hex head fits into the hex opening of the front plate. (*Chevrolet Motor Division of General Motors Corporation*)

of the front-plate hub. Remove the reaction disk from inside the front diaphragm plate. Slide the center plate off the hub of the front plate. The vacuum seal may stay in front of the center diaphragm plate. If the seal assembly is defective, the center-plate-and-seal assembly must be replaced as a unit.

Remove the diaphragms from the plates. If the rear-housing seal requires replacement, use a blunt punch or $1\frac{1}{4}$-inch socket to drive the seal out.

3. CLEANING AND INSPECTION Clean all parts with denatured alcohol. Blow out all passages and holes with compressed air. Air-dry parts. If slight rust is found on the inside surface of the power-cylinder housing, polish it with crocus cloth and clean with denatured alcohol.

CAUTION: Never use gasoline, kerosene, or other liquid to clean power-brake parts. These liquids will damage the rubber parts.

Rubber parts must be in good condition, or the brake will not work properly. Replace them if there is the slightest trace of damage.

4. REASSEMBLY Be sure all parts are clean. Rewash them before reassembly if there is any doubt about their being clean. Lubricate rubber, plastic, and metal friction points with special silicone lubricant.

If the rear housing seal was removed, press a new seal into place with the special tool (Fig. 16-7). Install reaction disk in front-plate hub, small tip side first. Use a rounded rod to seat it.

Clamp the special tool (Fig. 16-6) in a vise. Put the front plate on the tool with hex head of tool in front plate. Put the front diaphragm on the front plate with the long fold of diaphragm facing down. Install the seal protector over the threads on the front-plate hub (Fig. 16-8). Apply a light film of silicone lubrication on the seal, and then guide center plate, seal first, onto the front-plate hub. Remove the seal protector.

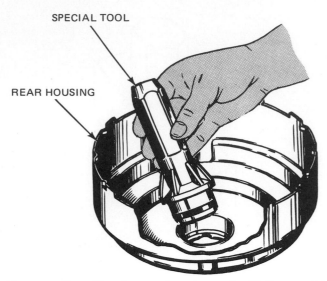

Fig. 16-7. Installing the rear-housing seal with the special tool. (*Chevrolet Motor Division of General Motors Corporation*)

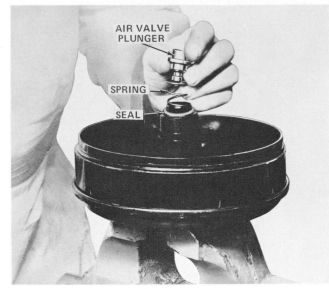

Fig. 16-9. Installing the air-valve assembly. (*Chevrolet Motor Division of General Motors Corporation*)

Apply a light film of silicone lubricant to the front and rear bearing surfaces of the air valve, but not to the rubber grommet inside the valve. Install the square ring seal on the front-plate hub. Then install the return spring and air valve in the base of the front-plate hub (Fig. 16-9).

Set the rear plate over the hub of the front plate. Use your hands only and screw the plate onto the hub, making sure that the valve and spring are properly aligned. Use your index finger to check travel of valve plunger. It should be free. Plates should be tight, but do not overtorque.

Assemble the rear diaphragm to the rear plate and put the lip of the diaphragm in the groove in the rear plate. Install the diaphragm retainer, using your fingers to press the retainer until it seats on the shoulder of the center plate (Fig. 16-10).

Apply talcum powder to the inside wall of the rear housing and silicone lubricant to the scalloped cutouts of the front housing and to the seal in the rear housing. Assemble the diaphragm-and-plate assembly into the rear housing. Bosses on center plate must align with cutouts in the rear housing during assembly. Work the outer rim of the front diaphragm into the rear housing with a screwdriver blade so that the rim is under the lances in the housing.

With the setup shown in Fig. 16-5, compress housings in the arbor press until the diaphragm edge is fully compressed with tangs on the front housing against the slots in the rear housing. Rotate the

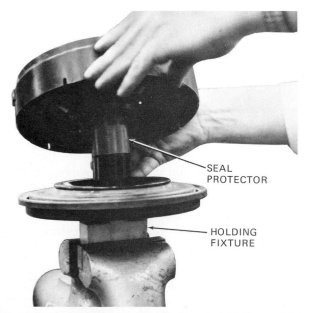

Fig. 16-8. Seal protector installed to protect the seal from threads on the front-plate hub. (*Chevrolet Motor Division of General Motors Corporation*)

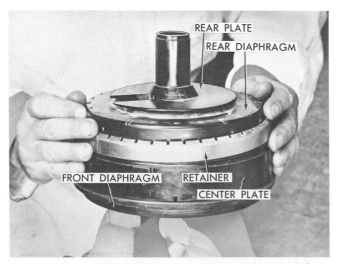

Fig. 16-10. Installing the rear-diaphragm retainer. (*Chevrolet Motor Division of General Motors Corporation*)

spanner clockwise until tangs butt against rear-housing stops.

Bend lanced areas in to secure the assembly. (If tangs break, that half of the housing must be replaced.) Remove the assembly from the press and detach tools.

Wet the poppet valve with denatured alcohol, install retainer inside the poppet, and put it into the hub. Install silencers and filters over the ball end of the pushrod (see Fig. 16-3). Put the spring over the end of the rod, then push the rod into place. Tap the end of the rod with a plastic hammer to seat the ball in the poppet. Seat the filters and silencers into the hub and install the retainer on the end of the hub. Assemble the silencer in the dust boot, wet the dust-boot opening with denatured alcohol, and assemble over the plate hub and rear-housing hub.

If the pushrod has a clevis, attach it. Dip a new check-valve grommet in denatured alcohol and install it in front housing. Dip a new check valve in denatured alcohol and install it in the grommet.

Apply silicone lubricant to the piston end of the piston rod and insert the rod into the front plate. Twist it to eliminate air bubbles between it and the reaction disk. Assemble the seal over the rod and press it into the recess in the front housing.

To adjust the piston rod, use the special rod gauge shown in Fig. 16-11 in the manner demonstrated in Fig. 16-12. To adjust, grasp the serrated end of the piston rod with pliers and turn the adjusting screw either in or out as necessary. The adjustment screw is self-locking.

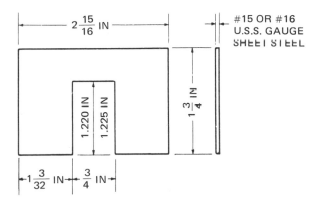

Fig. 16-11. Piston-rod gauge. (*Chevrolet Motor Division of General Motors Corporation*)

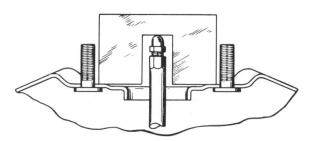

Fig. 16-12. Checking the adjustment of the piston rod with the gauge. (*Chevrolet Motor Division of General Motors Corporation*)

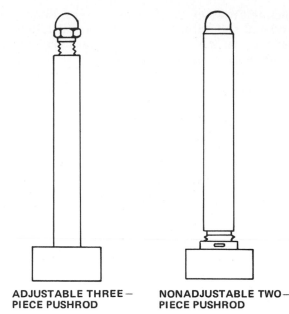

ADJUSTABLE THREE—PIECE PUSHROD   NONADJUSTABLE TWO—PIECE PUSHROD

Fig. 16-13. Some piston rods are adjustable, others are not. (*American Motors Corporation*)

Install the master cylinder and then install the assembly in the car. Bleed the hydraulic system after connecting the tubes to the master cylinder (⊘15-40).

⊘ **16-4 Adjustments of Other Power-brake Units** American Motors Corporation, Chrysler Corporation, and Ford Motor Company no longer supply overhaul instructions on power-brake units. They specify that if trouble occurs in the unit, it be replaced with a new assembly. Many do have a pushrod adjustment as shown in Fig. 16-12. However, some pushrods are not adjustable (Fig. 16-13). On these, if the height is not correct, the complete unit must be replaced.

CHAPTER 16 CHECKUP

Because power brakes have been widely adopted on automobiles in recent years, it will be of great value to you to understand not only how these units operate but also what troubles they might have and how they are serviced. The chapter you have just completed describes the trouble diagnosis and servicing of one of the most popular types of passenger-car power brakes. The checkup that follows will give you a chance to test yourself on how well you remember the important points covered in the chapter. Don't feel discouraged if any of the questions seem hard to answer. That simply means that you should read the chapter again. Taking the test, finding out what points are not clear in your mind, and then reviewing those points—this is a procedure that is very good for memorizing the important points in the chapter.

Correcting Troubles Lists This exercise helps you spot related and unrelated troubles on a list. In each list below, you will find one item that does not belong. Write each list in your notebook, but do not write the item that does not belong. Progress Quiz 15-1, in the middle of the previous chapter, explains in more detail how to take this test. Refer to it if you are not sure what to do.

1. Excessive pedal pressure required: defective vacuum-check valve, hose collapsed, vacuum fitting plugged, pedal linkage binding, air inlet clogged, faulty piston seal, vacuum pump stuck, piston stuck.
2. Brakes grab: reaction, or "brake-feel," mechanism damaged; air-vacuum valve sticking; ruptured diaphragm.
3. Pedal goes to floorboard: broken return spring, hydraulic-plunger seal leaking, compensating valve not closing.
4. Brakes fail to release: pedal linkage binding, faulty check-valve action, compensator port plugged, compensator valve hanging open, hydraulic-plunger seal sticking, piston sticking, broken return spring.
5. Loss of brake fluid: worn or damaged seals in hydraulic section, vacuum fitting plugged, loose line connection.

Servicing Procedures Write down in your notebook the servicing procedures that are asked for. Don't copy from the book; try to explain the procedures as you would to a friend, in your own words.

1. Explain how to disassemble the Bendix power-brake unit.
2. Explain how to assemble the Bendix power-brake unit.
3. Refer to a shop manual describing the servicing of a specific model of power brake and write down the step-by-step procedure of disassembly, assembly, and adjustment of the power brake.

SUGGESTIONS FOR FURTHER STUDY

If your local school automotive shop or automotive dealer service shop has power-brake units that you can examine, you will be able to see how the various parts work together. If you are able to disassemble, or watch an automotive mechanic disassemble, one of these units, the relationship of the parts will become clearer. Study any manufacturers' shop manuals you can find on these units. Be sure to write important facts in your notebook.

chapter 17

TIRES AND TIRE SERVICE

This chapter describes tires and tire service, including tire removal and replacement and tire and tube repair.

⊘ **17-1 Function and Types of Tires**   Tires have two functions: First, they interpose a cushion between the road and the car wheels to absorb shocks resulting from irregularities in the road. The tires flex, or give, as bumps are encountered, thus reducing the shock effect to the passengers in the car. Second, the tires provide frictional contact between the wheels and the road so that good traction is secured. This permits the transmission of power through the tires to the road for rapid acceleration, combats the tendency of the car to skid on turns, and allows quick stops when the brakes are applied.

Tires are of two basic types: solid and pneumatic (air-filled). Solid tires have very limited usage, their use being confined largely to specialized industrial applications. Only pneumatic tires will be considered here. Pneumatic tires are of two types: those using an inner tube and the tubeless type. On the type with an inner tube, both the tube and the tire casing are mounted on the wheel rim, with the tube inside the casing (Fig. 17-1). The inner tube is inflated with air, and this causes the tire casing to resist any change of shape. The tubeless tire does not use an inner tube. This tire is mounted on the rim in such a way that the air is retained between the rim and tire casing (Fig. 2-17).

The amount of air pressure used depends on the type of tire and the operation. Passenger-car tires are inflated about 22 to 30 psi (pounds per square inch) [1.55 to 2.11 kg/cm²]. Heavy-duty tires on trucks or buses may be inflated up to 100 psi [7.03 kg/cm²].

⊘ **17-2 Tire Construction**   Tire casings (and tubeless tires) are made up of layers of cord impregnated with rubber over which the rubber sidewalls and tread are applied (Fig. 17-2). The layers of cord (called the *plies*) are formed over a spacing device and rubberized, and the sidewall and tread materials are applied and vulcanized into place. The term "vulcanizing" pertains to a process of heating the rubber under pressure. This process both molds the rubber into the desired form and gives it the charac-

teristics required. The number of layers of cord (or plies) varies according to the use to which the tire will be put. Passenger-car tires usually have four plies. Heavy-duty truck and bus tires may have up to 14 plies, whereas tires for extremely heavy-duty service, such as earth-moving machinery, have been made with 32 plies.

⊘ **17-3 Bias vs. Radial Plies**   There are two ways to apply the plies: on the bias and radially (Figs. 17-2 and 17-3). For many years, most tires were of the biased type. These had the plies crisscrossed, with one layer running one way and the other running so the plies were more or less perpendicular. This gave a carcass that was strong in all directions be-

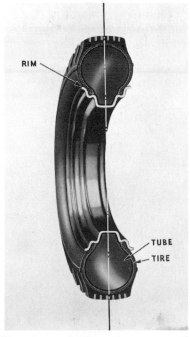

Fig. 17-1.   Tire rim and tire cut away so that the tube can be seen. (*Chrysler Corporation*)

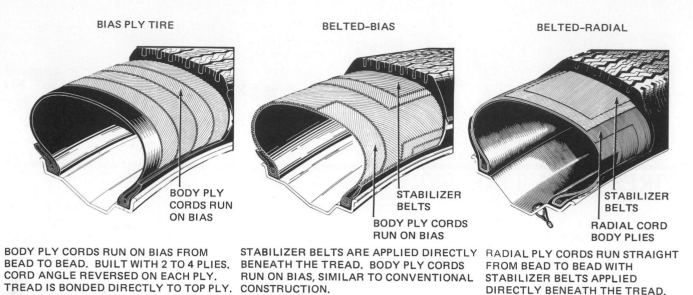

BIAS PLY TIRE	BELTED-BIAS	BELTED-RADIAL

BODY PLY CORDS RUN ON BIAS

STABILIZER BELTS

BODY PLY CORDS RUN ON BIAS

STABILIZER BELTS

RADIAL CORD BODY PLIES

BODY PLY CORDS RUN ON BIAS FROM BEAD TO BEAD. BUILT WITH 2 TO 4 PLIES. CORD ANGLE REVERSED ON EACH PLY. TREAD IS BONDED DIRECTLY TO TOP PLY.

STABILIZER BELTS ARE APPLIED DIRECTLY BENEATH THE TREAD. BODY PLY CORDS RUN ON BIAS, SIMILAR TO CONVENTIONAL CONSTRUCTION.

RADIAL PLY CORDS RUN STRAIGHT FROM BEAD TO BEAD WITH STABILIZER BELTS APPLIED DIRECTLY BENEATH THE TREAD.

Fig. 17-2. Cutaway views of the three basic tire constructions. (*Firestone Rubber Company*)

cause of the overlapping plies. The difficulty with these was that the plies tended to move against each other, generating heat, particularly at high speed. Also, the tread tended to "squirm" as it met the road, and this caused tread wear.

To remedy this problem, tires with radial plies were introduced (Fig. 17-3). On these, the plies all run parallel to each other and vertical to the tire rim. To provide strength in the direction parallel to the tire rim, belts are applied all the way around the tire. The tread is then vulcanized on top of the belts. The belts are made of rayon, glass fiber, or steel mesh. All work in a similar manner. They provide added strength to the circumference of the tire. In addition, several other claims are made for them. One is that the belted tire puts more rubber on the road. It is less stiff because of the radial plies and thinner sidewalls, and thus flexes more to apply a greater part of the tread to the road (Fig. 17-4). In

addition, because the sidewalls can be made thinner and more flexible, the tread has less tendency to heel up when the car goes around a curve (Fig. 17-5). This reduces skid tendencies on turns. Also, more gasoline mileage is claimed because the tire rolls on the road with less resistance, thus using up less horsepower. Evidence indicates that the belted-radial tire lasts considerably longer, too. A reason for this is that the grooves in the tread do not "squirm" or close up (which means sidewise movement of the tread parts) as the tire meets the pavement. This is in contrast with the bias-ply tire, on which the treads tend to pinch together (Fig. 17-6). Not only does this mean less wear, but also better traction, or antiskid action, during the longer life, too.

Bias-ply tires may also be belted (Fig. 17-7), but even some manufacturers who made the belted-bias tire openly recommend the belted-radial as being superior.

CAUTION: Car manufacturers strongly caution against mixing belted-radial and bias-ply (either belted or unbelted) on a car. If the car owner wants

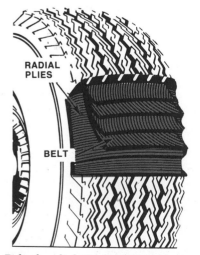

RADIAL PLIES

BELT

Fig. 17-3. Belted-radial tire, partly cut away to show radial plies and belt. (*B. F. Goodrich Company*)

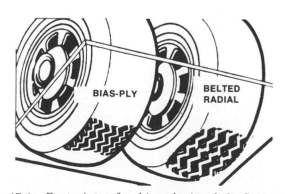

BIAS-PLY

BELTED RADIAL

Fig. 17-4. Footprints of a bias-ply (nonbelted) tire and a belted-radial tire on a flat surface.

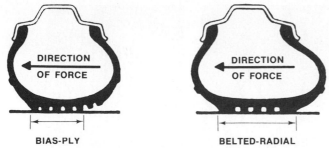

Fig. 17-5. Difference in the amount of tread a bias-ply (nonbelted) tire and a belted-radial tire apply to the pavement during a turn.

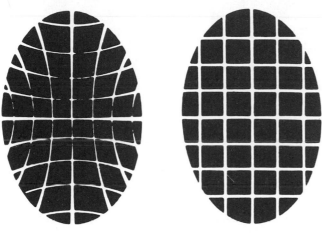

Fig. 17-6. Bias-ply tire treads tend to "squirm," or pinch together, as the tire meets the road. Belted-radial tire treads tend to remain apart.

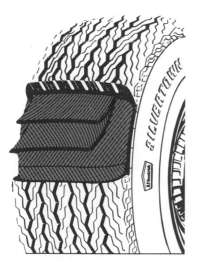

Fig. 17-7. Belted bias tire, partly cut away to show bias plies and belt. (*B. F. Goodrich Company*)

belted radials, five tires should be bought. It is especially important not to use radials on the front if snow tires are installed at the rear: this can result in oversteer and spins on wet or icy roads.

⊘ 17-4 Tread Design Various shapes of tread are used (Fig. 17-8). The tread designs provide traction and reduce the possibility of skidding. Snow tires have an especially heavy design, using relatively large cleats that can cut down through snow and provide greatly improved traction. There is also a snow-and-ice tire that has steel inserts, or studs, which help the tire to get a better "footing" on slick ice or snow. These special types of tires make driving much safer and easier in winter weather. They are, however, comparatively noisy on dry pavement.

⊘ 17-5 Tire Valve Air is introduced into the tire (or inner tube) through a valve that opens when the chuck on the air hose is applied to it. On a tire with an inner tube, the valve is mounted on the tube. On the tubeless tire, the valve is mounted on the wheel rim. In the closed position, the valve is held against its seat by spring pressure and the air pressure in the tube. Air can be released from the tube by pressing on the end of the valve stem. Some valves have a cap which is screwed down tightly over the end of the valve stem to provide an added safeguard against air leakage and to keep dirt from entering the valve.

⊘ 17-6 Types of Tires and Tubes We have already looked at some design features of tires, including plies, belts, and treads. Now let us look at some other specialized aspects of tires.

1. TIRE SIZES Tire sizes are marked on the side of the casing (Fig. 17-9). A tire might be marked 8.00 × 15, for example. This means that the tire fits on a 15-inch [381 mm] rim and that it is 8 inches [203.2 mm] larger in radius than the rim (when properly inflated but without load). Thus, the diameter of the tire, when inflated but unloaded, is 31 inches (8 + 15 + 8). In the metric system, this would be 787.4 mm (203.2 + 381.0 + 203.2).

Today's tires have several markings on the sidewall. The markings carry a letter code to designate the type of car the tire is designed for: D means a lightweight car, F means intermediate, G means a standard car, H, J, and L are for large luxury cars and high-performance vehicles. For example, some cars use a G78-14 tire. Here, the 14 means a rim 14-inches [355.6 mm] in diameter. The 78 indicates the ratio between the tire height and width (as shown in Fig. 17-9); that is, the tire is 78 percent as high as it is wide. On a 100 tire, the height and width would be the same. There are four aspect ratios: 83, 78, 70, and 60. The lower the number, the wider the tire looks, compared with its height. The 60 tire, for example, is only 60 percent as high as it is wide.

The addition of an R to the sidewall markings, such as GR78-14, indicates that the tire is a radial. Some radial tires are marked in the metric system. For example, a tire marked 175 R 13 is a radial tire which measures approximately 175 mm (about 6.9 inches) wide and mounts on a 13-inch-diameter wheel.

Fig. 17-8. Types of tire tread. (*B. F. Goodrich Company; Goodyear Tire and Rubber Company*)

2. *TUBELESS TIRES* Late-model cars are equipped with tires that do not use tubes. The rim used with this type of tire must be sealed, and it must have a sealed-in tire valve. The tire bead is so contructed that it seals tightly against the rim flange; thus the air pressure will be retained when the tire is inflated.

3. *PUNCTURE-SEALING TIRES* Some tubeless tires have a coating of plastic material in the inner surface. When the tire is punctured, this plastic material is forced by the internal air pressure into the hole left when the nail or other object is removed. The plastic material then hardens, sealing the hole.

4. *TUBES* Three types of rubber, one natural and two synthetic, have been used to make tubes. Today the most common tube material is butyl. You can identify a butyl tube by its blue stripe. The other synthetic rubber tube (GR-S) has a red stripe. Natural rubber is not striped.

5. *PUNCTURE-SEALING TUBES* Some tubes have a coating of plastic material which acts like the plastic material used in the puncture-sealing tire. It flows into and seals any holes left by punctures. In some tubes the plastic material coats the inside of the tube. In others the material is retained between an inner rubber diaphragm and the tube in a series of cells. This latter construction prevents the material from flowing as a result of centrifugal force and thereby from building up in certain spots in the tube. If the material were allowed to build up, it would cause an unbalanced condition.

6. *SAFETY TUBE* The safety tube is really two tubes in one, one smaller than the other and joined at the rim edge. When the tube is filled with air, the air flows first into the inside tube. From there it passes through an equalizing passage into the space between the two tubes. Thus both tubes are filled

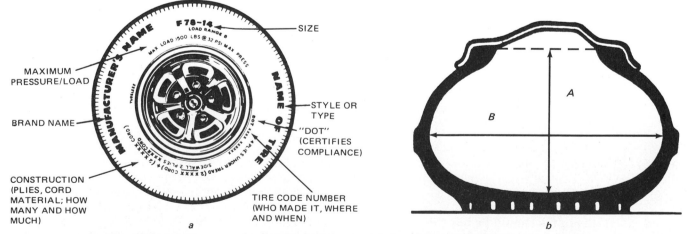

Fig. 17-9. (*a*) Every mark on a tire is important information. Note the location of the tire size and the pressure and load limits. (*b*) The aspect ratio of a tire is the ratio of the tire height to its width. In the illustration, this is the ratio of *A* to *B*.

with air. Now let us see what happens if a puncture or blowout occurs. In this case, the air is lost from between the two tubes. But the inside tube, which has not been damaged, retains its air pressure. It is sufficiently strong to support the weight of the car until the car can be slowed and stopped. Usually, the inside tube is reinforced with nylon fabric so that it can take the suddenly imposed weight of the car—without giving way—when a blowout occurs.

⊘ **17-7 Wheels** Figure 17-10 shows how wheels are made. The outer part, called the *rim,* is of one-piece construction and is welded to the wheel center. Note that the center of the rim is smaller than the rest, giving the rim the name "drop center." The drop center is necessary to permit removal and installation of the tire. The bead of the tire must be pushed off the rim flange and into the smaller diameter before it can be worked up over the rim. We discuss tire service later in the chapter.

⊘ **17-8 Mag Wheels** Wheels made of magnesium, termed "mag" wheels, are lightweight and strong. They are widely used on high-performance cars. The low weight is important because it reduces unsprung weight, and this improves handling performance.

⊘ **17-9 Split-Rim Wheels** Split-rim wheels are used on heavy-duty trucks, trailers, earthmovers, and so on. They are solidly made and require a different method of tire installation. The drop-rim wheel is

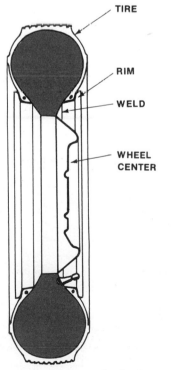

Fig. 17-10. Passenger-car tire and wheel cut away to show internal construction. Note that the rim is in one piece, with the center welded to it.

not satisfactory for heavy-duty tires. Two types of split-rim wheels are shown in Fig. 17-11. One split-rim wheel has two pieces, the wheel-assembly piece and the flange. The flange locks into the wheel assembly, as shown. The other kind also has these two pieces, but, in addition, it has a rim lock ring. With either type, the whole wheel and rim, with tire, are removed as an assembly for tire service. Then the lock rim and flange can be removed so the tire can be taken off the rim. These tires require tubes because the rim cannot be made airtight.

CAUTION: If you ever work on tires mounted on split-rim wheels, make sure all air pressure has been released from the tube before beginning to remove the lock rim or flange. If air pressure is still in the tube, it could blow the tire off the rim when the lock ring or flange is removed and seriously injure or even kill anyone nearby. Heavy-duty tires carry high air pressures.

⊘ **17-10 Tire Service** Tire service includes periodic inflation to make sure the tire is kept at the proper pressure, periodic tire inspection so that small damages can be detected and repaired before they develop into major defects, and tire removal, repair, and replacement. These services are covered in detail below.

⊘ **17-11 Tire Inflation and Tire Wear** As we have noted in previous chapters, incorrect tire inflation can cause many types of steering and braking difficulty. Low pressure will cause hard steering, front-wheel shimmy, steering kickback, and tire squeal on turns. Uneven tire pressure will tend to make the car pull to one side. ⊘ 6-12 covers, in detail, the effects of improper tire inflation on the tires themselves. Low pressure wears the sides of the treads (Figs. 6-9 and 17-12), causes excessive flexing of the sidewalls, and results in ply separation. A tire with insufficient pressure is also subject to rim bruises; this could break plies and lead to early tire failure. Excessive pressure also causes uneven tread wear; the tread wears in the center. Also, a tire that is excessively inflated will give a hard ride and is subject to fabric rupture, since the pressure may be so high that the tire does not give normally. Thus, when the tire meets a rut or bump, the fabric takes the shock and cannot give, or flex, in a normal manner. This can result in weakened or even broken tire fabric.

⊘ **17-12 Toe-in or Toe-out Tire Wear** Excessive toe-in or toe-out on turns causes the tire to be dragged sideways as it is moving forward. For example, a tire on a front wheel that toes-in 1 inch [25.4 mm] from straight ahead will be dragged sideways about 150 feet [45.72 m] every mile [1.60 km]. This sideward drag scrapes off rubber, as shown in Fig. 17-12. Note the feather edges of rubber that

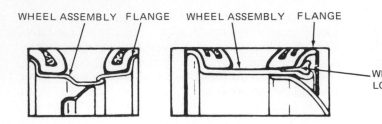

WHEEL ASSEMBLY FLANGE   WHEEL ASSEMBLY FLANGE

WHEEL-RIM
LOCK RING

Fig. 17-11. Two-piece and three-piece rims for heavy-duty applications. (*Ford Motor Company*)

appear on one side of the tread. If both sides show this type of wear, the front end is misaligned. If only one tire shows this type of wear, chances are that the steering arm is bent. This condition can cause one wheel to toe-in more than the other.

⊘ **17-13 Camber Wear** If a wheel has excessive camber, the tire runs more on one shoulder than the other. The tread will wear excessively on that side, as shown in Fig. 17-12.

⊘ **17-14 Cornering Wear** Cornering wear, shown in Fig. 17-12, is caused by taking curves at excessive speeds. The tire not only skids, but it tends to roll, producing the diagonal type of wear shown. This is one of the more common causes of tire wear. The only remedy is to slow down around curves.

⊘ **17-15 Uneven Tire Wear** Uneven tire wear, with the tread unevenly or spottily worn, is shown in Fig. 17-12. It can result from several mechanical problems. These problems include misaligned wheels, unbalanced wheels, uneven or "grabby" brakes, overinflated tires, and out-of-round brake drums.

⊘ **17-16 High-Speed Wear** Tires wear more rapidly at high speed than at low speed. Tires driven consistently at 70 to 80 miles [112.65 to 128.75 km] per hour will give less than half as many miles as tires driven at, say, 30 miles per hour [48.28 kmph].

⊘ **17-17 Checking Tire Pressure and Inflating Tires** To check tire pressure (Fig. 17-13) and inflate the tire, you must know the correct tire pressure for the tire you are servicing. You find this specification on the tire sidewall (on many tires), in the shop manual, in the driver's operating manual, and also on one of the door jambs (or at some similar place) on the car. Specifications are for cold tires. Tires that are hot from being driven or from sitting in the sun will have an increased air pressure because air expands when hot. Tires that have just been driven on a highway may show an increase of as much as 5 to 7 psi [0.352 to 0.492 kg/cm²].

As a hot tire cools, it loses pressure, so never bleed a hot tire to reduce the pressure. If you do, when the tire cools, its pressure could drop well below the specified minimum.

There are times when the tire pressure should be on the high side. For instance, one tire manufacturer recommends adding 4 psi [0.28 kg/cm²] for turnpike speed, trailer pulling, or extraheavy loads. But never exceed the maximum pressure specified on the tire sidewall.

If the tire valve has a cap, always replace the cap after checking pressure or adding air.

⊘ **17-18 Tire Rotation** The amount of wear a tire gets depends on its location on the car. For example, the right rear tire wears about twice as fast as the left front tire. To equalize wear, manufacturers recommend rotating the tires every 5,000 miles [8,046 km]. Figure 17-14 shows the recommended

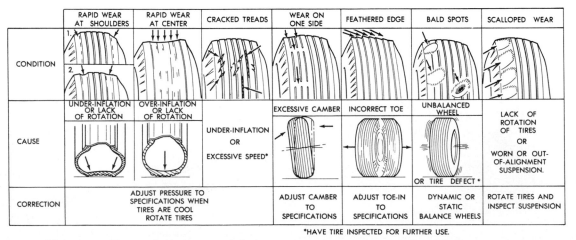

	RAPID WEAR AT SHOULDERS	RAPID WEAR AT CENTER	CRACKED TREADS	WEAR ON ONE SIDE	FEATHERED EDGE	BALD SPOTS	SCALLOPED WEAR
CONDITION							
CAUSE	UNDER-INFLATION OR LACK OF ROTATION	OVER-INFLATION OR LACK OF ROTATION	UNDER-INFLATION OR EXCESSIVE SPEED*	EXCESSIVE CAMBER	INCORRECT TOE	UNBALANCED WHEEL OR TIRE DEFECT*	LACK OF ROTATION OF TIRES OR WORN OR OUT-OF-ALIGNMENT SUSPENSION.
CORRECTION	ADJUST PRESSURE TO SPECIFICATIONS WHEN TIRES ARE COOL ROTATE TIRES			ADJUST CAMBER TO SPECIFICATIONS	ADJUST TOE-IN TO SPECIFICATIONS	DYNAMIC OR STATIC BALANCE WHEELS	ROTATE TIRES AND INSPECT SUSPENSION

*HAVE TIRE INSPECTED FOR FURTHER USE.

Fig. 17-12. Types of tire wear and their causes and corrections. (*Chrysler Corporation*)

Fig. 17-13. Checking tire air pressure.

procedure for bias-belted, bias-ply, and radial tires. Note that bias-belted and bias-ply tires can be switched from one side of the car to the other, but that belted radial tires should not be switched from one side to the other. Doing this would reverse their direction of rotation which could result in handling and wear problems (see Fig. 17-14).

NOTE: Always check tire pressures (Fig. 17-13) after switching tires. Many cars require that the front tires carry different pressures from the rear tires. Thus, when you switch tires from front to back, the pres-

sures will require adjustment to meet the specifications.

CAUTION: Studded tires should never be rotated. A studded tire should be put back on the wheel from which it was removed.

⊘ **17-19 Tire Inspection** Every automotive service mechanic or technician—everyone having anything to do with cars around the service station or garage—should try to inspect every tire of every car that is driven in. This does not mean that you go around jacking up cars and taking the tires off to inspect them. A quick glance can tell the trained tire technician a great deal about a tire. The technician can see in a moment the pattern of tread wear and determine from that whether there is some problem (see Fig. 17-12).

When inspecting a tire, remove all stones and so on from the treads to make sure they are not hiding some damage. Check for bulges in the sidewalls. A bulge is a danger signal, since it can mean that the plies are separated or broken and that the tire is about ready to blow out. A tire with a bulge should be removed from the rim so that it can be checked inside and out. If the plies are broken or separated, the tire should be thrown away.

Many tires have wear indicators, which are filled-in sections of the tread grooves. When the tread has worn down enough to show the indicators (see Fig. 17-15), the tire should be replaced. There are also gauges that can be inserted into the tread grooves to measure how much tread is left. A simple way to check tread wear is with a Lincoln penny, as shown in Fig. 17-16. If at any point you can see all of Lincoln's head, the tread is excessively worn.

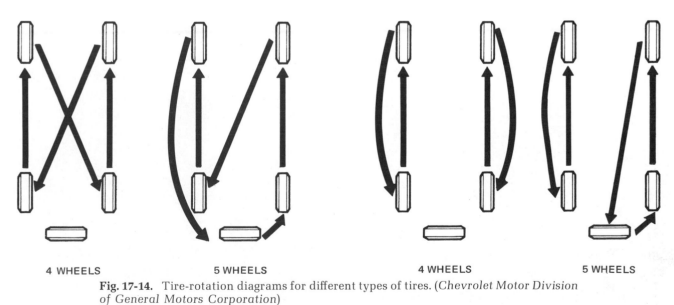

Fig. 17-14. Tire-rotation diagrams for different types of tires. (*Chevrolet Motor Division of General Motors Corporation*)

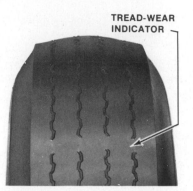

Fig. 17-15. Tire tread, worn down so much that the tread-wear indicator shows up. (*Chevrolet Motor Division of General Motors Corporation*)

Fig. 17-17. Loosening wheel nuts. (*British Motors Corporation, Ltd.*)

Some state laws require a tread depth of at least $\frac{1}{32}$ inch [0.79 mm] in any two adjacent grooves at any location on the tire. A tire with little or no tread has little holding power on the highway and will produce poor braking action.

NOTE: A tire can look okay from the outside and still have internal damage from rim bruises or fabric breaks. The only way to completely inspect a tire is to remove it from the rim and look at it closely inside and out.

⊘ 17-20 Tube Inspection   Tubes usually give little trouble if correctly installed. However, careless installation can cause trouble. For example, if the wheel rim is rough or rusty, or if the tire bead is rough, the tube may wear through. Dirt in the casing can cause the same trouble. Another condition that can cause trouble is installing a tube that is too large in the tire. Sometimes an old tube (which may have stretched a little) is put into a new tire. When this is done, the tube can overlap at some point; the overlap will rub and wear and possibly cause early tube failure.

⊘ 17-21 Removing a Wheel from the Car   To repair a tire, first remove the wheel from the car (except for small-hole repairs on tubeless tires). Loosen the

nuts before jacking up the car. It is easier to do it this way because the wheel will not turn if the car weight is on it. On many cars the lug nuts on the right-hand side of the car have right-hand threads, and the lug nuts on the left-hand side have left-hand threads. With this arrangement, the forward rotation of the wheels tends to tighten the nuts, not loosen them.

Figure 17-17 shows the use of a hand tool to loosen the lug nuts. In a well-equipped service shop, you will use a hydraulic jack to raise the car and an air-powered impact wrench to loosen or tighten the nuts (See Fig. 17-18).

CAUTION: When using an impact wrench, use the special socket with it. An ordinary socket is likely to break from the high twisting force of the impact wrench.

Fig. 17-18. Using an air-powered impact wrench to loosen a wheel-attaching nut. (*Mobile Oil Corporation*)

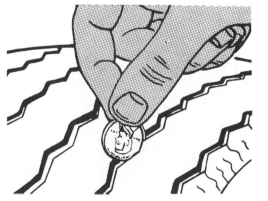

Fig. 17-16. Using a penny to check tire-tread wear.

Fig. 17-19. Removing the knock-off spinner, which holds the wheel on the hub. (*British Motors Corporation, Ltd.*)

Figure 17-19 shows removal of the knock-off spinner on a quick-change wheel. Knock the spinner loose with a hammer, and then spin it off, as shown.

⊘ **17-22 Removing a Tire from a Drop-Center Rim**
With the wheel off the car, make a chalk mark across the tire and rim so you can put the tire back in the same position. This preserves the balance of the wheel and tire. Next, release the air from the tire by holding the tire valve open or removing the valve core. Then remove the tire from the rim, using the equipment available in the shop. At one time tire irons—flat strips of steel—were used to remove and install tires on rims. Today, however, they are not recommended because they can damage the tire bead and ruin the tire.

⊘ **17-23 Demounting Tools** Instead of tire irons, use a special demounting tool, as shown in Figs. 17-20 to 17-22. First, place the tire-and-rim assembly in a special fixture to hold it, outside down. Then, push both beads down off the rim flanges into the drop-center well of the rim. Using the center post

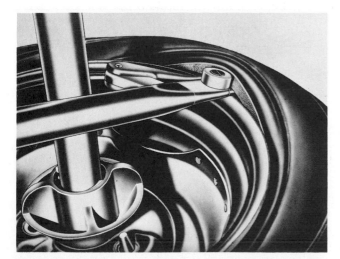

Fig. 17-20. Using a special tire-removing tool as the first step in removing a tire from a rim. (*Jack P. Hennessy Company, Inc.*)

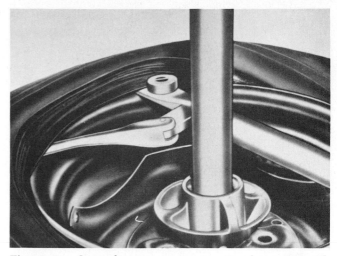

Fig. 17-21. Second step in removing tire from rim with special tool. The center post is used as a pivot as the tool is worked around the rim, raising the bead above the rim. (*Jack P. Hennessy Company, Inc.*)

as a pivot, move the tool around to lift the bead off the rim. Repeat the procedure to lift the lower bead up and off the rim (Fig. 17-22).

⊘ **17-24 Powered Tire Changers** Where many tires are changed, as in a tire dealer's shop, special powered tire changers are used. One is shown in Fig. 17-23. This has two major moving parts: the bead loosener and the rotating center post for demounting and mounting the tire. The bead loosener is brought down into position after the tire-and-rim assembly has been placed on the center post. The rim is held firm by a positioning pin and an adapter cup that screws down on the center post. When the bead loosener is operating, as shown in Fig. 17-24, a hydraulic cylinder is actuated to force the loosener

Fig. 17-22. Starting to raise the lower bead above the rim with the special tool. (*Jack P. Hennessy Company, Inc.*)

Fig. 17-23. Powered tire changer. (*Jack P. Hennessy Company, Inc.*)

Fig. 17-25. Using the powered tire changer to lift the upper bead above the rim. (*Jack P. Hennessy Company, Inc.*)

shoe down onto the bead, as shown. At the same time, a lower shoe pushes upward on the lower bead to loosen it. Next, the demounter tool is placed over the center post, as shown in Fig. 17-25, with the demounting end under the bead. Then, the operator starts the center post revolving, and the demounting tool is carried all the way around to lift the bead above the rim. The lower bead is lifted off the rim in the same way.

To remount the tire, use the same procedure but in reverse, also reversing the double-ended demounting-mounting tool (Fig. 17-26). As the center post revolves and carries the tool around with it, the bead is slid over the edge of the rim and down into place.

⊘ **17-25 Inspecting the Wheel**   When the tire is off

the wheel, check the wheel rim for any signs of dents or roughness. Use coarse steel wool to clean off rust spots, file off nicks or burrs, and clean the rim to remove all filings and dirt. A wheel or rim that has been bent by an accident or by slamming into a curb, for example, should be discarded. As a rule, it is not practical to try to straighten a bent wheel. Even if you do get the wheel straightened, it may be weakened so that it could fail when put under stress on the highway.

⊘ **17-26 Remounting Tires**   The tire using a tube requires one mounting procedure, the tubeless tire another.

1. TIRE WITH TUBE   Before replacing a tire that uses a tube, inflate the tube until it is barely rounded and put it into the casing. The inside and outside of the tire bead should be coated with a vegetable-oil

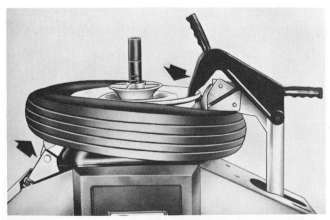

Fig. 17-24. Using the powered tire changer to push the bead off the rim. Note that both beads are being pushed off the rim at the same time, as shown by the arrows. (*Jack P. Hennessy Company, Inc.*)

Fig. 17-26. Using the powered tire changer to push the upper bead down over the rim. (*Jack P. Hennessy Company, Inc.*)

soft soap to make it easier for the beads to slide over the rim. Do not use a nondrying lubricant; this would allow the tire to "walk around" on the rim so that balance would be lost. Never use grease or oil—these will damage the rubber. In replacing the tire on the rim, install one bead first, following with the second. A special installing tool should be used, as shown in Figs. 17-26 to 17-28. After the tire is in place, make sure the beads are up on the bead seats in the rim and that they are uniformly seated all around the rim. Inflate the tube, making sure that it is properly centered in the tire and that the valve stem is square in the rim-valve-stem hole. Deflate and then reinflate the tube. This last operation ensures good alignment of the tire, tube, and rim.

CAUTION: If a tire has been deflated, never inflate it while the car weight is on the tire. Always jack up the car before inflating the tire so that the tube can distribute itself around the tire evenly. If this is not done, some parts of the tube will be stretched more than other parts, and this puts a strain on the tube that might cause it to blow out.

2. *TUBELESS TIRE* In mounting the tubeless tire, make sure that the rim flange, where the tire bead seats, is clean, smooth, and in good condition (⊘ 17-25). The tire bead seals the air in at this point, and so the rim flange must be smooth enough to permit a good seal.

If the valve in the wheel rim requires replacement, remove the old valve and install a new one. There are two types: the snap-in type, shown in Fig. 17-29, and the type that is secured with a nut. To remove the snap-in type, drive the valve into the rim with a soft hammer or cut the base off. Then use a valve installing tool to install the new valve. Lubricate the new valve with rubber lubricant. Then push the valve through the hole enough so that you can screw the tool onto the stem. Give the tool a sharp pull to seat the valve.

To replace the tire, install the two beads over the rim, as noted above (for a tire with a tube). (See Figs. 17-26 to 17-28.) Coating the beads and rim flanges with a vegetable-oil soft soap or a special lubricant such as Ruglyde makes the mounting procedure easier. Do not use a nondrying lubricant— this would allow the tire to "walk around" on the rim so that balance would be lost. Never use grease or oil, since they will damage the rubber. After mounting the tire on the rim, use a commercial tire-mounting band or a simple rope tourniquet to spread the beads (Fig. 17-30). Then give the tire a few quick bursts of air to seat the beads properly. After the beads are seated, inflate the tire to 40 psi [2.81 kg/cm²] (for most passenger-car tires).

CAUTION: Do not stand over the tire when inflating it! If it burst, you could be seriously injured!

If the bead-positioning rings on the tire (the outer rings near the sidewalls) are evenly visible all

Fig. 17-27. Using a special tire-mounting tool to force the lower bead down into place past the upper flange of the rim. (*Jack P. Hennessy Company, Inc.*)

Fig. 17-28. Using a special tire-mounting tool to force the upper bead down into place over the rim. (*Jack P. Hennessy Company, Inc.*)

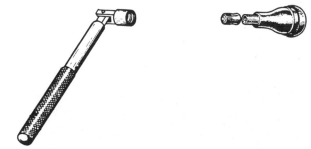

Fig. 17-29. Snap-in tire valve for a tubeless tire, and the tool used to install it. (*British Motors Corporation, Ltd.*)

around the rim, the beads are seated properly. If the positioning rings are not evenly visible, deflate the tire completely and then reinflate it.

After the beads are properly positioned, deflate the tire to the recommended pressure.

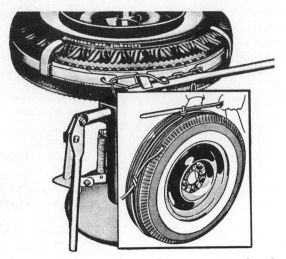

Fig. 17-30. Using a commercial tire-mounting band or a rope tourniquet to spread the beads during mounting of a tubeless tire.

⊘ 17-27 Tube Repair If a tire tube has been punctured but is otherwise in good shape, it can be repaired with a patch. First, you have to find the hole. Inflate the tube after it is out of the tire, then submerge it in water. Bubbles will appear where the leak is. Mark the spot with anything that will make a light scratch on the rubber. Deflate the tube and dry it.

There are two ways to patch a tube leak: the cold-patch and the hot-patch methods. With the cold-patch method, first make sure the rubber is clean, dry, and free of oil or grease. Then roughen the area around the hole, and cover the area with cement. Let the cement dry until it is tacky, then peel the back off a patch and apply the patch firmly. Recheck the tire for leaks by reinflating it and submerging it in water.

With the hot-patch method, prepare the tube in the same way as for the cold patch. Put the hot patch into place and clamp it. Then, with a match, light the fuel on the back of the patch. The heat ensures a good bond. After the patch has cooled, recheck for leaks by submerging the inflated tube in water.

Another kind of hot patch uses a vulcanizing hot plate, which supplies the heat required to bond the patch to the tube.

NOTE: The hot-patch method is superior to the cold-patch method.

⊘ 17-28 Tire Repair No attempt should be made to repair a tire that has been badly damaged. If plies are torn or have holes in them, the tire should be thrown away. Even though you might be able to patch up the tire to get a little more mileage out of it, using it would be dangerous and illegal. The tire might blow out at high speed and cause a fatal accident.

Repairing small holes in a tubeless tire is simple. First make sure that the object that caused the hole is removed. While the tire is off, check it for other

puncturing objects. Tubeless tires can carry a nail for miles without losing air.

NOTE: You find leaks from a tubeless tire the same way you find leaks from a tube. With the tire on the wheel and inflated, submerge the tire and wheel in water. Bubbles will show the location of any leaks. If a water tank is not available, you can coat the tire with soapy water. Bubbles will show the location of leaks.

If air leaks around the spoke welds of the wheel, you can repair the leaks as follows: Clean the area and apply two coats of cold-patching cement on the inside of the rim. Allow the first coat to dry before applying the second coat. Then cement a strip of rubber over the area.

⊘ 17-29 Repairing a Puncture with a Rubber Plug—Tire on Rim A temporary repair of a small puncture can be made with the tire still mounted on the rim, as described in the next paragraph. However, this repair is only a temporary fix. At the first opportunity, the tire must be removed from the rim and repaired from the inside, as explained in ⊘ 17-30.

Remove the puncturing object and clean the hole with a rasp. Apply the special vulcanizing fluid, supplied with the repair kit, to the outside of the hole. Push the snout of the vulcanizing-fluid can into the hole to get fluid inside the tire. There are different kinds of rubber plugs. The kind shown in Fig. 17-31 is installed with a special needle. To use this plug, first cover the hole with vulcanizing fluid. Then select a plug of the right size for the hole. The plug should be at least twice the diameter of the hole. Roll the small end of the plug into the eye of the needle. Dip the plug into vulcanizing fluid. Push the needle and plug through the hole. Then pull the needle out. Trim off the plug $\frac{1}{8}$ inch [3.2 mm] above the tire surface. Check for leakage. If there is no leakage, the tire is ready for service after it is inflated (Fig. 17-32).

Another type of plug and its applicator are shown in Figs. 17-33 and 17-34. When using this plug, first clean the hole with a rasp. Coat the hole on the inside with vulcanizing fluid. Then place the plug on the applicator, and coat the plug with vulcanizing fluid. Next insert the applicator through the hole, as shown in Fig. 17-33. Pull the plug back out enough to force the cap on the end of the plug to seat on the inside of the tire, as shown in Fig. 17-34. Finally, remove the applicator and cut off the plug about $\frac{1}{8}$ inch [3.2 mm] from the tire surface.

⊘ 17-30 Repairing a Tire—Removed from Rim There are three methods of repairing holes in tires: the rubber-plug, the cold-patch, and the hot-patch methods. Permanent repairs are made from inside the tire—with the tire off the rim.

1. RUBBER-PLUG METHOD Rubber plugs can be used in the same way as explained in ⊘ 17-29. The basic difference is that the repair is made from in-

Fig. 17-31. Tire cut away to show the needle being used to insert the rubber plug in the hole.

Fig. 17-32. Tire cut away to show the repair plug in place.

side the tire, and the inside area round the injury is buffed and cleaned. Then the plug is installed from inside the tire.

2. *COLD-PATCH METHOD* In the cold-patch method, first clean and buff the inside area around the injury. Then pour a small amount of self-vulcanizing fluid around the injury and allow it to dry for 5 minutes. Next, remove the backing on the patch, and place the patch over the injury, stitching it down with the stitching tool. Start stitching at the center and work out, making sure to stitch down the edges.

CAUTION: Be sure no dirt gets on the fluid or patch during a repair job. Dirt could allow leakage.

3. *HOT-PATCH METHOD* The hot-patch method is very similar to the cold-patch method. The essential difference is that heat is applied after the patch has been put into place over the area. This is done by lighting the patch with a match, or with an electric hot plate, according to the type of patch being used (Fig. 17-35). After the repair is done, mount the tire on the rim, inflate it, and test it for leakage, as explained in ⬡ 17-28.

⬡ **17-31 Recapping** Recapping is a specialized trade. The process involves applying new tread material to the old casing and vulcanizing it into place. Only casings that are in good condition should be recapped. Recapping cannot repair a casing with broken or separated piles or other damage. It requires a special machine, such as the machine shown in Fig. 17-36.

The tire is first cleaned and the tread area is roughened by rasping it or buffing it on a wire wheel. Then a strip of new rubber tread, called *camelback,* is placed around the tread. The casing with the camelback then goes into the recapping machine.

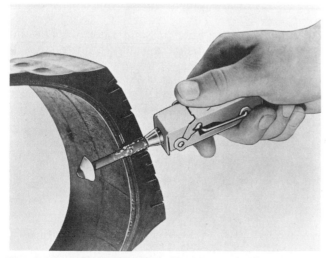

Fig. 17-33. First step in installing a repair plug in a tire. The plug has been inserted by the applicator far enough to allow the cup on the end to clear the inside of the tire. (*General Motors Corporation*)

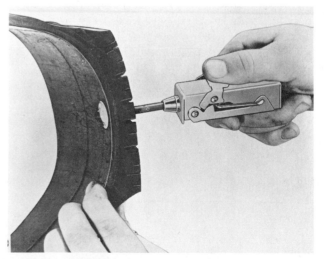

Fig. 17-34. Second step in installing a repair plug in a tire. The plug has been pulled out far enough to seat the cup on the inside of the tire. (*General Motors Corporation*)

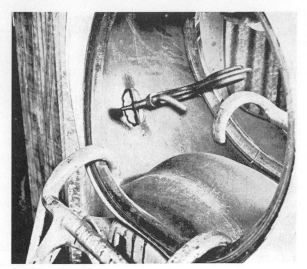

Fig. 17-35. Repairing a tubeless tire by the hot-patch method.

The machine is clamped shut, and heat is applied for the specified time. Thus, a new tread is formed and vulcanized onto the old casing.

⊘ **17-32 Repairing a Tire That Uses a Tube** If a tire that uses a tube has a small hole, nothing more than

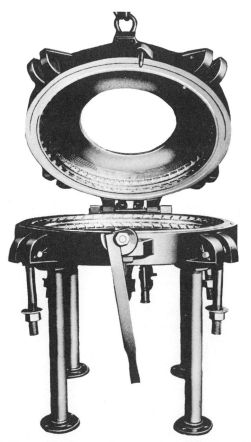

Fig. 17-36. One type of recapping machine. (*Akron Equipment Company*)

cleaning out the injured spot is necessary to make the repair. The tube will hold the air. However, if the hole is of any size, it should be repaired with a cold patch on the inside. This method prevents dirt or water from working in between the tire and tube and causing trouble.

⊘ **17-33 Balancing the Wheel** After a tire change or repair, the tire-and-wheel assembly should be checked for balance. Balancing is covered in Chap. 8.

CHAPTER 17 CHECKUP

Here is your checkup on the chapter you have just finished on tires and tubes. Today tires are more or less taken for granted (unless one goes flat). Yet a surprising amount of information on tires is of importance to the automotive service mechanic. Thus, you should know how to inflate a tire properly, the various ways in which tires may wear and what causes the different types of wear, and how to remove, repair, and replace tires. The test that follows will help you to review and remember these facts.

Completing the Sentences The sentences below are incomplete. After each sentence there are several words or phrases, only one of which will correctly complete the sentence. Write each sentence in your notebook, selecting the proper word or phrase to complete it correctly.

1. Three types of tires are bias, belted-bias, and: (*a*) radial ply, (*b*) belted-radial, (*c*) belted centrifugal.
2. The outside diameter of a 7.50 × 16 tire, when inflated but unloaded, is: (*a*) 16 in. [306.4 mm], (*b*) 23.50 in. [596.9 mm], (*c*) 31 in. [787.4 mm].
3. The most commonly used material for tire tubes today is: (*a*) natural rubber, (*b*) octane rubber, (*c*) butane, (*d*) butyl.
4. For a thorough inspection, a tire should be: (*a*) on the car, (*b*) on the wheel, (*c*) off the wheel, (*d*) inflated.
5. Of the four tires on a passenger car, the one that wears most rapidly is the: (*a*) right front tire, (*b*) right rear tire, (*c*) left front tire, (*d*) left rear tire.
6. To equalize tire wear, it is suggested that tires be rotated, or shifted from one wheel to another, every: (*a*) 50 mi [80.46 km], (*b*) 500 mi [804.6 km], (*c*) 5,000 mi [8,046 km], (*d*) 50,000 mi [80.460 km].

Servicing Procedures In the following, you are asked to write in your notebook the service procedures asked for. Don't copy from the book; try to explain the procedure in your own words, just as you would to a friend.

1. List the points to watch when inflating tires.
2. List types of tire wear and their causes.
3. Explain how to remove a tire from a wheel rim.
4. Explain how to repair a tube.
5. Explain how to repair a tire.

chapter 18

CHASSIS LUBRICATION

This brief chapter on chassis lubrication is included to emphasize the importance of this service.

⊘ **18-1 Periodic Lubrication** Various chassis units, described earlier in the book, should be checked periodically: some require periodic lubrication, others do not. The charts that follow (Figs. 18-1 to 18-3) provide typical examples.

In addition to performing the actual lubricating job, the lubrication technician performs other service jobs at the same time. Thus, it is customary to check the battery, tires, lights, fan belt, cooling system, distributor, brake action, clutch, transmission, muffler, spark plugs, and so on. Actually, most of the components of the automobile can be checked, to some extent at least, by the lubrication technician while "under the hood" or under the car. This is a form of safety insurance, since it is often possible to detect trouble in an early stage. It can then be "nipped in the bud" before it develops into serious trouble.

Various lubrication schedules are set up for different makes and models of cars. For best performance and long life of the car, these lubrication schedules should be carefully followed. Study the manufacturer's charts to learn where lubricant is required, how frequently, and the type and amount of lubricant to use.

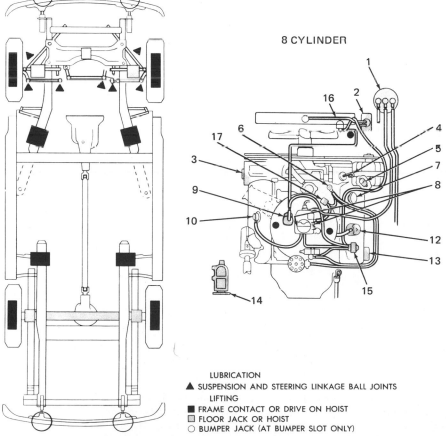

8 CYLINDER

1. Fuel-vapor storage canister
2. Coolant reserve system
3. Air-injection pump
4. Crankcase dipstick
   (other V8, opposite side)
5. Fuel filter
6. Thermal ignition control
   (some models)
7. Oil-fill cap
8. Carburetor choke shaft
9. EGR control valve
10. PCV valve
12. Crankcase inlet-air cleaner
13. Oil filter
    (other V8, left front)
14. Brake master cylinder
15. Vacuum amplifier
16. Vacuum thermal control (CCEGR)
17. Orifice spark-advance control
    (OSAC) valve
● Cooling system drains

LUBRICATION
▲ SUSPENSION AND STEERING LINKAGE BALL JOINTS
LIFTING
■ FRAME CONTACT OR DRIVE ON HOIST
▨ FLOOR JACK OR HOIST
○ BUMPER JACK (AT BUMPER SLOT ONLY)

Fig. 18-1. Lubrication and maintenance guide. Refer to Fig. 18-2 for required services and intervals. (*Chrysler Corporation*)

LUBRICATION AND MAINTENANCE SCHEDULE

REQUIRED SERVICES FOR EMISSION CONTROL AND PROPER PERFORMANCE

TIME OR MILEAGE INTERVAL
(Follow the interval which occurs first—Mileage in thousands)

Service	Time	Condition	4	8	12	16	18	20	24	28	32	36
ENGINE OIL—change	Every 3 months	or	•	•	•	•		•	•	•	•	•
OIL FILTER—change	Every second oil change	—		•					•			•
MANIFOLD HEAT VALVE (6 Cylinder)—apply solvent	Every 6 months	Time interval only										
CARBURETOR CHOKE SHAFT, FAST IDLE CAM and PIVOT PIN—apply solvent	Every 6 months	Time interval only										
DRIVE BELTS—check, adjust or replace	Every 12 months	or			•				•			•
CRANKCASE INLET AIR CLEANER—clean, lubricate	Every 12 months	or			•				•			•
PCV VALVE—check operation (replace every 2 years or 24,000 miles)	Every 12 months	or			•				•			•
CARBURETOR AIR FILTER—clean (replace every 2 years)	Every 12 months	or			•				•			•
EXHAUST GAS RECIRCULATION SYSTEM—check operation	Every 12 months	or			•				•			•
VAPOR STORAGE CANISTER—change filter	Every 12 months	or			•				•			•
ENGINE IDLE SPEED, IGNITION TIMING and MIXTURE—check, adjust as required	Every 12 months	or			•				•			•
TAPPETS (6 Cylinder Engine)—adjust if required	Every 12 months	or			•				•			•
SPARK PLUGS—replace, IGNITION CABLES—inspect	Every 18,000 miles	Mileage interval only					•					•
ORIFICE SPARK ADVANCE CONTROL—inspect	Every 24 months	or							•			
FUEL FILTER—replace	Every 24 months	or							•			
AUTOMATIC CHOKE—check operation (and adjust if required)	Every 24 months	or							•			
RECOMMENDED SERVICES												
POWER STEERING—check (pump) fluid level	Every 3 months	or	•	•	•	•		•	•	•	•	•
TIRES—inspect for wear	Every 3 months	or	•	•	•	•		•	•	•	•	•
BRAKE MASTER CYLINDER FLUID LEVEL—check	Every 6 months	Time interval only										
EXHAUST SYSTEM—check for leaks and damaged or missing parts	Every 6 months	Time interval only										
TRANSMISSION and REAR AXLE (ALL)—check fluid level	Every 6 months	Time interval only										
FRONT SUSPENSION BALL JOINTS, STEERING LINKAGE and UNIVERSAL JOINTS—inspect seals	Every 6 months	Time interval only										
COOLING SYSTEM and ANTI-FREEZE—check	Every 6 months	Time interval only										
AIR CONDITIONING—check sight glass and control operation	Every 6 months	Time interval only										
HEADLIGHTS—aim	Every 6 months	Time interval only										
MANUAL TRANSMISSION SHIFT MECHANISM (FLOOR MOUNTED)—lubricate	Every 6 months	or			•			•		•	•	
BRAKE HOSE AND TUBING—check for deterioration and leaks*	Every second oil change	or			•			•		•	•	
TIRES—rotate	Every second oil change	or			•			•		•	•	
RUBBER and PLASTIC COMPONENTS—inspect (See Below)*	Every second oil change	or			•			•		•	•	
BRAKE LINING—inspect	Every 12 months	or					•					•
FRONT WHEEL BEARINGS—inspect (and whenever drums or rotors are removed)	Every 24 months	or							•			
FRONT SUSPENSION BALL JOINTS and STEERING LINKAGE TIE RODS—lubricate	Every 3 years	or										•
SEVERE and/or TRAILER TOW—RECOMMENDED SERVICES												
UNIVERSAL JOINTS—inspect	Every 3 months	not to exceed	•	•	•	•		•	•	•	•	•
TRANSMISSION and REAR AXLE (ALL)—check lubricant level	Every 3 months	not to exceed	•	•	•	•		•	•	•	•	•
BRAKE HOSE and TUBING—inspect	Every 3 months	not to exceed	•	•	•	•		•	•	•	•	•
AUTOMATIC TRANSMISSION—change fluid, filter and adjust bands	Every 24,000 miles	Mileage interval only							•			
MANUAL TRANSMISSION—change oil	Every 36,000 miles	Mileage interval only										•
REAR AXLE—change lubricant	Every 36,000 miles	Mileage interval only										•

*UNDERHOOD RUBBER AND PLASTIC COMPONENTS
The following rubber and plastic components that are exposed to underhood temperatures should be inspected. Replace if inspection reveals deterioration that could result in failure.

BELTS, ACCESSORY DRIVE
CONTROL ARM BUSHINGS, UPPER AND LOWER (FRONT SUSPENSION)
ENGINE MOUNTS
HOSES—POWER STEERING, HYDRAULIC BRAKE, VACUUM BRAKE, COOLANT AND FUEL LINE.

Fig. 18-2. Chart of required services and time or mileage intervals at which the services should be performed. (*Chrysler Corporation*)

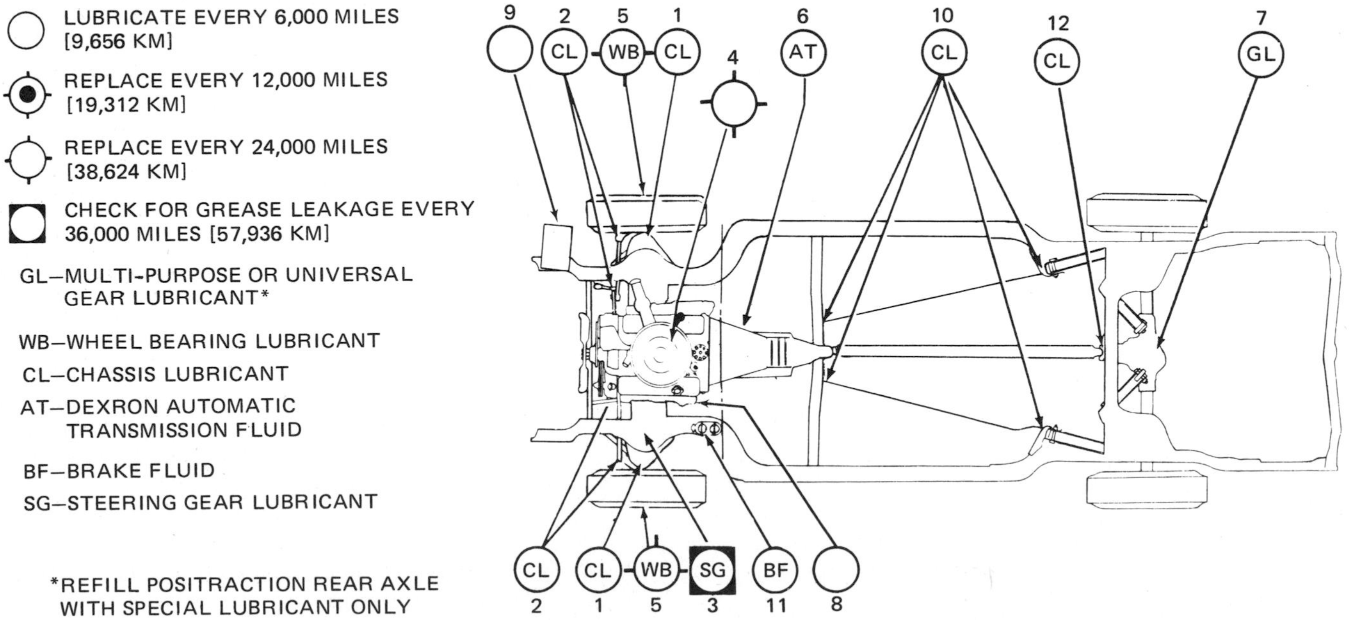

○ LUBRICATE EVERY 6,000 MILES [9,656 KM]

◉ REPLACE EVERY 12,000 MILES [19,312 KM]

◔ REPLACE EVERY 24,000 MILES [38,624 KM]

■ CHECK FOR GREASE LEAKAGE EVERY 36,000 MILES [57,936 KM]

GL—MULTI-PURPOSE OR UNIVERSAL GEAR LUBRICANT*

WB—WHEEL BEARING LUBRICANT

CL—CHASSIS LUBRICANT

AT—DEXRON AUTOMATIC TRANSMISSION FLUID

BF—BRAKE FLUID

SG—STEERING GEAR LUBRICANT

*REFILL POSITRACTION REAR AXLE WITH SPECIAL LUBRICANT ONLY

1. Front suspension
2. Steering linkage
3. Steering gear
4. Air cleaner
5. Front-wheel bearings
6. Automatic transmission
7. Rear axle
8. Oil filter
9. Battery
10. Parking brake
11. Brake master cylinder
12. Rear universal joint

Fig. 18-3. Lubrication chart for Chevrolet models. (*Chevrolet Motor Division of General Motors Corporation*)

CAR FRAME AND BODY

This chapter describes the construction, servicing, and repair of the car frame and body. Actually, this chapter should be considered as only an introduction to body repair, which is a complex subject. For a complete exposition of body repair, the reader is referred to one of the textbooks that have been published on the subject.

⊘ **19-1 Servicing Operations Required** To get an idea of the different kinds of service operations required, consider this. The body service manual issued by one car manufacturer for one model year contains 870 pages, about 250,000 words, and about 1,200 illustrations. It provides servicing information on glasswork, chrome, fabric and upholstery, door locks, manual and electric window openers, front-seat adjusters (manual and electric), hydroelectric convertible-top raisers, weatherstripping, etc. All this is specific servicing material describing specific service operations. The manual does not describe the straightening of doors and frames, sheet-metal work, and other fundamentals that the body mechanic must know. Some of these fundamentals are described below.

⊘ **19-2 Car Frame** The car frame is designed to support all body and engine parts and is in turn supported by the front and rear wheel springs. The frame is normally made up of specially formed channel or U-shaped members that are riveted or welded together. Figure 19-1 illustrates an automobile frame with the wheels, engine, and steering systems attached. This assembly is often referred to as the *chassis*. Figure 19-2 illustrates a typical frame. It will be noted that the frame members are designed to receive and support all attached parts.

⊘ **19-3 Frame Service** Almost the only service required on frames results from accidents in which the frame has been twisted or broken. It is possible to repair such damage, if it is not too severe, by straightening the bent members and replacing or welding those that have been broken. In order to determine whether the frame has been bent, frame alignment can be checked by any of several methods. One method of checking the frame for forward alignment is shown in Fig. 19-3. In using this method, frame gauges are hung from the car in three different places. If the pointers on the centers of the gauges do not line up, the frame is out of line. See Figs. 19-4 and 19-5.

A more accurate check can be made with a tramming tool—a tram gauge. This device can extend to 90 inches [2,286 mm] or more and has a series of vertical pointers that can be extended upward varying amounts. By use of the gauge, the various dimensions of the underbody, or frame, can be checked, as shown in Fig. 19-6.

If the frame is out of line, it can be straightened satisfactorily if the misalignment is not too great. The recommendations of the various car manufacturers differ in the matter of straightening frame members. Some state that frame members should be straightened cold, without the application of heat. It is their contention that application of heat weakens the frame members excessively. Other car manufacturers state that heat may be applied provided the temperature of the steel is kept below 1200 degrees Fahrenheit [648.9°C]. Steel, at this temperature, is a deep cherry-red color. Heat above this temperature will seriously weaken the steel. A torch can be used to apply heat to the member to be straightened. Special straightening tools are usually required, including heavy I beams placed alongside the distorted frame member, chains to be attached between the beam and the frame member, and jacks to apply straightening pressure on the chain against the frame member.

When frame members have been broken or so badly distorted that they require replacement, new members can be installed with either rivets or nuts and bolts. The hot-riveting method is usually preferred. In this method the rivet is heated and riveted into place.

When the front-suspension cross member has been damaged, the usual practice is to replace it. This part is manufactured to extremely close toler-

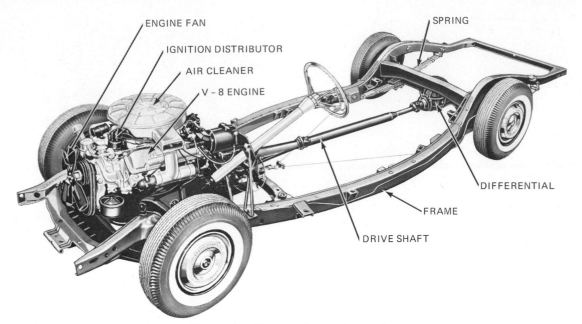

Fig. 19-1. Chassis of an automobile.

Fig. 19-2. Frame of a car.

Fig. 19-3. Checking frame alignment with frame gauges. Pointers will line up as shown by the white line if the frame has proper forward alignment. (*Bear Manufacturing Company*)

Fig. 19-4. Misalignment of pointers due to sideway, or bending of the frame sideways. (*Bear Manufacturing Company*)

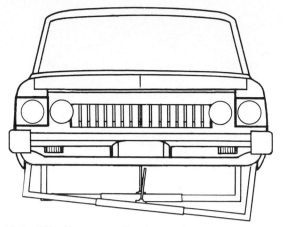

Fig. 19-5. Misalignment of pointers due to sag, or twisting of the frame. (*Bear Manufacturing Company*)

ances and, once bent, is practically impossible to restore to perfect alignment. If it is not in proper alignment, the front wheels cannot be properly aligned, and poor steering control and rapid tire wear are likely to result.

On vehicles that do not have independent front suspension, the front axle is bent to correct front-wheel alignment. This has already been discussed in ⊘ 8-9, item 7.

⊘ **19-4 Car Body** The car body is attached to the frame by numerous nuts and bolts (except on unitized construction), all the bolts being insulated with rubber washers or shims to prevent the transfer of vibration and noise from the frame to the body. A few of the various types of body bolts are shown in Fig. 19-7. With unitized construction, the body and frame are a single unit, welded together (Fig. 19-8).

The body is designed to contain and protect the

Fig. 19-7. Types of body bolts that attach the body to the car frame. (*Buick Motor Division of General Motors Corporation*)

engine and accessories, as well as the passengers. In addition, it is shaped to reduce the resistance to the air as it moves forward. This shaping of the car to reduce air resistance is called *streamlining*. Streamlining makes use of curves rather than angles and flat surfaces. In the early-model car, the vertical front sections of the radiator and the windshield offered considerable resistance to the car movement through the air. In addition, air eddies formed in back of the car, tending to produce a drag that im-

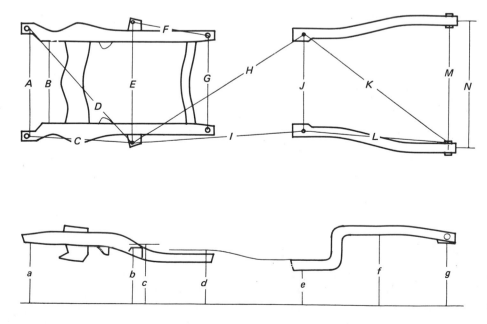

Fig. 19-6. Horizontal and vertical checking dimensions on stub frames on a vehicle with unitized construction. (*Fisher Body Division of General Motors Corporation*)

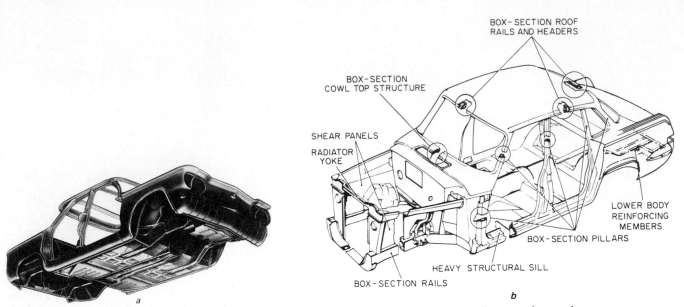

Fig. 19-8. Unitized construction of car body and frame (*a*) as seen from underneath, and (*b*) in partial cutaway view to show details of the separate parts that are welded together. (*Chevrolet Motor Division of General Motors Corporation and Chrysler Corporation*)

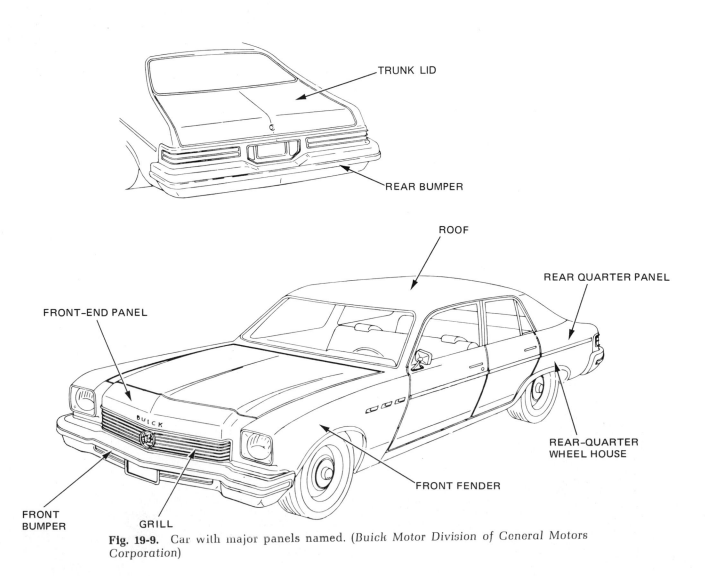

Fig. 19-9. Car with major panels named. (*Buick Motor Division of General Motors Corporation*)

peded forward motion. At intermediate and high speeds, considerable power was required to overcome this air resistance.

The streamlined car has sloping lines that permit the car body to move more smoothly through the air. The sloping lines tend to push the air up and around the car. Air eddies are not formed behind the car body as on the early-model car.

The car body is made up of a number of pressed-steel panels which are welded together to form the complete body (Fig. 19-9). Reinforcing members are placed at proper intervals in the body. Attachment brackets are welded to the body to attach the door, trim, instrument panel, hood, trunk lid, headlining, and so on. In case of accidents, panels can be replaced if they are so badly damaged that they cannot be straightened. Figure 19-10 shows the sheet metal for the front end of the car.

NOTE: Some body panels are made of molded fiberglass (see Fig. 19-11).

⊘ **19-5 Doors** There are two general types of doors: closed style (with upper frames) and hardtop or convertible style (without upper frames). Doors contain a variety of devices (Fig. 19-12), including window regulators (openers and closers), locks, cigarette lighters, windshield-wiper controls, seat-adjustment controls, rearview mirror and control, and door re-

inforcing strips. Window regulators can be mechanical with a hand crank, or electric, with a reversible electric motor. Door locks can be mechanical with a hand-operated button, or electric, with a two-way solenoid. Cigarette lighters and ashtrays may be found in any door. The windshield-wiper control is located, on some cars, in the front left-hand door, as is the rearview mirror and control. This location permits the driver to operate the controls as necessary.

1. DOOR ADJUSTMENT Many doors have provisions for adjustment (Fig. 19-13). That is, the holes in the hinges and the hinge-attachment points, are enlarged or elongated. Thus the door can be shifted up or down, or forward or back, in order to make it fit the door opening properly. The screws are loosened slightly to make the adjustment, and then the door is pried in the right direction with a padded pry bar. When the adjustment is correct, the screws are tightened. If shifting the door throws the striker plate out of alignment, the striker plate then has to be adjusted.

2. GLASS ALIGNMENT The doors have provisions for alignment of the glass in case it does not close properly. When a glass is raised, it should fit, watertight, on the top and two sides. If it does not, the two supports at the bottom of the glass can be adjusted to correct the fit.

3. WINDOW REGULATOR The window regulator

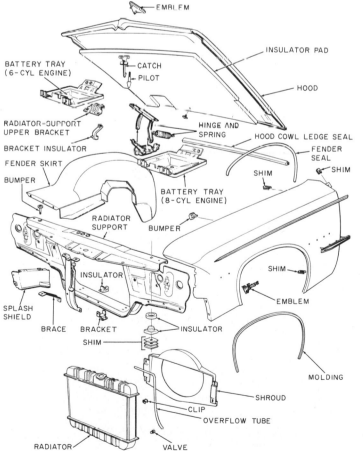

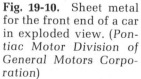

Fig. 19-10. Sheet metal for the front end of a car in exploded view. (*Pontiac Motor Division of General Motors Corporation*)

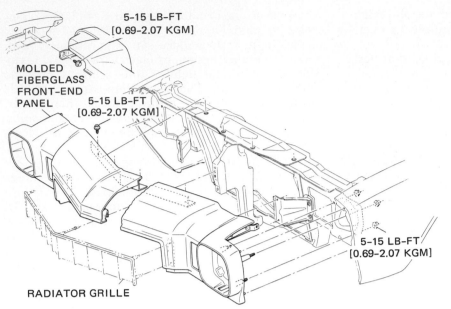

Fig. 19-11. Front-panel assembly, a one-piece molded fiberglass panel, with attachments. (*Buick Motor Division of General Motors Corporation*)

may be operated either by a hand crank or by an electric motor. If something goes wrong, the inner lining of the door must come off so the trouble can be corrected. There are many different arrangements. Figure 19-12 shows only one.

4. *DOOR LOCK* The door lock is operated by a push button in the upper sash of the door. Many cars also have an electric solenoid to lock or unlock the door. If the car has electric door locks, there is a master control in the driver's door. The master control can be flipped to prevent opening of any door, or to permit any of the doors to be individually controlled by the passengers.

5. *TRIM AND WEATHERSTRIPPING* Doors must have weatherstripping to seal them against the entrance of rain or outside air. The weatherstripping

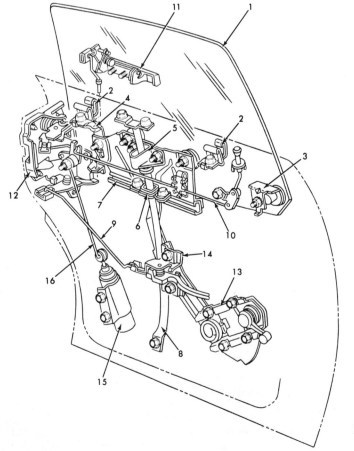

1. Window assembly
2. Belt trim support retainers
3. Front up-travel stop
4. Rear up-travel stop
5. Lower-sash upper guide
6. Lower-sash lower guide
7. Lower-sash guide plate assembly
8. Guide-tube assembly
9. Remote control to lock-connecting rod
10. Inside locking rod
11. Door outside lift-bar handle
12. Door lock
13. Window regulator (electric)
14. Door-lock remote-control handle
15. Door-lock solenoid
16. Rod inside locking to solenoid

Fig. 19-12. Rear-door hardware. (*Fisher Body Division of General Motors Corporation*)

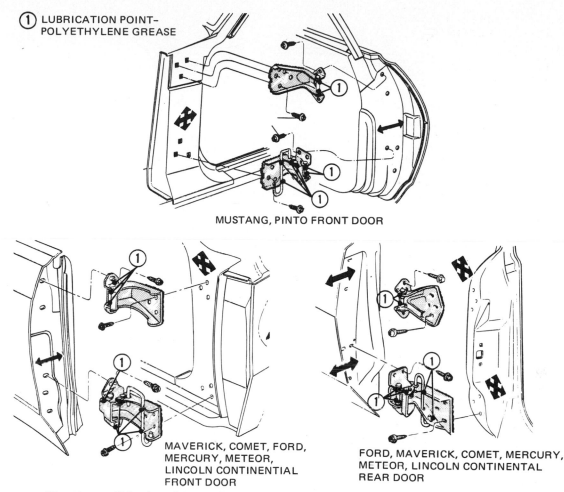

MUSTANG, PINTO FRONT DOOR

MAVERICK, COMET, FORD,
MERCURY, METEOR,
LINCOLN CONTINENTAL
FRONT DOOR

FORD, MAVERICK, COMET, MERCURY,
METEOR, LINCOLN CONTINENTAL
REAR DOOR

Fig. 19-13. Side door hinge adjustments on various models. (*Ford Motor Company*)

seals at all joints. Door trim includes handles and embellishment strips, attached by screws or locking catches.

⊘ **19-6 Trunk Lid** The trunk lid, or rear-compartment lid as it is also called, is attached at the forward end by two hinges. Many cars have a device to assist in opening the lid (Fig. 19-14). This device is called a *lid support assembly*. It includes a gas-filled cylinder. The gas is under pressure, and when the lid is unlocked, the device extends to raise the lid. If this assembly requires replacement, it must be removed from the car in the *fully extended position*. If it is detached with the trunk lid only partly open, it will instantly extend fully, and this could injure you or damage the car.

Trunk lids have a lock that must be operated by a key. In some cars, the lid may be unlocked by an electric solenoid and a push button in the glove compartment.

⊘ **19-7 Front Hoods** Front hoods (Fig. 19-15) are attached to the body by two hinges, usually spring-loaded. The springs make it easier to open the hood and hold it open. Elongated or oversize holes permit

the hood to be shifted as necessary to secure a good fit. In many cars the hood lock is at the front of the car. In others it is connected by a cable to a control lever inside the driver's compartment.

⊘ **19-8 Station Wagon Tail Gate** There are several styles of tail gate. In one, the tail gate is in one piece with a fixed window. With this arrangement, the tail gate is hinged at the top, just like the trunk lid. Another arrangement has the glass separate from the rest of the tail gate, which is hinged at the bottom. The glass can be retracted into the roof of the car by an electric motor. In some vehicles, the tail gate is hinged to swing down, or to swing to one side. The tail gate can contain a variety of devices: lock-release solenoid, defogger blower, and counterbalance support assemblies. In addition, it may have a warning system that turns on a warning light on the instrument panel if the gate is not closed when the ignition switch is turned on.

⊘ **19-9 Sun Roof** The sun roof is a metal panel in the roof of the car that slides back and forth on guide rails in the roof (Fig. 19-16). When it is slid back, the sun can shine down through the opening onto

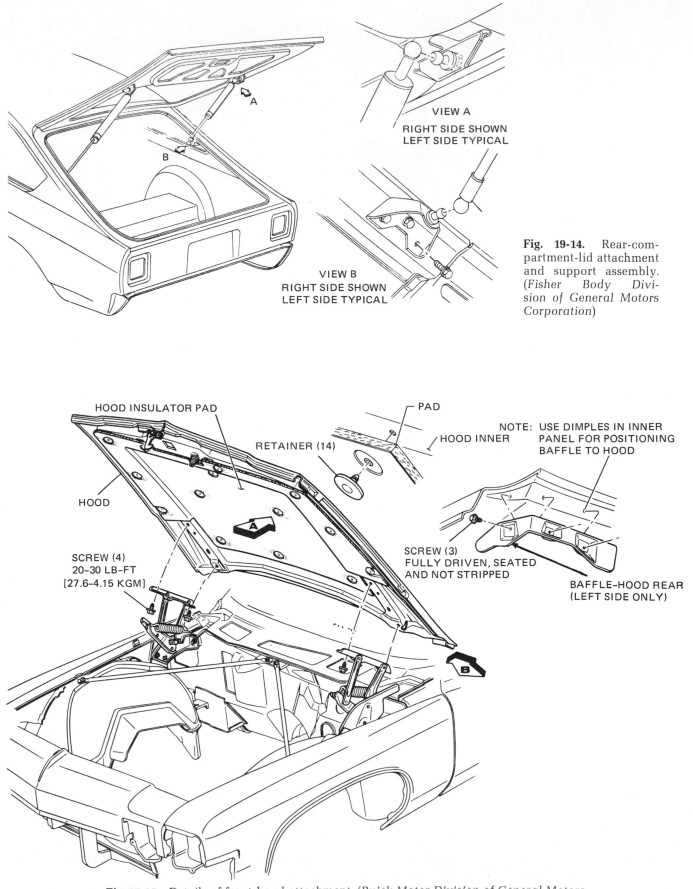

Fig. 19-14. Rear-compartment-lid attachment and support assembly. (*Fisher Body Division of General Motors Corporation*)

VIEW A
RIGHT SIDE SHOWN
LEFT SIDE TYPICAL

VIEW B
RIGHT SIDE SHOWN
LEFT SIDE TYPICAL

HOOD INSULATOR PAD

PAD

HOOD INNER

RETAINER (14)

NOTE: USE DIMPLES IN INNER PANEL FOR POSITIONING BAFFLE TO HOOD

HOOD

SCREW (4)
20–30 LB–FT
[27.6–4.15 KGM]

SCREW (3)
FULLY DRIVEN, SEATED
AND NOT STRIPPED

BAFFLE–HOOD REAR
(LEFT SIDE ONLY)

Fig. 19-15. Details of front-hood attachment. (*Buick Motor Division of General Motors Corporation*)

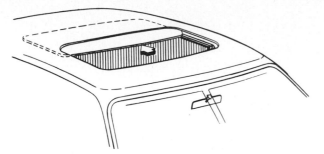

Fig. 19-16. Sun roof, partly open. (*Fisher Body Division of General Motors Corporation*)

the passengers. On some cars the sun panel is operated by a two-way electric motor; on other cars it is operated by a hand crank.

⊘ **19-10 Seats** Seats come in a variety of designs (Figs. 19-17 and 19-18). Some have a manual forward-and-back adjustment, others have electric motors to move them back and forth, or up and down. The latter are called *four-way seats*. Some seats are six-way—they have an additional control that changes the tilt of the seat. Figure 19-19 shows the major parts of a six-way seat adjuster.

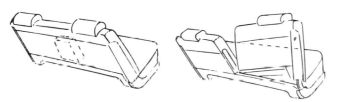

FULL-WIDTH BENCH SEATS BUILT-IN
CENTER ARM REST—SOME STYLES

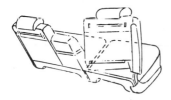

60–40 SEAT   FULL-WIDTH NOTCH-DOWN
BENCH SEAT

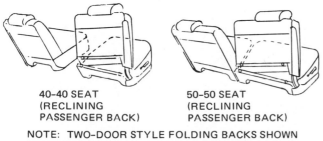

40–40 SEAT   50–50 SEAT
(RECLINING   (RECLINING
PASSENGER BACK)   PASSENGER BACK)

NOTE: TWO-DOOR STYLE FOLDING BACKS SHOWN
FOUR-DOOR STYLES HAVE NON-FOLDING BACKS

Fig. 19-17. Types of front seats (except bucket seats). (*Fisher Body Division of General Motors Corporation*)

STANDARD BUCKET   BUCKET SEAT WITH
SEAT   ADJUSTABLE BACK

SWIVEL-SHELL BUCKET   SALON BUCKET SEAT
SEAT   (RECLINING BACK)

CUSTOM-COMFORT BUCKET SEAT
(RECLINING BACK AND ADJUSTABLE LOMBAR SUPPORT)

Fig. 19-18. Types of bucket seats. (*Fisher Body Division of General Motors Corporation*)

⊘ **19-11 Optional Seat Belts** The purpose of seat belts is to restrain the driver and passengers if there is an accident. During a front-end crash, for example, the car is brought to a sudden stop. But everything inside the car continues to move forward until it hits some solid object. An unrestrained passenger would continue to move forward until he or she hit the windshield or the instrument panel. It is these so-called second collisions that hurt and kill people. However, if the passengers and driver are wearing seat belts, they will be restrained. They will not continue to move forward and will not hit some solid object in the car.

There are two different kinds of seat belts, lap belts and shoulder belts. The lap belt has been credited with saving many lives and injuries. The lap belt plus the shoulder belt is even more effective. The lap belt prevents the passenger or driver from being thrown forward. The shoulder belt keeps the passenger or driver from jackknifing. That is, the upper body is kept from bending at the waist and moving forward. The driver who jackknifes is thrown into the steering shaft. A passenger who jackknifes strikes the instrument panel with his or her head.

The seat belts installed on earlier-model cars were optional: the driver and passengers did not

Car Frame and Body   285

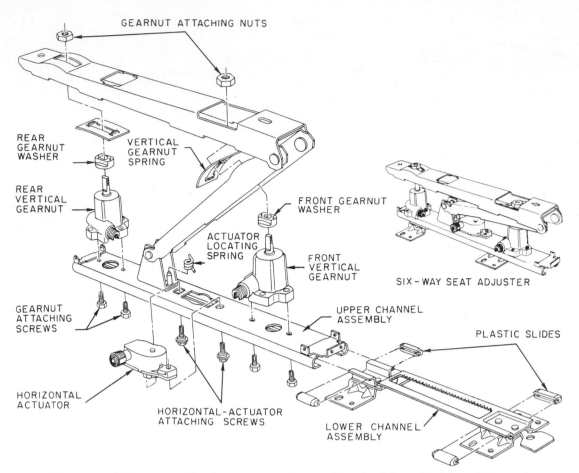

Fig. 19-19. Major parts of a six-way seat adjuster. (*Pontiac Motor Division of General Motors Corporation*)

have to use them. Then, on later-model cars, a warning buzzer was incorporated which sounded if the seat belts were not fastened. The latest arrangement is called the *seat-belt-starter interlock system*. It requires the driver and any front-seat passengers to buckle their seat belts before the engine can be started. The purpose of these devices is to urge, or require, the driver and front-seat passengers to use their seat belts, and thus protect themselves from injury or death in case the car is involved in an accident.

⊘ **19-12 Front-Seat-Belt Warning System** The front-seat-belt warning system includes a buzzer and a red warning light which remind the driver and passengers to buckle their seat belts. Figure 19-20 is a schematic drawing of the system. Figure 19-21 is a wiring diagram of the system. The reminder signals (light and buzzer) come on if the seat belts are not buckled and the driver starts the engine and then:

1. Releases the parking brake (manual transmission), or
2. Shifts into gear (automatic transmission).

The outboard seat-belt retractors have switches which are closed when the seat belts are retracted. When the seat belts are pulled out, and buckled, the

retractor switches open, thus preventing the buzzer and light from coming on.

There is a sensing switch under the passenger side of the front seat. This switch is interconnected with the right-hand seat-belt-retractor switch. The

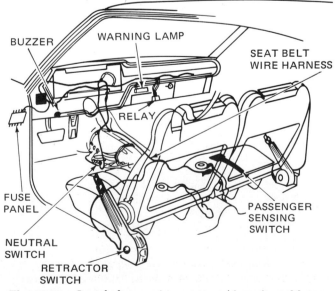

Fig. 19-20. Seat-belt warning system. (*American Motors Corporation*)

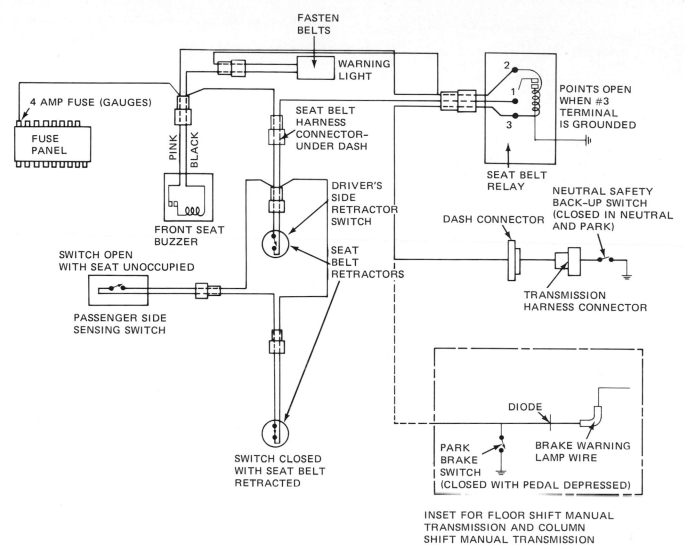

Fig. 19-21. Seat-belt warning-system wiring diagram. (*American Motors Corporation*)

sensing switch closes when a weight of more than a few pounds (a passenger) is placed on the seat. Then, if the passenger fails to buckle up, the retractor switch, also closed, completes the circuit to the buzzer and light. Now, when the driver releases the parking brake (manual transmission), or shifts into gear (automatic transmission), the reminders come on.

Some manufacturers supply adjusting information for the passenger-sensing switch. It works as follows. If the switch is too sensitive, apply your full weight on one knee directly above the sensing switch. When the cushion bottoms, the switch contacts will be bent. This should increase the amount of weight necessary to actuate the switch. Other manufacturers state that the switch should be replaced if it does not work satisfactorily.

⊘ **19-13 Seat-Belt-Starter Interlock System** The seat-belt-starter interlock system makes it necessary to buckle the front seat belts before the engine can be started. The sequence required of the driver is:

1. Get in the car and sit down.
2. Buckle the seat belt. If a passenger gets in, the passenger must also buckle up.
3. Insert the ignition key and turn the switch to START.

This is the only sequence that will start the engine. Figure 19-22 shows the parts in the system. Figure 19-23 shows how the shoulder belt, lap belt, and other parts are arranged.

If the seat belts are not buckled, or are buckled before the occupants are seated, a relay operates to activate the warning light and buzzer. The light and buzzer will also come on if any front-seat occupant unbuckles after the transmission has been shifted to a forward-drive position.

The light and buzzer will not come on if a front seat belt is unbuckled and the engine is running with the transmission in PARK or NEUTRAL (automatic and column-shift) or the parking brake is engaged (floor-shift transmission).

1. *BOUNCE* The logic module is under the front seat. It has a time delay that deactivates the interlock

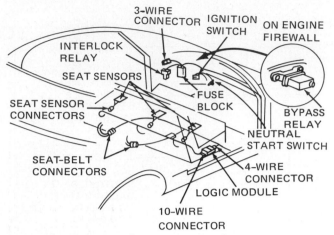

Fig. 19-22. Location of components in the seat-belt-starter interlock system. (*Chevrolet Motor Division of General Motors Corporation*)

system for a few seconds if a buckled-in occupant momentarily lifts off the seat. Without this feature, the logic module would sense that the occupant had left the car and then buckled the seat belt before being reseated; that would prevent starting. However, the time delay allows the system to ignore the momentary lifting of the occupant off the seat. But if the occupant is off the seat for more than 5 to 10 seconds, the seat belts must be unbuckled and then rebuckled before the engine will start.

2. RESTARTING Once the car has been started, if the correct sequence is followed as noted above, it can be restarted with the seat belts unbuckled as long as the driver remains seated. If the driver leaves the seat, the three-step sequence must be repeated to start the engine.

3. MECHANIC'S START The engine can be started with the seat belts in any position when the front seats are unoccupied. Simply reach inside the car and turn the ignition key to START without sitting on the front seat. The light and buzzer will come on if the front seat is then occupied and the transmission is shifted to DRIVE, but they will turn off as soon as the seat belts at the occupied positions are buckled up.

4. OVERRIDE RELAY An override, or bypass, relay is located on the firewall under the hood (Fig. 19-24). This relay can be used to start the engine when the interlock system has failed and is preventing starting. To use the relay, turn the ignition switch to ON. Then open the hood, and press and *release* the button on the relay. Holding the button in will damage the override mechanism. The engine can now be started by turning the ignition key to START. The relay will remain engaged until the ignition key is turned to OFF or LOCK.

⊘ **19-14 Seat-Belt-Starter Interlock-System Trouble Diagnosis** There are four possible troubles:

1. Starting motor will not crank the engine

2. Starting motor cranks with the seat belts unbuckled
3. Buzzer and light will not operate
4. Buzzer and light remain on

The service manuals of the automotive manufacturers supply step-by-step procedures to follow with any of these four conditions. Chrysler has developed an interlock tester which quickly checks out the system. It has a plug connector which is connected into the system. Then the tester switch is turned on, and the tester goes through an automatic testing sequence.

NOTE: Because so many people objected to the seat-belt-starter interlock system, federal law was changed so that the system is no longer required. Also, it is now legal to deactivate the system in cars now in operation.

⊘ **19-15 Body Electric Equipment** The body carries a considerable amount of wiring connecting the various electrically operated body devices. We have covered some of these—door locks, window regulators, sun-roof motors, seat adjusters, seat-belt-starter interlock systems, and so on. In addition, the body carries several lights—headlights, taillights, turn signal lights, and interior lights. Several other electrical devices include the open-door warning-buzzer system, the headlights-on warning buzzer, and the security alarm system, covered in following sections.

⊘ **19-16 Open-Door Warning-Buzzer System** The open-door warning-buzzer system operates a buzzer if the door in the driver's side is opened with the ignition key in the ignition switch. It makes no difference what position the ignition switch is in. Figure 19-25 shows the system. When the ignition key is left in the ignition switch, a warning switch, located in the ignition switch and connected to the door switch (see Fig. 19-25), is closed. Then, if the door is opened, the door switch is closed, completing the circuit to the horn relay. This relay now buzzes. The system warns the driver that the ignition key is still in the ignition switch and should be removed. An ignition key in the ignition switch of an unoccupied car is an invitation to thieves.

⊘ **19-17 Headlights-on Warning Buzzer System** The headlights-on warning-buzzer system is usually combined with the open-door warning-buzzer system (Fig. 19-26). When the headlights are on and the driver's door is open, a warning buzzer sounds. The system warns the driver to turn off the headlights before leaving the car.

⊘ **19-18 Security Alarm System** The security alarm system, shown in one version in Figs. 19-27 and 19-28 (on page 291), sounds an alarm if a thief tries

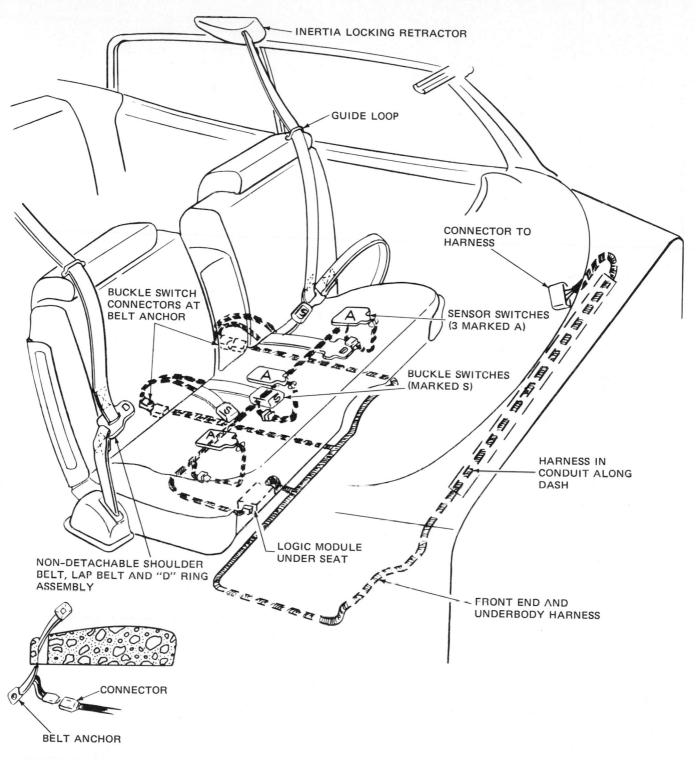

INERTIA LOCKING RETRACTOR

GUIDE LOOP

CONNECTOR TO HARNESS

BUCKLE SWITCH CONNECTORS AT BELT ANCHOR

SENSOR SWITCHES (3 MARKED A)

BUCKLE SWITCHES (MARKED S)

HARNESS IN CONDUIT ALONG DASH

LOGIC MODULE UNDER SEAT

NON-DETACHABLE SHOULDER BELT, LAP BELT AND "D" RING ASSEMBLY

FRONT END AND UNDERBODY HARNESS

CONNECTOR

BELT ANCHOR

SECTION AT BELT BUCKLE

Fig. 19-23. Location of components of the seat-belt-starter interlock system in the front-seat area. (*Fisher Body Division of General Motors Corporation*)

to force entry to any door, the hood, the trunk, or the tailgate. The alarm consists of the horn sounding at about 90 cycles per minute for 3 to 5 minutes. In addition, the headlights, taillights, and side marker lights flash on and off at the same rate.

When either front door is locked with the key, the system shown is armed: it is ready to sound the alarm if any attempt is made to force entry into the car. The system can be turned off by using the door key to unlock the door.

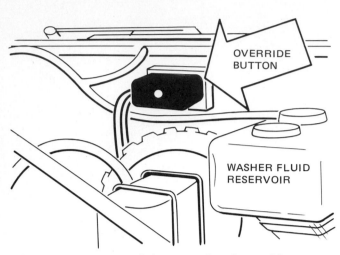

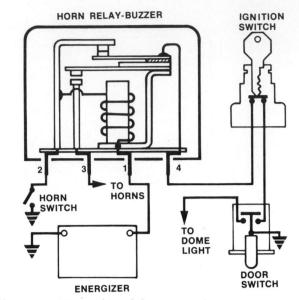

Fig. 19-24. Location of the override relay and button in the engine compartment.

Fig. 19-25. Horn relay of the type with a warning system.

⊘ **19-19 Air Bags** Air bags are a passive safety feature to protect the driver and passengers in an accident. "Passive" means that the driver and passengers do not have to do anything to be protected by the air bags. This is in contrast with seat belts, described above, that require an action—buckling up. Many people do not bother to buckle up because it is "too much trouble." As a result, there are far more highway injuries and deaths than there need be. Air-bag advocates believe that the air bag will save many lives and prevent injuries.

The principle is simple. At the instant that a

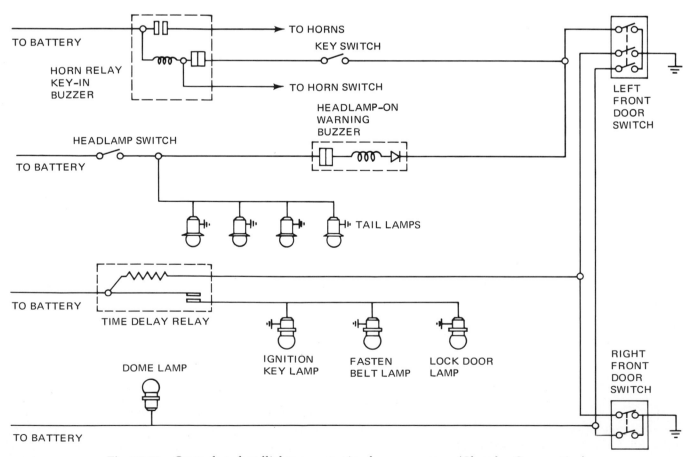

Fig. 19-26. Open-door-headlights-on warning-buzzer system. (*Chrysler Corporation*)

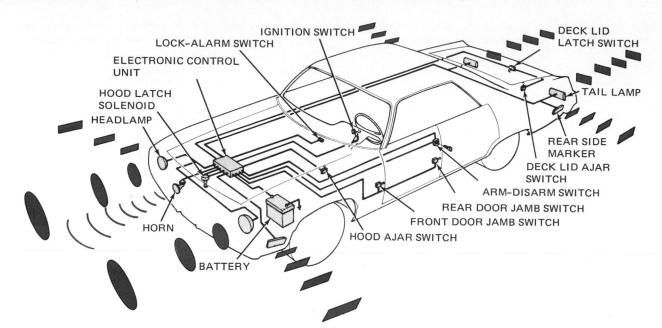

Fig. 19-27. Location of components of a security alarm system. The circles and rectangles indicate the flashing lights when the system is in action. The arcs represent the intermittent blowing of the horn. (*Chrysler Corporation*)

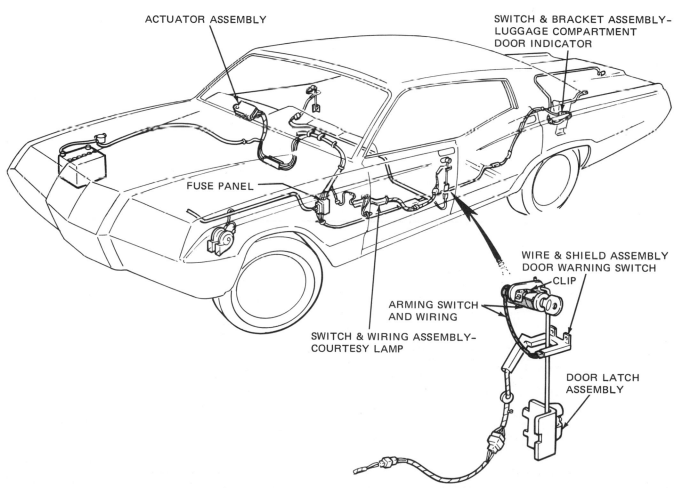

Fig. 19-28. Location of components and wiring circuit of a security or antitheft alarm system. (*Ford Motor Company*)

Car Frame and Body   291

crash occurs, the air bags are blown up. They then give the driver and passengers a cushion into which to move. The air bags absorb the forward motion of the occupants and save them from hitting anything hard that could injure them.

Figure 19-29 shows one arrangement for the passengers in the front seat. Figure 19-30 shows how the system operates. A dummy was used in this crash to show how fast the system works. At impact, the dummy is sitting back in the seat in a normal position. At $\frac{1}{30}$ second after the crash starts (upper right in Fig. 19-30), the air-bag system has actuated. The bag is already pushing out from its position in the instrument panel.

The system is actuated by a bumper detector. This detector contains a switch that is closed when the car is suddenly decelerated (when it is brought to a quick stop in an accident). When the switch closes, the air-vessel-and-inflater assembly is actuated (see Fig. 19-29). The air vessel is filled with compressed gas. When it is actuated, this gas is released, and it flows into the air bag. The action is almost instantaneous. Now see 3 at the lower left in Fig. 19-31. This is the condition $\frac{2}{30}$ second after

impact. Note that the air bag is almost fully inflated, and that the dummy has moved forward into the air bag. In 4 (lower right in Fig. 19-30), the dummy is all the way forward into the air bag. Now, a fraction of a second later, when the force of the dummy's forward motion has been completely absorbed, the air bag begins to deflate through relief holes. This quick deflation, after the air bag has done its job, permits the passenger to get out of the car.

The air-bag on the driver's side is located in the steering wheel. Figure 19-31 shows the complete system for the driver and passengers, and Fig. 19-32 shows the air bag inflated. Figure 19-33 shows the action with a dummy occupying the driver's seat. The times between the four parts of the picture, showing the inflation of the air bag and the forward motion of the dummy, are approximately the same as in Fig. 19-30.

⊘ **19-20 Energy-absorbing Bumpers** The energy-absorbing bumper is required by law on late-model cars. It will withstand collisions at low speed without damage to the bumper or car. Further, most of these bumpers resume their original position after

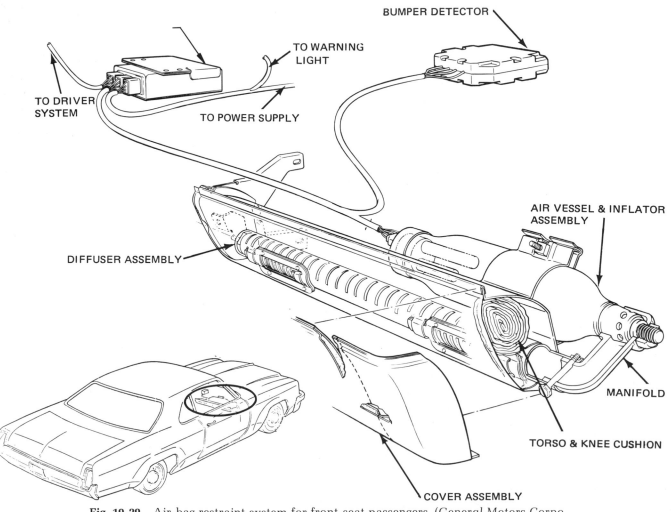

Fig. 19-29. Air-bag restraint system for front-seat passengers. (*General Motors Corporation*)

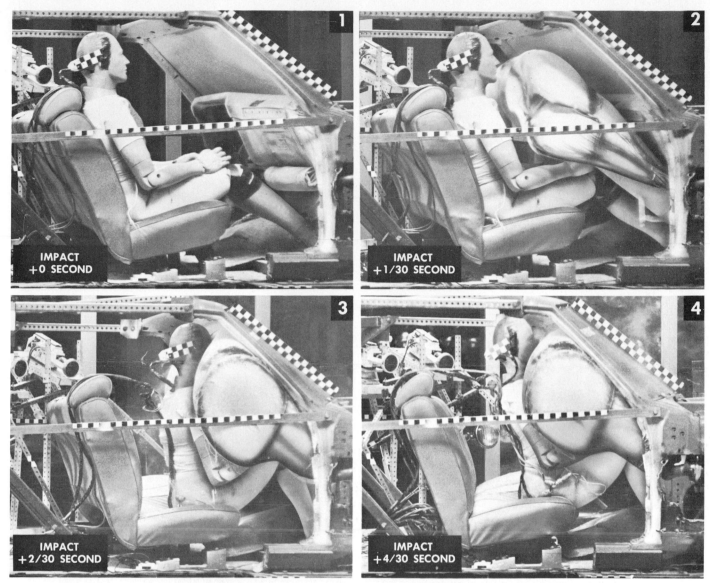

Fig. 19-30. Air-bag operation in a simulated front-end crash, using a test dummy in the passenger's seat. The entire sequence shown took place in $^4/_{30}$ second. (*General Motors Corporation*)

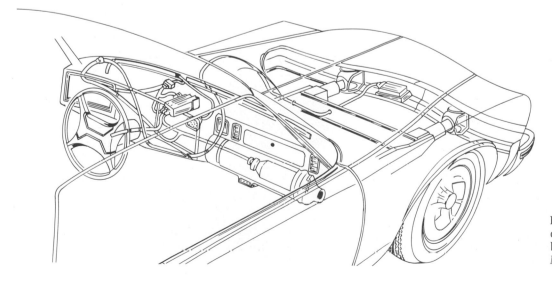

Fig. 19-31. Locations of components in an air-bag system. (*General Motors Corporation*)

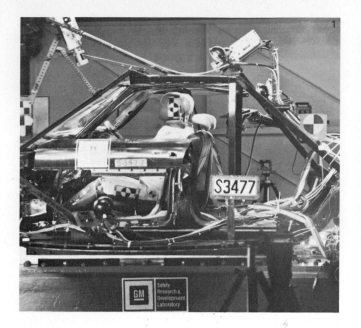

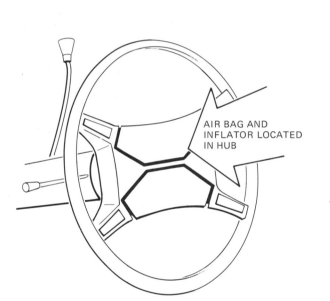

AIR BAG AND
INFLATOR LOCATED
IN HUB

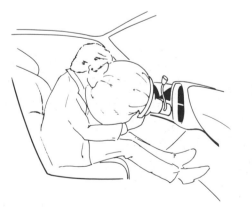

DRIVER'S AIR BAG

Fig. 19-32. Location of the air bag in the steering wheel. The lower picture shows the action when the air bag is inflated and the driver is thrown forward into it. (*General Motors Corporation*)

Fig. 19-33. Air-bag operation in a simulated front-end crash, using a test dummy in the driver's seat. (*General Motors Corporation*)

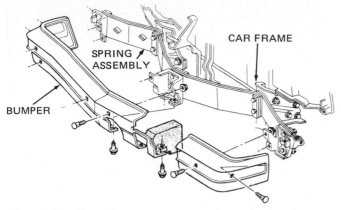

Fig. 19-34. Front-bumper system using a leaf-spring assembly to absorb the energy of a front-end impact. (*Chevrolet Motor Division of General Motors Corporation*)

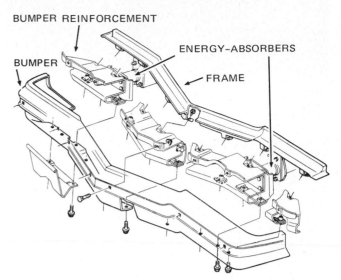

Fig. 19-36. Location of components in a front-bumper system using two energy absorbers of the shock-absorber type. (*Chevrolet Motor Division of General Motors Corporation*)

the collision. There are several types, used at both the front and the rear of late-model cars. One uses a leaf-spring assembly which supports the bumper as shown in Fig. 19-34. On impact, the spring gives and absorbs the blow. It then returns to its original position, if the impact was within the designed limits. If the impact was greater than the designed limits, damage may have occurred and repair may be required.

A second type uses a pair of special bolts and two bolt dies (Fig. 19-35). The dies are steel rings having an inner diameter smaller than the energy-absorbing bolts. During impact, the dies are pushed along the bolts. This action reduces the diameter of the special energy-absorbing bolts. In the system shown, the bolt diameters are reduced from 0.33

inch [8.38 mm] to 0.31 inch [7.87 mm]. The bolts are elongated about 1 inch [25.4 mm] during an impact that moves the bumper 3½ inches [88.9 mm]. If the impact is severe enough to elongate the bolts, the energy-absorbing-bolt assembly, dies, and related parts must be replaced. If the impact was greater than the designated limit of the system, other damage may have occurred which would require repair.

A third type of energy-absorbing bumper uses a pair of energy absorbers that are like shock absorbers. Figure 19-36 shows how the two absorbers are located between the frame and the bumper reinforcement. During a front-end impact, the energy absorbers shorten, just like telescope-type shock absorbers. Following the impact, if the impact is not beyond the designed limits of the energy absorbers, they return to their original length.

Figure 19-37 is an external view of an energy absorber. Figure 19-38 is a sectional view of the energy absorber in its normal extended position. Figure 19-39 shows the absorber action. At the top, the absorber is shown in the extended position at

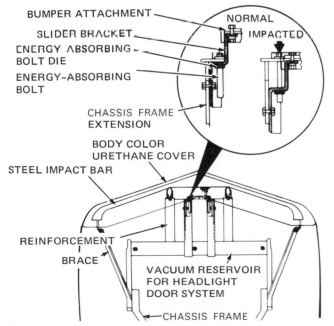

Fig. 19-35. Front-bumper system using a pair of special bolts and dies. The dies draw the bolts to a smaller diameter to absorb the energy of a front-end impact. (*Chevrolet Motor Division of General Motors Corporation*)

Fig. 19-37. Energy absorber. (*Chevrolet Motor Division of General Motors Corporation*)

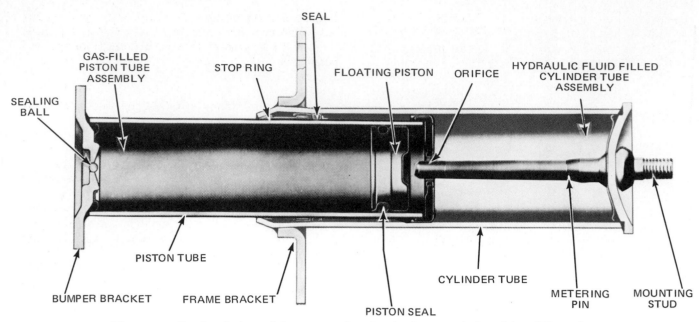

Fig. 19-38. Sectional view of the energy absorber in the extended position. (*Chevrolet Motor Division of General Motors Corporation*)

the start of impact. The impact forces the piston tube to the right (in Fig. 19-39). This action forces the hydraulic fluid to flow around the metering pin and through the orifice in the end of the piston tube. As the piston tube continues to move, the flow of hydraulic fluid into the piston tube pushes the floating piston to the left (in Fig. 19-39). This compresses the gas in the piston tube, as shown in the bottom picture.

At the conclusion of the impact, if it was within the designed limits, the compressed gas forces the piston tube out again to its original position. If the impact was greater than the designed limits of the system, damage may have occurred which would require repair work.

An energy absorber of a somewhat different design is shown in Fig. 19-40. The main difference

is that the energy absorber described above depends on a chamber filled with high-pressure gas for its action. But the unit shown in Fig. 19-40 uses a heavy return spring. In this design, when bumper impact loads reach about 10,000 pounds [4,535.9 kg], a valve in the absorber opens, allowing the hydraulic fluid to be forced through a set of small holes. Then, after the impact, if it caused no structural damage, the spring pushes the two ends of the absorber apart so they return to the normal condition.

⊘ **19-21 Servicing the Gas-filled Energy Absorber**
The gas-filled energy absorber is shown in Figs. 19-36 to 19-39. It is serviced by unit replacement. If a unit is to be scrapped, the internal gas pressure must be released as explained below.

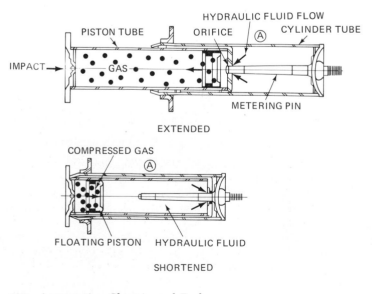

Fig. 19-39. Operation of the energy absorber during a front-end impact. *Top:* Action at the start of impact; the piston tube starts to enter the cylinder tube, and hydraulic fluid flows through the orifice. *Bottom:* The piston tube has reached the inner limit of motion; hydraulic fluid has flowed through the orifice, forcing the floating piston to compress the gas. (*General Motors Corporation*)

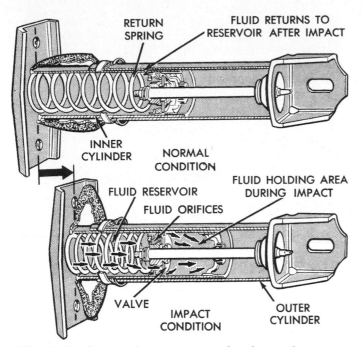

Fig. 19-40. Bumper-impact energy absorber with spring return. (*Chrysler Corporation*)

CAUTION: The energy absorber contains gas at high pressure. Under no conditions should you attempt to repair, weld, or apply heat to the unit. This could cause the unit to explode.

To relieve the gas pressure, put the energy absorber in a vise. Drill a small hole in the piston tube, as shown in Fig. 19-41. Use the caution label as a locator for drilling. Drill either in front of or through the label.

Fig. 19-41. Drilling a hole in the piston tube to relieve the gas pressure before discarding a defective energy absorber. (*Chevrolet Motor Division of General Motors Corporation*)

CAUTION: Wear safety glasses when drilling the hole. The gas, when released, can drive metal chips at high speed. One of these could enter an eye and put it out.

1. HANDLING THE BOUND-UP ENERGY ABSORBER When an energy absorber is bound up as a result of a collision, extra care must be used to remove it from the vehicle.

a. Stand clear of the bumper.

b. Use a chain or cable to apply positive restraint to the energy absorber, so it will not suddenly return to the original length.

c. Drill a small hole in the piston tube near the bumper bracket to relieve the gas pressure.

d. After the gas has escaped, remove the absorber from the vehicle.

2. CHECKING THE ENERGY ABSORBER ON THE CAR First examine it for leakage around the seal between the cylinder tube and the piston tube. A stain or trace of oil on the piston tube near the seal is normal. But if oil is dripping continuously from the seal or stud end of the unit, it should be replaced.

Examine the bumper bracket, piston tube, frame bracket, and cylinder tube for evidence of visible distortion. Scuffing of the piston tube, if the unit has been stroked, is considered normal. If there is obvious damage, the unit and associated damaged parts should be replaced.

The energy absorbers can be checked on the car. Each unit should be checked separately. The test is made with the engine not running, the transmission in PARK, the parking-brake set, and a brake-applying tool holding the service brakes. Any suitable barrier can be used, such as a pillar, wall, or post. Then install a device that can apply pressure. Apply pressure to see if the energy absorber will move in ⅜ inch [9.5 mm] or more. Then, when the pressure is released, the bumper should return to its original position. The pressure device can be a hydraulic or mechanical jack. Pressure must be applied squarely to the bumper to avoid slippage.

CAUTION: Driving into a post, wall, or other barrier to perform the test is not recommended.

3. CHECKING THE ENERGY ABSORBER ON THE BENCH A bench check can be made in a suitable arbor press. The unit should compress at least ⅜ inch [9.5 mm] and return to its normal length when the pressure is released. If it does not, discard the unit.

⊘ **19-22 Body Service** When you consider the variety of electrical and mechanical devices installed as part of the vehicle body, you realize that the auto-body technician has to be very versatile. Auto-body work includes not only handling the servicing of everything we have mentioned so far, but also sheet-metal and plastic work, painting, and glass replacement. Sometimes, scratches in glass can be polished

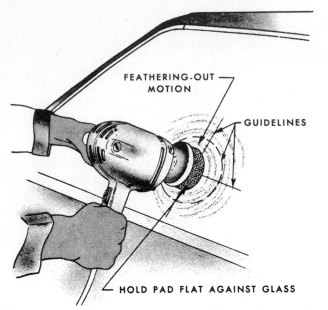

Fig. 19-42. Removing a minor scratch from glass. (*Fisher Body Division of General Motors Corporation*)

out with a special compound on a felt pad driven by a low-speed rotary polisher (Fig. 19-42).

⊘ **19-23 Glass Replacement** Fixed glass is held in place by synthetic self-curing rubber adhesive materials, or butyl tape. If fixed glass has to be replaced, the adhesive materials may or may not require replacement also. Where the original adhesive material remains on the body flange and appears in good condition, it can serve as a base for the new glass. But if the body is to be repainted, extensive metal work is required, or the original adhesive has lost its adhesion, new adhesive material must be used when the new glass is installed. The old glass can be removed by pulling a length of steel music wire along the edges of the glass (Fig. 19-43). This cuts

Fig. 19-43. Cutting adhesive in which glass is set with steel music wire. (*Fisher Body Division of General Motors Corporation*)

the adhesive so the glass can be taken out. If the glass is large, use rubber suction cups to handle it.

In preparation for installing the new glass, replace or reshape retaining clips as necessary. If the old adhesive has been removed, apply a bead of new adhesive. Prepare the glass for installation by cleaning it. Then apply a primer around the edges of the glass, ¼ inch [6.35 mm] in from the edge, on both sides. After 5 minutes, apply a continuous bead of adhesive over the entire inside edge of the glass where it was primed. Lift the glass into place, carefully centering it in the opening. Press the glass firmly down to provide a good seal. Avoid excessive squeeze out. If necessary, paddle additional adhesive into areas that do not seem to have enough.

Water-test the seal immediately with a soft, warm spray. If leaks show up, paddle in extra adhesive material. Cement a rubber spacer on both right and left sides of the glass to the body metal to ensure that the glass will stay put. Allow it to cure for 6 hours at room temperature.

Window glass can be replaced by detaching it from the regulator arms and installing new glass. The new glass may require adjustment, as previously mentioned (⊘ 19-5).

⊘ **19-24 Body Repair** If the body has been twisted or crushed but is still in good enough general condition to warrant repair, the first step is usually to straighten it. Figure 19-44 shows the use of hydraulic jacks to straighten the body.

When metal panels have been dented or distorted, they can be straightened and refinished (if the proper tools are available). If the damage is severe, the old panel can be removed and a new panel welded into place.

A variety of tools are available to remove dents from body panels (Fig. 19-45). The simplest are hammers and dolly blocks. Dolly blocks are steel blocks of various shapes and contours that are held on one side of the distorted panel while the other side is pounded with a hammer.

Air-driven body and fender reshapers are available which quickly and easily straighten out dents in body or fender panels. The reshaper consists of a pair of dolly blocks attached to a frame. The upper dolly block is operated by air as an air hammer, and the lower dolly block pivots on the frame to maintain alignment with the other block. When the two dolly blocks are placed on the two sides of a distorted panel and the air hammer is operated, the panel is quickly flattened out. Dolly blocks of various contours are available to fit different fender and body contours.

The hot-shrinkage technique is useful in straightening out panels with large dents. When distortion has taken place—for example, when a dent has been made in a panel—the metal has been stretched, and it must be shrunk to bring it back into shape. The hot-shrinkage method makes use of the fact that application of heat and then cold to the panel will cause the metal to contract, or shrink.

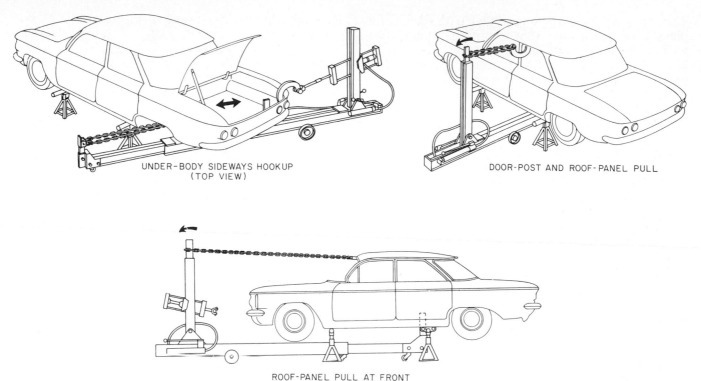

UNDER-BODY SIDEWAYS HOOKUP
(TOP VIEW)

DOOR-POST AND ROOF-PANEL PULL

ROOF-PANEL PULL AT FRONT

Fig. 19-44. Using a hydraulic jack and special straightening equipment to straighten the body. (*Bear Manufacturing Company*)

This method requires a rawhide or wood mallet, a special shrinking dolly block, and an acetylene torch.

The first step in hot shrinking is to rough out the dented section so that it bulges outward above the normal curvature of the surface. This operation can be accomplished with dolly block and a hammer. Then a small section in the center of the bulge is heated to a cherry-red color with the acetylene torch. Excessive temperature should be avoided, since this would make the metal brittle. When the spot reaches a cherry-red heat, place the shrinking dolly block under the hot spot and use the hammer to pound the outside surface of the heated spot down onto the low-crown surface of the shrinking dolly block. Only a few blows will be required.

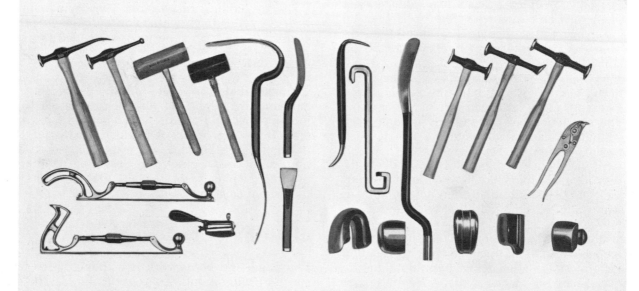

Fig. 19-45. Set of body tools including hammers, spoons, file holders, and dolly blocks. (*Kent-Moore Corporation*)

Then, quickly take a sponge filled with water and place it on the heated spot to cool it. This causes a decided shrinking of the metal sheet. The pounding and quenching must be performed quickly. Repeat this action of heating, pounding, and quenching over the entire surface of the bulge, but do not overlap the areas. Work from the center out. The bulge will be brought down to proper contour by this action. It will, however, be rough and will require further attention with a dolly block and a hammer before it is ready for finishing work.

When a body panel has been dented in not too deeply and without too much irregularity, it is sometimes possible to remove the dent without working from the inside. A piece of welding rod is welded to the center of the dent and formed into a handle, and the dent is pulled out while heat is applied with the torch. The welding rod is then cut off close to the body and the remaining stub driven in, level with the panel. The small remaining cavity can then be filled with surfacing material or solder, as explained below, and sanded smooth.

After a panel surface has been restored to its natural contour, rough places must be filed or sanded off. Shops doing considerable body work have power-driven sanders. The sanding disk can be changed for a buffing wheel for finish work.

If the panel surface is excessively rough, with deep file marks or gouges, a special surfacing material can be used to fill the gouges. This material will bond to the metal surface and can be sanded smooth. Paddle soldering also can be used where the marks or gouges are quite deep. To paddle-solder a surface, first clean it with muriatic acid to remove all paint and oil and then heat it with the acetylene torch. Apply solder and smooth with a wooden paddle or with rags. This not only fills deep gouges but will also fill small dents. Sand off roughness.

As an alternate to the above panel- and fender-repair procedure, a special plastic-type substance—supplied in rolls and somewhat like cloth—can be used for repairing these body parts. Unroll the substance and cut it with knife or scissors to fit the repair and then dip it into a special liquid. Next, apply it to the cleaned and sanded surface to be repaired and mold it by hand into approximately the original contour of the damaged surface. After a few hours, the substance has set and has become very hard and tough. It can then be sanded to a final finish and painted just as though it were metal.

If new panels are welded into place, the weld marks will stand up above the natural body contour. These weld marks should be driven below the contour surface and the channel filled with solder.

⊘ **19-25 Body Painting**   Before repainting a repaired panel, wash off all trace of soldering flux and then wash the panel with a metal conditioner. Before a body is painted, all traces of rust or scaling paint must be sanded off so that either well-bonded paint or the metal is exposed. First spray a primer coat on with a spray gun (Fig. 19-46); follow this with a

Fig. 19-46.   Spray gun for applying paint to a car body. (*Alexander Milburn Company*)

finish coat. Two general types of finish materials are used in the auto-body shop, lacquer and enamel. Enamel can be of the air-drying type or it can be baking enamel. Baking enamel is baked, after it is sprayed on, by application of heat; infrared lamps may be used for this purpose.

Where a shop has a special car-painting department that handles a number of cars each day, a special paint booth is required (Fig. 19-47). Note that this is an enclosed booth consisting of two compartments, the spray-painting enclosure and the drying chamber. Filtered and heated air enters to replace the air taken out by the spray-booth exhaust system. This protects the freshly painted car from dust particles that could ruin the job. The drying chamber has a traveling oven which can be moved from one section of the car to the next as needed to dry the paint.

⊘ **19-26 Fiberglass and Urethane Panels**   The amount of fiberglass in car bodies varies from a minor panel to a complete car body. Many panels are also being made of molded urethane. These panels are flexible and cannot be painted with lacquer as it would crack off. Servicing of fiberglass or urethane panels is a specialty that requires particular chemicals and paints.

CHAPTER 19 CHECKUP

Car frame and body work is a specialty for which specific training and tools are required. The body mechanic usually devotes full time to body repair and does not engage in other repair or servicing activities. Nevertheless, the mechanic with a well-

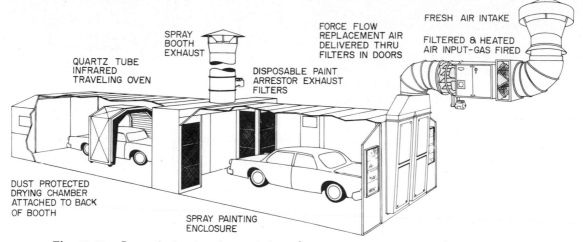

Fig. 19-47. Car-painting booth consisting of two compartments, one for painting the car and the other for drying the paint. (*Ford Motor Company*)

rounded education in the field of automotive techniques should have an understanding of how body-repair work is done. The chapter you have just completed gives you a brief introduction to the subject. The checkup that follows covers high points of the chapter. When you take the test, you will review these high points and at the same time find out how well you remember them.

Completing the Sentences   The sentences below are incomplete. After each sentence there are several words or phrases, only one of which will correctly complete the sentence. Write each sentence in your notebook, selecting the proper word or phrase to complete it correctly.

1. A rather complete check of frame alignment can be made with a: (*a*) frame gauge, (*b*) tram gauge, (*c*) carpenter's level, (*d*) carpenter's square.
2. The preferred method of replacing frame members is the: (*a*) hot-riveting method, (*b*) cold-riveting method, (*c*) welding method.
3. To improve the fit of an undistorted door, move it up and down, or back and forth, after loosening the: (*a*) frame bracket screws, (*b*) hinge-attaching screws, (*c*) window-regulator screws.
4. The steel block held on one side of a distorted panel while the other side is struck with a hammer is called a: (*a*) body block, (*b*) reshaper, (*c*) dolly block.
5. Where the metal in a panel has been stretched, it can be shrunk to bring it back into shape by the: (*a*) hot-shrinkage method, (*b*) cold-shrinkage method, (*c*) paddle-soldering method.
6. Two general types of body-finish paint are: (*a*) masking and enamel, (*b*) lead-base and enamel, (*c*) enamel and lacquer.
7. The latest seat-belt system is the: (*a*) seat-belt warning system, (*b*) air-bag system, (*c*) seat-belt starter interlock system.

8. During a front-end crash, the air bags will inflate in: (*a*) a few seconds, (*b*) a small fraction of a second, (*c*) around a minute.
9. Two types of energy absorbers for front bumpers are: (*a*) air-filled and gas-filled, (*b*) gas-filled and spring-return, (*c*) coil-spring and electric.
10. Devices that may be included in doors are window regulators, cigarette lighters, rearview mirror, and: (*a*) lid support, (*b*) locks, (*c*) spring-loaded raiser.

Servicing Procedures   Write in your notebook the procedures asked for below. Don't copy from the book; explain the procedures in your own words, just as you would to a friend.

1. Explain how to check frame alignment, and list important points to watch when straightening or replacing a frame member.
2. What are some important points the body designer must keep in mind?
3. Explain how to improve the fit of a door that is not distorted; a door that is distorted.
4. Explain how to check and correct body alignment with a measuring bar and body jack.
5. Explain how to use the hot-shrinkage method to bring a body panel back into shape.

SUGGESTIONS FOR FURTHER STUDY

There are many books devoted exclusively to frame and body repair and painting. If you are especially interested in this subject, you may find one or more of these books at your local public or school library. You can also purchase these books from your local bookstore. If you have a chance, you can spend some time at a local body shop, watching the body mechanics at work repairing and repainting bodies. Be sure you write important facts in your notebook.

chapter 20

AIR CONDITIONING

This chapter discusses the theory of refrigeration and air conditioning and the construction and operation of the air-conditioning equipment used in automobiles. Chapter 21 discusses the servicing and repair of this equipment.

⊘ **20-1 Air Conditioning** An air conditioner does two things when it "conditions," or treats, the air: (1) it takes heat from the air (by refrigeration), thus lowering the temperature of the air; and (2) it takes moisture from the air, thus drying the air. The air conditioner both cools and dries the air.

Air conditioners have been used for many years in public buildings, theaters, restaurants, and homes. A few installations of air-conditioning equipment were made on passenger cars a number of years ago. But only recently have the major car companies made air conditioning generally available, as accessory equipment, on their cars.

The terms "refrigeration" and "air conditioning" sound rather formidable. Of course, there is a lot of science and engineering behind them, but in essence they are not hard to understand. All of us are familiar with electric refrigerators. We see them in our homes, in restaurants, food stores, soda fountains, and so on. An air conditioner is nothing more than a refrigerator with an air-circulating system. But before we talk about the air-circulating system, let us discuss refrigerators.

⊘ **20-2 Methods of Cooling** If you hold a piece of ice in your hand, your hand gets cold. This is because the ice takes heat from your hand. Likewise, if you put a liquid such as water or alcohol on your hand, and then blow on it, your hand feels cold. Why? Because the liquid evaporates and removes heat from your hand. In the same way, when we are hot and perspire, the perspiration evaporates and removes heat from our body so that we are cooled.

Thus, to cool an object, you remove heat from it.

1. *COOLING BY EVAPORATION* We noted, in ⊘ 1-10, that heat, or the temperature of an object, is nothing more or less than the speed of molecular motion. When the molecules that make up an object move fast, the object is hot. When the molecules move slowly, the object is cold. In ice, the molecules

are moving rather slowly and in restricted paths. They "hang together," so ice is a solid. But if the ice is heated, it melts; the molecules move faster and break out of their restricted paths, and the ice turns into water. Further heating causes the water to boil. As this happens, the molecules are set into such fast motion that they "jump" clear of the water: the water turns to vapor.

When you put a liquid on your hand, it begins to evaporate; that is, the molecules forming the liquid begin to leave your hand. To jump clear, however, they must be moving rather fast. They cannot, of themselves, suddenly "decide" to begin moving fast. They must be given a push. This push comes from the molecules of the skin. The skin molecules are moving, too. Liquid molecules and skin molecules, both in motion, are constantly colliding. During such collisions, the skin molecules are slowed down and the liquid molecules are speeded up. This speeding up gives the liquid molecules enough velocity to allow them to jump clear: the liquid evaporates. But note that the skin molecules are slowed down. This means that the skin is cooled (slower molecular motion means a lower temperature).

2. *COOLING BY MELTING* When a solid is turned into a liquid, a cooling effect results. Ice, for example, is widely used as a cooling agent. When ice melts, as in a refrigerator, it takes heat away from the surrounding air, thus cooling the contents of the refrigerator. In the solid, ice, the molecules are moving slowly. But as the solid turns to liquid, the molecules move much more rapidly. This speedup must come from the air molecules around the ice; as the air molecules and ice molecules collide, the air molecules are slowed down and the ice molecules speeded up. In other words, the air is cooled and the ice is warmed. When the ice molecules are sufficiently speeded up, they break out of their restricted paths; the ice melts, or turns to water. This change of state (from solid to liquid) has a big cooling effect, since the air molecules lose a great deal of their velocity as they collide with the ice molecules.

Remember, cooling means that the molecules are slowed down.

⊘ 20-3 More on Evaporation

Since the refrigeration devices used in home refrigerators and car air conditioners operate on the principle of evaporation of a liquid, let us talk some more about evaporation. If you filled a glass of water and then watched it for a day or two, you would notice that the water level would gradually drop as the water evaporated. You could speed up the evaporation by applying heat to the water. When you apply heat, you speed up the molecular movement. The molecules become more lively; more of them "jump" clear and escape from the glass. If you heated the water to 212 degrees Fahrenheit [100°C] (at sea level), it would begin to boil; that is, the water molecules would begin to move so rapidly that the water would be violently agitated and the evaporation would go on at a lively rate.

You could also speed up evaporation by placing the glass of water in a vacuum. A vacuum is, as you will recall from ⊘ 1-6, an absence of air or other substance. During evaporation of water, as noted above, water molecules are constantly gaining enough speed to leave the water. With air above the water, some of the water molecules will collide with air molecules and, in effect, will be knocked back into the water (Fig. 20-1). But this would not occur if the air were removed from above the water. With the air removed, evaporation of the water would thus be speeded up.

Air can be removed from around the glass of water by sealing it into a jar (Fig. 20-2) and using a vacuum pump (⊘ 1-7) to draw the air from the jar. When this happens, the water begins to evaporate more rapidly. Soon, however, if the vacuum pump stops, the rate of evaporation slows down again. The reason is that the space around the glass

Fig. 20-2. Glass of water sealed into a glass jar. When air is pumped out of the jar, water evaporation increases.

becomes partly filled with water molecules. These free water molecules collide with molecules leaving the surface of the water, knocking some of them back into the water. After a time, the space will become so saturated, or filled, with water molecules that for every molecule leaving the water, another molecule gets knocked back into the water. In other words, evaporation, in effect, ceases.

But if the vacuum pump is started again, the free water molecules will be pumped out and evaporation will start once again.

Thus, evaporation of a liquid depends not only on the heat that goes into the liquid but also on the amount of pressure, or vacuum, above the liquid. When there is a high vacuum, there are few free molecules to block the escape of molecules from the liquid. But as vacuum decreases, more free molecules are present to block the escape of molecules from the liquid.

⊘ 20-4 Effect of Pressure on Evaporation

If we reversed the vacuum pump, and pumped free water molecules back into the sealed jar, we would create a pressure in the jar. This would produce a very curious result. For, under the proper conditions of increased pressure, water molecules would be forced *back into* the glass of water. Here is how that could happen. We pump free water molecules into the sealed jar. There are thus many water molecules moving about in the jar. Many collisions take place and, as a result, more water molecules get knocked *back into* the glass of water than leave the glass of water.

Actually, under such conditions, water would condense all over the inside surface of the jar and all over the glass itself. The water molecules would become so crowded (as more and more were pumped into the jar) that collisions would be more frequent. Soon molecules would begin to stick together in clumps (driven together by the collisions). These clumps would form the beads of condensed water on the inside surfaces of the jar.

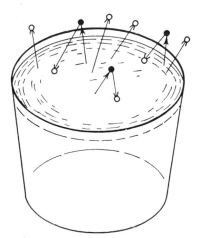

Fig. 20-1. Glass of water illustrating evaporation. The molecules of water (hollow circles) and the molecules of air (solid circles) are shown enormously enlarged. Molecules of water that collide with molecules of air may be "bounced" back into the water.

20-5 Heat and Pressure One more thing must be considered—the heat resulting from the increased pressure. We have already noted, in ⊘ 1-10 and 1-11, that increasing the pressure increases the heat. Whenever a gas—such as air or water vapor—is subjected to pressure, the molecules are moved closer together. More molecular collisions take place; the molecules are set into faster motion by these more frequent collisions. (Faster motion means higher temperature.) Thus, in the experiment described in the previous section, we would find that the temperature in the sealed jar would increase. The water molecules are set into fast motion. The walls of the jar are bombarded by these fast-moving molecules of water vapor. Thus, the molecules of the substance composing the jar are bombarded into faster motion, and the jar begins to get hot. However, there is air outside the jar. The air molecules, as they move about, come into contact with the outer surface of the jar. The jar molecules have been set into fast motion; they, in turn, set the air molecules into fast motion.

Now, what have we said? We have said that heat is produced inside the jar by compressing water vapor in the jar. Part of this heat passes to the jar itself. Then heat passes from the jar to the surrounding air. All this was described in terms of molecular motion in the previous paragraph.

Since the jar is cooler than the compressed water vapor, water molecules are slowed down as they strike the inner surface of the jar. In fact, many are slowed down so much that they are no longer vapor: they are water. Thus, water condenses on the inside of the jar, as mentioned above.

NOTE: The above discussion on heat and heat transfer is only part of the story. Heat also is transferred by radiation, which is movement of heat energy. Any modern physics textbook contains information on this subject.

20-6 Condensation Water may also condense on any cold surface. For example, all of us have seen moisture condense on the outside of a glass of ice water. On a damp day, so much water will condense that it will run off the glass. The same thing is happening here as that mentioned in the previous section. Water molecules in the air strike the cold surface of the glass. The water molecules give up part of their speed of motion (part of their heat) to the cold, or slow-moving, glass molecules. In giving up some of their speed of motion, they are slowed down so much that they cannot "get away" from the surface of the glass. Thus, water molecules collect on the cold surface of the glass. In other words, water condenses on the glass.

20-7 Boiling Points Water boils at 212 degrees Fahrenheit [100°C] at sea level. At higher altitudes, where the atmospheric pressure is lower (⊘ 1-5), the boiling point is also lower. Thus, water will boil at

187 degrees Fahrenheit [86.1°C] on the top of Pikes Peak, a mountain in Colorado that is 14,108 feet [4,300 m] high. The reason is that at the lower pressure there are fewer air molecules to knock water molecules back into the water. Water molecules can escape more easily (water can boil at a lower temperature). The lower the air pressure on the water, the lower the temperature at which the water boils.

Normally, we tend to think of a boiling liquid as being hot. This is only natural, since we boil water every day and, to us, boiling water is *hot*. However, many liquids boil at temperatures we would consider very cold. For instance, sulfur dioxide (SO_2) boils at a temperature of 14 degrees Fahrenheit [−10°C] at sea level. Below that temperature it is a liquid. If the pressure is reduced, its boiling point is lowered.

Pure ammonia (not the diluted ammonia used in households) boils at a temperature of −28 degrees Fahrenheit [−33°C], or 28 degrees Fahrenheit *below zero* (at atmospheric pressure). Another substance with a low boiling point is Freon-12, or dichlorodifluoromethane. It boils at −22 degrees Fahrenheit [−30°C] (at atmospheric pressure). We mention Freon-12 because it is the substance, the liquid, used in many refrigerators and in automobile air conditioners. It is called a *refrigerant*. Any substance used in a refrigerator to produce the cooling effect through a cycle of evaporation and condensation (as explained below) is called a refrigerant.

20-8 Refrigeration We have now covered the fundamentals of refrigeration. All we have to do is to put those fundamentals together to learn how a modern electric refrigerator operates. In learning this, we shall also learn how the car air conditioner works. The refrigerating unit in an automobile air conditioner works in exactly the same way as an electric refrigerator. There is only one additional device in the conditioner to circulate the air.

20-9 A Simple Refrigerator We could make a simple refrigerator that would work for a short time by putting a jug of refrigerant such as Freon-12 in the top of a closed compartment (Fig. 20-3). Note that the mouth of the jug is outside the cabinet, or refrigerating compartment. Since the Freon-12 boils at −22 degrees Fahrenheit [−30°C], as already noted, it will begin to boil as soon as it is put into the refrigerating compartment. The boiling action removes heat from the refrigerating compartment, since, as explained above, when a liquid is changed to a vapor, it absorbs heat. The only place the boiling Freon-12 can obtain heat is from the refrigerating compartment. It therefore cools this compartment by removing heat from it. The refrigerating action will continue as long as there is any refrigerant left to evaporate from the jug.

The refrigerator in Fig. 20-3 obviously has several drawbacks. In the first place, it is wasteful to let all the refrigerant escape. It is expensive and,

Fig. 20-3. A simple refrigerator. Evaporation of Freon-12 removes heat from the cabinet.

besides, it might be dangerous to have refrigerant gases floating freely about the house. Furthermore, since the Freon-12 boils at −22 degrees Fahrenheit [−30°C], it would try to pull everything in the refrigerating compartment down to this temperature, so all the food would be frozen.

To eliminate these drawbacks, actual refrigerators use the same refrigerant over and over again, taking the gas, or vapor, and turning it into liquid again. The liquid is then put back into the "jug" so that it can boil away once more. This is a more or less continuous action, controlled so that the refrigerant will not boil away too rapidly and thus cool the refrigerator too much.

⊘ **20-10 Refrigerator Operation** To provide continued use of the refrigerant, and also to control it so that the proper temperature will be maintained, a closed refrigerating system is used (Fig. 20-4). The "jug," or evaporator, is inside the refrigerator cabinet. It is connected by two tubes to a pumping mechanism driven by an electric motor (the pumping mechanism is driven by the engine in an automobile). There is also a temperature control inside the cabinet. The control has a set of contact points that close when the temperature goes too high. As this happens, the motor circuit is closed so that the motor starts and drives the pump and fan.

When the pump starts, it produces a partial vacuum in the upper part of the evaporator, and thus pumps off evaporated refrigerant. This reduces the pressure above the liquid refrigerant. The refrigerant therefore begins to boil. As it boils, it removes heat from the refrigerator cabinet. The vaporizing refrigerant is continually pumped from the evaporator, thereby maintaining the low pressure which permits the refrigerant to continue to boil. So long as the pump is working, it continues to remove

evaporated refrigerant, and thus heat, from the evaporator.

In the pump, the vapor is compressed, or put under pressure. Actually, the pressure may approach 200 psi [14.06 kg/cm^2]. This high pressure "pushes" the molecules close together. They are set into violent motion by the increased number of collisions. In other words, the vapor temperature is increased; it may go well above 100 degrees Fahrenheit [37.8°C]. The hot, compressed vapor then passes from the pump into the condenser. The condenser is a long tube, usually equipped with radiating fins or plates. As the hot vapor enters the tube, it begins to cool off (to transfer some of its heat—molecular motion—to the tube and radiating fins or plates). The refrigerator shown in Fig. 20-4 is equipped with a fan to help the cooling action.

By the time the vapor has passed through the condenser, it has cooled enough (molecules have slowed down enough) that it starts to condense, or turn to liquid. It then passes through the capillary tube and, in liquid form, enters the evaporator again. The capillary tube is simply a small-diameter tube through which the liquid can pass, but slowly. It acts as a sort of throttle to hold back the liquid. This means that the pressure is high on the pump side of the capillary tube but low on the evaporator side. The pump is allowed to build up a comparatively high pressure in the condenser while the pressure in the evaporator can remain comparatively low. Thus, the high pressure causes the refrigerant to condense in the condenser, and the low pressure in the evaporator permits the refrigerant to evaporate.

The above series of events continues as long as the control holds its contact points closed. However, as soon as the temperature falls low enough, the control opens its contact points, the motor shuts off, and the pumping action stops.

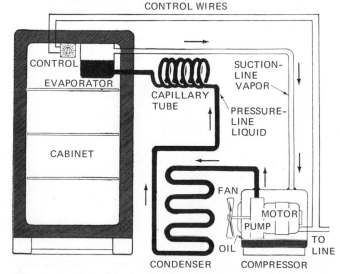

Fig. 20-4. Simplified schematic diagram of an electric refrigerator.

⊘ **20-11 Refrigerator Control** Figure 20-5 is a simplified drawing of a temperature control used in refrigerators. The bulb and bellows are connected by a tube. The bulb contains a liquid having a low-temperature boiling point. The bulb is placed in the refrigerator cabinet so that it is subjected to refrigerator temperature. As this temperature goes up, the liquid starts to boil, creating pressure in the bellows. The pressure expands the bellows, causing it to move against, and compress, the spring. As the bellows expands and the spring compresses, the movable contact is shifted toward the stationary contact. When the preset operating temperature is reached, the pressure due to the boiling liquid in the bulb is great enough for the bellows to close the contacts. Now the motor is connected to the main circuit; it begins to drive the pump, so refrigeration starts.

Note that the temperature setting can be changed by the adjustment knob. When the knob is turned so as to place more spring pressure on the bellows, the temperature must go higher before the contacts will close. This is because a higher pressure in the bellows will be required; that is, a higher bulb temperature is needed. When the adjustment knob is turned the other way, reducing the spring pressure against the bellows, the bellows can close the contact points at a lower temperature.

⊘ **20-12 Refrigerator Pump, or Compressor** A variety of pumps (commonly called *compressors*) have been used in refrigerators and air conditioners. The purpose of the compressor is to apply pressure to the vaporized refrigerant after it leaves the evaporator. This highly pressurized refrigerant then passes into the condenser, where it gives up heat and turns from a vapor into a liquid. The liquid refrigerant,

still under pressure, then passes to the evaporator, where it evaporates, picking up heat as it does so. The vapor then passes back to the compressor, where it undergoes the same process. This process continues so long as the refrigerator or air conditioner operates.

Check Your Progress

Progress Quiz 20-1 Before you continue your studies of air conditioners, let us stop and check up on the progress you have been making. Air conditioning is a new subject to many automotive mechanics. But it is very important. More and more cars are being equipped with air conditioning. Even though you do not plan to specialize in this field, you must have some knowledge of the subject. Here's the reason. Since the compressor and other conditioner units are mounted in and around the engine compartment, you may find it necessary to remove and reinstall these components when working on the engine. Removing the compressor is not quite the same as removing the alternator. There is more to it than merely disconnecting a couple of wires. Thus, you should know what air conditioning is "all about" before you attempt such jobs. The quiz that follows gives you a chance to check your memory on the important points covered in the past few pages. Reread these pages if you have any trouble answering the questions.

Completing the Sentences The sentences below are incomplete. After each sentence there are several words or phrases, only one of which will correctly complete the sentence. Write each sentence in your notebook, selecting the proper word or phrases to complete it correctly.

1. An air conditioner does two things to the air: it: (*a*) warms and dries the air, (*b*) cools and dries the air, (*c*) cools and moistens the air.
2. Essentially, the process of cooling means: (*a*) evaporation, (*b*) melting, (*c*) removal of heat, (*d*) removal of moisture.
3. From the molecular standpoint, cooling means that the molecules: (*a*) jump clear, (*b*) are slowed down, (*c*) stop, (*d*) turn to liquid.
4. Rate of evaporation of a liquid depends upon: (*a*) temperature and pressure, (*b*) vacuum and pressure, (*c*) heat and cold.
5. As the pressure on a liquid is lowered, the boiling point (or temperature) of the liquid is: (*a*) raised, (*b*) lowered, (*c*) held steady.
6. In a refrigerator, refrigeration is produced by a cycle of: (*a*) evaporation and condensation, (*b*) boiling and freezing, (*c*) refrigerant loss.
7. Heat is removed from the refrigerator by the evaporation of refrigerant in the: (*a*) condenser, (*b*) compressor, (*c*) evaporator, (*d*) control.
8. Heat that the refrigerant takes on in the evap-

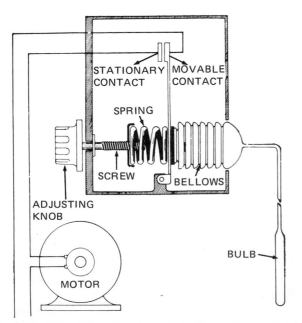

Fig. 20-5. Simplified drawing of a bellows thermostat for controlling refrigerator temperature.

oration-compression part of the refrigerator circuit is later disposed of when the refrigerant enters the: (*a*) condenser, (*b*) compressor, (*c*) evaporator, (*d*) control.

9. The high-pressure side of the system (in the compressor and the condenser) is separated from the low-pressure side (in the evaporator) by the: (*a*) control bulb, (*b*) bellows, (*c*) intake port, (*d*) capillary tube.

10. In the refrigerator control, expansion of the bellows and closing of the contacts are caused by: (*a*) increasing pressure in bulb, (*b*) falling pressure in bulb, (*c*) reduced temperature in evaporator.

⊘ **20-13 Automobile Air Conditioner** We have described the operation of a typical electric refrigerator. Now let us see how the various components of the refrigerator can be assembled into an automobile in order to "refrigerate" the occupants of the car. There are essentially only two differences in the operation of a refrigerator and a car air conditioner. First, we don't pull the car temperature down to 35 to 40 degrees Fahrenheit [1.7 to 4.4°C] as in the refrigerator. Second, we use a blower system to circulate the air in the car, moving it between the evaporator (where cooling takes place) and the passenger compartment of the car.

Figure 20-6 is a schematic view of an air-conditioner installation on a car. Figure 20-7 shows a similar installation as viewed from inside the car. The three essentials of the system we have already discussed: the compressor, condenser, and evaporator (see Fig. 20-4). There are certain additional elements, including the receiver, expansion valve, suc-

tion-throttling valve, sight glass, and air-circulation system. Let's see how these units operate.

NOTE: The air-conditioning system shown in Fig. 20-7 and discussed below is only one of several being used in automobiles. It is, however, typical and will serve to demonstrate how these systems function.

⊘ **20-14 Types of Systems** There are two basic types of automotive air-conditioner systems. One is the "factory-option" type. It is selected by the customer when the car is bought and is installed in the factory. The other is the "hang-on" or field-installed type. It is installed in cars not originally equipped with air conditioners.

The "hang-on" type, which is an air conditioner only, is called a "cycling-clutch" system. The factory-installed type, which includes a heater, is called an "evaporator-pressure-control-valve system." We shall explain these terms shortly.

⊘ **20-15 Magnetic Clutch** The compressor is a type of pump. It takes in low-pressure refrigerant vapor and sends it out at high pressure. The compressor is driven by a belt from the engine crankshaft pulley (Fig. 20-8). The compressor pulley is really two pulleys in one. Figure 20-9 is a sectional view of the assembly. The outer pulley is driven by a belt from the engine crankshaft pulley. The inner pulley is called the *armature* (Fig. 20-10). It is attached to the compressor shaft. The third part of the assembly is the clutch coil (Fig. 20-11).

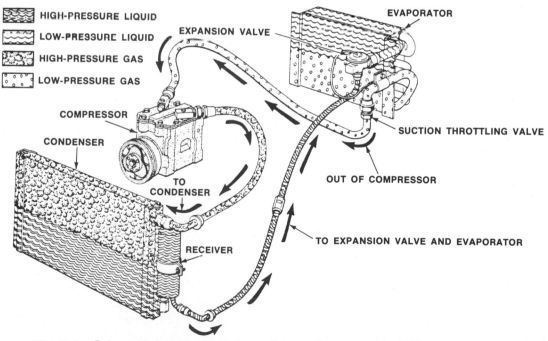

HIGH-PRESSURE LIQUID
LOW-PRESSURE LIQUID
HIGH-PRESSURE GAS
LOW-PRESSURE GAS

EVAPORATOR
EXPANSION VALVE
COMPRESSOR
CONDENSER
TO CONDENSER
SUCTION THROTTLING VALVE
OUT OF COMPRESSOR
TO EXPANSION VALVE AND EVAPORATOR
RECEIVER

Fig. 20-6. Schematic layout of an air conditioner for a car. (*Ford Motor Company*)

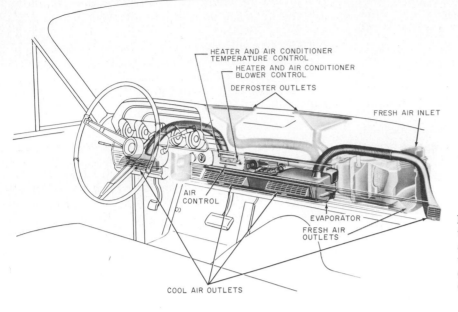

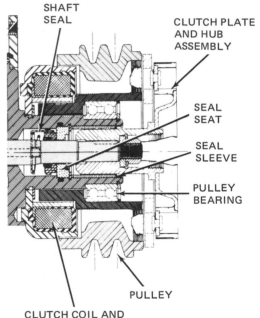

When the engine is running, the outer pulley is turning. This pulley is mounted on ball bearings so that it can turn independently. When no cooling is required, the pulley spins on the ball bearings. The armature and compressor shaft are not turning. This is the situation shown in Fig. 20-12.

However, when the control system calls for cooling, the armature and shaft turn together. A clutch coil is mounted on the compressor (Fig. 20-11). When the coil is connected to the car battery, it produces a magnetic field. The magnetic field locks the armature to the rotating pulley (Fig. 20-13) so both turn together. Now, the compressor operates and cooling takes place.

Fig. 20-9. Sectional view of the magnetic clutch. (*United Delco Division of General Motors Corporation*)

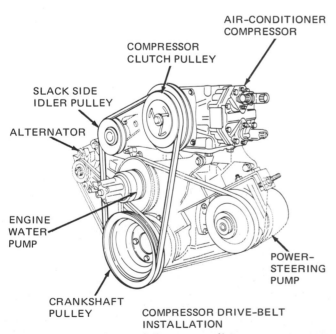
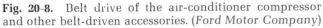

Fig. 20-8. Belt drive of the air-conditioner compressor and other belt-driven accessories. (*Ford Motor Company*)

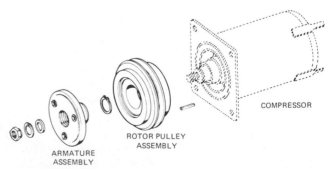

Fig. 20-10. Armature assembly and rotor pulley assembly of a magnetic clutch. (*Warner Electric Brake and Clutch Company*)

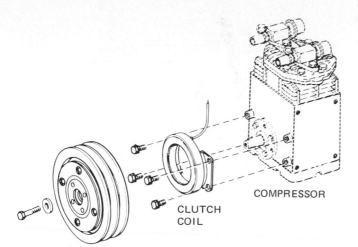

ROTOR PULLEY ASSEMBLY

Fig. 20-11. Clutch coil and rotor pulley assembly for a magnetic clutch. (*Warner Electric Brake and Clutch Company*)

⊘ **20-16 Types of Compressors** There are three general types of compressors: round, square, and V-shaped (Figs. 20-14 to 20-16).

1. *TECUMSEH OR YORK COMPRESSOR* Figure 20-15 shows the Tecumseh or York compressor. It has two pistons working in parallel cylinders (Fig. 20-17). Figures 20-18 and 20-19 show how each piston works. On the downstroke (Fig. 20-18), vacuum is produced, closing the outlet valve and opening the inlet valve. Refrigerant vapor from the evaporator is "sucked" into the cylinder. Then, on the upstroke, or compression stroke (Fig. 20-19), the pressure

OFF

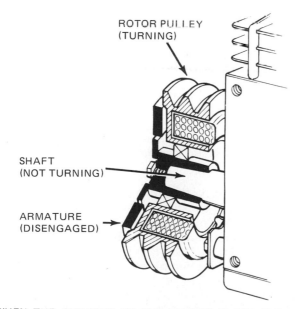

WHEN THE CURRENT TO THE CLUTCH IS OFF, THE ROTOR PULLEY IDLES FREE ON THE CLUTCH BEARING. THE COMPRESSOR SHAFT DOES NOT ROTATE

Fig. 20-12. Cutaway view of a magnetic clutch in the OFF position. (*Warner Electric Brake and Clutch Company*)

ON

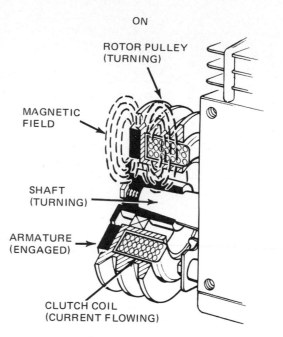

WHEN THE CURRENT FLOWS TO THE FIELD OF THE CLUTCH, THE ROTOR PULLEY AND ARMATURE (ATTACHED TO THE COMPRESSOR SHAFT) ARE "LOCKED" TOGETHER MAGNETICALLY. THE COMPRESSOR SHAFT ROTATES AND REFRIGERATION IS PROVIDED.

Fig. 20-13. Cutaway view of a magnetic clutch in the ON position. (*Warner Electric Brake and Clutch Company*)

closes the inlet valve and opens the outlet valve. The pressure compresses the refrigerant vapor and pushes it to the condenser.

2. *CHRYSLER COMPRESSOR* The Chrysler compressor (Fig. 20-16) also has two cylinders, but they are set at an angle to form a V. Figure 20-20 shows this compressor partly disassembled.

3. *ROUND (FRIGIDAIRE) SIX-CYLINDER COMPRESSOR* This compressor (Fig. 20-14) has three double-ended pistons, or six in all (Fig. 20-21). The compressor causes the pistons to move back and forth in their cylinders by means of a swash, or

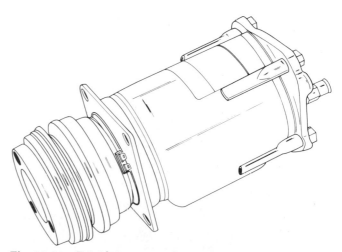

Fig. 20-14. Frigidaire type of compressor. (*United Delco Division of General Motors Corporation*)

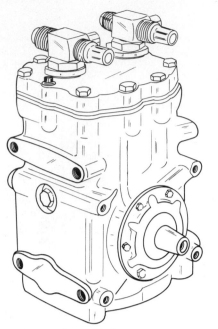

Fig. 20-15. Tecumseh or York-type compressor. (*United Delco Division of General Motors Corporation*)

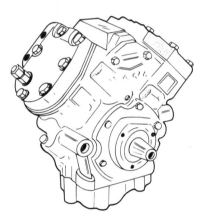

Fig. 20-16. Chrysler compressor. (*United Delco Division of General Motors Corporation*)

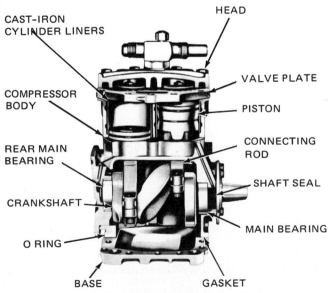

Fig. 20-17. Cutaway view of a parallel-cylinder compressor. (*Ford Motor Company*)

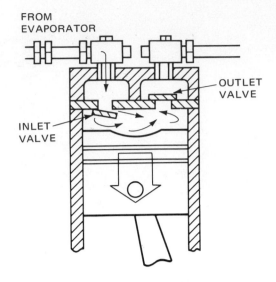

Fig. 20-18. During the downstroke, or intake stroke, the inlet valve opens to allow vapor to flow from the evaporator into the cylinder. (*Ford Motor Company*)

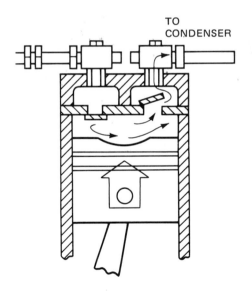

Fig. 20-19. During the upstroke, or compression stroke, the inlet valve is closed and the outlet valve is opened to allow compressed refrigerant vapor to flow to the condenser. (*Ford Motor Company*)

wobble, plate. As the shaft rotates, the plate wobbles (Fig. 20-22). The pistons fit around the plate as shown in Fig. 20-22. This arrangement forces the pistons to move back and forth, producing the pumping action.
4. *ROUND (FRIGIDAIRE) FOUR-CYLINDER COMPRESSOR* This compressor, known as the R-4 type, has four cylinders set radially around an eccentric on the compressor shaft (Fig. 20-23). As the shaft rotates, four pistons are moved back and forth in their cylinders. This action pumps the refrigerant from the evaporator to the condenser.

NOTE: All compressors have a sump for oil. The oil circulates through the compressor to produce adequate lubrication. Some of the oil also circulates

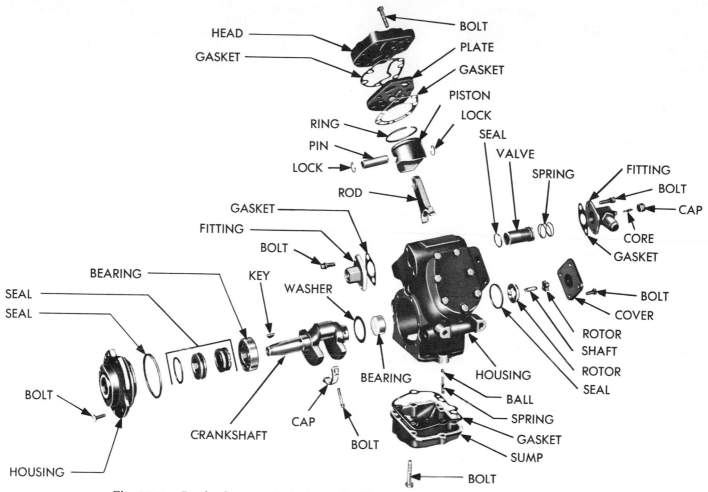

Fig. 20-20. Partly disassembled view of a V-type compressor. (*Chrysler Corporation*)

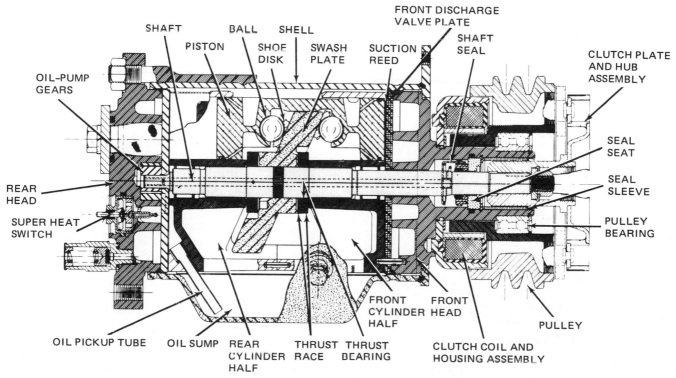

Fig. 20-21. Sectional view of a Frigidaire compressor. (*United Delco Division of General Motors Corporation*)

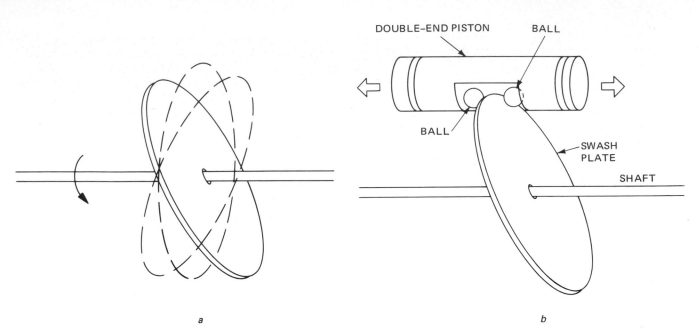

a *b*

Fig. 20-22. Simplified drawing of a swash plate. (*a*) As the shaft rotates, the plate wobbles as shown by the dashed lines. (*b*) as the swash plate wobbles, it causes the double-ended piston to move back and forth in its cylinders.

through the air conditioning system, but it returns to the compressor. This is an important point because all the components in the system, condenser, evaporator, receiver, contain some oil. Thus, when one of these components is replaced, the oil that the component retains must be measured so that the same amount of new oil can be put into the system.

⊘ 20-17 Cycling-Clutch Air-conditioning System

The cycling-clutch system gets its name from the fact that the clutch is repeatedly applied and released to control the flow of refrigerant in the sys-

tem. Figure 20-24 shows the system installed in a car. Notice that the condenser is installed in front of the radiator for the engine cooling system. The evaporator is located under the car instrument panel, and, when the system is operating, a blower sends air through the evaporator. The air is cooled and dried and then passes out into the passenger compartment.

The cycling-clutch system is controlled by a thermostatic switch located in the passenger compartment of the car. When the temperature goes too high, the thermostat closes contacts which connect the magnetic clutch to the battery. The compressor goes to work and cooling results.

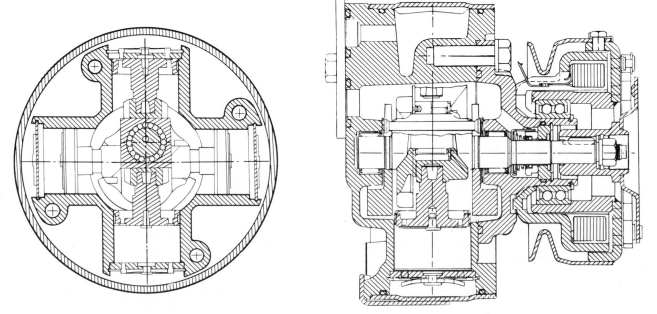

Fig. 20-23. End and side sectional views of the Frigidaire R-4 compressor. (*Pontiac Motor Division of General Motors Corporation*)

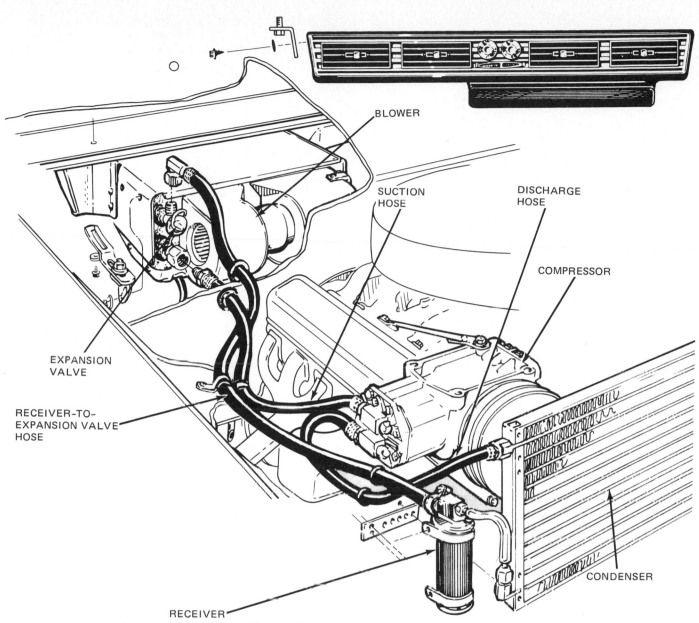

Fig. 20-24. Layout of a field-installed air-conditioning system. This is the cycling-clutch type. (*John E. Mitchell Company*)

⊘ **20-18 Expansion Valve** The system includes an expansion valve (Fig. 20-25) located in the line between the condenser and evaporator. It controls the flow of refrigerant from the condenser to the evaporator. The temperature-sensing bulb is attached to the top of the evaporator. If the evaporator temperature goes too high, the evaporator needs more refrigerant. The expansion valve takes care of this. The vapor in the temperature-sensing bulb expands with increasing temperature, putting more pressure on the diaphragm. The diaphragm moves down, forcing the valve to open to allow more refrigerant to flow to the evaporator. Now, the evaporator temperature goes down. The vapor in the sensing bulb contracts and releases pressure on the diaphragm. This allows the valve to close, reducing the flow of refrigerant. In operation, the valve is positioned to allow just the right amount of refrigerant to flow to maintain the proper evaporator temperature.

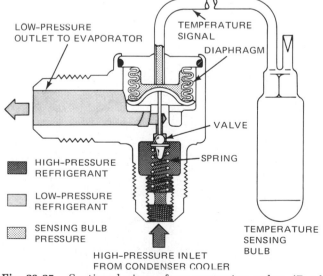

Fig. 20-25. Sectional view of an expansion valve. (*Ford Motor Company*)

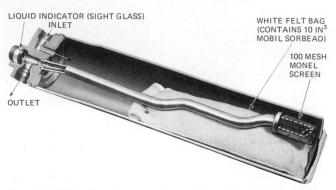

Fig. 20-26. Sectional view of a receiver-dehydrator assembly. (*Buick Motor Division of General Motors Corporation*)

⊘ 20-19 Receiver Dehydrator The receiver dehydrator (Fig. 20-26) is to ensure the supply of a solid column of liquid refrigerant to the thermostatic expansion valve. Any vapor that leaves the condenser gathers at the top of the receiver. The outlet is fed from a tube that goes to the bottom of the receiver. The receiver also contains a quantity of a water-absorbent material (in the white felt bag), and this removes any moisture that has gotten into the system during original assembly or charging.

⊘ 20-20 Sight Glass At the top of the receiver dehydrator there is a sight glass, or liquid indicator (Fig. 20-26), for the diagnosis of troubles. If bubbles or foam can be seen under the sight glass when the system is working, it means that air has gotten into the system or that there is insufficient refrigerant, so it is not condensing properly in the condenser.

⊘ 20-21 Evaporator-Pressure-Control Valve System The evaporator-pressure-control valve system is widely used as a factory option and, if ordered, is installed at the factory. The system includes the car heater. Figure 20-27 shows how the system fits into the car. The system contains the same components as does the cycling-clutch system. In this system, the compressor operates continuously as long as the dash controls are set for air conditioning. The amount of cooling the system produces depends on the position of the doors in the air passages and the actions of the control valves.

Figure 20-28 shows the system schematically. Note that the valves have been installed in the receiver. These valves are the expansion valve, already described, and a suction-throttling valve (called the *POA valve*). The expansion valve is somewhat different in basic construction, but it does the same job previously described (⊘ 20-18). You will recall that its job is to allow sufficient refrigerant to enter the evaporator to keep the evaporator temperature down.

The suction-throttling valve does quite the opposite. It keeps the evaporator temperature from falling too low. If it fell too low, moisture would freeze on the evaporator and cause ice to form. This would block the air flow and prevent normal air conditioning. The suction-throttling valve senses the pressure of the vapor coming from the evaporator. If the pressure goes too high, it opens to release pressure, increasing the cooling. If the cooling becomes too great, the valve partly closes to increase the pressure, and so the cooling is reduced.

⊘ 20-22 Controls The air-conditioning system is controlled by levers or buttons on the instrument panel. On some models the controls are vacuum-

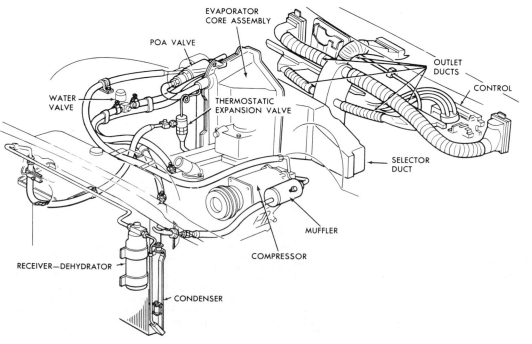

Fig. 20-27. Typical evaporator-pressure-control-valve air-conditioning system. (*United Delco Division of General Motors Corporation*)

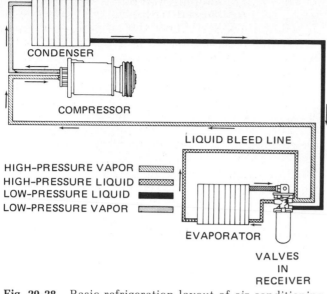

HIGH-PRESSURE VAPOR
HIGH-PRESSURE LIQUID
LOW-PRESSURE LIQUID
LOW-PRESSURE VAPOR

Fig. 20-28. Basic refrigeration layout of air-conditioning system with VIR (valves in receiver). (*Chevrolet Division of General Motors Corporation*)

operated. In one system the levers are set manually and adjusted by the driver for different conditions. In a fully automatic system, the driver simply sets the temperature desired, and the system takes over from there. The system will cool when cooling is needed and will heat when heating is needed to maintain the preset temperature.

20-23 Manual Temperature-Control System Figure 20-29 is a schematic drawing of the manual temperature-control system. Air enters either from outside or from inside the car, depending on the positions of doors 1 and 2. These are the outside-air door and the recirculating-air door. The position of these doors is controlled by the movement of the functional-control lever (see Fig. 20-29). When the lever is moved to the left—to MAX A/C—the outside-air door is closed and the recirculating-air door is opened. If the lever is set at FRESH A/C, fresh air from outside will be brought into the system.

The speed with which the air moves is controlled by the speed of the blower. The setting of

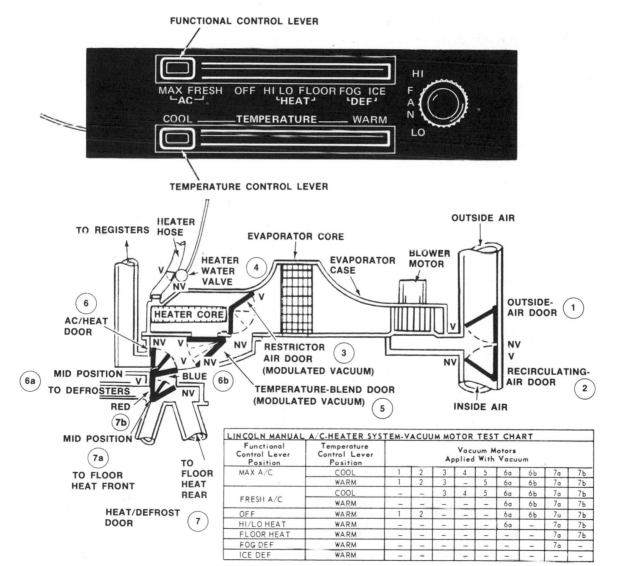

Functional Control Lever Position	Temperature Control Lever Position	Vacuum Motors Applied With Vacuum								
MAX A/C	COOL	1	2	3	4	5	6a	6b	7a	7b
	WARM	1	2	3	–	5	6a	6b	7a	7b
FRESH A/C	COOL	–	–	3	4	5	6a	6b	7a	7b
	WARM	–	–	–	–	–	6a	6b	7a	7b
OFF	WARM	1	2	–	–	–	6a	6b	7a	7b
HI/LO HEAT	WARM	–	–	–	–	–	6a	–	7a	7b
FLOOR HEAT	WARM	–	–	–	–	–	–	–	7a	7b
FOG DEF	WARM	–	–	–	–	–	–	–	7a	–
ICE DEF	WARM	–	–	–	–	–	–	–	–	–

Fig. 20-29. Manually controlled air-conditioning and heating system. (*Ford Motor Company*)

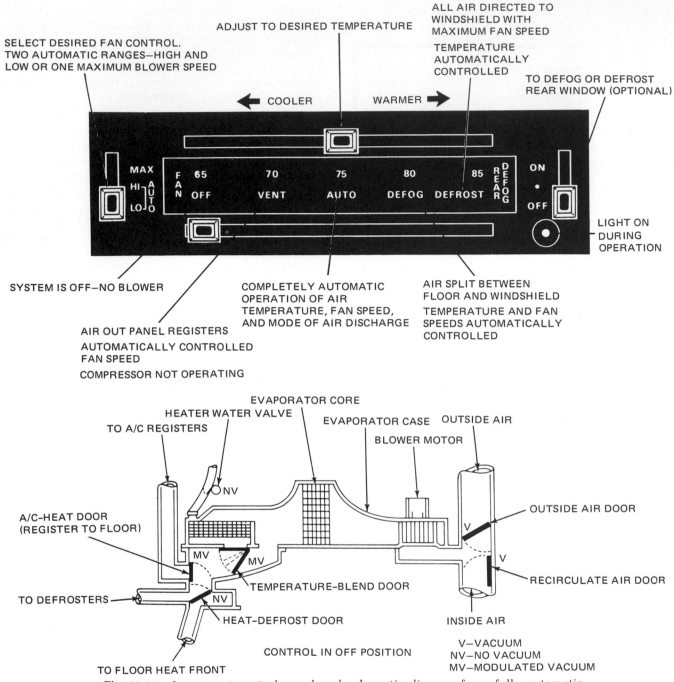

SELECT DESIRED FAN CONTROL.
TWO AUTOMATIC RANGES—HIGH AND
LOW OR ONE MAXIMUM BLOWER SPEED

ADJUST TO DESIRED TEMPERATURE

ALL AIR DIRECTED TO
WINDSHIELD WITH
MAXIMUM FAN SPEED

TEMPERATURE
AUTOMATICALLY
CONTROLLED

TO DEFOG OR DEFROST
REAR WINDOW (OPTIONAL)

← COOLER   WARMER →

MAX
HI AUTO
LO

FAN 65 OFF   70 VENT   75 AUTO   80 DEFOG   85 DEFROST   REAR DEFOG

ON
OFF

LIGHT ON
DURING
OPERATION

SYSTEM IS OFF—NO BLOWER

AIR OUT PANEL REGISTERS
AUTOMATICALLY CONTROLLED
FAN SPEED
COMPRESSOR NOT OPERATING

COMPLETELY AUTOMATIC
OPERATION OF AIR
TEMPERATURE, FAN SPEED,
AND MODE OF AIR DISCHARGE

AIR SPLIT BETWEEN
FLOOR AND WINDSHIELD
TEMPERATURE AND FAN
SPEEDS AUTOMATICALLY
CONTROLLED

EVAPORATOR CORE

HEATER WATER VALVE

TO A/C REGISTERS

EVAPORATOR CASE   OUTSIDE AIR

BLOWER MOTOR

NV

A/C-HEAT DOOR
(REGISTER TO FLOOR)

OUTSIDE AIR DOOR

MV   MV

TO DEFROSTERS

NV

TEMPERATURE-BLEND DOOR

V

V

RECIRCULATE AIR DOOR

HEAT-DEFROST DOOR

INSIDE AIR

TO FLOOR HEAT FRONT

CONTROL IN OFF POSITION

V—VACUUM
NV—NO VACUUM
MV—MODULATED VACUUM

Fig. 20-30. Instrument control panel and schematic diagram for a fully automatic
heater–air-conditioner system. (*Ford Motor Company*)

the FAN knob (Fig. 20-29) determines the speed of the
blower and the speed with which air is brought into
the system.

The air goes first through the evaporator core.
It may or may not be cooled, depending on the position of the temperature-control lever. If the lever is
set at A/C, the magnetic clutch on the compressor
will be actuated. The compressor operates, and cooling results. If the lever is set at HEAT or DEF (for
defrost), the magnetic clutch will not operate, and
no compressor action takes place. Thus there will
be no cooling.

After passing through the evaporator core, the
air meets the air-restrictor door (3 in Fig. 20-29). This

door can be swung up to admit air to the heater core
or swung down to prevent air from entering the
heater core. Hot water from the engine cooling system circulates through the heater core when the
system calls for heat to warm the car interior. The
temperature-blend door (5) can be moved varying
amounts to control the percentage of heater-core air
and evaporator-core air that mix at this point. Next,
the air meets the air-conditioner-heat door (6), which
can be moved one way or the other. In the *up* position, the passage to the registers is blocked, and the
air moves down into the defroster-floor-heat position. Now the air, which has been warmed, can
move to the defrosters or to the floor-heat out-

lets, depending on the position of the heat-defrost door (7).

The system also includes a water-heater valve (4). This valve shuts off the flow of hot water from the engine cooling system when the air conditioner is running. Both the water valve and the air door are operated by vacuum motors.

⊘ 20-24 Automatic Temperature-Control System

The automatic temperature-control system is simple from the standpoint of the driver, but it is complicated from the standpoint of the automotive technician. Figure 20-30 is a schematic layout of the system. Note that the control panel has two levers. The upper lever can be moved to select the desired temperature (65 to 85 degrees Fahrenheit) [18.3° to 29.4°C]. The lower lever can be moved all the way to the left to get automatic action in high, making the blower operate at the maximum speed until the desired temperature is reached. Then the blower will slow down and operate just fast enough to maintain the desired temperature. If slower action is desired, the driver can set the lever at LOW. If the driver wants only untreated outside air to enter, the lever is set at VENT. At this setting, the outside-recirculating door (1 and 2 in Fig. 20-30) is moved down so that outside air enters. To defog or defrost the windshield, the driver sets the lever at either of these positions.

The air passes through the evaporator core after it leaves the blower. Whether the air is cooled depends on whether the air conditioner is working. Next, the air either bypasses the heater core or passes through the heater core. If the system calls for heat, the air conditioner does not work but the heater core is hot because hot water from the engine cooling system is circulating through it. With this operating condition, the water heater valve (4) is open. Also, the bypass-air door (3) is closed, and the temperature-blend door (5) is open. The direction the heated air then takes depends on the positions of the high-low door (6) and the panel-defrost door (7).

NOTE: Many systems are of the "reheat" type in which the air conditioner operates continuously in the A/C mode. If this cools the air too much, some of the air is diverted through the heater core so that it is reheated. This reheated air then merges with the cool air to provide the proper temperature of air as required by the control setting.

CHAPTER 20 CHECKUP

With the widespread adoption of air conditioning for automobiles, everyone in the automotive field has become interested in the subject. Some, perhaps, plan to specialize in car air-conditioning service and will be taking special courses in the subject. Others maybe interested only to the extent of wanting to learn something about how the system operates. But everyone who works on cars should have a basic understanding of the system. They should know how various components are removed and reinstalled on the car. It is necessary for them to know this because, for example, the compressor must be removed before many service operations can be carried out on the engine. Regardless of your own personal plans for your future in the automotive field, you will want to make sure you understand how air conditioners work and also how the components are removed and replaced (as explained in the following chapter). Thus, you will want to check yourself on how well you understood the chapter you have just finished by taking the test that follows.

Unscrambling the Lists   When the two lists below are unscrambled and combined, they form a list of the components in the air-conditioning system and their functions. To unscramble the lists, take one item at a time from the components list, and then find the item from the functions list that goes with it. Write the results in your notebook.

COMPONENTS:
compressor
condenser
receiver
check valve
sight glass
bypass valve
expansion valve
evaporator

FUNCTIONS:
causes cooling by evaporation of refrigerant
storage tank for liquid refrigerant
prevents surging of refrigerant back to condenser
to check refrigerant for bubbles
controls refrigerant circuit
removes heat from condensed vapor
compresses refrigerant vapor
provides pressure drop at evaporator

Completing the Sentences   The sentences below are incomplete. After each sentence there are several words or phrases, only one of which will correctly complete the sentence. Write each sentence in your notebook, selecting the proper word or phrase to complete it correctly.

1. Other things being equal, the drier the air, the: (a) faster water will evaporate, (b) slower water will evaporate, (c) greater the air pressure.
2. Other things being equal, the lower the air pressure, the: (a) faster water will evaporate, (b) slower water will evaporate, (c) higher the temperature.
3. Condensation of a vapor on a cold surface is due to the vapor's losing some of its heat; that is, its molecules: (a) speed up, (b) slow down, (c) stop moving entirely.
4. In the refrigeration system, the pressure is relatively low in the: (a) compressor, (b) condenser, (c) evaporator.
5. When the compressor is operating, the pressure is high in the: (a) condenser, (b) evaporator, (c) cabinet.

6. The purpose of the receiver dehydrator in the car air conditioner is to ensure a solid column of liquid refrigerant to the: (*a*) condenser, (*b*) compressor, (*c*) expansion valve.

7. When the magnetic clutch is actuated, then: (*a*) there is no refrigerating action, (*b*) refrigerating action takes place, (*c*) the bypass circuit is open.

8. In the car air conditioner, the device that reduces the high pressure (compressor-condenser) to low pressure (evaporator) is called: (*a*) sight glass, (*b*) check valve, (*c*) bypass valve, (*d*) expansion valve.

9. In the air-conditioning system described in this chapter, air is circulated through the evaporator by the: (*a*) blower, (*b*) compressor, (*c*) diaphragm.

10. The thermostatic control starts and stops the refrigerating action by causing the closing and opening of the electric circuit between the battery and the: (*a*) compressor, (*b*) bypass valve, (*c*) check valve, (*d*) magnetic clutch.

Purpose and Operation of Components In the following exercise, you are asked to write the purpose and operation of various components in the air-conditioning system. If you have any difficulty writing your explanations, turn back in the chapter and reread the pages that will give you the answer. Don't copy; try to tell it in your own words, just as you might explain it to a friend. This is a good way to fix the explanation in your mind. Write in your notebook.

1. Explain, in terms of molecular action, how cooling is achieved by evaporation.

2. Explain, in terms of molecular action, why lowering the pressure increases the rate of evaporation.

3. Explain, in terms of molecular action, why compressing a vapor and then cooling it causes condensation.

4. Describe the complete refrigeration cycle, starting with the evaporation of the refrigerant in the evaporator.

5. Explain how a refrigerator control operates.

6. What is the purpose of the receiver?

7. What is the purpose of the check valve?

8. What is the purpose of the sight glass?

9. What is the purpose of the solenoid bypass valve?

10. What is the purpose of the expansion valve? Explain how it works.

11. Describe the operation of one of the air-conditioner controls described in the chapter.

12. Why does dry air feel cooler to us than moist air?

SUGGESTIONS FOR FURTHER STUDY

If you are especially interested in refrigeration and air conditioning, you should study *Automotive Air Conditioning*, another book in the McGraw-Hill Automotive Technology Series. For specific car air-conditioning information, refer to special manuals issued by the car and air-conditioner manufacturers. These manuals are supplied to the service people in the car-dealer shops. Your local school automotive shop may also be able to obtain these manuals. If you can borrow these manuals and study them, you will be able to find out the details of specific air-conditioning systems used on automobiles: how they are constructed, how they operate, and how they are serviced. Write in your notebook any important facts you learn.

chapter 21

AIR-CONDITIONER SERVICE

This chapter describes various troubles that might occur with automotive air conditioners, how to diagnose these troubles to find their causes, and how to correct the causes of trouble. Further, it explains how to remove various components of the system. Even though you might not plan on performing actual service operations on air-conditioning equipment, you may find it necessary to remove and replace certain conditioner components (such as the compressor) while you are doing other automotive work. For example, many engine-servicing operations require removal of the compressor. The following pages describe the various removal, servicing, and replacement procedures on air-conditioning equipment.

⊘ **21-1 Troubleshooting the System** *You must not attempt any service work on air conditioners and that includes diagnostic checks—unless you have the proper equipment and know exactly how to use it. Furthermore, you must be fully aware of the dangers inherent in working with high-pressure equipment and with liquid refrigerants (see ⊘ 21-2).*

Bearing the above caution in mind, the following chart will help you to locate possible causes of trouble in the air-conditioning system. Troubles (and their causes) are not listed in the order of frequency of occurrence.

AIR-CONDITIONING TROUBLE-DIAGNOSIS CHART

COMPLAINT	POSSIBLE CAUSE	CHECK OR CORRECTION
1. Poor cooling	a. Blowers not operating	Check electric system, switches, blower motors
	b. Relay on thermostat contacts stuck	Clean points or replace relay on thermostat
	c. Air flow through evaporator restricted	Check filter for dirt, and check scoops, air ducts, return grilles for restrictions
	d. Not enough refrigerant	Check for leaks, add refrigerant
	e. Too much refrigerant	Bleed off refrigerant
	f. Expansion valve out of adjustment or defective	Adjust or replace
	g. Power element (from expansion valve) defective or improperly mounted	Power element must mount tight on low-pressure line but must be insulated from high-pressure (liquid) line
	h. Receiver-to-evaporator line clogged	Replace line
	i. Insufficient air flow through condenser	Clean condenser core and radiator. *Do not use steam!*
	j. High engine temperatures	Check engine cooling system
	k. Air in system	Bleed off air
	l. Solenoid bypass valve stuck open	Repair or replace
	m. Clutch solenoid or clutch out of adjustment or defective	Adjust, repair, replace as necessary
	n. High-pressure line restricted	Replace line
	o. Compressor defective	Replace
2. Excessive cooling	a. Solenoid bypass valve stuck closed	Free plunger or replace valve
	b. Relay or thermostat points stuck	Clean points, replace relay or thermostat
	c. Temperature-control rheostat shorted	Replace

COMPLAINT	POSSIBLE CAUSE	CHECK OR CORRECTION
3. Noises	a. Tubing loose	Tighten clamps, make sure tubing does not rub
	b. Blowers	Check motor mounting, blower attachment screws (on shaft), motor bearings
	c. Compressor	If from mounting, tighten; if from pulley clutch (on units so equipped), replace clutch. If internal, replace compressor
	d. Expansion valve hisses	Shortage of refrigerant, or restrictions in line
4. Water leaking in trunk	a. Drain hose not connected	Connect
	b. Drain pan dirty	Clean
	c. Evaporator case sweating	Insulate case properly

NOTE: When pressures are checked with the special equipment described on later pages and incorrect pressures are found, possible causes and corrections may be as follows:

COMPLAINT	POSSIBLE CAUSE	CHECK OR CORRECTION
5. Excessive pressure on high-pressure side	a. Air or excess refrigerant	Purge air and refrigerant to remove excess
	b. Clogged condenser core restricts air circulation	Clean core with air or brush. *Do not use steam!*
	c. Line restricted (high side)	Replace line
	d. High engine temperature	Check engine cooling system
	e. Insufficient air flow through evaporator	Check as noted in item 1 c
	f. Expansion valve out of adjustment or faulty	Adjust or replace
6. Insufficient pressure on high-pressure side	a. Insufficient refrigerant	Add refrigerant
	b. Bypass valve stuck open	Free plunger, replace valve
	c. Bypass valve leaks	Replace valve if valve and seat are worn or defective
	d. Expansion valve out of adjustment or faulty	Adjust or replace
	e. Compressor faulty	Replace
7. Excessive pressure on low-pressure side	a. Expansion valve action faulty	Check power-element bulb contact (see item 1 g) Adjust or replace valve
	b. Bypass valve leaky or stuck open	Clear valve, replace if defective
	c. Compressor defective	Replace
8. Insufficient pressure on low-pressure side	a. Line restricted	Replace kinked or restricted lines
	b. Shortage of refrigerant	Add refrigerant
	c. Expansion valve out of adjustment or faulty	Adjust valve, replace if defective

⊘ **21-2 Essential Cautions You Must Observe**
There is no more danger in working with air conditioners than in working with any component of the car—provided you observe normal caution. Listed here are the things to look out for when you work on air conditioners or handle refrigerant:

1. UNDERCOATING Never apply undercoating to any connections in the refrigeration lines. Mask all flare joints and connections before applying undercoating.

2. STEAM CLEANING AND WELDING Heat in any form *must not be applied* to any refrigerant line or any component of the air-conditioning system. It must be remembered that the refrigeration system contains refrigerant under pressure. Heating the refrigerant increases the pressure excessively and may cause serious damage. Do not steam-clean any tube or component. When welding, remove components or move refrigeration tubing out of the way.

3. HANDLING THE REFRIGERANT The refrigerant normally used in automotive air-conditioning systems is Freon-12. It is considered to be about the safest refrigerant commercially available, but you can be hurt if you handle it carelessly. Note the following:

a. Always wear glasses or goggles when handling refrigerant or servicing air conditioners. You could damage your eyes seriously by getting refrigerant in them. If you get Freon-12 in your eyes, apply a few drops of sterile mineral oil as an irrigator. Wash eyes with boric acid solution if they still hurt. See an eye specialist at once.

b. Do not discharge Freon-12 in a room where there is an exposed flame. If Freon-12 vapor comes into contact with an open flame, it is converted into a dangerously toxic gas. Of course, small amounts would not be particularly harmful. But to be on the safe side, if you have to discharge Freon-12 from a system, it is best to do it outside in the open air. If you do discharge the Freon-12 in the garage, discharge it into the garage exhaust system. The refrigerant evaporates so quickly that it will displace all the air around the car. This could cause you to suffocate if the immediate area in which you are working is enclosed and is without ventilation!

c. Be sure to use only the Freon-12 especially prepared for air-conditioning systems. The kind used in such equipment as boat air horns and fire-alarm signals is not pure and can ruin an air conditioner. Freon-12 is supplied in small "one-shot" pressure cans and in larger high-pressure drums. There is no special danger if the drums are handled carefully. But remember the following:

Do not overheat the drum (by leaving it in the sun, applying hot water or a torch, putting it on a stove or radiator, and so on). An overheated drum may explode, and this could injure or kill you! The drum must never be heated above 150 degrees Fahrenheit [65.6°C].

For the same reason, do not drop the drum or handle it carelessly. Do not carry the drum around in the passenger compartment of a car. Do not leave the drum uncapped—the cap protects the valve and safety plug.

d. Do not allow refrigerant to touch bright metal. It will tarnish chrome and will damage any metal or painted surface it touches.

e. Always hold the refrigerant container upright when charging the system. If it is on its side, liquid refrigerant can feed into the system and will damage the compressor.

4. *HANDLING TUBING* Refrigerant tubing, or lines, should not be crushed or kinked; this would restrict the flow of refrigerant and reduce cooling action. Lines must be kept sealed and dehydrated in stock, just as received from the factory. Do not remove the caps until just before installation. When tightening fittings, use two wrenches to avoid damaging the tubes.

If lines have to be disconnected for any reason, close the ends of the lines with caps or masking tape.

5. *REFRIGERATING OIL* A special oil is used in the refrigeration system to provide lubrication of the compressor. This oil is sealed into the system and does not need replacement unless it is lost (by removing refrigerant, by accident, and so on). The new oil comes in special containers which are sealed to prevent the entrance of moisture. The new oil should not be exposed to the air any longer than absolutely necessary, since it will absorb moisture. Moisture in the system may freeze and clog the refrigerant flow.

6. *VACUUM PUMP* A special vacuum pump (shown in Fig. 21-5) must be used to remove any air or moisture that has entered the system when the system has been opened for replacement of any part.

⊘ **21-3 Service Operations** Service operations on the automotive air-conditioning system include periodic inspection checks, preparing the system for winter operation, preparing it for summer operation, evacuating the system before adding refrigerant, adding refrigerant, adding oil as necessary, purging the system of air or excess refrigerant, removing and replacing various components, repairing some of the components, and adjusting the expansion valve.

These operations on one specific system are covered in following sections. Other systems require different procedures. Always check the shop manual for the specific system to be serviced before starting the service job.

⊘ **21-4 Periodic Inspection** Periodically, the system should be checked to see whether it is operating normally. First, note whether the compressor drive belts are tight. If they are not tight enough, they will slip when the system is in operation. Then listen to the solenoid bypass valve to make sure it opens and closes when the cooling switch is turned on and off. (On models using a solenoid-operated clutch, note the clutch action.) If the car interior is too cool to permit operation of the air conditioner, heat it with the car heater.

A leak detector should be used to check the system for leakage of the refrigerant. There are two general types, flame and electronic. The device shown in Fig. 21-1 is the flame type. It is a small torch that burns a special fuel—anhydrous methyl alcohol. It has a long tube that is open at one end and connected to the base of the torch at the other. When the torch is lighted, air is drawn through the tube. If the open end of the tube is placed close to a point where refrigerant (Freon-12) is leaking, the refrigerant will be drawn through the tube and will pass through the flame. As the refrigerant passes through the flame, it will change the color of the flame. The flame will turn green, brilliant blue, or purple. By moving the open end of the tube around and holding it close to the connections in the system, you can locate any leak.

CAUTION: Do not breathe the fumes or black smoke that the torch gives off when a leak has been located; they are poisonous.

Fig. 21-1. Leak detector for detecting leakage of Freon-12 and locating the source of leakage. (*Oldsmobile Division of General Motors Corporation*)

The leak detector shown in use in Fig. 21-2 is the electronic type. It uses dry-cell batteries to operate an electronic "sniffing" device that quickly detects and locates the source of Freon-12 leaks.

NOTE: There is also a liquid leak detector which is used to check connections after they have been broken and reconnected. This liquid is daubed on the connection and will form bubbles if refrigerant is escaping.

Check both the blower fans and the control knobs to make sure they operate normally.

Set the control for maximum cooling so that the system will operate continuously. Operate on fast idle for 15 minutes. Remove the cover from or clean the sight glass and check for bubbles. Use a flashlight to make sure you can see the refrigerant passing under the sight glass. If there are bubbles, it means there is insufficient refrigerant in the system, so more should be added.

An absence of bubbles means that there is either too much refrigerant or no refrigerant at all. To determine which is the case, cycle the magnetic clutch on the compressor. This is done by moving the air-conditioner controls to OFF and then ON with the engine running. If there is no refrigerant, no bubbles will appear. This condition requires a leak test, leak repair, and recharging of the system with refrigerant.

⊘ **21-5 Air-conditioning Performance Test** To test the air conditioner for performance, you need a manifold gauge set (Fig. 21-3). This gauge set is connected to the system to measure the pressures. These measurements tell you if there is trouble, and where trouble causes are located. The gauge set is also used

Fig. 21-2. Using an electronic refrigerant leak detector.

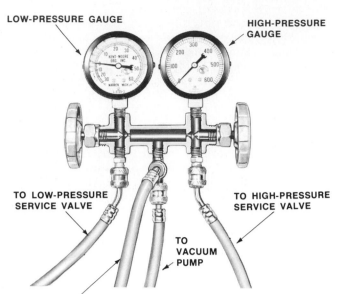

Fig. 21-3. Connections to the manifold gauge set to check and service the air-conditioner system. The manifold is shown in sectional view so the valves can be seen. (*Ford Motor Company*)

to pump down, evacuate, and recharge the system, as explained in following sections.

⊘ **21-6 Discharging the System** When replacing any component, the system must be discharged. To do this, connect the manifold gauge set as shown in Fig. 21-4. Open the valves slightly to allow refrigerant to discharge slowly. In the setup shown in Fig. 21-4, a container is being used to catch and measure any oil that comes out with the refrigerant. If the valves are opened too much, most of the oil will be blown out of the system.

CAUTION: Discharge refrigerant into open air or the shop ventilating system—never in a closed, unventilated area.

⊘ **21-7 Evacuating the System** To evacuate the system, connect a refrigerant supply tank and a vacuum pump to the manifold gauge set (Fig. 21-5). Note that the manifold gauge set is connected to the service valves. The refrigerant tank valve should be closed. Open both manifold gauge valves. Run the vacuum pump until the low-pressure gauge reads at least 25 psi [1.76 kg/cm²]. Continue to run the vacuum pump for 20 to 30 minutes. Turn off the pump and close both gauge valves.

⊘ **21-8 Charging the System** First, discharge and evacuate the system as outlined in previous sections. Leave the vacuum-pump valve closed. Set the low-pressure gauge valve at the full counterclockwise or open position. Set the high-pressure gauge valve at the full clockwise or closed position.

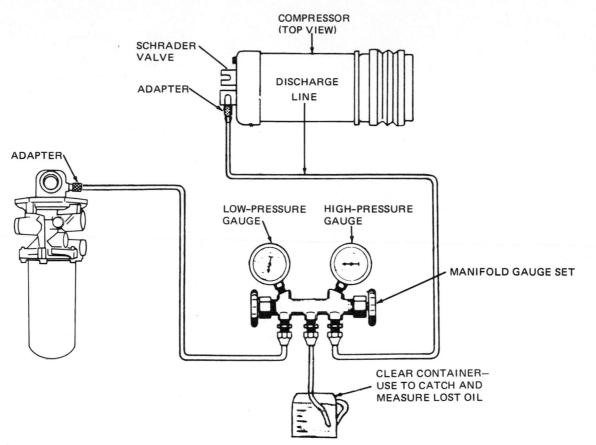

Fig. 21-4. Test setup for discharging the system. (*Buick Motor Division of General Motors Corporation*)

Open the refrigerant-supply-tank valve to allow refrigerant to enter the system. Watch the gauges. When both gauges reach 60 to 80 psi [4.22 to 5.62 kg/cm²] at about 75 degrees Fahrenheit [23.9°C], shut off the tank valve. Check for leaks with a leak detector.

Set the air-conditioner controls for maximum cooling. Start the engine and open the refrigerant-tank valve. Run the engine at 1,500 rpm and complete the charging until the specified weight of refrigerant has entered the system.

NOTE: If the refrigerant will not enter the system because of low temperature, Ford advises placing the supply tank in a container of hot water (at about 150 degrees Fahrenheit [65.6°C]). Never heat the tank with a torch; this could cause a deadly explosion.

During the charging, the high-pressure side may build up to an excessive value because of an overcharge of refrigerant, an overheated engine, or high air temperatures. Do not allow the pressure to go above 240 psi [16.87 kg/cm²]. If it does, stop the engine, determine the cause of the buildup, and correct it.

After the proper amount of refrigerant has been put into the system, close the refrigerant-tank valve. Check the system pressures. At 70 to 90 degrees Fahrenheit [21.1 to 32.2°C], pressures (in Ford systems) should be:

Low-pressure suction gauge: 4 to 25 psi [0.28 to 1.76 kg/cm²]
High-pressure discharge gauge: 120 to 170 psi [8.44 to 11.95 kg/cm²]

⊘ **21-9 Charging from Small Containers** A special valve and valve retainer must be used to connect the small cans into the system. Do not open the high-pressure-gauge valve on the manifold when a can is connected. The high pressure could cause the can to explode.

⊘ **21-10 Adding Oil** There must be a specific amount of oil in the system; the kind required is 525 viscosity special refrigerant oil. It circulates throughout the system, and there will be some oil in every component. If a component is removed, the oil that comes away with it must be replaced when a new component is installed. One method of doing this, recommended by Buick, is to measure the oil in the component removed and then add that amount of new oil when the replacement component is installed. Ford recommends that the following amounts of oil be added to replacement units:

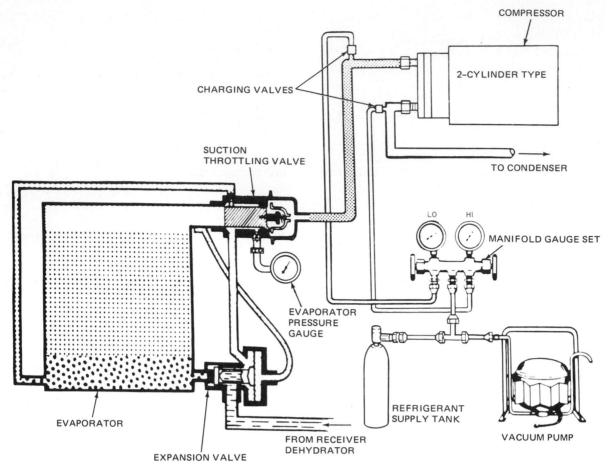

Fig. 21-5. Test setup for testing, evacuating, and charging the refrigerant system. (*Ford Motor Company*)

Evaporator: 3 fluid ounces [88.71 cc]
Condenser: 1 fluid ounce [29.57 cc]
Receiver: 1 fluid ounce [29.57 cc]
Condenser and receiver assembly: 2 fluid ounces [59.14 cc].

Pour the oil directly into the replacement component.

⊘ **21-11 Removing and Replacing Components** If any component is removed, the system must be discharged. New components come capped and sealed. The caps should not be removed until just before the component is installed. Then, the system must be evacuated and recharged as already noted.

New compressors come charged and with a full measure of oil. When they are installed, the charge must be bled off so the high- and low-pressure lines can be attached to the compressor.

⊘ **21-12 Repairing the Compressor** There are several varieties of compressor and thus several overhaul procedures are required. Inasmuch as these procedures require special tools and a special workspace that can be kept clean, most shops do not try to overhaul compressors. Instead, they purchase

new or rebuilt compressors to replace compressors that have gone bad.

CHAPTER 21 CHECKUP

The chapter you have just completed covers the highlights of servicing one type of car air conditioner. Although the basic servicing procedures cover all types, variations in design and construction make necessary some variation in servicing. If you do not plan to specialize in air-conditioning work, the main servicing procedure you should know about is how to remove and replace the compressor. However, if you do plan to specialize in this subject, you should know not only all the details covered in the chapter but the operation and maintenance procedures on other types of equipment. The material in the chapter gives you a good start in this direction. To find out how well you remember the material, take the following test.

Completing the Sentences The sentences below are incomplete. After each sentence there are several words or phrases, only one of which will correctly complete the sentence. Write each sentence in your notebook, selecting the proper word or phrase to complete it correctly.

1. When Freon-12 comes into contact with an open flame, it is converted into: (*a*) a harmless gas, (*b*) a dangerously toxic gas, (*c*) a liquid.
2. A drum of Freon-12 must never be heated above: (*a*) 150°F [65.6°C], (*b*) 175°F [79.4°C], (*c*) 212°F [100°C], (*d*) 300°F [148.9°C].
3. The purpose of the vacuum pump used in servicing the air-conditioning system is to: (*a*) pump down the system, (*b*) evacuate the system, (*c*) hydrate the system.
4. When the system is discharged, most of the refrigerant is released into the: (*a*) compressor, (*b*) condenser, (*c*) evaporator, (*d*) air.
5. The purpose of evacuating the system is to remove: (*a*) all traces of refrigerant, (*b*) all air and moisture, (*c*) all low-pressure refrigerant.
6. Before you charge a system, you must: (*a*) remove the compressor, (*b*) remove the ignition key so the engine cannot start, (*c*) discharge and evacuate the system.
7. If the expansion valve is out of adjustment and starves the evaporator, the result will be: (*a*) excessive cooling, (*b*) excessively low temperature of evaporator, (*c*) insufficient cooling.
8. The only servicing operation to be performed on the compressor discussed in the chapter is replacement of the: (*a*) rotor, (*b*) bearings, (*c*) complete unit.
9. When you remove the compressor to service it, you should: (*a*) purge it of refrigerant, (*b*) maintain pressure in it, (*c*) disassemble it completely.
10. High and low pressure in the system are measured by use of a special: (*a*) vacuum gauge, (*b*) pressure gauge, (*c*) gauge set.

Servicing Procedures Write in your notebook the servicing procedures that are asked for. Don't copy from the book; try to explain the procedure in your own words, just as you would tell it to a friend.

1. What are the main causes of poor cooling?
2. What would cause excessive cooling?

3. Make a list of possible causes of noise in the cooling system.
4. What could cause excessive pressure on the high-pressure side?
5. What could cause insufficient pressure on the high-pressure side?
6. What could cause excessive pressure on the low-pressure side?
7. What could cause insufficient pressure on the low-pressure side?
8. Explain how you check the pressures in the system.
9. List the essential cautions you must observe in working on an air conditioner and in handling refrigerant.
10. Explain how the two types of leak detector are used.
11. Explain how to pump down a system.
12. Explain how to evacuate a system (low-pressure side and complete system).
13. Explain how to charge a system (partially and completely).
14. Explain how to check the oil level and how to add oil.
15. Explain how to purge excess refrigerant or air from a system.
16. Explain how to remove and replace a compressor.
17. Explain how to adjust an expansion valve. How to remove and replace it.

SUGGESTIONS FOR FURTHER STUDY

If you wish to learn more about servicing automobile air conditioners, study the various car shop manuals and special manuals issued for this equipment by the car companies. If the service shop of a local car dealer is servicing air-conditioning equipment, try to be on hand so that you can observe how the various operations are performed. Be sure to write everything you learn in your notebook.

GLOSSARY

This glossary of automotive terms used in the book provides a ready reference for the student. The definitions may differ somewhat from those in a standard dictionary. They are not intended to be all-inclusive but to refresh the memory on automotive terms. More complete definitions and explanations of the terms are found in the text.

Abrasive A substance used for cutting, grinding, lapping, or polishing metal.

Accessories Devices not considered essential to the operation of the vehicle: radio, car heater, and electric window lifts, for example.

Adjustments Changes, either necessary or desired, in clearances, fit, or setting.

Air bags Balloon-type passenger safety devices that inflate automatically on impact, forming a passive restraint system.

Air brake A brake system which uses compressed air to supply the effort required to apply the brake.

Air compressor An engine-driven air pump used to supply air under pressure for operating air brakes and other air-powered devices on a vehicle.

Air conditioning An accessory system that treats passenger-compartment air by cooling and drying it.

Air impact wrench An air-powered hand-held tool that runs nuts and bolts on and off quickly with a series of sharp rapid blows created by pressurized air forced into the wrench.

Air line A hose, pipe, or tube through which air passes.

Air pressure Atmospheric pressure of 14.7 psi (pounds per square inch) [in the metric system 1.0355 kg/cm^2 (kilograms per square centimeter)] at sea level. The pressure on air produced by a pump, by compression in the engine cylinder, etc.

Air suspension Any suspension system that uses contained air for vehicle springing.

Allen wrench A type of screwdriver which turns a screw with a matching recessed hex-head.

Antenna The device used to pick up radio signals.

Antifriction bearing Name given to almost any type of ball, roller, or tapered roller bearing.

Antiskid system A system installed along with the brake system to prevent wheel lockup during braking and thus prevent skidding.

Asbestos A fiber material that is heat resistant and non-flammable, used for brake lining, clutch facings, and gaskets.

Aspect ratio The ratio of tire height to width. For example, a G78 tire is 78 percent as high as it is wide. The lower the number, the wider the tire.

Atmospheric pressure See "Air pressure."

Automatic level control A suspension system which compensates for variations in load in the rear of the car, positioning the rear at a predesigned level regardless of load.

Backlash In gearing, the clearance between meshing teeth of two gears. The amount by which the width of the tooth space exceeds the thickness of the tooth in that space; generally, the amount of free motion, or lash, in a mechanical system.

Ball-and-nut-steering-gear See "Recirculating-ball-and-nut steering gear."

Ball bearing An antifriction bearing with an inner and an outer race with one or more rows of balls between.

Ball check valve A valve consisting of a ball and seat. Fluid can pass in one direction only; when it attempts to flow the other way, it is checked by the ball seating on the seat.

Ball joint A flexible joint constructed with a ball and socket, used in front-suspension systems and valve-train rocker arms.

Ball-joint angle The inward tilt of the steering axis from the vertical.

Ball-joint suspension A type of front suspension which attaches the wheel spindle directly to the upper and lower suspension arms through ball joints.

Ball stud Stud with a ball on end, commonly used in the steering linkage to connect the pitman arm to the linkage, or to connect tie rods.

Battery An electrochemical device for storing energy in chemical form so that it can be released as electricity. A group of electric cells connected together.

Bead That part of the tire which is shaped to fit the rim, made of steel wires, wrapped, and reinforced by the plies of the tires.

Bearing The part which transmits the load to the support and, in so doing, takes the friction caused by moving parts in contact.

Bell-shaped wear Type of wear of an opening (such as a brake drum) where one end is worn most so that the opening flares out like a bell.

Belted-bias tire A tire in which the plies are laid on the bias, crisscrossing each other, with a circumferential belt on top. The rubber tread is vulcanized on top of the belt and plies.

Belted-radial tire A tire in which the plies run parallel to each other and vertical to the tire bead. Over this radial section, belts running parallel to the tire tread are applied.

Bevel gear A gear shaped like the lower part of a cone, used to transmit motion through an angle.

Bias-ply tire A conventionally constructed tire in which the plies are laid on the bias, crisscrossing each other at an angle of about 30 to 40 degrees.

Bleeding A process by which air is removed from a hydraulic system (brake or power-steering) by removing part of the fluid or by operating the system to work out the air.

Blower Name sometimes applied to a supercharger, or engine intake-air compressor. Also applied to the fan motor used with a passenger compartment heater or air conditioner.

Body The assembly of sheet-metal sections, together with windows, doors, seats, and other parts, that provides an enclosure for the passengers, engine, etc.

Body panels Sheets or panels of steel which are fastened together to form the car body.

Boiling point The temperature at which a liquid begins to boil.

Brake An energy conversion device used to retard, stop, or hold a vehicle or mechanism.

Brake drag A constant, relatively light contact between linings and drums when brakes are not applied. The result is a car that pulls, and brakes destroy themselves by burning up from the heat generated.

Brake-drum glaze Excessively smooth surface of the brake drum that lowers friction and, therefore, braking efficiency.

Brake drums Metal drums mounted on the car wheels which form the outer shell of the brakes; brake shoes press against the drums to slow or stop drum and wheel rotation for braking.

Brake fade A reduction, or fading out, of braking effectiveness caused by overheating from excessively long and hard brake application, or from a loss of friction between braking surfaces caused by water.

Brake feel The reaction of the brake pedal against the driver's foot that tells the driver how heavily the brakes are being applied.

Brake fluid A special non-mineral-oil fluid used in the hydraulic braking system.

Brake grab A sudden increase in braking at a wheel, usually caused by contaminated linings.

Brake horsepower (bhp) The power delivered by the engine which is available for driving the vehicle.

Brake lines The tubes or hoses connecting the master and wheel cylinders, or calipers, in a hydraulic-brake system.

Brake lining A high-friction material, usually a form of asbestos, attached by rivets, or a bonding process, to the brake shoe. The lining takes the wear when the shoe is pressed against the brake drum, or rotor.

Brake shoes In drum brakes, arc-shaped metal pieces lined with a high-friction material, or brake lining,

which are forced against the revolving drums to produce braking action. In disk brakes, flat metal pieces having brake lining which are forced against the rotor face.

Brake system A combination of one or more brakes and their related means of operation and control.

Butyl A type of synthetic rubber used in making tire tubes.

Bypass valve In an oil filter, the valve that opens when the filter has clogged to allow oil to reach the engine. In the car air conditioner, the solenoid bypass valve.

Calibrate To check or correct the initial setting of a test instrument.

Caliper A measuring tool that can be set to measure the thickness of a block, the diameter of a shaft, or the bore of a hole (inside caliper). In a disk brake, a housing for pistons and brake shoes, connected to the hydraulic system, which holds the brake shoes so they straddle the disk.

Camber Tilting of the top of the wheels from the vertical; when tilt is outward, camber is positive.

Camelback A strip of new rubber tread used to recap a tire.

Capillary tube A tube with a small inside diameter. In refrigerators, the capillary tube is used to produce a pressure differential between the condenser and evaporator.

Capacitor See "Condenser."

Car lift A piece of shop equipment, operated electrically, hydraulically, or by air, which can raise the entire vehicle or, in some cases, one end of a vehicle.

Caster Tilting of the steering axis forward or backward to provide directional steering stability.

Celsius In the metric system, a temperature scale on which water boils at 100 degrees and freezes at 0°; equal to a reading on a Fahrenheit thermometer of $\frac{5}{9}(°F - 32)$. Also called *centigrade*.

Centigrade See "Celsius."

Centimeter (cm) In the metric system, a unit of linear measure equal to approximately 0.39 inch.

Charging the system The process of adding refrigerant to the air-conditioning system.

Chassis The assembly of mechanisms that make up the major operating part of the vehicle. It is usually assumed to include everything except the car body.

Check valve A valve that opens to permit the passage of air or fluid in one direction only, or operates to check, or prevent, excessive pressure rise or other undesirable action.

Circuit The complete path of an electric current, including the current source. When the path is continuous, the circuit is closed and current flows. When the path is broken, the circuit is open and no current flows. This term is also used to explain hydraulic-system operations.

Circuit breaker A protective device that opens an electric circuit to prevent damage when overheated by excess current flow. Some circuit breakers contain a thermostatic blade that warps to open the circuit when maximum current is reached.

Clutch In the vehicle, the mechanism in the power train

that connects the engine crankshaft to, or disconnects it from, the transmission and thus the remainder of the power train.

Clutch pedal A pedal in the driver's compartment to operate the clutch.

Clutch solenoid In some car air conditioners, a solenoid that operates a clutch on the compressor drive pulley. When the clutch is engaged, the compressor is driven and cooling takes place.

Coil spring A spring made up of an elastic metal, such as steel, formed into a wire or bar and wound into a coil.

Cold patch A method of repairing a punctured tire or tube by gluing a thin rubber patch over the hole.

Collapsible steering column An energy-absorbing steering column design to collapse if the driver is thrown onto it by a severe collision.

Compensating port A small hole in each section of a master cylinder, closed by piston movement which traps fluid ahead of the piston and applies the brakes. When the pedal is released, the piston uncovers the compensating port, allowing the trapped fluid to return to the fluid reservoir.

Compressor In an air conditioner, the mechanism which pumps vaporized refrigerant out of the evaporator, compresses it to a relatively high pressure, and then delivers it to the condenser.

Condensation The change of state during which a gas turns to liquid, because of temperature, pressure, or other changes. Moisture, from the air, deposited on a cool surface.

Condenser In the ignition system, also called a *capacitor*. Connected across the contact points to reduce arcing by providing a "storage place" for electricity (electrons) as the contact points open. In an air-conditioning system, the radiatorlike device that allows the vaporized refrigerant to lose heat and return to a liquid state.

Cornering wear A type of tire-tread wear caused by taking turns at excessive speeds.

Corrosion A gradual eating or wearing away, as by the effect of chemical action.

Cubic centimeter (cm³) A unit in the metric system used to measure volume; equal to approximately 0.061 cubic inch.

Defroster That part of the car heater system, and ducts, designed to melt frost or ice on the inside or outside of the windshield.

Dehumidification The process of removing moisture, or drying. In the air conditioner, the air is dehumidified as it passes through the evaporator, since water condenses from the air onto the evaporator coils.

Dehydrator filter A filtering device in the line between the condenser and evaporator through which all liquid refrigerant must pass. The device removes dirt and moisture from the refrigerant.

Disk brakes Brakes using flat disks against which flat shoes are pressed to produce braking action.

Disk runout The amount that the brake disk wobbles during rotation.

Directional signal A device on the car which uses flashing lights to indicate the direction the driver intends to turn.

Disassemble To take apart.

Disk In a disk brake, the rotor, or revolving piece of metal, against which shoes are pressed to provide braking action.

Dolly blocks Blocks of metal, variously shaped and contoured, used to straighten body panels and fenders. The dolly block is held on one side of the panel while the other side is struck with a special hammer.

Drive line The driving connection, made up of one or more drive shafts, between the transmission and the differential; consists of the drive shaft with universal and slip joints.

Drop center wheel The conventional passenger car wheel, which has a drop in the center for one bead to fit into while the other bead is lifted over the rim flange.

Drop light A portable light, with long electric cord, used in the shop to illuminate the work area.

Drum brakes Brakes using curved brake shoes which press against the inner circumference of a metal drum to produce braking action.

Drum lathe A special lathe for turning brake drums; some can be used to resurface disk-brake rotors.

Dry friction The friction between two dry solids.

Dual-brake system A brake system that has two separate hydraulic systems, one operating the front brakes, the other operating the rear brakes.

Dynamic balance Balance of an object when it is in motion (for example, dynamic balance of a wheel).

Electric brakes Brakes which use an armature-electromagnet combination at each wheel; as the electromagnet is energized, the magnetic attraction between the armature and electromagnet causes the brake shoes to move against the brake drum.

Electric system In the automobile, the system that electrically cranks the engine for starting, furnishes high-voltage sparks to the engine cylinders to fire the compressed air-fuel charges, lights the lights, operates the heater motor, radio, and so on. Consists, in part, of the starting motor, wiring, battery, alternator, regulator, ignition distributor, and ignition coil.

Epoxy A plastic compound that can be used to repair some types of cracks in metal.

Evacuating the system A procedure required whenever any component in the air-conditioning system (except compressor) has been removed and replaced. The procedure uses a vacuum pump to remove air and moisture from the system.

Evaporation The change of state during which a liquid turns to a vapor, or gas.

Evaporator The device in an air conditioner in which refrigerant changes from a liquid to a gas (evaporates), taking heat from the surrounding air as it does so.

Exhaust system A group of parts consisting of the exhaust manifold, exhaust pipe, muffler, tail pipe, and resonator, if used.

Expansion valve A valve between the condenser and evaporator in an air conditioner, located at the evaporator, which provides a pressure differential; the high pressure on the condenser side is reduced to low pressure on the evaporator side.

Feeler gauge Strips of metal of accurately known thicknesses used to measure clearances.

File A cutting tool with a large number of cutting edges arranged along a surface.

Fixed-caliper disk brakes Disk brakes using a caliper which is fixed in position and cannot move; the caliper uses four pistons, two on each side of the disk.

Floating-caliper disk brakes Disk brakes using a caliper mounted through rubber bushings which permit the caliper to float, or move, when the brakes are applied; uses only one large piston in each caliper.

Floor jack A small, portable, hydraulically operated lifting device to raise part of a vehicle from the floor for repairs.

Flushing the brake system The washing out of the hydraulic lines and the master and wheel cylinders, or calipers, with clean brake fluid to remove dirt or impurities.

Four-wheel drive A vehicle that has driving axles that can be engaged on the front and rear so that all four wheels can be driven.

Frame The assembly of metal structural parts and channel sections that supports the engine and body and is supported by the car wheels.

Frame gauges Gauges hung from the car frame to check frame alignment.

Freon-12 A refrigerant widely used in air conditioners.

Friction The resistance to motion between two bodies in contact with each other.

Friction bearings Bearings having sliding contact between the moving surfaces. Sleeve bearings, such as those used in connecting rods, are friction bearings.

Front-end geometry The angular relationship of the front wheels, wheel-attaching parts, and car frame, including camber, caster, steering-axis inclination, toe-in, and toe-out on turns.

Fuel line The pipe or tube through which fuel travels from the tank to the fuel pump and from the pump to the carburetor.

Fuel tank The storage tank for fuel on the vehicle.

Fuse Device in an electric circuit to protect against excessive current flow which could overheat and damage the circuit.

Gasket A flat strip, usually of cork or metal, or both, placed between two machined surfaces to provide a tight seal.

Gearshift A linkage-type mechanism by which the gears in an automobile transmission are engaged.

Grease Lubricating oil to which thickening agents have been added.

Grinder A machine for removing metal by means of an abrasive wheel or stone.

Grinding wheel A wheel, made of abrasive material, used for grinding metal objects held against it.

Ground Connection of an electric unit to the engine or frame to return the current to its source.

Guide-matic An electronic device which automatically controls the headlights, shifting between upper and lower beams as conditions warrant.

Hacksaw A special form of saw with removable blade, used to saw metals.

Headlights Lights at the front of the vehicle designed to illuminate the road ahead when the vehicle is moving forward.

Heater A small radiator, or heater core, mounted under the instrument panel, through which hot coolant circulates. When heat is needed, a fan is turned on to circulate air through the hot core.

Hood That part of the car body which fits over and protects the engine.

Horn A noise-making electrical signaling device on the vehicle.

Hotchkiss drive The type of rear suspension in which the springs absorb the rear-end torque.

Hot patch A method of repairing a tire or tube by using heat to vulcanize the patch to the damaged surface.

Hub Center part of a wheel.

Hydraulics A branch of science dealing with the use of liquids under pressure to transfer force or motion, or to increase the force applied.

Hydraulic brakes A braking system that uses hydraulic pressure to force the brake shoes against the brake drums or rotors as the brake pedal is depressed.

Hydraulic press A piece of shop equipment used to develop a heavy force against an object by means of a hydraulic piston and jack assembly.

Hydraulic Pressure Pressure exerted through the medium of a liquid.

Hydraulic valve A valve in a hydraulic system that operates on, or controls, hydraulic pressure in the system.

Idling speed The speed, or rpm, at which the engine runs without load when the accelerator pedal is released.

Included angle Camber angle plus steering-axis inclination angle.

Independent front suspension The conventional front-suspension system in which each front wheel is independently supported by a spring.

Indicator A device used to make known some condition, by use of a light or pointer, for example, the temperature indicator or oil pressure indicator.

In-line steering gear A type of integral power steering, using a recirculating-ball steering gear to which are added a control valve and an actuating piston.

Inner tube See "Tire tube."

Kilogram (kg) In the metric system, a unit of weight, or mass, equal to approximately 2.2 pounds.

Kilometer (km) In the metric system, a unit of linear measure equal to 0.621 mile.

Kilowatt (kW) In the metric system, a measure of power. One horsepower equals 0.746 kilowatt.

Kinetic energy The energy of motion; the energy stored in a moving body as developed through its momentum, for example, the kinetic energy stored in a rotating flywheel.

Kingpin In older cars, and in trucks, the steel pin on which the steering knuckle pivots; it attaches the steering knuckle to the knuckle support or axle.

Kingpin inclination Inward tilt of the kingpin from the vertical. See also "Steering-axis inclination."

Knuckle A front-suspension part that acts as a hinge to support a front wheel and permit it to be turned to steer the car. The knuckle pivots on ball joints, or, in earlier models, on kingpins. Also called *steering knuckle*.

kW See "Kilowatt."

Leaf spring A spring made up of a single leaf or of a series of flat steel plates of graduated length assembled one on top of another to absorb road shocks by bending, or flexing, in the middle.

Leak detector A device or substance that can be used to detect leakage of gas or liquid.

Light An electrical device that includes a wire in a gas-filled bulb which glows brightly when current passes through it; also called a *lamp*.

Linear measurement A measurement taken in a straight line, for example, the measurement of crankshaft end play.

Lining See "Brake lining."

Linkage An assembly of rods, or links, to transmit motion.

Linkage-type power steering A type of power steering in which the power-steering units (power cylinder and valve) are part of the steering linkage; frequently, a bolt-on type of unit.

Liter (l) In the metric system, a measure of volume equal to approximately 0.264 U.S. gallon.

Locknut A second nut turned down on a holding nut to prevent loosening.

Lockwasher A type of washer placed under the head of a bolt or nut to prevent the bolt or nut from working loose.

Magnetic clutch A magnetically operated clutch used to engage and disengage the air-conditioner compressor.

Mag wheel A type of lightweight wheel, made from magnesium, usually very strong, shiny, and spoked, that does not use a hub cap. It is widely used in race-car applications and as a replacement wheel on passenger cars. Many similar wheels, made of metals other than magnesium, are often called mag wheels.

Manifold gauge set A high- and a low-pressure gauge mounted together as a set, used for checking pressures in the air-conditioning system.

Master cylinder The liquid-filled cylinder in the hydraulic-brake system or clutch where hydraulic pressure is developed by depression of a foot pedal.

Meter (m) In the metric system, a unit of linear measure equal to 39.37 inches. Also, the name given to a test instrument, such as an ammeter, that measures as a result of the substance being measured passing through it. Also, any device that measures and controls the discharge of the substance passing through it. For example, a carburetor jet is used to meter fuel flow.

Micrometer A precision device that measures small distances, such as crankshaft or cylinder-bore diameter, or the thickness of an object. Also called a *mike*.

Millimeter (mm) In the metric system, a unit of linear measure equal to approximately 0.039 inch.

Motor vehicle Any type of self-propelled vehicle mounted on wheels or tracks.

Needle bearing Antifriction bearing of the roller type; the rollers are very small in diameter (needle-sized).

Neoprene A synthetic rubber that is not affected by various chemicals harmful to natural rubber.

Nut A removable fastener, used to lock pieces together on a bolt, made by threading a hole through the center of a piece of metal which has been shaped to a standard size on the outside.

Odometer The device, usually set in the speedometer, that measures the distance the vehicle has traveled in miles or kilometers.

One-wire system On an automobile, the practice of using the car body, engine, and frame as a path for the grounded side of electric circuits, allowing the attached electric circuits to be of the one-wire type.

Open circuit A break, or opening, in an electric circuit which prevents the passage of an electric current.

O ring A type of sealing ring, made of special rubberlike material, which is compressed into grooves to provide sealing action.

Oversteer The built-in characteristic of certain types of rear-suspension systems which causes the rear wheels to move toward the outside of a turn.

Parallelogram linkage A steering system which uses a short idler arm on the right side, mounted so that it is parallel to the pitman arm.

Parking brakes Mechanically operated brakes that work independently of the foot-operated service brakes on the vehicle; they are set when the vehicle is parked.

Passage A small hole or gallery in an assembly or casting, through which air, coolant, fuel, or oil flows.

Pedal reserve The distance from the brake pedal to the floorboard after the brakes are applied.

Performance test The use of a manifold gauge set to test the air conditioner for performance by checking pressures in the air-conditioning system.

Piston A movable part, fitted to a cylinder, which can receive or transmit motion as a result of pressure changes (fluid, vapor, gas) in the cylinder.

Pitman arm In the steering system, the arm that is connected on one end to the steering-gear-sector shaft and on the other end to the steering linkage, or tie rod; it swings back and forth for steering as the steering wheel is turned.

Pivot A pin, or short shaft, upon which another part rests or turns.

Plastic gasket compound A plastic paste in a tube which can be laid in any shape to make a gasket.

Plies The layers of cord in a tire casing, each of which is called a *ply*.

Power brakes Brakes that use vacuum and atmospheric pressure to provide most of the effort required for stopping the vehicle.

Power cylinder Operating cylinder which produces power to actuate a mechanism. Both power brakes and power-steering units have power cylinders.

Power steering A device that uses hydraulic pressure from a pump to multiply the driver's effort as an aid in turning the steering wheel.

Power take-off An attachment for connecting the engine

to devices or other machinery when its use is required.

Preload In bearings, the amount of load originally imposed on a bearing before actual operating loads are imposed. It is imposed by bearing adjustments and ensures alignment and minimum looseness in the system.

Pressure bleeder A piece of shop equipment that uses air pressure to force brake fluid into the brake system for bleeding.

psi Abbreviation for pounds per square inch; often used to indicate pressure of a liquid or gas.

Pull A movement in a particular direction as the result of an unbalanced condition. For example, an unbalanced braking condition at the front brakes will cause the car to swerve, or pull, to one side when the brakes are applied; can also be caused by unequal front-wheel alignment.

Puller Generally, a shop tool that permits removal of one closely fitted part from another without damage. Often contains a screw or screws which can be turned to apply gradual pressure.

Pulley A metal wheel with a V-shaped groove around the rim which drives, or is driven by, a belt.

Pulsation A surge, felt in the brake pedal during low-pressure braking.

Pump A device that transfers gas or liquid from one place to another.

Puncture-sealing tires and tubes Tires and tubes coated on the inside with a plastic material. Air pressure in the tire or tube forces that material through holes made by punctures. The material hardens on contact with the air to seal the puncture.

Race The metal rings on which balls or roller bearings rotate.

Rack-and-pinion steering gear A type of steering gear using a pinion on the end of the steering shaft which is meshed with a rack on the major cross member of the steering linkage.

Radial-ply tire A tire in which the plies are laid on radially, or perpendicular to the rim, with a circumferential belt on top of them. The rubber tread is vulcanized on top of the belt and plies.

Reamer A metal-cutting tool with a series of sharp cutting edges that remove material from a hole when the tool is turned in it.

Rear-end torque Reactionary torque applied to the rear-axle housing as torque is applied to the wheels; rear-end torque attempts to turn the axle housing in a direction opposite to wheel rotation. See also "Torque."

Recapping A form of tire repair in which a cap of new materials is placed on the old tread and vulcanized into place.

Receiver In a car air conditioner, a metal tank for holding excess liquid refrigerant. The liquid refrigerant is delivered from the condenser to the receiver; from there, it passes to the evaporator as needed.

Recirculating-ball-and-nut steering gear A type of steering gear which has a nut (meshing with a gear sector) assembled on a worm and has balls circulating between the nut and worm threads.

Refrigerant A substance used in an air conditioner which circulates between the condenser and evaporator to produce cooling through a cycle of evaporation and condensation. Freon-12 is the refrigerant most widely used in automobile air conditioners.

Refrigeration Cooling by removal of heat.

Relief valve A valve that opens, when a predetermined pressure is reached, to prevent excessive pressure.

Return spring A "pull-back" spring, often used in brake systems.

Rotary-valve steering gear A type of power steering gear.

Runout Wobble.

Safety rim A type of wheel rim having a hump on the inner edge of the ledge on which the tire bead rides. The hump helps hold the tire in the rim in case of a blowout.

Scored Scratched or grooved; a cylinder wall may be scored by abrasive particles moved up and down by the piston rings.

Screw A metal fastener that can be turned, usually with a screwdriver, having threads that fit into a threaded hole. There are many different types and sizes of screws.

Seal A material, shaped around a shaft, used to close off the operating compartment of the shaft, preventing oil leakage.

Sealer A thick, tacky, compound, usually spread with a brush, which may be used as a gasket, or sealant, to close small openings or surface irregularities.

Seat The surface upon which another part rests, such as a valve seat. Also, the process of a part wearing into fit; for example, piston rings seat after a few miles of driving.

Seat adjuster A device to permit forward or backward (and sometimes upward and downward) movement of the front seat.

Sector One section of a gear; specifically, the gear sector on the pitman shaft, in many steering gears.

Self-adjuster The mechanism used on drum brakes to compensate for shoe wear by automatically keeping the shoe adjusted close to the drum.

Servo A device in a hydraulic system that converts hydraulic pressure into mechanical movement. It consists of a piston which moves in a cylinder as hydraulic pressure acts on it.

Shackle Swinging support by which one end of a leaf spring is attached to a car frame.

Shim A slotted strip of metal used as a spacer to adjust front-end alignment on many cars and to make small corrections in the position of body sheet metal and other parts.

Shimmy Rapid oscillation; in wheel shimmy, for example, the front wheel tries to turn in and out alternately and rapidly. This causes the front end of the car to oscillate, or shimmy.

Shim stock Sheets of metal of accurately known thickness which can be cut into strips and used to measure, or correct, clearance.

Shock absorber A device placed at each vehicle wheel to regulate spring rebound and compression.

Shoe In the brake system, the metal plate that supports the brake lining and absorbs and transmits braking forces.

Short-arm, long-arm suspension Name given to the conventional front-suspension system which uses a short upper control arm and a longer lower control arm.

Sight glass In a car air conditioner, a viewing glass set in the refrigerant line; it provides for a visual check of refrigerant passing from the receiver to the evaporator.

Skid control A device to prevent wheel lockup during braking and thus skidding.

Snap ring A metal fastener, made in two types: external, to fit into a groove in a shaft, and internal, to fit into a groove in a housing. Snap rings must be installed and removed with special snap-ring pliers.

Soldering The uniting of pieces of metal with solder, flux, and heat.

Solenoid switch A switch which is opened and closed electromagnetically by movement of a core. Usually, this core also causes a mechanical action, such as the movement of a drive pinion into mesh with flywheel teeth for cranking.

Specifications The measurements, usually as recommended by the manufacturer, for the vehicle being serviced.

Speed The rate of motion, usually measured in miles per hour [kilometers per hour].

Speedometer Instrument that indicates vehicle speed, usually driven from the transmission.

Spline Slot or groove cut in a shaft or bore; a splined shaft onto which a hub, wheel, gear, etc., with matching splines in its bore is assembled so that the two must turn together.

Spongy pedal A term applied to the feel of the brake pedal when air is trapped in the hydraulic system.

Spring An elastic device which yields under stress or pressure but returns to its original state or position when the stress or pressure is removed. The operating component of the automotive suspension system which absorbs the force of road shock by flexing and twisting.

Spring rate The load required to move a spring or a suspended wheel a given distance. An indicator of the softness or firmness of a given spring or suspension.

Sprung weight The weight of that part of the car which is supported on springs; for example, the frame and body.

Squeak A high-pitched noise of short duration.

Squeal A continuous, high-pitched, low-volume noise.

Stabilizer bar An interconnecting shaft between the two lower suspension arms which reduces body roll on turns.

Starting motor The electric motor in the electric system that cranks the engine, or turns the crankshaft, for starting. Also called *cranking motor.*

Static balance Balance of an object while it is at rest or not moving.

Static friction Friction between two bodies at rest.

Steering and ignition lock A device that secures the ignition switch in the OFF position and also secures the steering wheel so it cannot be turned.

Steering arm The arm attached to the steering knuckle to turn the knuckle, and wheel, for steering.

Steering axis The centerline of the ball joints in a front-suspension system.

Steering-axis inclination The inward tilt of the steering axis from the vertical.

Steering gear That part of the steering system, located at the lower end of the steering shaft, that carries the rotary motion of the steering wheel to the car wheels for steering.

Steering geometry See "Toe-out on turns."

Steering kickback Sharp and rapid movements of the steering wheel as front wheels encounter obstructions in the road; the shocks of these encounters "kick back" to the steering wheel.

Steering knuckle The front-wheel spindle which is supported by upper and lower ball joints and the wheel; the part mounting the wheel which is turned for steering.

Steering shaft The column extending from the steering gear to the steering wheel.

Steering system The mechanism that enables the driver to turn the wheels for changing the direction of vehicle movement.

Steering wheel The wheel at the top of the steering shaft in the driver's compartment which is used to guide, or steer, the car.

Stepped feeler gauge A "go no-go" gauge; a feeler gauge which has a thinner tip and is thicker along the rest of the gauge.

Streamlining The shaping of an object that moves through a medium (such as air or water), or past which the medium moves, so that less energy is lost by the parting and reuniting of the medium as the object moves through it.

Strut A bar that connects from the lower control arm to the car frame, used when the lower control arm is of the type having only one point of attachment to the frame. Also called a *brake reaction rod.*

Stud A headless bolt that is threaded on both ends.

Suction throttling valve In an air conditioner, a valve located between the evaporator and the compressor to prevent freezing of moisture on the evaporator.

Surface grinder A grinder used to resurface flat areas, such as cylinder heads.

Suspension The system of springs and parts which supports the upper portion of a vehicle on its axles and wheels.

Suspension arm In the front suspension, an arm pivoted at one end to the frame and at the other to the steering-knuckle support.

Sway bar See "Stabilizer bar."

Thermistor Heat-sensing electric device with a negative temperature coefficient of resistance. That is, as temperature increases, resistance decreases. Used as the sensing device for engine-temperature-indicating instruments.

Thermometer An instrument for measuring temperature.

Thermostat A device that operates on, or regulates, temperature changes. Several thermostats are used in engines.

Threaded insert A threaded coil put into a hole that has damaged threads. The process involves restoring the original-size threads to a hole with damaged threads by drilling the hole oversize, tapping it, and inserting the threaded coil.

Tie rods In the steering system, the rods that link the pitman arm to the steering-knuckle arms.

Tilt steering wheel A type of steering wheel which can be tilted at various angles by means of a flex joint in the steering shaft.

Tire The casing and tube assembled on a car wheel to provide pneumatically cushioned contact and traction with the road.

Tire casing Layers of cord, called *plies,* shaped in a form and impregnated with rubber, to which the tread is applied.

Tire rotation The interchanging of the running location of tires on a car to minimize noise and to equalize tire wear.

Tire tread That part of the tire which comes in contact with the road.

Tire tube The inside rubber tube assembled in the tire casing; it maintains the air at sufficient pressure to inflate the casing and adequately support the weight of the vehicle.

Tire-wear indicator Extra rubber molded into the bottom of the tire tread groove, which appears as a strip of smooth rubber ½ inch [12.7 mm] wide extending across the tire when the tire tread depth decreases to 1/16 inch [1.59 mm].

Toe-in The amount, in inches or millimeters, that the front of the front wheels point inward.

Toe-out on turns Difference in angles between the two front wheels and the car frame during turns. The inner wheel in a turn turns out, or toes out, more. Also called *steering geometry.*

Torque Turning or twisting effort, usually measured in pound-feet or kilogram-meters.

Torque wrench A special wrench that indicates the amount of torque being applied to a nut or bolt.

Torsion-bar spring A long, straight bar, fastened to the frame at one end and to a suspension part at the other. Spring action is produced by the twisting of the bar.

Torsion-bar steering gear A rotary valve power-steering gear.

Tracking The following of the rear wheels directly behind, or in the tracks of, the front wheels.

Tramp Up-and-down motion or hopping of the front wheels taking place at higher speeds because of unbalanced wheels or excessive wheel runout. Also called *high-speed shimmy.*

Trouble diagnosis The detective work necessary to run down the cause of a trouble. Also implies the correction of the trouble by elimination of the cause.

Tubeless tire A tire that holds air without use of a tube.

Twin I-beam A type of front-suspension system used on some trucks.

U bolt An iron rod, with threads on each end, bent into the shape of a U, fitted with a nut at each end.

Unitized construction A type of automotive body and frame construction in which the frame and body parts are welded together to form a single part.

Unsprung weight The weight of that part of the car which is not supported on springs; for example, the wheels and tires.

Vacuum An absence of air or other substance.

Vacuum motor A small motor, powered by intake manifold vacuum, used for raising and lowering headlight doors and for other similar jobs.

Vacuum-suspended power brake A type of power brake in which both sides of the piston are subjected to vacuum; the piston is "suspended" in vacuum.

Valve A device that can be opened or closed to allow or stop the flow of a liquid, gas, or vapor from one place to another.

Valve spool A spool-shaped valve in the power-steering unit.

Vaporization The change of a liquid into a vapor, often by the application of heat.

V-8 engine A type of engine with two banks of four cylinders each set at an angle to each other to form a V.

Vise A gripping device for holding a piece while it is being worked on.

Voltmeter An electric meter for measuring the voltage of an electrical device, such as a battery or alternator, or for measuring the voltage between two points in an electric circuit.

Vulcanizing A process of treating raw rubber by heat and pressure; the treatment forms the rubber and gives it the desired characteristics of toughness and flexibility.

Welding The process of joining pieces of metal by fusing them together with heat.

Wheel balancer A device that checks a wheel, either statically or dynamically, for balance.

Wheel cylinders In the hydraulic-brake system, hydraulic cylinders placed in the brake mechanisms at the wheels; hydraulic pressure from the master cylinder causes the wheel cylinders to move the brake shoes into pressure contact with the brake drums for braking.

Wheel tramp Tendency for the wheel to move up and down so it repeatedly bears hard, or "tramps," on the pavement. Sometimes called *high-speed shimmy.*

Window regulator A device for opening and closing the windows; usually operated by a crank.

Windshield wiper A mechanism which utilizes a rubber blade to wipe the windshield; it is operated either by vacuum or electrically.

Wire feeler gauge A round wire gauge used for checking clearances between electric contacts, such as distributor points and spark-plug electrodes.

Wiring harness A group of individually insulated wires wrapped together.

Worm Type of gear on the lower end of the steering shaft.

Zip gun An air-powered cutting tool often used for work on the exhaust system.

INDEX

A

The answers to the questions in the progress quizzes and chapter checkups are given here. In chapter checkups, you may be asked to list parts in components, describe the purpose and operation of components, define certain terms, and so on. Obviously, no answers to these could be given here since that would mean repeating substantially the entire book. Therefore, you are asked to refer to the book to check your answer.

If you want to figure your grade on any quiz, divide the number of questions in the quiz into 100. This gives you the value of each question. For instance, suppose there are 8 questions: 8 goes into a hundred 12.5 times. A correct answer gives you 12.5 points. If you answered 6 correct of the 8, your grade would be 75 (6 × 12.5).

If you are not satisfied with the grade you make on a quiz or checkup, restudy the section and retake the test. This will help you remember the important facts.

Remember, when you take a course in school, you can pass and graduate even though you make a grade of less than 100. But in the automotive shop, you must score 100 percent all the time. If you make 1 error out of 100 service jobs, for example, your average would be 99. In school that is a fine average. But in the automotive shop that one job you erred on could cause such serious trouble (a ruined engine or a wrecked car) that it would outweigh all the good jobs you performed. Therefore, always proceed carefully in performing any service job and make sure you know exactly what you are supposed to do and how you are to do it.

CHAPTER 1

Progress Quiz 1-1
Completing the Sentences 1. (c) 2. (b) 3. (d) 4. (c) 5. (b) 6. (b) 7. (b) 8. (c) 9. (b) 10. (b)

Progress Quiz 1-2
Completing the Sentences 1. (b) 2. (a) 3. (c) 4. (a) 5. (c) 6. (c) 7. (c) 8. (a) 9. (b) 10. (c)

Chapter 1 Checkup
Completing the Sentences 1. (c) 2. (a) 3. (a) 4. (a) 5. (b) 6. (b) 7. (c) 8. (b) 9. (c) 10. (c)

Problems 1. 2,880 psf 2. 20 3. 200 4. 600 lb 5. 100 lb 6. 2,400 lb 7. 25 lb 8. 0.5

CHAPTER 2

Chapter 2 Checkup
Correcting Parts Lists 1. windshield 2. coupler 3. fan belt 4. engine cylinders 5. piston

Picking Out the Right Answer 1. (c) 2. (c) 3. (b) 4. (c) 5. (c)

CHAPTER 3

Chapter 3 Checkup
Correcting Parts Lists 1. frame 2. levers 3. suspension gears 4. snugger 5. distribution valve

Completing the Sentences 1. (c) 2. (d) 3. (a) 4. (b) 5. (a) 6. (c) 7. (a) 8. (b) 9. (c) 10. (a)

CHAPTER 4

Chapter 4 Checkup
Correcting Parts Lists 1. connecting rod 2. dust shield

Completing the Sentences 1. (c) 2. (b) 3. (a)

CHAPTER 5

Progress Quiz 5-1
Completing the Sentences 1. (a) 2. (c) 3. (b) 4. (c) 5. (a) 6. (a) 7. (a) 8. (a) 9. (a) 10. (a)

Progress Quiz 5-2
Completing the Sentences 1. (c) 2. (b) 3. (a) 4. (a) 5. (c) 6. (b) 7. (b) 8. (a) 9. (a) 10. (c)

Chapter 5 Checkup

Correcting Parts Lists 1. toe-up 2. caster angle 3. propeller shaft 4. oil pump 5. valve-centering block 6. rotary valve 7. friction clutch 8. valve spool

Unscrambling the Lists (Front-End Geometry)

FACTORS:	CONDITIONS:
camber	tilting of wheels from vertical
steering-axis inclination	inward tilt of steering axis from vertical
included angle	camber plus steering-axis inclination
caster	forward or backward tilt of steering axis
toe-in	turning in of front wheels

CHAPTER 6

Chapter 6 Checkup

Correcting Troubles Lists 1. excessive caster 2. tight U bolt 3. engine mounting tight 4. wheels out of balance 5. defective shock absorbers 6. steering gear binding 7. grabbing brakes 8. caster too low 9. power steering inoperative 10. wheel aligned with axle 11. underinflation 12. binding in steering linkage 13. underinflation 14. tight wheel bearing 15. caster too low

CHAPTER 7

Chapter 7 Checkup

Completing the Sentences 1. (b) 2. (c) 3. (b) 4. (c) 5. (a) 6. (c) 7. (a) 8. (c) 9. (a) 10. (b)

CHAPTER 8

Chapter 8 Checkup

Completing the Sentences 1. (b) 2. (c) 3. (b) 4. (b) 5. (c) 6. (b) 7. (a) 8. (c) 9. (a) 10. (a) 11. (c) 12. (b) 13. (c) 14. (c) 15. (a)

CHAPTER 9

Chapter 9 Checkup

Completing the Sentences 1. (c) 2. (b) 3. (a) 4. (c) 5. (b)

CHAPTER 10

Chapter 10 Checkup

Correcting Troubles Lists 1. pump pressure above 700 psi [49.216 kg/cm²] 2. excessive caster 3. engine idles too fast 4. tires overinflated 5. steering gear tight on car frame

Completing the Sentences 1. (b) 2. (b) 3. (c) 4. (b) 5. (c)

CHAPTER 11

Chapter 11 Checkup

Correcting Troubles Lists 1. fluid level high 2. engine idle excessive 3. excessive oil pressure 4. pump valve stuck 5. gear-shaft adjustment too tight

Completing the Sentences 1. (c) 2. (a) 3. (c) 4. (a)

CHAPTER 12

Chapter 12 Checkup

Completing the Sentences 1. (c) 2. (a) 3. (b) 4. (c) 5. (b) 6. (a) 7. (b) 8. (c) 9. (b) 10. (c)

CHAPTER 13

Chapter 13 Checkup

Correcting Troubles Lists 1. tight pump drive belt 2. low tire pressure 3. excessive oil in cylinder 4. oil pressure low 5. high oil level

Completing the Sentences 1. (b) 2. (a) 3. (c) 4. (d)

CHAPTER 14

Progress Quiz 14-1

Completing the Sentences 1. (b) 2. (c) 3. (a) 4. (b) 5. (c) 6. (b) 7. (a) 8. (b) 9. (b) 10. (a)

Progress Quiz 14-2

Completing the Sentences 1. (b) 2. (b) 3. (c) 4. (b) 5. (c) 6. (a) 7. (b) 8. (c) 9. (a) 10. (b)

Chapter 14 Checkup

Correcting Parts Lists 1. cable linkage 2. activating pin 3. pushrod 4. rocker plate 5. drum

Completing the Sentences 1. (a) 2. (b) 3. (c) 4. (c) 5. (c) 6. (a) 7. (b) 8. (b)

CHAPTER 15

Progress Quiz 15-1

Correcting Troubles Lists 1. brake line clogged 2. master cylinder defective 3. brake lining soaked with oil 4. master cylinder defective 5. brake lining water-soaked drums scored 7. linings soaked with oil 8. air in es high fluid level in reservoir 10. mismatched linings

pter 15 Checkup
gnosing *Brake Complaints* 1. (b) 2. (c) 3. (c) 4. (a) 5. (d) a) 7. (c) 8. (c)

ompleting the Sentences 1. (b) 2. (c) 3. (b) 4. (b) 5. (c) . (b) 7. (b) 8. (c)

CHAPTER 16

Chapter 16 Checkup
Correcting Troubles Lists 1. vacuum pump stuck 2. ruptured diaphragm 3. broken return spring 4. compensator valve hanging open 5. vacuum fitting plugged

CHAPTER 17

Chapter 17 Checkup
Completing the Sentences 1. (b) 2. (c) 3. (d) 4. (c) 5. (b) 6. (c)

CHAPTER 18

Chapter 18 Checkup
Refer to lubrication charts

CHAPTER 19

Chapter 19 Checkup
Completing the Sentences 1. (b) 2. (a) 3. (a and b) 4. (c) 5. (a) 6. (c) 7. (c) 8. (b) 9. (b) 10. (b)

CHAPTER 20

Progress Quiz 20-1
Completing the Sentences 1. (b) 2. (b) 3. (b) 4. (a) 5. (b) 6. (a) 7. (c) 8. (a) 9. (d) 10. (a)

Chapter 20 Checkup
Unscrambling the Lists

COMPONENTS:	FUNCTIONS:
compressor	compresses refrigerant vapor
condenser	removes heat from condensed vapor
receiver	storage tank for liquid refrigerant
check valve	prevents surging of refrigerant back to condenser
sight glass	to check refrigerant for bubbles
bypass valve	controls refrigerant circuit
expansion valve	provides pressure drop at evaporator
evaporator	causes cooling by evaporation of refrigerant

Completing the Sentences 1. (a) 2. (a) 3. (b) 4. (c) 5. (a) 6. (c) 7. (b) 8. (d) 9. (a) 10. (d)

CHAPTER 21

Chapter 21 Checkup
Completing the Sentences 1. (b) 2. (a) 3. (b) 4. (d) 5. (b) 6. (c) 7. (c) 8. (c) 9. (a) 10. (c)